EVIL SISTERS

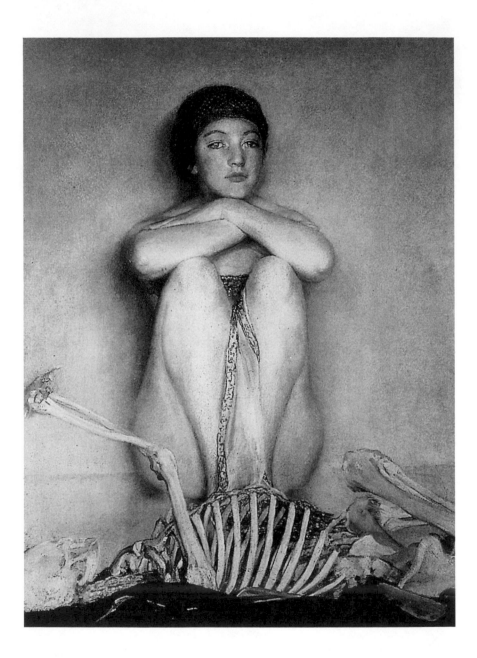

William Sergeant Kendall (1869–1938),
A Sphinx, *oil on canvas, 48 x 36 inches, ca. 1915 (dated 1914 on reverse)*

EVIL
SISTERS

THE THREAT OF FEMALE SEXUALITY
AND THE CULT OF MANHOOD

BRAM DIJKSTRA

ALFRED A. KNOPF   NEW YORK   1996

This Is a Borzoi Book
Published by Alfred A. Knopf, Inc.

Copyright © 1996 by Bram Dijkstra

http://www.randomhouse.com/

Library of Congress Cataloging-in-Publication Data
Dijkstra, Bram.
Evil sisters / Bram Dijkstra.—1st ed.
p. cm.
Includes bibliographical references and index.
ISBN (invalid) 0-394-56945-8
1. Women in popular culture—History.   2. Femmes fatales—History.
3. Sexism—History.   4. Racism—History.   I. Title.
HQ1122.D55 1996
305.42'09—dc20   96-7448   CIP

Manufactured in the United States of America
First Edition

THIS BOOK IS FOR MY THREE SISTERS—
YOKA, ADRI, AND MARIJKE—WHO TAUGHT
ME EARLY THAT TO UNDERESTIMATE WOMEN IS TO
PLAY THE FOOL; AND, AS ALWAYS, THIS BOOK IS ALSO
FOR SANDRA, WHOSE ACCOMPLISHMENTS
NEVER CEASE TO AMAZE ME!

ACKNOWLEDGMENTS

Several superbly qualified readers, in particular Sandra Dijkstra, Marilyn Yalom, and Victoria Wilson, my editor at Knopf, took pencil in hand and showed me how to paint this forest of horrors better by trimming its trees. Without their efforts this book would have been longer and less.

A book such as this cannot be written in an isolation chamber. The work of hundreds of other recent researchers has had an indelible impact on my own understanding of the continuities of gender prejudice in twentieth-century culture. As I emphasized in *Idols of Perversity,* without the extraordinary historical studies of such scholars as Richard Hofstadter, John and Robin Haller, Sandra Gilbert and Susan Gubar, G. J. Barker-Benfield, Stephen Jay Gould, Anne Fausto-Sterling, Sander Gilman, Klaus Theweleit, and numerous others, my understanding of the materials presented in this book could not but have been much narrower. It is a laudable practice in scholarship to acknowledge such influences by means of citation in the text. Lately, however, this practice has threatened to become almost the main focus of certain scholarly studies, requiring the reader to wade through a morass of abstruse arguments about the fine points of interpretation. That this should be so is almost inevitable, for every citation properly invites discussion, qualification, and debate. This book, however, is primarily an effort at historical synthesis and reportage, taking as its point of departure an important trove of largely forgotten original sources.

It has been my primary concern to let this important material speak for itself. The absence of references to, or citations from the work of other researchers who have dealt with this material therefore does not imply an absence of indebtedness on my part. Every work in the Bibliography has contributed to my understanding of the issues involved—as is true of others I no doubt have omitted inadvertently. Unless they were truly essential to my presentation, I have, for the sake of concision, not again included the many texts already listed in the Bibliography to *Idols of Perversity*. But the very nature of this study clearly puts the concept of originality in doubt, and I have no intention to claim as my own what is part of a collective exploration. To search for history is to travel in company. Only fools and ideologues would profess to be able to set out on such a journey alone.

CONTENTS

C O N T E N T S

EVIL SISTERS

INTRODUCTION

Du-ring the first thirty years of this century scientists and artists became obsessed with speculation about woman's indelible
link with humanity's "bestial" origins. The revolutionary late-
nineteenth-century reorganization of all scientific thought according to
the tenets of evolutionary theory virtually required the development of
schemes positing "man's" ability to transcend the deadly cycles of "mere
nature." At the same time, the period's wholesale denigration of women
as little more than baby-making machines effectively placed a premium
on "manhood" and a curse on feminine identity. Propelled by such
notions, many of those still counted among the heroes of modern science—biologists, medical researchers, and psychologists—were encouraged to formulate some of the twentieth century's most pernicious and
durable fictions of race, class, and gender: fictions that helped shape
every facet of twentieth-century life.

The later nineteenth century used Darwin's discoveries to transform
the scattershot gender conflicts of earlier centuries into a "scientifically
grounded" exposé of female sexuality as a source of social disruption
and "degeneration." At the opening of the new century, biology and
medicine set out to prove that nature had given *all* women a basic instinct that made them into predators, destroyers, witches—evil sisters.
Soon experts in many related fields rushed in to delineate why every
woman was doomed to be a harbinger of death to the male.

A "latent vampire" lay "concealed under thoroughly respectable inhibited womanhood," as William J. Fielding, author of numerous, and very influential, books on sex and socialization, stressed in 1927, in a widely distributed pamphlet with the lurid title *Woman: The Eternal Primitive.* Under every apparently saintly skin throbbed the hungry flesh of a sinner. Whenever given "the opportunity to gratify a fundamental craving of her nature," woman could be counted upon to give free rein to "an unconscious instinct that is deeply rooted in the primitive feminine mind." (37–41) Such apparently "scientific" rhetoric encouraged the general public to regard women as biological terrorists out to deplete the creative energies of every civilized male.

Female sexuality had come to be seen as a degenerative disease. Women were nature's secret weapon against manhood's valiant efforts to triumph over mortality. "What have you done?" exclaimed one dignified gentleman, appalled at Marie Stopes's efforts in support of birth control: "You have let women know about things which only prostitutes ought to know; once you give women a taste for these things, they become vampires." A brood of sexual women, Stopes's interlocutor exclaimed, could only lead to "a race of effeminate men." (*Enduring Passion,* 6)

In the closing paragraph of *Idols of Perversity* (1986) I suggested that late-nineteenth-century erotic *fantasies* about the deadly nature of female sexuality had a significant influence on the development and dissemination of racist thinking in our own century: "The images of the viraginous woman and the effeminate Jew—both equally eager to depredate the gold, the pure seed of the Aryan male—began to merge. The deadly racist and sexist evolutionary dreams of turn-of-the-century culture fed the masochistic middle-class fantasy in which the godlike Greek, the führer, the lordly executioner, would kill the vampire and bring on a millennium of pure blood, evolving genes, and men who were men." Twisted "erotic" fantasies of gynecide had opened the door to the realities of genocide. *Evil Sisters* shows how this deadly shift occurred.

The extravagant speculations of science provided the rapidly expanding field of popular culture—and particularly the early movie industry—with a ready-made set of crowd-pleasing themes. These, in turn, helped shape the worldview of the millions who flocked to that cheap, new, easily accessible and digestible form of entertainment. A single image, effectively exploited, often proved to be worth far more than a triple-decker novel. Much like discarded fashions the ghosts of poorly considered scientific theorems tend to float through our fantasies long after they have been formally discredited. In our imagination everything is real. Thus, when, toward mid-century, in the aftermath of World War II, the biologists finally got around to discarding some of their own formerly "incontrovertible truths," the media had already turned those mistakes into cultural commonplaces—into "natural laws" of the entertainment industry. Culture has many historical sources— most of them forgotten, and what we remember often only a dim haze of ghostly imagery on a defective picture tube. In this book I set out to reconfigure a few such historical ghosts—particularly those relating to the early twentieth century's remarkable fear of female sexuality and the scientists' attempts to fetishize manhood as a gateway to immortality.

The "discoveries" of early-twentieth-century biology saddled Western culture with a vicious eroticism centered on images of the sexual woman as vampire. This book traces the cultural pedigree of the vampires so pervasive in our popular media today. It also provides a genealogy for the cat women, tiger women, praying mantises, snake-fanciers, and man-eating tarantulas still prowling about our movie theaters, television screens, best-seller lists, and comic-book stores. Batman, the X-Men, and a horde of other superheroes (with a few impossibly buxom, barely thonged female sword-fighters and monster-bashers thrown into the mix to satisfy contemporary adolescent taste) have their hands full trying to control this ever-burgeoning feline, insect, and rodent population. On Broadway, the deadly kiss of the spider woman is one of the milder afflictions addling men's minds. In the fashion magazines, jean designers display an endless succession of anorexic models who try their best to look as hungry and dangerous as possible. Dorothy's Kansas has been overrun by monsters.

Most of us appear to accept these images as a normal part of social life, as an "inherent" expression of human nature. After all, psychoanalysis discovered long ago that love "is" death, and that somewhere deep inside each man there is a hungry hunter desperately trying to keep up with the whirlwind of women who run with the wolves. In our popular culture the long-standing nature-versus-nurture controversy appears to have been all but resolved in favor of the call of the wild. This is, of course, a great convenience to our marketeers, for if sex as violence is truly "archetypal," why should the entertainment industry have any qualms about providing our nature with nurture?

Biology's renewed fascination with genetics disturbingly retraces the vicious configurations of early-twentieth-century sex and race theories. Until this *deus ex machina* of modern biology came along, human history had been cluttered with inconvenient, low-yield concepts such as "moral responsibility," "social concern," and "community." Since no one could quite figure out how to combine the subjective complexities of humane social behavior with the exigencies of getting ahead in the world, genetics came along at just the right time to show us that we are all helplessly caught in the molecular mechanics of primal drives. What better way to keep the qualms of humanism at bay? The conveniently mechanistic eugenicist premises of early-twentieth-century biology proved that inequalities of gender, race, and class were scientific absolutes rooted in the dynamic truths of species evolution. Absolutist minds breed absolutist solutions, just as our metaphors come to dictate our realities as soon as we forget that they are merely fanciful representations of the fictions in our minds.

The scientists of a century ago were as variegated a lot as they are today. Many had a complex and far more nuanced perspective than I will be able to convey in what follows. This is the chronicle of only *one*—though a very central—current in early-twentieth-century thinking. *Of course* there were opposing currents, and *of course* the ideas delineated here had their vociferous opponents. The idea-structure of Western culture was, as yet, anything but monolithic during the early years of this century. But in our rush to celebrate the "triumphs" of twentieth-century thought, we have tended to overlook the destructive facets of our inheritance. This book attempts to provide a counterbalance.

It also goes without saying that there is far more to the work of writers such as Joseph Conrad (or Fitzgerald, or Faulkner) than the antifeminine imagery highlighted here. At the same time it would be foolish to deny that the early-twentieth-century metaphors of sexual depredation these authors' works helped to legitimize were used to justify a wide range of monstrously inhuman political practices. In a similar fashion, sociologists and politicians used the scientists' subjectively determined findings to give their own tendentious arguments the flavor of "truth." No doubt scientists lose control over the public's perception of their findings in much the same way poets or artists do. But it is as irresponsible not to hold these scientists accountable for the implications of their theorems as it is to excuse the artist for the affective impact of the imagery s/he produces. My aim is to delineate a crucial facet of the psychosocial development of Western culture during the first thirty years of this century, and to show that the follies of scientific speculation can lead to social paranoia just as easily as the positive discoveries of science can serve to brighten our lives. Others, more qualified for that task than I am, will have to separate fact from fiction in the scientific research saga that turned nineteenth-century notions about man's "vital essence" into biology's subsequent fascination with "germ plasm" and today's scientific magic show of DNA.

Our actions in everyday life are guided by what we *assume* to be true in human experience—by speculation, not by scientific reality (except when reality happens to impinge directly on our ability to survive). The late twentieth century continues to exploit gender, class, and race conflict through its updating of the early-twentieth-century's fantasy-image of the vampire as a "medical" phenomenon (which, I shall demonstrate, always translates—even where it concerns seemingly heterosexual, nominally masculine figures such as Dracula—into the nineteenth century's male-generated image of *woman* as vampire). And though fragments of the theme of the vampire can be traced back to virtually the beginnings of recorded history, even the most "archetypically" focused historians of this predator must readily admit that it was not until the very end of the nineteenth century that the image of the vampire gained widespread currency in Western European and American popular culture. Our continued, and, it would seem, even increasing, fascination with the vampire as a creature of sexual depredation is a disconcerting indication of the renewed popularity of sadomasochistic concepts of sexual interaction. Our uncritical acceptance of this imagery as erotic rather than as abusive is a powerful indicator of the cynical disparities between official social policy and the destructive metaphors of the entertainment industry.

We need to change the nature and the quality of our fantasies before we can change the quality (as opposed to the fetishized desire-structures) of our social environment. In the end only our imagination can change the world, for our social reality is a product of the dreams and fears we hold in common. But fantasies are never linear. Dreams would not be dreams, nor would they have the power to make us act like monsters, if, in psychological terms, their origins were not vastly overdetermined. Still, once we become willing to recognize the ghosts of the past as the spectral imagery of our socialization rather than as the guardians of our predestined fate within nature, we can at last begin the daunting task of exorcising the vampires of misogyny and race-hatred from our infinitely variable imagination—that exasperating and exhilarating source of good and evil in the world.

Theda Bara, publicity still, ca. 1916–17
You are next: the vampire's appetite for public consumption.

I. THE LORDS OF CREATION
BATTLE THE VAMPIRES OF TIME

T all, delicate, and graceful, her loving eyes soft with pity, she stands in the doorway. The light of day embraces her as with a halo. Her mere presence radiates warmth into this dank and gloomy drawing room. Repelled and agonized by what she sees, but conscious only of the demands of love and duty, she rushes toward the stumbling, besotted figure of the man who was once, and therefore must forever be, her husband.

The man, his ability to stand alone long gone, shivers in a stupor of dark shame. Gently, yet strong in courage and determination, she helps him stand. Forgetting past maltreatment, and visibly grateful to be re-united with him, she at once becomes a pillar of pure strength and courage. Tears glisten in her gentle eyes. In the gloomy half-light that surrounds them, they embrace.

Firmly supporting the man within her angel wings, she slowly guides his trembling steps toward the open door—toward the wedge of light promising escape from this dark world of sin. But just before they reach that beckoning gateway to redemption, its radiance is blighted by a shadow.

In the doorway looms the Woman. Searing eyes, white sparks of fury in coal-black sockets, illuminate her ice-cold beauty. She is a creature scorched by livid sin. The force of her hypnotic gaze and her cool, possessive arrogance instantly drive the reeling forms of man and wife asunder.

When the Woman steps into the room, wedging herself between them, the wife recoils in horror from this unclean presence. The husband, left to his own uncertain footing, slumps helplessly against the wainscoting. Bravely the angel of mercy's radiant eyes confront the glaring stare of evil; "Pity him, leave him be," they beg wordlessly.

A brazen grin fires the harsh beauty of the worldly woman's features. Icy in her contempt, she glances at the slumping man. Then, sinuously, lasciviously, she walks toward him. As he sinks away in panic, she presses him into a corner, voluptuously curving her body against his. Utterly self-possessed, she leans her hands against the wall, trapping his head between them. Then, a cat no longer playing with her prey, her predatory face ablaze with hatred, she kisses him full on his mouth. The obscene pleasures of her lust etch themselves brutally into the yielding features of the man. The wife, devastated by the sight of so much sin, collapses.

Harsh, satanic laughter marks the triumph of the Woman. He who was once a man slips to his knees before her. He reaches out, and in abject, desperate submission, kisses her disdaining hand. Blinded by tears, the wife stumbles out of the darkened room into the light of day. The Woman grins again as she watches her flee. Once more the unruly tides of lust have triumphed over the sacred bonds of love.

This climactic scene from *A Fool There Was,* Theda Bara's extraordinary 1915 film debut, is nearly as chilling today as it must have been at the time of its first screening. Even in our environment of casual household eroticism, in which scenes of explicit sex are only as far as the nearest magazine rack or video store, the hateful predatory intensity of that kiss continues to be shocking beyond words.

In *A Fool There Was,* John Schuyler, a successful businessman, model husband, and pillar of the community, falls victim to the enticements of a calculating woman, played by Theda Bara, who throughout the film is identified only as "the Vampire." As the story unfolds, the Vampire efficiently strips Schuyler of judgment, restraint, dignity, financial acumen, and friends. Soon, however, she abandons him for a new beau, and he, broken and alone, a pitiful shadow of his former self, stumbles about drunkenly in his town house, abandoned and despised even by his once obsequious male secretary.

His spurned wife, Kate, meanwhile, has never flagged in her devotion to the man she married. Hopeful that someday he might recognize the error of his ways, she has kept herself occupied in her suburban mansion with the proper education of their adorable little daughter. She staunchly tolerates every slight to her own dignity. "Love often means a cross," she humbly instructs her daughter, who seems puzzled by the masochistic intricacies of grown-up behavior.

When, from a friend, Kate hears that the Vampire has left the man of her life for a younger victim, she knows exactly what she must do. "My place is with him," a title flashes. She goes to the town house, which her modesty and womanly virtue have forced her to shun until now. The subsequent dramatic confrontation between this angel of modern marriage and the sexual vampire of primordial chaos sent a chill of sheer horror through much of the world.

Audiences saw the vampire woman triumph with what must still be one of the most graphically sexual kisses ever recorded on screen. The scene's stark melodrama and silent intensity may have dated, but its visual power is undiminished. Clearly there continues to be a direct connection between the lurid, bestial intensity of that single kiss and our own lingering suspicions about the function of human sexuality in a civilized environment. This was not merely the bite of a fantasy vampire. Instead, it was an evocation of sexual intercourse as the deadly attack of a cannibalistic usurper. It showed vividly that to get involved with a sexual woman was equivalent to death itself.

It is difficult to imagine what the scene's effect must have been on an audience for whom the public spectacle of a woman kissing a man on the lips was still largely taboo. Even in books by physicians for physicians, descriptions of specific sexual practices were usually still written in Latin, so that only responsible professionals and men of comparable dignity might know what was being discussed. Film kisses, if there were any, tended to be restricted to pecks on the cheek or a very fleeting touch of lips. Theda Bara's brazen and prolonged depredation of this civilized man's mouth, therefore, was a violation of more than a dramatic taboo. In depicting a woman's absolute erotic power over a man, this kiss also became a violation of the principles of manhood itself: here was a woman who was, in essence, raping a man.

The scene climaxing in the vampire kiss was thus a filmic episode of extraordinary power in 1915 precisely because it was a shrewd exploitation of the dominant psychological currents of gender politics. No wonder the massive crowds who went to see the movie decided that they had discovered a true devil's disciple in the female lead. Though Theda Bara's debut was by no means the first filmic representation of the generic, erotic predator audiences of the period had come to hold responsible for the moral and social failure of middle-class males, the ferocious energy she brought to her role was destined to bring almost overnight currency to a new word in the English language. For "the Vampire" of *A Fool There Was* became a popular model for the characterization of all women who used their bodies as lures to attract able-bodied and financially secure males. To say "She's like the Vampire in *A Fool There Was*" provided far more information than the average moviegoer needed. "She's a vampire" did well enough. But Americans love to abbreviate anything with two or more syllables. Time is money, after all. Therefore, within a few months after the release of *A Fool There Was,* such women had come to be designated as "vamps."

Theda Bara's subsequent, oft-repeated, and highly influential screen performances as a sexual predator soon also made "vamping" into a widely recognized verb for antisocial feminine behavior of a sexual nature. Thus her actions gave a generic name as well as a new profession to the thousands of future cinematic vamps whose task it would be to crawl through screendom in dualistic opposition to the ever diminishing ranks of virginal heroines styled after Lillian Gish and Mary Pickford. Cinematic vamps came to lord it in very unequal fashion over the "virgin" wives of the filmic bourgeois household. The angels of domestic mercy whose task it was to tend lovingly to an unending procession of straying husbands were effectively relegated to the periphery of most screenplays, to make way for a new category of female predators eager to lead civilized men of business astray.

A Fool There Was had proved uniquely responsive to a wide range of gender, class, and socioeconomic preconceptions current in Western European and American culture during the time of its first release. The film offered a shrewd distillation of many of the period's most popular theses about the inherent nature of gender conflict. Evolutionary biologists, sociologists, economists, and physicians had all made it a point to emphasize the wondrous, but precarious, achievement of the civilized, highly acculturated white woman, the much lauded household nun who starred in the late-nineteenth-century male's dreams of domestic glory. A creature of magnificent self-negation, she was, precisely because of her high level of evolutionary development, constitutionally incapable of countering the depredations of the sexual woman, the stalking temptress, the destroyer of family fortunes, the pre-Bolshevik economic vampire of early-twentieth-century capitalist society.

A Fool There Was, Porter Emerson Browne's 1909 novelization of his highly successful Broadway drama of that same year, had virtually been written as if it were meant to be a movie script—which was not surprising, given the author's experience as a dramatist. Frank Powell, the shrewd actor-director of the 1915 film version, clearly recognized the cinematic nature of the book's descriptive passages, and followed Browne's narrative very closely when he came to revisualize John Schuyler's edifying fall for the screen. Browne's novel, filled with chatty authorial commentaries on his characters' every action, is an invaluable source of information about the social philosophy underlying the imagery of Powell's film.

Browne had made it absolutely clear to his readers that the pitiful male victim of his narrative was a member of America's most genetically privileged ruling class. From the outset he let them know that his story would trace the inevitable fate of those among this group who, through overconfidence or lack of moral vigilance, failed to adhere to the rules of continence in the crucial biological struggle between evolution and degeneration.

"Perhaps," Browne speculated in the opening paragraph of his novel (announcing himself as a committed evolutionist), the beginning of Schuyler's story should be set "a hundred years ago—perhaps a thousand—perhaps even ten thousand; and it may well be, yet longer ago, even, than that." Browne wanted his readers to know that the lamentable antihero belonged to the most remarkable evolutionary elite of Western civilization: "John Schuyler came from a long line of clean-bodied, clean-souled, clear-eyed, clear-headed ancestors; and from these he had inherited cleanness of body and of soul, clearness of eye and of head."

All these exemplary rosy-cheeked, well-scrubbed ancestors, "these honest, impassive Dutchmen and—women—these broad-shouldered, narrow-hipped English," had, Browne emphasized, done just about anything members of the ruling white race could do to make Schuyler the fittest of the fit in the "struggle for life": "They had amalgamated for him their virtues, and they had eradicated for him their vices; they had cultivated for him those things of theirs that it were well to cultivate; and they had plucked ruthlessly from the gardens of heredity the weeds and tares that might have grown to check his growth."

Schuyler, then, was the finest flower of Aryan manhood, cultivated in the era's Mendelian laboratories of genetic engineering. This future backslider grew up in "a big house—big in size—big in atmosphere—big in manner" on Fifth Avenue in New York City. He was, we are told, the child of intensely "upright," affluent parents, a family devoutly guided by the light of the world's most perfect economic system: the social Darwinism formulated by Herbert Spencer and popularized in the United States by William Graham Sumner, John Fiske, and a host of others. These writers on social and economic theory insisted that the principles of biological evolution proved that "natural selection" as an intuitive form of genetic engineering had made fundamental inequalities between races and social classes, even between men and women, not only a practical reality but an essential feature of the future evolution of the human race.

In his book *The Destiny of Man* (1884), Fiske, for instance, had argued that in highly evolved human beings the physical body was no more than a temporal vehicle for the immortal soul. But he gave this perfectly orthodox religious argument a new twist. The human brain, he insisted, was God's tool for the separation of the Good, the Bad, and the Ugly in the realm of evolution. The more rarified the human intellect, the closer it came to immortality. The brain was the storehouse of the soul. The more densely packed this storehouse became, the more certain its owner could be of his election to eternal life.

Thus the processes of evolutionary development were no longer a slow and laborious movement of species adaptation to environmental necessities. Instead, evolution had become a matter of urgent personal responsibility—an individual moral choice. It wasn't the shape of the casket that counted but what you put in it:

> In the human organism physical variation has well-nigh stopped, or is confined to insignificant features, save in the grey surface of the cerebrum. The work of cerebral organization is chiefly completed after birth, as we see by contrasting the smooth ape-like brain-surface of the new-born child with the deeply-furrowed and myriad-seamed surface of the adult civilized brain. (56–7)

The evolutionary superman should leave the body to its own devices: for "whereas in its rude beginnings the psychical life was but an appendage to the body, in fully-developed Humanity the body is the vehicle for the soul." (65)

Clearly those who spent much of their time on earth focused on the body had remained on a far lower level of evolutionary development than those who had cultivated their minds. Those who had failed to improve themselves on the "psychical" level had, therefore, in a very real sense, remained animals, and this had eliminated them from the competition for immortality. Such moral weaklings did not even deserve to be classified as human. Indeed, said Fiske, "in many respects the interval between the highest and the lowest men far surpasses quantitatively the interval between the lowest men and the highest apes." (71)

Arguments of this sort, which became extremely popular around the turn of the century, had done much to make "genetic" justifications of racial prejudice an integral part of late-nineteenth-century "scientific" truth. Fiske and numerous others helped make these ideas part of religious orthodoxy as well. Soon the exploitation of those who were "racially inferior" to "civilized man" ceased to be perceived as maltreatment of God's creatures, as earlier religious doctrine had maintained. It now came to be seen as a divinely willed punishment for those who had failed to make use of their God-given opportunity to better themselves: "Original sin," Fiske maintained, "is neither more nor less than the brute inheritance which every man carries with him, and the process of evolution is an advance toward true salvation." (103)

"Primitives"—poor whites, laborers, and peasants, as well as all the "mentally inferior" races—were clearly evil: their social inferiority was due to their sinful lack of concern for the preservation of their spiritual capital and their indulgence in the lewd pleasures of the body. This, in turn, proved them to be more like the animals than like "civilized" humanity. If, therefore, they were treated like animals, they were getting merely what they deserved for having failed to mortify their flesh.

In his best-selling novelization of *A Fool There Was,* Browne made it a point to follow his exposition of the evolutionary superiority of John Schuyler's ancestors with a scathing account of the frightful genetic sources of the Vampire, who was about to destroy his hero. The author was evidently certain that his readers would be fully aware of the scientific legitimacy of the theories of social Darwinism.

The Vampire, instead of having been born into the "clean" Anglo-Dutch stock of the American elite, came from the "noisome" environment of "a little hut on the black Breton coast." That location instantly made Browne think of ethnic cleansing: "In it it were perhaps better to die than to live," he remarked charitably. Signs of the inevitable genetic inferiority of the denizens of such a habitat were everywhere: scattered through the hovel in which the Vampire's mother lies dying are "a number of broken and greasy dishes, filled with fragments of food. And all about on the floor lay the litter of the sick-room." The absence of the inhabitants' genetic urge to utilize generous quantities of Dutch Boy cleanser is sadly evident.

The Vampire's mother, we are told, could have "been pretty once, in an animal way." The dying woman's own mother is also present and serves as her primitive nurse. She observes her daughter with "the sullen ferocity that is of beast rather than of man." In the midst of this middle-class nightmare we catch our first glimpse of the third generation of this degenerative peasant stock, the Vampire-to-be: "a little, pink, puling thing that whimpered and twisted weakly—a little, naked, thing half covered by roughly-cast sacking." (19–21)

Browne had neither sympathy nor hope for the potential economic and social improvement of "degenerates" of this sort. Their poverty was self-inflicted, a mark of their moral inferiority. Poverty bred filth, filth bred parasites, and parasites bred the Vampire. Browne was certain that the genetically privileged would automatically distinguish themselves from the chaff of humanity. They would pull themselves up by their own bootstraps, because their bootstraps were directly attached to a pulley in their evolving brains. You had to be smart, inventive, agile, better than the rest, on top of the heap, to be able to survive in the Darwinian world; those who made the most money thereby proved conclusively that they also had the densest, most evolved, most "concentrated," most elaborately "creased"—to use John Fiske's picturesque term—gray matter.

It was common among late-nineteenth-century intellectuals to think of the evolution of the human brain as a "distillation process." Fiske, like most of his contemporaries, measured human achievement in terms of the size and density of the brain: "The cranial capacity of the European exceeds that of the Australian by forty cubic inches, or nearly four times as much as that by which the Australian exceeds the gorilla." (48) The denser the brain, the more elaborate its "creases":

> The cerebral surface of a human infant is like that of an ape. In an adult savage, or in a European peasant, the furrowing is somewhat marked and complicated. In the brain of a great scholar, the furrows are very deep and crooked, and hundreds of creases appear which are not found at all in the brains of ordinary men. (49)

Such brilliant wrinkles in the development of the elite's cranial capacity were due to many centuries of rigorous genetic selection. The rich should not help the poor, for to do so would be tantamount to contaminating a superior gene pool with inferior matter. The elite should mingle only with other members of the elite, and let all others attempt to rise from the incoherent homogeneity of the mass of humanity by their own devices. The "simple but wasteful process of survival of the fittest, through which such marvellous things have come into being," (23) became for Fiske and his contemporaries a justification for even the most extreme forms of social depredation.

Indeed, the psychic growth of humanity was to a large extent dependent on evolutionary "warfare." Fiske had no doubt that in the long run humanity could reach perfection in this world. "The future is lighted for us with the radiant colours of hope. Strife and sorrow shall disappear. Peace and love shall reign supreme." (118) Ultimately prosperity would trickle down to all who survived the "desperate struggle for existence." (27)

But it was now time for "Man" to take over the reins from mother nature. Her methods of selection had been anything but foolproof to begin with, for they had been based, as Darwin had pointed out, more on woman's unreliable instinctive desire to choose the best available mate than on scientific, intelligent, masculine reason. The elite's revulsion from the "filth" of the "lower orders," so well exploited by Browne in his description of the squalor that had bred his vampire, had been the initial impetus in separating it from the mass, and had created a species of humanity instantly recognizable as both mentally *and* physically superior to all others.

Browne brought in a physician for the express purpose of emphasizing this point. Two of the elite's young men ("did you ever see better shoulders—better shaped heads—better carriages?") are interested in the same young woman ("the right sort—no frills, or airs, or bluffs. Sensible, natural"). As an evolutionary technician, the doctor is proud to see how they've all turned out: "If I'd have had a few more patients like them, I'd have starved to death long ago. Why, they didn't have even a single measle—not one whooping cough out of the lot." Though he dimly recognizes that romance might be a factor in deciding which of the boys should get the girl, he sees that as a mere detail: "As long as one of 'em marries her, that fixes it, doesn't it? And it doesn't make any difference which one; they're equally fine boys, both of 'em." (49)

Browne's point of reference for scenes such as this was the separate, and proudly unequal, world of turn-of-the-century social Darwinism. The future of evolution should no longer be entrusted to the imperfect administrative talents of nature. Instead, it had become the sole respon-

sibility of "Man." The spirit of God was in the decisions the evolutionary elite were making every day. "The destinies of all other living things
are more and more dependent upon the will of Man," (33) Fiske insisted. "Natural selection itself will by and by occupy a subordinate place
in comparison with selection by Man." (33–4) This made the evolutionary male the sole adjudicator of God's will in the world. In effect, it was
he who, having been gifted with God's greatest creation, the scientist's
infallible brain, must determine who should live and who should die.

To reach the pot of spiritual gold at the end of the evolutionary
rainbow, Fiske argued, it was essential that man concentrate on eradicating those elements within the human environment which kept him
from progressing toward his goal: "Man is slowly passing from a primitive social state in which he was little better than a brute, toward an ultimate social state in which his character shall have become so
transformed that nothing of the brute can be detected in it. The ape and
the tiger in human nature will become extinct." (103)

Words such as "eradication," "elimination," and "extinction" were
the stock-in-trade of the turn-of-the-century social Darwinist theorists.
A few decades later they would give shape to the genocidal ambitions of
Adolf Hitler and the Nazis. Porter Emerson Browne's novel set out to
show why it was needful for the elite to contemplate such drastic measures. His vampire lived to prey on the elite because the rules of separation had been breached in her conception. A product of miscegenation,
she was the misbegotten fruit of a tryst between the woman from the
hovel and a dissipated French aristocrat (a "latin," and hence not a member of the sturdy Anglo-Dutch elite, but "a bit too graceful . . . a bit too
well groomed" [23]—obviously a sensualist).

In setting up his drama of the warring factions of evolution and degeneration, Browne was following the thinking of William Graham
Sumner, the most influential American social theorist of the years
around 1900, and regarded by many of his contemporaries as an even
greater thinker than Herbert Spencer. Sumner is still generally acknowledged to be the "father" of American sociology. His 1907 study *Folkways,* long regarded as a classic of social anthropology, remained required
reading in university courses well into the 1970s.

Like Fiske, Sumner argued that nature was justly wasteful of those
who could not keep their heads above water in the struggle for existence. Science, not morality, was the key to a better future. His disdain
for the misguided concerns of lily-livered moralists was so fierce that he

makes today's hyper-right-wing social commentators seem like faint-hearted liberals.

Sumner's voice was quite self-consciously that of Wotan, the Norse God of War, the Exterminator, the Righteous Thunderer, who demanded human sacrifice in the name of Universal Order. The humanists' foolish attempt to mix "ethics into economics and politics, is utterly ignorant and mischievous," Sumner insisted; only policies "tested by all the criteria which science provides" were valid. (*Social Darwinism* [*SD*] 2) Americans needed to learn that there was a "great gulf between all the sentimental, ethical, humanitarian, and benevolent views about social matters and the scientific view of the same." (*SD* 4)

In 1909, the year of the first publication of *A Fool There Was,* Sumner, confident that his point of view had prevailed in the society around him, declared with ominous prescience that "the mores of the twentieth century will not be tinged by humanitarianism as those of the last hundred years have been." (*War and Other Essays* [*WOE*] 163) An elite corps of supermen engineered by evolutionary science would rule the world through vast personal economic and intellectual monopolies. Social inequality would be a sacred covenant that, if kept to religiously, would ultimately provide for the improvement of living conditions for all through the principles of trickle-down economics. However, "the dogma that all men are equal is the most flagrant falsehood and the most immoral doctrine which men have ever believed." (*Earth-Hunger* [*EH*] 362–3) The realities of evolution required that "masses of men who are approximately equal are in time exterminated and enslaved." (*Folkways* [*F*] 48)

Sumner was a vociferous advocate of nonmoral social expediency and economic opportunism. Humanism was a dirty word—not because it implied religious doubt, but because its values were community oriented and hence "anti-individualistic." Economic egotism was the will of God. The father of American sociology had an unshakable confidence in the practical superiority of all things new and improved, and he was cheered by the realization that "the mores of the latter half of the nineteenth century were marked by the decline of the dominion of the classical culture which had prevailed since the Renaissance." (*WOE* 158) The arts were for sissies and mama's boys—the accumulation of wealth was culture enough for him.

Sumner, in fact, considered anyone with an interest in traditional arts and crafts to be the victim of a primitive and unmanly voodoo mentality, for "in the minds of primitive people all which is archaic is sacred and all which is novel is questionable." (*F* 552) There was little one could learn from the past. "History is only the tiresome repetition of one story." The only thing it might teach a modern entrepreneur was how to avoid the stupid superstitions of past generations concerning the supposed values of altruism. Otherwise history was bunk. Sumner's resolute disdain for the past clearly set the tone for mainstream twentieth-century American values. He was the chief ideological engineer of the dominant patterns of later American social and economic thought.

A ruthless disregard for the well-being of others was, Sumner insisted, the only valid means to power in the world of evolutionary economics. War was the model for all forms of human advancement. In the struggle for life, whether for sheer physical survival or for the conquest of a commercial monopoly, the best of humanity would inevitably rise to the top. Therefore, "the assertion that all men are equal is perhaps the purest falsehood in dogma that was ever put into human language." (*SD* 12)

The emergence of the evolutionary elite had been a function of their ability to succeed over others in the struggle for life, and this, in turn, was clearly a direct result of their manly appetite for war. Compromise, concern for others, and humane thought were signs of weakness, a return to the effeminate concerns of more primitive minds. Sumner's social philosophy, though brutally materialistic, was a simple page out of the Puritan's Bible: hard work, frugality, and determination were his keys to success. "There is no boon in nature. All the blessings we enjoy are the fruits of labor, toil, self-denial, and study." (*SD* 111)

A Fool There Was, in its various incarnations as play, novel, and movie, provided a dramatic warning to the ruling class of early-twentieth-century America that it must not give in to the enticements of the flesh. Man must use the cross of capital accumulation to ward off the vampire of economic dissipation, and chant "*apage Satana*" to her erotic blandishments. Men such as John Schuyler, Browne suggested, had been brought up in a world so perfect, so ideally balanced between ambitious men and compliant women, that they had lost their will to fight: their insulation from the conflicts of the jungle had softened their will, had "feminized" them, and had thus made them vulnerable to the lewd enticements of the sexual woman, that vampire of nature nourished by the degenerate lusts that had kept back the lower orders of organized society.

The weakling males of *A Fool There Was* are, to be sure, sexual toys to the Vampire, but first and foremost they are the fools of economic dissipation. Their lack of continence in the erotic realm is of concern to us primarily because it causes them to bleed in economic terms. The movie makes this point in a particularly dramatic fashion very early on. We are shown the Vampire in her apartment. Having just awakened, she stretches, catlike, to remind us of her animal nature. She is brought the newspaper by a servant. In it she reads that "John Schuyler, wealthy lawyer and statesman," has been appointed special presidential envoy to Britain. Discovering that he is to sail the next day "on the 'Gigantic,' " she rudely orders her servants about (she is, after all, only a woman of the people, and therefore knows little about the proper etiquette of master-servant relationships). Still in her nightgown, loose-fitting (and hence suggestive of undisciplined freedom), she throws some things in a suitcase. It is our first good look at the Vampire: high cheekbones, sunken cheeks, dark, eerie eyes—a voluptuous body, dangerous.

Suddenly a man rushes in. He is still young, but he looks like someone ravaged by the agonies of age. Though tall and handsome, he seems stunted. Once, no doubt, he was wealthy; the elegant cut of his unpressed clothes tells us that. He rushes to the Vampire, who stands before him with an air of regal authority. But, uncorseted, she seems oddly vulgar, even in comparison to the distraught young man. He: "You have ruined me, you devil, and now you discard me!" She moves toward him and hangs her arm onto his shoulder, casually. It is an almost masculine gesture. Among men it would have signified the familiarity of friend to friend. Here, however, it is a clear gesture of ownership. She embraces him, consoles him, promises not to leave. There is wild abandon in their kiss. Then suddenly, she seems flustered, indisposed. Clearly she wants to be rid of him. Reluctantly, at her bidding, he leaves. Grimacing at him behind his back, the vampire finds his wallet on the floor, examines it closely, and sees that it is filled with money. Demonic laughter distorts her beautiful face and turns her dark eyes into flashing sparks. In theaters everywhere males watching the film no doubt checked to see whether their own wallets were still in their pockets.

A scene or two later we are dockside. The Vampire steps out of her cab. A man, crabbed, hunched over, miserable, skinny, and, quite literally dirt-poor, accosts her: "See what you made of me, and still you prosper, you hell cat!" She grins and calls a policeman. The poor man is chased away while the Vampire saunters to the ship, her long satin gown flashing like a peacock's tail. As her broken victim stumbles away, another cab races up. The walletless lover stumbles out. The beggar shouts to him: "I might have known you'd follow her, Parmalee! Our predecessor, Van Dam, rots in prison through her! Look what she has done for me—look what she is doing to you!"

One woman, so many economic fools! The Vampire walks on, a big smirk of triumph on her face. She totes one of the giant roses emblematic of the obscene sexual prowess of this man-eating woman. Unconcerned, she walks onto the ship for her self-appointed rendezvous with John Schuyler, wealthy lawyer and statesman, doting husband, model father, leading member of the Anglo-Dutch Aryan-American evolutionary elite, and future victim of this vampire emanating from the lower orders.

In the cinematic world dominated by William Graham Sumner's conceptions about the nature of human relationships, men such as Schuyler and Parmalee merely got what they deserved within the natural order of things, for they had broken the first rule of monopoly capitalism: they had sought to share pleasure with another. The most extremist conception of the self as private property had fueled Sumner's disdain for the concept of equality. The concept of self and the concept of sharing formed an insurmountable, universal dichotomy, as fundamental as the differences between men and women. What weaklings such as Schuyler did not realize was that any form of social sharing— whether economic, sexual, or even merely emotional—was a subversion of the most basic principle of evolution: "The unlucky will pull down the lucky. That is all that equality ever can mean. The worst becomes the standard." (*SD* 113)

Any attempt, therefore, whether public or private, to help the strugglers for existence escape the hardships of survival simply brought out the worst in humanity. Even to offer charity was to give in to prostitution, for to share one's money was to squander one's manhood: "A drunkard in the gutter is just where he ought to be. . . . Gambling and less mentionable vices all cure themselves by the ruin and dissolution of their victims." (*SD* 267–8)

Social pleasure was a betrayal of evolutionary necessity: "All of us are only more or less idle, vicious, and weak. We all have to fight the same temptations, and each one has enough to do to fight his own battle." (*EH* 97) Only those who stood the test of steely self-control by ignoring the expiring bodies of others had Sumner's wholehearted approval: "The achievements of the human race have been accomplished by the *elite* of the race; there is no ground at all in history for the notion that the masses of mankind have provided the wisdom and done the work." After all, "only the elite of any society, in any age, think."

(*F 206*) *Homo sapiens* must use the bodies of the cranial homunculi littering the gutters of the cities as stepping-stones to the light.

This was a principle certainly not lost on Sumner's European contemporaries. The German proto-fascist artist Fidus, for instance, in a design for a book cover, demonstrated to the thinking man of his time the proper form for such an ascension. The stepping-stones Fidus's evolutionary male was determined to hold underfoot were importunate, grasping, naked women, sexual women, vampires, primitives—outwardly enticing creatures who had crawled out of the hovels of the working class, determined to stand in the way of the advancing male.

Fidus (Hugo Höppener, 1868–1948),
design for a book cover, ca. 1910
How to cope with feminine temptation
while striving for the light

They were, as such, the unwitting storm troops of socialism. Sumner made the link between the "erotic" mentality and socialism quite clear. Most people, he emphasized, "are subjects of passion, emotion, and in-stinct. Only the *elite* of the race has yet been raised to the point where reason and conscience can even curb the lower motive forces. For the mass of mankind, therefore, the price of better things is too severe, for that price can be summed up in one word: self-control." (*What Social Classes Owe to Each Other* [*WSC*] 65) Inevitably those who failed would attempt to find succor in the bosom of socialism, a system that, Sumner was convinced, had been designed to glorify human weakness.

Socialism was like a "third sex"—an offense against nature and sci-ence alike—neither truly male nor truly female, an attempt to suspend the fundamental gender dichotomy established by the evolutionary ad-vance. It was as much a subversion of the feminine spirit of dutiful re-productive service as an assault upon the "virile," creative will of the male. Any attempt to establish a dialectical synthesis of these two funda-mentally opposed principles signaled a first step toward the total collapse of civilized society, for only "social degeneration" could be the result of "the decline of virile virtues." (*F* 106)

Women such as the Vampire of *A Fool There Was* were, in their bla-tant sexuality, clearly masculinized creatures, predators hiding in women's bodies, social degenerates: socialists. There was an immediate parallelism between a man's sexual history and his social fate. Capital was the vital essence of society: "Civilization is built on capital; it is all the time using up capital; it cannot be maintained, unless the supply of cap-ital is kept up." (*SD* 36) "Every bit of capital, therefore, which is given to a shiftless and inefficient member of society who makes no return for it is diverted from a reproductive use." (*WOE* 248) To waste capital on the poor and the vicious was to squander the lifeblood of civilization—was to let a vampire steal your vital energy.

Hence it was pointless to try to save the Schuylers of the world. "Al-most all legislative effort to prevent vice is really protective of vice, be-cause all such legislation saves the vicious man from the penalty of his vice. Nature's remedies against vice are terrible. She removes the victims without pity." In the promulgation of vicious temptations within a highly developed civilization, nature had, in effect, set up a "self-cleansing" mechanism. Only those already predisposed to vice would be susceptible to its temptations. Hence only the weak could fall victim to vice, and any man with vicious habits deserved what he got. Nature had established an efficient "process of decline and dissolution by which she removes things which have survived their usefulness." (*WOE* 252)

However, there was good reason to prevent the vampires of social-ism and mob rule from invading the hallowed grounds of the ruling class. The lower orders should be dominated ruthlessly. The concept of liberty was a product of evolutionary civilization, Sumner maintained, and therefore was a principle that made sense "only for the rich." (*SD* 40) To protect the freedom of the economic elite, Sumner, the strict laissez-faire evolutionary libertarian who otherwise despised any regula-tory interference of government in the accumulative efforts of individ-ual men, saw a useful purpose for even the harshest forms of social legislation. There could be "no liberty but liberty under the law. Law does not restrict liberty; it creates the only real liberty there is—for lib-erty in any real sense belongs only to civilized life and to educated men." (*SD* 53)

Liberty as the exclusive right of those who had power over others was a core principle of the turn-of-the-century international system of economic imperialism. Race stratification was the result of scientifically identifiable, constitutional defects in the mental and physical endow-ment of those not part of the evolutionary elite. (The term "genetic in-feriority" was to come into common usage only after the convenient and timely "rediscovery," in 1900, of the botanist Gregor Mendel's laws of heredity by Hugo de Vries and others.)

Fundamental constitutional inequalities, identified by the level of performance of various races in the evolutionary struggle to reach fi-nancial (and hence spiritual) dominance, had established the inalienable right of the fittest to dominate all others by whatever means necessary—be it intimidation, violence, or extermination: "There can be no rights against nature, except to get out of her whatever we can, which is only the fact of the struggle for existence stated over again." (*WOE* 257)

The fittest had transcended the realm of nature altogether through steel-edged self-control and strict adherence to the principles of human science. Nature, the realm of the emotions, of waste, and of mob rule, had become an obstructive force to the further flowering of civilization. The social Darwinists despised Rousseau and all Romantic notions of nature as a gentle nurturer. As Edgar Rice Burroughs was to show in the October 1912 issue of *All Story* magazine, when he created the figure of Tarzan, only a white member of the evolutionary elite could still be seen as a "noble" savage. When Sumner urged the evolutionary ape-men of capitalism to plunder nature and "to get out of *her*" (italics added) whatever they could, he was not simply using a conventional anthropomorphic figure of speech; he was using this gender-specific designation quite deliberately. For as everyone knew, woman and nature were one. If nature was the enemy, then the enemy was woman (at least in her natural state) and everything identified with her.

At the turn of the century only inferior minds could have questioned the absolute truth of the first law of evolution: that men were the lords of creation, and women a lower order of humanity—volatile, emotional, reproductive tools of nature's chaotic, and hence wasteful, efforts to keep life going at all cost. Woman, the feminine principle of nature, was the thief of progress. She was interested only in quantity, in species survival, in maintaining life in all its forms. She had no interest in "quality," in the "virile," elitist principles of the evolutionary advance. She made time stagnate and drained the energy from the upward thrust of manly achievement. But, as Henri Bergson argued, progress was movement, change, action. Therefore the feminine principle, nature, woman, was the vampire of time.

The "lower orders" of humanity were inferior because they had not been able to shed the dominance of the feminine principle in their mental and physical constitution. In them this feminine principle manifested itself as indecision, logical inconsistency, sentimentality, volatility, and a lack of concern with time—which was nothing but a constitutional incapacity for scientific thought. Worst of all, and most directly indicative of the dominance of the feminine in their nature, was their obsession with the reproductive functions of the body—with the frivolities of eroticism.

Because the feminine principle was so intent upon maintaining life at all cost, it was directly obstructive to the evolutionary advance. The masculine principle alone was creative. No man who considered himself to be among the fittest, Sumner argued, should feel even the slightest guilt while engaging in the economic plunder of less evolved members of the human community:

> We are rebuked for the wrongs of the aborigines, the vices of civilization, the greed of traders, the mistakes of missionaries, land-grabbing, etc., yet we Americans and others are living today in the enjoyment of the fruits of these wrongs perpetrated a few years ago. The fact is, as history clearly shows, that the extension of the higher civilization over the globe is a natural

process in which we are all swept along in spite of our ethical judgments. Those men, civilized or uncivilized, who cannot or will not come into the process will be crushed under it. (*WOE* 272)

Such considerations led Sumner with chilling consistency to thoughts of eugenics and genocide.

The sociologist is often asked if he wants to kill off certain classes of troublesome and burdensome persons. No such inference follows from any sound sociological doctrine, but it is allowed to infer, as to a great many persons and classes, that it would have been better for society, and would have involved no pain to them, if they had never been born. (*WOE* 187)

Sumner's "scientifically based" racist formulations spoke with special force to his contemporaries, who were only too happy to shed the burden of humanist social theory in favor of the "natural inequalities" of evolutionist thought. In 1898 Sumner himself commented on the remarkable change in public sentiment he had witnessed in recent years toward issues of race: "For thirty years the negro has been in fashion. He has had political value and has been petted. Now we have made friends with the Southerners. They and we are hugging each other. We are all united. The negro's day is over. He is out of fashion." (*WOE* 328) Sumner used the burgeoning racism among America's middle, lower-middle, and skilled laboring classes to emphasize his antihumanist position and to play to the sympathies of the middle-class male, whom Sumner regarded as the "forgotten man," the indispensable backbone of the nation.

The change of attitude toward blacks that Sumner identified as having taken shape during the last thirty years of the nineteenth century ran parallel to the change of attitude toward women that was taking place throughout European and American society during that same period. Indeed, Sumner encouraged his readers at every turn to draw direct parallels between racial inferiority and the dominance of "feminine" characteristics. Even by being merely passive, the "dregs" of society and the non-Aryan "barbarians" who encircled the camp of the evolutionary elite were likely to have a negative influence on American society: "The penalty of ceasing an aggressive behavior toward the hardships of life on the part of mankind is, that we go backward. We cannot stand still." (*WSC* 60) Like women, the inferior races were vampires of time. Respect for individual achievement, as manifested by private property—the sign of manly fitness—was rarely a feature of the barbarian's constitutional makeup: "Primitive races regarded, and often now regard, appropriation as the best title to property," (*WSC* 60) he warned. Races low on the evolutionary scale could be counted on to attempt to sap the strength of the evolutionary elite by appealing to the sentimentalist side of civilized society. The capitalist elite must maintain eternal vigilance against the primitive humanist appeals of these degenerate segments of American culture. "Where population has become chronically excessive, and where the population has succumbed and sunk, instead of developing energy enough for a new advance, there races have degenerated and settled into permanent barbarism." (*WSC* 55)

The parallelism between "the feminine principle," sexuality, "barbarism," and "degeneration" implicit in Sumner's thinking provides a very precise key to the ideological significance, and hence the prescriptive narrative content, of both the novel and the film of *A Fool There Was*. Browne's narrative was a particularly instructive parable about the economic responsibilities of the ruling class, and of the subversive force of the "regressive" feminine principle aligned against the evolutionary male.

The screen version, in particular, became a bellwether of popular sentiment, as is indicated by the simple fact that it was responsible for introducing several words and phrases that remain in common usage. Even today Hollywood and popular culture are overrun by "vamps." As a verb, "to vamp" came to be used to describe the sundry predatory activities of man-hungry women, and the phrase "Kiss me, my fool!"—with which Theda dispatched her victims—became a favorite line in the repertoire of several generations of pop-culture wits.

In Browne's original those words were almost as heavily weighted with ideology and politics as the Vampire's final kiss itself. Her arrogant order was a witch's incantation permitting the feminine principle to call up and command whatever degenerative, self-destructive impulses still remained within the evolutionary male. Frank Powell, in his screen version, demonstrated how well he understood the importance of this scene by using Browne's text almost unchanged as a shooting script.

The scene in question immediately follows the Vampire's walk past the wrecks of her discarded lovers before boarding the ocean liner on which Schuyler, her next victim, is to sail to Europe. The camera shows us that wealth abounds on the deck of this mobile playground of the evolutionary elite, who are unaware that they are about to set sail with a pestilent monster on board. We witness a scene happily abustle with friends toasting friends. Among these Parmalee, the Vampire's most recently depleted victim, moves with slinking gait, eyes looking out, as Browne describes him, "from hollows in his face. His cheeks were sunken. His lips were leaden." He is a broken man, but still a man, seeking retribution.

> Coming down the deck was a woman, a woman darkly beautiful, tall, lithe, sinuous. Great masses of dead black hair were coiled about her head. Her cheeks were white; her lips very red. Eyes heavy lidded looked out in cold, inscrutable hauteur upon the confusion about her. She wore a gown that clung to her perfectly-modelled figure—that seemed almost a part of her being. She carried, in her left arm, a great cluster of crimson roses.

Almost exactly twenty years later, in 1936, James M. Cain—a young man of twenty-three when the movie version of *A Fool There Was* first appeared—must have had this scene in mind when, on the final page of his novel *Double Indemnity*, he described the climactic appearance of his own economic vampire, Phyllis Nirdlinger, woman of death:

> She's made her face chalk white, with black circles under her eyes and red on her lips and cheeks. She's got that red thing on. It's awful-looking. It's just one big square of red silk that she wraps around her, but it's got no armholes, and her hands look like stumps underneath it when she moves them around.

Theda Bara's Vampire clearly was to have a terrifying reach—one that even today threatens us through every new "film noir" release based on the pulp-fiction principles of the middle years of this century.

In both the novel and the film of *A Fool There Was,* we see how Browne's "very old young man," Parmalee, his body trembling, racked by an inner fever, drawn as by a magnet and gaining sudden force, moves rapidly toward the Vampire.

> "You thought you'd throw me over," were the words that tore from his shrivelled lips, "but it won't work—you Vampire!"

Swiftly, he tore from his right hand the handkerchief that covered it. There was in it a revolver. The bright mouth of the weapon sprang to the white forehead of The Woman.

Yet she did not start—she made no sound, no movement. The smile still dwelt upon her lips. It was only in the eyes that a difference came—in the black, inscrutable eyes. They gleamed now, heavy-lidded as before. Their gaze was fixed straight into the sunken, hate-lit eyes of the man before her, a man who, but for her, might still have been a boy. She bent forward a little. Her forehead, between the eyes, was now touching the bright muzzle of the weapon. The finger on the trigger trembled—trembled but did not pull.

Came slowly, sibilantly, from between the smiling red lips:

"Kiss me, My Fool!"

Her eyes still fixed him. The hand holding the revolver trembled more violently. Slowly the mouth of the weapon sank to lips—to chin—to breast. It hovered there a moment, just over the heart—the finger twitched a little—twitched but did not pull. It was a finger governed by a vanished will in a shrivelled brain.

Then, suddenly, the revolver leaped—the finger pulled. With a shrill screech of hopeless, hideous imprecation, a shriek that died still-born, the bullet pierced flesh and bone and brain; and that which had been a man that should have been a boy, lurched drunkenly and lay a crumpled nothing upon the deck. There was blood upon the deck—beside the hem of the crimson gown, near to the crimson heel of her shoe. And the gown was caught beneath the body of the boy that was.

She looked down upon him. The smile not even yet had left her lips. With a lithe movement, infinitely graceful, she drew away, disengaging the hem of her crimson garment. A crimson petal from the great cluster in her arms fell upon it, to lie upon the hollow whiteness of the upturned cheek. And that was all. (111–14)

It was a classic scene—an archetypal cinematic set piece. The audiences of the play that had been one of Broadway's biggest hits of 1909, the many readers of Browne's novelization of that play, and the millions of viewers who came to thrill to Theda Bara's evil nature in *A Fool There Was* never forgot its chilling impact. Powell, in his screen imagery, had followed Browne's description step by step. As a result, for decades to come, timid young women, giggling with embarrassment and probably not even aware any longer of the origin of the words they were using, would draw their hesitant lovers to them with the Vampire's words on their lips. Modifying the famous quote, and thereby unconsciously softening its proprietary intent, they would murmur: "Kiss me, you fool!" By doing so they could feel appropriately outrageous, more than a little sinful, and most certainly aroused by the thought of the seductive power popular myth attributed to them. In *The Beautiful and Damned* (1922) F. Scott Fitzgerald disparagingly described one of his minor characters, Muriel, as trying to "resemble Theda Bara, the prominent motion picture actress. People told her constantly that she was a 'vampire,' and she believed them. She suspected hopefully that they were afraid of her, and she did her utmost under all circumstances to give the impression of danger." (83)

The social impact of the scene of Parmalee's suicide in *A Fool There Was,* then, illustrates the powerful influence the movies can have on our sense of social relationships   how we recast our world even without knowing it by subtly shifting our views to accommodate the "reality" of what we see on-screen. Clearly, what this scene did better than anything comparable in earlier movies was to bring popular currency to the intellectuals' contention that constitutionally—genetically—the sexual woman was no more than a tool of the forces aligned against evolution, a predatory animal, "a woman who is beast turning human" and who was therefore no more than "the infected carrier of the past," as, in 1936, Djuna Barnes was to put it in *Nightwood* (37). The sexual woman, the scene taught millions of viewers, was an actual vampire whose depredations meant death to the evolutionary male.

Browne had emphasized that point directly in his text. The family friend, upon noticing Schuyler's fascination with the woman of death, tries to stave off the inevitable by asking him if he has read Rudyard Kipling's poem "The Vampire" (1897, the acknowledged inspiration for Browne's narrative): " 'Why, yes, of course,' returned Schuyler. 'Almost everyone's read that.' " The Vampire's soon-to-be next victim thereupon conveniently recites the first few lines of the poem for those readers whose memory was a little rusty:

> *A fool there was, and he made his prayer,*
> *(Even as you and I)*
> *To a rag and a bone and a hank of hair.*

We called her the woman who did not care.
But the fool, he called her his Lady Fair—

The family friend, pointing dramatically to a pool of Parmalee's blood still on the deck, now completes his exposition of Browne's Sumner-inspired social message:

> "There's the fool," he nodded toward the drying spot upon the deck. "And there," he indicated, with a backward toss of his wellshaped head, the corridor down which had passed the woman, "is his lady fair. I've even heard," he went on, "that she used to call him her 'fool,' quoting the poem. Pretty little conceit, eh?" His jaw, firm, square, set tight. Then, with a touch of deeper feeling. "She murdered that boy just as surely as if she had cut his throat; and the worst of it is that she can't be held legally guilty—morally, yes, guilty as sin; but legally——" He shook his head. "The laws that man makes for mankind are a joke." (130–31)

Who could be more Aryan than this family friend with his well-shaped head and his square jaw? Who could possibly question his forceful implication that a well-ordered society should not hesitate to exterminate such vermin as this vampire emanating from the lower orders to wreak havoc among the evolutionary elite—this murderous, regressively sexual woman? Who could question the suggestion of Browne's melodrama that the sexual urge so crudely exhibited by the lower orders must be forcibly controlled? Certainly not Frank Powell, and his boss, the (at this time still rather minor) movie producer William Fox. Fox and Powell had succeeded in identifying so closely with both Browne's ideological intentions and the general public's preoccupations that the success of their movie adaptation, in the very year of its first release, provided the producer with enough capital to establish the Fox Film Corporation—which, twenty years later, in a famous merger, became 20th Century-Fox. (This complex pattern of influence and exploitation prefigured the chameleonic sequence of multimedia mergers that today often rewards those whose fantasies speak with particular force to the public's largely unarticulated social and economic concerns.)

Clearly, then, like all such phenomena of popular culture, *A Fool There Was* had an ideological importance far beyond its surface function as an entertainment. It was a crucial early-twentieth-century weapon in the struggle for the hearts and minds of the American middle class, a prime example of how the predatory economic principles of Sumner and his followers were absorbed into the everyday experiences of average folk.

Most of Sumner's observations about women and the family had been written during the first decade of the century, and they were collected for general publication at virtually the same time as Browne's 1909 novelization of his Broadway hit. Sumner, as the acknowledged leader of American social and political thought, and revered as such by most of his contemporaries, undoubtedly articulated the opinions of the majority of educated American males concerning the role of women in society. It is therefore no coincidence that Browne's melodrama should have been virtually a direct dramatization of those ideas.

Sumner cautioned his readers not to assume that the privileged, protected position women had obtained in the civilized world as helpless and weak creatures unable to cope with the tensions of masculine economic and social aggression was one that had prevailed throughout history. Indeed, it was a common mistake to think that primitive women had been physically inferior to the male. There was ample anthropological evidence to suggest that they might once even have been the stronger sex. Their misery was due to their "inferiority in the struggle for existence on account of maternity." (*WOE* 44–6) Woman's subjection to her reproductive function had made her destined to be enslaved forever to the will of man. Thus, in historical terms, the issue was one of divergent aptitudes rather than of unequal strength.

The weakness and helplessness of civilized women was, in fact, a wonderful side effect of the processes of evolution. The more primitive the social environment, the more its women were likely to exhibit independence and strength. The continuing barbarism of the lower races was to a large extent due to their inability to avoid what Sumner had designated as "sex-vice"—their invidious enjoyment of sexual relations beyond such as were necessary to produce the next generation. Sexual pleasure had sapped their will to advance. Civilized societies had been wise to eliminate all emphasis on such wasteful indulgences by stressing the reproductive duty of woman, and by turning her into a highly specialized—and hence, in genetic terms, an also particularly highly evolved—organism.

Like most of the intellectuals of his time, Sumner was convinced that Darwin had established once and for all that men and women were fundamentally different. Darwin had pointed out that humanity had evolved from primitive organisms that contained within themselves both male and female sexual characteristics. The first step on the road to human civilization had been taken when these bisexual organisms had given way to species in which the sexual functions had been separated— a brilliant move on the part of nature, which through this development for the first time had acted according to the principles of functional specialization by permitting the two genders to develop the patterns of behavior to which each was best suited.

As with everything in nature, these developments were slow and imperfect, leaving the various organisms plenty of possibility for reversion to earlier, more primitive patterns of sexual behavior. But slowly, over the course of hundreds of thousands of years, the precisely defined, separate existential responsibilities of the human male and female had established themselves as ironclad laws of nature, and as civilization had progressed, humanity had learned to distinguish efficiently between what belonged to man and what to woman in the world. This was unquestionably due in large part to a phenomenon Darwin had pointed to in his *Origin of Species*. "Peculiarities" developed by one sex, and supportive of their survival as the fittest of their species in the struggle for existence, would "become hereditarily attached to that sex." (93) In other words, "maleness" and "femaleness" could be characterized within the evolutionary master plan as exponentially developing and ever more decisively diverging essential functions.

Sumner and many of his contemporaries, as a result, religiously emphasized the idea that the closer a species came to reaching perfection, the greater, too, would become the *divergence,* within that species, of the primary qualities that defined a person as male or as female. "According to the current applications of the evolution philosophy," Sumner stressed in *Folkways,* quoting the British physician Harry Campbell, " 'inheritable characters peculiar to one sex show a tendency to be inherited chiefly or solely by that sex in the offspring.' " (*F* 344)

Evolution, therefore, made an ever widening gap between the roles of men and women in society inevitable. The more civilized the male, the more economically aggressive, assertive, and individualized he would be. A woman proved herself to be part of the crown of creation by being as passive, malleable, and focused on motherhood as she could possibly be.

In *The Descent of Man* Darwin had already pointed out that while men were forever driven by the urge to create, the urge to expend en-

ergy to overcome opposition, women were governed only by the passive, instinctive compulsion to re-create, to reproduce, to repeat themselves, until the end of time. Woman was, therefore, for good reason, the
enemy of time. The closer women came to ideal femininity, the more
retentive of the status quo—and hence also the more hostile to
change—they became. That was why they were instinctively averse to
conflict, as well as gregarious, uncritical, and anti-individual, intent
upon gathering and breeding rather than upon entering into competition for anything other than the attention of men. A woman's hostility
toward other women had only one motive: to protect her own reproductive efficiency or that of the female offspring she had produced.

Sumner, like most of his contemporaries, accepted these principles
as natural laws, and everything he had to say about the status of women or
the family and social change in his exploration of "folkways" was based
on this demarcation of the functions of the two genders and their consequently very divergent potentialities and limitations in society. Although
he was too sophisticated to be blatantly gender specific in the majority
of his pronouncements, his underlying assumptions about the conflict-
ing instinctual motivations of men and women inform every aspect of
his worldview. He was not even sure that one should consider men and
women to be part of the same species. "The sexes differ so much in
structure and function, and consequently in traits of feeling and character, that their interests are antagonistic," he insisted. (F 345) The battle of
the sexes was, for Sumner, a simple and unchangeable fact of nature.

In the very distant past, at the very dawn of civilization, Sumner
said, women had not only been the equals of men; they had been in
charge of the family unit as well. As a result, they had, in effect, controlled primitive society. During this dark period, human motivations
had been governed by the principle of "woman-descent." The world
had stagnated during this period.

> This much can be said with confidence about the family under
> woman-descent: it was the conservative institution of that form
> of society and in it traditions were cherished and education was
> accomplished. It did not encourage change or cherish reforms,
> but preserved what had been inherited and protected what
> existed. (WOE 48)

As a model early-modernist intellectual, Sumner, as we have seen,
regarded "tradition" as a dirty word and saw education as a waste of

time unless it led directly to knowledge that was of immediate use in the "struggle for existence." A classical education, with its effeminate emphasis on idealism and altruism, was rubbish. Civilization was finally shaking off the shackles of its feminine past. By getting rid of humanist sentimentalism and traditional values, society had finally cleared the way "for the dominion of materialistic standards and ideals." (*WOE* 158)

The gender-specific subtext underlying the cultural dualism of Sumner's reasoning thus begins to reveal itself. A culture that was humane and egalitarian in focus, that set stock in tradition and emphasized a wide-ranging education in the arts rather than a narrow focus on practical and immediately marketable skills, was static and effeminate. Its cultural preoccupations were a holdover from the "pre-evolutionary" dawn of a civilization still paralyzed by matriarchy—by "woman-rule"—and hence such weakling concerns should be eradicated in the muscular universe of monopoly capitalism that was getting set to shape the future of man.

In Sumner's mind socialism, with its concern for the underdog, its emphasis on an egalitarian society, and its advocacy of community values, was clearly the archetypal example of a primitive cultural concept, a leftover from the dark ages of effeminate humanism, a product of the barbaric world of "woman-rule." He was convinced that the shift from matriarchy to patriarchy, "the change from mother-family to father-family," had been "by far the greatest and most important revolution in the history of civilization." (*WOE* 49) It had turned stasis into progress. Sumner wrote *Folkways,* his most ambitious and most famous book, largely to prove the validity of this axiom. Had men not been able to struggle out from under the yoke of femininity, the world today would still be caught in the unproductive communal life of that distant past when men and women lived side by side "on an equality of personal rights." (*WOE* 47)

The progressive separation of men and women into different species had made the ascendancy of the male a foregone conclusion. It had been man's reward for his revolt against the static collectivism of matriarchy. The male's indomitable will to order and individual expression had led to the invention of progress: "Our ways of property, inheritance, trade and intercourse have all been created by or adjusted to the system of man-descent. We can see what a great revolution had to be accomplished to go over from woman-descent to man-descent."

Sumner remained remarkably uncommunicative about the details of

this revolution, but he hints that it was accomplished when the male finally took control over his mate's unbridled reproductive profligacy and
began to husband the family's economic resources in a constructive and
creative fashion. To illustrate what would otherwise have remained the
fate of man, he sketched out a lurid tale of masculine sexual woe among
the Iroquois under woman-rule: "A husband had to satisfy not only his
wife, but all her female relatives if he was to be in peace and comfort."
No wonder, then, that any society in which the mother-family continued to hold sway exhibited signs of masculine weakness and racial degeneracy. For in such societies men had failed to assert their natural
evolutionary primacy and had succumbed to sensualism instead: "They
accept custom and tradition and make the best of it as they find it."
(*WOE* 46–50) In a world guided by equality between the sexes, even the
inverted harem arrangements of the Iroquois were likely to be reinsti-
tuted. It was a thought that apparently gave Sumner and his contemporaries many sleepless nights.

A *Fool There Was* dramatized John Schuyler's submerged but not yet
properly conquered "effeminate" sensual weakness: his regressive inability to ward off the degenerative incursions of the sexual vampire of
matriarchy. Obviously this otherwise exemplary member of the evolutionary elite had become far too dependent on the humane feminine
impulses personified by his wife. The nuclear family was evolution's
greatest invention, but only if man and wife both knew their place.

Certainly there can be no question that Schuyler's Kate is a model
heroine of divergent gender evolution. She is as passive and tractable as
any man could require his wife to be. She is modest ("her voice was low
and deep, and very soft"), infantile ("she was like her child grown up,
glorified into womanhood"), and concerned only with her husband and
daughter (in that order). In short, she is "the perfect figure of perfect
womanhood." She therefore cannot be at fault—Schuyler himself is to
blame, for he has allowed himself to be drawn too far into the realm of
the "mother-family." As a result, Schuyler's masculine mettle, his will to
fight, has been weakened.

Though "agile, alert, thrilling with vitality and virility," Schuyler
has become weak in ambition: his family has become his only universe.
To a friend he admits: "My world is right here; and it's all the world I
want, Tom." A residue of ambition has made him accept the job as presidential envoy to the Court of St. James: "I'm ambitious in a way; but
when that way requires me to leave the people—the things—that I love,

then ambition chameleonizes and I become ambitious antithetically." Describing how happy he is in his little corner of the world, he admits that he nearly turned down his appointment, and now "I'm sort of sorry that I didn't." Insulated from the outside world and isolated from harsh reality, Schuyler has become engulfed by woman-rule, seduced by stasis. As Kate says, "It will be the first time we've been apart for more than a day or two since we were married." A true woman, content in her passivity, she remarks: "I'd rather have peace than all the honors there are." Yielding to the comforts of domestic bliss, Schuyler has taken on his wife's way of thinking. Instead of remaining God's personally delegated lord of creation over his private domestic monopoly, he has allowed himself to become "feminized." (90–101)

Kate, being the Ideal Wife, realizes that she "mustn't stand in the way of his advancement." But she knows all too well that a gentle, nonaggressive male such as her husband, used to being coddled in the warm bosom of his family, must become a prime target for predators in the world outside. And, of course, Porter Emerson Browne hastened to show his readers that she was right. Even while the ship that is to take Schuyler to England is still in harbor, and while he is still surrounded by doting wife, loving child, and devoted family friend, the die has already been cast for his undoing: "Take good care of them while I'm gone, won't you old man," he instructs the family friend. And then he admits:

> "By Jove, I'd like to chuck it all, even at the last minute as it is, and stay at home—"
> Facing his wife, child and friend, his eyes were up the broad deck. Came toward him The Woman—The Woman Known of the Man Who Knew, and of Young Parmalee. Schuyler's voice died in his throat. Her eyes were upon him. His eyes were upon her. She made no movement. She paused not in her indolent, sinuous walk. Her eyes were upon him; and that was all—dark eyes, glowing, inscrutable, beautiful with the beauty that was hers. And his eyes were on hers. (126)

From this point on all is lost. The voice of masculine reason has died in the throat of this man already seduced by femininity. Eros has captured him. His manly senses, weakened by his sojourn in the bosom of acculturated womanhood, are no longer sufficient armature against the dangerous lure of brute sexuality. Schuyler proves to be an easy prey to the vampire of degeneration. Had he but dared to venture earlier into the world of evolutionary strife, he might have understood that, to protect his marital monopoly, he should have thrust the stake of manhood into the Vampire's breast instead of abandoning himself to the dark ocean of her eyes!

The movie version of this scene conveys this message in a succinct sequence of images. On board ship, we see the Schuyler family at play—almost as if we were watching a home movie of an outing. We watch the Vampire watching them through a circular porthole. She takes out a circular mirror-compact (symbolic of the chaotic, uroboric stasis of primitive feminine sexuality). She looks at herself and primps. We see the happy family saying good-bye. We see the Vampire grin into the mirror. Then, the grin still on her face, she looks through the porthole, and we see her mockingly observe the fond farewells. As he embraces his wife, Schuyler sees her looking at him. He is visibly distracted.

The ship is about to leave. The warning sounds. The Vampire is on deck now. Panting, chest heaving, her eyes glittering, she watches the heavy-hearted husband say his last good-byes to his doting wife and ever-adorable little daughter. We see them next as, with tears in their eyes, they stand, waving, on the receding quay.

Suddenly we see the Vampire standing next to Schuyler at the ship's railing. He waves forlornly into the distance, clutching the nosegay of modest flowers his wife has given him: it is a symbol of her virtue—a plea: forget me not! The Vampire knows all too well how to counter such simple domestic magic. She drops her single, bold, obscenely oversized, luridly open-petaled (obviously crimson) rose. Schuyler, still thinking only of his wife, remains oblivious to her gesture. Undaunted, the Vampire taps him on the shoulder and asks him to retrieve the rose. The perfect gentleman, Schuyler does her bidding.

The image on-screen is dramatic and precise: in a close-up we see Schuyler's manly hand, still holding his wife's modest nosegay—the meek bouquet of the acculturated feminine—as it reaches for the engulfing petals of the Vampire's extravagant erotic emblem. The viewer instantly recognizes that a modest nosegay cannot compete against the gigantic rose's voluptuous regressive force. The victim, still unaware of what's in store, hurriedly turns his eyes back to the harbor, seeking a last glimpse of his wife and child. The Vampire, however, smiles and walks away, visibly certain that she has conquered.

At stake in these scenes, as virtually every viewer in 1915 would have

understood, was the future of humanity itself. The choice between evolution and degeneration, William Graham Sumner had told his contemporaries, was predicated upon the outcome of the internecine struggle
between the collectivist, static, and indiscriminately sexual chaos of the
mother-family structure (in which, as we have seen, any male who happened to be handy might serve to feed the ruling woman's libido) and
that greatest achievement of evolution: patriarchy, the father-family,
"pair marriage"—the monogamic union of a man and a woman.

The concept of pair marriage (today we would call it "the nuclear
family") was by its very nature an expression of the masculine will to individual power. Hence, Sumner insisted, "pair marriage is monopolistic." Moreover, it was "interwoven with capital," because it was an
expression of the true masculine will to ownership. No form of social
arrangement was more directly designed to express the monopolistic
destiny of man: "It is the barrier against which all socialism breaks into
dust." (F 376–7)

Since pair marriage was the ultimate testing ground of masculine
monogamic fortitude, no male unable to rule such a personal monopoly
rightfully belonged to the evolutionary elite. In pair marriage the male
learned once and for all how to govern and subject. A man's wife was an
integral part of his working capital. Thus capitalism and monogamy
would stand or fall together as the greatest achievements of the masculine will to individual mastery. Therefore, Sumner exclaimed ecstatically,
"the grandest and most powerful monopoly in the world is the family,
in its monogamic form." (SD 196)

Sumner sketched a glowing picture of the nuclear family as an island
of personal privilege and salvation in a world of constant depredation
and danger—a bulwark against economic destruction. The evolutionary
millennium, therefore, would announce itself in the triumphant proliferation of such personal monopolies within society. The nuclear family
was an outpost of civilization against the predatory agents of primitive
feminine sexual license who still roamed the world outside, a massed
army of degenerates, including not only all still self-consciously sexual,
and hence fundamentally uncivilized, women, but also the hordes of inferior males still subject to these wild women's siren call.

Monogamy intensified a "man's feeling of cohesion with his own
wife and his own children, aside from and against all the world." (SD
198). This remark provides an exact key to John Schuyler's failure as the
leader of his family monopoly: Schuyler had properly *separated* himself
from the rest of the world in his marriage, but he had failed to regard his

house and home as an armed bulwark *against* the outside world. He had failed to circle the wagons of his personal monopoly; and by not maintaining constant vigilance against the incursions of the vampire of otherness, he had left himself vulnerable to her depredations. He was no longer an economic warrior; he had lost his will to fight. An excess of humanist deference to his wife had made him unfit to maintain himself among the evolutionary elite.

How, then, should a man deal with his wife, if regarding her as an inspiration and an equal was tantamount to inviting the Vampire into your house and hearth? The father of American sociology did not hesitate to give his readers sound marital advice: within a properly organized family monopoly, with the husband firmly in control, the sex-tortured vampire female of yore could finally be laid to rest, and the acculturated woman, meekly shadowing her personal lord of creation, could at last gain a dignity women had never known before. The "father-family" had finally been able to make woman understand that her existential status was, and must always be, that of "an inferior whose status and destiny came from her position as an adjunct." Today's evolutionary male had been able to soften the harshness of that fate somewhat by kindly lifting his wife upon a pedestal; "the moral inferences however, remain, and we regard them as self-evident and eternal. Loyalty to her husband is the highest virtue of a woman, and devotion to her family and sacrifice for it are the field of heroism for her." (*WOE* 51)

The nineteenth century, Sumner exulted, had finally given the civilized male the upper hand in his principled struggle against brute nature—which was always squarely on the side of the sexual woman and matriarchy. During that century man had at last been able to convince woman to abandon her wasteful, indiscriminate campaign to obtain as much of the male's vital essence as she could. The civilized male had taught her to accept only as much as she needed to fulfill her maternal duties. Thus man had finally been able to wean woman from her natural tendency toward "sex-vice and heathenism." (*WOE* 78) In the long run woman had recognized how advantageous her subjection to the male could actually be: "When a woman came to be considered a 'toy' she ceased to be drudge; when she came to be esteemed as a woman she lost value as a slave whose labor could be productively employed." (*SD* 205)

The marital subjection of woman to monopolistic patriarchal authority, then, had been evolution's greatest achievement to date: "It is the lot of every woman to stand beside some man, and to give her strength and life to help him in every way which circumstances offer opportunity for. Out of this relation come her ideas of her honor, duties and virtue." (*F* 357)

No one who has spent even a few moments listening to the popular music of this century, whether that of today or of thirty, fifty, or eighty years ago, will find anything unusual in Sumner's exhortation to America's women to "stand by your man" and "give him all the love you can." Very few of us realize anymore that the ideological justification for such exhortations originated in the high-flown theories of William Graham Sumner and his fellow turn-of-the-century social philosophers. However, two-bit versions of million-dollar ideas catch on only when the public decides they make sense. The spate of films, starting with *A Fool There Was,* in which the world of Lillian Gish, the eternal virgin of acculturated femininity, was pitted against that of Theda Bara, the regressive Vampire of "woman-rule," did much to "normalize" the "scientific" basis for Sumner's principles of domestic monopoly. There is no question that the silent-movie industry provided the all-important image structures underlying most twentieth-century American race and gender relationships.

For Sumner and many of his male contemporaries, then, there were only two kinds of women. The "good girls" were those who had been properly acculturated to their subservient role in the monogamic monopoly structure of the nuclear family, and who were content to be governed in all things by the superior judgment of their imperial mate. These were the evolved, genetically privileged child-women of modern society, who, having submitted for many generations to a rigorous mortification of the flesh, had internalized the meritorious "inherited feminine characteristic" of passivity and subservience to the masculine will. The bad women were those who continued to insist on their personal independence as human beings and who, therefore, continued to deny the cultural benefits of their monogamic subservience. These women were easy to identify, for they were invariably lewd and provocative, and clearly driven to erotic excess by their bestial need for the male's vital essence. These were women who had remained mired in the feminine world of collectivism, of primitive polyandrist promiscuity.

The scene immediately following the Vampire's initial floral seduction of John Schuyler in the movie version of *A Fool There Was* left its audiences in no doubt that the Vampire was one of these, in evolutionary terms, still ignorant matriarchal animals. Onto the screen flashes another passage from Kipling's poem:

Oh, the years we waste and the tears we waste
And the work of our head and hand
Belong to the woman who did not know
   (And now we know that she never could know)
And did not understand.

Immediately after this the camera opens on the Vampire, lying down amid a setting of exotic, tropical splendor. Her hand is on Schuyler's chest; his head is resting near her midriff. We see the Vampire offer him a drink: clearly they are wallowing in the most decadent luxury imaginable. Schuyler downs his drink. Slow, excruciatingly languorous movements highlight their sinful pleasure. When he passionately places her hand over his heart, the Vampire flashes an evil grin.

Soon Schuyler falls asleep: clear evidence of his dissipation, his depletion, his abandonment. The truly extraordinary scene that follows must have sent mixed waves of arousal and consternation through the males in the audience: With the sleeping man nestled under her bosom, the Vampire very slowly raises both arms from her lap, in an almost perfectly rounded curve, until they hover ominously above her head like the bat wings of a pterodactyl. Her hands droop down oddly from this upward curve to suggest the claws of a predator about to pounce. Then, like a cat, she stretches her arms behind her head in a gesture of utter contentment. Clearly she has already had her fill but is about to go back into action. Another good man gone, the audience realizes, another victim fallen to the sexual woman. After this the action shifts to far more mundane events, as if to allow the viewer time to recover. Publicity stills capitalized on the shock this image sent through the movie's audiences by showing Theda Bara in a similar pose, with her arms raised, but this time lifting her hair above her head as if to form bat wings.

Sumner never tired of pointing out that civilization was a product of man's struggle *against* nature: "The whole retrospect of human history runs downwards towards beast-like misery and slavery to the destructive forces of nature." (*WOE* 179) A sexual woman, being a primitive woman, was not "above," but part of, nature. One could go even further and insist that she was nature itself. In consequence, man's struggle against nature expressed itself first and foremost in his struggle against the sexual woman. Men like Schuyler, who could not withstand the enticements of women, could not be expected to hold on to their capital either. Economic and sexual continence were clearly interchangeable factors of a single principle of evolutionary self-control.

But Sumner also saw great danger in the successes of man's campaign to eradicate female sexuality: "it is now not believed that women are more sensual than men, but decidedly the contrary." (*WOE* 106–7) He cautioned that it was unwise to let the nineteenth century's admirable idealization of woman blind man to her negative origins:

> It seems clear that pair marriage has finally set aside the notion which, in the past, has been so persistently held,—that women are bad by nature, so that one half of the human race is permanently dragging down the other half. The opposite notion seems now to be gaining currency,—that all women are good, and can be permanently employed to raise up the men. These fluctuations only show how each sway of conditions and interests produces its own fallacies. (*F* 376)

Man's vigilance in his struggle against nature should not slacken this late in the game. It should be understood by every male that under the skin of even the most perfectly acculturated female, the repressed impulses of nature still lurked. Inevitably woman's "badness," her natural compulsion to indulge in reproductive promiscuity, and her inherent tendencies toward socialistic primitivism and stasis remained a dangerous source of potential "reversion" for society. Therefore the apostles of evolution needed to be constantly on their guard against any evidence of the resurgence of primitive woman-rule in civilized society. Sentimentalist egalitarian tendencies were always a dead giveaway of such a resurgence. "The law of the survival of the fittest was not made by man and cannot be abrogated by man. We can only, by interfering with it, produce the survival of the unfittest." (*WOE* 177) Thus, even in social realms not directly related to sexuality, the eternal feminine was, through its invidious egalitarian schemes, out to drain the evolutionary male, if not of his vital essence, then of his capital. As we have seen, the Vampire of *A Fool There Was* left no wallet unturned to convey precisely such a message.

In his enthusiasm for the family as a training ground for the principles of monopolistic capitalism, Sumner was even tempted to abandon his earlier doubts about the need for an active role on the part of evolutionary civilization in eliminating the "unfit." Even now, he admitted, "science has to fight so hard against tradition that its authority is only

slowly winning recognition." (*WOE* 179) But at last science, basing itself on the higher principles of eugenics, was wisely beginning to demand that the evolutionary elite ought to police American marriages:
"If we are not prepared to interfere in any way at all with freedom of
marriage or the continuance of family life between two people who are
not fit to be parents," he decided, we should be prepared for "a policy
by which society continually uses up its best members, while it preserves
and stimulates the reproduction of its bad ones." (*EH* 98) Perhaps, he intimated, strict eugenicist prohibitions and even a judicious eradication
of those who were totally useless might lead to an *endlösung* of the problem of "reversion."

Sumner and most of his contemporaries were absolutely convinced
that the evolutionary capitalist male should allow only the most passive,
most perfectly acculturated of women to become part of his marital
monopoly. To forge ahead in the struggle for existence, a man must be
able to rule his own household first and foremost. Monogamic marriage,
"like other monopolies . . . wins an advantage for those who are included at the cost of depression to those who are excluded; and millions, of course, in trying to attain to the heights of a monogamic
marriage, fail. If they fall, they fall far lower than they would be under
lower forms of marriage." (*SD* 197) Divorce, discord, and marital failure
were clearly fates worse than death. A man who was unable to maintain himself at the head of such a monogamic marriage was visibly
sliding back down the evolutionary ladder to a level of personal
degradation comparable to that of the lowest among the lower orders of
humanity.

Within this context it becomes easy to understand the ideological
significance of the climactic scene in *A Fool There Was,* in which the
Vampire, with a single kiss, a single act of sexual assertion, bluntly and
irrevocably snatches a prosperous and hence "intellectually evolved"
man from the bosom of his nuclear family. The scene was clearly much
more than merely another campy instance of early movie melodrama.
Theda Bara's contemporaries knew that they were watching the social
vampire of female sexuality depredate civilized society. Once we know
this was the movie's immediate subtext as a social document, the scene
of Theda Bara's predatory kiss is restored to its original function as the
visual dramatization of a central test of manhood essential to the survival
of evolutionary civilization—a test, it is worth emphasizing, to which
late-twentieth-century society still adheres, to a disturbingly large ex-

tent, although we have forgotten its direct ideological justification. That is why we still register the episode as one of emblematic force; that is why it still has a special capacity to shock us.

As a dramatic illustration of the ongoing battle between civilization and nature, of the choice between evolutionary capitalism and social degradation, the scene has perhaps no equal in the annals of the silent film. Yet today the film is completely unknown, except among film historians, who, often without ever having seen it, dismiss it as the artistically forgettable screen debut of Theda Bara, whom they also tend to regard as merely an odd, rather negligible phenomenon of the silent screen's infant years.

That attitude is dramatically indicative of the code of silence our culture tends to impose on those of its historical productions that have become too blatantly indicative of the sources of our contemporary mores. Our systematic forgetting of the meaning of *A Fool There Was* is a striking example of the elusive yet pervasive propagandistic control the visual media of the twentieth century were beginning to exert over the structures of the human imagination. For every time Theda Bara's Vampire kiss made her audiences shiver, the continuing social misery and personal suffering of generations of women to come was made more inevitable. The good woman or the bad, the virgin or the vampire—submission or a stake through the heart—those were to be the choices for twentieth-century women. The screen debut of a young actress from the Midwest had established the central gender dualism of the new century in no uncertain terms.

A Fool There Was was obviously not the first product of mass culture to present audiences with such pat choices. Inevitably, such melodramas had, partially as the result of several decades of pervasive evolutionist propaganda, become standard fare in the American and European cultural environment of the early twentieth century. But rarely before had they been presented in as striking, graphic, and visually categorical a fashion. The public immediately recognized the sociopedagogic function of the film's central confrontation scene, and accepted its message that an irrevocable evolutionary choice between vice ("socialist," woman-ruled promiscuity) and virtue ("capitalist," masculine, paternalistic monogamy) confronted every male.

The early twentieth century's ever expanding cultural documentation of the confrontation between the sexual woman and the would-be continent male, her habitual victim, was linked to a growing conviction among physicians, biologists, and other such theologians of the scientific age, that *all* women were, in fact, "real" vampires, driven by nature to depredate the male, and hence creatures who were, even if only in medical terms, dangerous to a man's health even when they were virtuous, submissive, monogamous wives. Theda Bara's name, it had been rumored, was an anagram for Arab Death; but as the men of the early twentieth century were beginning to discover, even the most seemingly compliant household nun could be deadly!

Arthur Lange, The Source of Strength;
exhibited Grosze Berliner Kunstausstellung, 1909
Superman struggles to be born: the evolutionary male's
sublime effort to overcome earthly vulgarity.

II. VITAL ESSENCE AND BLIGHTING MILDEW: DIMORPHIC GENDER EVOLUTION AND THE NATURAL PHILOSOPHY OF LUST

She stood there. Red lips were parted in a little, inscrutable smile. White shoulders shimmered. Lithe muscles rippled beneath her gown with every movement of her delicate body. She was beautiful—beautiful as an animal is beautiful. And her eyes were upon his." Lured by the Vampire's long, flowing hair, sensuous, snakelike limbs, and blood-red mouth, John Schuyler, in both the book and movie versions of *A Fool There Was,* became an abject slave to beauty, a pitiful victim to the feminine world of sight. It was a clear case of nature reasserting herself—of death, waste, and genetic chaos conquering the selective, individualistic, masculine spirit yearning for immortality.

The early twentieth century's scientific community considered it a matter of great urgency to inform the world at large about nature's terrifying habit of siding with the regressive feminine. Lurid, anthropomorphizing descriptions of mating rituals in the animal and insect world were the order of the day among naturalists. The popular imagination, thus encouraged by the leaders of the evolutionary advance, seized upon these descriptions and made them into exemplary illustrations of the inevitable battle of the sexes. Remy de Gourmont, a prominent French novelist and poet whose influence on English-speaking intellectuals was dramatic and far-reaching during the early years of this century, set the tone. Science had shown, he said, that the male entered the feminine world of perpetual rut with great reluctance, and only in response to the insistent call of the reproductive instinct. Once there, he became a pitiful victim, his vital energy unequal to the demands of woman.

Gourmont used the writings of the biologists of his time to draw a none-too-subtle image of the fate men faced in the realm of the reproductive feminine. Too often, he insisted in his 1903 book *The Natural Philosophy of Love (Physique de l'amour—essai sur l'instinct sexuel),* the innocent male, deluded into thinking of woman as an appetizing fruit, suddenly found himself sucked dry by the vampire of vital essence:

> The male cochineal has a long body with very delicate transparent wings. . . . One sees him flying over the nopals, then suddenly alighting on a female, who resembles a fat wood-louse, round and puffy, twice as stout as the male, and wingless. Glued by her feet to a branch, with her proboscis stuck into it, continually pumping sap, she looks like a fruit. . . . In certain species of coccidae the male is so small that his proportion [to the female] is that of an ant strolling over a peach. His goings and comings are like those of an ant hunting for a soft spot to bite, but he is seeking the genital cleft, and having found it, often after long and anxious explorations, he fulfils his function, falls off and dies. (27–8)

The "humanized" emotions attributed to insects in this passage were analogous to those found in descriptions of insect encounters by many of the "naturalists" of the late nineteenth and early twentieth centuries. These provided Gourmont with a boundless field of moralizing exempla. Being a skilled novelist, he was able to add a virtually cinematic sense of drama to the naturalists' accounts of male reproductive sacrifice.

Inevitably, spiders and the praying mantis were among Gourmont's favorite denizens of the vampire world of gender relationships:

> The mantis who eats her husband is an excellent egg-layer who prepares, passionately, the future of her progeny. . . . The male is bashful; at the moment of desire he limits himself to posing, to making sheep's eyes, which the female seems to consider with indifference or disdain. Tired of parade, he finally decides, and

with spread wings, leaps trembling upon the back of the ogress. The mating lasts five or six hours; when the knot is loosed, the suitor is, regularly, eaten. The terrible female is polyandrous. (98–9)

Today we assume that to hold up a cross to the vampire before us is to force the creature to fear God. But in the early years of this century the cross, as the symbol of sacrificial Christian manhood, as man's sword in the battle for spiritual transcendence, functioned first of all as a shield against the frightful world of visual temptation represented by woman, that world of the eyes into which the intellectuals of the period saw generation after generation of innocent, unthinking insect males being drawn, to be eaten alive by the monstrous agents of brute nature. Gourmont's excursions into entomology were clearly designed to demonstrate that "the feminine" in nature—woman—had been programmed to be a reproductive machine, whose workings were fueled by the masculine vital essence:

The spermatophore of the ephippiger is enormous, nearly half the size of the animal. . . . The female, having consumed the leather-bottle spermatophore, adds thereto the poor emptied male. She does not even wait until he is dead; she chops him up as he is dying, limb by limb: having fecundated her with all his blood, he must feed her with all his flesh. (96)

The manner in which the female insect devoured the male (the larger his spermatophore the better, obviously) clearly proved that manhood was mere mincemeat to woman, nature's designated spermatophage—the vampire of reproduction. This point was by no means lost on Porter Emerson Browne. For the benefit of the naturalists among the readers of *A Fool There Was,* Browne described his fallen bourgeois antihero as little more than the Vampire's own still marginally ambulant but already direly depleted spermatophore—an obvious dead ringer for the biologists' hapless insect adventurers. Schuyler, Browne wrote, had become "a palsied, shrunken, shriveled caricature of something that had once been human," a "sunken-eyed, sunken-cheeked, wrinkled thing . . . that crawled, quiveringly" with "nerveless, shaking talons."

Schuyler had already delivered a similar analogy. "What is there of me to save?" he exclaimed at one point to the family friend who was trying to make him see reason: "I am a husk—squeezed dry." When the Vampire tells him that she is about to move on to a better-endowed sperm carrier, he mutters: "Squeeze him dry, won't you, you Vampire! . . . Squeeze the honor and the manhood and the life and the soul out of him, won't you?"

Analogies of this sort functioned to mitigate the male's responsibility for his carnal weakness. Men who had given in to the feminine, who had innocently permitted themselves to be drawn into the world of visual temptation, of arousal and abandon, of insect lures and erotic traps, could not really be blamed for their excursions into the land of the vampire, for nature had loaded the dice in favor of the spermatophage. Ever supportive, all-suffering, and perfectly colonized, Schuyler's wife knows that better than anyone. Indelibly part of the eternal feminine, Kate intuitively understands the rule of nature: "I can forgive, John, dear. I do forgive. It was not your fault. Is it the fault of the bird that he goes to his death when the eyes of the snake are upon him? It was not that you were weak, even; it was that—she was strong, strong in the one way in which she leads."

The world of nature meant death to the men of steel who were forging the principles of twentieth-century genetic salvation. "There was," Schuyler tries to explain to the steadfast family friend at the time of the latter's last attempt to save him, "something—her eyes, it was— eyes that burnt and seared!" Understanding that the insolence of the untamed woman lies in the analytic acumen of her eyes, Schuyler's wife tries to show him that she is different, that she is properly acculturated: "She rose. Violet eyes were moist. She turned away, a little, that he might not see." But this gesture of dutiful self-effacement was no longer meaningful at this point, for Browne wanted to make it clear to his readers that once a man had sunk into the engulfing depths of the feminine eye, not even the most invisible wife could rescue him from the monstrous libations of the sexual vampire, nature's spermatophage.

To emphasize this point, Browne made the Vampire reappear once more to break up the wife and the friend's joint final attempt to rescue Schuyler: "She looked on him with eyes that revealed only amusement—amusement, and power." Schuyler—that crawling, quivery insect that had once been a man—pleads with her to allow him his "little, pitiful" last chance at redemption. He is now no more than a male mantis, praying: "He was on his knees now, thin hands raised in beseeching. She looked down upon him from where she sat, upon the desk, little feet swinging. She raised delicate brows."

Then—we can almost hear this predator's mandibles clicking—"she leaned forward, eyes heavy lidded, white arms extended, white teeth glowing, white shoulders shimmering. She hissed, sibilantly: 'A kiss, My Fool!'" Schuyler makes a last, desperate attempt to gather the remnants of his manhood—but "her lips curved. Her breast heaved. Her arms glowed. And her eyes were on his." Inevitably, he capitulates: "He was not a man now. He was a Thing, and that Thing was of her. Hands hung slack, loose, at his sides: jaw drooped; lips were pendulous. Only, in his eyes was that light that she, and she alone knew how to kindle—he was hers, soul, and body, and brain." Another hapless cochineal had bit the dust. Browne's male readers at this point no doubt nervously crossed their antennae.

In a final, futile effort to escape the bite of nature and regain the world of masculine monopoly, Schuyler tries to strangle the Vampire, to kill the beast, but the effort is too much for this human wood louse's wasted body: "His head fell back. His body, inert, rolled from hers, turned again as it struck the chair, and fell, a thing crushed and dead, at her feet."

Schuyler's death is the Vampire's ultimate triumph; primitive matriarchy has gained the day once more. The world of the eye, of the senses, has killed the world of the spirit. Having consumed his spermatophore, the Vampire has added "thereto the poor emptied male": primitive sin has withered man's hope forever. It was clearly the sexual woman's ultimate goal to deprive the male of all his gray matter. This human spermatophage was a brain-vampire, first and foremost. Porter Emerson Browne had left his readers no room for doubt in this respect: "Haven't you a spark of manhood left? No brains?" the family friend calls out, appalled, upon seeing Schuyler in the final stage of his degeneration. The friend realizes "that if this time he failed to arouse whatever of latent, atrophied manhood there might be in the breast of the other, that never again, probably, would the shrivelling brain come within call." Earlier, Browne had already made it a point to identify Parmalee, the Vampire's previous victim, as a man consumed by cranial rot: that young man's suicide had been the inevitable outcome of "a vanished will in a shrivelled brain." Schuyler knows the abominable physiological effects of sexual pleasure better than anyone: "Save me from her—from myself," he begs his friend: "My blood has turned to water, and my bones to chalk! My brain has withered!" (278–301)

These amazing feats of biochemical degeneration could not have come as a surprise to the early-twentieth-century readers of *A Fool*

There Was. Indeed, any suggestion that sex might *not* rot the brain would have been far more controversial to them. Biologists, physicians, sexologists, and common folk were united in the conviction that a man's "vital essence" was the most precious commodity the world had ever seen, and that its conservation or expenditure was the absolute key to all processes of evolution and degeneration. Every teenage male of 1915 knew that the quickest way to Sumner's gutter was to let a woman lay waste to his store of vitality (next to an indulgence in solitary vice, of course). Frank Powell, in directing the movie version of Browne's melodrama, knew he could count on this knowledge when he telescoped that author's heavy-handed moral disquisitions into a single, supremely powerful image: in the final scene of the film, after the Vampire's final depredation, we see Schuyler in his town house, literally an animal now, on all fours, crawling down a staircase that, as we know all too well, leads to the Vampire's bedroom. Here, truly, was a man devolving, an insect crawling down the face of nature.

"The individual who leads a licentious life," the physician John Cowan had pointed out in his *Science of a New Life* some forty-six years earlier, "causes a great drain on his vitality—such a drain as required the whole life-force of his system to supply." As a result, the seminally spendthrift male "does, in part or in whole, weaken his nervous system . . . and dyspepsia, rheumatism, apoplexy, paralysis, and a score of other diseases, assert their sway."

In both its book and movie versions, *A Fool There Was* had been careful to highlight precisely these physiological symptoms of Schuyler's escapade into the arms of the Vampire. Indeed, Schuyler was clearly a textbook case—perhaps even a case Browne had taken directly out of *Cowan's* textbook; for Cowan had stressed that such a man's "intensely animal and selfish elements" will "disorganize his brain-tissue—memory is weakened, perceptive and reflective power is weakened, as seen in imbecility of plan and purpose, and indecision of thought and action; the moral sentiments are debased, the soul blighted."

Such a man, said Cowan, "arrests his growth, and brings on premature old age." Worse, indulgence "destroys his manhood, and the offspring propagated by him are sickly, scrofulous, deformed, and die prematurely." Schuyler had fortunately been able to produce his adorable daughter well before he fell into the arms of the Vampire, but Browne's antihero exhibited every other symptom of incontinence on Cowan's list.

Chastity and strict abstinence bore far more luminous fruit: "The nervous system is invigorated and strengthened. The special senses—the sight, hearing, etc.—are strong, delicate and acute." The continent man grows old but does not age, he promised:

> for the last days, in their pleasurable enjoyment of good health and a sound mind, are as were the days of his childhood. The brain is enlarged and perfected, memory grows strong, the perceptive and reflective faculties increase in power, as shown in the ability to originate and execute, the calm, self-possessed strength to endure, and gentleness, courage, generosity and nobleness of character. The moral sentiments are elevated, love grows and ripens, and the soul, in its exercise, reaches up and commingles with the spirit of God.

Finally, but certainly not least, "the reproductive element is preserved in all its life-renewing and life-giving power, until full ripeness of years."

Doctor Cowan was not a man who dabbled in half measures: "It is a popular opinion that a healthy man who is continent should occasionally have seminal emissions." Wrong, wrong, wrong: "A perfectly healthy, continent man, living a right life socially, morally and physically, does not and cannot have seminal emissions." (118–20) It was not that Cowan wanted all sexual intercourse to cease immediately; he merely wanted to impress upon his readers that *any* loss of semen was a significant loss of vital essence to a man, and therefore every incidence of carnal concourse should be orchestrated to take place under optimal conditions, specifically geared to facilitate a wife's (nearly) immaculate conception.

Our tendency might be to assume that Cowan must have been a conservative fringe figure even in 1870—but exactly the opposite was the case. He was not only a highly respected centrist member of the medical establishment of his day, but a major advocate of abolition ("out of slavery comes superstition, imbecility, weakness, degradation, and a lapse backward into the shadowy depths of hell" [379]) and of equal rights for women. In a publicity section appended to *The Science of a New Life,* important public figures, such as William Lloyd Garrison and Elizabeth Cady Stanton, sang the author's praises. Garrison believed that "licentiousness and foul disease" were infecting "the very life-blood of the people," and noted that "the essential remedy for these great evils is to be found in Dr. Cowan's work." Stanton said she had used Cowan's work as a textbook in lectures "for several years" and recommended it for study "to every mother in the land."

Why all this emphasis on "seminal continence"? Why should men have regarded even modest expenditures of seed with alarm? The physicians of the later nineteenth century had responded to the political ascendancy of Herbert Spencer's and William Graham Sumner's evolutionary elite by placing renewed and newly urgent emphasis on an age-old medical theory that could be traced back at least as far as Aristotle. The nineteenth-century version of this theory became an ingenious tool in the service of the dominant socioeconomic power structure. Sumner used it to explain why the radical inequality of races and classes was an expression of the Divine Will. As a result, humanist social reformers found themselves running into brick walls over and over again. They found few of their contemporaries willing to accept the notion that "degenerates" who had frivolously wasted their "vital essence" should be considered "equal" to the "continent" (because wealthy) members of the power elite.

Each human being, so the theory went, was sent into the world with a carefully measured, modest allotment of "vital essence," which was an almost magical potion of "energy." The quality of this energy, as an obvious prelude to the ascendancy of genetics, was generally regarded as a product of inheritance. As science marched into the twentieth century it often came to be described as a quasi-electrical "current." How you used this vital essence was entirely up to you, but one thing was certain: your store of vitality was as precisely circumscribed as the wax of a candle. Consequently, if you "burned your candle at both ends," you could not expect to live very long. To waste your vital essence, then, was to waste your life—and, by extension, that of your offspring. If, on the other hand, you husbanded your life-energy carefully—if you economized on your expenditures, so to speak—you and your children could expect to live and prosper.

Since the exact constituents of this vital energy were God's secret, science could only speculate upon the optimum trajectory of its expenditure. But long tradition and personal experience had made late-nineteenth-century medical researchers certain of one thing: human life-energy was, first and foremost, concentrated in the blood. A person's blood was the primary conduit for the dissemination of his—or her—vital essence.

Physicians of the day had no doubt whatever that the human generative fluid was an almost pure distillate of the vital essence stored by the blood: What, after all, could be more logical than that the fluid that created life also contained the greatest measure of a man's "life force"? Thus the key to a man's well-being, as Cowan had pointed out already, was his ability to hold on to as much of that precious fluid as possible. For, as Augustus Kinsley Gardner, M.D., pointed out in his *Conjugal Sins Against the Laws of Life and Health* (1870), "The sperm is the purest extract of the blood, and according to the expression of Fernel [1497–1558; one of the first modern physiologists], *totus homo semen est* ["man is all semen," or "semen makes the man"]. Nature in creating it has intended it not only to communicate life, but also to nourish the individual life." (163)

By the second decade of the twentieth century speculative science had determined rather precisely how the body distilled its vital essence for productive use. In what was already no less than the tenth edition of their 1911 book *The Science of Sex Regeneration,* A. Gould and Dr. Franklin L. Dubois described the process in detail: Certain arteries brought "fresh blood" to the sexual organs, which distilled the seminal fluid from the blood. Other arteries carried away the blood that had "been drained of its vital essence" and was therefore no longer of use. The authors emphasized that since this distillation process "requires a great deal of the vitality of the body as well as its richest blood, the great danger of wasting this precious material will be at once understood." And they continued:

> Normally, up to the time a boy is twelve years old, not a drop of this semen has passed from the spermatic cord into the urethra . . . because the child needs every particle of his material forces to build up and strengthen his growing body; the semen secreted is therefore re-distributed throughout the body to nourish brain, muscles, bones, and sinews. It will thus be seen that secretions of the testes have other and most important functions beside propagation. In full maturity, when not used for purposes of procreation, this important fluid, a true elixir of life, should never be wasted, but allowed to be reabsorbed by the system as fast as it is secreted.
>
> It will readily be seen how weakening any practice would be which would cause a waste of this material. If the vital essences are drawn from the blood and brain and body, deprived of their

natural nourishment, they become weakened in proportion to
the waste. The re-absorption of the semen strengthens the boy;
its waste causes weakness and degeneration. (94–5)

If, then, man were indeed "all semen," it would obviously take
buckets of the precious fluid to build *mens sana in corpore sano,* a healthy
mind in a healthy body. Indeed, most scientists were convinced that the
brain's gray matter was nothing but a wonderfully concentrated accumulation of manly continence. Each seminal emission quite literally
caused one to spend one's genetic endowment. "An uncontrolled sex
life," said Gould and Dubois, wasted "the physical resources which
should be used to build up new brain cells." A variety of still widely
popular expressions and superstitions attest to the continuing (if, fortunately, steadily diminishing) influence of these theories, which were almost universally accepted during the first few decades of this century.
The teenager, or "young adult," today who still, in describing a sexual
encounter, brags of having "screwed his, her, or the other's brains out"
surely does not have a clue that this expression had its justification in the
most serious researches of early-twentieth-century medical science. On
the other hand, the football coach who demands that his team keep
away from sexual activity for at least forty-eight hours before a big game
no doubt consciously continues a tradition he inherited from his own
coach at college—who, of course, in turn had learned this bit of scientific theory about the conservation of aggressive energy from the up-to-
date sports-medicine textbooks he read while a student during the
Twenties.

Gould and Dubois also made a direct link between the vital-essence
theory and social Darwinism—a link that had remained largely implied
in the writings of the earlier seminal philosophers. "Life has become
one big battle," they emphasized. In the hectic, dog-eat-dog world of
contemporary society, a man who wanted to reach the top could not afford to lose even a pinch of that precious vital essence his brain needed
so desperately to maintain its advantage over the rest of the upward-
striving masses: "The man who will not control his sex impulse is courting defeat, as this is a day when fitness counts and the weaklings are soon
brushed aside and sink in the mire." (191–3)

Medicine and capitalism had thus joined forces to impress upon the
men of the early twentieth century that their financial solvency would
be dependent on their ability to invest their vital energy wisely. Clearly
the principles of seminal management were crucial to the triumph of

Sumner's plutocracy. The man who held on to his semen could expect to see his capital grow—and capital, as Sumner never tired of pointing out, was the lifeblood of the evolutionary elite. The seminal economists emphasized that in all essential respects blood and semen were one. As Gould and Dubois put it, "The spermatozoa is the most highly vitalized form of living matter called protoplasm and is the most precious nutriment of the blood"; (208) therefore blood, brain cells, and money were parallel reflections of a man's true grit, "and as the richest part of the blood is used in the manufacture this is all lost when it is secreted." (218)

Consequently, as Schuyler discovered to his sorrow in *A Fool There Was*, loss of semen meant loss of money, meant loss of manhood, meant loss of self. The true evolutionary male had no business messing with emission, for the capitalist plutocracy, the imperialist ruling class, the flower of Aryan manhood, was a direct product of reabsorbed masculine potency: "The powerful muscles, the vigor of nerve and brain, the manly form, the qualities of will, initiative and courage, idealism, the social instinct, sex love, etc., are all dependent for their normal development on the sex organs." (211)

Many therefore thought that the superman of the evolutionary future would be something of a privileged spiritual spermatophore, whose large and impressive cranial cavity would be filled with the precious gray matter of a superior brain compacted from the seminal production of a pair of well-guarded testes. No wonder, then, that the physicians of the later nineteenth and early twentieth centuries railed furiously against what they saw as sensual "effeminacy" among males. Such effeminacy was clearly the melancholy result of youthful incontinence—either of the solitary sort or in submission to the libations of a vampire woman.

The period's researchers were obsessed with the identification of the physical signs of "mental" weakness, much as their spiritual heirs today are determined to identify a malformed gene for every perceived social aberration or offense. The pseudoscience of phrenology and cranial measurement (the bigger the brain, the manlier the man) had already led to a new equation of true genius with muscle: "Avoid accepting an effeminate man," women's-rights advocate Cowan had urged his female readers in 1869,

> for he, lacking the requisites that go to make a perfect man, and lacking the formation for a perfect woman, approach[es] the mediocre, and is as small and effeminate in soul and mind as in body. A full or large and well-built man approaches to the noble,

generous and perfect in mankind, and is always the most desirable for a husband. (68)

Fifty years later many had accepted the notion that a "real" man
must also make an effort to *look* manly. The Hollywood cowboy was
saddling up, and Tarzan had begun his efforts to clean up the jungle. The
ideal figures of Conan the Barbarian and Superman were about to be
born into the fantasies of boys painfully aware of their own inability to
be as masculine as their fathers wanted them to be. The rippling muscles
of Rodin's entirely idiomatic *Thinker* of the 1880s became emblematic
of seminal continence. Said Gould and Dubois:

> The physical state has a great influence on morality. It is gener-
> ally believed today that whatever affects the body affects the
> mind and whatever affects the mind affects the body. The phys-
> ical passions clamor most strongly in the physically weak. Their
> uncontrolled passions make them weak. When the energy is low
> and the nerves worn out, the lower or animal part of man
> springs into control. Flabby muscles and a bad stomach are the
> results of abuse. Those allowing themselves to get in this condi-
> tion will find it hard to lead a clean life. (196)

By 1926, Earle Liederman, a leader in the bodybuilding movement,
had gone into the breach to explain to his followers *The Hidden Truth
about Sex*. "I have received thousands of questions from my students per-
taining to sex," he acknowledged. He therefore felt called upon to explain the link between "vitality" and true "virility" once and for all. To
be "superbly sexed" meant "to have supreme vitality, and *vice versa*." But
sexual health and sexual spending were two very different matters. Virility and continence went hand in hand: "Without the benefit of the internal secretion during youth, the resulting undeveloped 'man' is
soft-muscled and light-boned, mentally vacillating, neurotic and hysterical or childishly (immaturely) emotional" (27–30)—all, quite obviously,
typically "feminine" conditions.

Sexual spending spelled the difference between "virile" muscle and
degenerate flab: "An illustration of this can be had in the case of twins,
both of whom were 18 years of age, who became my pupils simultaneously. They both were practically the same weight and size and possessed
about equal strength." While "one of them in less than six months

Auguste Rodin, The Thinker, *ca. 1885*
The original monument to *mens sana in corpore sano*

gained many inches around his chest, arms, thighs, etc.," the other, of
course, turned out to be a solitary sinner: "The God-given life that was
placed in his body to nourish his nerves, bones and tissues, was wasted.
In that case, how could he expect to physically compete against his
cleanminded and careful living brother?" (7–8) No wonder the greatest
challenges to Edgar Rice Burroughs's Tarzan were always to be women
rather than wild animals or vicious natives.

Thus flabby effeminacy came to be the mark of the erotomaniac.
(Think of waddly Robert Morley, with blubbery cheeks, enacting a
Fifties take on Oscar Wilde.) Men everywhere rushed out to invest in

one or more of the many muscle-building devices advertised in the magazines and newspapers of the Teens and Twenties, hoping to hide the effects of their youthful indiscretions. Charles Atlas was about to make millions by teaching the ninety-pound weaklings of the next generation that only major additions to their musculature would help them catch the attention of the girl next door.

Where was the woman's part in all this seminal accumulation? Clearly she did not have the proper ductless glands to help her build a better brain. It was almost universally accepted that women's mental capacities were stunted in comparison with those of men. The womb was the distillery of woman's "vital essence." Blood flowed to it just as it flowed to the testes. But the female factory of cerebral matter was much more inefficient: even the measly monthly manufacture of a single ovum, compared with millions of dapper sperm whipped up by men in a single day, was sufficient to indicate the primitive nature of her production apparatus. In addition, much of the blood that might otherwise be distilled to build little gray cells was lost during her menses, or otherwise used to feed the next generation developing in her womb. In consequence, woman was, both in mind and body, inherently feeble, and at best no more than a "defective" man, as many scientists of the period liked to point out.

It had not been until late in the nineteenth century that medical science had once again picked up the thread, first so elaborately spun by the medieval church fathers, of women's vicious hunger for men's precious seminal fluids. Mid-nineteenth-century physicians had, in general, still recognized that, in the realm of seminal depletion, the male tended to dig his own grave. In 1855, for instance, the prominent physician Henry Wright, while admitting that "woman sometimes approaches man as the blighting mildew to his best affections and the richest fruits of his manhood," was still unwilling to see this as a process she had instigated herself. For woman, Wright maintained, notwithstanding her potentially deadly fungal parasitism,

> embodies a saving power essential to man. She may err in her modes of manifestation, through ignorance or a bad organization. She may coarsely and clumsily fulfil her holy and delicate mission. But that she so often comes as the harbinger of death, is in a great degree owing to the unnatural conditions of him to whom she comes, and to his erroneous views of the purposes of her mission.

If a man "resolutely set to work to correct his own tendencies to un-natural, sensual indulgences," he would find that "woman will come to him only as a purifying and ennobling influence." (152–4)

This philosophy of personal responsibility did not sit well with the generation of 1870, who thought it unfair to have to shoulder the blame for the failures of their manly resolve all by themselves. Scientists every-where set out to reveal the reasons why women should most certainly be held fully accountable for the sexual temptation of men. The greatest failure of the household nun of the mid-nineteenth century had been, as physicians later in the century concluded, her inability to curb the in-sistent call of her womb—and this had inevitably produced an epidemic of hysterical symptoms.

Augustus Gardner, who was a professor of the "Diseases of Women and Clinical Midwifery" at the New York Medical College, pointed out in 1870 that Plato had already insisted that "the womb of woman is an animal which has an intense desire to conceive, and which is a fury if it does not conceive." (53) Though Gardner believed that Plato had erred in attributing to the womb a protomasculine (and hence obviously primitively bisexual) capacity to produce a kind of seminal fluid of its own, our professor of clinical midwifery clearly believed in the basic ac-curacy of the image. Fortunately woman's animal womb had been lulled to sleep by civilization. Any attempt to reawaken the slumbering beast could not but be an unmitigated disaster. Gardner was convinced that uncontrolled infusions of the male's vital essence were bound to jar this predator out of its hibernation.

Gardner argued that while some misguided researchers were posit-ing the theory that hysteria was a normal feminine response to seminal deprivation, his own research had indicated that the womb would slum-ber peacefully as long as it was left unstirred by man—particularly, and that was the crux of his argument, if it had never been called to active duty by woman herself. For the key most immediately likely to unleash hysteria, that veritable black panther of feminine sexual evil, was not to be found in man's measured and dutiful acts of impregnation, but in the dreaded and, according to Gardner, all-too-widespread practice of "per-sonal pollution" among the teenage women of his time. (53–64)

Gardner was certain that "self-abuse" accounted for "woman's pres-ent degeneracy," especially among American women, who had recently taken to this habit at an alarming rate. To "a far greater degree, probably than among the women of any other country in the world," he insisted, "personal abuse lies at the root of much of the feebleness, nervousness, pale, waxen-facedness and general good-for-nothing-ness of the entire community." (221)

The relentlessly probing physicians of the generation of 1870 thus taught their sons to fear the unspeakable evil hidden behind their sisters' bedroom doors. Those weak and fainting creatures who had seemed so undemanding in their ostensible compliance with the demands of civilization had been unmasked as Dracula's daughters. Soon these sons would produce a second wave of gender ideologues, led by figures such as Remy de Gourmont, intent upon completing the demonization of woman by identifying her as a voracious entomological entity emanating out of the preevolutionary past. Every woman, this new generation argued, contained within herself the destructive potential of the woman-vampire, the sexual woman, the woman of death, who had allowed the animal inside her womb to roam free and become a devouring *vagina dentata*. Artists and illustrators inevitably rushed in to document the link between woman and the devouring maw of reproductive nature in a wide variety of apposite juxtapositions that were to become a standard feature of twentieth-century pop-culture iconography.

The theory of evolution, given its emphasis on "natural selection" and its assumption of the existence of inherent hierarchies of inequality among all beings, gave a dramatic ring of truth to the period's imagery of women as prowling sexual animals, veritable spermatophages in search of nourishment, whose appetites had begun to obstruct humanity's development into two dimorphically divergent genders.

Thus the evil sisters of the masculine imagination, unleashed by the physicians of the previous generation, needed only to be compared to the insect vampires, devouring spiders, and prowling panthers of the naturalists to be unmasked as blind slaves to their female function. They were soon given a place among the cannibals of nature Remy de Gourmont had unmasked in his "poetic" paraphrases of the already tendentious accounts of the biologists.

For with the speculative daring characteristic of much of turn-of-the-century post-Darwinian science, Gourmont had used the biologists' flights of anthropomorphizing fancy as a basis for his deliberately provocative antihumanist treatise positing the general pointlessness of all idealism in the realm of human relationships. This allowed him to argue that it was absurd to regard love as anything other than a rather messy and inefficient expression of the human animal's participation in nature's blind schemes of perpetual self-reproduction.

Rolf Armstrong, "Some Bears" cover of Puck, *March 27, 1915*
Domesticating the *vagina dentata*

"We must abandon the old ladder whose rungs the evolutionists ascended with such difficulty," he insisted. "Man is not the culmination of nature, he is *in Nature,* he is *one* of the unities of life, that is all." (2–3) No reader could have doubted Gourmont's insistence on the essential similarity of motives between humanity and the insect and animal worlds. He deliberately and sardonically used the most affective and "poetic" language he could muster each time he fell into one of his dramatic accounts of the deadly "amours" of beasts or insects.

The "courtship" of dragonflies, for instance, he described as a ritual in which the male "pursues the desired mistress" in a vain attempt to gain a transcendent experience:

> No gesture of love can be conceived more charming than that of the female slowly bending back her blue body, going halfway toward her lover, who erect on his fore-feet bears, with taut muscles, the full weight of the movement. It is so pure, so immaterial, one would say that two ideas were joined in the limpidity of ineluctable thought. (93)

But hidden within all this coital lyricism was a biological theory as gynephobic as any produced at the turn of the century, and quite as simplistically dependent on "idealistic" evolutionary theory as those of others whose "unrealistic" expectations Gourmont disdained. He returned time and time again to the love-death equation that pervaded late-nineteenth-century culture. "In most animal species," he insisted, "coition is but a prelude to death, and often love and death work their supreme act in the same instant." (84) Thus he tried to coax his readers into visions of Tristan and Isolde while reading of praying mantises and spiders.

Nature's love-death was at all times the result of the male's sexual response to the female. Woman was nothing but a monstrous breeding mechanism. Her only reason for existence was reproduction: "The sole aim of the couple is to free the female from all care that is not purely sexual, to permit her the most perfect accomplishment of her most important function." (39) Indeed, "she is sexed throughout all her parts: *tota femina sexus.*" (43) Combine this remark with that other Latin declaration of Fernel's, *totus homo semen,* quoted by Gardner, and we discover the "scientific" origins of the early-twentieth-century male's fascination with the concept of woman as vampire: the male was a container filled with vital fluids, and woman, the sexual animal, longed to gather these into her deadly womb. The biologists had proved this to be a scientifically correct description of the physiology of love. Gourmont's anthropomorphizing accounts of the reproductive cannibalism of the female spider, cochineal, and praying mantis were thus specifically constructed to turn the findings of the biologists into an entomological soap opera:

The white-fronted dectic is, like all the locustians (grasshoppers), a very ancient insect; it existed in the coal era, and it is perhaps this antiquity which explains its peculiar fecundative method. Like the cephalopoda, his contemporaries, he has recourse to the spermatophore; yet there is mating, there is embracing; there are even play and caresses. Here are the couple face to face, they caress each other with long antennae. . . . The male disentangles himself and escapes, but a new assault masters him, he lies flat on his back. This time the female, lifted on her high legs, holds him belly to belly; she bends back the extremity of her abdomen; the victim does likewise; there is junction, and soon one sees something enormous issue from the convulsive flanks of the male, as if the animal were pushing out its entrails. . . .

The female receives this leather bottle, or spermatophore, and carries it off glued to her belly. . . . She breaks off little pieces, chews them carefully, and swallows them. . . . The male has begun to sing again, during this meal, but it is not a love-song, he is about to die; he dies. Passing near him at this moment, the female looks at him, smells him, and takes a bite of his thigh.

Cannibalism, Gourmont implied, pervaded feminine nature and was not restricted to the deadly encompassment of her *vagina dentata*.

Using every bit of poetic license he could muster in his determination to draw none too subtle analogies between the predatory mating of insects and the fate of the human male who succumbs to the enticements of love, Gourmont called "the enigmatic female" of the green grasshopper a "cannibal Marguerite de Bourgogne" (a woman infamous for her reputedly unbridled sexual appetite), implying that in the realms of human and insect love alike, woman's hunger for the male essence was an intrinsic aspect of "the serenity of nature, which permits all things, wills all things, and for whom there are neither vices nor virtues, but only movements and chemical reactions." (96–7)

Thus Gourmont fed fires of sadomasochistic fascination about the cannibalistic nature of the reproductive processes that were also being fanned by such revelations as those offered by the celebrated American sociologist Lester Ward in his *Pure Sociology*—like Gourmont's *Natural Philosophy of Love,* first published in 1903. "No fact in biology is better established than that reproduction represents a specialized mode of nutrition through the renewal of the organism," Ward insisted, (290) thus directly echoing Gourmont's remark that "fecundation belongs to the general phenomena of nutrition." (96) Like Gourmont, Ward was fascinated by "the gynaecocentric theory" of the importance of material survival in the organic world,

> the view that the female sex is primary and the male secondary in the organic scheme, that originally and normally all things center, as it were, about the female, and that the male, though not necessary in carrying out the scheme, was developed under the operation of the principle of advantage to secure organic progress through the crossing of strains.

Ward, who claimed to have been the first to formulate this idea (though "in a humorous vein") at a debate attended by prominent feminists, including Elizabeth Cady Stanton, in 1888, stressed that science had since caught up with him. New research in biology had legitimized his levity, and had proved it to be truth. He emphasized the turmoil all this was likely to cause in the masculine breast: "This theory is not only new but novel, and perhaps somewhat startling." (296–7)

Citing Lamarck, Comte, Schopenhauer, and Haeckel as his precursors, Ward, like Gourmont, stressed that from a reproductive point of view the male was "a mere afterthought of nature." Darwin and T. H. Huxley had pointed to "the parasitic nature of the male in certain cases, the male being attached to the female and living at her expense." Such discoveries had shown that the male's only function among the lower forms of life was to be a sperm bearer. In those primitive contexts, "the males are reduced to the role of spermatophores." Inevitably, like Gourmont, Ward got around to the habits of female spiders—and what he had to say about them was bound to add to the reproductive anxiety of his male readers:

> While the behavior of the relatively gigantic female in seizing and devouring the tiny male fertilizer when he is only seeking to do the only duty that he exists for, may seem remarkable and even contrary to the interests of nature, the fact of the enormous difference between the female and the male, is, according to the gynaecocentric hypothesis, not anomalous at all, but perfectly natural and normal.

With a dramatic show of masochistic self-pity, Ward next quoted a letter from the prominent entomologist L. O. Howard, first published in 1886 in the journal *Science*. In its graphic details this missive topped even Gourmont's account of the love rituals of the praying mantis:

A few days since I brought a male of *Mantis carolina* to a friend who had been keeping a solitary female as a pet. Placing them in the same jar, the male, in alarm, endeavored to escape. In a few minutes the female succeeded in grasping him. She first bit off his left front tarsus, and consumed the tibia and femur. Next she gnawed out his left eye. At this the male seemed to realize his proximity to one of the opposite sex, and began vain endeavors to mate. The female next ate up his right front leg, and then entirely decapitated him, devouring his head and gnawing into his thorax. Not until she had eaten all of his thorax except about three millimeters did she stop to rest. All this while the male had continued his vain attempts to obtain entrance at the valvules, and he now succeeded, as she voluntarily spread the parts open, and union took place. She remained quiet for four hours, and the remnant of the male gave occasional signs of life by a movement of one of his remaining tarsi for three hours. The next morning she had entirely rid herself of her spouse, and nothing but his wings remained. (315–16)

This dramatic symbolic narrative of the destruction of the male's transcendent dreams of intellectual flight "on account of the rapacity of the female" must have cooled the erotic ardor of many among the human spermatophores who read this and other such accounts in the popular-science magazines of around 1900, or in the tendentious disquisitions of social theorists such as Ward and Gourmont. Ward, by and large, still made an effort to retain scientific objectivity in the matter, but Gourmont's underlying antifeminine purpose was perfectly transparent: in the realm of reproduction the male existed merely as an appetizer. With his talent for openly politicizing the findings of the biologists in terms of the "eternal battle of the sexes," Gourmont thus helped make the hidden gender-ideological motives underlying the biologists' findings explicit.

The union of male and female in sexual congress thus came to be an indication of the male's forced return to a state of primitive hermaphroditic unity with the ur-feminine in nature. As the male was reabsorbed into nature's primal reproductive frenzy, the creative achievements of progress were in effect being reversed. Thus sexual congress with a woman canceled one of evolution's primary achievements: that creative, productive "individual autonomy" the male had been able to establish at long last through the progressive accentuation of gender differences, the dogged pursuit of "dimorphic gender evolution," the radically divergent evolutionary development of men and women in diametrically opposite directions.

It was, Gourmont argued, within the context of this grand evolutionary scheme, the duty of a being "to persevere in its being and even to augment the characteristics which specialize it." (40) Among the organisms that were at the origin of all life, the feminine impulse reigned supreme. Therefore the basic *concept* of femininity was, even in terms of its primary purpose, unchangeable; it was the very essence of the endlessly self-reproductive, and hence inherently conservative, motive of nature. In primitive, hermaphroditic organisms, Gourmont asserted, the masculine, generative element was automatically engulfed and dwarfed by the reproductive feminine element. Women's-rights activists—who, after all, were determined to "reabsorb" the unique abilities men had struggled to obtain—were thus far more a part of the primitive motives of nature than they realized, for they were merely acting in accordance with the "singular feminism which one normally finds in nature. For feminism reigns there, especially among inferior species and insects." (19–20)

The biological development of species, Gourmont said, was characterized by a sequence of more or less haphazard changes. The masculine, though generally cowed by the overwhelming preponderance of the reproductive motive in nature, had, in certain situations, accidentally retained some of its essential being—some of the genetic ur-matter of creative evolution. While the dominant feminine halves of the original bisexual organisms had been busy reproducing, some of the masculine vital essence had snuck away into a new, embryonically self-assertive corner, and had thus become a heroic speck of individualist difference in a sea of collectivist femininity.

Bravely struggling against reabsorption, masculinity, in the long run, had succeeded in differentiating itself into a separate, male organ of generation. Residual traces of this development could still be found in the growth of the human masculine embryo: "The female is primitive. At the third month, the human embryo has external uro-genital organs clearly resembling the female organs. To arrive at the complete female estate they have to undergo but a very slight modification; to become male they have to undergo a considerable and very complex transformation." (18) Freud and penis envy were clearly waiting in the wings of Gourmont's theater of evolution.

At last the male had gained a certain measure of morphological autonomy in nature—a root requirement for the development of individual identity, of ego—but only after a long, drawn-out evolutionary struggle against the dominance of reproductive femininity. For "while hermaphroditism demands a perfect resemblance of individuals . . . the separation of the sexes leads, in principle, to dimorphism, the role of the male and his modes of activity differ from those of the female."

Masculinity must therefore be regarded as the triumph of the intellect over nature itself: "It is almost only among mammifers and in certain groups of birds that the male is equal or superior to the female. One would say that he has slowly attained a first place not intended by nature for him." (20) Thus from his origin as a generative spermatozoid, through his development into an autonomous masculine organ, to his ultimate transformation into the ultimate rebel form of human masculine individualism, the male's triumphant development into a separate organism should really be seen as an affront against the purposes of nature itself. Indeed, the concept of masculinity, the core of the principle of dimorphic gender evolution, was the true source of man's triumph over nature. Masculinity and evolutionary progress were two terms for a single principle. (33)

No wonder, then, that Tarzan and his numerous pulp-fiction clones in twentieth-century pop culture found themselves perpetually caught in deadly altercations with demonic emissaries from the world of entomology, or with ferocious denizens of primal nature's numerous prehistoric Jurassic Parks. The wild women these heroes encountered were equally predictably teamed with the most intimidating saber-toothed predators to be found in the jungle of primitive bisexuality. The "good girls" who accompanied the masterful musclemen of masculine species evolution into the wilds of nature in turn always had their hands full trying to keep the monstrous *vagina dentata* of primal instinct at bay while their men went about the business of saving the world.

Meanwhile Gourmont's remarkable and fanciful outline of the creation of masculinity out of the fluids of generation provided the more intellectually inclined with a pseudological explanation for the physiologists' contention that the human brain was, in essence, a coagulate of seminal fluids, a storehouse of "essential manhood." To Ezra Pound this aspect of his French mentor's odd prose poem of misogynist invective clearly spoke with particular force, and Pound took it upon himself to translate Gourmont's 1903 treatise into English in 1921.

The American edition, together with a postscript by Pound, was published by Boni and Liveright in August 1922, and thereafter continued a long life of its own as a vaguely salacious compendium of sexological information for intellectuals, a status probably largely inspired by its graphic delineations of the large assortment of "prongs" and other bestial accoutrements used by insects in their various attempts at reproduction. The book had gone into a third printing by 1925 and was published in England in 1926 before being republished privately by the Rarity Press in New York in 1931 as a "careful scientific inquiry into the subject of sex in relation to man and the lower animals." After that, various pirated and semilegitimate editions continued the book's educational mission well into the 1950s.

As late as 1958, Pound included his postscript to Gourmont's opus in his essay collection *Pavannes and Divagations.* Neither the book nor Pound's postscript can therefore be dismissed as merely an odd and fugitive item in the annals of twentieth-century culture. Pound clearly found in the Frenchman's heavily metaphoric study of animal sexuality one of the main keys to his own theory of creativity—and of male-female relationships.

In his pompous "Translator's Postscript," Pound, who loved to palm off secondhand notions as his own ideas, suggested that "it is more than likely that the brain itself is, in origin and development, only a sort of great clot of genital fluid held in suspense or reserve." Moreover, he continued, obviously excited by his own inventive brilliance as he repeated this medical commonplace of his time, "species would have developed in accordance with, or their development would have been affected by, the relative discharge and retention of the fluid." (169)

Pound had, of course, cribbed this "new idea" from his mentor, but he could just as well have based his version on numerous other contemporary sources. By the time he translated Gourmont's book, the notion had been accepted by most intellectuals. It certainly was not the peculiarly Poundian fantasy it has been made out to be by recent scholars. Instead, it was one of the central principles of the early twentieth century's ideology of gender.

However, most of the physicians and intellectuals of his time danced around the notion with elaborate garlands of decorous circumlocution, and Pound's bluntness therefore represents an invaluable and rare instance of expressive candor. But the fact is that during the 1910s the idea that the *male* brain (women's essential contribution to that region was negligible, after all) was a "great clot of genital fluid" had become a widely accepted subtext underlying the period's gender-ideological disquisitions. It was undoubtedly also a spur to the discovery, by its medical researchers, that *all* women were, in essence, doomed by nature to be "brain vampires"—a discovery that was itself to be a logical extension of the seminal-continence theories that had led to the idealization of "muscular virility" as the outward indicator of evolutionary "superiority."

In light of the widespread currency of this biomedical assumption during the early years of this century, Freud's concept of sublimation loses some of its gloss as a product of innovative thinking. Indeed, his proposition that the creative impulse was "generated" by the libido had clearly found its origin in the vital-essence theory of the brain. Gourmont had already insisted that all intellectual activity was a product of the sexual impulse. Theorems of this nature could have held no surprises for scientists and lay persons who had already determined that man's gray matter was, in principle, a product of the testes.

The theory of evolution's popularity among the vast majority of turn-of-the-century intellectuals, coupled with dreams of Aryan economic grandeur such as William Graham Sumner delineated, had fostered a wide range of fantasies concerning man's (read: "the male's") imminent transcendence to a higher level of intellectual (and hence also physical) consciousness. The expectation that man would soon reach true supermale status informed the ruminations of philosophers, scientists, and artists alike, from Nietzsche to Nordau, from Lombroso to Freud, and from Wagner to Alfred Jarry, on up well into the twentieth century to the likes of Ezra Pound and, ultimately, Adolf Hitler. Often, as in the case of Remy de Gourmont, those superman dreams manifested themselves negatively, in the form of an ironic denial of the likelihood of such a further development, given the obstructive power of the female reproductive element in nature. Still, evolutionary idealism, whether posited as an imminent possibility or as a pipe dream made unattainable by the grim realities of man's links to the animal world, was in virtually all cases at the center of argument among intellectuals.

The sudden blossoming of vampire themes in the popular culture of the period after 1870 now reveals its own logical inevitability as a transmutation of the economic principles of social Darwinism into the metaphoric realm of gender conflict. Reasonable men everywhere had learned to shudder at the realization that woman was driven by instinct to go after the "vital fluids" the male needed most to survive in the dog-eat-dog economic world detailed by Spencer and Sumner and widely identified as the staging arena for the inevitable imperialist "struggle for life among nations." At the same time scientists had begun to assert that humanity, rather than occupying a special position above the animal world on the great chain of being, as religion insisted, was propelled by motives that were, through the fragile and easily reversible processes of "dimorphic gender development," linked directly to the destructive passions of nature's predators.

It had not been nearly as easy to make such assumptions until the ascendancy of the theory of evolution to a position of virtual law among the educated strata of Western society. This fundamental transformation of cultural attitudes had been all but completed by the year 1900. Darwinism seemed to attack the very concept that humane coexistence was either feasible or, for that matter, desirable. Earlier the conviction that there existed an absolute and fundamental God-created difference between humanity and the animals had seemed to many the very foundation upon which all personal moral responsibility toward others was predicated. Now Darwin had come along to insist that through a process of natural selection man was "descended from some less highly organized form" in nature. Instead of having been made in God's image, he was, of all things, descended from "a hairy, tailed quadruped, probably arboreal in its habits." (*Descent of Man,* 696) Darwin understood very well what this meant: "The belief in God has often been advanced as not only the greatest but the most complete of all the distinctions between man and the lower animals. It is, however, impossible . . . to maintain that this belief is innate or instinctive in man." (700)

To Darwin's contemporaries these revelations had come as a source of great hope as well as of immense fear. For if man's "godlike intellect" was a product of evolution, rather than the result of an act of creation directly willed by God, this meant that humanity need not maintain the static position Christian doctrine had assigned to it, somewhere between the angels and the animals. Instead, he was clearly free to orchestrate his own evolution into a true "superman," a creature with intellectual powers analogous to those previously given only to the angels. But Darwin had also included a rather terrifying hitch to this evolutionary scenario: he had insisted that the animal past had remained encoded in "the embryological structure of man." The scientist could thus "partly recall in imagination the former condition of our early progenitors." This was not at all a comforting intellectual exercise for man, since it brought to the fore all too clearly "the homologies which he presents with the lower animals—the rudiments which he retains—and the reversions to which he is liable." (696)

In consequence, fear of "reversion," of a return of the repressed "animal impulses" in man, became a widespread obsession. If Darwin's contentions were correct, there were only two roads left open to man: either he could continue to add gray cells to his cranium until he reached superman status, or he must descend into an inescapable spiral of degeneration by squandering his vital essence. Burroughs's Tarzan, always known for his excellent timing, had come onto the pop-cultural scene in 1912. Being a principled, morally and physically superior white man in the ape-infested world of primal Africa, he rapidly revealed himself to be the perfect symbolic-metaphoric representative of higher civilization's never-ending quest to transcend the limitations placed upon modern man by the brutal demands of predatory nature.

Gourmont, Pound, and the vast host of others who liked to sketch out nightmarish scenarios of the regressive role of the feminine in nature were thus in fact rather ordinary members of that oversubscribed men's club of turn-of-the-century intellectuals perhaps best designated as the league of prurient prudes: men both fearful of and yet endlessly fascinated by the enticements of human sexuality. They set out to destroy their "Puritan" parents' "sentimental" ideas about the special angelic nature of their sisters, not to liberate them, but to demonize the very concept of femininity itself.

They were determined to show the world that women were "inherently evil," that they represented nature's entrance into the cave of primal depredation. But when it came to having to decide between virtue and the dreams of promiscuity the suspect passions of these "evil sisters" evoked in their fevered brains, they quickly scurried back into the Victorian fold.

Gourmont, for instance, after regaling his readers with countless lurid and terrifying tales of sexual promiscuity and cannibalism in the insect world, concluded that "one need not scorn chastity nor disdain asceticism," since "asceticism, of which humanity alone is capable, is one of the means which may lift us above animality; but by itself it is insufficient to do this; by itself it is good for nothing, save perhaps to excite sterile pride; one must add to it an active exercise of the intelligence." (143) An ever intensifying dimorphism separating the social functions of men and women constituted humanity's only hope of escaping the backsliding sexual machinations of brute nature represented by the feminine. Gourmont intimated that "a notable difference, morphological and psychological, between the two sexes," was "one of the very conditions of civilization." The greater that difference, the higher the evolutionary status of a culture. The twain ought never to meet again, for "masculine work diminishes femininity, while feminine work feminizes the males." (36-40)

Thus, only man's intelligence could free him from the tyranny of sex. The brain, Gourmont argued, again following popular scientific assumptions, would become so intent upon conserving its capacity for primary intellection that it would henceforth refuse to release any but the most minimal measures of that seminal matter of which it was composed. That was why "superior human specimens are nearly always sterile, or capable of only mediocre posterity." (167)

This last remark, to us so apparently extravagant and outrageous, had by 1915 gained virtually the status of folk wisdom. Few questioned its universal truth. Though it has since gradually lost its position of prominence as a biological axiom, it helped shape the conceptions of a generation of artists and intellectuals whom we still regard as near-contemporaries.

In Ernest Hemingway's *To Have and Have Not* (1937), for example, we find the following dialogue between the book's most manly man, Harry Morgan, and his doting wife, Marie. They are discussing their disappointing daughters: "Those girls aren't much, are they?" Harry observes. His wife dutifully replies: "No, Hon." "Funny we couldn't get no boys," Harry ruminates. Marie counters by remarking: "That's because you're such a man. That way it always comes out girls." (126)

What Marie is saying here would have made a lot of sense to Hemingway's readers of the 1930s. They would have understood the statement as an effective, simply worded, but basically accurate expression of the "scientific" discovery that "superior" males were inherently unwilling to "spend" enough of their vital essence to allow the production of adequate male offspring. This was, in fact, a breakthrough in medical knowledge frequently used at the time to explain why "great minds" so often produced children who—though provided with every genetic advantage imaginable—ended up being intellectual "disappointments" to their parents.

Hemingway's original readers, then, doubtlessly accepted as normal a viciously antifeminine dialogue we today might be tempted to read as a satirical exposé of the medical ignorance of working-class people. But Hemingway wanted us to sympathize with these two "genuine" human beings who were trying to survive in a world the author regarded as having become effeminate and ruled by predatory females. There is little doubt that he was speaking for himself through Marie—a point we might be hard pressed to accept unless we understand the historical "ordinariness" of Marie's seemingly so extraordinary remark. By having the good woman Marie praise Harry's manhood in this fashion, Hemingway consciously chose to reinforce the invidious gender-ideological implications of the vital-essence theory so popular during the period of his apprenticeship as a writer.

In the postscript to his translation of Gourmont's *Natural Philosophy of Love,* Ezra Pound, as a matter of fact, demonstrated that working-class Marie was as up-to-date in her physiological speculations as the most avant-garde among her intellectual contemporaries. Pound had speculated that increases in the relative intelligence or debility of animals as well as of men and women were determined by their ability to retain enough seminal fluid to let the proper "brain-silting" occur:

> Some animals profiting hardly at all by the alluvial Nile-flood; the baboon [frequently used as an example of notorious promiscuity in nature] retaining nothing; men apparently stupefying themselves in some cases by excess, and in other cases discharging apparently only a surplus at high pressure; the imbecile, or the genius, the "strong minded." (169)

Ironically, given Pound's often expressed hatred for the bourgeois mentality and its pursuit of the "cash-nexus," his concept of the formation and growth of the brain is based on exactly those Puritan principles of personal "containment, control and development" that gave impetus to Spencer's and Sumner's capitalist economic imperialism. To grow and prosper, one should preserve at least one's principal and "spend" only surplus capital. To the Puritan that had been a sign of one's election by God. To contain oneself morally and economically was to be "strong-minded." He who squandered his principal, his "seed"-capital, was, on the other hand, clearly an "imbecile" incapable of self-control, one of those whom God had rejected.

Ideas of this sort, usually hidden behind metaphors of a more decorous nature than Pound had been willing to find, underlie the production of most of the twentieth century's literary lights. Thus we can be sure that F. Scott Fitzgerald counted on his readers' understanding of both the physiological and economic principles of spermatic expenditure and female vampirism when, in 1922 in *The Beautiful and Damned,* he wrote that "Gloria had lulled Anthony's mind to sleep." (191) At the age of thirty-two, the novel's male hero had thus become "a bleak and disordered wreck," (406) clearly one of Gourmont's emptied spermatophores.

Fitzgerald's terminology is, of course, exactly analogous to that used by the long forgotten Porter Emerson Browne in his description of the effects of Schuyler's descent into the lair of the Vampire. Indeed Fitzgerald was no doubt strongly influenced by at least the movie version of *A Fool There Was.* Like the average moviegoer of 1915, he would have seen in that film what a man could expect from the energy vampirism to which women were prone. It was precisely this ambient knowledge (still festering in the late-twentieth-century viewer as a sub- or semiconscious cultural prejudice) that Theda Bara personified in her film debut. It was this knowledge that served to turn the climactic single kiss with which she reclaimed her prey into such a shocking and paradigmatic visual event.

The act of depredation thus depicted in *A Fool There Was* was, then, though sexual and financial, first of all a depiction of women's instinctual "energy vampirism." As such it represented the cultural identification of a new existential hazard: injudicious seminal "spending." By ending up "a bleak and disordered wreck" in the arms of a sexual vampire, Schuyler paved the way for the decline and fall of Fitzgerald's Anthony Patch seven years later.

By the time *A Fool There Was* came to be filmed, nineteenth-century prohibitions concerning the public display of sexual themes had largely disintegrated. Nudity (though usually covered with diaphanous gauze) was not uncommon, even on the "legitimate" stage. Academic artists had mostly given up pretending that the lusciously proportioned, unclothed woodland waifs they painted were philosophically or historically motivated; and in the movies, Roman orgies heaving with robustly endowed feminine bodies were becoming a staple.

But to watch two people kiss, to express not simple affection but raw sexual desire, still fell well beyond what had become casually acceptable. Our erotic sensibilities have become jaded by decades of explicit scenes of voyeuristic exploitation, yet even from our vantage point that 1915 kiss remains lewd. The ideological energies underpinning

Theda Bara's action, though today they may have precipitated into our subconscious, have nonetheless remained an integral element of our conception of gender relationships.

We still realize that this kiss is not a kiss but the embrace of a primitive, regressive-feminine emanation of nature, a spider, a praying mantis, a deadly insect whose embrace illustrated the scientists' contention that aggression was the deciding force in all interpersonal relationships. This was an iconic kiss, and as such it is still emblematic of the social ideology that has dominated our consciousness ever since.

The opportunistic new conceptualization of the nature of economic relationships delineated by William Graham Sumner and numerous others had served both as source and fuel to the turn of the century's attempts to identify the motivational implications of humanity's newly discovered animal instincts and animal origins. Biology, anthropology, and sociology were daily discovering further analogues between human motivation and the "laws of the jungle." Descriptions of the ruthless gender wars of insects were soon being matched by equally graphic descriptions of horrific primitive human sex practices and tendentious accounts of the "lower races'" bestial disregard for human life.

All these shocking revelations were clearly intended to help the generation of 1900 get over its "religious" prejudice that there might be a qualitative difference in the basic motivations of humans and animals. The road to perfection is ever elusive. It is, on the other hand, much less difficult to delineate the failures we encounter on our voyage to the ideal. Most of us acquire ample experience in that realm.

The typical intellectual of the early twentieth century, therefore, while affirming humanity's need for higher spiritual goals, tended to concentrate on delineating, in Nietzsche's words, "the vast distance between himself and his aim." Most were content to see themselves as merely responding defensively to the predatory nature of the world around them. The evolutionist credo demanded that each rugged warrior in the trench warfare of natural selection "must be," to quote Nietzsche again, "an enemy to the men he loves and the institutions in which he grew up; he must spare neither person nor thing, however it may hurt him; he will be misunderstood and thought an ally of forces that he abhors; in his search for righteousness he will seem unrighteous by human standards." (351)

Evidences of the necessary inhumanity of each man toward all others could be found everywhere. Indeed, the inexorable course of civi-

lization demanded that one be predatory, and content to be so, for to
flinch from that task was to demonstrate one's evolutionary inferiority,
and hence the probability that one was to fall by the wayside in the
"struggle for life." Social theories that extolled the splendid achievements of predatory individualism and the virtues of imperialism as a
"civilizing" factor were the order of the day. These encouraged the
person to rejoice not only in the domination of others but also in the
domination of nature itself through phenomenal feats of virtuous
self-control. War came to be considered a glorious feature of man's creative evolution, and aggression seemed a key to the very meaning of life.

World War I was the inevitable result of the ascendancy of this
predatory mentality. The half-century to follow was to see the cultural
dominance of a boundless range of theories all positing the evolutionary necessity of unrelenting belligerence. This cultural glorification of
hatred helped prepare Western culture for a second worldwide orgy of
destruction in what was to prove to be a century of mass murder in the
name of higher civilization.

The dominant ideology of the turn of the century expressed itself
in a series of strict dualistic choices. "Being" meant being in control;
nothingness was to be controlled by another. Selfhood was dominance;
submission signified loss of self—death. If love was an expression of selfhood and the nonself was death, then to love another meant to expand
one's love of self. On the level of social metaphor, to love was therefore
an act of incorporation. You preyed, or you were preyed upon. Love and
depredation went hand in hand. That is why Freud, to almost universal
acclaim, had come to the conclusion that love and death were pretty
much one and the same thing, especially if you happened to be the one
being incorporated rather than the one doing the incorporating.

It was a foregone conclusion that within such a social environment
love and sex would come to be seen as forms of deadly vampirism. The
men of the early twentieth century considered it their birthright to do
the incorporating. If the woman refused to become a passive subject, or
if she used strategies of her own to make the male emotionally dependent on her, she was branded an engulfer, an incorporating vampire.

The movie version of *A Fool There Was* distilled the dominant
worldview of 1915 into a singular confrontation between a man and a
woman. Theda Bara's kiss was emblematic of the triumph of sex over
love, of degeneration over evolution, of negative aggression over creative incorporation—of woman over man. But the movie's success had

been predetermined by its cultural antecedents, for the sociology of aggression was a direct response to the practical needs of the economics of
accumulation. The origins of modern vampire imagery in the late-
nineteenth-century imagination were very precise. The primitive male
inside the eternal female was baring his invasive fangs. Dracula was on
the move.

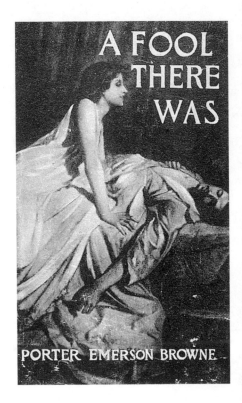

Philip Burne-Jones (1862–1926), "The Vampire," ca. 1897, and
Cover of Porter Emerson Browne's A Fool There Was
(The H. K. Fly Company, Publishers, New York, 1909)

III. FOR THE BLOOD IS THE LIFE: HYSTERIA, FREUD'S JEWEL BOX, TRANSCENDENT MANHOOD, AND THE MARK OF THE BEAST

A scandalously suggestive painting made London art lovers whisper in April 1897. Titled *The Vampire*, it luridly delineated the soul-destroying consequences of feminine lust. Exhibited at the New Gallery, it was the work of Philip Burne-Jones, usually forced to work in the shadow of his far more illustrious father, Sir Edward Coley Burne-Jones.

The painting showed a young man prone and lifeless upon his bed, his pale features bloodless, his body drained of all its energy and manhood. The vaguely bohemian nature of his bedroom and the flamboyant cut of his nightdress suggested that the victim was an artist. A dark spot, almost like a bullet wound, was visible on his half-bare chest. Hovering above him, leaning on bare arms in a catlike, half-crouched position, sharp teeth flashing with a steely glint between thin lips, the woman.

Her eyes are as dark as coals, smoldering above high, hollow cheeks and ringed by the ashes of hell. Her torso and loins are outlined starkly by the flowing gauzes and clinging folds of her gown. Long, dark hair undulates over her shoulders; white skin and the agile curves of hip and thigh proclaim her youth. She is a nightmare image of physical hunger and hot passion, an enticing female version of Henry Fuseli's monstrous *Incubus* of a hundred years earlier. The tensile strength of her slender limbs contrasts dramatically with the artist's prostrate inanition. Her body, we realize, has gained what his has lost.

Burne-Jones's message was clear: the womb of woman was indeed an animal. Hysteria burned in this young woman's eyes—a direct consequence of what Augustus Gardner had called the "exciting erethisms" she must have employed in the "super-excitation of the uterus." (54) By 1897 everyone knew that women who had reawakened the beast were doomed to slide back down the evolutionary ladder until they reached the hunting grounds of primitive humanity, for in them, nature yearned for savage rituals: "The least impression is redoubled like the sound of a *tam-tam,*" Gardner had said. A young woman so affected would seek out "emotions still more violent and more varied. It is this necessity, which nothing can appease, which took the Roman women to the spectacles where men were devoured by ferocious beasts, and which now actually attracts them to bull-fights and capital executions." (72) In such cases, a woman soon lost the veneer of civilization and could be counted upon to degrade "the nuptial couch by copying the foulness of the bagnio."

These women were the direct ancestors of Ernest Hemingway's Brett Ashley, always seductively in motion, creatures kissed by the devil, daughters of Dracula. The awakened woman was out of control, driven only by the vampire within her: her lion's mouth, her *vagina dentata.* Swept up in the hysteria of her reproductive impulse, she became a destroyer. The animal womb was the cannibal mouth of the primordial praying mantis, the spider, the primitive spermatophage. Hysteria had very sharp teeth.

Alerted by hordes of physicians such as Gardner that "these nervous women are pale, wan and languishing; the skin is dry and cold or burning; the eye is cast down or haggard, timid or caressing, the complexion cloudy; the physiognomy languishingly expressive and very mobile," (71–3) the young men of 1897 could not help but recognize the debilitating activity of the animal womb in the pose of the woman in Burne-Jones's painting. Indeed, in their scissorlike separation, her thighs recalled the praying mantis's jaws of death. A slight realignment of the two bodies—one no censor of the period would have tolerated—would have shown her straddling her victim, to apply the evil teeth of her bestial nature directly to the feast of seminal extraction here so obviously intimated by the artist.

It would have been impossible for Burne-Jones to have devised a more topical shocker. Like many other cultural icons that gain their notoriety by tapping directly into the mainline of a period's ideological preoccupations, this painting struck a chord whose fickle sonances would reverberate far and wide. For Burne-Jones's scandalous painting had an international influence that far exceeded its artistic merits. Its popularity became emblematic of the popularity—and hence the social significance—of the vampire theme as it began to unfold from the late nineteenth century up to the present.

At the time of *The Vampire*'s exhibition, it was widely rumored that the artist's motivation for painting this denunciation of predatory womanhood had been an infatuation with the prominent London actress Mrs. Patrick Campbell. The painting's stagelike visual setting certainly suggests a direct link with theatrical mise-en-scène. The larger cultural motive for this melodrama in paint, however, was the remarkable confluence of aggressive sexual, racial, and economic obsessions characteristic of the fin de siècle, which also drove Bram Stoker to publish his novel *Dracula* at virtually the same historical moment Burne-Jones first displayed *The Vampire* in public.

Stoker's preoccupation with vampirism may or may not have had any influence on Burne-Jones's selection of this theme. The two were friends, and there was most likely an exchange of ideas, but it was the socioeconomic environment of the 1890s that had made the ascendancy of vampire themes inevitable during this period. The institutionalization of an imperialist economic agenda required that "others" be conceptualized as evil, inferior, or both. Under the tutelage of Herbert Spencer, William Graham Sumner, and other social Darwinists, predatory social relationships had come to seem inevitable. Aggression was an expression of "natural law." The "rugged individualist" showed his mettle by obliterating those who stood in his way. The reigning dichotomy of evolution and degeneration had created a need for a symbolic opponent who embodied the evils of the nonself and who could become the scapegoat for all failures of nerve, self-assertion, and personal "continence" to which the not yet perfect warriors of imperialism were prone. The vampire, the archetypal shape-shifter, the protean predator who could never be pinned down, was an embodiment of the general sense of unease and personal danger that must characterize the state of mind of those who live in a culture that glorifies aggression.

Burne-Jones's female vampire was, in any case, clearly an evil sister, a Lucy Westenra who had fallen under Dracula's influence by responding to the call of the wild, the call of her womb. That this was the painting's message few would have doubted, for *The Vampire* was what was called in its day a "problem picture." That meant it contained an underlying philosophical message that might not be apparent at first glance to the average viewer. Artists had developed the practice of exhibiting such works with apposite quotations from literary texts. Philip Burne-Jones's painting, however, was able to dispense with such cumbersome research. It was one of the first British entries into the field of painted modern "moral documentaries," a genre that had only recently become popular in Western European academic art. These works did not call upon the viewers' knowledge of history, classical literature, or myth but on their knowledge of modern medical research, biology, and psychiatry.

Burne-Jones, in painting his image of woman as vampire, thus played quite as deliberately on the newest revelations of science as Bram Stoker did when, in *Dracula,* he cited Charcot, Lombroso, and Nordau—the period's leading experts on hysteria and degeneration—to characterize the primitive nature of his vampire-predator. Both the painting and the novel are therefore dramatic reflections of the popular reception given to the scientific truths of the imperialist era. To them the usually unspoken but widely understood equation of blood, semen, and economic potency, which had preoccupied the generation of 1870, had become an issue of life and death.

The Montreal clergyman W. J. Hunter, for one, worried that the world might lose its evolutionary momentum in a morass of foolishly spilled seed. In his book *Manhood Wrecked and Rescued* (1900), he repeatedly quoted prominent medical authorities to drive home the cautionary message that "loss of semen is loss of blood." We should never forget, he warned, paraphrasing familiar knowledge, that

> the semen, or male principle, is composed of the elements which form brain, nerve, muscle, bone—in short, every tissue of which the body is composed; and by parting with it a portion of the life principle is lost; and a constant loss of the life principle, whether for purposes of generation or otherwise, must invariably drain the system of a vast amount of life force, and render it an easy prey to the innumerable diseases to which humanity is subject. (119)

"Blood," "loss," "drain," and "prey": these were, of course, all key words in the vampire equation.

Ironically, the Reverend Hunter's remarks, so easily dismissed by

today's readers as foolish and naive, help to explain the premises underlying the writings of the early-twentieth-century grand masters of psychoanalysis, writings that often still remain unquestioned as legitimate
analytic sources for the treatment of our own sense of social imbalance.
It may at first seem foolish to attempt to link the fears of a minor Cana-
dian religious writer to the ideas of Freud, the father of modern psychoanalysis. But Hunter's desire to keep his manful readers from killing
themselves through sexual expenditure helps us understand Freud's insistence on linking eros and thanatos. Freud's discovery of that odd mental configuration he came to regard as the "death instinct" is a logical
extrapolation from the late-nineteenth-century socioeconomic mentality that had come to see destructive, aggressive, and suicidal tendencies
as normal expressions of the degenerative inroads of eros into the God-
given life of man.

Well before Freud formulated his notion of the death instinct, his
student Otto Weininger, in his widely influential book *Sex and Character*
(1903), had already suggested that since sexual activity involved the loss
of vital energy, it should ultimately be seen as an act of violence:

> Since Novalis first called attention to it, many have insisted on
> the association between sexual desire and cruelty. All that is born
> of woman must die. Reproduction, birth, and death are indis-
> solubly associated; the thought of untimely death awakens sex-
> ual desire in its fiercest form, as the determination to reproduce
> oneself. And so sexual union, considered ethically, psychologi-
> cally, and biologically, is allied to murder; it is the negation of
> the woman and the man; in its extreme case it robs them of
> their consciousness to give life to the child. (248)

Freud, Weininger, and virtually everyone else growing up during
the later nineteenth century had been bombarded with speculations
concerning the link between semen and blood, and most had unquestioningly accepted these as scientific truths. Once we strip Freud's pos-
tulate of the "death instinct" of the technical jargon with which he
surrounded his discovery, we realize that the notion is, frankly, no more
than a complex restatement and justification of the long-standing medical declaration that every time a man ejaculated he died a little, and that
therefore eros and thanatos were two sides of the same coin.

The increasing popularity of narratives about vampires was also related to the medical establishment's virtual equation of semen and

blood. Guard your blood, for it is your capital—your genetic inheritance—as well as your life, was the message of Stoker's *Dracula*. Dr. Seward, the thoroughly modern alienist who is one of the heroes of the book, reports that Renfield, the madman in Dracula's thrall, sees blood as a unique source of renewal: "He was lying on his belly on the floor licking up, like a dog, the blood which had fallen from my wounded wrist." As if hypnotized, Renfield repeats "over and over again: 'The blood is the life! The blood is the life!'" (149)

The Reverend Hunter, of course, was in a better position than most to appreciate the biblical authority of Renfield's utterance. He knew very well that religion *and* medicine stood in massed authority behind him when, a scant three years after Renfield, he too stressed the eros-thanatos equation: "loss of semen is loss of blood. The blood is the life, and if you drain off a sufficient quantity life becomes extinct." (118) The seminal ecology movement of the age of Spencer and Sumner clearly did not fool around with half measures.

Recent critics have learned to point with amusement to the supposedly "subconscious" sexual imagery of the early vampire narratives. But the artists and writers who developed the twentieth century's image of the vampire were not at all naive about the link between vampirism and sexuality. To them, however, the link did not so much represent a psychological equation as a direct medical truth. Even marginally educated males of the period would have recognized these tales as cautionary directives against sexual incontinence. The turn of the century, after all, was the age of symbolism. Readers then were used to reading between the lines when it came to sexual matters. Today we expect to be shown everything related to sexuality in minute detail. What might seem like extraordinarily sophisticated symbolism to us would have been crystal clear to the well-informed reader of 1900—though he would have been too well-bred to prattle about it in talk-show fashion.

During the fifty years around 1900, many were, instead, still trying to cope with the apparent contradictions between scientific and religious truths. Biblical exegesis had been placed under a good deal of strain, but in its semen-blood equation science had clearly helped illuminate the Bible and the Mosaic laws against the ingestion of blood: "Only be sure that thou eat not the blood: for the blood *is* the life; and thou mayest not eat the life with the flesh." (Deut. 12:23) The Bible held that to ingest blood was to ingest life, and science had now shown that semen was blood. The man's part in the reproductive process, ejaculation, must therefore be an actual "bloodletting," truly a step toward death—a *petit mort*, a "little death," as the French insisted.

It would, then, seem almost impossible for the more imaginative men of the turn of the century *not* to have come up with an up-to-date version of the vampire of folk legend. Medical science demanded it. Stoker, for instance, used Renfield's lucid moments to convey the "logical" motive underlying his madman's actions: thus Renfield admits that he attacked Seward in an attempt to short-circuit the biblical injunction against appropriating "the life" of others: "I tried to kill him for the purpose of strengthening my vital powers by the assimilation with my own body of life through the medium of his blood—relying, of course, upon the Scriptural phrase, 'For the blood is the life.' " (240)

Even to non-Bible-reading contemporary moviegoers that scriptural phrase should still sound quite familiar, for Dracula—not Renfield—utters it in Francis Ford Coppola's film version of Stoker's book, in a scene in which the satanic vampire blasphemously parodies the Roman Catholic sacramental communion ceremony. It is a logical transference, for the phrase calls attention to the religious origins of the vampire's depredation of the blood of ordinary people. Through the faithful flows "the blood of Christ," offered to them during the ceremony of the Eucharist to maintain the spiritual bond between God and His worshipers. This symbolic bond of blood, this gift of God's blood-sacrifice, the essence of God ingested by the faithful, holds the promise of eternal life. Among those given to blasphemy, this holy ritual (which undoubtedly can be traced to an origin in analogue pre-Christian ceremonies) could easily be mistaken for a form of "energy vampirism" through which the communicants would gain immortality by ingesting the "blood" of the Son of God.

Within this context Dracula, as an incarnation of Satan, is clearly, as he always is within the Christian context, an arch parodist, a blasphemous, Oscar Wildean inverter of the will of God. It was God's intention to elevate the faithful through holy communion to the status of eternally living cells in His celestial body, provided they show themselves worthy in the material world through species evolution, efficient economic management, and the consequent accumulation of sufficient wealth. The collective religious imagination is ecumenical, blending Puritan ideas with Catholic ones and those of every denomination in between. Therefore it clearly would be Satan's delight to vampirize the faithful. Dracula and his minions thus became the predatory shock troops of the Devil, invading the world of the living, drinking the blood of God's anointed, and gaining invidious immortality from the theft of the God-given vital energies of the faithful. Thus they would turn the radiant cells of the living God into the viral pestilence of the undead Devil. These "Draculoids," symbolic self-polluters preying on the continent male for illegal sustenance, now became the cause of death itself—crawling beasts of sexual predation, deliberately abandoned by God in the evolutionary advance.

Vampires, then, were the resentful fallen angels of Darwinian species degeneration—erotic, and hence racial and economic inferiors—who circled the globe, eager to bring death to the men of steel, the evolutionary elite of the age of imperialism. In our own day, the "scientific" specificity of these cultural commonplaces has been lost. Now the apparent "symbolism" of the period's vampire narratives has come to be seen as reflective of an "archetypal" pattern embedded in the "collective unconscious." Thus the underlying political motives of the sexual superstitions of a hundred years ago continue to influence our own time on an even more insidious level: as natural and "instinctual" impulses. Propaganda that disguises itself as "scientific truth" is hard to counter. The ultimate irony of this train of events is that entirely different medical realities are making it easy for today's media to exploit even the early-twentieth-century vampire tale's underlying contention that sex "diseases" the blood. A generation terrorized by the thought of AIDS is now being guided to think of sex as a "disease" of the blood in a far more literal sense than early-twentieth-century moralists such as Bram Stoker and the Reverend Hunter could have imagined.

Given the confluence of these themes at the turn of the century, it can also come as no surprise that the vampire was usually a woman with sex on her mind—and her victims' gold in her pocket. True, the most persistent vampire of them all was Dracula, a man, but male vampires were always immediately recognizable as degenerate aristocrats, effete foreigners. They were almost always sexually ambiguous and hence "unmanly." If they were the acknowledged leaders of the vampire pack, that was primarily because, being, after all, still marginally male, they were inevitably smarter than their female counterparts. Natural selection thus required that they lord it over their feminine minions. Dracula, for instance, behaves like a stern older brother to the evil sisters in his castle, authoritatively establishing hierarchies of depredation in a matter-of-fact extension of the bourgeois world's normal male responsibilities. In

Dracula there is no indication that women would even think of leaving the vampire family household. They did not accompany Dracula on his voyage to England, for overtly sexual women were not "presentable" in polite society.

Stoker, however, gives us an elaborate delineation of the making of a female vampire in the figure of Lucy Westenra. Lucy, as a not yet awakened but emphatically sexual woman, cannot understand why society won't let "a girl marry three men, or as many as want her." (68) Stoker played the blood-semen equation popular among his contemporaries for all it was worth by making Lucy the direct conduit between Aryan manhood and Dracula, the emissary of degeneration. While being preyed upon by the vampire, she receives, in the form of transfusions, the blood, the symbolic manhood, of no less than four men. Carmilla, in Le Fanu's 1870 novella, is an incarnation of the lubricious countess Mircalla, whose sexual exploits were infamous during her lifetime. Thus, like Lucy, she became an easy prey to one of Dracula's brood. Before 1900, in other words, female vampires were rarely self-starters but needed a male to "awaken" them to their hunger for blood. These early writers about female vampires clearly agreed with Otto Weininger, who remarked in *Sex and Character* that "there is not a single woman in the history of thought, not even the most man-like, who can be truthfully compared with men of fifth- or sixth-rate genius." (69)

The male vampire almost always remained a metaphoric monster, a creature of the imagination, whose insistence on flashing his fangs gave him away as a primitive predator. But beginning with Burne-Jones's portrayal of a shop girl turned vampire to an unsuspecting artist, female predators were not so readily identifiable. The sexual woman as vampire did not need to flaunt the rapacious efficiency of her all-consuming mandibles; her seductions were far more subtle.

By 1915, given the period's obsession with the "science of blood," the physicians' emphasis on the debilitating effects of any form of sexual spending had been instrumental in turning any woman who exhibited even the slightest independent interest in sex into a vampire, whose *vagina dentata* extracted a man's very lifeblood. By this time, indeed, blood, not metaphorically but in its most literal sense, had come to be seen as the key to humanity's future. Pure, healthy, "thick" blood would lead to a race of superbeings, while "unclean," "bad," genetically contaminated, "thin" blood was the key to species degeneration.

But the men of the time wanted instant rewards for the careful husbanding of their blood. They wanted to see themselves as the vanguard of a new, genetically nearly perfect species of men. Why work toward a millennium they could not be a part of? In consequence, Joseph Le Conte, professor of geology at the University of California, Berkeley, gained international fame during the 1890s when he declared in *Evolution and Religious Thought* (1888) that "life-force is certainly correlated with, transmutable into, and derivable from, physical and chemical forces. . . . It becomes naught else than *conservation of energy*, and not, as we had hoped, conservation of *self-conscious personality*." (312) Rodin's *Thinker* was about to find scientific justification for his formidable musculature, for Le Conte argued that the density and quality of the materials of which you were made were far more important in your formation as a human being than your "moral" inheritance: the health, the material "mass," of the body—your genes, we would now say— shaped the mind. It was Cowan's refrain: *mens sana in corpore sano.*

Le Conte's argument that the physical excellence of a man's body was thus ultimately the key to his spiritual genius was, in fact, exactly analogous to Sumner's contention that financial genius was an expression of the mental health that accrued to the continent man. Both theorists had, in essence, reformulated the arguments of the phrenologists to fit evolutionary theory. Thus they helped give further credibility to this pseudoscience, whose premises came to dominate race and gender theory after 1870 and ultimately led to the "physical culture" fetish of Hitler's Aryan Reich.

"The spirit of man," Le Conte had said, "was developed out of the *anima* or conscious principle of animals, and . . . this, again, was developed out of the lower forms of life-force, and this in its turn out of the chemical and physical forces of Nature." (313) The physical makeup of each species reflected its rank on the ladder to evolutionary perfection, to immortality.

The image of a ladder, rather than a smooth, unbroken upward motion, represented most accurately the steps humanity must undertake in its quest for immortality. For, said Le Conte, evolution manifested itself through "the sudden appearance of new powers and properties," one after the other, powers that were not attainable without recourse to the steps previously taken. Indeed, "force and matter may be said to exist *now* on several distinct planes raised one above another. There is a sort of taxonomic scale of force and matter." Between these evolutionary planes there were distinct breaks: "the passage from one plane upward to another is not a gradual passage by sliding scale, but *at one bound*. When the necessary conditions are present, a new and higher form of force at once appears, *like a birth* into a higher sphere." Le Conte's implication was clear: physiognomy and physical behavior were immediate manifestations of the spiritual "force levels" attained by each species on the ladder of evolutionary development. Consequently material beauty and, by extension, material power were the outward signs of superior evolutionary potency.

The merging of William Graham Sumner's "continence" theories of social evolution with Le Conte's biological ladder provided the turn-of-the-century Aryan male with plenty of motives for self-congratulation. All he needed to do was look into the mirror and see a man standing on the highest rung of the ladder to perfection. But he also knew that mirrors were emblematic of feminine vanity. Woman stood in the line of sight between him and immortality. For if man's evolutionary development occurred in a series of sudden "bounds," of sudden steps up the ladder of species development, reverses in the evolutionary process, patterns of degeneration, could just as easily and suddenly force him to follow the same trajectory down. Given the fact that man's "material density," his "life-force," had proven to be visibly quantifiable, it stood to reason that spiritual degeneration would also manifest itself in sudden steps in the "degeneration," the "downward" transformation of the physiological characteristics of the body during a person's lifetime. Suddenly the cultural assumptions underlying Oscar Wilde's *The Picture of Dorian Gray* take on a new clarity: the life force of Wilde's lubricious hero has come to lodge in his portrait, and this displacement makes it possible for Dorian to escape exhibiting the outward signs of his own degeneration.

Indeed, Le Conte's theory of the physical basis for humanity's spiritual evolution clarifies the premise driving many of this period's popular narratives featuring monstrous "downward" physiological transformations of persons of dubious moral rectitude. The vampire's theft of the blood of others, for instance, is a ruthless appropriation of their life force, their moral *and* physical being, a theft that permits this predator to maintain, like Dorian, an outwardly civilized appearance. But while Dorian's degeneracy was temporarily "isolated" in his portrait, the vampire continues to incorporate the bestial—that is what makes him or her capable of shape-shifting, of becoming a wolf or a bat at will. On the other hand, Lucy Westenra, whose already shaky moral being had been further soiled by Dracula's libations, degenerates completely into a licentious animal in her undead state:

> When Lucy—I call the thing that was before us Lucy because it bore her shape—saw us she drew back with an angry snarl, such as a cat gives when taken unawares; then her eyes ranged over us. Lucy's eyes in form and colour; but Lucy's eyes unclean and full of hell-fire, instead of the pure, gentle orbs we knew. At that moment the remnant of my love passed into hate and loathing; had she then to be killed, I could have done it with savage delight. As she looked, her eyes blazed with unholy light, and the face became wreathed with a voluptuous smile. Oh, God, how it made me shudder to see it! With a careless motion, she flung to the ground, callous as a devil, the child that up to now she had clutched strenuously to her breast, growling over it as a dog growls over a bone. (217)

Bereft of her own life force and in need of that of others, Lucy has degenerated into a predatory voluptuary, a sexual animal, unable to hide her evil from others.

If a fundamental transformation of this sort could take place in a sweet young thing such as Lucy, it becomes clear that the sudden, temporary transformation of a seemingly normal human being into a werewolf could be the logical effect of a temporary imbalance in the affected person's physical-chemical store of vital energy. Thus the on-again, off-again transformations of Robert Louis Stevenson's civilized Dr. Jekyll into the brutal, licentious, Cro-Magnon Mr. Hyde undoubtedly made perfect sense to informed turn-of-the-century readers. Hyde takes on the "normal" features of a member of the "lower orders." Stripped of the physical superiority of the evolutionary elite by the chemical imbalance Dr. Jekyll induced in his own body to determine its capacity to maintain—and, if possible, improve—the elite's sociobiological advantage over all others, he "reverts" to near-animal status. In today's parlance, Dr. Jekyll was experimenting with instantaneous genetic mutation. Deprived of the superior life force of the Anglo-Saxon elite, Dr. Jekyll's body was logically and scientifically driven back into bestial forms of physiognomic and spiritual deformation directly representative of Hyde's far lower working-class standing on the ladder of human evolutionary development.

The many fanciful narratives of downward transformation and mutation produced during the years around 1900 were therefore not at all intuitive responses to "archetypal" impulses lodged since time immemorial in humanity's "collective unconscious," as some recent critics have suggested. They may since have *come to seem like* subconscious expressions of the existential fears produced by our culture, but that is so only because we fail to recognize that our social and psychological assumptions are still largely based on the prejudicial premises of early-twentieth-century science. We may have outgrown the "truths" of our great-grandparents, but their invidious sadomasochistic conceptions of race, class, and gender have precipitated unchecked into our subconscious through the uncritical mediation of popular culture.

These turn-of-the-century mutation fantasies were, in fact, examples of what their authors considered to be a thoroughly fact-based form of narrative, an early incarnation of a genre that was soon to become designated as "science fiction." Novels such as H. Rider Haggard's *She* (whose two-thousand-year-old heroine both Jung and Freud thought to be an almost perfect personification of the feminine impulse in nature), Stevenson's *Dr. Jekyll and Mr. Hyde,* Wilde's *The Picture of Dorian Gray,* Stoker's *Dracula,* and a host of lesser-known but often equally influential late-nineteenth-century fictions were not naive, spontaneous, or unconscious fantasies—they were instead knowledgeable adaptations of the scientists' prejudicial theories concerning the inherent and necessary inequalities of gender, class, and race.

The monstrous creatures stalking through these narratives were meant to strike fear into their readers' hearts and thus make them more determined than ever to maintain the "vital balance" of their genetically superior physical endowment. Degenerates surrounded the master race, ready to prey on the elite's "intellect" and to diminish its economic vitality. Degenerates were thus mental and physical parasites who were trying to obtain by unlawful means the social and personal equilibrium they had been unable to attain as a result of their Hyde-like physiological excesses. The early-twentieth-century human-turned-monster was always a creature who had failed the crucial test of "biological self-control." He was a personification of the Aryan male's fear of the "debilitating" effects of sexual activity of any kind. Such phobias were rarely recognized as economically motivated. Instead they were regarded as realistic assessments of the hazardous rule of nature in the physiological constitution of all living organisms. Sexual violence, whether real or imagined, was thus taken outside the realm of personal responsibility.

All these issues are succinctly brought together in Rudyard Kipling's celebrated story "The Mark of the Beast," first published in 1890. A masterpiece of dualist doublethink and doublespeak, the tale establishes a clear contrast between the actions of the British (and, by extension, all Westerners) as the agents of progress and species evolution, and those of the genetically retarded "lower orders" that populate the East. The story is a dramatic anticipation of Kipling's infamous poem of 1899, "The White Man's Burden," which was to warm many an imperialist heart with its exaltation of "the savage wars of peace" waged by the White Man (consistently capitalized in the text), who only wanted to "serve" the "new-caught sullen peoples, / Half devil and half child" (emphatically kept lowercase throughout), so lamentably incapable of recognizing what was good for them.

In "The Mark of the Beast," Kipling had already mapped out the serious dangers members of the evolutionary elite must face in their efforts to liberate the East from its "dark Egyptian night" (and, of course, its natural resources). The colonialist had to descend into a cauldron of preevolutionary dangers to his soul when he left the protective confines of the civilized West: "East of Suez, some hold, the direct control of Providence ceases," the story began, thus providing the cliché mongers of the first half of the twentieth century with one of their favorite bons mots. There, Kipling continued, "Man" is "handed over to the Gods and Devils of Asia." For Europeans, too deep an immersion in such a primitive environment could be fatal. The story's purpose was to show that the struggle between evolution and degeneration must always be of primary concern to every colonialist.

The narrator informs us that during a boisterous New Year's Eve get-together of several colonial gentlemen, a man named Fleete became roaring drunk. Though the narrator is tolerant of such a minor failing in an Englishman, the reader is immediately alerted to the likelihood that ill must befall such an uncontrolled tippler. The narrator and Strickland, another friend, take it upon themselves to escort Fleete home. Their journey becomes tinged with Darwinian significance almost immediately: "Our road lay through the bazaar, close to a little temple of Hanuman, the Monkey-god, who is a leading divinity worthy of respect." The author's ironic inflection is palpable here. People who worshiped man's "hairy quadruped" ancestor could not be up to any good.

Still, the narrator knows enough about the tropics to be cautious in the presence of the forces of degeneration. But Fleete, less knowledgeable and totally besotted, desecrates the idol of Hanuman. Revenge is swift. A leper, quite literally faceless as a result of his physical condition (which, of course, in accordance with the healthy mind–healthy body equation, also reflects the condition of his psyche), comes forward and, "making a noise exactly like the mewing of an otter," bites Fleete's breast.

The leper's bite is the mark of the beast. Through it the animal world invades Fleete's body and unleashes the forces of devolution upon this Westerner who, in a moment of "excusable" levity, has let his civilized guard down. In the East, in India, the realm of the monkey god, such mistakes are punished swiftly. What more obvious way to begin a slide back to the Darwinian origins of human life than to have your blood infected by a vampire bite from a physically decomposing devotee of Hanuman the monkey god? No wonder Fleete's dark journey of reversion begins almost immediately after this. Kipling describes an etiology of degeneration that was to become a standard feature of twentieth-century horror fiction: Fleete's senses take on a new, animal-like acuity. "Can't you smell the blood?" he asks ominously as his friends take him through a "native" market. "Higher" animals such as horses, who instinctively trust humans (just as the better sort of natives instinctively trust their colonial masters), become distraught with fear in his presence. In *Wolf,* a recent Hollywood contribution to the perpetuation of Kipling's "sexuality is animalism" proposition, Jack Nicholson has the same effect on these peaceable quadrupeds soon after having received a nip on the wrist by one of the leper's unregenerate offspring. Again like Kipling's incautious Brit, he thereupon develops a tendency to "wolf down" a variety of uncivilized vittles.

Indeed, the first thing Fleete does when he arrives home is to order raw meat. Then he opens his shirt and his friends see just over his left breast a mark that resembles the "irregular blotches arranged in a circle—on a leopard's hide." Already Fleete has reverted to the evolutionary level of the predators. When his servant brings in the chops he has ordered, "all red and juicy," he bolts "three in a most offensive manner," directly imitating the feeding habits of a leopard: "He ate on his right grinders only, and threw his head over his right shoulder as he snapped the meat." The animal in Fleete has come forward and soon takes over completely. He starts to prowl for food, and his friends find him "grovelling about the garden."

They bring him back to his room and guard the premises. "Presently from the room came the long-drawn howl of a wolf." Soon "Fleete could not speak, he could only snarl, and his snarls were those of a wolf, not of a man." His friends and the doctor they call in try to act as if

Fleete's strange condition were merely an extraordinary case of "hy-drophobia," or rabies, instead of a full-blown case of lycanthropy, but they know better. They know that the true responsibility for Fleete's condition lies with the leper. To counter the forces of degeneration and save the world, they, too, must now shed part of their humanity in a per-ilous descent to the level of their enemies.

To kill an animal, Kipling wants us to understand, you must become an animal yourself: civilization cannot defend itself against the lower or-ders unless it is willing to take on the bestiality of those lower orders to subdue them. Thus we see a century's worth of Anglo-European impe-rialist foreign policy taking shape in the pages of Kipling's story. To save Fleete, the highly evolved British must take brutal action. They capture the leper, the Silver Man devoted to the monkey god (silver is the metal of the moon, the refracted feminine light of masculinity's nocturnal satellite). Soon the British find themselves in the usual position of white men burdened by their colonial responsibility: "Strickland knocked his legs from under him and I put my foot on his neck. He mewed hideously, and even through my riding boots I could feel that his flesh was not the flesh of a clean man."

Once again it is civilization's responsibility to exorcise the vampire. Fleete's mind and body have been taken over by the degenerate native. To save him, they must destroy the bestial creature's primitive will. What they subsequently do, Kipling remarks delicately, "is not to be printed." But he tells us just enough to make it clear that the civilized Englishmen torture the helplessly bound leprous native with a red-hot gun barrel until he agrees to "take away the evil spirit."

"We watched the face of the beast, and saw the soul of Fleete com-ing back into the eyes." The East has been subdued; the beast has been conquered; evolutionary man has triumphed. Kipling's lesson in colonial management was certain not to fall on deaf ears among the millions of boys and young men who read his stories and were about to become the next generation of husbands, fathers, and colonial administrators.

But such a major confrontation with the forces of degeneration, such a strenuous journey into the heart of darkness, must take its toll on the emissaries of evolution, Kipling emphasized. After the ordeal is over, and after it becomes clear that Fleete has been saved and will be his old self again, Strickland suddenly goes "into an amazing fit of hysterics." Loss of manliness, of "self-control," is the effect of contact with the enemy, no matter how noble the cause. "It is terrible to see a strong man overtaken with hysteria," the narrator admits. The colonial struggle takes its toll on manhood: "It struck me that we had fought for Fleete's soul with the Silver Man in that room, and had disgraced ourselves as Englishmen for ever, and I laughed and gasped and gurgled just as shamefully as Strickland, while Fleete thought that we had both gone mad. We never told him what we had done." Contamination by the Silver Man, the minion of the Moon, the still largely "female" male of the lower races, dims the sunlight of the English Man, the Golden Man, the creature of God's blood.

In details such as these we see the racist and antifeminine scenarios of turn-of-the-century evolutionist ideology merge once again. The traits of the degenerate native, of the less evolved non-Western species, were also those (if to a slightly less obvious degree) of all women, regardless of their racial origin. The men of the evolutionary advance had come to understand that women must be treated in much the same way the Empire treated the degenerate non-Western male. The cause of their inferiority was the same—they, too, were slaves of the monkey god. Women, too, needed to be colonized, controlled, and subdued by violence—even, if necessary, obliterated—if they did not accept their secondary evolutionary status as grown children, upper household servants in a world made for men.

This fundamental analogue in the positions of all non-Western races and all women—an analogue tirelessly emphasized by the early-twentieth-century evolutionary theorists—forms one of the basic themes of the period's adventure fiction, much of which had been shaped by H. Rider Haggard's fantasies of "eternal" women who ruled "primitive" African, Asian, or South American empires. Narratives of this sort gave numerous authors whose entertainments we still read their start. In February 1914, for instance, Rex Stout (author of many best-selling Nero Wolfe detective novels) published a "lost civilization" novel in *The All Story Magazine. Under the Andes* contained all the clichés of that genre, including an international adventuress named Desirée le Mire, who "is all things to some men, and some things to all men. She is a courtezan among queens and a queen among courtezans" (7) and an "entrancing mixture of Cleopatra, Sappho, Helen of Troy, and the devil." (20)

As soon as this temptress is transported to the primitive, womblike subterranean world under the Andes discovered by the heroes of the story, she becomes an object of worship for the natives of this realm, who are textbook cases of the "missing link" between humanity and the monkeys:

They were men; I suppose they must have the name. They were about four feet tall, with long, hairy arms and legs, bodies of a curious bloated appearance, and eyes—the remainder of the face was entirely concealed by thick hair—eyes dull and vacant, of an incredibly large size; they had the appearance of ghouls, apes, monsters—anything but human beings.

Uncritically thrilled by the abject worship she receives from this race of evolutionary backsliders, Desirée proceeds to dance for them. It is obvious that she is intimately in tune with their needs: "her white, supple body . . . glided across, back and forth, now this way, now that, to the very edge of the dizzy height, with wild abandon, or slow measured grace, or the rushing sweep of a panther." (79–81)

The October 1912 issue of the same magazine had seen the first publication of Edgar Rice Burroughs's *Tarzan of the Apes—A Romance of the Jungle*. In the many Tarzan narratives that were to follow upon the extraordinary success of this first tale, Burroughs was to provide the world with numerous stunning, knife-wielding, primitive, masculinized white women of the Desirée variety. One of these was his princess La, who makes her appearance in *Tarzan and the Jewels of Opar* (1916): "physically a creature of perfection," but

a cold and heartless creature, daughter of a thousand other cold, heartless, beautiful women, who had never known love. And so when love came to her it liberated all the pent passions of a thousand generations, transforming La into a pulsing, throbbing volcano of desire, and with desire thwarted this great force of love and gentleness and sacrifice was transmuted by its own fires into one of hatred and revenge. (65)

Passages of this sort were to become standard fare in the pulp fiction of midcentury. They allowed the genre's (mostly male) readership to indulge in erotic fantasies of violent sexual temptation and domination while they waited for the hero to reject these degenerate temptresses in a decisive show of superior masculine self-control.

These wildly dancing, "throbbing volcano[s] of desire" were obviously the evil white African sisters of the domesticated Janes of civilized society. They served as a warning that under the acculturated skin of every "good girl," nature's reversive tendencies were lying in wait to crawl forth at the first possible opportunity. That was why they were also always white. They did not have to "slide back down the evolutionary scale" like the Dr. Jekylls and Dorian Grays. As in the case of La, "by some queer freak of fate, aided by natural selection," these princesses never participated in the "physical degradation" that turned their male subjects habitually into "frightful men with hairy bodies and gnarled and crooked legs." (64) Degeneration did not affect their bodies, because their bodies were "naturally primitive," examples of the primordial "enticement to reproduction" placed in the way of every evolutionary male.

Vampires one and all, these African queens were invariably intent upon luring the blond "perfect, godlike figure" (69) of Tarzan, or one of his numerous lordly Aryan counterparts of the pulp magazines of the first half of this century, into sexual perdition: "She pressed her cheek close to Tarzan's shoulder. Slowly she turned her head until her hot lips pressed against his flesh." But their prey unfailingly (though, for prurience' sake, usually only at the very last moment) would recognize the danger these women's freely roaming African wombs spelled to his vitality, and reject their advances. Such rejection invariably turned the African queens into furies from hell:

> A strange anomaly was La of Opar—a creature of circumstance torn by conflicting emotions. Now the cruel and bloodthirsty creature of a heartless god and again a melting woman filled with compassion and tenderness. Sometimes the incarnation of jealousy and revenge and sometimes a sobbing maiden, generous and forgiving; at once a virgin and a wanton; but always a woman. (75)

Men who failed to domesticate such "creatures" were doomed to end up dancing or howling to the moon along with the throngs of other degenerate men who always formed these bestial, primal women's abject entourage.

Even to *want* to dance was a sign of effeminacy in men. Hysteria was the sound of the tam-tam in civilized humanity, Gardner had said. Dance represented loss of control, loss of masculinity. Men who danced had caved in to the lure of sensuality, had been caught in the perpetual ring dance of feminine lust, the junior hop of reproductive hysteria. For what was of the beast in man was what he yielded to woman.

Early-twentieth-century pop culture, in consequence, devised numerous ways to show women dancing. Their light-footedness was a surefire indication of their light-headed nature. After all, women, given their inferior capacity to hold on to their vital essence, were almost universally thought to have "thinner" blood than men. That condition not only had a major impact on the size and density of their brains, but it also made them, like La, volatile and unpredictable. Their blood was quite literally untrustworthy. When, for instance, in *Dracula,* Van Helsing desperately needed a donor to perform a blood transfusion to save Lucy Westenra's life, he ruled out all the available women. His motive was unambiguous: "I fear to trust those women, even if they would have courage to submit." (156) But what Van Helsing really feared to trust was the purity of these women's blood. As women servants in the Westenra household they were even less likely to have "reliable" blood than the women of Lucy's own class. Van Helsing's verdict is decisive: "A brave man's blood is the best thing on this earth when a woman is in trouble." (157)

Within the antifeminine parameters of turn-of-the-century culture, issues of blood were thus also issues of gender. "Good" blood was synonymous with masculinity and "bad" blood with all things feminine. The purification of men's blood was regarded as of crucial importance to the survival of the human race itself. Sexual contact with a woman was, quite literally, an act of "pollution." Sociobiologists such as Spencer, Fiske, and Sumner saw the physical evolution of the human brain, its literal growth in size and density, as the key to any further human development, both in the realm of racial genetics and as a prerequisite to national social coherence. For them the economic progress of a nation was in the long run entirely dependent on the increasing prevalence, among its best and brightest men, of commodious cranial cavities fully packed with as purely concentrated a seminal distillate of gray matter as a well-organized civil society could hope to cultivate in its financial elites.

If the quality of a man's brain was dependent on seminal continence, on the purity of the blood that brought nutrients to his gray matter, then it stood to reason that his economic potential could also be equated with his ability to hold on to and to husband this precious fluid. Even in this respect the science of the day was able to link continence and evolution in the popular mind: in charts documenting the evolution of man from the animals, superior manhood was always portrayed as standing up straight, in full erection, as it were, whereas the "lower orders" were shown in increasingly depressing "bending" postures, clearly losing their vitality as they found themselves closer to the earth. Today most of us have the good sense to regard such pronouncements as crack-pot notions; but they were centrally important in shaping the worldview of even the most "progressively thinking" early-twentieth-century men and women, and through the cultural production of these earlier generations, the impact of such notions is still widely apparent.

The biological, medical, and psychological commonplaces of the theory of evolutionary inequality established what seemed to most to be a brand-new justification of the theories of Giambattista Vico and his followers: the kinetic energy of progress was coming to be defined as the very motive for existence. The evolutionary elite lived in a Bergson-ian universe in which conscious being was determined by the experience of directed energy as an end in itself. In a world that had lost its faith in God as the all-knowing Father, a new, economically productive motivation was needed to keep the work ethic "healthy" and to provide "moral" justification for the exploitation and subjugation of most of humanity. Where once monarchs were "chosen" by God, Puritans "elected," and virtue rewarded, now the phenomena of Nature (emphatically capitalized) became, in Le Conte's words, "naught else than objectified modes of divine thought." (301)

In this manner a brave new world of scientific-pragmatic absolutist thinking, emphasizing the universal, unchanging demands of Nature, could do away with all humane concerns (without, however, also dispensing with the rhetoric of humane values), all community-oriented personal responsibilities (while steadfastly sentimentalizing the values of community), and all belief in the intellectual, physical, and emotional equality of the sexes (though romanticizing man and woman as indelibly "one"). Instead Nature now challenged each individual man to do whatever he could to become one of the evolutionary elite. Evolution was the kinetic impulse at the core of Nature, the life force. Whatever stood in the way of progress must be destroyed. Sumner had already made it very clear that altruism, moral considerations, respect for others—humanist concerns—were mere superstitions, foolishness designed to keep the evolutionary elite from attaining its transcendent potential. The twentieth century was getting set to follow the lead of Fidus's upward-striving *Homo sapiens* and trample on anyone who stood in its way.

Within this new world of predatory antihumanist values, the imagery of the vampire presented a virtual microcosm of the existential fears the new system of economic imperialism had spawned. As if disseminated by a plague of emissaries from a mythical Transylvania, that imagery has since come to pervade the twentieth-century popular imagination. The Reverend Hunter's old equation "loss of semen is loss of blood" was giving way to another, even more terrifying one: "loss of semen is loss of economic potential."

For the early-twentieth-century male, then, the conviction that there was a virtually exact parallelism between money, brainpower, semen, and blood had come to define the meaning of life itself. To him that string of equations was no laughing matter but a biomedical truth, a matter of life and death. No wonder chaos had been thrown into the world of evolutionary manhood by the simple introduction of that predatory, semen-hungry entity, woman. Clearly there was something of the vampire in every female. Just to look at her was a source of temptation, an invitation to "loss of semen," and hence an invidious invitation to let oneself be vampirized.

There is perhaps no more celebrated delineation of the period's equation of semen, capital, and blood than the *Fragment of an Analysis of a Case of Hysteria* Freud first published in 1905, which has since come to be known as *Dora*. Freud's frustrating confrontation with the regressive tendencies of modern femininity forced him to deal explicitly, though quite delicately, with what he saw as the sexual woman's oral fixation on the priceless jewelry of masculinity. In the process Freud revealed the mixed sexual and economic symbolism the men of the period read into woman's lust for the "coffers" of man's essence.

Freud had begun his analysis of Dora in 1900 when, upon entering her eighteenth year, his unwilling subject was brought to him by her father. Right from the start Freud determined that Dora must be regarded as a particularly poorly acculturated young woman, a characteristic representative of the girls Augustus Gardner had written about, who heard the sound of a tam-tam every time they cracked open a lubricious book: "She used to read Mantegazza's *Physiology of Love* and books of that sort" and tended to get "over-excited" by such stimuli, (41) Freud noted. Paolo Mantegazza's *Trilogia dell' amore,* consisting of *The Physiology of Love, The Hygiene of Love,* and *The Sexual Relations of Mankind,* had been something of a *Kinsey Report* for the later nineteenth century. In the volume Dora had been reading, Mantegazza had revealed to his contemporaries, in the words of an advertisement for a 1935 American edition, "the methods which human beings have used to arouse the sense-tingling delights of erotic ecstasy."

Oddly, Freud, even after divulging that she had been reading a number of such stimulating works of sexual enlightenment, still seemed a bit surprised that "Dora knew that there was a kind of getting wet involved in sexual intercourse." An avid reader of the "scandalously explicit" works of Mantegazza could not have avoided an awareness of such details. But what Freud was trying to establish in describing Dora as hovering between "innocence" and "lust" was the inevitable, constitutional "hysteria" of a young woman on the verge of sexual awakening. At such a point, Freud clearly believed, the erotic affections of a young woman were likely to attach themselves to any available masculine object. Freud appears to have had a good deal of confidence in his own appeal as the focus of such an awakening, for he rapidly came to the conclusion that during the course of her analysis Dora must have begun to lust after him. Thus, when she broke off the analysis of her own accord, he was certain that she was trying to punish him for not having "given in" to her:

> I knew Dora would not come back again. Her breaking off so unexpectedly, just when my hopes of a successful termination of the treatment were at their highest, and her thus bringing those hopes to nothing—this was an unmistakable act of vengeance on her part. Her purpose of self-injury also profited by this action. No one who, like me, conjures up the most evil of those half-tamed demons that inhabit the human breast, and seeks to wrestle with them, can expect to come through the struggle unscathed.

Could he, Freud wondered, have prevented Dora from resorting to her rude form of analytic coitus interruptus ("just when my hopes of a successful termination" were highest)? Should he have played the lover's part and "shown a warm personal interest in her—a course which, even after allowing for my position as her physician, would have been tantamount to providing her with a substitute for the affection she longed for? I do not know." (131)

Freud's dispassionate tone here could not have been more disingenuous, for he knew the answer to his own question: he would have become Dora's great masculine hero, her father substitute, on whom she would have lavished all "those half-tamed demons" that inhabited a young girl's breast. "The transference took me unawares, and because of the unknown quantity in me which reminded Dora of Herr K. [the first of Dora's 'father substitutes'], she took revenge on me as she wanted to take her revenge on him, and deserted me as she believed herself to have been deceived and deserted by him." (141)

The men of Freud's generation were convinced that "sexual awakening" came to a young woman in a blindly instinctual fashion, and was likely to take the form of an indiscriminate attachment to whatever male member she was first exposed to. Men therefore needed not feel guilty about engaging in acts of "therapeutic rape" in order to awaken women to their reproductive duties. Mantegazza, for example, sentimentalized the molestation of young girls by libertines, by intimating that such incidents were a normal stage in preparing the female animal for her maternal duties:

> Anyone who has visited the Museum of the Louvre at Paris must have found his eyes coming to rest upon a young satyr, who, in addition to his sensual lips, has an incomparable expression of cynical and lascivious laughter. His mouth is distorted, his nostrils are wide and flaring, while his eye is intent upon contemplating a longed for object. This expression is, to tell the truth, one of the most natural and terrible of those which, as a matter of course in the physical realm, precede the sexual embrace; a woman who is conscious of being gazed on in such a manner must feel an irresistible fascination, such as would hurl her, willing or not, into the arms of the man. I am acquainted with a certain young girl who, innocent of everything sexual, upon having a virile member thrust into her hand by a libertine, experienced so great a degree of lascivious emotion that she was led to cry out, as many female animals do at first rude contact with the fecundating male. (39)

In Freud's imagination, Herr K.—whose wife (with whom Dora's father was having an affair) had introduced Dora to the joys of reading Mantegazza—had been involved in a very Mantegazza-like incident of molestation with Dora. "I have formed in my own mind the following reconstruction of the scene. I believe that during the man's passionate embrace she felt not merely his kiss upon her lips but also the pressure of his erect member against her body." (45) Being a man of his time, Freud expected no less than the first sounding of the call of the wild in Dora's response. He therefore concluded that "the pressure of the erect member probably led to an analogous change in the corresponding female organ, the clitoris." (46) The father of psychoanalysis took it for granted that she must have been swept up in primordial desire for Herr K.'s member. One of the "hysterical" symptoms that had caused Dora's

father to bring her to Freud had been a recurring sore throat. By factor-
ing in the "normal" repressions of a civilized young woman, and by
combining Dora's assertion (her "sensory hallucination") that "she
could still feel upon the upper part of her body the pressure of Herr K.'s
embrace," (45) with his own fantasy about Herr K.'s phallic contribution, he decided that Dora's sore throat must be a clear indication that
she was trying to repress the "excessively repulsive and perverted phan-
tasy of sucking at a penis." (69)

All this because "the erotogenic oral zone . . . had been
overindulged in Dora's infancy by the habit of sucking for pleasure"
(breast-feeding). The structural analogue between a woman's nipple and
a man's penis was, of course, self-evident. (46) But Freud would not
have been Freud if he had not had a little more up his sleeve. Dora was
really lusting after her own father, as Freudian little girls were wont to.
Extrapolating from this assumption, he decided that Dora had come to
the conclusion that both her mother and Frau K. had engaged in fellatio ("sexual gratification *per os*") with her father—although he admitted
with a typical analyst's disdain for the opinions of his subject that "she
would not hear of going so far as this." (46–7)

Dora's sore throat now became for Freud a dead giveaway that she
"was clearly putting herself in her mother's place," as well as reacting
"like a jealous wife" toward Frau K., her mother's substitute in her father's affections:

> If we have rightly guessed the nature of the imaginary sexual
> situation which underlay her cough, in that phantasy she must
> have been putting herself in Frau K.'s place. She was therefore
> identifying herself both with the woman her father had once
> loved and with the woman he loved now. The inference is obvi-
> ous that her affection for her father was a much stronger one
> than she knew or than she would have cared to admit: in fact
> that she was in love with him. (73)

Thus, with the help of a sore throat, Freud was able to turn a single
unwanted kiss, forced upon a girl who was fourteen at the time, into the
displaced, vampirelike oral obsession of a young woman for her father.
Freud's own erotic fantasies about Dora led him to assume that no male
could possibly give Dora a kiss without experiencing a dramatic erection. But Herr K.'s phallus probably loomed much larger in Freud's mind
than it ever did in Dora's. He jealously imagined that he too must be the

focus of such oral desires on Dora's part—was he not also one of Dora's father substitutes? Thus Freud had already decided what *he* could have expected from Dora had he "allowed her" to project her desire for her father onto him. The sex-crazed oral demons awakened in this young woman would have moved in to vampirize *him*.

But the remedy he imagined Dora to be seeking for her dry throat obviously frightened him on an intellectual level, no matter how appealing it might have seemed to him as an erotic fantasy. A predator in the making such as Dora must therefore be given a still more complex motivation to make her depredations less seductive to her analyst. Consequently Freud, once more the consummate man of his time, established a specific analogy between semen and wealth as the locus of transference for Dora's suppressed oral desires. Dora believed, he reported, that Frau K.'s interest in her father was motivated by his being "a man of means." But Dora also knew that her father was "a man of no means," that he was impotent. Indeed, it had been Freud's knowledge of this fact that had led him to speculate that Frau K. and Dora's mother had resorted to fellatio to insure the continued quasi-economic depletion of their prey. Freud's intimation was that Dora was jealous of the two older women because they were "spending" the seminal inheritance she had determined to be rightfully hers.

The turn of the century's insistence on drawing analogies between semen storage and earning power made it inevitable that the economics of sexual spending should remind Freud of boxes, jewelry, and deposits. Thus Freud's discovery that Dora knew "that during the act of copulation the man presented the woman with something liquid *in the form of drops*" (109) led him to conclude that the young woman had intuitively established a homology between these "drops" of semen and a set of pearl-drop earrings characteristic of "the jewellery [*Schmuck*] that Dora's mother wanted to have." In one of Dora's recurrent dreams, a jewelry case of her mother's had figured prominently. Freud saw this as a clear indication of Dora's jealousy for her mother's "semen gathering" abilities. Dora had said, he reported, that her mother was "very fond of jewellery and had had a lot given her by father." (86) Indeed, her father had obviously been so liberal in his expenditures on jewelry (in symbolic terms, his expenditure of the pearl drops her mother craved) that, in line with the sex-economic laws of early-twentieth-century medicine, he had become impotent in the process. Dora, meanwhile, Freud intimated, was painfully aware that her own "jewel-case" was still empty:

"Is not 'jewel-case' [*Schmuckkästchen*] a term commonly used to describe female genitals that are immaculate and intact?" (109–10)

Whether or not Freud's analysis of Dora has any continuing psychoanalytic value need not concern us here. But his delineation of her case unquestionably remains invaluable as a direct expression of the symbolic importance given by him and his contemporaries to the parallelism between "treasure"—jewelry, wealth, gold, money—and semen. No one at all familiar with contemporary slang needs to be reminded of the continued widespread currency of derogatory male references to a woman's "box," a lingering misogynistic reference to the dangerous "jewel-drop"-gathering capacity she exhibited to the males of the turn of the century.

But to understand Freud's motives for his jewel-box analysis, we need to analyze the analyst still further. His account of the nature of Dora's "repressed desires" was obviously influenced by the fact that he felt strongly attracted to her. Freud saw Dora as "in the first bloom of youth—a girl of intelligent and engaging looks." Having already determined that young girls were destined to lock their sights onto their fathers upon their sexual awakening at puberty, it became easy for Freud to make himself Dora's object of desire by suggesting that through the process of transference he "was replacing her father in her imagination." (140) But actually it was Freud who had unconsciously wished that transference into being. Even from his own account it becomes clear that Dora never exhibited any active interest in him.

But upon determining, just as Augustus Gardner would have, that Dora's "hysteria" had found its origin in the fact "that she had masturbated in childhood," Freud's own erotic imagination shifted into overdrive. Here was a brazen "sexual woman" in the bud—and a very attractive one at that! Surely she must be casting her erotic spermatophagic antennae about for the nearest wood-louse to land upon! Herr K.'s kiss, "against whose seductive influence the little 'suck-a-thumbs' had defended herself at the time by the feeling of disgust," had done its work: the vampire in Dora had come forward. Herr K., whose ostentatious display of affection had presumably caused Dora to choose him as her first erotic father substitute, was a smoker. Lascivious "suck-a-thumbs" Dora had intuited the oral-phallic potency of cigars as symbols of masculinity, particularly after she had felt the importunate pressure of his nether cigar against her body when she was fourteen. The inference, Freud thought, was obvious: "Since I am a smoker too—

I came to the conclusion that the idea had probably occurred to her one day during a sitting that she would like to have a kiss from me." (92) No doubt one of those euphemistic, all-encompassing, turn-of-the-century kisses. After all, how could this attractive young woman whose vampire proclivities already had been unleashed not lust after him, the internationally celebrated analyst? Was there anyone with a more capacious spermatophoric cranium? Clearly it pleased Freud's ego mightily to have come to the realization that Dora must have been driven to distraction by thoughts of the size of his own cigar.

But a wealth of fears must also have come over this man who, prodded by the sadomasochistic preoccupations of his contemporaries, was soon to determine that the death instinct and the pleasure principle were coextensive. The cave of earthly delights was also a sinkhole of intellectual and economic degeneration. Dora's syphilitic father was a prime example of the debilitating effects of uncontrolled spermletting. And now Dora seemed to want Freud to take the role of her dad. No one knew better than he that syphilis rotted the brain. Freud's brain was his capital. He must overcome the disturbing attraction he felt within himself for this remarkable, worldly-wise, far-too-attractive young woman, if only to protect his financial potency. But he needed to do so without damaging his ego. He must make Dora take the blame for his lust. What better way to do this than to prove that she was no more than an instinctual spermatophage? Freud's elaborate exposition of Dora's need to fill her empty jewel box with pearl drops was the result.

Dora, was, by Freud's own admission, a particularly intelligent and sensible young woman. She probably soon caught the drift of her analyst's fevered erotic fantasies concerning her imagined proclivity for oral depredation and therefore wisely decided to break off the "treatment." Deeply hurt by his imagined sexual vampire's lack of interest in his seminal pulchritude, Freud reacted to her decision with the emotional despondency of a jilted lover. The language with which he described the event betrays his state of mind. It is couched in all the melodrama of popular fiction: "She said good-bye to me very warmly, with the heartiest wishes for the New Year, and—came no more." The "most evil" of the "half-tamed demons" within her had driven her to this "act of vengeance." He had lost her because he had not given her the erotic satisfaction she needed: "Might I perhaps have kept the girl under my treatment," Freud wondered, "if I . . . had shown a warm personal interest in her . . . ?" He had been too dignified in his approaches, he concluded.

Thus what happened became all Dora's fault. There was something mean, something unnatural in her, he decided, that had made her take her revenge on him. She was a cheap young thing who had confused her lust for pearl drops with a yearning for real pearls. Dora's decision to break off the analysis, he speculated vaguely, "had to do with money." (141) Did he think she thought he was "cheap"? For, like her father, he had withheld his treasure from her, the pearl drops she so desperately wanted. His tightness, his apparent lack of material wealth, had driven her into a hysterical state of deprivation, into the sort of infantile, vengeful tantrum women were prone to if they were denied what they wanted most from a man. Ultimately Freud took his own emotional revenge on this intelligent young woman who had rejected him, by writing and publishing his "dispassionate scientific case-study" of her "classic" case of feminine "hysteria," thus proving to his own satisfaction that he had been blameless in the affair.

Freud's exposition of his assumptions in the Dora case highlights the complex confluence and confusion of the issues of money, intellect, and seminal potency in the thinking of early-twentieth-century intellectuals. Since nature had made it impossible for a woman not to covet a man's semen, all women were clearly "jewel-gathering" vampires, intent upon syphoning off not only the vital essence of a man's being but also his intellect and his wealth.

In Freud's mind, therefore, Dora's imagined depredations quite specifically came to have a "vampire" motive. Her "hysteria" was clearly a result of her personal (ontogenetic) revolt against her normal existential fate, and indicative of her desire to revert to the human species' phylogenetic stage of primitive bisexual promiscuity—a desire that had manifested itself first in her habit of masturbation. Until that point, she had been able to keep up with her brother in her studies. This was normal, since prepubertal male and female children were, ontogenetically, still in the bisexual, preevolutionary stage of human development. The dimorphic physiopsychic divergence of males and females into warring species began in earnest only at the onset of puberty. But at this point Dora's masturbatory habits had begun to take their toll by commandeering whatever vital essence her reproductive system might otherwise have been able to contribute to her development into a properly acculturated woman:

> It was as though she had been a boy up till that moment and had then become girlish for the first time. She had in truth been a wild creature; but after the "asthma" she became quiet and well-

behaved. That illness formed the boundary between two phases of her sexual life, of which the first was masculine in character, and the second feminine. (101)

Freud's insistence on putting quotation marks around the word "asthma" proves that he was certain the illness was more a matter of Dora losing "vital essence" as a result of her "masculine" behavior than a case of "real" illness. Dora's fascination with gathering metaphoric jewels for her still-empty box, too, was an instinctive attempt on her part to regain the "boyish" health, the "life-force," she had lost when her masturbatory habits had driven her into feminine invalidism. Dora, Freud maintained, had made an analogy between her father's habit of spending money on Frau K. and the latter's seminal depredations:

> There could be no doubt that she had taken money from him, for she spent more than she could possibly have afforded out of her own purse or her husband's. . . . And, while previously Frau K. had been an invalid and had even been obliged to spend months in a sanatorium for nervous disorders because she had been unable to walk, she had now become a healthy and lively woman. (49)

Thus, clearly, Frau K. had benefited in both a financial and a physical fashion from her liaison with Dora's father. Freud's implication was that Dora realized that her father was giving the precious pearl drops of his vitality to Frau K., and that the latter had regained her health by depredating his lifeblood. Dora, despising the "normal" stage of feminine invalidism the hysteria of her pubertal years had imposed on her, had decided to go in search of the lost "masculinity," the prepubertal health, of her childhood by finding a seminal victim of her own. Hence her presumed oral obsession. Dora was jealous of the wealth/health her father had spent on Frau K., a treasure she felt was rightfully hers. Freud knew perfectly well that Dora's desire for her father was a stand-in for the hunger she would, in due course, transfer to the lovers of her adult life. Thus Freud saw in her the classic symptoms of a newly sexually awakened young woman in search of an opportunity to fill her empty jewel box. In Dora, through the transference mechanisms of Freud's imagination, this hunger had been shaped into an oral obsession that had made her into a budding vampire of men's vital essence in her desire to regain the health and "masculine potential" she had lost during her bouts of adolescent "self-pollution."

Freud had put himself in the place of Dora's father—and he was imagining himself in the role of her lover. He desired it and feared it. He feared it because it meant that his own "masculine integrity," his own seminal potency, was on the line. He might lose what Dora's father had lost. No wonder, then, that Freud's analysis of Dora, while purporting to be a cool and scientific account, abounded with self-revelatory "Freudian slips." At one point, for instance, describing his demanding intellectual sparring with his very intelligent and recalcitrant (hence obviously "masculinized") young female opponent, Freud remarked, "My powers of interpretation had run dry that day" (76)—not the best choice of words for a dispassionate analyst convinced of the oral-vampiric sexual fixation of his client. Who was the "hysteric" and who the analyst here?

As a historical document, Freud's account of the Dora case is thus a fascinating delineation of the complex but ultimately circular logic that helped turn economic obsessions into evidence of the "economics of sexual spending." Once the "vital" link between sexuality and "instinctual reversion" had been determined, it became easy to demonstrate woman's "natural" desire to make the male "spend" the intellect with which he had been entrusted in the service of evolution. Economic forces thus created the period's politics of gender in direct parallel to the imperialist politics of race.

Freud was, in matters relating to the psychology of sex, unquestionably one of the more enlightened men of his time. If he was willing to accept the semen-brain-wealth equation uncritically in 1905, it cannot be surprising that ideologues such as William Graham Sumner deemed it the main responsibility of every acculturated and evolved modern woman to become as asexual as possible—that she should do everything she could to take men's minds away from sexual arousal and its attendant dangers of wasteful ejaculation. As the Reverend Hunter had stressed, civilized women must remain sexually invisible. The sinful woman lived in the realm of material things, in the world of the visual, of sight: "Eve's looking at the forbidden fruit let sin into the world and laid the family of man beneath the curse. . . . The eye is the inlet of lust and sin, and if you would keep out evil thoughts and cherish good ones you must make a covenant with your eyes that you will not look upon any thing that is immodest or impure." (189–90)

Thus, in the manly world of turn-of-the-century evolutionary ide-alism and manifest economic destiny, only sexually invisible virgins and immaculate mothers could have a constructive role to play. But, of course, for every believer in a good woman's self-effacive abilities, a cyn-ical detractor could be found, ready to point out that evolutionary the-ory and the physical laws of blood clearly indicated that woman was incapable of significant improvement, and that sex-antagonism between men and women was therefore an unalterable law of nature, making it impossible for woman to be anything but a vampire to man.

Women who had not permitted themselves to be turned into passive-receptive, invisible mother-women were sexual predators by in-stinct, intent upon depleting men's economic potency as well as their vi-tality. The renewed currency of the biblical exhortation to remember that "the blood is the life" sent swarms of predators into the fantasies of most early-twentieth-century males. One of the most striking products of the blood-semen-wealth equation was a story by the American nov-elist Francis Marion Crawford that actually used the biblical phrase as its title.

First published in the December 16, 1905, issue of *Collier's Magazine,* "For the Blood Is the Life" was reprinted in Crawford's posthumous collection of horror stories, *Wandering Ghosts* (1911), (167–94) just in time for Theda Bara's decade. Since then it has become a staple of an-thologies dealing with the vampire theme, amply proving its durability as an expression of men's fear of female sexuality and providing us with an excellent example of the lines of descent through which the scien-tific and intellectual verities of the years around 1900 precipitated into later pop culture.

During the last two decades of his life, Crawford, who died in 1909, had become one of the most commercially successful novelists writing in English. He was an elegant and facile stylist and a superb storyteller. A friend of international stars such as Sarah Bernhardt and of women of wealth and influence such as Isabella Stewart Gardner, Crawford, who had grown up in Italy, was a prominent member of the international group of literati who helped shape the cultural consciousness of the twentieth century. His writing reflected the most up-to-date aesthetic and social prejudices of the European and American intelligentsia.

Crawford's narrative unfolds in a strikingly cinematic manner. It ex-isted in and for the world of the senses, and its opening section is a close verbal analogue to Philip Burne-Jones's painting *The Vampire.* The paint-

ing, in fact, could almost function as a still from the mental movie
Crawford's tale conjures in its readers. Like Burne-Jones, Crawford
equated sex and violence. His story featured a characteristic early-
twentieth-century emphasis on masochistic autoerotic fantasy. Manhood is "wrecked and rescued" in an innocent man's naive encounter
with the bloodthirsty depredations of the feminine.

Crawford surrounded his message with the decorous trappings of
upper-middle-class morality (a sophisticated narrator, a foreign setting,
irony), and the story was published without noticeable public protest on
the part of the large middle-class readership of *Collier's,* even though it
contained at least one dramatically bloody scene. The mass-market
"family" magazines of the day were remarkably tolerant of graphic gore
in service to the public order. Vampire stories habitually romanticize
rape, and, like Freud's *Dora* (also first published in 1905), Crawford's
story was particularly effective in paraphrasing the new, implicitly violent psychology of gender. But as long as the biological findings of the
scientists were couched in decent language, the editors of magazines
such as *Collier's* permitted their authors to venture surprisingly close to
explicit forms of sadistic pornography.

The narrator of "For the Blood Is the Life" purports to recount
a sequence of events that actually occurred in Calabria. These involved
"a wild, good-looking creature called Cristina, who was more like a
gipsy than any girl I ever saw about here. She had very red lips and very
black eyes, she was built like a greyhound, and had the tongue of the
devil." Alario—a miser who, in time-honored predatory mercantile
capitalist fashion, "made his money by selling sham jewelry in South
America"—is dying, but he stays alive long enough to arrange a marriage between his son Angelo ("a much better sort than himself") and
"the daughter of the richest man in the village," a "nice plump little
creature, with a fat dowry," just the sort of acculturated mother-woman
a middle-class father would want for his son. Angelo and his betrothed
behave as middle-class sons and daughters behave only in the dreams of
their parents and in educational narratives: they are happy with the
arrangement. Indeed, "the young people were said to be in love with
each other." However, there is danger on the horizon, for Cristina, red-
lipped, greyhound-shaped, earthy, and working-class, secretly lusts after
Angelo.

When Alario dies, a pair of workmen hired to make improvements
to the house he lived in—and, like Cristina, typical representatives of

the untrustworthy "lower" classes—steal "a small but heavy iron-bound box" containing his entire fortune. Angelo, "rather a simple-minded fellow," is thus shown to be unable to guard his inheritance properly at this crucial juncture.

The workmen dig a deep hole into the ground to hide the box of treasure, and just as they are doing so, hot-blooded Cristina happens to pass by. "She knew them, of course, and they knew her, and understood instantly that they were in her power. There was only one thing to be done for their safety, and they did it. They knocked her on the head, they dug the hole deep, and they buried her quickly with the iron-bound box."

The introduction of this box cannot help but remind us of Freud's own instructional tale featuring a jewel box and a semen-hungry woman. Thus the fate of Crawford's Dora, the primitive, animal-like, blood-red-lipped Cristina, takes on a certain ideological inevitability. Psychosexual analogues must have floated like shadows, like the ghost of Cristina herself, through the minds of the story's original readers. This young woman, buried in the primal earth together with a box containing the entire "worldly savings" of a man who had just spent his very last drop of vital essence, was a thinly veiled personification of feminine sexuality.

Angelo, the virtuous son of the predatory merchant, Crawford's narrator tells us, finds himself alone in more ways than one after the disappearance of his inheritance. "So long as his father had been alive and rich, every girl in the village had been in love with him; but that was all changed now." Even "the nice plump little creature who was to have been his turned up her nose at him in the most approved fashion." The blood was the life, but money was just as surely the life of the blood in the eyes of such early-twentieth-century women.

The dead Cristina, buried in an archetypal fertile vaginal "gorge" of the primal earth mother herself, thus became the undead guardian of the stolen jewel box the working-class thieves had left with her and that they, oddly enough, never attempted to reclaim. This latter detail is an easily explainable authorial oversight: Crawford did not need the thieves for his subsequent symbolic narrative development.

Inevitably Cristina, whose only crime had been to be a lusty and hence all too visible working-class woman, now turns into the personification of death itself. She has already metaphorically "absorbed" Alario's worldly wealth (Angelo's rightful masculine inheritance). Now, returned to ghostly existence, in the womb of the earth and caressed by the light of the moon (the early twentieth century's preferred symbols of the feminine), she becomes a vampire in earnest who, after having robbed Angelo of his social essence, his money, is about to rob him of his vital essence as well.

In the "lonely twilight hours," Angelo finds himself drawn to the area "where the narrow path turns down the gorge." Here he encounters the undead Cristina. Soon, "whenever he went near the gorge after sunset she was already there waiting for him." At first "he had only been sure of her blood-red mouth, but now each feature grew distinct, and the pale face looked at him with deep and hungry eyes."

Those eyes, of course, are the doorway into the feminine world of sight. The story's narrator, in fact, had introduced his tale with an account of a "sighting" of Cristina on her immemorial burial "mound." Cristina's ghost could still be seen winding her white arms around those who stood on her earthen *mons veneris*. This was a characteristic male fantasy image of the period, well illustrated by numerous paintings in which nubile young women desperately cling to the knees of serious men striving for spiritual transcendence. The narrator, too, had stood on Cristina's mound, and he knew "that those white, misty arms had been round me." But, being a sturdy member of the evolutionary elite, he had known better than to give in to the enticements: "I had felt the sudden conviction that there was something after all if I would only look behind me. I remembered the strong temptation to look back, a temptation I had resisted as unworthy of a man of sense." Our narrator, stronger than Lot's wife, stronger than Orpheus, and stronger than Angelo, was thus able to withstand the lure of sight, and this makes him the right man to caution us about the addictive lure of the vampire's eye, designed to lead a man "down the gorge out of which the vision rose," away from masculine spiritual concerns and the judicial conservation of his vitality.

Cristina, Angelo's Eurydice, is a needy creature: "Her cheeks were not livid like those of the dead, but pale with starvation, with the furious and unappeased physical hunger of her eyes that devoured him. They feasted on his soul and cast a spell over him, and at last they were close to his own and held them." Cristina has Dora's disease. Thus Angelo, his eyes caught by the woman's eyes, the eyes of the vampire, the hypnotic gaze of the phallicized cobra, is drawn into the material world of the maenads, those hungry women who had decapitated and dismembered Orpheus with more enthusiasm than a swarm of praying mantises. In the gorge, on Cristina's mound (her Wagnerian *Venusberg*), Angelo gives in to the vampire: "When the moon rose high that night the shadow of that Thing was not alone down there upon the mound."

Angelo, the decent, formerly wealthy middle-class man, robbed by working-class stiffs of his social essence, his money, can now add "formerly healthy" to his list of losses, for now, in a protracted *Liebestod,* Cristina deprives him systematically of his blood, his physical strength, and his intellectual essence. "She had him fast now, and he could not escape her, but would come to her every evening at dusk until she had drained him of his last drop of blood." Cristina is a true entomological specimen—a ruthless spermatophage: "As his blood failed, she grew more hungry and more thirsty every day." Even the people of the village remark that "he was 'consuming himself' for love," though they are still unaware of the literal truth of their metaphor.

Fortunately Angelo is saved from Orpheus's fate by another local man, Antonio, who happens along and, looking out "toward the mound," catches the lustful Cristina at her libations. He runs to the priest and puts in an urgent call for a Bible and some holy water: " 'I have seen an evil thing this night,' he said; 'I have seen how the dead drink the blood of the living. And the blood is the life.' " Sexual women were "undead" emissaries of brute nature, vampires. To save such women from themselves, men must selflessly take on "the white man's burden" and consent to "kill" them. Their wills must be broken; they must be beaten down by the foot soldiers of the evolutionary elite, tortured mentally and physically like the leprous Silver Man, who dared to pit his native culture against the superior force of the colonial landowner. Like him, the sexual woman must be branded into submission and voiceless compliance. Destroyed, banished beyond the boundaries of pleasure, these formerly undead vampires of sensuous temptation could then safely be reborn into social death as the silent, invisible automatons of an orderly world controlled by cigar-smoking psychoanalysts. The sexual woman could be reclaimed only through the permanent suppression of her lust—she must be taught to fear the phallus: she must be raped with the stake of masculine vengeance.

From Le Fanu's *Carmilla* through Bram Stoker's *Dracula* to Crawford's "For the Blood Is the Life," the ritual execution of female vampires always takes the form of a sadistic rape scene blended into a ritual of symbolic female castration. Carmilla, the earliest among the fin de siècle's beasts of feminine lust, is, in fact, made to undergo as graphic an analogue to clitoridectomy as the "moral" strictures of the time permitted Le Fanu to depict:

> Her eyes were open; no cadaverous smell exhaled from the coffin. The two medical men, one officially present, the other on the part of the promoter of the inquiry, attested the marvellous fact, that there was a faint, but appreciable respiration, and a corresponding action of the heart. The limbs were perfectly flexible, the flesh elastic; and the leaden coffin floated with blood, in which to a depth of seven inches, the body lay immersed. Here then, were all the admitted signs and proofs of vampirism. The body therefore, in accordance with the ancient practice, was raised, and a sharp stake driven through the heart of the vampire, who uttered a piercing shriek at the moment, in all respects such as might escape from a living person in the last agony. Then the head was struck off, and a torrent of blood flowed from the severed neck.

As Freud made clear, the head was the true locus of the vampire's *vagina dentata*. Her ritual castration, the excision of her phallic tooth, her clitoridectomy, must therefore take the form of a decapitation.

In Stoker's *Dracula* the ritual rape of Lucy, the most infamous child-destroying, polyandrous sexual vampire woman in European history this side of Elizabeth Báthory, the original Transylvanian "blood countess," took the concerted efforts of all four men who had previously unwittingly sacrificed their precious essence to her lust in the blood transfusions administered by Dr. Van Helsing. Still, Lucy's actual punishment is—quite appropriately, in Stoker's carefully structured world of male middle-class British dignity—left to Arthur, the man Lucy had chosen to be her husband and who is therefore forever her master by natural right. Stoker brought a new sadistic lasciviousness to his description of Lucy's violation:

> Arthur took the stake and the hammer, and when once his mind was set on action his hands never trembled nor even quivered. Van Helsing opened his missal and began to read, and Quincey and I followed as well as we could. Arthur placed the point over the heart, and as I looked I could see its dint in the white flesh. Then he struck with all his might.

The Thing in the coffin writhed; and a hideous, blood-curdling screech came from the opened red lips. The body shook and quivered and twisted in wild contortions; the sharp white teeth champed together till the lips were cut, and the mouth was smeared with a crimson foam. But Arthur never faltered. He looked like a figure of Thor as his untrembling arm rose and fell, driving deeper and deeper the mercy-bearing stake, whilst the blood from the pierced heart welled and spurted up around it. His face was set, and high duty seemed to shine through it; the sight of it gave us courage so that our voices seemed to ring through the little vault.

And then the writhing and quivering of the body became less, and the teeth seemed to champ, and the face to quiver. Finally it lay still. The terrible task was over.

For Stoker, this description was obviously a source of great erotic satisfaction. The account outlines an orgasmic experience of masculine self-assertion that reaches its climax with the woman's final submission to the force of the avenging phallus. Yet we are to believe that arousal had nothing to do with it: "high duty" was these men's motive, Stoker hastened to assure his readers, an exorcism of the foul energies of feminine sexuality. And indeed, once the therapeutic rape has been completed, Lucy gains new status as a proper woman: a woman dead to her senses. "No longer," asserts Van Helsing, self-professed "student of the brain" and follower of "the great Charcot," is Lucy "the devil's Un-Dead. She is God's true dead, whose soul is with Him!" Arthur—Thor himself, the Aryan god of thunder—has liberated the tree of life from its sexual parasite. The four men's stern punishment of sensual Lucy, the undead, has proved sufficient as an exorcism, and Lucy has achieved the nirvana of feminine virtue, for she is now stone dead. Although the masculine avengers don't omit the subsequent beheading, the reader is told about this secondary "clitoridectomy" only in passing, as if it were a matter of course: "Then we cut off the head and filled the mouth with garlic." (222–3) Thus, unlike Carmilla, whose symbolic castration became the central event, Lucy is brought to order by the avenging rapist's virtuous assertion of his phallic superiority over the material lusts of his victim.

Crawford's narrative, though clearly influenced by both Le Fanu and Stoker, brings a new twist to this last part of the "conversion" ritual used to subdue the vampire of feminine lust. Crawford transforms the ritual from a decapitation scene into a form of sexual assault that calls up odd symbolic echoes of a hysterectomy. He insisted upon the complete excision of the sexual woman's jewel-box, the removal of the very source of her deadly fertility and of her ability to "steal away" the evolutionary stability of middle-class economic continence. Thus, in a desperate effort to save the moribund Angelo, Antonio takes on the task of eradicating Cristina's "deep, dead eyes that saw in spite of death," her "parted lips redder than life itself," and her "gleaming teeth on which glistened a rosy drop." To destroy the sexual woman, to rape and neutralize "that Thing which is neither alive nor dead, that Thing that will abide neither above ground nor in the grave," Antonio must descend into the earth itself, into the primal mother's destroying womb—a realm into which the celibate priest cannot follow him:

> Antonio had brought something with him which the priest had not noticed. He had made it that afternoon—a sharp stake shaped from a piece of tough old driftwood. He had it with him now, and he had his heavy pick, and he had taken the lantern down into the grave. I don't think any power on earth could make him speak of what happened then, and the old priest was too frightened to look in. He says he heard Antonio breathing like a wild beast, and moving as if he were fighting with something almost as strong as himself; and he heard an evil sound also, with blows, as of something violently driven through flesh and bone; and then the most awful sound of all—a woman's shriek, the unearthly scream of a woman neither dead nor alive, but buried deep for many days. And he, the poor old priest, could only rock himself as he knelt there in the sand, crying aloud his prayers and exorcisms to drown these dreadful sounds. Then suddenly a small iron-bound chest was thrown up and rolled over against the old man's knee, and in a moment more Antonio was beside him, his face as white as tallow in the flickering light of the lantern, shoveling the sand and pebbles into the grave with furious haste, and looking over the edge till the pit was half full; and the priest had said that there was much fresh blood on Antonio's hands and on his clothes. (192–4)

The iron-bound treasure chest, Cristina's jewel box, the womb of death, has been cut out of the woman of earth, and its unlawfully buried contents can now be returned to their rightful owner. The predator has been subdued. From now on she can only stretch her yearning white arms toward the evolutionary males who surround her, and impotently paw at them from the denatured mound her feet can no longer leave. Being a man of the people, Antonio could allow himself to edge much closer than Stoker's Arthur to complete loss of self-control in his therapeutic rape of the sexual vampire. Arthur was the figure of Thor, Wotan's helpmate in the war against emasculation waged by the Nordic lords of creation. Antonio, the proletarian, is Thor's trusty servant, the middle-class executioner's assistant, the man who did the dirty work. We find him "breathing like a wild beast" where Stoker's middle-class gentleman remained unmoved. Antonio, as a loyal representative of the properly servile "lower orders," is obviously no stranger to the vile material desires of the sexual woman, and is therefore the right man to defang the vampire and return the jewel box of economic transcendence to its rightful middle-class owner.

It may seem extravagant to suggest that most early vampire narratives were organized around fantasies of middle-class males as "therapeutic" rapists, rightfully reasserting their control over the offending body of the sexual female. But one need only compare the passages quoted here with Stoker's account of the destruction of the only male vampire of any significance among this brood: Dracula himself. This primitive, medievally hypersexed male, who was patently unable to adjust his erotic hunger to the lofty standards of the European and American middle classes of 1900, must, of course, also be destroyed. He must be prevented from further infecting gullible, though otherwise civilized, females with the virus of his sexuality. But his destruction did not arouse any erotic fervor in Stoker, who was obsessed with maintaining the heterosexual proprieties among his predators. Thus he dispatched Dracula in a few laconic sentences whose clinical efficiency bears little resemblance to the graphic sexual violence with which he and his contemporaries documented the destruction of the vampire woman.

After hundreds of pages devoted to the meticulous documentation of Dracula's atavistic depredation of Lucy and Mina, and a detailed account of how his civilized opponents chased the monster across continents in dogged pursuit, Stoker's description of his male master vampire's final destruction is a distinct anticlimax. We see the event through the eyes of the virtuous Mina: "On the instant, came the sweep and flash of Jonathan's great knife. I shrieked as I saw it shear through the throat; whilst at the same moment Mr. Morris's bowie knife plunged into the heart." Not even a stake symbolizing the avenging phallus is necessary to secure Dracula's demise. His executioners, after all, were dignified heterosexual males. Therefore they needed only a few skillfully wielded, manly hunting utensils to dispatch their troublesome opponent. Compared with the lengthy and graphically detailed violence necessary to subdue a female vampire, it was, as Mina indeed emphasizes, a nearly miraculous, and almost clinically antiseptic procedure: "Before our very eyes, and almost in the drawing of a breath, the whole body crumbled into dust and passed from our sight." (380) That is all we hear about the destruction of the most infamous male vampire of all time. No coffins full of depredated blood, no Thor-like hammer blows, and certainly no elaborate rituals of decapitation. Instead, within seconds, all that is left of Dracula is a handful of dust.

It is, of course, quite obvious that there is a strong element of sexual sadism in all vampire narratives. The standard conventions of the vampire tale as we know it today were established in the late eighteenth and early nineteenth centuries, virtually contemporaneously with Sade's own narratives. Indeed, that period's literary environment was rife with material illustrative of Western society's elaborate psychosexual adjustment to the aggressive rituals of exploitation gradually being institutionalized throughout Europe in conjunction with the ascendancy of the principles of predatory mercantile, and early industrial, capitalism.

But in the late nineteenth century's focus on the female vampire we find a new component of virulent gender paranoia reflecting the period's active "scientific" and philosophical endorsement of violent pat terns of economic expansion and social inequality. The new availability of inexpensive print and visual media facilitated the immediate dissemination of popular parables reflecting the ideologues' equation of intellect with manhood, manhood with evolutionary dominance, evolutionary dominance with wealth, and wealth with intellect. Thus the early twentieth century came to codify the violent forms of gender hostility on which most sexual relationships are based even today as psychosocial laws of "nature."

Our society still tends to equate wealth with intellectual achievement, a direct legacy of the years around 1900, when readers were assaulted by a bewildering barrage of sociological, biological, anthropological, and psychoanalytic treatises—all, of course, equally "value-free" and scientific in focus—admonishing the middle-class male to face up to an ever expanding group of equations linking economics and sexuality.

The theory of evolution had demonstrated once and for all that the Western white male, and specifically the Aryan, was at the summit of creation. His outstanding intellectual achievements and his ability to build commercial empires proved it. Hence he had a right to rule the many races who were less evolved—those benighted creatures, "half devil and half child," who could not be trusted to keep their sexual impulses in check, and who were therefore the white man's burden.

Extravagant fantasies about the genital "hypertrophy" of the "lower races" had been cultivated by numerous suggestive "anthropological" descriptions, which were meant to convince the "evolved races" that their presumably much more minimal genital endowment was a laudable by-product of their lofty intellectual status. Mantegazza's remarks were typical in this respect:

> Observations as yet are very scarce with regard to the varying forms and dimensions of the sexual organs in the various races; but it has been proved that negroes as a general rule have a virile member much larger than that of other peoples; and I myself, while practicing medicine for a number of years in South America, have been able to verify this fact with my own eyes. Corresponding to this greater size of the male's genitals, the vagina in negresses is likewise unusually large. Falkenstein found the negroes of Loango to have a very large penis, their women finding little satisfaction in embracing a European, because of the annoying small size of our implement. (41)

Such information probably served to bring a minor measure of relief from performance anxiety to the leaders of the Aryan advance, by showing that brain and reproductive brawn were inversely proportioned. Indeed, during the 1930s the artists of the Third Reich, mindful of the racial implications of genital size, almost invariably took great care to show that the master race was, at least in this respect, extremely modestly endowed. But ideas concerning the formidable negative female sexual capacitance of the "lower races" probably also caused these weary warriors to have fearful early intimations of the Attack of the Fifty-foot Woman.

If an outstanding intellect was the result of seminal continence and a prerequisite to the attainment of wealth, then a man's drops of semen must indeed be regarded as his "jewels." Properly invested, this "seed-money" must therefore inevitably lead to wealth and a position among the vanguard of the evolutionary elite. "Money begets money," Daniel Defoe had declared almost two centuries earlier. Now science had shown that this was not just a metaphor but sound medical fact.

The main obstacle to the male's ascension was woman. Dora. Pan's Dora. Pandora's box was the primitive source not only of life but also of man's mortality. Woman was the primal earth from which every man came and into which he must return. Cristina's mound was the prehistoric lair of the serpent of primal chaos, the coffin into which the woman-vampire gathered the blood of living men: primal woman was the heart of darkness, Africa.

Alfred Kubin (1877–1959), The Ape, 1903–1906, mixed media 14 x 9⅜ inches;
Graphische Sammlung Albertina, Vienna
King Kong's Congo Song

IV. A CONGO SONG IN THE HEART OF DARKNESS: THE VAMPIRE-WOMAN'S AFRICAN GENESIS

"She walked with measured steps, draped in striped and fringed cloths, treading the earth proudly, with a slight jingle and flash of barbarous ornaments. She carried her head high; her hair was done in the shape of a helmet; she had brass leggings to the knees, brass wire gauntlets to the elbow, a crimson spot on her tawny cheek, innumerable necklaces of glass beads on her neck; bizarre things, charms, gifts of witch-men, that hung about her, glittered and trembled at every step. She must have had the value of several elephant tusks upon her. She was savage and superb, wild-eyed and magnificent; there was something ominous and stately in her deliberate progress. And in the hush that had fallen suddenly upon the whole sorrowful land, the immense wilderness, the colossal body of the fecund and mysterious life seemed to look at her, pensive, as though it had been looking at the image of its own tenebrous and passionate soul."(100–101)

Never before had there been a praying-mantis woman quite like this, complete with stalklike ornaments, an annelid's body rings along her extremities, and the glittering surfaces of a horned coleopteron's casings. Still, this is neither a fragment of a lost Tarzan novel, nor yet another scene from *A Fool There Was*. Instead, it is a key passage from Joseph Conrad's *Heart of Darkness* (serialized 1899; published 1902). Woman and brute nature were one, Conrad was saying; Africa's teeming fecundity found in woman its mirror image. The celebrated novelist's totemic African woman was a characteristic entry among the host of primal females produced by the writers of the Age of Imperialism. In *She* (1887), for instance, H. Rider Haggard's She Who Must Be Obeyed is "a tall and lovely woman, instinct with beauty in every part, and also with a certain snake-like grace which heretofore I had never seen anything to equal. When she moved a hand or foot her entire frame seemed to undulate, and the neck did not bend, it curved." (149) And later: "This woman had confounded and almost destroyed my moral sense, as indeed she must confound all who looked upon her superhuman loveliness." (239)

In *Tarzan and the Jewels of Opar* (1916), Edgar Rice Burroughs's La is a thinly disguised, linguistically Frenchified "She" who is the "Queen and High Priestess of the degraded remnants of the oldest civilization upon earth," an "almost naked woman, beautiful beyond compare." (64–5) Nemone, another predatory white African queen, whose carnal desires loom large in *Tarzan and the City of Gold* (1933), has a figure that "required no embellishments other than those with which nature had endowed it." She wears clothing only to emphasize her role as a missing link, biologically poised between bestiality and civilization:

> A girdle about her hips was of gold mesh. It supported another ivory triangle the slender apex of which curved slightly inward between her legs and also her scant skirt of black monkey hair that fell barely to her knees, conforming perfectly to the contours of her body. . . . Her movements seemed to Tarzan a combination of the seductive languor of the sensualist and the sinuous grace and savage alertness of the tigress. (66–7)

These irresistible women with simian wombs proliferated during the early decades of this century. Like a debilitating virus poised to eat through the carefully contained muscle and blood of the Aryan elite, the sexual woman's all too enticing image fanned out through the fantasies of numerous generations of adolescent boys. She was always an intolerably ambiguous and endlessly treacherous creature (Haggard's She was both "wisdom's daughter" and a deadly serpent, and Burroughs's La was "at once a virgin and a wanton"). These African queens were to have an indelible impact on the twentieth-century white male's erotic imagination. They still make their appearance in costumes, appetites, and entomological undress often directly inspired by Conrad, Haggard, and their contemporaries. The simian womb's repellent attraction was calculated to confuse and terrify the budding spermatophores of Western Europe and the United States, who frequently received their first intimations of nature's deadly mating dance from these sources. No wonder they looked around their neighborhoods and found a new brood of evil sisters where the spirited tomboys of their childhood used to play.

In this manner early-twentieth-century culture attempted to neutralize the dangerous erotic appeal of intelligent women who were self-reliant and sexually assertive—women like Freud's Dora, who had made a conscious effort to break out of the prison of passive domesticity envisioned for them by theorists such as Spencer and Sumner. Strong women came to be seen as "regressive bisexuals," holdovers from the era of "woman-rule," who sought to reverse the divergent evolutionary patterns of men and women. Today these images are frequently presented as clear proof of the existence of inalterable psychological states, of "archetypal" masculine responses to women's "sexual nature." The social scientists' prejudicial manipulation of the theory of dimorphic gender evolution thus became fodder for those who, even today, would convince us that men are from Mars and women from Venus.

Emile Durkheim, one of the giants of early-twentieth-century sociology, whose writings continue to carry substantial authority among academics, wrote his influential study *The Division of Labor in Society* (1893) essentially as a meditation on the theory of dimorphic gender evolution. This principle was the "ur-example" of all forms of specialization, he contended: "The sexual division of labor is the source of conjugal solidarity, and that is why psychologists have very justly seen in the separation of the sexes an event of tremendous importance in the evolution of emotions." (56) Ultimately Durkheim concluded that the division of labor presented not only "the character by which we have defined morality; it more and more tends to become the essential condition of social solidarity." (400)

Each further advance in the division of sexual labor was for Durkheim a significant event in the evolution of humanity. He marshaled the fin de siècle's usual evidences to show that women with "masculine" capabilities were "regressive":

The woman of past days was not at all the weak creature that she has become with the progress of morality. Prehistoric bones show that the difference between the strength of man and of woman was relatively much smaller than it is today. Even now, during infancy and until puberty, the development of the two sexes does not differ in any appreciable way: the characteristics are quite feminine.

The progressive accentuation of sexual differentiation at puberty reflected the achievements of evolutionary specialization in the human species: the individual's development, his ontogeny, thus truly came to recapitulate the phylogenetic history of masculinity's brave escape from the homogeneous bog of primal femininity:

If one admits that the development of the individual reproduces in its course that of the species, one may conjecture that the same homogeneity was found at the beginning of human evolution, and see in the female form the aboriginal image of what was the one and only type from which the masculine variety slowly detached itself. Travelers report, moreover, that in certain tribes of South America, man and woman, in structure and general appearance, present a similarity which is far greater than is seen elsewhere.

Getting down to phrenological brass tacks, Durkheim quoted the famous sociologist and brain-weight enthusiast Gustave Le Bon:

The volume of the crania of man and woman, even when we compare subjects of equal age, of equal height and equal weight, show considerable differences in favor of the man, and this inequality grows proportionately with civilization, so that from the point of view of the mass of the brain, and correspondingly of intelligence, woman tends more and more to be differentiated from the male sex.

Durkheim extrapolated from all this that "the state of marriage in societies where the two sexes are only weakly differentiated thus evinces conjugal solidarity which is itself very weak." The twentieth century was about to enter center stage intoning a Wagnerian leitmotif of dimorphic divergence:

Long ago, woman retired from warfare and public affairs, and consecrated her entire life to her family. Since then, her role has become even more specialized. Today, among cultivated people, the woman leads a completely different existence from that of the man. One might say that the two great functions of the psychic life are thus dissociated, that one of the sexes takes care of the affective functions and the other of intellectual functions.

Thus "the sexual division of labor" would lead to new forms of "conjugal solidarity" based on the progressive retreat of the feminine gender from all forms of intellectual endeavor. Durkheim maintained that Le Bon's discoveries had proved that

> with the progress of civilization the brain of the two sexes differentiates itself more and more. According to this observer, this progressive chart would be due both to the considerable development of masculine crania and to a stationary or even regressive state of female crania. "Thus," he says, "though the average cranium of Parisian men ranks among the greatest known crania, the average of Parisian women ranks among the smallest observed, even below the crania of the Chinese, and hardly above those of the women of New Caledonia." (56–61)

Clearly large oaks of social theory from tiny pseudoscientific acorns grow, as long as they are appositely prejudicial. Le Bon's and Durkheim's celebration of the highly civilized Parisian woman's shrinking brainpower was matched by similar passages in the writings of most of the prominent social scientists of the early twentieth century. Time and again they sang the praises of "highly evolved" females whose childlike mental incapacities demonstrated the advanced level of their dimorphic evolutionary development, and they concluded that "masculinism" in a woman could only be indicative of her reversion to primitivism, to the "bisexual" origins of mankind. Uncritical acceptance of the idea systems of social scientists such as Durkheim is likely to perpetuate the prejudicial concepts of gender on which those idea systems were built.

In *The Female Offender* (1893) Cesare Lombroso, the period's undisputed leader in phrenological research, had stressed that in a woman intellectual activity was a sign of criminal abnormality, of degenerate reversion to an earlier stage of human evolutionary development. Such women had remained caught in the near-bestial preevolutionary stage of the "lower orders" of contemporary humanity. "The criminal being only a reversion to the primitive type of his species, the female criminal necessarily offers the two most salient characteristics of primordial woman, namely, precocity and a minor degree of differentiation from the male."

In fact, the more physically beautiful the woman, the more primitive her impulses were likely to be. "The very precocity of prostitutes—the precocity which increases their apparent beauty—is primarily attributable to atavism." Nature's primary purpose for this beauty was to lure the human spermatophore back into the jaws of death. Hence sexuality was the source of "the virility underlying the female criminal type." To avoid the *vagina dentata* of nature, therefore, what civilized men should "look for most in the female is femininity." Men attracted to the quasi-virile beauty of women driven by strong sexual appetites ought to realize "that virility was one of the special features of the savage women." (112–13) Publishers of science-fiction materials as well as advertisers still pay constant tribute to Lombroso's theories.

The Female Offender had been the joint effort of Lombroso and his disciple, the historian Guglielmo Ferrero, who had married the criminologist's daughter, Gina Lombroso-Ferrero, M.D. The latter must have felt the weight of dimorphic gender evolution upon her shoulders as the female link between two such illustrious masculine minds. She therefore elaborated on the issues raised by her mentors in a book called *The Soul of Woman,* published in an English translation in 1923. This book, like numerous comparable ones published by women intellectuals during the early decades of this century, took the form of a handbook for other women on how to fit into the brave new world of dimorphic gender evolution. In the process she developed a theory still popular today among "femininist" feminists. It was not that "normal" modern women should aspire to having no intelligence at all, Lombroso-Ferrero suggested; it was just that female intelligence was fundamentally different from that of men. Woman's was guided by her reproductive function, for "maternity gives to woman's mind an imprint of altruism that colors her whole life. It marks her mind as well as her heart with a distinctive stamp."

"This instinct," she insisted, "is what makes woman's intelligence so keen in regard to everything that touches on the real, living and concrete world, so languid and capricious in regard to everything theoretical or general. The real world is the object of her passion; the theoretical world does not interest her." (114) Women who tried to do a man's job or think a man's thoughts would lose their "superior" position among the highest specimens of civilization: "In trying to imitate man, woman is denaturing herself and has retrograded considerably." (179)

During the early years of this century, women who—like the physician Gina Lombroso-Ferrero—found themselves doing "a man's job" often seemed intent upon doing penance for their own "aberrant" behavior by championing the cause of dimorphic gender evolution even more vociferously than their male colleagues. Beginning in the 1890s, for instance, Arabella Kenealy, a prominent British health professional, published a steady stream of essays railing against what she saw as modern woman's regressive tendency to engage in the pursuit of masculine concerns. In 1920 she summed up her position in *Feminism and Sex-Extinction,* a book designed to strike fear into the hearts of all gender benders.

To Kenealy, as to Durkheim, sexual dimorphism was the basis for all further evolution. Those who wanted to turn back this tide were female freaks. "Feminism," she declared with finality, "is Masculinism." The "development in woman, of male characteristics, as shall equip her to compete with the male in every department of life; academic, athletic, professional, political, industrial," would be the death of humanity, nullifying "all that civilisation has secured." Such masculinized women would "transform the impulse of Progress into one of Decadence." The greatest achievement of human evolution had been to widen the differences between men and women in an exponential fashion, so that today they were "constituted wholly different in body, brain and bent." (v–vi)

Kenealy, like Remy de Gourmont and virtually all other early-twentieth-century intellectuals, had become obsessed with the Darwinian revelation that the most primitive living organisms had been "bisexual" in the sense that they had contained within themselves both "male" and "female" generative functions. During the early years of this century, elaborate philosophical and psychological theories were constructed on the assumption that "residues" of this primitive bisexuality still manifested themselves in the contemporary psyche in the form of "degenerate" atavistic recurrences. When, in 1903, Otto Weininger, in his *Sex and Character,* argued that even in the modern world sexual differentiation was still incomplete, and that vestiges of primitive bisexuality existed to a greater or lesser degree in every human being, he even sparked a heated round of bickering between Freud and Wilhelm Fliess. Letters in their published correspondence document that Fliess believed Weininger had stolen this "intellectual property" from him. Freud hinted that this "property" was common to most of the scientists of their time. Weininger, he pointed out, "could have gotten the idea of bisexuality elsewhere, because it has figured in the literature for some time," and he readily admitted that in his own practice, the topic of residual bisexuality and its effect on the average person came up "in every treatment." (463–4)

The fuss the intellectuals of the day made over the human species's potential to "revert" to earlier stages of its development, as Darwin had suggested, inevitably led to fantasies about humanity's capacity to revert to its bisexual origins. These would-be scientific, tendentiously alarmist reversion theories had an indelible impact on the direction of twentieth-century thought. Very few had anything positive to say about the "primitive remnants" of the opposite gender that might still linger in the modern individual. "Masculinism" was almost invariably seen as the mark of the beast in women, and so was any sign of "effeminacy" in men. The resulting biological, psychoanalytical, and philosophical schemes to extirpate such presumed remnants from the social, cultural, and psychosexual structure of humanity have shaped most of our present ideas about the social function of gender.

The dynamics underlying twentieth-century theories of gender difference cannot be understood properly within their historical context unless we acknowledge that the ideas promulgated by figures such as Weininger and Kenealy, no matter how obscure their names may seem to us today, are still the bedrock of our own sense of sexual identity. When Arabella Kenealy contended that feminism, or as she put it, feminine "masculinism," undermined Western civilization's "all-important racial purpose of creating ever higher and more potent living species," (14) she was not voicing a fanatic's obsession, but an idea central to the mainstream of then-current thought. This idea is still in constant dialogue with our imagination, for the imagery derived from it gives form to much of the early twentieth century's cultural production—and, as we shall see, particularly to many of the works still used to teach schoolchildren and college students "fundamental truths" about "human nature."

Kenealy's delineation of dimorphic gender evolution and the primitive impulse behind feminine "masculinism" usefully summarizes the commonplaces of this theory. Her remarks also reveal the ideological parallelism of its racist and sexist components. Though she certainly was not a household *name* even during her lifetime, her book remains invaluable as a compendium of the household *thoughts* of early-

Franz von Stuck, Inferno, *1908*
The Hell of "feminine masculinism" documented by one of the period's
principal students of woman's reversive phallicism

twentieth-century science. "The differentiation and intensification of
Sex-characteristics" had been "the main feature in Human advance,"
the result of

> centuries of increasing differentiation and intensification of two
> opposite orders of impulse and faculty.
> In savages and in all the less civilized races, the personal and
> temperamental differences between the sexes are but slight, and
> last for no longer than a few years of life. As with other faculties,
> Sex-differentiations become ever further intensified and more
> complexly defined as development rises in the scale. Man be-
> comes more man, Woman more woman.

This development was far more notable "in the higher races and organisms." Kenealy saw it as indicative of the "degeneration of tissue which
sets in with on-coming age" that even in civilized society "the old man
becomes womanish, the old woman mannish."

Kenealy, the woman (like Weininger, the Jew, who had committed suicide, Freud speculated, "out of fear of his criminal nature"—that is, out of fear of the "feminine" within himself), went to incalculable lengths to denigrate her own kind, so that she might demonstrate her loyalty to her imperial master: the evolutionary Aryan male. "The best types of men differ far more from the best types of women than inferior men and women differ from one another," she declared, echoing Weininger. Inferior males, and even normal ones "when called upon to exercise for any length of time the functions of a woman," tended to become "emasculate." A degenerate male took on typically female characteristics: he "grows soft and sensitive, uncontrolled and emotional, loses energy and initiative; lapses in outlook and temperament from the masculine normal. In abnormal states of physical development, men are puerile or womanish." Such ideas were the basis for numerous old Hollywood movie caricatures of "colored folk" as squeaky, skittish, hysterical, wide-eyed, uncontrolled, and childish—the "scientific truths" of imperialist evolutionary theory.

Kenealy stressed that "man has, so to speak, a woman concealed in him; woman has a man submerged in her." However, such residuals needed to be kept under tight control. Like many of her contemporaries she had formulated an animus-anima theory well before Carl Gustav Jung, for although she considered "the emergence in the one sex of the characteristics of the other, when appreciable and permanent, . . . abnormal and unpleasing" and "obviously degenerative," she emphasized that such manifestations, when properly dominated and kept in check by the person's body and mind, could have a positive influence as well:

The woman in man endues him with intuitive apprehension of the Woman-nature; of its needs and modes, its disabilities, its sufferings and aspirations. The man in woman informs her of the intrinsic values of his sterner calibre, and thus lends her patience with his impatiences, moves her tenderness and care for him in his rougher, more arduous lot, wins her admiration of his enterprises and ambitions. Moreover the man in her strengthens and intelligises her mental fibre, stiffens and renders more stable and effective her more pliant will and softer, more delicate aptitudes.

Still, "man is at his best when the woman in him is dominated by his natural virile traits. Woman is at her best when the man in her is sheathed within her native womanliness." (26–9)

Kenealy's "anticipation" of Jung's theories was by no means surprising. It is far more surprising that Jung's notions have managed to maintain their aura of originality for so long. Kenealy, like Jung, merely took her arguments from the dominant trends in early-twentieth-century biomedical theory. In recent years we have been inundated with Jungian animus-anima symbolism designed to make us run with the wolves, beat the drum of manhood, or find the child within. Such projects represent a last-ditch effort by contemporary psychoconservatives to maintain gender-ideological control over the behavior of the men and women of late-twentieth-century society.

Jungian models force their adherents to accept the numerous deliberately prejudicial categories developed by the exponents of turn-of-the-century imperialist science as expressive of a system of "archetypal," and hence eternally recurring, human traits. In other words, the pop psychology of today is built on a foundation of biomedical assumptions that have long been transcended by the subsequent discoveries of science itself, but that still dominate the popular imagination in the form of a prejudicial imagery that is in turn used as conclusive evidence for the existence of a static and unchangeable "human nature."

Kenealy took her cue from Herbert Spencer's theory that evolution required the development of increasing heterogeneity among human races. She foresaw an "ever closer and more intricate association of the contrary factors of Maleness and Femaleness." (44–5) Thus, under wary masculine supervision the increasing dimorphic divergence of the sexes would continue, creating separate but equal spheres of influence for the sexes in which white women might breed without distraction while their Anglo-Aryan men could concentrate on the conquest of the universe. Like many of her contemporaries, she based her vision on what she called the "Mendelian factor" in sexual selection.

The Austrian botanist Gregor Johann Mendel (1822–84) had been a pioneer in the creation of hybrid species of plants and had developed a set of "laws" regarding the transmission and subsequent retention in plants of certain hereditary characteristics. His discoveries led to the gene studies of twentieth-century science, as well as to a wide range of racist/sexist speculations by hordes of "Mendelian biologists" who were certain they could identify and classify the biological traits that determined human excellence and inferiority. Today's genetic researchers often still unquestioningly accept the premises of these early speculators, who based their conception of the fundamental principles of human behavior on the mating habits of spiders, lice, and weeds. A receptive lay public subsequently helped turn such speculations into the folklore of twentieth-century science. As a result, the bedroom behavior of black widows and praying mantises became the basis for a new mythology of gender and race.

Kenealy, for instance, supported her theories by anthropomorphizing Mendel's experiments in the hybridization of plants just as Gourmont had tried to "humanize" the behavior of spermatophagous insects. She described how "dwarfish" and "tall" parental couples in the world of plants had shown Mendel how "the Dominant and the Recessive traits of the original parents reappear in the offspring." Mendel had, sensibly, styled as "dominant" those traits that had recurred in the hybrid and designated as "recessive" the traits that did not recur. However, these "recessive" traits had not been lost, Mendel had argued, they had merely been "submerged" and had been "neither impaired in their values, nor destroyed." These recessive traits were hibernating, only to reappear in a later generation "under different conditions of mating." (37)

Monstrous trees grow from small seeds. The concept of atavism, the basis for the late nineteenth century's justification of all manner of legislation prohibiting "miscegenation," had found its scientific legitimation in the Austrian botanist's laws. But Kenealy and many other members of the new Mendelian school of biologists that sprang into being around 1900 also extrapolated a gold mine of other racist and sexist "laws of nature" from his horticultural experiments. Mendel, for instance, had declared that no single "sex-cell" could bear both dominant and recessive traits. For Kenealy the implications of this were simple: the male was aggressive; hence, dominant traits were male traits. Women were passive; hence, recessiveness characterized the feminine. Further human evolution, then, clearly depended on the privileging of male characteristics. Clogging the human system with recessive feminine traits was a surefire step on the road to degeneration. Men could be expected to develop their full evolutionary potential only if women were quarantined in a world of their own, where they could recess to their hearts' content.

Even so, these dimorphically quarantined women should be required to transmit whatever "dominant" sex cells they had left directly to their male offspring, so that these could become ever more male, leaving the wimpy, still largely recessive, and hence decidedly inferior half-males of the "lower orders" in the dust of carnal desire.

Kenealy's "fully evolved" Anglo-Aryan woman would thus become a completely passive creature, bereft of all "dominant" traits and recessively content to breed. In the lower organisms "the two groups of Traits are but crudely differentiated," but "progressive evolution" gradually "reveals two contrary trends in physiological and psychical inherences." (44)

Kenealy clearly favored Joseph Le Conte's evolutionary literalism. Her arguments, as a result, took on a dramatic sense of urgency. A single generation of recalcitrant females might stop evolution cold in its tracks and send humanity reeling headlong into degeneration. She regarded the feminists of her time as perverse backsliders who sought "a reversion to earlier cruder states" (45) by recultivating the primitive bisexual masculinity they should be happy to have left behind. A truly evolved "girl's transition to womanhood" should be "one almost entirely of adaptation, physiological and psychical, to the functions of wifehood and child-bearing." The Anglo-Aryan woman needed to regard herself as a passive tool of nature, characterized only by altruism and a delight in self-sacrifice. (110–11)

Kenealy's remarks about gender difference represent an uncanny anticipation of hip late-twentieth-century left brain/right brain TV talk-show psychobabble:

> The left, Female-half of the body, with its allied half-brain, is inhibitive, and engenders the evolution and the preservation, physical and mental, of The Type; sustaining health and vital power by way of the female attributes of rest and conservation. The right, Male half, with its allied half-brain, is executive, and energises the development (Adaptation) of The Type in its relation to Environment, and, disbursing and applying the vital resources, generates and differentiates potential faculty in terms of living function. (57–8)

Women (or men) whose left brain/right brain equilibrium did not get pushed into the appropriate gender-direction during the crucial ontogenetic years of adolescence ended up short-circuited and gender-confused and were therefore pitifully degenerate.

The individual's vital essence was a complex form of physiologically generated and distributed "electricity," a certain amount of which was used up in every form of physical or intellectual activity. Women's wombs were the smithy of future evolutionary advance. Any part of a woman's allocation of vital essence squandered on activities unrelated to reproduction therefore served to undermine the human species, "to nullify all that civilization has secured, and to transform the impulse of

Progress into one of Decadence." To forestall any backsliding, women must retain as much as possible of their vital energy in its "latent" form and convert it only to its "functioning" state to produce healthy male offspring.

The future of "creative evolution"—Kenealy gratefully acknowledged the French philosopher Henri Bergson's influence on her thinking—was therefore entirely dependent on women's removal from the world of activity, be it physical or intellectual, and their willing cultivation of their "Recessive Woman-traits." The more latent vital energy a woman was able to tap during pregnancy, the more strapping, healthy, and creatively evolved her male babies were bound to be. Woman should regard herself as a passive physiological conductor of the superior paternal genes. A woman who engaged in any form of activity, from field sports to running a business to using her brain, wasted the "male-characteristics" within her

> at the cost of the masculine potential she bore in trust for male offspring. A woman who wins golf or hockey-matches may be said therefore to energise her muscles with the potential manhood of possible sons. With their potential existence indeed, since over-strenuous pursuits may sterilise women absolutely as regards male offspring. Thus it is that muscular and otherwise masculine women produce weakling males. (64)

Clearly Hemingway's Marie, who in *To Have and Have Not* had reassured her husband, Harry Morgan, that he was "such a man" they had only been able to have girls, had been studying the same biological textbooks that had served Arabella Kenealy. For Marie, Hemingway implied, was a little too sexual, a little too "masculine," to have been able to let her "recessed masculinity" make up for Harry's retentive tendencies. She had obviously spent the allotment she had been given in her nights of dalliance with her husband, not to mention during her earlier years as a prostitute. After all, a good woman must regard herself only as a safe-deposit box for the masculine "sex-cells," as Kenealy had stressed: "She holds these powers in trust merely, they are not hers to spend. To expend them is to despoil her sons; to make paupers and bankrupts of them, humanly speaking." (33)

Kenealy's imagery of deposits, bankruptcy, holding in trust, and spending shows once again how completely the early twentieth century had come to equate human biology, and in particular the politics of gender, with the principles of capitalist economics. She was certain that the "new" women, with their "masculinist" pretensions, would force the world into gender-bankruptcy. Such feminists ("feminine masculinists") were squandering the potential superpowers of the next generation of evolving males. "By developing into abnormal dominance the *male* potential in her the mother de-vitalizes sons more than she de-vitalizes daughters." Thus "the boy is puny and emasculate because his impoverished maleness is too feeble to dominate the Female traits inherent in him. . . . The girl is big and crude and masterful because her impoverished Womanliness is inadequate to inhibit and refine her inherent Male traits."

Masculinized mothers had therefore engendered a generation of evil sisters. "These crude hoyden-sisters of the weakly boys" produced by feminism were precipitating a new spiral of degeneration "by producing an ever increasing number of neurotic, emasculate men and boys." (77–9)

Strong women, then, engaged in a very real form of "virility vampirism." They were biological predators, "hoyden-sisters" of the Anglo-Aryan elite, who broke "into the Racial Trust Fund" (289) and betrayed the "altruistic responsibilities of motherhood" to become deep waste pits of misappropriated masculine potential. For every vampire-feminist brought into the world by a sexualized woman, the modern state lost economic ground to the forces of degeneration. These evil creatures, sisters to the predator of *A Fool There Was,* made "men the instruments and the victims of their feminine defects." "Cold-blooded, clever, and emotionless," they were "sensual in a fashion purely male (in keeping with their other male proclivities)," crude "adventuresses, spies, poisoners, adulteresses, monsters." (108)

Primitive women had been no better than predatory animals in their refusal to let themselves be consumed: "The tigress is only less fierce, less strong, and less savage than the tiger. Primal woman was only less fierce, less strong, and less savage than the male. It is only, indeed, in the maternal function and relation that the female traits of both tigress and primal woman awake." (47) The gaping-mouthed predators who invariably accompany the "jungle girls" of pop culture find in remarks such as this their immediate ideological raison d'être. When a woman's maternal instincts were permitted to remain dormant, when female "egotism" made her compete with men in the realm of sexuality—as she always did in such "primordial" adventure settings until the proper male-dominant hero came along to turn her into an adoring mother-to-be—

the forces of degeneration were bound to triumph: "Physical passion in woman is derived from the Male-traits in her." (167) Therefore the more "sexually promiscuous" a woman was, the more she drew from the male. Such a woman appealed only to "effeminate" men. Voicing one of the central clichés of her time, Kenealy insisted that "the province of the male" in reproduction was "but slight and brief" and exacted "so little from him as to interfere not at all with those other masculine activities which are the function of his sex." (8) However, once a man had been drawn, like Schuyler in *A Fool There Was*, into the sexual woman's sphere of influence, he was likely to descend further and further into the maelstrom of "spending." Thus vampirized, he rapidly became "emasculate."

The sexual woman thus became the agent of the Anglo-Aryan's "racial decline," forcing decent Brits back into the jungle of degeneracy, "to artificial, abnormal and evil conditions of living, environmental and personal." Hand in hand, effeminate men and mannish women were rushing back into the dark ages of bisexual savagery. They would, in the long run, most likely even return to the primitive habits of spiders and other organisms far down on the evolutionary scale.

For indeed, like Gourmont, Lester Ward, and virtually every other social critic of the early years of this century, Kenealy was obsessed with the primitive "feminism" of the entomological universe: "Insect-females are seen increasingly to have emancipated themselves from mother-instincts and maternal functions, as regards nurture or affection for their young." Instead, "reproduction, here in this disintegrating world of Devolution, functions without welding spark, or lighting gleam of parent-altruism." These hoyden insect females showed "a repulsive rapacity" in their reproductive efforts: "This secured, they straightway sting the craven male to death, or tear him limb from limb and ghoulishly devour him." (91–2) Kenealy was convinced that the same fate awaited the husbands of human feminists.

Twentieth-century science fiction, as no one familiar with the genre needs to be told, was to make analogous extrapolations its stock-in-trade. Jack Williamson's story "The Wand of Doom" is a nearly perfect example of this dark legacy. Published in the horror fiction pulp magazine *Weird Tales* in 1932, it is a young man's fantasy born of the older generation's "science." Williamson was twenty-four at the time of its publication. He had grown to adulthood in the Twenties, reading such guidebooks to the psychology of human sexuality as *Tarzan of the Apes* and the pulp magazine *Amazing Stories*, as he acknowledged much later in his autobiography, *Wonder's Child* (1984). He and Edmond Hamilton, a friend, were to become two of the world's most widely read writers of science and fantasy fiction during the following two decades. When Williamson wrote his story, the two young men were, by the author's own admission, "equally ignorant and apprehensive of sex. We seldom talked about women, but [Hamilton] saw them as predators, marriage as a trap into some dull job that would threaten his chosen lifestyle." (73–4) Williamson's own point of view was clearly not much different.

Written in patent emulation of the narrative style of Edgar Allan Poe but sprinkled liberally with words and ideas taken from the biologists of the period, "The Wand of Doom" turns the "scientifically grounded" gender theories of the early years of the century into the half-understood fantasies of young men whose heads were filled with contradictory "technical" information about the dichotomous angel-vampire nature of the human female.

The story recounts the sad fate of Paul Telfair, appropriately the son of a professor of biology—a geneticist, for Williamson includes much scientific-sounding talk about "the unexplored recesses of the germ-plasm." Paul's father obviously studied the feminine in nature, being a specialist in arachnids. Not surprisingly, Paul grows up with "an obsessive atavistic phobia": an "unnatural fear of spiders." This fear is "a race-memory of some stark jungle tragedy of the dawn-ages," inherited from "the things that wallowed and devoured one another in the ooze and slime of the primordial mud flats where life began."

Paul has been scarred by memories of the "spiders, tarantulas and scorpions" his father left running about the house. The resulting phobia keeps him "riveted helpless, while the formless, devouring terror from the past wakened in him." Even so, Paul becomes a scientist himself, with a flair for "electrical research." But his chances for marital bliss are dashed early. In Poe-like fashion, the love of his teenage years, a perfectly acculturated specimen of the sexless, passive ideal of womanhood, "a frail, lovely girl," who had become "an invalid before the wedding, died within the year." Paul is fated to have "hideous dreams of gigantic spiders" instead of finding solace in the arms of a paragon of virtue.

Like every scientist in early-twentieth-century fantasy fiction, he has grandiose dreams, and he sets out to realize them with the help of his brother Verne (as in Jules). In a bayou in Cajun country, they begin to materialize objects created in the human mind. It all has to do with modern electronics: they are tapping into the primeval memory circuits of the human brain. Paul calls the machine they have built for this purpose the "wand of creation." (Metaphors are everything in fantasy fiction—especially obvious ones.) With his wand Paul can materialize whatever he thinks about: "The mental energy is picked up, amplified, fixated in the form of matter." Phallic power can go no further: wave your wand and the world appears at your doorstep. Unfortunately nothing is perfect, all wands detumesce—and Paul's mental realizations disappear as soon as the electrical power is shut off.

But the eternal feminine is about to mount a counterattack against the inventions of science. The primordial swamp and ideal beauty forge an unholy alliance to undermine Paul's world when he materializes the image of his deceased fiancée with a few bursts of electricity. She is "slender, tall, with pale lovely skin" and "large eyes, limpidly dark." In addition, she has "dark hair, long, luxuriously heavy." Paul should have been forewarned about the fickle nature of dark-haired women.

At first the electrically resurrected Elaine seems like a timid young man's fondest erotic fantasy come true. She is more than happy to let Paul admire "the innocent, burgeoning beauty of her white body." Grateful for his attention, and "with childish eagerness," she kisses "his weary face with full, delicate red lips." All she wants is to "make him happier." She is a grateful love slave, for she knows that "Paul made me." In short, she knows that her existence can be revoked at any point by her master.

A habitual sleepwalker, Paul wanders into his laboratory one night, the dutiful Elaine anxiously in tow. Wands of creation, as is common knowledge, tend to be hyperactive during sleep, and Paul's is no exception. The evidence is in plain sight: Elaine was "breath-taking. Richly curving, erect, white-skinned, her fine body was almost bare. Her abundant hair fell in glistening waves, parted by the soft curves of her white, upturned breasts. Her full red lips were parted a little, and her limpid eyes were filled with anxious concern." But such erotic electricity sparks dangerous lusts in a young man, and Paul's wand of creation now becomes nature's rod of correction.

Elaine's feet produce "a soft, scratching shuffle upon the rough concrete." The sound triggers an atavistic nightmare of spiders in Paul's sleeping head. Elaine changes accordingly:

> Her fair body seemed to melt and flow in a shining vortex. It thickened and swelled, and became dark. Her limbs grew long and black, with dreadful swiftness; additional ones were thrust out, like pseudopods. Limbs and body were covered suddenly

with a rough black hair. Her head sank, her white teeth became
enormous and hideous fangs. Her limpid dark eyes grew scarlet,
glowed insanely with implacable evil. With the swiftness of a
dream, the innocently lovely woman was transformed into a gigantic tarantula!

Millennia of species evolution fall away as Paul is turned into a common spider-male, a mere menu item to his formerly submissive mate.
"The gigantic spider had seized him in its hideous jaws," and the insect
ritual made infamous by the anthropomorphizing biologists Williamson
read (or read about) in his teens commences. "Screaming and laughing
in the jaws of the monstrous spider," Paul meets primal masculinity's archetypal fate: "The great fangs closed with a sickening sound upon his
head . . . and his shrieks came mercifully no more."
    Williamson's account of the traumatic sexual initiation of a young
scientist of high ideals, a believer in the benefits of creative evolution, is
typical of the vast quantities of pulp horror fiction that were produced
during the Twenties and Thirties, in direct response to the early-
twentieth-century scientists' many metaphoric tales of sexual terror in
the natural world. These accounts of the trials of masculinity in the entomological cosmos were obviously tailor-made to serve as a basis for
the development of fantasy fiction.
    The scenario of "The Wand of Doom" was repeated over and over
again, at various levels of sophistication, in literally thousands of narratives written during the pulp era of American culture until, by midcentury, such fantasies came to be regarded as perfectly idiomatic,
"sophisticated" expressions of the "archetypal imagery of the battle of
the sexes" embedded in the human collective unconscious, and hence as
worthy of serious intellectual attention as Franz Kafka's *The Metamorphosis* (itself—though on a rather more elevated level—also a product of
the turn of the century's fascination with entomology). In line with the
new level of psychosocial credence given to humanity's reversive yearning for insect sexuality, Philip José Farmer's novella *The Lovers* caused a
sensation of sorts among cognoscenti of science fiction when it was
published in 1952 in the pulp magazine *Startling Stories.*
    In Farmer's narrative, a space-traveling earthling is seduced by a gor-
geous woman from the planet Ozagen, who approaches him with an
"open proposal—much like that of the Scarlet Woman in the Western
Talmud." (42) He accepts her invitation to sleep with her and falls passionately in love with his seducer. In the long run, however, he learns,

to his horror, that she is a shape-shifter, a "mimetic parasite," part of a breed of all-female "arthropodal insects," beetles who were clearly odd versions of Haggard's She, for they remained immortal as long as they did not become pregnant. Once fertilized, however, these "pseudo-women" became "womb tombs," for nature had condemned them to a gruesome fate in pregnancy: they must die in giving birth to (all-female) larvae who survived by eating their mothers' cocoonlike bodies.

Until that eventuality—which, quite understandably, they studiously avoided—these parasitic female insects, called *lalitha*, infiltrated humanity to live off the vital energies of (male) human hosts, whom they drove to sexual ecstasy and, by extension, to "war, liquor, depraved religious rites, falling birth rate, graft, corruption," and ultimately extinction. Moreover, "being always very beautiful, they mated with the most powerful men—the leaders, the rich, the poets, the thinkers. They competed with women and beat them at their own game, hands down, because in the *lalitha* Nature wrought the complete female." (59) In 1980, on the cover of a paperback reprint of a longer version of this narrative, Robert Bloch, an even more influential pulpster than Farmer, hailed *The Lovers* as "the book that turned science fiction around and headed it in the direction of a mature approach to sexual themes."

To the young men whose minds were filled with fragments of the ideas Gourmont, Ward, Kenealy, and a host of others had constructed in response to the deliberately anthropomorphizing "discoveries" of the biologists, the links between insects, predatory animals, and humans had come to seem all too real. Standardized assumptions about sex as a form of cannibalism, which had been inspired by descriptions of the love life of a variety of predatory insects and animals, were everywhere. An endless procession of gigantic spiders, vampires, cats, tentacled monsters, snake-bedecked women, women with (or better yet, turning into) wolves, black panthers, gorillas, bats, cobras, and whatever other gaping-mouthed predators these youngish men could imagine, were thus to become the most lasting cultural heritage of turn-of-the-century biological "science."

But most prevalent of all was the ultimate temptress, the bestially beautiful, primitive African queen, who made men lust after her against their better judgment. She held within herself the preevolutionary powers of all the mythical monsters and "lower races" combined, and hence rendered men virtually defenseless against her intemperate depredations. Novelists had come to take the public's awareness of the iconographic details of the evolutionary struggle for granted. They therefore began to

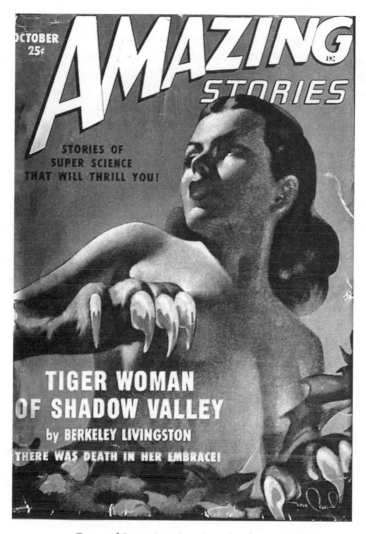

Cover of Amazing Stories, *October 1949*
The biology of female reversion revealed by the pulps.

produce elaborate "scientific" confrontations between the forces of evolution and degeneration in which they widely exploited the mesmerizing erotic attraction of the ultimate praying mantis, the woman with the
African womb. Their narratives of civilization's struggle against primitivism, of progress against feudalism, of man against woman in the dark
continent of the Western racist imagination, virtually always featured at
least one of these creatures born of the misalliance between entomology
and eros.

Since the middle years of this century, however, cultural critics have progressively forgotten the self-consciously gender-ideological motivations underlying many of these narratives. This has made it possible to read them as exemplary expressions of "universal psychological truths." A good case in point is Conrad's *Heart of Darkness*. This work's antifeminine content, so directly characterized by the description of Kurtz's African demon-woman quoted at the beginning of this chapter, has been largely ignored in favor of "existentialist" interpretations. The narrative has also been cast as an exposé of the evils of colonialism and is widely taught in schools as a moral disquisition on the deformations of humanism by racism. But such messages can be extracted from the book only if we ignore its underlying scenario, which declares in no uncertain terms that the soul of Africa is the soul of woman.

Conrad's story pits a properly evolved, properly gender-organized, modern, male-dominant civilization against a preevolutionary, female-dominant world of animal passions and brute nature. Kurtz's overly celebrated last words, "The horror! The horror!" are today habitually read as a weighty reflection upon man's existential fate. But Conrad meant them to represent no more than Kurtz's recognition of the appalling depth of his own moral weakness and vice in giving in to the primitive sexual temptations of the Congo.

Conrad's point of view, moreover, was not only antifeminine but also brutally racist. Speaking through his narrator, Marlow, the author portrayed Africa and the Africans as responsible for the colonialists' violence toward them, for the land and its people evoked in the emissaries of civilization levels of aggression these highly evolved men thought they had transcended:

"The earth seemed unearthly. We are accustomed to look upon the shackled form of a conquered monster [i.e., a 'Western' world 'tamed' by evolutionary advance], but there [in Africa]— there you could look at a thing monstrous and free. It was unearthly, and the men were—No, they were not inhuman. Well, you know, that was the worst of it—this suspicion of their not being inhuman. It would come slowly to one. They howled and leaped, and spun, and made horrid faces; but what thrilled you was just the thought of their humanity—like yours—the thought of your remote kinship with this wild and passionate uproar. Ugly. Yes, it was ugly enough; but if you were man enough you would admit to yourself that there was in you just the faintest trace of a response to the terrible frankness of that noise, a dim suspicion of there being a meaning in it which you—you so remote from the night of first ages—could comprehend. And why not? The mind of man is capable of anything—because everything is in it, all the past as well as all the future." (69)

Marlow here voices the turn-of-the-century evolutionists' favorite credo: "ontogeny recapitulates phylogeny." In the unrestrained passions of savages, modern man, though far removed from such bestial temptations, recognized the "primitive childhood" of civilization. But he also saw in their behavior the fearful potential in every person for "reversion" to, or "arrested development" at, this primitive stage. This theme was to be the source of a steady stream of tendentious twentieth-century narratives featuring a "return to savagery"—works such as William Golding's *Lord of the Flies.* Conrad's story was, like these later narratives, an exposition of the primitivist potential still simmering in the breast of civilized man. It was *not* a critical exposé of colonialism. Marlow, Conrad's voice in the narrative, is unabashedly racist in his observations about the "comic" attempts of Africans to adapt to a level of civilization that is far beyond them. About the fireman on his riverboat Marlow says: "to look at him was as edifying as seeing a dog in a parody of breeches and a feather hat, walking on his hind legs." (70)

Marlow prefers an undiluted confrontation with precivilized "savages" who "still belonged to the beginnings of time—had no inherited experience to teach them, as it were." (75) These quasi-prehistoric creatures force him to acknowledge the brutal origins of civilized humanity: that "bestial," preevolutionary, prehuman physiological abandon—that "wild and passionate uproar"—that heart of darkness that, Marlow insists, is the heart of Africa itself.

Conrad established the disparity in evolutionary achievement between the British and the Africans by pointing out that "nineteen hundred years ago" Britain, too, had been a place of darkness. But the Romans, who brought the beginnings of civilization, had been "men enough to face the darkness . . . the savagery, the utter savagery," around them—"all that mysterious life of the wilderness that stirs in the forest, in the jungles, in the hearts of wild men." (31) Thus nineteen hundred years of evolution, of growth into intellectual manhood, of the suppression of physiological self-indulgence, stood between the British and the Africans.

Conrad clearly saw Africa as the phylogenetic womb of humanity transported into the civilized present. Turn-of-the-century intellectuals took it for granted that the psychic childhood of mankind, while it was still ruled by its bisexual origins (the precivilized stage William Graham Sumner had designated as that of "woman-rule"), was, in gender-ideological terms, dominated by the body of woman. Woman, after all, was childlike and incapable of intellectual evolution. To Marlow, therefore, Africa was a woman. This womb of humanity was the heart of darkness, the source of blind lust, of the still masculine feminine, the phallic snake of unbridled feminine sexuality. Fliess reminded Freud at just about the same time that the latter had recognized primitive bisexuality in a "woman who had dreams of gigantic snakes. At the time you were quite impressed by the idea that undercurrents in a woman might stem from the masculine part of her psyche." (465)

Africa, then, was the soul of woman, and the Congo River her snake, the primal phallus, "the masculine part" of the primitive feminine psyche. The river thus offers Marlow entry into the primal womb. Conrad reminded his readers that even as a child Marlow had been fascinated by water—the sea—symbol of the feminine, "the mistress of his existence," (30) as well as by the Congo, phallus and uroboric vaginal entrance in one:

> "a mighty big river, that you could see on the map, resembling an immense snake uncoiled, with its head in the sea, its body at rest curving afar over a vast country, and its tail lost in the depths of the land. And as I looked at the map of it in a shop-window, it fascinated me as a snake would a bird—a silly little bird." (33)

Marlow's journey on the river into the heart of darkness therefore becomes the male's journey back to the origins of civilization, to the womb of lust. Symbolically Marlow rides the phallus of desire into the body of Africa, into the eternal feminine, poised to drag him back toward the phylogenetic childhood experiences buried within every male. But Marlow's motive for his journey back was as honorable as such a motive could possibly be: no less than to shield modern, evolved, desexualized womanhood from the atavistic recurrence of its precivilized impulses. To succeed, Marlow must be man enough to face the darkness—more civilized than Kurtz, who failed miserably at that task.

Conrad intimated that Marlow was a soldier of evolutionary manhood recruited by modern femininity to keep the atavistic snake of primal feminine sexuality from escaping out of Africa and back into the civilized world. Even as an adult, Marlow is still hypnotized by the river ("fascinating—deadly—like a snake" [36]). He therefore tries to have himself appointed skipper of a steamboat navigating its serpentine realm. "The men said 'My dear fellow,' and did nothing. Then—would you believe it?—I tried the women. I, Charlie Marlow, set the women to work—to get a job." (34) In Brussels, at the company's headquarters, he encounters two women, heavily symbolic guardians of "man's fate." The elder of the two seems to Marlow to know all about him: "An eerie feeling came over me. She seemed uncanny and fateful. Often far away there I thought of these two, guarding the door of Darkness." (37)

The two women guarding the primal womb, classical fates appointed to scrutinize its entrants, are well aware of the darkness ahead. They are midwives to modern femininity as well as sacred prostitutes, emissaries of the feminine sexual past. But Marlow knows that most other modern women live in a Kenealy-style nursery of benevolent physical and intellectual incapacitation: "It's queer how out of touch with truth women are. They live in a world of their own, and there had never been anything like it, and never can be. It is too beautiful altogether." (39)

To protect this world of beauty brought into being by the wonders of dimorphic gender evolution, Marlow must risk his own soul. He forges into Africa, the symbolic body of the eternal feminine, characterized by imbalance, hysteria, and madness. It seems to him "as if Nature herself had tried to ward off intruders." (41) The true mettle of civilization is to be tested in the figure of Marlow. The evolutionary advance must prove that it has better men to place against the temptation of primal sensuality than Kurtz, the near mythical station chief he sets out to rescue from the heart of darkness. Kurtz had ventured there before Marlow to serve as "an emissary of pity, and science, and progress." As a colonial cynic remarks to Marlow: "You are of the new gang—the gang of virtue. The same people who sent him specially also recommended you." (55) But as it turned out, Kurtz was a sensualist at heart, a weakling, a disappointment to the new order. Marlow must attempt to redeem the cause of contemplative, cerebral masculinity.

With "the smell of mud, primeval mud," in his nostrils, "the high stillness of primeval forest" before his eyes, and illumined by the light of a moon that had "spread over everything a thin layer of silver," (56) Marlow sets out to find Kurtz. "Going up that river was like travelling back to the earliest beginnings of the world," he remarks. "Clinging to the skirts of the unknown"—a far too benign, maternal image of Africa, as we soon discover—are tiny outposts of civilization. Everywhere he finds "the stillness of an implacable force brooding over an inscrutable intention. It looked at you with a vengeful aspect." Africa is the sphinx, half animal, half woman, always poised to lead the body's revenge against man's burgeoning intellect. "We were wanderers on prehistoric earth. . . . We could have fancied ourselves the first of men taking possession of an accursed inheritance, to be subdued at the cost of profound anguish and of excessive toil." (66–8) Atavism once again poises itself to overwhelm the emissaries of evolution. In the case of Kurtz, atavism has already won.

And yet Kurtz had been regarded as among the best civilization had to offer. Conrad cast him as a heavily symbolic figure: "His mother was half-English, his father was half-French. All Europe contributed to the making of Kurtz. . . . The International Society for the Suppression of Savage Customs had entrusted him with the making of a report, for its future guidance." (86) The author's irony here becomes heavy: the do-good organizations of sheltered society don't know what they are up against in their attempts to bring "culture" to the "lower orders." But Kurtz's civilized side is poised precariously over the primitive forces within him. He is all talk—his intellect is separated from his body—"he was very little more than a voice." (85) Dissociated from his physical self, his intellect becomes incapable of ruling his passions.

For Kurtz "lacked restraint in the gratification of his various lusts, there was something wanting in him." Indeed, as Marlow remarks sententiously: "he was hollow at the core." (97) As a result, Africa the wilderness, the primal feminine, "had caressed him, and—lo!—he had withered; it had taken him, loved him, embraced him, got into his veins, consumed his flesh, and sealed his soul to its own by the inconceivable ceremonies of some devilish initiation." (84)

But Conrad was not about to keep his delineation of the degenerative powers of the primal feminine purely in the always somewhat ambiguous realm of symbolism and metaphor. In the heart of darkest Africa, on the edge of the river basin of the primal womb of humanity, Marlow, therefore, like Kurtz before him, encounters, in the flesh, the African queen of aboriginal sin, that "wild and gorgeous apparition," the unmistakable birth mother of Kenealy's degenerative masculinized feminists, who stalked through the erotic dreams and the socioeconomic fears of so many early-twentieth-century males.

This African praying mantis, upon whom "the immense wilderness,

the colossal body of the fecund and mysterious life seemed to look . . .
as though it had been looking at the image of its own tenebrous and
passionate soul," is, Conrad makes clear, solely responsible for Kurtz's
"exalted and incredible degradation." It is she who has precipitated his
descent into that

> "heavy, mute spell of the wilderness—that seemed to draw him
> to its pitiless breast by the awakening of forgotten and brutal in-
> stincts, by the memory of gratified and monstrous passions. This
> alone, I was convinced, had driven him out to the edge of the
> forest, to the bush, towards the gleam of the fires, the throb of
> drums, the drone of weird incantations; this alone had beguiled
> his unlawful soul beyond the bounds of permitted aspirations."
> (107)

Conrad's primal woman, a nameless She/La, stands at the edge of
the jungle, "looking at us without a stir, and like the wilderness itself,
with an air of brooding over an inscrutable purpose." The "formidable
silence" of the world of visual seduction hangs over the scene. She is,
Conrad makes clear, the ultimate primal spermatophage of reproductive
sexuality, unevolved, masculine in her aggressive power, "savage and superb, wild-eyed and magnificent," the eternal woman of death whose
monstrous enticements are nature's revenge upon evolutionary masculinity, upon that brave new world of the intellect that had dared to de-
tach itself from the endlessly recurring cycles of destructive chaos and
waste dominating the world of "woman-rule."

Summoned one last time by She Who Must Be Obeyed, Kurtz now,
quite literally, slips back down the evolutionary ladder. He escapes from
the riverboat, and Marlow, suffering a "moral shock, altogether monstrous, intolerable to thought and odious to the soul" when he realizes
the depth of Kurtz's enslavement to primal femininity, discovers the
backslider "crawling on all-fours" back into the jungle, in an attempt to
regain the paradise of unlawful physical abandon represented by the
African woman. "Do you know what you are doing?" Marlow asks him.
"Perfectly," Kurtz answers, his voice echoing down the ages of evolutionary development, "far off and yet loud, like a hail through a speaking trumpet."

As the riverboat steals away from the heart of darkness with Kurtz
on board, the primal woman rushes out of the jungle and shouts something. "Do you understand this?" Marlow asks. Kurtz remains silent,

"looking out past me with fiery, longing eyes, with a mingled expression of wistfulness and hate. He made no answer, but I saw a smile, a smile of indefinable meaning, appear on his colourless lips that a moment after twitched convulsively. 'Do I not?' he said slowly, gasping, as if the words had been torn out of him by a supernatural power." As the riverboat withdraws from the primal womb, "the barbarous and superb" African woman, knowing that once more she has been denied, "stretched tragically her bare arms after us over the sombre and glittering river."

Given Kurtz's weakened and depleted condition—he has, after all, lost the bulk of his vital essence to the unspeakable temptations of primitive femininity—it is soon time for him to utter his famous last words: "The horror! The horror!" And while there will always remain in those words an element of the generalized existential pessimism the post–World War II critics came to read into them, Conrad's main intention was to convey that, in extremis, Kurtz had finally recognized the abominable nature of his own degeneration into physical license. Marlow, indeed, says so quite specifically when, upon being notified of Kurtz's death, he remarks that in those last words Kurtz "had pronounced a judgement upon the adventures of his soul on this earth." (112) Indeed, as if in an attempt to forestall the existentialist readings to come, Marlow emphasizes that Kurtz's recognition is a conventional moral one: "It was an affirmation, a moral victory, paid for by innumerable defeats, by abominable terrors, by abominable satisfactions." (113)

Marlow himself, having completed his journey into the womb of the world without succumbing to the erotic temptation of degeneration, has come to understand the value of civilized self-control. Abstinence is not merely a personal goal, a private transcendence, but a prerequisite for the further evolution of mankind. The primitive lure the Congo river had over him as a child has been broken. He now understands that the imperial superiority of Britain is the result of nineteen hundred years of progress in the realm of seminal containment. After all, Marlow is a true Anglo-Saxon; Kurtz was merely vaguely Germanic—a generalized European.

Just as Marlow's entry into the primal womb of darkness was facilitated and "guarded" by women, so Conrad's final reckoning of his journey takes the form of a crucial confrontation with Kurtz's "Intended" upon his return to Brussels. In a flash Marlow realizes that to keep civilization on its evolutionary course, he must protect the salutary, civilized, innocuous, fantasy world of the modern woman against the harsh realities of nature. Kurtz's Intended proves to be a prime example of Kenealy's hyper-evolved, ultrapassive, altruistic mother-woman. She seemed, Marlow notes, to be "floating toward me." When they meet, Kurtz has been dead for more than a year, but "she seemed as though she would remember and mourn forever." She has, Marlow observes approvingly, "a mature capacity for fidelity, for belief, for suffering." The room darkens around her "as if all the sad light of the cloudy evening had taken refuge on her forehead. This fair hair, this pale visage, this pure brow, seemed surrounded by an ashy halo." Her eyes are "guileless, profound, confident, and trustful." Marlow recognizes that she is "one of those creatures that are not the playthings of Time"; she is one of the household angels created by evolution, as close to actual disembodiment as she could possibly get: even in the gathering darkness "her forehead, smooth and white, remained illumined by the unextinguishable light of belief and love." (118)

This is what civilization means, Marlow recognizes: the angel of altruism, the mother of the human soul, whose "fair hair seemed to catch all the remaining light in a glimmer of gold." She is the counterforce man has created against the African devil-woman. The Intended is the virgin-mother of man's disembodied future, and she must therefore be protected at all cost. To tell her about Kurtz's weakness would be to destroy her, would represent another step back. To protect the future of civilized society, Marlow lies to her, making it seem as if Kurtz died with her name on his lips:

> "I said [it] with something like despair in my heart, but bowing my head before the faith that was in her, before that great and saving illusion that shone with an unearthly glow in the darkness, in the triumphant darkness from which I could not have defended her—from which I could not even defend myself." (119)

Conrad's main point in *Heart of Darkness* thus virtually coincided with the argument Kenealy developed in *Feminism and Sex-Extinction*. If today most critics still read the narrative as primarily a tale of imperialism, greed, and existential anguish, that is because we tend to overlook the gender-ideological fervor of turn-of-the-century evolutionary theory. Numerous other themes certainly remain structural elements of the story, but Conrad made it very clear that Kurtz's materialistic excesses, his hunger for gold, and his sadistic methods of gathering his wealth were factors secondary to his abject capitulation to Africa, to Woman, that eternal primitive prostitute enthralled by her predatory bisexual womb.

The daughters of Conrad's African goddess of lust, and of such other primal temptresses as H. Rider Haggard's Ayesha, "She Who Must Be Obeyed," who only needed to glance at an Englishman to make him feel "utterly cowed, as if all the manhood had been taken out of him," (234) proliferated throughout Western European and American culture during the first forty years of the twentieth century like bats out of the caves of Africa, digging their claws with special ferocity into the pages of the comics and pulp magazines of the Thirties, Forties, and Fifties. But there were also interesting new developments in the role of the woman with the African womb.

Conrad's savage goddess had still been a creature to be avoided at all cost, no matter how outwardly attractive she might seem. Her seduction was the dance of feral eroticism, "the beat of the drum, regular and muffled like the beating of a heart—the heart of a conquering darkness." Her very existence, Marlow had recognized when he was about to comfort Kurtz's Intended in Brussels, "was a moment of triumph for the wilderness, an invading and vengeful rush which, it seemed to me, I would have to keep back alone for the salvation of another soul." (116) Similarly, Haggard's Ayesha, in the end, is consumed by the fires of the masculine intellect, a vampire who "opposed herself to the eternal law, and, strong though she was, by it was swept back into nothingness— swept back with shame and hideous mockery." (309)

The African goddesses of the pulps of the early twentieth century, however, were beginning to behave far more like Kenealy's "hoyden- sisters," who were merely instinctual victims of the eternal feminine within them, and who only needed to be brought down a peg. More and more these young women learned that, no matter how seductive they might be to the average Joe, there were manly men out there able to withstand their every temptation. In the presence of such sterling specimens of manhood, these temptresses learned to give up their tomboy masculinity, the atavistic umbilical cord connecting them with the African womb, and to become decent, passive, Kenealyan house- wives instead. Tarzan and his ilk fell into an extremely predictable habit of withstanding them, but always only after these heroes, and the read- ers who followed their exploits, had had ample opportunity to ogle the evil sisters at length. After numerous ferocious attempts at seducing the hero, the lustful but basically incompetent temptresses of pop culture almost invariably underwent a major motivational crisis, usually either ending up sacrificing themselves to save the masculine hero while shedding floods of Wagnerian tears, or otherwise becoming model Kenealyan Intendeds who settled down modestly while they waited for their neglectful heroes to return from their muscular adventures. These conflicted pulp temptresses became forerunners to the countless Hollywood tough girls of the Thirties and Forties, who always started life as intrepid, "masculinized" reporters, sportswomen, gun molls, or gold diggers, only to be ratcheted into dutiful domesticity and impending motherhood by the last reel.

Toward the advent of World War II, the evolutionary male had become so thoroughly habituated to these brave renunciations that the "tomboy meets boy and settles into domestic bliss" solution of the movies was threatening to penetrate even the primal jungle. The vampire woman with the African womb was poised to meet up with Doris Day. She did so, in scandalous fashion, in Stuart Cloete's *Congo Song* (1943), a self-conscious updating of Conrad's *Heart of Darkness*. *Congo Song,* a huge best-seller when it was first published and continuously in print for almost two decades, selling millions of copies, was an extremely odd and repulsive, but for its time entirely characteristic, display of turn-of-the-century biological science presented as universal "existential truth." The book demonstrated that in gender-ideological terms very little had changed since 1900.

Cloete, as the dust jacket announced in proud acknowledgment of the international stature of the author's racist and misogynist credentials, "was born in Paris, was educated in England, served as an officer in the Coldstream Guards, and spent fifteen years farming in South Africa. Since coming to America he has lived in Florida, Wyoming, New York City, New Orleans and the Bahamas." During these years of travel Cloete obviously spent most of his free time reading not just Conrad but a plethora of the early twentieth century's leading biosexists and gender mythologists: Freud, Jung, Adler, and Frazer's *The Golden Bough* formed Cloete's acknowledged psychoanalytic sources. Remy de Gourmont and Otto Weininger were his unacknowledged, but often almost directly plagiarized, gurus in the field of gender ideology.

Though *Congo Song* is ostensibly a novel, it is primarily a disquisition on "the relations of the sexes," the only subject Channel, the physician who functions as Cloete's principal mouthpiece in the novel, appears to consider worth talking about. And talking about women and sex is the main theme of *Congo Song*. There is a desultory subplot about Nazi sab-

otage in Africa, but all Hitlerite rascals are summarily dispatched before
they have a chance to interfere with the main focus of the author's concerns. Their presence only served to demonstrate that during World War
II it was just as easy to be anti-Nazi and antifeminine as to be pro-Nazi
and antifeminine.

Congo Song centers on the multifarious sexual affairs of Olga le
Blanc—Cloete's version of Conrad's personification of the African
womb. Olga is a She/La of French-Polish extraction living in the Belgian Congo with her superannuated Swiss botanist husband. In addition
to the German spy whom she beds, she is surrounded by Channel, who
is French; Wilson, a British-American; Retief, a Belgian; and a handful
of males of various other nationalities, all of whom become her mates
pretty much indiscriminately whenever her womb calls for them. The
arrangement loudly spells "microcosm," as the author repeatedly emphasizes: "Scientist, painter, hunter, playboy, adulteress, and priest,"
(392) the gang's all here. Africa is "the dark forest of Freudian obsession,"
(63) the "womb of the world . . . her dark moist womb. This was a
breeding place, a spawning place, lush, dark, hot, fetid." (111) Here even
the European men are "driven by atavistic desires" (65) that make them
yearn for "sexual extinction." (82) In Africa sex was a bestial act that was
"atavistic, and must be atavistically performed without reservation."
(146)

Among all these men, "Olga was woman. So much so that she became representative, generic, symbolic, diffusing a sexual aura." (11)
Wilson, the British-American, recognizes right away that "Olga was all
women." (130) No wonder, then, that she is also a personification of the
African womb: "This was a brutal subhuman place. . . . And Olga, the
height of sophistication, was, by some reversal in time, by some completion of a psychological and biological combination, allied to this
atavistic world." (268) Cloete proclaims Olga's status as the world's
womb over and over again:

> She lay back in bed, lost in a geo-sexual dream. This was the
> centre of Africa: its tropical, equatorial heart . . . a primeval
> place: a hopeless place dark with age . . . where the dark pulse of
> life beat out a rhythm of its own. A woman waiting. A centre,
> pulsating, coreless. The earth rich, waiting for the rain. The
> field, waiting for the random sower. What had the field to do
> with the ploughman, the sower or the reaper? The field went on
> forever. A hundred sowed, a hundred ploughed. They came and

went. What was man to woman but this? His penetration of her
secrets but the planting of a seed. Her desire for him but the call
of the earth to the plough. (176)

Drunk with this realization, the sophisticated Olga, who is mother
Africa herself, lets herself be plowed by just about every man who happens to come near her. It is all due to the fact that she can't seem to separate "the masculine side to her character" (171) from her maternal
drive. "No woman was entirely woman. No man entirely man. Together, added up in a hormonic sum, the couple totalled a complete
man and woman," (132–3) Cloete remarked, cribbing directly from
Otto Weininger. The primitive man in Olga had made her into a "beautiful nymphomaniac." (201) She was, however, a maternal nymphomaniac: for "woman was, by her nature, a mother: very near to the
earth. . . . Mother coming out of mother, all beads of an endless umbilical cord that stretched back without a single break in the sequence to
the infinite prehuman past." Gourmont, too, is all over these passages:
"What was the male but an incomplete female? What was he but a wanton fertilizer of the female soil?" (114)

Channel, an interminable talker, is the all-knowing sage of Cloete's
sexual universe: "Beautiful women are fools. . . . It is a provision of nature that they have no brains." Consequently, "the abstract conception is
only possible to woman in exact proportion to her lack of femininity.
Mentally sterile and physically potent, she challenges man to fecundate
her, intriguing his mind with the pseudo-activity of her intellect, yet
fearing his mind, since by it he can negate her." (223) Concluding this
perusal of Weininger, Cloete's physician-mouthpiece asserts: "Women
are less civilized than men: interested only in the immediate, in the conservative, in the reproductive." A man's "sexual impulse is irregular" and
"the result of a metabolistic glandular irritation, whereas a woman is
continually sexual. She is sex, and on rare occasions she is beautiful."
The male was the evolutionary entity: "He may be motivated by sex,
but he dissociates himself from it. That's the big difference." (183–4)

To complete his Weiningeresque characterization of Olga, of
"Woman," as the African womb, Cloete included a sensational missing-
link relationship between his heroine and her "pet" gorilla, Congo, another entry in that long line of simian inamorati also including King
Kong, who were expressive of pop culture's conviction that apes and
women belonged in the same erotic arena. Congo, whose name once
again demonstrated Cloete's admirable attention to the subtleties of

symbolic representation, formed the bridge between animalism and woman's "instinctive maternity." He also served as a strict Freudian feral Oedipus *ex machina* whose thwarted fatal instincts were to bring his song to an improbably hopeful close. For Cloete wanted Congo also to be symbolic of "the bestial Nazi mentality," and his destruction therefore achieves both the death of Africa in Olga and the promise of a new world order guided by American capitalism. On the back slipcover of *Congo Song* Cloete emphasized that his readers should buy war bonds as a vote of confidence "in our capacity to drive on, to break all opposition, and then to reconstruct upon a new, a better design, a world that will be different."

But how did Olga, the woman who was all women, get hooked up with this jungle Nazi? Some years earlier she had given birth to a child who had died almost immediately from a tropical disease. At just that time a baby gorilla had been rescued from the womb of its dying mother. Olga's indiscriminate maternal instinct had embraced the baby gorilla, and she had suckled it at her breast, letting it grow into young gorillahood as if it were her own child. Cloete's readings of Freud, coupled with the "evolutionary leap" theories of Le Conte, determined the inevitable outcome of his tale of Oedipus in Africa: "Congo in his loves and hates was a primitive man; for if by heredity he was an anthropoid ape, by the environment Olga forced upon him he had made a jump from one geological era to another, and mentally must have corresponded to the Neanderthal man at least. And he was in love with Olga." Beating his Freudian drum loudly, Cloete added: "Superficially his attitude towards Olga was that of an affectionate child. He clung to her hand, held her skirts. Putting his arms about her neck, he would kiss her lips with his mouth. The rest was only to be seen in his eyes when he thought himself unobserved." (219)

To make sure that those among his readers who had not yet seen any of the King Kong films would find it impossible to misread the portentous significance of this mother-son relationship, Cloete's characters repeatedly remind themselves "of the folklore of gorillas among the natives: tales of their raping the women." Even though "none were substantiated, . . . all seemed possible." (270) Cloete therefore orchestrates a prurient air of anticipation: Will he or won't he? In the end, of course, Congo does what every Freudian son is supposed to dream of doing: "The ape had run amok. The balance between Olga's psychological power over Congo and Congo's fury had reached the final crisis." (361) Congo therefore kills his "father," the professor, Olga's titular husband (as well as Retief, another of her lovers), and is about to haul the lady off to Oedipal fulfillment when Channel, the philosophical physician, happens by and manages to kill the beast in the nick of time. "Congo threw his arms toward Olga and fell." (361–3)

But in wartime even prurience needed a patriotic edge; Cloete therefore included a happy ending, which intimated that the economic war that had started between the Nazis and the "civilized" nations was bound to conclude in an entirely analogous manner. For even Olga, frightened for once by Congo's uncontrolled sexual Nazism, at last comes to understand that she must abandon the precivilized, polyandrous stage of her ontogenetic development. She shows a new determination to grow up into acculturated adult femininity: "She saw the death of her gorilla as a turning point in her life. Her association with Congo had merely been the acceleration of a process begun in childhood and his going out of it had ended a phase of her life that had been purely physical." (376) At last realizing that she loves only Wilson, the true leader of humanity, the British-American whose race is in evolutionary terms miles ahead of the homoerotic Nazis, Olga awakens to postsexual womanhood. World War II is about to begin. She will become the nurturer and muzzle her *vagina dentata*. She realizes that she must transcend Africa, for she is needed on the home front: "Man was plunging into the abyss. He would come out of it fully humanized or remain in it a beast." He was "bursting out of bondage, out of the womb of a time that had been warm, darkened with false security. Now he must gamble all to gain all . . . or lose all." (389)

Cloete's abyss-and-womb imagery, as always, made everything perfectly clear: woman was the key to both evolution and degeneration. The primitive masculine in woman, the African womb, the vampire, must be destroyed by the stake of monogamy. Man "seeks not quantity, not women; but quality, the woman. This selectivity is part of his humanity, part of the superiority that raises man above the beasts, differentiating him; it is therefore of the spirit and not of the body." But man was also dependent on woman's choices, for "beyond the portal of her thighs he cannot go. Her thighs are of brass. To go there is the little death." (159) Woman must therefore learn to curb her maternal nymphomania and settle down to a life of true motherhood and recessive domestic sexual modesty: "The woman was the stabilizing factor . . . ; world regeneration when it came—if it came—must come through woman, as life came through her. She was the source." (138)

But even so, hidden inside each woman there remained the siren song of the Congo—of Africa, the "giantess, the dark, spawning womb where all men were Pigmies dwarfed by her immensity." Hers was the song of the "throbbing drums, of the ripe fruits falling"; hers was "the song no white man would ever sing." (398–9) At the conclusion of *Congo Song*, therefore, Olga, woman on the verge of acculturation, re-nounces her longing for the African gorilla. She puts a lock on the brass doors of her thighs. The next stage of mankind's evolutionary advance beckons with its kitchens full of convenient appliances: "The moment had come. She was here. In his arms, close to him. Warm and soft against him, her lips on his. 'It has been a long time, Henry.' 'A long time,' he said. 'A very long time.' " (390)

It had been forty years since Conrad published his cautionary para-ble about the consequences, for civilized man, of entering the raging African womb. Now Cloete's Wilson, his model Anglo-American male, had at long last succeeded in colonizing and subjecting that fearsome

Gustav Klimt, Beethoven Frieze, *end wall: "Hostile Forces," 1902,
casein paint on plaster; Austrian Gallery, Vienna*
Africa ("the giant Typhoeus") surrounded by "the dark spawning womb"
of universal feminine seminal vampirism

vampire queen. No longer would it be necessary to hide her from Kurtz's Intended. She had herself become the Intended, for she had freely given up her predatory will. For the good of mankind. For a Nazi-free future. The Fifties were just ahead. Doris Day was waiting in the wings to sing Gus Kahn's thoroughly modern Twenties lyrics with renewed fervor:

> Love me or leave me, and let me be lonely,
> For you won't believe me and I love you only;
> I'd rather be lonely than happy with somebody else . . .
> There'll be no one unless that someone is you . . .
> For my love is your love, there's no love for nobody else.

Congo Song shows how the sociobiology of the first few decades of the twentieth century precipitated into the popular culture of the Forties and Fifties, bifurcating into the contradictory moods of cynicism and maudlin sentimentality about gender relationships that characterized the period. Cloete's Olga was only one of thousands of fictional white women who had to learn to attach civilization's brass lock to their predatory loins before they could be allowed to sing along with Doris Day and Debbie Reynolds, sentimental serenaders who were ever glad to be unhappy while confessing their secret love for the boy next door, and who had learned to prefer singing in the rain or riding through the countryside by the light of the silvery moon over the wilding of their African wombs.

The gender attitudes that were to dominate our century were codified during years around 1900. Conrad's disquisition on the horror of the African womb was repeated endlessly by many other, less talented writers, who often modified the theme to highlight the beneficial influence of the Imperial Anglo-Saxon male's highly concentrated vital essence on the She/Las they encountered. But the scientists' terrifying revelations about the fundamental parallels between insect amours and human sexuality almost always dominated the metaphoric structure of these narratives.

Elinor Glyn's potboiler romance Three Weeks, for instance, caused an international scandal in 1907. It sold over two million copies in England and the United States alone. On the surface it might seem that Glyn's melodramatic and shoddily symbolic representation of a primitive masculine/feminine seductress was sufficient reason for the book's popularity. Glyn had an uncanny ability to capitalize on the intellectual fads of her time—a talent that was soon to land her a lucrative tenure as Hollywood's first famous madam of gossip and media gimmickry. But *Three Weeks* is particularly interesting because Glyn proved to be a lot more tolerant of the sensuous vampire whose maternal depredations she outlined in the book than the male medical leadership of the time would have considered acceptable. Her narrative suggested that it was part of the Imperialist White Man's Burden to gain carnal knowledge of such primitive queens, who, in turn, were driven to their seminal collection rituals only by an entirely honorable maternal desire to have their offspring benefit from the genetic superiority of Anglo-Aryan seed.

In *Three Weeks* events of momentous importance to the future of civilization motivated the sexual encounter of a Russian queen (Africans were a little too far down the evolutionary ladder for Glyn's taste) and an upstanding, standard-issue scion of the British middle class. Glyn gained instant notoriety by combining her advocacy of human Mendelian hybridization with three parts run-of-the-mill romance writing and one part *Prisoner of Zenda*–like adventure and intrigue (the Eastern queen has an ogre of a husband). To make the mix seem particularly exotic, Glyn added a generous helping of self-consciously "Frenchified" symbolist imagery laced with erotic innuendo.

The Russian queen was an early incarnation of Cloete's Olga. She has an African womb, but she is also a Kenealyan mother-woman. Her role in the narrative, moreover, is constructive rather than destructive. Glyn played both sides of the fence: she liberally used the popular imagery of the sexual woman as vampire, but hastened to reassure the British male that he was being pursued so doggedly only because his vital essence represented the cream of evolutionary promise. Even the queens of primitive societies longed for ordinary British men's seed. Thus Glyn provided moral motives for enticingly immoral acts. No wonder Hollywood loved her.

Paul, the young, blond, innocent middle-class hero of *Three Weeks,* while on his first solo excursion to the Continent, encounters a striking older woman ("well over thirty") with characteristic vampire features: a face "startlingly white, like a magnolia bloom," and "a mouth worth looking at again. It was so red . . . straight and chiselled and red, red, red." (17) Her "heavy black hair" is remarkably "thick—enough to strangle one, if she twisted it round one's throat." (20) Any man of worldly experience, after a mental association of this sort, would have gone to the North Pole until this danger had passed, but Paul knows only acculturated, civilized women: sweet simpletons like his mother and the girl next door who is his "intended," textbook examples of Conrad's beautiful dreamers of genteel civilization.

Paul is hypnotized by this serpent of sex: "The woman and her sinuous, sensuous black shape filled the space of his mental vision." (27) Inevitably, she maneuvers herself straight into the young man's arms: "She leant back among the purple cushions, her figure so supple in its lines, it made him think of a snake. She half closed her eyes again." (47–9) Those hypnotic eyes turn out to be almost chameleonic in their ability to match his own arousal: "She looked down straight into his face, as he gazed up at her, and to his intense surprise he could have sworn her eyes were green now! as green, as green as emeralds. And they held him and fascinated him and paralysed him, like those of a snake." (67)

Soon Paul, "even though subjection was in no way part of his nature," falls completely under the spell of "this strange foreign woman thing." She "lay in his arms, and purred love-words to him, and nestled close like a child." In her voice "now and then there was a savage echo which made him think of things barbaric." (124–6) Nature soon takes its course, modestly left to its sinful ways unaided by any further authorial description. For three weeks, the fertile period of woman's monthly and, Glyn insisted, moon-controlled reproductive cycle, the affair is to continue. " 'See, this is our moon,' said the lady, 'and as she waxes, so will our love wax.' " Later, in advance of a carnal embrace, she repeats: "We go on together, you and I and the moon." Almost immediately "a madness of tender caressing seized her. She purred as a tiger might have done, while she undulated like a snake." She plies Paul with "strange, subtle kisses, unlike the kisses of women. And often, between her purrings, she murmured love-words in some strange language of her own, brushing his ears and his eyes with her lips the while." (134) This is evidently a moon lady in full reproductive heat.

Paul is rather bewildered by the whole affair—he knows he is having quite a wonderful time, but his moral and his physical strength are waning. At the same time his strange lover's motives remain a mystery to him—he is, after all, young, innocent, and British. Much too dignified to spell out the doings of the birds and the bees directly, Glyn has her Russian queen speak to her young lover in transparent riddles: "Your very phrases are altered, Paul, and will alter more yet, while our moon waxes and our love grows." Paul responds: " 'Yes, it can grow until it is my life—my very life.' 'Yes Paul,' she said, 'your life'—and her strange eyes narrowed again, the Sphinx's inscrutable look of mystery in their chameleon depths." (143) Glyn wants us to understand that this queen bee of an Eastern country, "half barbaric, half advanced," (151) knows exactly what she's after: Paul's life—reproduced, in the form of a child—and she will stop at nothing to achieve her purpose. "The women of your country," she says, "are sweet and soft, but they know not the passion I know, my Paul—the fierceness and madness of love." (158)

The strange woman has chosen Paul because he is an unspoiled specimen of Anglo-Aryan manhood. "Life, for you," she points out, "was just eating and sleeping and strengthening your muscles." (143) *Mens sana in corpore sano.* As a bodybuilder, a man like Rodin's muscular *Thinker,* Paul is fertile ground for a forward-looking Russian queen, unlike her husband, who is "a useless vicious weakling, too feeble to deserve a fine death—a rotting carrion spoiling God's world and encumbering my path." (156)

Glyn emphasizes that her Eastern queen's motive for shunning her official mate is genetic, not "moral." Such trifling shortcomings as inhumanity and sadism do not trouble her: Discriminating women, she teaches Paul, will accept anything in a man except seminal weakness. Since genetic superiority manifested itself in a man's muscular endowment, the man should make his woman

> feel that there is no use struggling because he is too strong to resist. A woman will stand almost anything from a passionate lover. He may beat her and pain her soft flesh; he may shut her up and deprive her of all other friends—while the motive is raging love and interest in herself on his part, it only makes her love him the more.

Glyn's heroine was a tailor-made product of early-twentieth-century popular science. The author's casual adoption of this point of view shows that the period's "scientific" justification of women's "natural" tendency toward masochism was developing into an intellectual, psychoanalytically sanctioned justification of sadistic violence toward women. A man's physical strength was, after all, objective evidence of his self-control, of his ability to conserve his vital essence. Such a man would, therefore, force himself on a reluctant, acculturated woman only out of kindness. For it stood to reason that subconsciously she would want him to offer her proof of his exceptional talents as a supplier of the seminal fluids all women craved. Since a woman instinctively understood that violent and sadistic behavior in a man were manifestations of his sexual potency, she moreover often deliberately invited such displays of violence to test her partner's manhood. Nature, the argument went, had implanted the masochistic tendency in woman's sexual makeup to help her endure—and, indeed, to enjoy—such evidences of masculine potency. The many movie heroines for whom being beaten ("playfully spanked") by Clark Gable, Cary Grant, or Gary Cooper proved to be a predictable prelude to wedding bells in scores of Hollywood comedies of the Thirties and Forties were direct descendants of Glyn's joyfully masochistic Russian queen.

If this pop mythology of feminine masochism as an instinctual reflex in the service of natural selection had not become such a generally accepted feature of our "entertainment" industry, it might be easier to be amused by the numerous passages from *Three Weeks* that directly instruct Anglo-Saxon males to overcome their civilized "inhibitions" in the sexual arena. During the course of one of these, for instance, Paul learns that his lady's response is to "love him the more" the more frequently he consents to "beat her and pain her soft flesh." In the end he comes to recognize, although it goes against his grain as a British gentleman, "that he could always affect her when he pretended to dominate her by sheer brute force." Such "scientific" expositions of patterns of sadistic and masochistic behavior as "instinctive" inevitably continue to have an almost incalculably tragic effect on gender relationships even today.

All along, Paul's lady makes it quite clear that she has an immediate eugenicist motive for her depredations. She is horrified at the thought that the future of her people might continue to depend on a lurid degenerate such as her actual husband, who is clearly an Eastern European equivalent to the leper in Kipling's "Mark of the Beast." Paul must therefore take on his white man's burden and bring true manhood to her primitive world: "I have a right to find an heir as I will, a splendid heir who shall redeem the land," she exclaims. Her next speech must have made the heart of every good British imperialist beat faster: " 'I love the English,' she whispered, 'I have known the men of all nations—but I love the English best. They are straight and just—the fine ones at least. They are brave and fair—and fearless.' " (204–5) Here, for once, was one of the less evolved who actually *wanted* to lead her people out of that "dark Egyptian night."

Glyn habitually compared her erotically "masculinized" (and, perhaps because of this, surprisingly articulate and intelligent) semidomesticated maternal vampire to a tiger, a snake, a cat, or a child. To drive home the difference between this imperfectly evolved creature and the civilized, unsexed, and hence highly evolved women of England, the author had her heroine lecture Paul on these two faces of Eve in evolution, until, incongruously, she began to sound as if she were Arabella Kenealy in disguise.

Evolved women were fortunate to have attained the role of glorified domestics, household nuns, breeders who conserved their energies strictly, in the service of the evolutionary advance. The ancient Greeks, precursors of Western civilization, had already understood as much: "They were perhaps too practical to have indulged in the mental emotions we weave into it now—but they were wise, they did not educate the wives and daughters, they realised that to perform well domestic duties, a woman's mind should not be over-trained in learning." (212)

Being only partially evolved, Glyn's Eastern queen was still an efficient sexual vampire—but, given the period's characteristic genetic-exchange theories, that also meant that she was more likely to produce a female child (she was, after all, by being sexual, holding on to the masculine essence she held "in trust" for her potential male offspring). As (unlike, for instance, Hemingway's Harry Morgan) a truly continent Englishman Paul could be trusted to supply her with vital essence of such remarkable potency that it would overwhelm her propensity to produce females, and thus push her offspring into the male column.

Glyn's maternal vampire was therefore, in contradistinction to the run-of-the-mill vampire-women of early-twentieth-century history, motivated not by vulgar sensual feminine egotism but, rather, by a rare desire to fulfill her evolutionary destiny—to produce, for her primitive nation, an heir who might bring her culture with one bound into the forefront of the evolutionary advance. Her fierce "masculine" sexuality—which was the source of all Glyn's similes involving tigers and snakes—guaranteed that she had an especially impressive amount of "maleness" to transfer to her son-to-be. If she would only let go of the "male-traits" within her, this still semisavage woman could become mother to Superman himself, Glyn argued.

The author tried to make her description of this portentous evolutionary encounter between the emissaries of nature and culture as pregnant with significant symbolism as possible. The fateful consummation takes place during the time of the full moon. Paul's lady senses instinctively that this is the high point of her monthly fertility curve, and she murmurs ecstatically in her lover's ear:

"When a woman's love for a man rises to the highest point there is in it always an element of *the wife*. However wayward and tigerish and undomestic she may be, she then desires to be the acknowledged possession and belonging of the man, even to her own dishonour. She desires to reproduce his likeness, she wants to compass his material good."

To get Paul into the proper reproductive mood, "she undulated about, creeping as a serpent over her lover, and kissing his eyelids and hair." Her body clearly yearns for his seed: "Oh! my beloved, to-night I shall feast you as never before. The night of our full moon! Paul, I have ordered a bower of roses and music and song. I want you to remember it the whole of your life." (208–12)

The moment is at hand. The primitive past and the civilized present are to be fused to create a harmonious future of fertile mother-women and intellectual supermales. Soon the Russian queen's undulations begin to have their effect: "The exaltation of Paul's spirit had reached its zenith. . . . And the moon flooded the loggia with her light, and the roses gave forth their scent." Paul's orgasm is clearly elemental, and the woman in his arms knows instantly that she need not tap her lover's "spirit" any further: she has achieved what she set out to do. "This is our souls' wedding," she tells Paul. "In life and in death they can never part more."

Now that she is with child—she does not doubt it for a moment—she understands, like any good early-twentieth-century mother-to-be, that her sexual pleasures must end forthwith. Her soon-to-be-motherly (if extramarital) duties require that she no longer squander her "male-traits" recklessly and that she concentrate them instead on the nurturing of her superchild. While Paul sleeps—"the languor of utter prostration was upon him"—his lady gazes "at him, an anguish too deep for tears in her eyes. For was not this the end—the very end. Fierce, dry sobs shook her. There was something terrible and tigerish in her grief. And yet her will made her not linger." She writes her lover a note, indicating that henceforth her responsibility must be to the child he has brought her: "Now you are my life, and for this I must leave you, to save that life." Urging him not to follow her, she fades into the morning.

At this point in her narrative Glyn efficiently conflated the traditional requirements of romance and those of evolutionary science. As soon as Paul, already seriously weakened by the depletion of a considerable portion of his generative energies, discovers that his Eastern queen has left him, he faints like a woman. His muscles have lost their strength. Soon he lies "'twixt life and death, madly raving with brain fever." These three weeks of generative involvement with a maternal vampire have taken their toll: for weeks to come he will find himself to be "as weak as an infant. All his splendid youth and strength conquered by this raging blast." His "enfeebled brain" is still enslaved to lust: "It was sad to have to listen to his ever-constant moan: 'Darling, come back to me—darling, my Queen.'" Paul has clearly been "feminized" by his sexual spending.

Paul's father, a worldly-wise man, rushes to his bedside. When he sees his son, he realizes instantly that he has become the victim of a vital-essence vampire. Indeed, the young man looks just like an actual vampire victim: he lies

> nerveless and white, blue shadows on his once fresh skin. And most pitiful of all were his hands, now veined and transparent, falling idly upon the sheet. But at least the father realised it could have been no ordinary woman whose going caused the shock which—even after a life of three weeks' continual emotion—could prostrate his young Hercules. She must have been worth something—this tiger Queen.

For a protracted period of convalescence, Paul is "effeminated" by his encounter: "Paul's apathy seemed paralysing." His days passed "in one unending languid quietude. He expressed interest in no single thing. He was polite, and indifferent, and numb." He has become, in essence, an "invalid." (226–36)

But when Paul at last receives word from his soulmate that she is to be a mother and that his sacrifice of vital essence has not been squandered, he begins to revive and rebuild his strength. Then comes a message: "Beloved, he is so strong and fair, thy son, born the 19th of February." (263) England has triumphed once again: it has given of its best and brightest essence. Kicking and screaming, one more backward nation will be brought into the forefront of evolutionary civilization. Paul's Eastern queen has also had to expend all her own "male-traits" in the process of birthing a son: her letters to him are written in a "feeble and shaky" hand, and Paul learns that for a while she "had indeed been very ill . . . at death's door." But in return, maternity has made her into a civilized, Kenealyan mother-woman, who has given her all to her child. Thanks to the combined physical sacrifices of the evolutionary couple, their love child is, she writes proudly, "thy image, my Paul! English and beautiful, as I said he would be—not black and white like me."

For once a primitive country has been saved by judicious feminine self-sacrifice, by intuitive Mendelian genetic hybridization. For once a less evolved woman has understood that she must allow her body to be colonized and harvested by evolutionary necessity, that she must be plowed and seeded by the British Empire. Glyn's Eastern queen has proven to be no silver leper, eager to bite the conquering soldiers of the evolutionary advance and transform them into backsliding werewolves of bestial passion. Instead, she has offered herself in maternal self-sacrifice to the inseminating imperialist, the selfless superman of species evolution. Glyn's implication was quite clear: if the colonized people of the world would only act as wisely as Paul's lady and allow themselves to be "mastered" into pregnant submission, the "white man's burden" could be lightened immeasurably. The benighted colonized peoples of the world might then, in due course, join the New World Order, in which their children would be "not black and white," not half civilized, like their mother, but "beautiful" like Paul himself, and ruled by "the inherent manly English spirit." (305)

Glyn stressed that her heroine's timely enslavement to her civilized reproductive purpose had served to avert her country's return to the dark ages of primitive bestiality: "A most difficult political situation had been avoided by the birth of this child." The resolution of Glyn's imperialist theme is now at hand: in a jealous rage, the "evil-living King" runs a dagger through Paul's lady's heart, but the ogre is himself slain by one of the queen's loyal servants. This useful plot device conveniently removes the last remnants of the country's primitive nativism, thus preventing any future backsliding of the heroic maternal vampire into the direction of what Weininger and Lombroso would have called her "inherent tendency toward prostitution." As Glyn gleefully emphasizes, "a fair, rosy-cheeked, golden-haired English child" can now become the "never-to-be-sufficiently-beloved baby King" of this Eastern country. A bright future is at hand, guided by England's civilizing seed. As a stern English captain says to Paul's proud English father: "We're not here to judge the morals of the affair, Charles; you and I can only be thundering glad your grandson will sit on that throne all right." (275)

Glyn thus showed her readers that the imperialists' principal weapon in the battle for a New World Order was the womb of the colonized woman. After *Three Weeks* became a huge international best-seller, how-

ever, she was quite distressed to discover that her readers, in their enthusiasm for the lurid details of her story, had shown a tendency to overlook its sociopolitical moral. In the preface to a 1916 reprinting of her
novel, she therefore complained "that a great number of people are so
thrilled with the actual story of The Lady and Paul that they do not
analyse the meaning of the end after her death, and so miss the whole
intention of the work."

In *Three Weeks* Glyn succeeded in domesticating the woman with
the African womb who had still been the blackest enemy of civilization
in Conrad's *Heart of Darkness*. She had made her instead into a culturally
ambiguous "black and white" figure who, though immoral, became a
willing intermediary between the forces of darkness and light—a sexual
woman, to be sure, but also a cultivated one, whose "masculinity" manifested itself in her worldly wisdom, learning, and ironic disdain for
moral posturing. In that sense Cloete's French-Polish Olga was a linear
descendant of Glyn's Russian queen. To her millions of female readers
Glyn's Eastern woman of mystery served to domesticate the early-
twentieth-century male's fearful, sterile, and deadly masculine-feminine
predator into a creature they could understand much better: an intelligent, privileged woman who redeemed her admittedly retrograde impulses by turning them into a "constructive" desire for motherhood.

However, as Glyn made clear in delineating the fate of her brave
evolutionary frontierswoman, even when she sought to redeem herself,
the sexual woman must be prepared to "pay the price" (302) for being
in the forefront of the evolutionary advance. In order to become a
mother of "kings," even a "vampire" woman must let her sexuality and
her intellect be "vampirised" in turn by her offspring, either by virtuously turning herself into a doltish domestic or—if she was morally beyond all help—by exiting the stage altogether, like Paul's lamented
Eastern queen or, for that matter, Philip José Farmer's outer-space beetles.

Glyn's otherwise so seemingly "modern," and decidedly prurient,
handling of the depressing dualism of dead-end choices that were available to the intelligent young woman of her day thus ultimately only
served to reinforce the perception that these were the only two choices
available, two thoroughly distasteful alternatives: she could be a maternal vampire or a maternal virgin. *Three Weeks* told the millions of young
women who read it that they could choose to be either "old-fashioned,"
and become virtuous and sacrificially mindless mothers, or "modern
and liberated," and acknowledge their own sexuality at the risk of
dooming their male children to debility. Thus, whether the evolution-

ary male's sister chose to be evil or good, she was destined to remain colonized by her lord and master. She must either become the executioner's
masochistic assistant, begging for her master's attention by being mal-
treated, beaten, and used as a domestic slave, or she must remain shackled to the picture window of her suburban home. The only alternative
to that fate, if one believed the intellectual trendsetters of the period,
was to become a terrorist against the colonizer, to counter aggression
with aggression, to stop being merely a minor link in the food chain of
masculine ambition, and to adopt the men's image of the primitive "bisexual" predator—in other words, to become a living counterpart to the
regal She, the ruthless La, the lordly African woman, a cold and manipulative, sadistic-ingestive emissary of nature's African womb, a male-
trait-ridden, lust-driven prostitute, a sterile sexual vampire, a parasitic
insect in the jungle of love.

No doubt there were quite a few real women who chose to explore
that "third way" as a revenge against the dead-end street in which their
environment had placed them. But their choice could also be attributed
to the perverse appeal such women seemed to have among middle-class
males. The baroque windings of early-twentieth-century masculine
fears about the regressive effects of the feminists' assault upon his world
of domestic and economic privilege were starting to blend into a single
weave of race, class, and gender prejudice. The eugenicists warned him
that he must counter the depredations of the roaming hordes of degenerates who were knocking on the household nun's walled garden of sexless virtue. Every sexual vampire's lurid kiss further undermined
civilization's defenses against the emissaries of degeneration. The future
of species survival itself threatened to fall victim to the mark of the
beast. Worst of all, the physicians had discovered that even domestic relations made a man bleed.

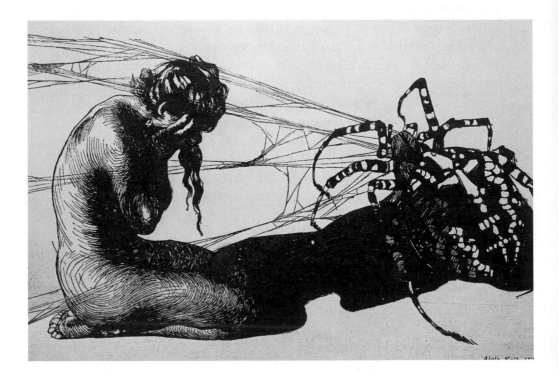

Alois Kolb, "Sex and Character," in Jugend, *1903, no. 51, p. 937*
Sisters under the skin: Weininger's revelations about Woman's helpless enthrall-
ment to the spider within, depicted by one of the favorite illustrators of *Jugend*—
Germany's leading avant-garde weekly of the early years of this century

V. THE PHYSIOLOGY OF VAMPIRISM: THE ROOT OF ALL EVIL AND THE WOMB OF PRODUCTION; SEMINAL ECONOMICS AND SPERMATOPHAGY

T he early twentieth century most commonly characterized sex as a communicable disease. In that spirit the Reverend F. B. Meyer strongly cautioned the public in 1920 against sexual intercourse during pregnancy. He worried that pregnant women, whose "sexual sense" should normally "become quiescent" during this period, would, if aroused, transmit a depraved lust for animal pleasures to their unborn offspring. "The effect of sexual indulgence at that time is likely to develop abnormally the sexual instinct in the child," he declared. Meyer's caution was recorded in a fascinating collection of essays on the social and economic implications of birth control by some of Britain's most "distinguished scientists, economists, and leaders of religious thought." The collection, titled *The Control of Parenthood,* was published simultaneously in London and New York by G. P. Putnam's.

Meyer was certain that in the prevalence of prenatal stimulation science would find "the key to much of the sexual precocity and depravity which curse humanity." (144) Nature herself, he argued, abhorred this regressive subversion of the principles of dimorphic gender evolution: "To those who obey her, Nature distributes her rarest gifts with prodigal generosity, but she chastises with a whip of scorpions all who ruthlessly offend against her conventions." (141) To awaken and energize the African womb even while it ought to be slumbering peacefully through its period of gestation was evidently to imprint the mark of the beast on the unborn. But at the same time psychoanalysis was beginning to posit a positive correlation between moderate sexual activity and mental health. The moralists were becoming confused.

Toward the end of the second decade of this century, therefore, the "maternal virgin or sexual vampire" dichotomy was reaching an ideological impasse. In his *In Defense of Women* (1918), H. L. Mencken, who, as the influential editor of the journal *The Smart Set,* had by this time already become one of the United States' most important cultural critics, complained that this dichotomy had become a vulgar commonplace: "What emerged in the end was a sort of double doctrine, first that women were devils and secondly that they were angels." This "preposterous dualism" had recently been turned "into a compromise dogma" that "held on the one hand, that women are unintelligent and immoral, and on the other hand, that they are free from all those weaknesses of the flesh which distinguish men. This, roughly speaking, is the notion of the average male numskull to-day." (163)

Mencken was not about to be fooled by such shilly-shallying. He had no doubt that behind every feminine mask of innocence a sexual vampire was lying in wait: "What these virtuous beldames actually desire in their hearts is not that the male be reduced to chemical purity, but that the franchise of dalliance be extended to themselves. The most elementary acquaintance with Freudian psychology exposes their secret animus." (141) The issue was simple. All women were sexual predators, and that was that. The "devil or angel" controversy had been concocted by warring factions of religious fanatics and masculinized feminists. The latter were, he contended, "simply women who, in their tastes and processes of mind, are two-thirds men." (142) Mencken had read his Weininger carefully. Against this brood of vampires the American male had one powerful prophylactic: his common sense.

How a woman behaved in response to sexual stimulation (whether during pregnancy or before) was a clear indication of her status in the evolutionary realm. Enjoyment was a sign of the prowling animal womb, while resigned, passive toleration of "masculine admiration, however violently expressed," as Mencken put it, was indicative of her successful acculturation to the requirements of dimorphic gender evolution. Mencken, however, doubted that any such acculturation was more than skin-deep: "No girl in her right senses has ever been actually seduced since the world began," he asserted. Women recognized instinctively that "nine men out of ten" would be quite happy "if there were no women in the world, once they had grown accustomed to the quiet." It was always the "women who seduce them from such celibate doings." (134–5)

Like Kipling, Conrad, Glyn, and a host of other early-twentieth-century chroniclers of the battle of the sexes, Mencken advocated the immediate colonization of woman's African womb. His heavily ironic "defense" concluded that women could not be blamed for being nature's tool in the battle of the sexes. Men were dolts who allowed themselves to be led by the nose. Instead, they should treat women the way the Western nations treated their colonial empires. Women, after all, were not "romantic political and social invalids" but "free competitors in a harsh world" (199) who needed to be kept under authoritarian control. Woman's main weakness was her addiction to sex and money. "It is always forgotten that this weakness is not confined to prostitutes, but runs through the whole female sex." (192) Any woman, Mencken said, once provided with such basic necessities, longed to be dominated: "The woman of true discretion, I am convinced, would much rather marry a superior man, even on unfavourable terms, than make John Smith her husband, serf and prisoner at one stroke." (202)

One of Herbert Spencer's most influential contributions to social Darwinism had been his assertion that societies were organisms that moved from a simple structural homogeneity to complex heterogeneity. Quantity and quality moved in opposite directions. Quality, the natural realm of the "superior man," was the evolutionary elite's weapon in its efforts to transcend the inherent mediocrity of nature. In fact, Mencken suspected that "nature is secretly against the superman, and seeks to prevent his birth." (106) In *The Control of Parenthood*, J. Arthur Thomson, one of the period's most prominent genetic biologists, spelled out Spencer's argument:

> Genesis decreases as individuation increases, the two varying in inverse ratio. Individuation means complexity, integration, fullness, and freedom of life. The tapeworm with its degenerate body and drifting life of ease has its millions of embryos; the Golden Eagle with its differentiated body and controlled life has two eaglets at a time. The less individuated organisms tend to

the spawning solution; the more individuated to economised reproduction.

True to established practice, Thomson, in delineating his economics of reproduction, made liberal use of implied parallels between the sexual habits of humans and animals. His comparison established direct affinities between "better" humans and "good" animals, such as the "Golden Eagle," and invidious homologies between "lesser" humans (the ones who "spawned" a lot) and tapeworms. To economize was essential to *gaining* individuation, while spending was the key to loss of selfhood. Thomson even insisted that "men of great ability, who illustrate inborn individuation, are often childless." (9–10) *Cogito ergo sum continens*. Worldwide empire was to be the thinking man's reward, but only if he found a way to keep the evolutionary elite from self-destructing in the reproductive realm.

Thomson hastened to acknowledge that a "differential decline in fertility with increase of individuation is unproved." (20) But he probably knew that such a caveat would have little effect on what the lay readership targeted by *The Control of Parenthood* would think he thought. He therefore provided this readership with an irresistible sample of his thinking by noting that he shared "the view of Mr. Havelock Ellis that birth-control within limits makes for progress and is likely to continue to do so, being not 'race suicide' but race-saving." (25)

This comment referred to a dilemma widely perceived as pressing by those who considered themselves part of the Anglo-Saxon or Aryan evolutionary elite. For if indiscriminate spawning brought out the tapeworm in a man, its civilizing alternative, continence, must be considered a potential source of "race suicide." The "inferior races" were spawning all around, and the evolutionary elite must therefore pay close attention to the productive efficiency of its seminal expenditure to maintain its position of economic leadership and avoid being overrun by hordes of erotic degenerates.

The biologist Leonard Hill, whose remarks followed Thomson's contribution to the collection, weighed in with an impassioned attack on contraception. Rounding up the usual suspects from the insect world, Hill sketched a natural environment of sexual warfare replete with incidents of masculine humiliation in the woman-dominant world of spiders, where "the male is so small that he has to warily approach the gross-bellied female or he is caught and eaten for his awkward gallantry." Hill stressed that in nature "the acme of life is reached when breeding takes place, and many insects after fertilisation and egg-laying die." Noting that among insects "the drive of the sexual instinct may lead to death in the very act of fertilisation," he sketched for his readers the tragic plight of the drone (the ultimate "socialist" worker of the insect world), "whose sexual organs are torn from him when he mates with the queen bee at the zenith of the nuptial flight into the azure of the sky, and dies as the reward of winning the race." (34–6)

Hill wanted his readers to remember that the human male had escaped the murderous cycles of reproductive femininity only by learning to survive the rigors of sexual intercourse. Today, therefore, as a reward for the male's achievements in continence, "the sexual glands modify the growth and development of the whole body and character." The continuation of evolutionary development depended on that process. The British Empire required men with well-protected testicles. Therefore man must always keep woman in subjection or be content to return to being no more than a meal in the world of woman-rule. The evolutionary male animal must be "of an active, fighting nature, so that the best stock should win the female and propagate the race." (34–6)

The key to Anglo-Aryan world domination was therefore a regime of *self*-control interspersed with brief episodes of sexual conquest, not *birth* control: "The boy who aims at excelling at athletics and at work, who has his energy fully taken up and recognises the need of keeping perfectly fit, is not troubled with overpowering desire. Overfeeding and laziness are great incentives to sexual immorality." Hill's implication was that the "steeled" young man, who could keep woman in her place, was also the soldier who could keep Britain on top in the economic struggle for life among nations. Adolf Hitler was to pay very close attention to such admonitions. Five years later, in *Mein Kampf,* he closely echoed Hill's remarks: "The neglect of physical training," Hitler worried, favored "in much too early youth the formation of sexual conceptions. The boy who, by sports and gymnastics, is brought to an ironlike inurement succumbs less to the need of sensual gratification than the stay-at-home who is fed exclusively on intellectual food." (346)

Hill contended that love was war in the evolutionary realm, and that therefore the soldiers of empire need not pity women for the harsh part nature had given them in the logistics of nation building: "If woman had been evolved as an egg-laying animal like a bird, how easy and simple the control of population, and what a different world—women free from menstruation, pregnancy, and the pangs of birth, the eggs selected and hatched in incubators!" (46–8) To encourage quality over quantity, nature had instead deliberately made human reproduction more painful and more costly in physiological terms. But that challenge had also produced the phenomenon of the unnatural woman who shied away from the rigors of reproduction. This had imposed a new "white man's burden" on the male. It was his duty not to let any woman slip by unfertilized, for "in consequence of the non-fulfillment of desire and the physiological functions of the sexual organs the sexual processes become deranged in many, and painful menstruation occurs, the breasts atrophy, the beauty is lost. In the case of the unmarried, the rose blushing uncared for fades away." Thus the circle of predatory gender relationships once more closed in upon itself, setting off a cycle of devolutionary masculinization among otherwise civilized women. For these atrophied females had a tendency to "become factory hands, approximating to the sterile workers of the bee community. Some few become sexual perverts and feminists, and like the worker bees come to hate the drones." (33)

The complexities of male dominance in the age of empire thus required steel-plated self-control. This, combined with a carefully monitored but authoritative program focused on the insemination of reluctant females, would lead to a new imperialist utopia: "There are vast tracts of the British Empire waiting to be populated by the British race. Let the youth of the overcrowded cities then emigrate and secure room for a healthy, natural sexual life, a more virile character, and far greater happiness." (52)

The contributors to *The Control of Parenthood* thus gave very serious thought to the "Imperial and Racial Aspects" of modern life, as one of the subsections of the book was titled. Harold Cox, editor of the *Edinburgh Review*, pointed out what many feared: "that if we reduce our population, there is a danger of our being overwhelmed by more prolific races." Cox considered this argument "superficially plausible but effectively valueless as a plea for an increased birth-rate" and trotted out the quality-over-quantity argument once again: "If the birth-rate were the test of racial strength the peoples of China and India would long since have overrun the world." The ease with which Britain had conquered India was a case in point: "The higher type of manhood that is developed by control of the birth-rate will always be able to take care of itself against the lower types produced by unlimited procreation." (78–80)

However, Mary Scharlieb, a prominent physician, worried that birth control would bring the ascendancy of unbridled "sensuous gratification." She was certain that "countries which practiced such self-abuse would rapidly degenerate, and would show a lack of physical vigour and of moral greatness." (95–6) She, too, saw the solution as residing in "athleticism and self-control." (118) These qualities would lead to a society governed by "eugenics, patriotism, and enlightened self-interest." (113) Nature, however, must be given its tithe: Every woman of childbearing age should "have a child about once in two years." This production schedule would lead to families blessed with five or six children. "A family of this size would be none too big for the necessities of the Empire." Parts of that empire, she feared, were "so sparsely populated that they offer almost overwhelming temptations to their neighbors." (124–5)

H. Rider Haggard, in reward for the massive popularity of *She* and other such epics chronicling a British imperialism beset by feminine wiles, had been made a Knight of the British Empire by this time. In *The Control of Parenthood* he therefore spoke with new authority when he alerted his readers to the dangers of genetic subversion. He insisted that birth control would force the "White Man's Countries" to "import such foreigners as they could get, until finally the original blood was watered away and they were overtaken by whatever destiny might be appointed to them." He did not need to spell out the nature of that destiny, for every reader could be expected to understand that the words "watery blood" were synonymous with "effeminacy" and "degeneration." (172) On recent visits to South Africa Haggard had been horrified by "the number of persons of mixed origin whom I saw walking about the streets of the cities." He considered "this miscegenation" an entirely new form of "racial suicide."

To reverse this pattern, "the refreshment of the Dominions with British blood" was absolutely essential. "Should the British Empire begin to decline, it will be a terrible event, since its ultimate fall would mean the greatest loss that the known history of the world records—a truth that even our rivals, yes, and our enemies, will, I believe, admit." But "the white races are, in the slang phrase, not the only pebbles on the beach. There remains the East. On the fringe of the East, also, there remains Russia, herself half Oriental." Most threatening of all, however, was the Far East, "animated by morals, rules, and standards utterly different from our own. The East is polygamous and in it there are, I believe, few unmarried women."

It was thus a world of unbridled eroticism and therefore dangerous. For

> while all these dim Eastern myriads were unarmed and helpless,
> they did not greatly matter to the arrogant white races. But as

Japan has taught us within our own generation, they are no longer unarmed or helpless, and what Japan has become today the peoples of China and of other places may, and probably will, become tomorrow.

The werewolf was at the white man's door. These undifferentiated masses were about to fan out over the world to attack the Empire's colonial holdings and "exterminate or subdue the handful" of brave Aryans who, though dramatically outnumbered, were bound to defend such territories. "Well do I remember," Haggard mused, "that wise and prescient man, my late friend, ex-President Roosevelt, discussing this matter with me." The two of them had tried to determine which of the Western world's colonial holdings would be the first to be overrun, for they had agreed that a global race war was inevitable. (179–87)

The imperialist rhetoric of blood, war, and depredation, of racial purity and degeneration, was thus the central theme of *The Control of Parenthood*. By 1920, that theme had become one of the dominant obsessions of Western culture. Even the issue of birth control was not cast in the "pro-choice/pro-life" dichotomy we have since become used to. The individual person's duty was first and foremost to country (duty to God ran a distant second). Haggard summarized the issue succinctly: "The best thing that we can do is to appeal to the women of the Empire to save the Empire, and to impress upon them the fact that great nations are not destroyed: they commit suicide." (188) The collection was deliberately designed to reflect the opinions of the widest possible spectrum of authorities. Rider Haggard was a celebrity, a religious authority, the bishop of Birmingham, wrote the introduction, and Marie Stopes, who had the last word, was as prominent as Margaret Sanger in the field of birth control.

If a popular book on birth control could approach its subject as a matter of international imperialist policy, involving issues of "race suicide" and "racial vampirism," it should come as no surprise that the well-to-do in the business community, the middle-class "aristocracy" of money, who had been anointed as the evolutionary elite by Sumner and his cohorts, were beginning to see sex as a racial battleground and the family as an outpost of the empire of economic mastery. This was, of course, also the issue that most fascinated the huge readership of Thomas Dixon's 1905 best-selling novel of racist diatribe, *The Clansman,* and the even larger audiences for the equally racist film by D. W. Griffith it inspired, *The Birth of a Nation* (1915).

Dixon's novel delineated the world of race wars Teddy Roosevelt and H. Rider Haggard imagined to be just around the corner. Instead of being ruled by muscular, godlike, blond, middle-class supermen, as it should have been, Dixon's mythical post–Civil War agrarian South had been overrun by an ungodly alliance of miscegenating, effeminate Northern aristocrats and half-breed women with "catlike eyes" and "full lips." This reign of horror had unleashed a "vulture army of the base, venal, unpatriotic, and corrupt," which had swept down like "a black cloud" over the Aryan South. The leader of this vermin was Stoneman, a decadent old Northern radical with "ape-like" arms and an "eagle-beaked nose breathing rapacity, sensuality throbbing in his massive jaws, and despotism frowning from his heavy brows." (99) Lombroso had, of course, already alerted Dixon's readers to the fact that a man with such features could not help but be a born criminal. This stone-hearted degenerate was, in turn, led by his—from a phrenologist's point of view, tellingly Semitic—nose by a monstrously miscegenated woman, an American version of Conrad's African queen:

> No more curious or sinister figure ever cast a shadow across the history of a great nation than did this mulatto woman in the most corrupt hour of American life. The grim old man who looked into her sleek tawny face and followed her catlike eyes was steadily gripping the Nation by the throat. Did he aim to make this woman the arbiter of its social life, and her ethics the limit of its moral laws? (94)

Of course he did. What else could be expected of Jews and of half-breeds who were, Dixon made clear, like the Africans who had spawned them, creatures "half-child, half-animal"? (292)

Dixon wanted to show that Stoneman and his effeminate Northern cultural elite had rigged the vote in Congress to ensure that post–Civil War Reconstruction would be a dance of degenerates. The Aryan South's lofty Christian principles were about to be betrayed and overrun by opportunists who would set themselves up as "absolute monarchs" by forging an alliance with the "scum of the earth." The "half-animal" woman with the African womb triumphed: "In the moment of ominous silence which followed" the vote, Dixon writes, "a yellow woman of sleek animal beauty leaned far over the gallery rail and laughed aloud." (145) Porter Emerson Browne's Vampire and Dixon's mulatto were clearly two of a kind: sexual women who had slithered out from among the lowest dregs of the lowest orders of humanity to infect the Aryan world with their lusts. The "yellow woman" laughs so loudly because she knows that now "ape-like black beasts" will be given free rein to range through the South and rape its highly evolved white women at will. Were this to happen, Dixon's implication was, hordes of other degenerate yellow women, the tainted fruit of these lustful encounters, could be expected to fan out over the North American continent and depredate the surviving middle-class Aryan males. Species evolution would grind to a halt.

What Dixon's villainous contaminator of white blood has not counted on, however, is the Southern white woman's iron will to purity and her virtuous submission to Anglo-American manhood. Dixon makes it abundantly clear that these meek women, elected of God to be the cradle of mankind's evolutionary advance, would rather kill themselves than allow their genetic contamination by the blood of degenerates. Dixon's miscreant has also erroneously discounted the evolutionary fervor of Southern white men. These rise up as one against the bestial hordes invading their earthly paradise, organize the Ku Klux Klan, "God's Army," and wreak swift and deadly vengeance upon the brutal but cowardly Africans. Even Stoneman, the lust-deformed leader of the effeminate Northern cultural elite, dying, finally sees the light: "When I first fell a victim to the wiles of the yellow vampire who kept my house, I dreamed of lifting her to my level." But instead she has dragged him down: "I felt myself sinking into the black abyss of animalism, I, whose soul had learned the pathway of the stars and held high converse with the great spirits of the ages———." (371) Stoneman wisely expires in the midst of this realization. Had the phrase not already been claimed by Conrad's Kurtz, Stoneman at this point might well have exclaimed: "The horror! The horror!"

The Clansman—like Marlow always a man of moderation and moral restraint—has the last word. In the novel's concluding chapter, triumphantly and biblically titled "Vengeance Is Mine," he is able to declare, hot on the heels of Stoneman's demise, that "Civilization has been saved, and the South redeemed from shame." The racially miscegenated sexual-woman/female-man/Jew-monster that was destined to stalk through the twentieth century in a virtually endless series of incarnations had encountered its first phalanx of fearless vampire killers: as Dixon promised in his introduction, "one of the most dramatic chapters in the history of the Aryan race" had come to a happy ending amid the light of flaming crosses and the smell of burning flesh.

Dixon's inspiration, like Porter Emerson Browne's for *A Fool There Was,* had been Kipling. His subtitle to *The Leopard's Spots* (1902), the first volume of his racist/sexist "Trilogy of Reconstruction," which continued with *The Clansman* and concluded with *The Traitor* (1907), was "A Romance of the White Man's Burden." Dixon was convinced that imperialism was the South's Manifest Destiny. The Ku Klux Klan was the military arm of "the Invisible Empire" of white supremacy. In *The Clansman,* a Dr. Barnes, portrayed by Dixon as a knowledgeable moderate and an "objective" scientist, anticipated Harold Cox's argument in *The Control of Parenthood:* "The breed to which the Southern white man belongs has conquered every foot of soil on this earth their feet have pressed for a thousand years. A handful of them hold in subjection three hundred million in India. Place a dozen of them in the heart of Africa, and they will rule the continent." (186) Clearly only the blood-watering, muscle-weakening genetic poison of the "yellow vampire" of miscegenation could keep the Aryans from remaining the masters of the universe.

Compared with Dixon's vicious racist hatemongering, soon to be replicated faithfully in D. W. Griffith's much overcelebrated *Birth of a Nation,* the "racial" implications of the theme of the vampire were a good deal more subdued in Browne's *A Fool There Was,* which was staged and novelized a mere two years after Dixon had concluded his trilogy of race, sex, and class parallelism, but Browne's intentions were clearly the same. Dixon's scope was meant to be "epic," whereas Browne's melodrama was "domestic." Browne's generic Woman, as Vampire, was white, but she was born into a "filthy" French peasant environment as the miscegenated daughter of the European version of the African womb: the effeminate remnants of the feudal aristocracy of the "dark ages" who had, by this time in history, become the swishy, licentious Draculas of middle-class economic pornography. Browne's "Woman" and Dixon's equally generic, miscegenated "Yellow Vampire" were therefore both presented as proof of the sexual woman's genetic ties with the "lower orders"—all those creatures "half devil and half child" whose reluctance to enter the brave new world of virtuous subjection to their Aryan masters expressed their perverse lack of appreciation for the white man's burden of evolutionary capital development.

Browne had set out to demonstrate that the destructive incursions of the sexual vampire and the colonized masses' resistance to progress were parallel facets of the tapeworm mentality—the effeminate collectivist "spawning" impulse that was a manifestation of species degeneration.

But he could not portray "the Vampire" of his novel simply as a daughter of the "lower classes," for most bourgeois readers would have found it hard to believe that such a creature could have had the grace and beauty necessary to make her into a truly fatal woman. It was a given of early-twentieth-century melodrama that such a woman must be a racial "defective"—a woman of mixed heritage. In *Three Weeks,* in her most positive incarnation, she had been an Eastern aristocrat with "modern" ambitions; this had made it possible for Elinor Glyn to portray her not only as physically refined and desirable but even as admirable, a woman with "positive" instincts. Still, the information that this queen was of Eastern origin was perfectly sufficient to make Glyn's readers accept the notion that this elegant lady could be capable of "immorality" and "animal lust." Such a woman, in turn, could be killed off with little fanfare.

Dixon's "yellow woman" similarly owed her "catlike" physical erotic power to the "tragedy of miscegenation," which had given her the outward beauty of the white race. But behind this facade of beauty, "the beast" of degeneration lay hidden. "The Woman" in Browne's novel completed the triad of mixes habitually used by early-twentieth-century authors to alert their readers to the appearance of a fatal woman. As the spawn of a liaison between the old European aristocracy and the barely evolved "lower orders" of Western civilization—bestial farmers and barely human laborers—she was truly one of Dracula's daughters.

In 1925, in *Mein Kampf,* Adolf Hitler spelled out the mathematics of miscegenation: "Any crossing between two beings of not quite the same high standard produces a medium between the standards of the parents. That means: the young one will probably be on a higher level than the racially lower parent, but not as high as the higher one." Hitler had understood perfectly the point Dixon, Browne, and Griffith were trying to make: "The stronger is to rule and he is not to amalgamate with the weaker one, that he may not sacrifice his own greatness." The weakling must be sacrificed to the strong: "If this law were not dominating, all conceivable development toward a higher level, on the part of all organically living beings, would be unthinkable for man." (390) The step from "excluding" the weakling (bred "in the swamp of a generally spreading softening and effeminacy" [386]) to exterminating him is small—and organic.

Browne's "Woman," then, was, like those of Dixon, Conrad, and many other novelists of this period, a sociopolitical construction intended to demonstrate the disastrous but, in a woman, not immediately

recognizable effects of miscegenation. An ocean full of social and economic implications churned ominously beneath the vampire's kiss. No
wonder Theda Bara's phrase "Kiss me, My Fool!" made a whole generation of men want to run for the exits. The period's reigning platitude
was that loss of money and loss of vital essence were more than merely
metaphoric consequences of the sexual vampire's incursions. They were
the source of species degeneration itself. A man's loss of vital essence directly *caused* the loss of his money, but the erotic depredations of the
African womb did more: they weakened a man's intellect. His weakened
intellect made him lose his capacity to conserve capital, and this in turn
undermined his capacity to make money. Thus, in the end, any Aryan's
seminal profligacy undermined the economic strength of the Aryan nations, and hence their ability to triumph in the coming race wars.

The social Darwinist teachings of Spencer and Sumner, the colonialist mythology of the empire builders, and the prejudicial dimorphic
gender evolutionism of the biologists, physicians, and theologians had
thus, by 1915, become a single issue in the minds of most educated
males. With the economic boom of the Twenties, their fears of seminal
depletion were gradually to be overtaken by financial euphoria. The
evolutionary ideology that had posited the genetic primacy of a capitalist meritocracy and, in the process, developed the image of the sexual
woman as vampire, thus also encouraged the development of a viciously
antihumane racist "patriotism," which took its cue from the rhetoric of
masculinity and effeminacy already developed within the context of
"the battle of the sexes." Now, slowly, the horrid usurpative ambitions
of the "lower orders"—the "black mob," the "yellow peril," and the
"red hordes"—began to take center stage. Soon the sexual woman
would no longer be seen as the primary cause of economic and species
degeneration. Instead, she would gradually become merely a "natural"
ally to the "lower orders," one more weapon in nature's war on the
lordly Aryan.

Easy money at the same time exerted a relaxing effect on sexual
mores. During the Twenties and Thirties the "real" vampire of the earlier decades underwent a parthenogenetic evolution. Her primitive, bestial half seamlessly shifted its shape into the pervasive erotic temptress,
the "Mata Hari" figure impersonated in Theda Bara's wake by actresses
such as Nita Naldi, Pola Negri, Garbo, and Dietrich. These ruthless seductresses were to blame for a staggeringly high death rate among their
suitors. The once secondary financial appetite of the earlier vampire,
meanwhile, spawned the gold digger—who was almost always an irre-

sistibly attractive working-class woman whose ambitions were more economic than amorous. But such modern, spunky (preferably blonde) bedroom capitalists soon came to exhibit an endearing tendency to fall in love against their better judgment and to renounce their ticker tapes for aprons. The daughters of such marriages made on Wall Street were to become the tomboys next door of the Fifties, whose only direct genetic connection with their vampire grandmothers consisted of gravity-defying breasts emblematic of their twin-set erotic pliability and maternal amplitude.

The demise of the "real" vampire of the early decades, however, also required the development of a new, this time far more metaphoric, vampire brood. In the cinematic revival of the vampire beginning with Tod Browning's *Dracula* of 1931, we therefore see the scientific "reality" of the 1910s transforming itself into the social mythology of today. That symbolic metamorphosis also transmuted the portentous socioeconomic meaning of the sexual woman's command to man: "Kiss me, My Fool!" The "kiss" out of wedlock that had once represented the "real" vampire's ruthless, degenerative appropriation of the lifeblood of the Aryan nation thus, under the influence of psychoanalysis, gradually took on the bland sociosymbolic "universality" of its current cultural function as an only vaguely predatory act of erotic convergence.

But before the political specificity of the vampire's kiss began to fade, it had succeeded in establishing a wide range of metaphoric equations that still dominate our erotic imagination. Popular culture today perhaps more than ever encourages acceptance of the Freudian dictum that love and death are two sides of the same coin. However, when Freud posited a "death instinct" that drives people "beyond the pleasure principle" in search of a dimly remembered prenatal condition of "inanimate stasis," and when he, in consequence, accepted the notion that "the aim of all life is death," he was merely being a man of his time, a man brought up in an environment in which all sexual encounters were seen as sadomasochistic depredations, and where, by the highest scientific authority, each instance of ejaculation had been declared to be indeed that infamous "little death" of French folklore, a chemical and economic disaster contributory to each man's progressive loss of self.

As long as psychoanalytic assumptions of this sort, whose perceived validity is intimately linked to specific historical conditions, continue to be taken seriously, there is little reason to assume that we have rid ourselves of the social influence of the early twentieth century's moral economy of sexual depletion. Culture and entertainment could not exist in their present form without the assumption that love and death are coextensive. In a Hollywood movie, to make love to an openly sexual woman is still a misstep virtually guaranteed to result in death, unless, like Michael Douglas—the reigning role model for all recuperating tempted men—the sinner can square his jaw against temptation and kill the offending woman instead.

The persistence of such fears can be attributed at least in part to what was certainly the oddest among the discoveries of turn-of-the-century medicine in the field of human sexuality. Researchers convinced of the miraculous properties of properly retained "testicular matter" argued that there must be a specific organic cause for the sexual woman's perverse descent into nonreproductive seminal theft. Certainly there was no mystery about the cause of a man's depletion. The loss of his vital essence was explanation enough. But why, conversely, should the woman thrive? That too, they decided, must have to do with the generous infusions of the masculine essence she received from her sexual partners. The male's "catabolic," creative drive clearly fell victim to the "anabolic," recessive needs of the woman.

One pseudoscientific assumption usually invites another, and the image of the sexual woman as a vampire who deprived the male of his vital essence inevitably helped scientists to conclude that the male's precious seminal fluid must literally have a role in "feeding" a woman's body. Women, the argument went, needed the male seminal extracts even for purposes quite apart from the process of impregnation. By the early 1920s this idea had become so widely current that Marie Stopes, in her book *Contraception* (1923), claimed (quite inaccurately) that the medical profession should have credited her for having discovered this earthshaking theorem. She insisted that in her book *Wise Parenthood* (1918) she had been first to have "explicitly enunciated" the "very important consideration" of "the beneficial *Absorption* by the vagina from the ejaculatory fluid" as a determining factor of the physical well-being of women. Since then she had "watched opinion about it pass the stages from hostile criticism to the adoption of my facts."

As is typical of so many of the quarrels about "being first" in the world of science, Stopes had merely enunciated an idea that was already widely in the air since at least the early 1890s. She was, however, correct in asserting that by 1923 the notion had become a medical commonplace. Moreover, Stopes was certainly one of the most committed and insistent advocates of this idea, which held that "women absorb from the seminal fluid of the man some substance, 'hormone,' 'vitamine,' or

stimulant which affects their internal economy in such a way as to benefit and nourish their whole systems." (81) The British birth control advocate's many books on sex, marriage, and contraception were hugely
influential during the Twenties and Thirties. Though antiabortion
groups and the followers of antipornography campaigner Anthony
Comstock managed to keep most of them from being published in the
United States until the late Twenties, they sold millions of copies in Europe. Many of these were smuggled into the United States with even
more zeal than copies of *Ulysses.* Her book *Married Love* (1918) became
a true publishing phenomenon.

The idea itself, however, had been floating around the edges of the
medical establishment since at least the eighteenth century, and, as
Havelock Ellis and other sexual anthropologists were fond of emphasizing, claims about the restorative qualities of various seminal and testicular extracts had been part of folk medicine for thousands of years. But
during the first twenty years of this century, probably as a logical out-
growth of the renewed widespread popularity of the vital-essence theory, the medical establishment was all abuzz over a variety of recent
discoveries that had lent an aura of scientific legitimacy to earlier speculations about the nutritive potency of the life-energy contained in a
man's vital fluids. After all, if these fluids were responsible for the size
and intellectual potency of his brain (that "great clot of genital fluid" of
Ezra Pound) and were transported to that location through the blood (or
the spinal marrow, as some suggested), a direct infusion of the fluid was
likely to have a dramatic impact on the physiological constitution of
women—who were, after all, poorly supplied with gray matter from the
start. Researchers suggested that any evidence of particularly vigorous
health among the grateful female recipients of the male's seminal fluid
should be attributed directly to its nutritional properties.

In 1869, at the height of the medical revival of interest in the vital-
essence theory, Charles-Edouard Brown-Séquard had begun to explore the rejuvenation potential of genital extracts. Brown-Séquard
(1817–1894) was a truly international pioneer in the field of neurophys-
iology and endocrinology. Born on Mauritius of an Irish-American father and a French-African mother, he had a British passport and spent
most of his life moving restlessly from place to place, an early example
of the gypsy medical researcher in pursuit of funding. He had worked
with Charcot and was a close friend of Paul Broca, the famous French
surgeon who was a moving force in the development of craniology and
modern brain research. He had been brought to the United States by

Louis Agassiz, the famous Swiss-American Harvard geologist whose study of fossilized human skulls had led him to posit a theory of the polygenesis of human races—a simple way to legitimize the argument that there were dramatic inequalities of evolutionary development among the various branches of the species.

Paris, Philadelphia, London, New York, Cambridge (Harvard), and Geneva were some of the locations where Brown-Séquard pursued his research on the localization of function in the brain. Convinced, like most of his contemporaries, that there was a direct link between the re-absorption of testicular secretions and physical health (not to mention cranial potency), he spent the summer of 1875 in the laboratory of Agassiz's summer home near Boston, transplanting the testes of young guinea pigs into guinea pigs that were at the end of their life cycle to see if this would produce significant improvement in their vitality. Brown-Séquard had been made much aware of human mortality around this time. His second wife had died in 1874; Agassiz a few months earlier, in December 1873; and his first wife just seven years before that. In 1869, during a stopover at the Faculty of Medicine of the Sorbonne, he had proposed, as J. M. D. Olmsted reported in a 1946 biography, "that if semen were injected into the blood of old men, they would probably show signs of renewed vigor."

Though his 1875 experiments with guinea pigs had seemed promising, he appears to have abandoned them at this time. A third marriage, in 1877, may have diverted his attention. But late in life, when he had gained phenomenal fame in medical circles and had been appointed professor at the Collège de France, his own infirmities caused him to return to his earlier experiments. In his early seventies, plagued by illness, he became, in Olmsted's words, determined to "prove correct this idea of the possibility of restoring the powers of the aged by injection of testicular extracts." (138)

In 1889 Brown-Séquard gave himself "six subcutaneous injections of small quantities of a water extract of ground-up testicles of dogs or guinea pigs." He reported that for many years he had been "so tired" after a few hours in the laboratory "that I had to go to bed almost as soon as I had taken a hasty meal." But after the injections all that "changed and I have regained at least all the force which I possessed a number of years ago." His capacity "to run up stairs, to stand for hours in the lab, to lift heavy objects," had all improved miraculously. (206–7)

Unfortunately, the vital essence of assorted animals proved insufficient to keep this pioneer of seminal tonics alive. Even the force of autosuggestion did not prevent him from falling into a series of progressively more debilitating illnesses. Still, Olmsted reported,

> from the moment of his announcement of the effects of his extracts on himself, the medical world was in furor. His tremendous reputation, recognized all over the civilized world, was a guarantee of good faith, and the wonder-working extract was tried out for almost every debility known to man. From outposts like Bucharest and St. Petersburg enthusiastic reports began to come in; the extract hastened transmission of sensory impulses; an overwhelming number of locomotive ataxia victims were helped; there was immunization against tuberculosis, augmentation in the vigor of the foetus of a syphilitic mother, and twenty-one cases of cancer had been ameliorated. Before the end of the year more than twelve thousand physicians were administering the extract to their patients. (209)

During the early 1890s various "elixirs" and "salts of spermine" were brought onto the market "and thus became the first endocrine product to be commercialized." Sales of such products "soon reached even the outposts of the British Empire, and a doctor in South Africa is reported to have laid down in his cellar barrels of the stuff which were never opened." (214–5) In 1893, the year before he died, Brown-Séquard, a true believer still, delineated "the physiological and therapeutic effects of a liquid extract of the male sex glands" in the house organ of the Académie des Sciences. This report became the basis for numerous subsequent investigations and experiments by others.

Though the brain researcher's seminal extracts failed to rejuvenate the blood of aging human spermatophores, the furor over the restorative potential of vital essence did not die down with his death. Debates for and against his findings proliferated in medical circles, and among those able to retain and recycle the bulk of their semen, the invocation of his name called up dreams of perpetual youth. But often the lure of woman loomed even larger. The mere thought of her could lead to a reckless expulsion of the precious fluids of rejuvenation. No wonder that images of spermatophagous insects began to gnaw at these men's brains.

Marie Stopes's cheerful descriptions of blissful young women growing into strapping young mothers on a diet of their husbands' endocrine secretions did not help to allay men's fears. Many, convinced that they were sliding further into cranial and physical infirmity each time they attended to their wives' reproductive needs, must have begun to draw direct analogies between their spouses and the female vampires rampant in fiction, who had taken to consuming Brown-Séquard's testicular extract in its undistilled form—as blood—rather than following approved medical procedure by letting themselves be injected with it "subcutaneously."

Though there were storms of controversy about the matter in the medical establishment, nearly everyone had become convinced that semen was a substance with potent nutritive qualities entirely separate from its reproductive function. These were directly related to the life-giving qualities of blood—of which semen, after all, was "the most rarified distillate." After rounding up the evidence supplied by a wide variety of folkloric and primitive medical practices, and highlighting the alimentary customs of the infamous spermatophages of the insect world, these men of science pronounced seminal fluid to be an effective tonic against numerous forms of female "hysteria"—particularly cases of adolescent anorexia.

In 1905 Havelock Ellis gave wide publicity as well as his unqualified stamp of approval to such findings in the fifth volume of his *Studies in the Psychology of Sex* (republished over and over again without the slightest modification in numerous subsequent editions well into the Fifties). Ellis's easily accessible summary of the medical literature on the subject helped it gain wide currency among the intellectuals of the period. He asserted that though semen had already been credited with being something of a magic potion by "the highest medical authorities in Greece," as well as by those "in India and Persia," scientific proof of the wholesome, invigorating qualities of this masculine brain food had been uncovered only very recently: "The positive action of semen, or rather of the testicular products, has been much investigated during recent years, and appears on the whole to be demonstrated." He stressed that an entirely new field of therapeutics had been opened up after "the notable discovery by Brown-Séquard, a quarter of a century ago, that the ingestion of the testicular juices in states of debility and senility acted as a beneficial stimulant and tonic." Investigators all over the world had found

that testicular extracts, and more especially the spermin as studied by Poehl, and by him regarded as a positive katalysator or accelerator of metabolic processes, exert a real influence in giving tone to the heart and other muscles, and in improving the metabolism of the tissues even when all influences of mental suggestion have been excluded. (178–9)

Ellis discussed the key findings of the seminal nutrition theorists at some length. He stressed the traditional nature of the belief "that semen might, when ingested, possess valuable stimulant qualities, a discovery which has been made by various savages, notably by the Australian aborigines, who, in many parts of Australia, administer a potion of semen to dying or feeble members of the tribe." Noteworthy was "that in Central Africa the testes of the goat are consumed as an aphrodisiac." Ellis then gave a thumbnail sketch of the matter's "scientific" history:

In eighteenth century Europe, Schurig, in his *Spermatologia,* still found it necessary to discuss at considerable length the possible medical properties of human semen, giving many prescriptions which contained it. The stimulation produced by ingestion of semen would appear to form in some cases a part of the attraction exerted by *fellatio;* De Sade emphasized this point; and in a case recorded by Howard semen appears to have acted as a stimulant for which the craving was as irresistible as is that for alcohol in dipsomania. (172)

Ellis also brought renewed attention to the eighteenth-century physiologist John Hunter's remark (first published posthumously in 1861, in his *Essays and Observations on Natural History, Anatomy, Physiology, Psychology and Geology*) that "when held some time in the mouth," semen "produces a warmth similar to spices, which lasts some time." Together with Ellis's suggestion that fellatio could become a physical addiction analogous to "dipsomania," this quote clearly caught his colleagues' attention with particular force. It was repeated over and over again by others as proof that seminal fluid had special properties as a stimulant. Theodore Besterman judged it so significant that he inserted it in his 1927 "enlarged" edition of Ernest Crawley's influential anthropological study *The Mystic Rose.* Marie Stopes, of course, used it as conclusive proof of her "original" theorem (making certain to quote from the 1920 edition of Ellis's remarks, not from the first edition of 1905). But inevitably the dissemination of these suggestive bits of medical and anthropological lore did not succeed in making men feel more wanted. The "man's blood as semen is food for woman" medical theory merely added yet another mixed signal of fear and arousal to the average early-twentieth-century male's sexual paranoia. Moreover, Ellis's suggestion of a link between the "stimulant" qualities of semen when ingested and the potentially addictive properties of fellatio gave a particularly erotic new specificity to the image of woman as vampire.

The American physician O. A. Wall, in his monumental 1918 treatise *Sex and Sex Worship (Phallic Worship)*, summed up the current thinking. He followed the period's standard practice of shoring up a paucity of medical proof with the liberal usage of "scientifically obtained" folkloric antecedents. The vampire of folklore who sapped the strength of its victims, he said, could be interpreted as a symbolic thief of sperm. "By 'strength' sometimes is meant semen; the vampires are also nocturnal demons who sucked the strength from the penises of their victims." Wall emphasized the ritual significance of fellatio in "primitive times," identifying it with a search for "strength": "In modern times Brown-Séquard's elixir was made from the testicles of slaughtered animals, and a proprietary medicine made from testicles is also on the market." He noted that "sucking the fresh semen is sometimes now considered a sovereign remedy for wasting disease, or, as in the houses of prostitution, an unfailing cosmetic remedy to produce a fine complexion," and he concluded that "fresh (vital) semen" had long been "considered a wonderful remedy for 'loss of vitality,' and sucking it from the penises of men has been a practice of both men and women for ages, antedating Brown-Séquard's theories for many centuries." (363–4)

By the early 1920s a whole new industry had developed, which had as its goal the "replenishing" of men's beleaguered vital essence by means of glandular infusions of all sorts, mostly of animal origin. In a 1922 issue of *The New Republic*, Nicholas and Lillian Kopeloff warned that "the term gland, in its magical omnipotence, is the fairy wand of today. Age fades at its touch. No longer would Ponce de Leon need to breast the stormy wave—a little ether, a little technique, a monkey's gland—and the Elixir of Life could be any home brew." The Kopeloffs were referring specifically to experiments staged by the French surgeon Serge Voronoff in the wake of Brown-Séquard's disclosures. This inventor of the "orchitic elixir" had been one of Voronoff's predecessors at the Collège de France. By 1919 Voronoff had begun to experiment with the transplantation of monkey testes to human subjects. As the

Kopeloffs' remark indicates, the public was fascinated more by the suggestive implications of the experiments themselves than by their disastrous results.

In a preface to Voronoff's *The Conquest of Life* (1928), the book's translator, Georges Gibier Rambaud, "former director of the New York Pasteur Institute," gave a useful chronology of Voronoff's rejuvenation experiments:

> The first announcement of that discovery was made by its author on October 18th, 1919, in the great amphitheater of the Paris Medical Faculty, before the 28th French Surgical Congress. It could be resumed in a few words: I have found a remedy for old age. I have already rejuvenated a number of animals.

Three years later Voronoff presented his first "rejuvenated" human patient "before a large audience gathered at the Laboratory of Experimental Physiology of the Collège de France." Rambaud noted that "the press of the whole world published echoes of that communication and a flood of comments was set loose." (9–10)

Voronoff's rejuvenation procedure was intended to "correct" a negative feature of dimorphic gender evolution in humans: "Many of the lower animals have retained the faculty of rejuvenating themselves, of entire rebirth from any part whatever of the body." But the positive value of primitive parthenogenesis had been lost to man. As we "follow the evolution of beings towards more and more perfected forms, we shall see that the cells of the body definitely lose this power to regenerate the whole organism." (21)

Even so, the human male's reproductive organs, as a source of the most advanced developments in species evolution, were the crown of creation. "These glands," said Voronoff, "transmit to the species the creative energy held by the individual. At the same time, however, they secrete a liquid which, passing direct into the blood, carries to all the tissues the stimulus and the energy necessary to the individual himself." Thus "in a single organ Nature has united the source of the life of the individual and that of the species." (44)

Unfortunately, these magically productive glands were also "the first to weaken and become atrophied" in time. Experiments had shown conclusively that "the removal of these glands reacts as much on the brain as on the heart, the muscles, the bones and all the other organs.

The moral and physical energies both diminish, the peculiarly masculine qualities fade out of existence, youth disappears." Voronoff shared his contemporaries' conviction that like stallions he had observed a man "in losing his genital glands . . . loses at the same time much of his intelligence." Signs of feminization were everywhere in castrated animals: "All the bones are slimmer. The cranial cavity is diminished, the face narrower, the chest contracted, while the legs are thinner and longer than those of normal animals. The muscles are less developed. Fat invades the body." Human brains, after castration, became effeminate pap: Frenchmen who had been "surgically deprived of their genital glands" had soon "noticed that they were suffering from defective memory, difficulty in concentrating their thoughts and in pursuing intellectual effort over a certain period." In prohibiting emasculated men from becoming priests, the Roman Catholic Church had long ago recognized "that a man who has been deprived of his genital glands loses not only his faculties for reproducing his species, which it is not the duty of a priest to exercise, but also some part of his intellectual faculties, which on the contrary, are very necessary to the pursuit of the sacerdotal office." (46–9)

Therefore, Voronoff concluded, the orchitic glands "certainly act as a general stimulant of our physical and intellectual energy." (51) And though women's ovaries had a roughly analogue function, they were, from a productive point of view, clearly inferior. The physical resemblance between a castrated male and the normal female made that very clear. Man's deathless future lay in the realization that "all human progress is due to the triumph of Man over Nature. Thus Man demonstrates his superiority over the rest of creation, and it is thanks to this superiority that he has arrived at his present stage of evolution." Immortality was the ultimate reward: "We aspire to bring Life itself under the domination of our will." (64)

Voronoff paid tribute to his predecessor Brown-Séquard as an "inspired savant" but pointed out that his researches had been hampered by nineteenth-century dogma. As a result, "the universal application of the Brown-Séquard method did not result in the success expected from it and is now almost completely abandoned." This was due, however, not to a faulty principle but to a faulty product. Orchitic extracts of the Brown-Séquard variety had to be "injected in small doses, several times a day, throughout the rest of life." (71–2) Voronoff felt he could build a better mousetrap. His own method would permit men to remain young to the age of 150. He suggested gland grafting: the substitution of new glands for old. This would guarantee a continuous intravenous flow of seminal nutrition. He proudly indicated that the world's governments had become very interested in the commercial and military implications of his method—and with good reason, for Voronoff sketched a generalized future of organ transplantation that has since indeed come to pass.

> Special hospitals should be created in the large towns, where fatal accidents are so numerous and so varied, in which people, to whom the grafting of a new gland or of an organ could ensure the restoration of strength or the re-establishment of a function, might be assembled. Any man who had died by accidental means, would also be immediately transported to this hospital, where his organs, after careful examination, would be removed for grafting purposes. (128)

But Voronoff's heart did not belong to organ transplantation; he had given it to monkey glands. Endocrinologically speaking, he considered these a close match to the human male's. Hence "monkeys, being precious beings from which we can borrow fresh supplies of vital energy when it becomes necessary," should be bred the way we breed sheep, goats, bullocks, and horses. Monkey farms would permit all humanity to benefit from the remarkable seminal productivity of these primitive humanoids' hyperactive testes. Still, Voronoff cautioned, it should be understood that genital grafting

> in no way is an aphrodisiac remedy, but acts on the whole organism by stimulating its activity. When the secretion from a youthful grafted gland gets into an aged man's blood, all the cells feel its effect, but those which react first are the most refined, the most delicate, the most sensitive, in other words: the brain cells. (150)

Much of the endocrinologist's book was devoted to case studies, complete with before and after photographs of newly brain-active males who had been "cured" of seminal malnutrition by means of monkey-gland grafts. Voronoff's glandular ambition knew no bounds. The ascendancy of the master race was at hand: "Why should we not also go so far as to graft intelligent and really gifted children, in order to intensify the qualities of their organisms?" (178)

And what about women? Voronoff had anticipated the question. There was good reason for sexual dimorphism, and he did not recommend that women try "the grafting of a man's interstitial gland. This would probably endow them with fresh vigor, but what they would gain in strength they would lose in gracefulness and in feminine sentimentality." In animals such grafts had produced "a sort of perversion of the maternal instinct; that is to say, an alteration in their psychic condition, in their sentiments of affection."

Thus what was brain food for the male was a masculinizing aphrodisiac for women. Voronoff believed that seminal irrigation would give a woman much more masculine "strength" than would be good for her. The orchitic infusion theory thus provided an "organic" explanation for "nymphomania." Ordinarily a civilized woman should promptly ovulate and become pregnant in response to what Ezra Pound had termed man's "alluvial Nile-flood." However, women who diverted man's brain food to nonreproductive uses—women with a masculinized tendency toward primitive bisexuality—would, with each potent seminal infusion, become less motherly and more sexual. This clearly was the sliding scale between the virgin mother and the whore that science had been looking for: excessive appropriation of the masculine orchitic elixir would tip the balance toward a "perversion of the maternal instinct." No wonder the fatal women of Hollywood's early days were always deep-voiced heavy smokers with tiger's eyes. Voronoff believed that to keep women from becoming masculinized, ovarian grafts were clearly the ticket: "Monkeys again furnish the grafting material, but, in this case, I borrow the youthful ovaries from the female chimpanzee." (185)

The line between legitimate pharmacology and quackery is usually razor thin. In the field of medicine in particular, a promising theorem is often rapidly transformed into a wonder cure. Voronoff's findings were highly controversial, but this counts less in historical terms than that he became a prominent public figure. Testicular grafts and seminal potions were on everyone's mind (though few were so uncouth as to discuss the issue directly). In their *New Republic* article of 1922, Nicholas and Lillian Kopeloff called for moderation and quoted the cautionary words of R. G. Hoskins, editor of the respected journal *Endocrinology:*

Only one group stands to gain in any case, namely the vendors of the endocrine preparations. The mere fact that hundreds of physicians and thousands of patients have testified to having profited by the use of this or that endocrine preparation carries no conviction of its actual value to one who reflects that the pharmacopeias are filled with useless medicaments of which the same can be said. (211)

The researches of Voronoff and the many other scientists who were experimenting with the "elixir of life" did immeasurable harm to thousands before they were finally abandoned. Even Hoskins had initially been an enthusiastic supporter of experiments such as those performed by L. L. Stanley at San Quentin, in which the testes of younger prisoners who had just been executed were transplanted into older, living inmates. David Hamilton, in his account of the work of Serge Voronoff, *The Monkey Gland Affair,* notes that "in the 1920s the San Quentin prison administration were proud of Stanley's achievement, and for some years after, press releases described this work, including the creditable performance of the transplanted patients at the annual prison sports." (26) Hamilton also points out that testicle transplantations became the order of the day during the early Twenties:

> In February 1921 a Chicago chef, Otto Trobach, issued a plea to be considered for a testis transplant operation. Both his testicles had been destroyed in a car accident, and he appealed to the prison authorities in Cook County to provide the glands of the next criminal to be executed in their institution. Another news story told of a thirty-nine-year-old physically frail American, George Hauser, who received a gland graft from an executed criminal in 1920. An author, Irvin R. Bacon, had a similar transplant carried out in the Majestic Hotel, New York, the cost of which was paid by the *New York American* newspaper. (43)

Throughout the Twenties Voronoff's revelations about the miraculous rejuvenating effects of monkey testes kept the rumor mills of the intellectual world abuzz—and most, as Voronoff himself readily admitted in *The Conquest of Life,* misunderstood the high moral intentions of the experimenter: "My method of regenerating failing organisms by the grafting of simian glands proved to be good material for the authors of theatrical yearly 'Revues' and for the song-writers of Montmartre." Voronoff deplored the humorous tone of such productions, and their implication that "the object and result of my grafting is to reawaken the amorous ardor that has been abolished by age." The cocktail-party circuit had clearly reduced the importance of his work to jokes about sexual potency: "There are many people who go into peals of laughter at the mention of the word 'grafting', and who immediately begin to tell you some story regarding the remarkable feats of prowess of certain rejuvenated old men." (149)

With the therapeutic and aphrodisiac qualities of semen a major topic of sotto voce small talk among the well-informed during the first twenty or thirty years of this century, a dramatic change took place in these men's subjective understanding of the nature of their relationship to the women in their lives. The portentous and flattering importance of their role as providers of "orchitic nutrients" clashed with their fears that too liberal a transfer of this magic potion would leave them brain-dead and effeminate, while the object of their affections would grow stronger, healthier, wealthier, and wiser in "a masculine fashion." No wonder the image of the sexual woman as vampire became a cultural norm around this time.

Once again Havelock Ellis had been among the first to draw a direct analogy between the restorative effects attributed to Brown-Séquard's potions of testicular extracts and the likely benefits to women of more traditional infusions of this manly tonic. He wrote (again in the fifth volume of his *Studies in the Psychology of Sex*): "If semen is a stimulant when ingested, it is easy to suppose that it may exert a similar action on the woman who receives it into the vagina in normal sexual congress." He pointed to medical evidence that "the vagina possesses considerable absorptive power" and concluded that

> if the vagina absorbs drugs it probably absorbs semen. Toff, of Braila (Roumania), who attaches much importance to such absorption, considers that it must be analogous to the ingestion of organic extractives. It is due to this influence, he believes, that weak and anemic girls so often become full-blooded and robust after marriage, and lose their nervous tendencies and shyness. (177–8)

Bernard Talmey, who was undoubtedly among the most influential American gynecologists of the first twenty years of this century, echoed Ellis directly in his highly technical book *Love: A Treatise on the Science of Sex-Attraction* (1915). Copulation, he wrote,

> involves the transmission into the female organism of certain fluids from the man, which have a beneficial effect upon the

woman. This is often demonstrated by the helpful effect marriage has upon weak and anaemic girls. A happy union is the
charm with which to banish chlorosis and many other female
ailments and irregularities.

But he insisted that "the influence of the seminal excitation is quite different from the copulative excitation. If the latter is induced while the
former does not follow, the practice will cause in the woman debility
and sometimes even nervous prostration." Therefore Talmey opposed
any form of birth control: "Any device to prevent the entrance of the
sperm into the vagina or uterus, such as condoms, cervical obturators or
sponges, for the same reason, ha[s] an injurious effect upon the woman's
general health." (362–3)

The period's odd discovery of the male's wet-nursing responsibility
toward his wife did not fail to produce appropriate analogues between
the male and female mothering functions. Havelock Ellis, indeed, went
so far as to compare the man's role in the care and feeding of his wife directly to that of a mother feeding her child:

> The mother is indebted to the child for the pleasurable relief of
> her distended breasts; and, while in civilization more subtle
> pleasures and intelligent reflection render this massive physical
> satisfaction comparatively unessential to the act of suckling,
> in more primitive conditions and among animals the need of
> this pleasurable physical satisfaction is a real bond between the
> mother and her offspring. The analogy is indeed very close: the
> erectile nipple corresponds to the erectile penis, the eager wa
> tery mouth of the infant to the moist and throbbing vagina, the
> vitally albuminous milk to the vitally albuminous semen.

In a lengthy footnote Ellis belabored this analogy further. He quoted
"Rafael Salillas, the Spanish sociologist," who had shown "that the analogy has been detected by the popular mind." Salillas maintained, Ellis
wrote, that

> "a significant anatomico-physiological concordance supposes a
> resemblance between the mouth and the sexual organs of a
> woman, between coitus and the ingestion of food, and between
> foods which do not require mastication and the spermatic ejac
> ulation; these representations find expression in the popular

name *papo* given to women's genital organs. *Papo* is the crop of birds, and is derived from *papar* (Latin, *papare*), to eat soft food such as we call pap. With this representation of infantile food is connected the term *leche* [milk] as applied to the ejaculated genital fluid." (vol. I, part II, 1913, 18–19)

"Dispassionate" and "scientific" observations of this order must have had a remarkable effect on the imaginations of the thousands of intellectuals who studiously perused each of Ellis's books. An interesting example of their impact can be found among the manuscript diary notes of the physician-poet William Carlos Williams, preserved at the State University of New York at Buffalo, in which, at one point, he compares the nipple of a woman's breast to a little penis.

Marie Stopes, in the revised American edition of her *Married Love* (1931), also cited the sources Ellis had used to arrive at her conclusion that "it can confidently be stated that women *do* absorb and benefit from some ingredients of the masculine ejaculate." (56) In her book *Enduring Passion* (1928), she had already translated the fragmented suppositions underlying Ellis's assertions into an ironclad law of nature: "A woman's need and *hunger* for nourishment in sex union," she insisted, "is a true physiological hunger to be satisfied only by the supplying of the actual molecular substances lacked by her system." To maintain their physical and mental health, women should not attempt to deprive themselves of "the seminal and prostatic secretions which they ought to have, and crave for unconsciously." She reported that she had thoroughly researched the effect of such deprivation and had concluded that "the chemical and complex molecular substances found in the accessory glands of the male" could be harvested and "supplied to women who unconsciously feel their need and show it in the apparently irrelevant but really quite direct way of inviting sex union in what appears excessive amounts from their mates. Or, sometimes, from lovers in addition to their husbands." In this manner nymphomania could be nipped in the bud.

Stopes's motives were compassionate and progressive:

Such women are constantly sneered at or laughed at or made the butts of ignorant and vulgar jokes—but who has studied and helped them? Just a few medical men have "cured" a few of them as private patients by giving them certain glandular extracts. I know of no fair and kindly and open consideration of their needs. I think a frank and fundamental statement of the facts will do something to alter public opinion and clean up the foetid atmosphere round the whole subject.

She hoped that, to help such seminally deficient women, a "molecular compound" of these "glandular extracts" could be developed "and presented in such a way that they can be swallowed by the mouth in ordinary gelatine capsules."

Stopes cautioned that "we cannot by any human process exactly simulate the way these glandular extracts naturally enter the blood and lymph streams by infinitesimal amounts *continuously*. The best we can do," she suggested, was "to swallow a capsule three times daily, and carry this on for several months." Stopes let it be known that she was not talking about a treatment analogous to the controversial monkey-gland experiments of Voronoff and Steinach, which had caused such "vague and hysterical talk," but that she was advocating oral ingestion of capsules of the real thing, to counter an organic deficiency in certain women. She regarded her program as analogous to a vitamin treatment:

> The sex-starved woman, in my opinion, is one whose system is not supplied with the necessary amount of certain complex chemical molecules produced in the prostatic glands. If then she will swallow the properly prepared extracts of these glands in suitable quantities for her own requirements, she should, by nourishing her system properly as it demands, not only enhance its general physiological condition, but mitigate the distressing *social* symptoms involved.

Different women had different needs:

> For some sex-starved women the prostatic extract alone is very effective, sometimes prostatic and orchic extract should be mixed. For others, those for instance with a markedly "run down" condition, the addition of chemical compounds of glycero-phosphates of calcium and other elements are useful. (42–8)

It should be emphasized that the principal intention of Stopes's writings was always to defend female sexuality as natural and beautiful, whether or not it involved procreation. Her writings were controversial

not as a result of her ideas about the nutritive value of semen, but because she defended birth control as a contribution to women's mental
health. Her advocacy of the seminal-nutrition theorem allowed her to
dramatize the psychological and physiological benefits to women of
sexual intercourse, which, in contradistinction to most medical authorities, she saw as "the most magical key to peace, joy and strength." In her
advocacy of sexual pleasure as a woman's right she clearly set out to
countermand the prevalent notion that the sexual woman was "diseased." But she also had a direct, far less liberal gender-political ulterior
motive for her insistence that women must have semen to stay healthy.
She wanted to steer her readers away from the "disastrous homosexual
entanglements" she had observed among wives whose husbands failed
to provide them with the level of physical stimulation they needed. Her
detailed exposition of women's physiological need for the infusions of
prostatic fluid they received in heterosexual intercourse clearly proved,
she insisted, "that women can only *play* with each other and *cannot* in
the very nature of things have natural union or supply each other with
the seminal and prostatic secretions which they ought to have, and crave
for unconsciously." Therefore, "homosexual excitement does not really
meet their need."

She put the blame for women's lesbian "aberrations" squarely on the
shoulders of the many males who, misguided by generations of misogynistic, ascetic idealists, had become incapable of abandoning themselves to the pleasures of the body for fear of losing an essential part of
their "vitality." The typical male still believed that sexual intercourse, although it was "a natural physiological demand of his body, necessitates
an expenditure rather than a gaining of energy on the part of the man,
and has left him with his forces temporarily reduced." (4)

These men's consequent reluctance to share their precious vitality
had made their women more inclined to satisfy their bodies' hunger in
encounters with their female friends. But, said Stopes,

> lesbian love, as the alternative is NOT a real equivalent and
> merely soothes perhaps and satisfies no more than the surface
> nervous excitement. It does not, and by its nature it can never
> supply the actual physiological nourishment, the chemical mol-
> ecules produced by the accessory glandular systems of the male.
> These are supplied to the woman's system when the normal act
> of union is experienced, and the man's secretions are deposited
> in her body together with the semen. (43)

In her otherwise remarkably progressive campaign to legitimize women's enjoyment of sexual intercourse as a necessary element of their psychological and physiological health, Stopes thus chose to overlook the extremely coercive and manipulative implications male researchers had built into the seminal-nourishment theory. Judging from her contribution to the debate concerning the effects of birth control on the functioning of the British Empire, Stopes's censure of same-sex relationships may have been inspired, at least in part, by an economically motivated concern that such relationships would undermine the "productive" role of the nuclear family. Fewer children would mean healthier and better empire builders, she had argued. The empire did not need quantity but quality. Her position was that, though "normal" women must, by nature, want to have offspring, they should at least have the right to enjoy sexual intercourse to the fullest by being able to decide *when* to get pregnant. If they spent their time in the pleasurable accumulation of the male's nutritive fluids, their bodies would grow ever more healthy, and this, in turn, would improve the genetic configuration of their offspring. In pursuit of that ideal Stopes turned her male colleagues' reasoning back upon itself. How can you insist, she argued, that a woman who enjoys sex thereby proves herself to be "abnormal," "sinful," and "primitive" if you also show that nature requires her to nourish her body with a man's semen to remain healthy?

But it was precisely this unresolved paradox that created more worry than relief among Stopes's millions of readers of both sexes, as well as among the male lay public—far and away the largest percentage of the readership of authorities such as Havelock Ellis. Indeed, Ellis's lofty reputation guaranteed that the seminal-nourishment theory would gain a special aura of legitimacy. His advocacy of a rigorously guarded expenditure of the precious substance certainly puts an entirely new spin on anthropologist Bronislaw Malinowski's assertion, in 1931, that "Havelock Ellis has been a personal experience to most thinking men and women of our age—a personal experience which lasts." (*Sex, Culture, and Myth*, 129) As Stopes had pointed out, most men still believed that they were gifted by nature with only a very finite measure of this vital essence. The discovery that they had an actual physiological responsibility to share their allotment with their wives was tantamount to an admission that even the most "normal" woman was as much a "real" vampire as the vampires of myth.

The analogue between the girl next door and the vampires who were, as Wall stressed, held to account in folklore for "wasting diseases, as tuberculosis, etc." (362) became frighteningly direct if a man's stock of vitality must diminish in proportion to the manner in which, as Ellis put it, "weak and anemic girls" became "full-blooded and robust after marriage." Clearly the continuous depletion of that tonic that made the girl next door into a strapping physical specimen must have just the opposite effect on the donor and was bound to turn him, like the vampire victim in days of yore, into a tubercular wreck.

Stopes was not much help to these men by extolling the spermal "nuclear plasm" in *Married Love* as "the most highly specialized and richest substance in our bodies." If only in deference to their wives' needs, men must not be profligate with it. Therefore, masturbation was still a no-no. "A strong will" to keep from "wasting the semen in an ejaculation" was needed by those so tempted. (43–6) Havelock Ellis's position also did little to reassure a generation of men who had grown up believing that "self-abuse" led to "headache, dyspepsia, costiveness, spinal disease, epilepsy, impaired eyesight, palpitations of the heart, pain in the side, incontinence of urine, hysteria, paralysis, involuntary seminal emissions, impotency, consumption, insanity, etc." (Cowan, 354) A man's "testicular products," Ellis asserted, should not be released to the throngs of still-anemic young women out there without serious reflection:

> If these glandular secretions are so valuable when administered as drugs to other persons, must they not be of far greater value when naturally secreted and poured out into the circulation in the living body? It is now generally believed, on the basis of a large and various body of evidence, that this is undoubtedly so. (*V,* 179–80)

For most reasonably informed males the whole matter of sexual contact was thus becoming fraught with responsibilities of an astonishingly complex nature. No wonder that this was a period in which male postcoital depression was considered direct evidence of the physiological cost of the male's compliance with nature's reproductive arrangements. Marie Stopes, in pursuit of her own agenda, tried hard to ridicule men who felt that, in sexual congress, "the woman had robbed them of something." She boldly attacked the notion that *post coitum omne triste*—the universally quoted old saw suggesting that loss of his precious vital essence made every man feel a letdown after ejaculation:

I challenge, not that it is generally considered to be a fact: that is obvious! I challenge the very existence of the fact itself. I deny that it is a *fact* in a scientific sense. It is a phenomenon based on ignorance and folly and the hypnotism of custom. It is *not* an inherent physiological and inevitable result of the unions of an enlightened and instructed race of lovers. (*Enduring Passion,* 7–8)

The "post-coital happiness" of a couple of long standing, she insisted, could only increase with the knowledge that each properly absorbed ejaculation would cause husband and wife to become, quite literally, more "at one." But Stopes's positive outlook on the "absorption theory" (which had also caused her to advocate the exclusive use of cervical caps as a method of birth control) did little to make her male contemporaries more cheerful about their role in sexual encounters with women.

The world-renowned Dutch gynecologist Th. H. van de Velde, who wrote some of the most widely influential sex manuals of the Twenties and Thirties, also weighed in on the issue of women's seminal-energy vampirism. Van de Velde was, particularly in the United States, regarded as a progressive force in sexology until well into the Fifties. His *Ideal Marriage* (1926) was the sort of book enlightened parents gave to their children to prepare them for their wedding day. In his 1928 follow-up, *Sex Hostility in Marriage: Its Origin, Prevention and Treatment,* published in an American edition in 1931, he had the following to say about the issue:

> Owing to the seminal absorption, the woman's whole body is penetrated by the masculine materials, while, as far as the man is concerned, no such process occurs. In every union that takes its natural course, the woman experiences a sensation that may be compared, in many ways, to the effect on the body of the injection of a small quantity of serum. The duration of this effect cannot be estimated, but we know that it cannot be short.

This said, van de Velde, whose books were first published in Germany, touched upon a hotly debated issue that was soon to become a cornerstone of the miscegenation policies of Nazism. Was it possible, he asked, that this "serum injection" of the male's vital essence could have such a direct physiological influence upon the beneficiary and be "so powerful that it is capable of influencing a child born subsequently through coitus with another man?" Van de Velde wisely decided to stay out of the fray: "I can come to no definite opinion on this point." (106)

In fact, many proponents of the seminal-absorption theory argued that if the woman's body was actually being nourished by her partner's semen, that must, following the "you are what you eat" principle, also mean that each woman must retain a lifelong "imprint" of every man with whom she has had sexual intercourse. Long-term marital relations with one man would therefore make a woman quite literally more "at one" with him, as Marie Stopes had already emphasized. This principle was even used to explain the popular observation that a husband and wife began to resemble each other physically during the course of a long life together. Science, it appeared, had at last been able to validate the centuries-old conception that a man and his wife together were one entity in the eyes of God and therefore shared a single soul.

Consequently the racial eugenicists of the early twentieth century used the seminal-absorption theory to terrorize Aryan women into refraining from any form of physical contact with genetically "inferior" males. Taking their cue once again from the meager "scientific experiments" Ellis had cited, they declared that a man's blood, converted into semen and introduced into the woman's body, was there reconverted into blood and in this manner directly absorbed into her bloodstream. Thus the male's seminal injection was in essence a "blood transfusion," and each woman with whom he had sexual intercourse in this manner became "blood of his blood." Stoker's Van Helsing had evidently been medically correct when he had remarked that the blood transfusions Lucy Westenra received from four different men had made her into a "polyandrist." (*Dracula*, 182) During the later 1910s and throughout the Twenties, therefore, in perfect synchrony with the heyday of the sexual vampire in the movies, sexologists used this concept of the literal—and "specific"—transfer of the male's vital essence into the bloodstream of the woman as justification for a wide range of "eugenicist," antifeminine, and viciously racist prejudices.

In 1902 Ernest Crawley, in *The Mystic Rose*, had already noted the popularity of this belief among his contemporaries: "In ordinary human thought the seed is the strength, as much as the blood is the life." (226) No doubt this principle was also the inspiration for F. Marion Crawford's vampire tale of 1905. The more a woman engaged in sexual intercourse with a particular man, the more of that man's "blood" she could be said to draw into her own veins. It stood to reason, then, that by thus absorbing the man himself with his seminal matter, a woman was liable to become more like the donor with each transfusion.

Conversely, the man, who, after all, "lost strength" with each ejaculation, became a little "less" each time. Losing "manhood," he, though in a different sense, also came to resemble his woman, by becoming more "effeminate"—particularly if he attended too assiduously to her needs. But since the woman was the beneficiary of the man's seminal munificence, only she was "genetically" affected by promiscuous behavior. Masculine promiscuity was certainly not to be recommended, for its effects were wasteful depletion, dissipation, and "feminization." But a promiscuous woman was another matter altogether. A wide range of sexual partners would make her blood reflect a cauldron of "mongrel" genetic influences. The woman certainly gained "masculine strength" in promiscuity, but that strength, mixed with her feminine reproductive impulse, made her ever more "sexual" and lustful, and hence also more primitive in her desires.

It was widely thought that whenever a woman's inclination to promiscuity became so strong as to include a willingness to absorb the "blood-traits" of racial inferiors, she was likely to take on the physiological markers of the "mongrels" whose degenerate vital essence she had accepted. Arabella Kenealy, a true believer in this principle, declared that "sex-promiscuity" created a direct "adulteration of personality," producing in such a woman "eventually that which has been styled a 'composite face'—the face resulting when a number of portraits of different persons are printed one over another on the same photographic plate." (178)

Bernard Talmey also used this reasoning to make a case for the "natural origins" of the double standard of marital fidelity for men and women. In *Love,* he cited recent physiological studies by the biologists Waldstein and Ekler (who had gained their wisdom from experiments with rabbits) in support of his eugenicist point of view. The crux of the matter was that a woman's physiology was affected by "every copulation, no matter whether fertilization has taken place or not. Thus a part of the male circulates within the blood of the female, even after copulation without fertilization," and this left an indelible "blood imprint" on the woman. She was consequently forever changed, in a quite literal, physical sense, by each of her sexual partners. "Through her veins circulate material parts of her lover." When, therefore, at some later date, another man impregnates her, she still maintains "a perennial impression left by her former mate. This is the reason why aesthetic and fastidious men refrain from marrying a widow or a divorced woman." Indeed, Talmey added, the woman's "permanent" absorption of her former partners' blood "accounts for the observation not seldom made in the cases of

widows that the children of the second husband bear a certain resemblance with the first dead one." (160)

Arabella Kenealy characteristically reduced the principle to its lowest common denominator. She saw "odious and startling evidence" that
woman's "nature retains ineffaceable vestiges of all that has happened to
her" in the sexual realm. Indeed, "a woman's children by a second husband may resemble her first husband far more than they resemble their
father." This produced

> a significant and repulsive adulteration of type, and one so in-
> trinsic that a woman who had been previously wife to a negro
> or a Chinaman will present her second husband, typically Euro-
> pean, with offspring of negroid or of Mongolian type. That
> husbands and wives come to resemble one another in physiog-
> nomy and characteristics, is further indication of the subtle and
> potent temperamental fusion and implications of the mysterious
> sex-union. (173)

Obviously, "scientific" findings of such a provocative nature could
not fail to fascinate the public. The notion that their semen made an indelible "imprint" on the bodies of women endowed men with a new
sense of power and proprietorship over the women they had slept with,
since it had now been proven that a woman could never overcome the
residues of her involvement with her former lovers. The men in her bed
had quite literally become flesh of her flesh. At the same time those men
became thereby perpetual competitors with the woman's subsequent
lovers in not only a psychological but also a direct physiological sense.
This gave the issue of a woman's previous sexual experiences—and particularly that of her "racial" orthodoxy in choosing her partners—a dramatic new importance to the Aryan elite. It enormously expanded the
woman's responsibility, and hence her potential for failure, in the realm
of eugenics. She could now be held solely accountable for any deficiencies in evolutionary excellence her children might exhibit. The theorem
thus played directly into the hands of racist-evolutionist ideologues, and
simultaneously opened up a monstrous new range of motives for the
browbeating and abuse of wives "imprinted" with other men's sperm.

Thus the seminal-absorption theory provided conclusive proof that
a strict and exclusive form of monogamy was the evolutionary bourgeoisie's only defense against the "mongrelization" of the superior
Aryan gene pool. Marriage between "racial equals" became a primary

responsibility of the evolved human couple. But in a world that threatened to be overrun by degenerates and barbarians it was not merely the
Aryan's responsibility to marry an uncontaminated Aryan woman; he
must also recognize his duty to the race by liberally sharing with his wife
"the profound effects of physiological copulation," (156) as C. W. Malchow, M.D., put it in his book *The Sexual Life* (1907).

Malchow, whose book had reached its twentieth printing by 1923,
was, like the contributors to *The Control of Parenthood,* worried about the
falling birthrate among the "evolved" segment of society. He, too,
blamed his male contemporaries' fear of spending. Excessive moderation was causing a deterioration in the Aryan woman's capacity to produce a strapping future crop of racial superiors. Signs of this tendency
had become "so plainly evident that the guardians of the nation are
forced to confront them, and the question of 'race suicide' has agitated
the minds of the thoughtful." Among these latter not the least was
H. Rider Haggard's good friend, president Theodore Roosevelt, whom
Malchow quoted as having remarked to "a committee of the inter-
church conference on marriage and divorce," that "for the race as for the
individual no material prosperity, no business growth, no artistic or scientific development, will count, if the race commits suicide." Roosevelt
gave as his main proof of the Aryan nation's burgeoning death wish,
"the diminishing birth rate and the loosening of the marital ties among
the old native American families." (151-2)

No wonder, then, that Ezra Pound and the men of his generation
should have come to regard the brain, that "great clot of genital fluid,"
as something on the order of a limited checking account in nature's
great energy savings bank. Sexual vampires were women who insisted
that they should be permitted to make substantial withdrawals at will.
Such women were economic vampires as well, indiscriminate "socialist"
mongrels. To give of yourself liberally in marriage was one thing (you
were, after all, morally obliged to take care of the physiological needs of
your reproductive companion), but to allow your vital essence to be
drained by semen-hungry sexual women outside of wedlock was clearly
both racial and economic suicide.

Such women were real-life vampires, plain and simple. Science had
shown that they were indeed spermatophages, just like their insect sisters. The entomologists' anthropomorphizing descriptions of the love
affairs of praying mantises and black widow spiders had proved to be directly analogous to the effects of the sexual woman's depredations in the
human environment. No wonder the visual arts and popular culture

Alfred Kubin, Each Night a Dream Visits Us, *ca. 1903,*
india ink on paper; Albertina, Vienna
Woman as spider

spawned hordes of these sexual gourmands who were part insect, part
woman. Their predatory mastications have had an indelible influence on
our perception of the feminine.

In the Twenties this focus on the entomological prehistory of the
human female culminated in the work of the German physician Bernhard Bauer, whose weighty, two-volume study *Woman and Love* was

published in the United States in 1927 by Horace Liveright, the foremost American publisher of such gynentomological literature of that
decade, and hence not surprisingly also the producer of a stage version
of *Dracula* that opened on Broadway the same year. This production,
liberally decorated with spider webs (so no one would forget the link
between the spider and the vampire), became the first step toward the
quintessential 1931 Tod Browning movie (in which the principals were
also forever wading through webbing) and hundreds of subsequent
vampire melodramas.

Bauer's study of the female psyche opened, appropriately, with an
encomium to Remy de Gourmont and an updated restatement of the
theory of dimorphic gender evolution. Though Bauer acknowledged in
passing that "the love-life of other animals is very different from that of
men and women," (I, 12) he immediately moved to a direct appropriation of Gourmont's most lurid descriptions of female "sexual cannibalism" in the insect world, starring, once again, the spider and the praying
mantis. Bauer's argument, too, was essentially that of Gourmont: "the
purpose of life is the perpetuation of life." (I, 1) What we might regard
as "apparent cruelty" in the animal world "fulfills a natural demand. We
must suppose that the female does not only need the spermatozoa of the
male, that will fertilise her ova; she also requires the whole body of her
spouse to provide nutriment for the offspring that is about to develop,
and that is why she eats him up." Clearly such imagery had, toward the
end of the Twenties, with the widespread acceptance of the seminal-
absorption theory, acquired a truly mordant significance, deftly cali-
brated to fan the fires of misogyny. At every turn Bauer reiterated that
"the amatory life of mankind cannot be understood, cannot even be
properly described, without a knowledge of similar processes in the
lower animals. This applies to the love-life of mankind in general; but it
applies, above all, to the love-life of women." (I, 16)

In the course of an eight-hundred-page perambulation of the early
twentieth century's favorite clichés about the bestial sources of human
sexuality, Bauer, predictably, ended up exactly where he began: in the
realm of "brute nature," "animal instinct," and, of course, the world of
"the garden spider and the praying mantis." But Bauer's book reached its
true climax in his identification of the satanic horde that had so terrorized the endless parade of biologists, anthropologists, psychologists, and
sexologists of the first twenty years of this century: the Aryan male's evil
sisters.

Alfred Kubin, The Egg, *ca. 1902, india ink on paper;*
Graphische Sammlung Albertina, Vienna
The reproductive woman as deadly spermatophagous beetle

The sexual woman (every woman, Bauer had shown) had at last
been revealed once and for all as the vampire, the spider, the praying
mantis of nature. "The unsatisfied woman," Bauer stressed, "is bad-
tempered and virulent, always ready to vent her dissatisfaction in every
possible way, and in the same way we find that in the animal kingdom
lack of sexual satisfaction causes the female to manifest a generally hostile temper toward her environment." But if the unsatisfied woman was
a danger, the self-consciously sexual woman, the "insatiable woman,"
was the ultimate vampire, an evil sister grown to spidery proportions,
who meant death itself to her mate. Praying mantises and spider-women
ate their mates to absorb their strength:

> The female is not satisfied with one germ-cell from the male,
> but takes all the cells within her body in order to ensure the per-
> petuation of the species. Thus we have cannibalism among ani-
> mals, with the female as the active party. We often hear similar

expressions among human beings. For instance, some one will describe an insatiable woman as "sucking the life out of the man." Even though the phrase "sucking out" is not intended literally, it means that the insatiable woman who lives only for sex, can wreck not only one man, but many. Physically, mentally and morally, but especially morally. This vampirism among human beings is very serious, because it may destroy not only one man, but the happiness of whole families or even whole peoples. Honour, reputation, wife, family, parents—all will be sacrificed by a man mad with desire, when he is in the clutches of such a vampire, who is sucking the life out of him. (II, 311–12)

Bauer's rhapsodic masochism thus succinctly indicated how, toward the second half of the Twenties, the alimentary, economic, and racial implications of Western culture's obsession with the sexual woman as vampire had reached their inevitable metaphoric nexus.

The sexual woman was a predator, that was clear. William J. Robinson, M.D., chief of the Department of Genito-Urinary Diseases at the Bronx Hospital, former president of the Berlin Anglo-American Medical Society, author of more than two dozen widely read books on human sexuality, and friend and supporter of Margaret Sanger, had already been adamant in his condemnation of the "hypersensual woman," the woman who put an undue strain on her husband's rational faculties. In *Woman: Her Sex and Love Life* (1917) he had warned that to such a woman "the name vampire can be applied in its literal sense. Just as the vampire sucks the blood of its victims in their sleep while they are alive, so does the woman vampire suck the life and exhaust the vitality of her male partner—or victim." Robinson warned that "no age is exempt, sexual vampires may be found among girls of twenty as well as among women of sixty and over." (178–80)

But what galled many of the men of the period most was that the sexual woman, the vampire of seminal essence, sought to deplete the male not only in the purely physical realm but also in that special male sphere: the world of the intellect and of capital gain. Women who attempted to enter these fields of manly achievement were shirking their duty in the dimorphic realm of the evolutionary advance. They were appropriating the "lifeblood" of the male, not only in their nonreproductive, and hence "race-suicidal," seminal depredations, but also in their attempts to usurp the "creative" world of business, finance, and material production. Many feared that once women gained a foothold there, men might as well pack their bags and permanently move to Mars.

It became thus progressively less difficult to believe that these "unnatural" women had forged a perverse alliance with the "lower races" and with the primitive, anti-individualistic working-class upstarts who had inexplicably begun to insist on a bigger piece of the economic pie—on precisely that piece that was continuing to elude the middle-class male. These women, then, were allied with the great antievolutionary conspiracy of the colonized races and the degenerate erotomaniacs who called themselves socialists and communists. These were clearly all charter members of a political conspiracy concocted by effeminate Jews. The Aryan races were in danger of being overrun by swarms of subhuman monsters. The silver leper of racism and the predatory vampire of female sexuality were about to be wedded in the devouring fires of hate.

C. Allan Gilbert (1873–1929), Vanity, *popular print*
Woman as death personified

VI. AND FOOLS THEY WERE:
THE BIOLOGY OF RACISM AND
THE IRON LAW OF THE JUNGLE;
LOVE RITUALS OF THE
SOCIALIST VAMPIRE

Whenever the sexual vampire of early twentieth-century culture sank her teeth into still another backsliding businessman, the evolutionary dreams of an entire generation lost more of their bite. The attack of the saber-toothed woman metaphorized and personalized—turned into a "woman problem"—the economic worldview historian Brooks Adams had succinctly identified in *McClure's Magazine* in 1899 as "the new struggle for life among nations."

Biology, sociology, anthropology, speculative medicine, physiology, and psychology all joined in to help construct a coherent new mythology of gender directly in tune with the profitable economics of racial inequality. Virtually all aspects of human behavior and motivation came to be explained as forever determined by the categorical imperatives of the Western male's genetic election to superman status. The Aryan was "God's man," and all others were the Devil's disciples. Sanctimonious prattle by scientists about the "inalterable" processes of "evolution," "dimorphism," and "sexual selection" gave social acts of brutality an aura of inevitability, and even made them seem charitable. Plunder and mass murder were justified as a form of euthanasia. Otherness became evidence of "degeneration." Racial and sexual "deviance" became proof of atavistic recurrence of the beast in man. Archaeologists, sociologists, anthropologists, and sexologists found binding "patterns of culture," "symbols of transformation," and "archetypal structures of human behavior" everywhere.

In 1949 the eminent Harvard anthropologist Clyde Kluckhohn stressed in his collection of essays *Mirror for Man* that "after the end of World War I, pseudo-scientific racism was systematically used for political demagoguery." (136) The underlying motives for this development were clearly economic. The imperialist politicians of Western Europe and the United States, whose expansionism had been sanctioned by the predatory theories of social Darwinism and evolutionary racism, had run out of new territories worth colonizing by the 1910s. The "laws of nature" now required that the strong take from the weaker. World War I had been fought as a first skirmish in the industrialized nations' biological war to maintain the existing economic hierarchies. Politicians forcefully argued the social significance of genetic pride of place. The struggle for existence required the Tarzans of evolution to defend each triumph of natural selection against the forces of degeneration.

Like sex, racial "inferiority" came to be seen as an infectious disease, a contaminant affecting one's capacity to thrive in the economic arena. As Thorstein Veblen observed in his *Theory of the Leisure Class* (1899):

> It is a matter of common notoriety that when individuals, or even considerable groups of men, are segregated from a higher industrial culture and exposed to a lower cultural environment, or to an economic situation of a more primitive character, they quickly show evidence of reversion toward the spiritual features which characterize the predatory type. (136)

Early-twentieth-century sociobiology habitually pitted orthogenesis (linear evolutionary development) against the reversive (atavistic) pollutants racially "inferior" admixtures would bring into a nation's gene pool.

The equation of wealth and virtue, identified by Veblen as a system of "invidious comparison" that required the moral "valuation of persons in respect of worth," also created a "race for reputability" in which "no approach to a definitive attainment is possible." This in turn produced an ever deepening sense of personal frustration among the vast majority of those who found themselves on the wrong side of an "invidious pecuniary comparison with other men." (39–40)

The "racial inferiors" whose erotic "effeminacy" threatened to contaminate the Western male's high economic seriousness with frivolous suggestions of nonproductive pleasure were obviously to blame for the humiliation the average middle-class male had to suffer in these ever recurring invidious comparisons. As Kluckhohn pointed out, "Aversion is not very active unless there is a real or imagined conflict of interests." As long as things go our way we tend to be magnanimous, but "when the security of individuals or the cohesion of a group is threatened, scapegoats are almost always sought and found." Evolutionary biology, anthropology, and sexology provided answers no one wanted to find in the economic realm. Failure was due to the reversive influence of degenerates, the lower orders, and the sexual women who drained the striving male of his vitality and thus caused him to miss out on the evolutionary advance of civilization.

In the United States in particular, Kluckhohn pointed out, "where great emphasis is placed upon success, but where many individuals fail to achieve it, the temptation to blame an 'out-group' for one's own failure 'to measure up' is especially strong." (136–7) During the first two decades of the twentieth century, the Anglo-Aryan core of the American ruling class responded in precisely this manner to the waves of immigration from Eastern Europe and Italy, which reached their peak between 1910 and 1913 with the arrival of more than ten million. In 1914, in his book *The Old World in the New,* Edward Alsworth Ross, then professor of sociology at the University of Wisconsin, noted with approval the increase in anti-Semitism in New York: "The line is drawn against the Jews in hotels, resorts, clubs, and private schools, and constantly this line hardens and extends." His explanation was that "the Gentile resents being obliged to engage in a humiliating and undignified scramble in order to keep his trade or his clients against the Jewish invader." (164)

The period's men of science were frequently inordinately proud of their own evident superiority. Their genetic excellence had already been proved, and that permitted them to sit in judgment over the rest of humanity. As Kluckhohn pointed out, the discoveries of Darwin, Mendel, and a host of other advocates of "invidious comparison" in the realm of genetics had "put everything on a new footing. From the popular point of view, laws had been evolved that stated immutable and watertight connections between biological processes and all sorts of other phenomena. A magic key had been created which unlocked all previous perplexities about human behavior." (106)

The scientists' sense of their own worth was palpable. In *Idiot Man,* an arrogant collection of essays on the inferiority of most humans, the winner of the 1913 Nobel Prize for physiology, Charles Richet, professor at the Faculté de Médecine of the University of Paris, jeered: "For about thirty thousand years the Black races have dwelt in Africa, and during these thirty thousand years they have done nothing to raise themselves above the level of the monkeys." Richet emphasized their regressive "non-adaptability": "Even amongst white men they continue to live a vegetable existence, producing nothing except carbonic acid and urea." (9) The Chinese Richet considered "small and ugly" and "unable to emerge from the semi-barbarous state which they achieved ages ago." (14)

Richet bewailed the fact that the stupidity of mankind had led it to accept the leadership of "idiot" rulers over that of truly great men such as Galileo, Leibnitz, Kant, or—it was easy to infer—the Nobel Prize–winning author himself, who quickly revealed himself to be a true believer in Sumner's economic plutocracy: "Nothing is more lawful than acquired wealth; nothing is more iniquitous than hereditary wealth." Socialism was "a strange idea of progress which crushes out all intellectual superiority." Darwin had proved once and for all that "absolute equality is so gross an error that it has only been able to sprout in the befogged brains of theorists." The Darwinian logic for the coming race wars was perfectly obvious to Richet:

> Those who succumb deserve to go under because they have less powerful weapons. Their inferiority explains and justifies their ruin. In the same way in our human societies, the most intelligent, the strongest and the bravest deserve to triumph over the soft, the effeminate and the slow witted. (46–9)

The concept of war itself, on the other hand, was an atavistic holdover of the most ignorant and imbecilic stage of humanity's evolution—a holdover of the spirit of woman-rule, and therefore best personified as a woman: "a dirty old hag, abject, blear-eyed, a walking skeleton. . . . She is violent, full of lies and fury, given to fits of frenzied rage; she foams and bites. She roars instead of speaking. Even from afar she stinks. She is War." (77) Richet, who wrote his diatribe in the wake of World War I, here fell directly in line with a practice that had taken hold among editorial cartoonists and "socially concerned" artists during that war, to personify destruction as primitive femininity personified. By 1938 this imagery had even reached the cover of one of the popular new picture magazines, *Look.* An otherwise sober account of the continuing buildup of belligerence across the world during the twenty years since the end of World War I was advertised with an eye-catching color plate of a full-breasted blonde woman, an obvious sexual temptress, who was smoking a cigarette labeled YOUTH and whose head was a grinning skull.

The period's intellectuals had decided that these forces of reversion had to be confronted on their own turf and that a "race war" against "the soft, the effeminate and the slow witted" was therefore just around the corner. In *Pure Sociology* (1903) Lester Ward considered it "a waste of breath to urge peace, justice, humanity." Instead, he insisted, war would rightly continue until "the highest type of man shall gain dominion over all the lower types of man." There was little doubt in his mind who be-

Cover of Look *magazine, November 8, 1938*

longed to this elite: "The inhabitants of southern, central and western Europe, call them Aryan, Indo-Germanic, or anything you please," he said, are "the repository of the highest culture."

Ward conveniently provided a thumbnail sketch of the "modern" achievements of the Aryan master race, which, he pointed out, had just about completed

> the work of extending its dominion over other parts of the earth. It has already spread over the whole of South and North America, over Australia, and over Southern Africa. It has gained a firm foothold on Northern Africa, Southern and Eastern Asia, and most of the larger islands and archipelagos of the sea.

But Ward stressed that the final triumph of the Aryan was dependent upon the ascendancy of the manly values of this master race over the mental effeminacy that had taken hold of many otherwise civilized societies. This was a condition characterized by "maudlin sentimentality and inconsistent sympathy, thinking on problems of the world without discrimination or perspective, incapacity to scent the drift of events or weigh the relative gravity of heterogeneous and unequal facts." (238–40)

The scientific community's sudden enthusiastic legitimation, beginning in 1900, of Mendel's hybridization experiments dating back to 1865 showed that the new century was eager to tackle the social implication of the Austrian monk's discoveries. Genetics thus became almost immediately a political science. Many were convinced that new, universal laws of social stratification had been discovered. Equality as a political issue was dead, they argued. Socialism was a concept spawned by degenerate minds. Social compassion was a manifestation of effeminacy.

Even so, there remained some who opposed these Sumnerite rationalizations of the ascendancy of "power elites" at the expense of the less fortunate in society. Most of the opposition, inevitably, came from scientists who leaned toward socialism or Marxism. Paul Kammerer, a researcher at Vienna's Institute for Experimental Biology, for instance, was a Mendelian geneticist who supported a minority viewpoint championing Lamarck in his book *The Inheritance of Acquired Characteristics* (1924). Kammerer lectured in the United States in 1923 and 1924, denouncing the right-wing political use made of Mendel. As he wrote:

> The race theory boasts of the rigid unchangeability of national character, but nevertheless professes to be convinced of the the-

ory of evolution. Abusing the name of Darwin, the race theorists claim that the pitiless struggle for existence is their only
guide, but at the same time they coquette with an international
religion of love. The race theorists claim to shun the mixing of
politics and science, but they creep around the throne and altar,
and even sometimes "color" the truth for partisan advantage.
(267)

Kammerer, a Jew, was responding to the increase of virulent anti-
Semitism in the world around him, which had been so sudden and dramatic that he (obviously mistakenly) believed it to be a result of the
recent global hostilities: "Only the World War achieved the sad distinction of creating anti-semitism" in the United States, he insisted. That
Kammerer could think so is itself a striking indication of the sudden
exponential increase in racial antagonism in the wake of the marriage between imperialist economics and evolutionary biology. He
was, moreover, certainly correct in noting the increased exploitation of
"anti-semitism, panslavism, jugoslavism, pangermanism, and other
'isms,' as a platform of independent and influential political parties." (281)
    Unlike most of his colleagues, Kammerer insisted that there was as
much historical evidence for the existence of a human tendency toward
peaceful coexistence as there was for one of mutual depredation:

> This social stimulus—or to express it practically the same—this
> ethical will adds to individual regeneration, regeneration in gen-
> eral. The individual will to help gradually develops into the gen-
> eral will to help. *Symbiosis,* or the organization for mutual aid
> between individuals, develops into *pansymbiosis; i.e.,* an organi-
> zation for mutual aid *en masse.* (285)

The various races all had superb, if sometimes divergent, sets of acquired
characteristics, which, when united, would create a new transracial
humanity far better than that produced by the principles of "racial
purity." "Unadulterated Darwinism," he said, "teaches of the transmutation of the species, the metamorphosis and intermingling of races and
classes." In its pure form Darwinism was "a doctrine of natural, world-
embracing humaneness." (265)
    But the prevailing political mood of the Twenties was fiercely anti-
Marxist, and most biologists extended that hostility directly to Kammerer's politically incorrect take on the evolutionary future. He was

subjected to a relentless series of attacks, spearheaded by the prominent Cambridge University Mendelian William Bateson. Soon Kammerer's colleagues proved to their own satisfaction that he had faked the appearance of an acquired physical characteristic on a midwife toad. Though he insisted that his specimen had been tampered with, he was discredited and declared a scientific fraud. Devastated by these developments, Kammerer committed suicide on September 23, 1926. In a note found on his body he offered his remains to science, remarking with bitter irony: "Perhaps my worthy academic colleagues will discover in my brain a trace of the qualities they found absent from the manifestations of my mental activities while I was alive."

In his book *The Case of the Midwife Toad* (1971), Arthur Koestler paid tribute to Kammerer, whom he described as "one of the most brilliant and unorthodox biologists of his time." (2) He delineated the vicious and quite unscientific political rancor of a scientific community unwilling to countenance any divergence from its narrow, politicized Darwinist orthodoxies. Kammerer's undoing was his revolutionary antiracist opposition to the Mendelians' theories concerning "race hygiene"— not the dubious validity of his experiments, for if rigorous scientific accuracy were to have been his colleagues' principal criterion, the ranks of celebrated early-twentieth-century scientists would have diminished precipitously overnight. Kammerer's fate demonstrates chillingly what happens to those who attempt to alter the conditions of the narrow symbiosis between science and the propaganda needs of the politicians.

Kammerer's scornful delineation of the forces of racial antagonism aligned against his own position is, in fact, prophetic in light of what was in store for Western civilization. In the debate on race, he pointed out, most of his colleagues considered "all measures for human welfare, such as medicine and hygiene," to be "obstacles to progress." Many deemed it "naive optimism to expect favorable effects, in future generations, of such measures as the protection of the laborer, the shortening of working hours, the betterment of the economic situation, and the bodily, mental and cultural training of the young." Others saw "tuberculosis, venereal diseases, alcohol, and war" as " 'friends of the race' because they make for a weeding-out process." (261–2)

But though Kammerer was remarkably enlightened in the field of race theory, not even he could avoid the siren song of semen. "The capacity of our brain," he argued, "is limited." There was therefore an ever expanding need for gray matter: "Consciousness is unable to absorb again and again all the traditions of posterity and to add to it, if the organic foundation is not correspondingly enlarged." Eugen Steinach, one of his colleagues in Vienna and, with Voronoff, a reigning champion of rejuvenation research, had invented a method that would send the beneficial nutritive qualities of semen straight to the brain. As Kammerer delineated the process, the lucky men involved were given a "ligation (vasoligature), followed by a severing (vasectomy) of the spermatic duct." This caused a "readjustment between generative and interstitial tissue." The resulting "incretion" of "hormones" could subsequently "mix uninterruptedly with the blood circulation." Sweeping undiluted through the body in this fashion, the seminal fluids would provide "a strong chemical influence not only in the development of sex differentiations, but also in the preservation of general vitality." To ensure that human reproduction would not come to a screeching halt in man's rush to perpetual youth, Kammerer suggested the "ligation of only one spermatic duct."

The natural inheritance of acquired characteristics, Kammerer argued, would see to it that "males (young as well as old) whose youth and general vitality were intensified by a unilateral vasoligature" produced "a progeny strengthened in the same way right from the start." (321–7) But such a transmission of inherited characteristics would not automatically produce a new species of geniuses. Kammerer was that rarest of phenomena among biologists: a left-wing eugenicist. He argued that, though genius was undoubtedly an acquired characteristic, a combination of genetic *and* environmental conditions needed to be in place to allow the brain to flower. Not least among the impediments to the development of a race of supermen, moreover, was the genius's unfortunate habit of mating with women of substantially inferior intellectual endowment—itself an organic condition of the feminine that was as much a given to Kammerer as it was to his more conservative colleagues.

He complained that by using the term "negative eugenics" to designate "the weeding out of detrimental characteristics," he had come to be portrayed as "criticizing and condemning eugenics as it stands today." But nothing was further from the truth. He merely hoped to combine this practice with "productive eugenics," the active encouragement (through surgery, if necessary) of the genius traits in man. He wanted to combine the practice of "negative" and "productive" eugenics, and this caused him to give enthusiastic support to the practice, spreading like wildfire through the United States at this time, of "the sterilization of inferior individuals."

It should be obvious that there was nothing wrong with this procedure, he reasoned, for "very often this sterilization has a curative effect on the individual in question, changing him into a useful member of society, even though he is robbed of his propagative powers." Through the beneficial "incretion" effected by the vasoligature, "the ductless gland system arrives at a new dynamical equilibrium, with the result that the individual in question recuperates both psychically and physically." (352)

The faddish seminal-nutrition theories of the 1910s and Twenties thus played directly into the hands of the "negative eugenicists," who came to dominate biology and the medical profession throughout Western Europe and the United States in the years leading up to World War II. These scientists, who instigated a wide range of brutal experiments on "mental and racial inferiors" during this period, were the true intellectual architects of Germany's genocidal policies. Demagogues like Hitler could not have developed their race-cleansing policies with impunity if it had not been for the enthusiastic "scientific" legitimation of such practices by the large *international* tribe of geneticist millenarians. But today we tend to dismiss those experiments as merely a minor aberration of scientific judgment, an overzealous application of the legitimate premises of genetic research. Politics and science still share the same narrow bed.

"Scientific" racism had already become the dominant thread in such alarmist treatises as Max Nordau's enormously influential *Degeneration* (1893, translated from the German in 1895); Houston Stewart Chamberlain's *The Origins of the Nineteenth Century* (1899)—which became the historical bible of the Nazis; and Gustave Le Bon's *The Psychological Laws of the Evolution of Peoples* (1894), based on the categorical racism of Gobineau's *The Inequality of Human Races*—the latter a watershed book in the history of prejudice, which, though first published in France in 1854, was conveniently reprinted in a (much shortened) American edition in 1915, just a few months after the release of D. W. Griffith's *The Birth of a Nation.*

The effectiveness of these writers' tracts against effeminates, hysterics, and craniologically deprived racial degenerates depended on their readers' ability to imagine a future in which such horrid creatures might come to rule Western culture and drag it back into the Stone Age. They pictured a society in which such "vitally incapacitated" defectives would lord it over the superior Aryan, and they hinted at monstrous futures whose horrors clearly demanded fictional elaboration. As Nordau insisted: "We stand now in the midst of a severe mental epidemic; of a sort of black death of degeneration and hysteria, and it is natural that we should ask anxiously on all sides: 'What is to come next?' " (*Degeneration,* 537) This dark imagery of a world at the mercy of roaming bands of lascivious degenerates eager to rape and kill the scattered remnants of a more civilized society was, of course, soon to become the stock-in-trade of speculative fiction, from Ignatius Donnelly's *Caesar's Column* (1891) and H. G. Wells's *The Time Machine* (1895) through countless "lost world" tales in the pulp magazines of the Twenties and Thirties, as well as numerous post–atomic war melodramas of the Fifties, right up to the *Star Wars* series and the recent Hollywood fad for the dystopic futures of films such as *Blade Runner, Road Warrior,* and *Waterworld.*

Nordau's militant language about the need for civilization to "eradicate" degeneracy was characteristic of the fashion for "tough thought." This aggressive rhetoric would soon inspire Thomas Dixon and D. W. Griffith, as well as a horde of other early-twentieth-century advocates of racial purity. "The normal man, with his clear mind, logical thought, sound judgment, and strong will, sees, where the degenerate only gropes," Nordau wrote. This was why "degenerates must succumb." Only the strong survived. The weak "can neither adapt themselves to the conditions of Nature and civilization, nor maintain themselves in the struggle for existence against the healthy." (541) Nordau knew for certain that sexuality was a major factor in the creation of degenerates: "He who places pleasure above discipline, and impulse above self-restraint, wishes not for progress, but for retrogression to the most primitive animality." (554)

Progressives, socialists, and other such political radicals were degenerates deliberately scheming to undermine civilization: "Retrogression, relapse—this is in general the idea of this band who dare to speak of liberty and progress." But what they were really advocating was a return to "the most forgotten, faraway past." They wanted to "confound all the arts and lead them back to the primitive forms they had before evolution differentiated them." This cultural socialism was a clear sign of an "atavistic" yearning for collectivist homogeneity, and everyone knew that "atavism is one of the most constant marks of degeneracy."

Nordau had dedicated his book to Cesare Lombroso, who had "developed with so much genius" the "notion of degeneracy first introduced into science by Morel" (a French "alienist" of the mid-nineteenth century, who had delineated the "reversions" in human evolution Darwin was soon to identify as the distaff side of species development in *The Descent of Man*). Lombroso had shown, Nordau said, that the ontogenetic evolution of certain individuals in a civilized soci-

ety was aborted before they could reach the appointed heights the phylogenetic trajectory of their race required them to scale: "The disease of
degeneracy consists precisely in the fact that the degenerate organism
has not the power to mount to the height of evolution already attained
by the species, but stops on the way at an earlier or later point. The relapse of the degenerate may reach to the most stupendous depth." Indeed, in devolutionary terms such a failure of evolutionary stamina
manifested itself not infrequently in the "atavistic recurrence" of feminized behavior. The degenerate, said Nordau, in a passage that may
well have set Philip José Farmer's creative juices flowing in *The Lovers,*
could easily sink "somatically to the level of fishes, nay to that of the
arthropoda, or, even further, to that of rhizopods not yet sexually differentiated." Nordau directly identified the "effeminate male"—the
ephebe—and the "masculinized female"—the gynander—of fin de siècle symbolist art as genetic defectives: "They are not the future, but an
immeasurably remote past. They are not progress, but the most appalling
reaction." Such creatures were manifestations of "the most exhausted
senility, the starless winter night, the grave and corruption." (555–6)

This last sentence clearly identifies the intellectual lineage of Bram
Stoker's Dracula, the original turn-of-the-century vampire of degeneration. Nordau's diatribe may indeed even have given Stoker the idea for
his novel, for the latter had clearly read *Degeneration* with bated breath
before embarking on the composition of *Dracula.* To solidify his claim
to scientific expertise in the delineation of his predator, he had Van
Helsing, who is the Dutch-Aryan composite stand-in for Stoker's scientific mentors, remark that "the Count is a criminal and of criminal type.
Nordau and Lombroso would classify him, and *qua* criminal he is of imperfectly formed mind." (346)

Dracula and his minions—the mentally inferior peasants and the
working classes, the insane (Renfield), the "lower races," the primitive
"bi-sexual" masculinized women (Lucy Westenra), the socialists and
egalitarians—were, Stoker wanted to show in emulation of Nordau and
Lombroso, poised to overrun the world, eager to infect the evolving
Anglo-Aryan with the dread blood disease of lust. Nordau had pointed
out that it was "the sacred duty of all healthy and moral men" to exterminate these vampires and rescue "those who are not already too deeply
diseased." He had described degeneration as an "invading mental malady" and had called upon the Jonathan Harkers and Minas of Western
culture, and in particular upon the Van Helsings of evolutionary biology
and medicine, to destroy the invader by any means necessary: "Whoever

looks upon civilization as a good," Nordau exclaimed, "must mercilessly crush under his thumb the anti-social vermin." (556–7)

Pronouncements such as this called in no uncertain terms for the reign of the Iron Heel. Ironically, Nordau, arch-hunter of degenerates, like Lombroso, ruthless cataloguer of the phrenological traits of "moral inferiors," and Weininger, scourge of "semitic effeminates," was a Jew. Theorists can never control how politicians will exploit their theorems. Doctrines that advocate "final solutions," as Franz Kafka would demonstrate brilliantly in his 1914 story "In the Penal Colony," have no respect for their designers. Even so, it would be absurd to suggest that Jewish intellectuals such as Nordau, Lombroso and Weininger *created* genocidal racism. They merely collaborated in the general movement toward anti-humane "tough thought" dominant among the majority of "Aryan" scientists and intellectuals.

Gobineau had already defined "the word *degenerate,* when applied to a people," as applying to any race that had been vampirized by aliens: "continual adulterations having gradually affected the quality of [their] blood." (25) And years before Darwin's theories opened the door to the theory of dimorphic gender evolution, Gobineau had determined that the struggle between evolution and degeneration was gender-specific:

> Every human activity, moral or intellectual, has its original source in one or other of these two currents, "male" or "female"; and only the races which have one of these elements in abundance (without, of course, being quite destitute of the other) can reach in their social life, a satisfactory stage of culture, and so attain to civilization. (88)

Equilibrium between the male and female currents represented stasis to Gobineau. Thus he gave the apostles of progress their reason to hate "primitive bisexuality" even before this concept had been articulated.

Gobineau, however, was an aristocrat not yet fully in tune with the gender-specific division of mind and body already developed by bourgeois culture. He failed to establish a clearly defined "invidious comparison" between masculinity and femininity. He even committed the ideological faux pas of identifying the intellectual element in culture as feminine and the material element as masculine. But Gobineau had otherwise, de facto, invented the science of race inequality, and he could therefore be forgiven for this biological misunderstanding. His followers quickly corrected his error (which Gobineau, after all, had incurred by borrowing his categories from the inferior Hindus). Soon, in accord with the correct principles of dimorphic gender evolution, the races that had followed the "feminine" path were identified as the inferior ones. Those whose inspiration had been "masculine" were the cradle of the evolutionary elite.

The "universal truths" of our culture are often built on the skimpiest of scientific platforms. Gustave Le Bon showed how easy it was to construct such a platform. Pointing to what he saw as the vast differences in mental capacity between superior and inferior races, he remarked that one need not do a lot of traveling to come to that conclusion, since racial differences were exactly analogous to the mental differences between "the civilized man and woman even when the latter is highly educated. The man and the woman may have common interests and sentiments, but never like chains of thought." (36) Le Bon proved the truth of this contention by quoting from his own "scientific" speculations in the field of craniology. Scholars such as Emile Durkheim and Lester Ward cited this very passage to establish the legitimacy of the concept of the master race.

Le Bon contended that in comparing the skulls of

the various human races, belonging to the past and the present, it is found that the races in which the volume of the skull presents the greatest individual variations are the most highly civilized races; that in proportion as a race grows civilized, the skulls of the individuals composing it become more and more differentiated.

This was obviously a clear example of Spencer's "progressive heterogeneity" in action. Thus, by discovering exactly what ideology had taught him to look for, Le Bon was able to conclude that civilization tended "not to intellectual equality, but to an inequality that is always growing more and more pronounced. Anatomical and physiological equality only exist in the case of individuals of quite inferior races."

Le Bon then used this scientific "evidence" to "prove" the existence as well as the need for dimorphic gender evolution: "Among inferior peoples or the inferior classes of superior peoples the man and the woman are intellectually on much the same level. On the other hand, in proportion as peoples grow civilized, the difference between the sexes is accentuated." Again his craniological research had proved all this beyond doubt.

The volume of the male and female skull, even when the subjects compared, as in my investigations, are strictly of the same age, height, and weight, presents differences that increase rapidly with the degree of civilization. Very slight in the case of the inferior races, these differences become immense in the case of the superior races. In these superior races the feminine skulls are often scarcely more developed than those of the women of very inferior races. (48–9)

On the basis of such "facts" Le Bon established a parallelism of motives between the feminine principle in nature and the "antiindividualism" of the socialists. If the higher masculine civilization wished to survive, the collectivist impulse (Sumner's "woman-rule") must be eradicated like an infectious disease, for "when Socialism shall have become master in Europe, its only chance of enduring will be to exterminate all the individuals without exception endowed with a superiority capable of raising them, however slightly, above the most humble level." (44)

D. W. Griffith was heavily influenced by the warnings of masterrace theorists such as Le Bon. *The Birth of a Nation* (1915) was his contribution to the further dissemination of their ideas. He was particularly impressed by Nordau's call to the supermen of Western civilization to crush the anti-social vermin of social and erotic degeneracy. The vampire brood that was threatening the future of the Aryan by swarming out over the globe must be destroyed. This suggestion—not the subsequently much touted technical innovations of *The Birth of a Nation*— galvanized the film's audiences and made it into the most successful cinematic spectacle yet created. Griffith's tendentious portrayal of pure and virtuous white womanhood beset by ignorant, rampaging "African savages" intent upon sowing "miscegenation" wherever they ruled had tapped directly into the favorite obsession of most early-twentieth-century race theorists.

Film historians have generally whitewashed the viciously racist and sexist nature of Griffith's film by stressing the importance of its contribution to the technical development of the cinema. But whether those contributions were as significant as they have been made out to be is highly debatable. Most of the film's innovations were mechanical rather than structural, and often closely echoed what other filmmakers were doing already. In terms of narrative sophistication there is, for example, little difference between *A Fool There Was* and *The Birth of a Nation*. But the metaphoric contexts of the "battle of the sexes" inevitably change far more rapidly than those that focus on "the struggle for life among races." The issue of "technique" became a decorous veil used by critics to obscure the negative historical importance of the ideological content of Griffith's scurrilous diatribe. In the real world of politics and propaganda, of ideology and the manipulation of consciousness, aesthetic arguments that glorify form over content are an indelible part of the processes of control, a convenient way to avoid having to acknowledge the propaganda function of cultural artifacts.

In fact, *The Birth of a Nation* constitutes probably the most relentless and vicious conflation of fashionably "evolutionist" rhetoric about the evils of "miscegenation" before the advent of Nazi Germany. The very first caption of the movie said it all: "The bringing of the African to America planted the first seed of disunion." Griffith's formulation was inspired by race theorists such as Edward Alsworth Ross, who had, the year before, in *The Old World in the New,* railed against the discordant influence of "the Jewish invader."

The imagery with which Griffith followed his declaration was a direct visual evocation of Max Nordau's catalogue of degenerates: social radicals, hysterics, half-breeds, masculinized women, and the ultimate beneficiaries of the evil deeds of all evolutionary backsliders: childish, half-witted Africans. Griffith's film pictured the ideological principles of Dixon's *The Clansman* in excruciating detail. The end of the Civil War, Dixon had argued, had also threatened to bring an end to the march of Western civilization:

> No sculptor ever dreamed a more sinister emblem of the corruption of a race of empire-builders than this group. Its black figures, wrapped in the night of four thousand years of barbarism, squatted there the "equal" of their master, grinning at his forms of Justice, the evolution of forty centuries of Aryan genius. (171)

But though Dixon's incendiary rhetoric was the immediate inspiration for Griffith's visual assault on all Americans of African heritage who were not content to bow and scrape before their Aryan "masters," the racism of *The Birth of a Nation* was even more manipulative and destructive than that of its source text. For while a reader's personal life-experiences and accumulated knowledge generally serve as a moderating influence and interfere with any writer's ability to make fiction be accepted as reality, film—particularly during the 1910s, when it was still a novelty—traded on the viewers' assumption that what they were seeing was "real." In the cinema the book reader's temporary "suspension of disbelief" was supplanted by the viewer's unshakable faith in the veracity of the seen.

Even Griffith's use of white actors to portray the worst of the Africans—presumably because he refused to allow his white actors to be "contaminated" by real African-Americans—must have been calculated for effect. For in several "mass" sequences he *did* use African-American extras. But his systematic use of whites in blackface in all but the most marginal of *personal* confrontations actually helped strengthen the alarmist, genocidal message of his film. By having his viewers register the evil (and even the few cringingly subservient "good") Africans of his tale as swarthy, rough-featured, charcoal-smudged, scumble-faced, and hence clearly, in Lombroso's terms, "phrenologically degenerate" whites, he indirectly reinforced the visual "truth" of his "evolutionist" thesis. The implication was that to mingle with Africans was to be contaminated with inferior genetic matter, with "the disease of degeneracy." The blackfaced whites were easily recognizable to the audience as having horrid, "lower," "diseased," "sullied," versions of the Aryan master's superior features. The issue here was not even that blacks should be regarded as "separate but equal" or that they were "different" and hence to be feared. Instead, the blacks of Griffith's film presented the "criminally diseased" future of the white race if it were to give in to the forces of degeneracy by being content, as Nordau had said, to "live, like parasites, on labour which past generations have accumulated for them." (540) Griffith's blacks were thus degenerate whites slowly devolving in a fog of effeminate sensualist dissipation.

Progress was "the effect of an ever more rigorous subjugation of the beast in man," (560) Nordau had contended. Progress must therefore also depend on the proper subjugation of man's lust for woman. In all his films Griffith made it clear that because animalism was always hovering below the surface of a woman's life (given the constitutional "primitivism" of her reproductive nature), death was her only avenue of escape if she wanted to avoid the mark of the beast, the bite of the vampire in heat. In *The Birth of a Nation* the potential for a "black death of degeneration and hysteria" (Nordau, *Degeneration,* 537) among women is sparked by the Northern anti-individualist socialist radicals' insane belief that bestial African men would be able to maintain their feeble near-humanity within the proximity of white women. *The Clansman* had sketched what must happen under such circumstances. Dixon showed his virtuous white heroine Marion being accosted by Gus, a black man whose bulging "bead eyes" begin to gleam "ape-like" the moment he sees her. The man's degenerate loss of self-control is virtually instantaneous: "A single tiger-spring, and the black claws of the beast sank into the soft white throat and she was still." (304)

Griffith's adaptation of this scene proved him to be a sufficiently orthodox gender ideologue to bypass its obvious prurient cinematic potential in favor of a treatment that foregrounded his sacrificial heroine's awareness of her responsibility to the future of the white race. If woman brought out the beast in primitive man, that was obviously because "the beast" prowled restlessly just underneath her alluring skin. The Griffith heroine (most often Lillian Gish), heedful of that consideration, was always a creature whose physical near-invisibility would preclude the arousal of the beast in the white men around her. Instead, she inspired paternalistic condescension and dreams of virgin-motherhood. But Griffith was also convinced that in male "degenerates" the beast of sexual primitivism lurked even closer to the surface than in women. No amount of feminine self-effacement could keep the beast from stirring in such inherently animalistic males. A good woman's only defense against such degenerates was the protective vigilance of the Aryan males around her. It was their responsibility to prevent any contact between the lower orders and white womanhood.

But since drooling liberal Northern politicians had prevented the sturdy Aryan representatives of Southern manhood from exercising this protective role in Griffith's fictional take on history, a good woman's only escape from the mark of the beast was to efface herself in earnest by committing suicide before any degenerate could touch her. In *The Birth of a Nation* this self-sacrificial ardor of white Southern womanhood is sufficient to spark a rebirth of the Aryan's evolutionary fervor.

Griffith was clearly convinced that racial equality would forever destroy civilized society's greatest creation: the asexual woman. To force this point upon his audiences, Griffith showed them that any liberalization of the African's slave status would lead to the wholesale molestation of white womanhood by leering black animals. He tried to emphasize the inevitability of such a fate in a vicious parody of a civil rights demonstration, in which, for once, he quite deliberately used not whites in blackface but a group of actual African-Americans, on whom the camera lingers to "force" the audience to confront these "near-animals'" terrifying "degeneracy." He made them carry signs prominently displaying the slogan: EQUALITY, EQUAL RIGHTS, EQUAL POLITICS, EQUAL MARRIAGE. The last word was, of course, the rabble-rousing kicker. Griffith wanted his audiences' reaction to be: "Good God, not *my* daughter! Over my dead body! Where is my shotgun?" Griffith's incitement to violence was deliberate and deadly. Nothing in the infamous Nazi propaganda films of Leni Riefenstahl was ever quite this blatant, simplistic, and vicious.

The film's genocidal scenario now moves to its inevitable conclusion. Flora, a true flower of white Southern womanhood and little sister to Ben Cameron, the man who has just created the Ku Klux Klan, must be sacrificed to awaken Aryan manhood to its cleansing task. We therefore follow Ben's angelic, floral sister as she goes "alone to the spring" to fetch a pail of water. The sexual symbolism of this scene could have escaped no educated viewer familiar with the prurient symbolic representation of woman in late-nineteenth-century academic painting as *la source,* the wellspring of life, or with the closely related imagery of *The Broken Pitcher,* signifying the loss of virginity.

She is, of course, accosted almost instantly by the luridly blackfaced renegade Gus. All he has to do is mutter: "You see I'm a captain now and I want to marry . . ." and our courageous calyx of white womanhood instantly knows what to do. Without even a hint of hesitation she dashes off to a nearby cliff. Griffith made certain to prolong her desperate run for maximum effect, so that when, at last, Flora jumped, every Aryan heart in the audience could fill with genocidal fervor. Brother Ben arrives just in time to have her expire in his arms. He vows eternal revenge on the forces of degeneration. For intellectually impaired Aryans a moralizing caption helped make Griffith's intention explicit: "For her who had learned the stern lesson of honor we should not grieve that she found sweeter the *opal gates of death.*"

A miscegenated sexual awakening was tantamount to a life of progressive degeneracy, and hence worse than death. Griffith's moral was: Don't let our women go to the spring unprotected, or they will perish in the coming race wars. In *The Clansman* this realization had still come to the woman only *after* she had been "defiled." Therefore, instead of showing white womanhood executing a preventative strike against the monster of sexuality, Dixon had presented his readers with a cleansing ritual: the double suicide of mother and daughter. Bathed in typical turn-of-the-century gender symbolism, this scene showed dawn, the morning star (evolving masculinity), revitalized by the death of night (the moon, the "Woman-spirit"):

> They stood for a moment, as if listening to the music of the falls, looking out over the valley faintly outlining itself in the dawn. The first far-away streaks of blue light on the mountain ranges, defining distance, slowly appeared. A fresh motionless day brooded over the world as the amorous stir of the spirit of morning rose from the moist earth of the fields below.
>
> A bright star still shone in the sky, and the face of the mother gazed at it intently. Did the Woman-spirit, the burning focus of the fiercest desire to live and will, catch in this supreme moment the star's Divine speech before which all human passions sink into silence? Perhaps, for she smiled. The daughter answered with a smile; and then, hand in hand, they stepped from the cliff into the mists and on through the opal gates of Death. (307–8)

Thus Dixon showed acculturated Aryan womanhood dutifully sacrificing itself to the higher eugenicist requirements of the godly star of masculine transcendence.

The Clansman and The Birth of a Nation were instrumental in the rebirth of the Ku Klux Klan. The imagery of these two works gave the arguments of the new gender-based evolutionary racist ideologues a very precise frame of reference: protection of the principles of dimorphic gender evolution through the extermination of the vampire of sexuality wherever she might rear her predatory head. The early-twentieth-century racist agenda, by taking its justification from the rhetoric of the battle of the sexes, established a particularly volatile and potentially murderous emotional environment. Griffith helped establish the century's racist image of the African-American male as a polysexual animal forever intent upon reawakening the slumbering African womb in Aryan womanhood. The African-American male thus became, in many white men's fantasies, the masculine counterpart to Conrad's archetypal African woman, who had inspired Kurtz's exclamation "The horror! The horror!" because she carried within herself the mark of the beast that would drag the evolutionary male back into the heart of darkness. In The Birth of a Nation Griffith set out to show that only the Ku Klux Klan, the avenging spirit of the Aryan nation, could ward off this bestial creature of reversion. He made his heroes adopt the instruments

Bram Stoker had already designated as the only weapons strong enough to subdue Lucy, the monster of reawakened female sexuality: the burning cross, the stake, decapitation, and immolation. These now became the weapons of choice of the genocidal lynch mobs of Aryan racism.

Griffith's gender-ideological framework is apparent everywhere in *The Birth of a Nation.* Blacks are invariably portrayed within the context of Nordau's definition of degenerate effeminacy: "All persons of unbalanced minds—the neurasthenic, the hysteric, the degenerate, the insane—have the keenest scent for perversions of a sexual kind, and perceive them under all disguises." (*Degeneration,* 451) Griffith used this formulation to heighten his audience's fear of the "prowling African." Gus is by no means the only offender in this respect. The "mulatto" Lynch (who gratuitously strangles dogs with his bare hands when they get in his way) is also given a central role in Griffith's portrayal of the sadistic degeneracy of the African. In his *The Psychological Laws of the Evolution of Peoples,* Gustave Le Bon had helped formulate the prevailing Aryan opinion about such miscegenated creatures: "All the countries inhabited by too large a proportion of half-breeds are, solely for this reason, given over to perpetual anarchy, unless they are ruled by an iron hand." Le Bon supported this viewpoint by citing Louis Agassiz, who had maintained that such "cross-breeding" produced "an indescribable type whose physical and mental energy suffers." (53)

Griffith's Klansmen, in contrast, are superior along standard eugenicist lines. Nordau anticipated the characteristics of the filmmaker's heroic whites perfectly. "The normal man, with his clear mind, logical thought, sound judgment, and strong will, sees, where the degenerate only gropes; he plans and acts where the latter dozes and dreams." The manly man could not be expected to share the same ground with woozy effeminates: "In possession of all the good things of this earth, he leaves to the impotent degenerate at most the shelter of the hospital, lunatic asylum, and prison, in contemptuous pity." (541) Once again this was to be the exact scenario of *The Birth of a Nation.* As soon as Aryan manhood, provoked beyond further tolerance by the black man's constitutional degeneracy, takes up arms to drive the demon out, its impotent opposition scatters. Griffith shows his Klansmen riding rigidly upright and manly through the South, sternly exterminating the cringing interlopers wherever they go.

Gustave Le Bon had repeatedly urged white Americans to reassert their manliness in "the land of liberty," which, for that very reason, could never be the land of equality nor of fraternity, those two Latin chimeras which the laws of progress do not recognize. In no country on the globe has natural selection made its iron arm more rudely felt. It is unpitying; but it is precisely because it ignores pity that the race it has contributed to form retains its power and energy. There is no room for the weak, the mediocre, the incapable on the soil of the United States. By the mere fact that they are inferior, isolated individuals or entire races are destined to perish.

He commended the American white male for having taught the rest of the world the practical uses of mass murder: "The Redskin Indians, because useless, have been shot down, or condemned to die of hunger. The Chinese workmen, whose labor constitutes a vexatious source of competition, will soon undergo a similar fate." As for the blacks: "They are almost tolerated because they fill none but subordinate positions which no American citizen would consent to accept. Theoretically they have rights; practically they are treated like semi-useful animals, who are got rid of as soon as they become dangerous." (146–8)

Griffith agreed wholeheartedly with Le Bon. The American Aryan's "brilliant" genocidal actions against the effeminate principles of "European Socialism" must be celebrated, and the Aryans must form a unified national front against the agents of miscegenation. The requisite happy ending of *The Birth of a Nation* therefore takes the form of a ritual of national unification after the benighted Northerners have come to see the light of reason and freely join the heroic Southerners in their program of ethnic cleansing. A cross-matched, heaven-blessed, double marriage of purebred Northern and Southern Aryan males and females served to send Griffith's audiences contentedly into the streets to seek out African-Americans to exterminate in emulation of these cinematic models of manly behavior.

Thus Griffith's message prefigured the one Alfred Rosenberg, Adolf Hitler's favorite genocidal philosopher, directed toward the United States in his National Socialist manifesto of 1930, *The Myth of the Twentieth Century:* "An America true to its Northern-European heritage, cleansed of Black, Yellow and Jewish contaminants, would be a thousand times more powerful than one that remains weakened by such infusions of alien blood." (671) In the writings of such racial theorists as Rosenberg, there was also never any doubt that the main conductor of both good and bad blood must always be woman. She was the key, both to the glory of the evolutionary elite and to its potential downfall. In his delineation of "good" and "bad" women, Griffith held steadfastly to the principles of *Blut und Ehre* (blood and honor—words that would become the title of a 1936 Rosenberg book). Rosenberg had begun to articulate these principles by 1919 in direct emulation of the same turn-of-the-century evolutionary theorists of race and gender whose notions had inspired the hatemongering productions of Dixon and Griffith.

Like most of his contemporaries, Griffith did not separate the issues of gender and race. To him they were interlocking elements of the great struggle between human evolution and bestial degeneracy. Moreover, *The Birth of a Nation* was by no means an isolated instance of racist sermonizing in his career as a filmmaker. It was merely the central statement of a proto-fascist racial and gynephobic ideology that pervaded every aspect of his work. Most of his contemporaries saw nothing unusual or reprehensible in his beliefs. Indeed, the popularity of *The Birth of a Nation* is a clear indication that Griffith's ideas were the norm rather than the exception among white Americans. His phenomenal influence on the narrative practices of subsequent filmmakers is therefore by no means a good reason to celebrate his work. We do not excuse Hitler for being a genocidal demogogue because he was also an artful orator. Neither should Griffith be held any less responsible for his views because he made cleverly constructed films.

In fact, such permissive modernist attitudes toward the radical separation of form and content came into vogue only after Griffith's heyday. Specialization was still a new concept during the early years of this century. Few thought it necessary or feasible to segregate economic, social, ethical, sexual, and even physiological concepts into separate fields of study. As a result, the misconceptions and prejudices developed in one branch of science were unhesitatingly used to prove the validity of prejudicial assumptions in other fields. The reigning myths of gender, class, and race had invaded virtually every field of research, sometimes directly, but often in the form of tendentious metaphors. Serge Voronoff's delineation of dimorphic gender evolution as the element in species development that, though absolutely necessary, had, in effect, brought death into the world was a case in point.

Voronoff, following the precepts of Freudian psychology, had used a set of metaphors that evoked images of death as the primal form of woman. Starting from this premise, he subsequently sketched a biophysical world of internecine struggle in which an elemental evolutionary social contract (freedom, masculinity) was perpetually threatened by the feminine (an onslaught of Bolshevik protozoan reversion cells).

The individual human being, Voronoff maintained, was a community of cells whose life "is ensured only by the mutual help of all the others in the organism. They form a society, a state, in which each one fills a special role destined to ensure the life of the whole." The more evolved cells exhibited a Spencerian heterogeneity: "the more per-

"They have killed my friend": drawing, dated
October 12, 1914, made by an unidentified French
soldier in the trenches during World War I.
Death as the triumph of the feminine in the fears
of early-twentieth-century males

fected" they were, "the further they diverge from the primitive type and the more they depend on the work of the less delicate cells of other organs." This was clearly the proper model for a highly developed human society as well, but as in the larger world, the body's lower orders were always seeking to infiltrate the body politic: "These cells, which are little differentiated, are the connective tissue cells. They creep in everywhere, and are . . . the plebeians, a hardy and vigorous race which reproduce themselves with great facility." Physically stronger than the more highly evolved cells, these worker-cells "continually encroach upon the places occupied by the noble cells." Autopsies of the bodies of old people invariably revealed "the disappearance, the atrophy, of the differentiated and specialized cells, which are replaced by conjunctive cells."

Death was a result, Voronoff maintained, of the brain's invasion by these conjunctive cells, which gradually usurped the place of the "cerebral cells" and in this manner deprived the human body of the guidance it needed to survive. Voronoff had clearly set up a dramatic metaphoric "battle of the sexes" in which the masculine, individualistic, semen-fed brain cells were progressively destroyed—their life-force "atrophied"— by invasive, plebeian, primitively bisexual (though predominantly female) cells. Thus death was the triumph of the feminine, a yearning of the organism to return to its inorganic origins, a factor of the primitive collectivist principles of nature: "namely, the predominance of conjunctive cells replacing highly differentiated cells—a veritable triumph of anarchy, an ephemeral reign of inferior elements—from which results the disorganization of all the functions and the final death of the organism." (23–7)

Such a melodramatic portrayal of "the struggle for life among cell structures," no doubt strongly influenced by concepts such as Freud's "death instinct," could not help but reinforce the period's suspicions that there existed a primitive alliance between the lower orders and the feminine. Ideas of this nature were certainly on Djuna Barnes's mind when, in her novel *Nightwood* (1936), she characterized her bisexual (and hence "masculinized") heroine, Robin Vote, as "a woman who is beast turning human" and remarked that "such a woman is the infected carrier of the past: before her the structure of our head and jaws ache—we feel that we could eat her, she who is death returning, for only then do we put our face close to the blood on the lips of our forefathers." (37)

To fall into the clutches of such a woman, particularly one who had emanated from the "lower classes"—not to speak of the unspeakable twice-doomed women of the "lower races"—was to condemn oneself to an early death. No man of any sense would knowingly let himself be invaded by such a plague of death-dealing "conjunctive cells." But where the brain alone could easily have combated the incursion of these deadly cells with its superior capacity for intellection, the seductions of the eye were man's main portal to the collectivist cell structure of primitive nature, to the plebeian world of feminine lust.

To look upon the sexual woman, the visible woman, was to look upon the Medusa and to be turned to stone by the birth mother of man's mortality. To see her was to drown in the deadly night of the senses—to be forced to face an otherness that could never be subsumed by forcible incorporation. The sexual woman could be paid, but she could not be owned. Her self-possession challenged the immortality promised by the cash nexus, and her pursuit of pleasure turned the bitter sadomasochistic dirge of masculine spending into a siren song of unreproductive joy. Sex for the sake of pleasure undercut the laws of

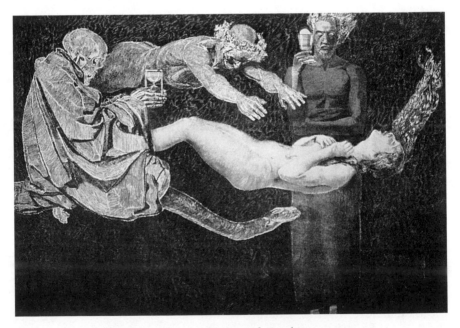

August Brömse, "Fleeting Life," etching, ca. 1910
The fantasies of the surrealists lose much of their apparent "originality"
when placed in the context of early-twentieth-century science,
and the symbolic imagery it spawned.

creation. It revealed that pleasure was beauty and beauty truth. True pleasure made any other truths purposeless. To look upon the sexual woman was therefore to abandon the organized promises of immortality for the fragmentary orgasms of a fleeting life—and to celebrate life was to look into the eyes of death.

By the mid-1920s Carl Gustav Jung had effectively codified these perceptions into an archetype of masculine psychology. In his contribution to *The Book of Marriage* (1926), Hermann Keyserling's star-studded symposium on the future of this institution, Jung remarked that

> *every man bears in his heart the image of woman,* not the image of *this* particular woman, but of *one* particular woman. This image is in reality an unconscious primeval inheritance, engraved on the living system, a "type" (archetype) of every ancestral experience of woman, the residue of all impressions left by women, a hereditary psychic system of adaptation. If there were no women, this unconscious image would make it possible to describe what a woman spiritually should be.

The "image of woman" Jung found in the soul of man was, of course, the anima. But even if we ignore Jung's schoolboylike cribbing of the Platonic "Idea" to develop his theory of the existence of universal psychological states, it becomes clear that his anima archetype was anything but an "eternal" construct. She was a perfectly average figment of early-twentieth-century male social psychology, a *femme moyenne fatale*. Jung's mind was filled with the images of nineteenth-century art:

> There are types of women whom Nature seems to have fashioned purposely for the reception of the projection of the anima. One might even speak of one certain type. The so-called "sphinx" nature belongs to it most indispensably: a certain ambiguous and equivocal character, not a vagueness into which nothing can be put, but a vagueness full of promise, with the speaking silence of the Mona Lisa; a being both old and young, mother and daughter, of a questionable purity; childish, yet with a naive wisdom, disarming to men. (358–9)

Jung's anima figure was the ideal bourgeois wife with a touch of the vampire thrown in to lend her an air of mystery. She was a product, not of a "universally inherent archetypal memory" in the male psyche, but of a century of socioeconomic indoctrination: a cultural construct, not a "psychic necessity." But that is precisely why she became such an oppressive reality in everyday life. Jung's anima was both "the" woman: the early-twentieth-century male's submissive, infinitely malleable wife, and "this" woman: the sexual vampire, the woman as colonized other, demanding her share of reality, demanding *her* reality—the collectivist invader: one of Voronoff's "conjunctive cells" lying in wait to gobble up the male's cerebral tissue. But she was "this" woman made tolerable to the period's culturally deformed erotic sensibility. No wonder, then, that Jung's dream woman still haunts our culture. She is the "Cosmo Girl" of today—the word made flesh of masculine erotic economics: virgin *and* whore, mother *and* child, goddess *and* slave, wisdom's daughter *and* nature's idiot, a fusion of the pleasure principle and the death instinct.

The Jungian anima figure is, as Jung himself pointed out, *She Who Must Be Obeyed,* the sadomasochistic fantasy construction of H. Rider Haggard's imperialist mind, a purportedly timeless creature who spawned a million pulp-fiction and comic-book imitations throughout the twentieth century. As the dead-end product of this closed system of the bourgeois imagination, the Cosmo Girl of today is perhaps *twice* as invisible as she was at the beginning of the century, for then she had at least attained a certain amount of negative visibility as the dangerous vampire of men's existential fears. Today she has become merely a chameleonic plaything of a thousand uses, ever compliant in her attempts to adapt herself to the latest fashions of the male imagination: a junior executive in a Wonderbra.

From the vantage point of many of today's twice-marginalized women, the sexual woman of the early years of this century becomes a particularly appealing figure, whose emotional independence from men, sexual confidence, pleasure in the seductive authority of her body, and "masculine" economic depredations gave her a centrality in that period's cultural imagination of which today's manufactured "sex symbols" can only dream. The early twentieth century's sexual woman had at least gained "invidious" visibility: from the vantage point of those made twice invisible, her ability to destroy the men around her makes her seem strong. To those living in the Cosmo Girl's world of enforced economic nonentity, she may indeed seem to be a veritable demon of "empowerment." But in fact she was, even then, the negative, mirror image of the dreams of mastery of the imperialist male. She was the nightmare inversion of his social sense of self, and though she *appeared* other, she remained, and still remains, a construct of the male imagination, the "anima" of the imperial male's inability to live up to his evolutionary dreams.

Those among today's theorists of "feminine identity" who are trying to reanimate her as a "positive" force are likely to find themselves ultimately also retracing the social trajectory of the sexual vampire of the early years of this century. This may lead to sadomasochistic fantasies of power, but it cannot lead to peace—for to accept the vampire image of feminine sexuality as a positive model also requires acceptance of the aggressive-reactive principles of the turn of the century's gender wars. Such an acceptance must also lead to a return either to the vulnerability of the colonized leper forcibly subdued by his imperial master or to the equally restrictive usurpation of the master's whip. Neither of these polar alternatives will allow its participants to break through the closed circle of gender imperialism.

The false dichotomy between absolute virtue and deadly vice established in the nineteenth century had, by the early years of this century, in fact already become virtually impossible to maintain, yet there were compelling economic reasons to do so, not least to protect the concept of the righteous subjection of the "lower" races to the "higher" morality and God-ordained new world order of imperialism. For if the men of the evolutionary advance could not keep their women in line, how could they expect to control the seething colonized masses or even the effeminate socialism of the invasive Jew?

To accept the sexual vampire's temptation of pleasure as a positive option for living was therefore also to accept the possibility that Kipling's leper was not a werewolf but a victim of the Western world's moral self-righteousness. To accept physical pleasure as a good was to undermine the fiscal rigidities of the robber barons, who blithely stepped on the human "offal" Sumner wanted to see die in the streets so that the Aryan race might be cleansed of the weak. "The Woman," man's anima, was the threat of "otherness" made visible. If the Aryan brain must succumb to her conjunctive cells, if the white man must be bitten by the leper, then at least let the pleasure be painful, let the "victim" agonize in his joy, make him cringe at his own weakness. He must be taught that to love the vampire was to lose his "manhood," was to let otherness triumph, was to allow Western civilization to be trampled by the "yellow peril," the "barbarian hordes" of Eastern Europe, and to be contaminated by the African womb.

Thus, ultimately, to glorify the aggressive violence of the early twentieth century's sexual vampire is *still* to deny pleasure, is to perpet-

uate the sadomasochistic deformations of the principles of human community, to internalize the "death wish" imposed on women by the men
who invented the image of the vampire. That the image of the vampire
should have strong appeal among today's women in search of an independent voice in a society still largely organized along principles of masculine dominance is inevitable, for she was always a woman in revolt
against the system of masculine intellectual paternalism. But she was a
woman of straw. An evil sister. A "witch." Not a woman of real power,
but one whose transgressions gave her opponents a license to commit gynecide. Her revolt was that of the period's monstrous backsliding "feminists" intent upon reestablishing the intemperate passions of the era of
"woman-rule." In her, as Otto Weininger had insisted, "a smouldering,
irrational and intemperate Socialism" revealed the homologies between
sexual degeneracy and racial inferiority. The "red road" of erotic dissipation Porter Emerson Browne's Schuyler took is the "red flag" of Arabella
Kenealy's "chaotic and disintegrating forces," the blood-thinning "semitic" effeminacy of the "lower orders" of the world.

Early-twentieth-century audiences saw analogues between the con-
flicting intentions of the various political movements, the clash of "race-
interests," and the depredations of the sexual woman as representative of
existential realities. The dark red blood of the capitalist superman was
much thicker than the watery gruel irrigating the bodies of genetic "inferiors." Lothrop Stoddard, one of the period's leading "race theorists,"
declared in his book *The Rising Tide of Color Against White World-
Supremacy* (1920) that the "Nordic" capitalist bourgeoisie of the United
States, the Schuylers of the world, were the guardians of one element

> fundamental to all the compoundings of the social pharma-
> copoeia. That element is *blood*. It is clean, virile, genius-bearing
> blood, streaming down the ages through the unerring action of
> heredity, which, in anything like a favorable environment, will
> multiply itself, solve our problems, and sweep us on to higher
> and nobler destinies. (305)

Prescott Hall had argued in the March 1919 issue of *The Journal of
Heredity,* in a passage that was dutifully quoted by Stoddard, that the genetically inferior creatures of the world were mounting a major campaign of regressive contamination against the Nordics: "Just as we isolate
bacterial invasions, and starve out the bacteria by limiting the area and
amount of their food-supply, so we can compel an inferior race to re-

main in its native habitat." But that process of "genetic starvation" also meant that the evolutionary elite must maintain "self-control" at all times when faced with erotic temptation. (260)

In a preface to Stoddard's book, Madison Grant, chairman of the New York Zoological Society, insisted that "Asia, in the guise of Bolshevism with Semitic leadership and Chinese executioners," (xxxi) was organizing precisely such a bacterial assault upon the Nordic race. Stoddard himself added that "Bolshevism is, in fact, as anti-racial as it is anti-social. To the Bolshevik mind, with its furious hatred of constructive ability and its fanatical determination to enforce levelling, proletarian equality, the very existence of superior biological values is a crime." Bolshevism saw miscegenation, sexual "pollution," as a primary tool in its conquest of the world: "Bolshevism is the renegade, the traitor within the gates, who would betray the citadel, degrade the very fibre of our being, and ultimately hurl a rebarbarized, racially impoverished world into the most debased and hopeless of mongrelizations." (220–1)

The vampire, the sexual woman, then, represented not only the return of the "primitive" visual world of arousal, which the "evolved" male had (or should have) repressed; she also symbolized the political threat of the economically exploited social classes whence she most often emanated. Her vulgar and politically subversive origins, however, were obscured by her physical beauty—by what Kipling, in "The Vampire," had designated as "a rag and a bone and a hank of hair." These lures served to seduce otherwise continent "Nordic" middle-class males who "did not know" that a materialist aesthetic and evolutionary intelligence could not, and should not, coexist. The seduction of the vampire woman represented the weakening of the white race's imperialist control over the world; therefore she must be isolated and destroyed like a "bacterial invasion" wherever she was found.

The sexual woman, as Porter Emerson Browne had made clear in *A Fool There Was*, drained the evolutionary male both morally and physiologically. Schuyler, for instance, literally sensed the Vampire sucking the "brains" out of him to feed her own physical health: she was a case study of the seminal-nutrition theory. As he grew weaker, she grew stronger and more powerful. Browne tells us that her mouth and cheeks bloomed into fiery health and beauty in proportion to her depredations of Schuyler's vital essence. This woman of the people thus also becomes emblematic of the social demands of the "inferior races." Madison Grant warned his contemporaries that sexual democracy and racial equality were two sides of the same coin. The advocacy of democratic ideals among an homogenous population of Nordic blood, as in England or America, is one thing, but it is quite another for the white man to share his blood with, or intrust his ideals to, brown, yellow, black, or red men. This is suicide pure and simple, and the first victim of this amazing folly will be the white man himself. (xxxii)

The sexual vampire, therefore, was a racial vampire as well. A Nordic man's submission to the vampire of sex was a first step toward racial suicide. It was to immerse oneself in the chaotic, unclean world of "collective" existence, of "socialist anarchy." In *A Fool There Was* Schuyler was shown degenerating directly to the brutal level of the sexual vampire's "noisome" working-class origins, which Browne, early in the novel, had described as strewn with "broken and greasy dishes, filled with fragments of food." A visitor who enters Schuyler's once impeccable town house after the Vampire has taken her fill of him encounters there "the very essence of dirt and disorder." Every piece of furniture in the apartment was askew, and "over all lay a pall of dust, dank choking." (265)

Browne wanted to show his readers that a descent into the world of the body was a descent into sloth and chaos, into socialist anarchy. Five years later Edward Alsworth Ross, in *The Old World in the New* (1914), pointed out that the Nordic could identify the invading bacteria of otherness by its horror of soap: " 'The Slavs,' remarks a physician, 'are immune to certain kinds of dirt. They can stand what would kill a white man.' " This was, Ross insisted, because they came "from a part of the world in which never more than a third of the children have grown up. In every generation, dirt, ignorance, superstition, and lack of medical attention have winnowed out all but the sturdiest." (291) Nordic men should not mingle with such creatures; to do so would "thin the blood of the American people" and bring on "race suicide." (297–9)

The Crimson Tide, a novel by the hugely popular writer of romance fiction Robert W. Chambers, published in 1919, directly in the wake of the Russian Revolution, provocatively announced on its cover that it was "A Story of Bolshevism in New York." Chambers once again described the lair of the socialist beast as a refuge of germs: "The bedroom, which smelled of sour fish, was very cold, very dirty, and very blue with cigar smoke. The remains of a delicatessen breakfast stood on a table near the only window, which was tightly shut, and under the sill

of which a radiator emitted explosive symptoms of steam to come."
(196) The (clearly Jewish) Bolsheviks who live in this mess are completely oblivious to their environment. They wear greasy raincoats and
soiled collars and use dirty red handkerchiefs. Perfect exemplars of degeneracy, they are contemptible advocates of socialism, equal rights for
women, and birth control.

Chambers sketched a monstrous future if America were to relax its
allegiance to cleanliness:

> The Crimson Tide, washing through Russia, eastward, seethed
> and eddied among the wrecks of empires, lapping Poland's
> bones, splashing over the charred threshold of the huns, creep-
> ing into the Balkans, crawling towards Greece and Italy, menac-
> ing Scandinavia, and arousing the stern watchers along the
> French frontier—the ultimate eastward barrier of human liberty.

But the agents of effeminacy and reversion were already busy subverting even these last bastions of Aryan culture, disguised as unwashed
immigrants:

> Everywhere, among all peoples, swarmed the stealthy agents of
> the Red Apocalypse, whispering discontent, hinting treason,
> stirring the unhappy to sullen anger, inciting the simple-minded
> to insanity, the ignorant to revolution. For four years it had been
> a battle between Light and Night; and now there threatened to
> be joined in battle the uttermost forces of Evolution and
> Chaos—the spiritual Armageddon at last, where Life and Light
> and Order must fight a final fight with Degeneracy, Darkness
> and Death. (294–5)

Chambers's implication—that the struggle between the forces of
progress and reversion was a struggle between "manliness" and "effeminacy"—would have escaped few among his contemporaries. Evolution,
Life, Light, and Order, they all knew, represented the masculine, the intellectual realm, whereas Chaos—the primal uroboros—was the world
of primitive reproductive feminine sexuality, the vampire's world of Degeneracy, Darkness, and Death.

In *The Slayer of Souls,* a science fiction fantasy Chambers published a
year later, he elaborated this analogy even more directly. Now he

showed the red vampire as already involved in an Aryan-American brain-drain in direct emulation of the sexual vampire of *A Fool There Was:*

> Over the United States stretched an unseen network of secret intrigue woven tirelessly night and day by the busy enemies of civilization—Reds, parlour-socialists, enemy-aliens, terrorists, Bolsheviki, pseudo-intellectuals, I.W.W.'s, social faddists, and amateur meddlers of every nuance—all the various varieties of the vicious, witless, and mentally unhinged—brought together through the "cohesive power of plunder" and the degeneration of cranial tissue. (113)

The parallel appetites of the vampires of socialism and sex had, by 1920, clearly become a matter of public record.

For Chambers's readers a hopeful ending was requisite. The clean-cut American heroes who save the day in *The Crimson Tide* therefore live to exult in the imminent defeat of the vampire of socialism: "You of the Bolsheviki can not come among us dripping with human blood, show-ing us your fangs, and expect from us anything except a fusillade." (356) Chambers also included a spirited defense of the evolutionary male's salutary "marriage law," which he defined in words taken directly from William Graham Sumner: "A race is worthless and contemptible if its men cease to work hard and, at need, to fight hard; and if its women cease to breed freely. If the best classes do not reproduce themselves the nation will, of course, go down." Sexual dimorphism ruled: "The woman who shrinks from motherhood is as low a creature as a man of the professional pacifist, or poltroon, type, who shirks his duty as a sol-dier." The further evolution of Anglo-Aryan civilization depended on the strict avoidance of all forms of "miscegenation": "Only that nation has a future whose sons and daughters obey the primary laws of their racial being." (244–5)

These were not the words of a minor figure in American culture. Chambers (1865–1933), a close friend of Charles Dana Gibson, was per-haps the most popular novelist of his time, and his works were routinely serialized first in large-circulation general-interest monthlies such as *Cosmopolitan, Scribner's,* and *The Atlantic Monthly.* His first book, *The King in Yellow* (1895), is still highly prized among aficionados of horror tales, and its title story continues to be a mainstay of fantasy-fiction antholo-gies. A true superman of romance fiction, Chambers wrote faster than a

speeding bullet and had already published some sixty extremely successful novels, most of them sprinkled with similar sentiments, before the
appearance of *The Crimson Tide*. If the "Gibson Girl" represented the
preflapper standard of emulation for young women, the typical middle-
of-the-road, petit-bourgeois Anglo-American manner of thinking
about the world of politics and gender difference prevalent during the
first twenty years of this century ought to be identified as the "Chambers Mind."

The sexual vampire of *A Fool There Was* and of numerous other narratives and films from this period used her beauty to undermine America's future just as surely as Chambers's raging Red Bolsheviks or the
Black, Brown, and Yellow Peril of Stoddard's "rising tide of color."
Thus racial, sexual, and political prejudices converged during this period
to make the sexual woman into one of the most terrifying human monsters of all time. In the "regressive" passions of the vampire woman a
world of race, sex, and class prejudice found its overarching expression.
She was ultimately not a human being but the female "Beast of the
Apocalypse" of Chambers's Crimson Tide: "the woman was beautiful as
an animal is beautiful."

Porter Emerson Browne's descriptions of the "medical" symptoms
Schuyler exhibited as a result of his submission to the sexual vampire directly foreshadowed the "degeneration of cranial tissue" Chambers was
to diagnose as a symptom of Anglo-Aryan submission to the incursions
of the Crimson Tide. Schuyler had wasted his allotment of vital essence
irrevocably, as Browne made him acknowledge quite bluntly: "I'm a
husk—squeezed dry." Blake, his best friend, is overwhelmed: " 'My
God, this is awful!' he exclaimed. 'Haven't you a spark of manhood left?
no brains?' " Obviously fully apprised of the latest medical discoveries,
"Blake knew that if this time he failed to arouse whatever of latent, atrophied manhood there might be in the breast of the other, that never
again, probably, would the shriveling brain come within call." (276–8)
And Schuyler self-diagnoses: "Save me from her—from myself—My
blood has turned to water, and my bones to chalk! My brain has withered!" The sexual vampire and the Crimson Tide of the lower orders:
two versions of a single disease of the blood.

Like that other monster hit of 1915, *The Birth of a Nation,* the movie
version of *A Fool There Was* skillfully tapped into these elements of so-
ciomedical paranoia. What could be more topical, in the early days of
1915, with World War I already raging in Europe, than the theme of the
domestic invader? Chambers's terrorist web of economic spoilers intent

upon undermining the peaceable imperialist world order, with its neat evolutionary stratifications, was personified just as much by Theda Bara, the sexual vampire, as by the monstrous political meddling of the mongrel temptress of *The Birth of a Nation*. The Black Menace, The Crimson Tide, the Yellow Peril, the Leering Semite: all were creations of the African womb. All had been bitten by the leper of reversion, and all, in turn, were poised and eager to infect the Aryan with their disease.

In the years surrounding the release of both films, American anti-immigrant paranoia had reached a new virulence. "Scientific" sociological treatises such as Ross's *The Old World in the New*, which had claimed that the influx of immigrants would "thin the blood of the American people," (297) were legion. Thus 1915 was indeed the perfect time for an American edition of Gobineau's *The Inequality of Human Races*. The "father" of "scientific racism" found an eager new audience for his contention that wherever "the Aryan blood is exhausted stagnation supervenes." (212)

Many thought that the tide of immigration that reached its peak during the early years of this century threatened to "mongrelize" Aryan-American civilization. Unwashed immigrants with alien concepts of community were set to pollute the middle-class household with unclean thoughts of sexual liberation. Andrew Carnegie claimed as much in his essay collection *Problems of Today*, published in November 1908, only weeks before the first appearance of the play and the novelization of *A Fool There Was*: "Just as Socialism goes back to the savage past and urges man to return to Communism, so seemingly it contemplates the return of man and woman to barbarism in their holiest relations."

Carnegie begged his readers to remember that the dimorphically evolved household had at last weaned woman of her primitive erotic ardor: "In the happiest and holiest homes of to-day, it is not the man who leads the wife upward, but the infinitely purer and more angelic wife whom the husband reverently follows upon the heavenly path as the highest embodiment of all the virtues that have been revealed to him." In contrast to the Socialist vampires of free love, "throughout the English-speaking race as a rule to-day, it is the wife and mother who sanctifies the home. If all the dreams of the wildest Socialist were realities purchasable at the cost of the present happy home of Individualism, with wife and children, the sacrifice were too great—the blow to our civilization would be fatal." (169–70)

Rhetoric of this sort increased in vehemence throughout the first thirty years of this century. Toward the end of his long career, Gustave

Le Bon warned his American followers in *The Psychology of Peoples* (the American edition of his *The Psychological Laws of the Evolution of Peoples* appeared in 1924 under this title) that the "new barbarians" who had burdened the United States with "a gigantic invasion of inferior elements" were poised to unleash a new civil war "between races which have reached different levels of evolution." (161–2) The nation's "large and flourishing middle class," Edward Alsworth Ross emphasized in his highly influential *Principles of Sociology* (1920), was its "guaranty of social health." But if this group of social superiors "should become luxury-loving and soft, their traits might gradually sap the manhood of the people." (523–4)

As works of propaganda and of ideological indoctrination, *A Fool There Was* and *The Birth of a Nation* could therefore not have been more timely, or more effective. Though *A Fool There Was* has been forgotten because it did not cater to the public's love of grandiose spectacle, it was precisely its emphatic foregrounding of the everyday world and its emphasis on a bourgeois, commonplace environment that made this film, in its own way, as innovative and determining in its influence on the development of filmmaking as Griffiths's bible of visual pomp. No running, jumping, horse riding, dueling, clowning, casts of thousands, titanic struggles, or strange historical customs and costumes here; simply a modern, well-to-do, upper-middle-class family everyone could recognize, living in a suburban house of the sort every member of the audience had at least seen. Here the fate of a darling Aryan family, living in a familiar world of business dealings, hard work, and playful leisure—the sort of life every American wanted to achieve or to maintain—was shown desecrated by a vile sexual agent of the socialist hordes.

Elements of self-consciously Freudian sexual symbolism played a central role in the mise en scène of the movie version of *A Fool There Was*. The dramatic "gunplay" of Parmalee's prophetic suicide was a case in point. The movie showed the young man's gun clearly to be a symbol of his waning manhood. The "psychological" role of the young man's weapon was made obvious to all: When Parmalee sees the Vampire on the ocean liner's deck, he pulls out his gun, then puts it back in his pocket. The gesture was quite obviously meant to symbolize a momentary erotic stimulus, quickly suppressed. In the boys' world of dime novels and action films, guns were (as they still are today) always blazing, always ejaculating, always ready to kill—totemic expressions of the uncontrollable erections of adolescent boys. But far more than today, in addition to being an expression of unbridled male potency and aggressive power, the phallic gun, in the "grown-up" world of early-twentieth-century "psychological dramas," also symbolized death to the user, for the man with the gun was sure to find it turned back upon him by the vampire of temptation. Indiscriminate discharge of the sacred gun represented a descent into the world of catabolic excess; it was a sign of seminal incontinence. Frequent use was an admission of profligacy, a return to adolescent seminal bravado, and hence a clear sign of physiological "effeminacy," of moral—and even actual—suicide.

The sexual mythology of the time required that the adult masculine eros conquer death through the judicious husbandry of the body's vital essence. In the symbolism of popular culture, that meant that a man's gun must "slay" the sexual woman by driving her into helpless economic dependency and a state of abject reproductive passivity: the domestic ideal of the men of 1915. These socioeconomic implications of the theory of gender dimorphism were unambiguous. Leslie Mortimer Shaw, former United States Secretary of the Treasury and governor of Iowa, spelled out the reigning laws of nature in his book *Vanishing Landmarks: The Trend Toward Bolshevism* (1919): "None of us admire either 'mannish' women or 'sissy' men. Woman does not get her happiness from her creatorships or sovereignties. The normal woman prefers that her husband be the sovereign, and she his queen. Woman gets her happiness from her sacrifices." Love made woman man's footstool: "If told sufficiently often, she is even proud to be a slave to the man who loves her and sometimes is without ever receiving a single post-nuptial word of endearment." (74–6)

Nearly all medical and biological authorities working in the imperialist nations were in agreement around 1915 that the future of humanity was best served by urging the male to move toward true masculinity and material immortality. The fully acculturated dimorphically evolved woman, meanwhile, presumably would become the absolute embodiment of thanatos, and in an ultimate act of evolutionary self-effacement, allow herself to implode into nonexistence.

It would, of course, be absurd to suggest that the inherently gynecidal logic of this train of "scientific" reasoning concerning the divergent existential responsibilities of the sexes was actually understood as such by most of the lay public in 1915. But snippets of the philosophers', scientists', and psychologists' theorems inevitably made their way into the culture at large in the form of commonplaces about the "battle of the sexes," and aspects of the dominant theory of evolutionary gender dimorphism were on almost everyone's mind.

"The Infernal Feminine": the trend toward
Bolshevism depicted on the January 19, 1922, cover
of Life, *a popular American humor magazine*

Both *A Fool There Was* and *The Birth of a Nation* therefore presented their viewers with a picture of "collectivism," the deadly feminine instinct, in action. The Vampire with the African womb was, like the African male and the effeminate collectivist immigrant, an emissary of chaos. All were representative of a single alien force intent upon undermining the American male's hard-won economic equilibrium, determined to take him out of the reach of immortality and into the house of death, determined to reverse the binary poles of the sadomasochistic undercurrent of twentieth-century dualist thought.

Thus the two films are, certainly in historical terms, equally important as expressions of the newly discovered social function of the motion picture as a tool of mass indoctrination. With the advent of cinema, the social function of mass communication changed dramatically. Until then the (relatively) "rational" (because verbal, and hence potentially dialectical) dispersal of ideas in Western European and American culture had remained a slow and ineffective process, undermined in all its attempts to universalize gender and race prejudice by annoyingly tenacious patterns of reasoned counter-argumentation. Now, almost at once, the element of rational thought had been eliminated from the equation. *The Birth of a Nation* showed its public that the African was a degenerate interloper, a "dysgenic" element in American public life, while *A Fool There Was* proved that the sexual woman was the dysgenic emissary of socialism in domestic life. The very *silence* of the early motion picture made its images available to all—not limited to the well-to-do, or even the merely literate, but readily understandable to anyone able to scrape together the few pennies it cost to gain admission.

And bring in their pennies the audiences of 1915 most certainly did. As Upton Sinclair reported in his 1933 biography of William Fox, *A Fool There Was* made the future mogul's fortune. In 1914 gross rentals of Fox Film Corporation productions had amounted to $272,401. In 1915 that figure jumped to $3,208,201—a nearly twelvefold increase in revenue. Much of that increase came from the earnings of *A Fool There Was.* The popularity of *The Birth of a Nation* is too well documented to need further reiteration here.

Films rapidly became indispensable tools in the psychosocial reorganization of culture. The sexual vampire and the vampire of socioeconomic conflict were beginning to merge into a single, "racially inferior" predator. The metaphors of gynecide that had taught the early-twentieth-century male to excise the "feminine" impulses within himself to gain "immortality" gradually became the basis for a primarily *racial* imagery of "gendered" inequality. Even as the medical basis for masculine "seminal continence" was being undercut by more reliable methods of endocrinological research, the unreason of racism found "rational" refuge in the metaphor of the vampire. The imagery of the sexual woman began to blend with notions positing the "predatory effeminacy" of the "inferior races." Domination and submission are the cornerstones of any dualistic system. To kill the vampire who refuses to be dominated, to drive a stake through her heart, is to kill death, take back the immortality she stole from us. Mass murder eroticizes killing by turning the sword of vengeance upon the "agents of death," just as the sadist gains "life" through domination and the masochist a motive for revenge through submission. Killing is a displacement of our fear of nonbeing. Thoughts of genocide become "realistic" when the very existence of another is seen as the cause of our death.

In the years since Theda Bara's heyday, the cultural link between the depredations of the vampire and the male's sexual spending has been lost. When the medical theories on which the concept was based gradually came to be discredited, the public's *conscious* understanding of the "medical" truth of woman as vampire also disappeared. It was only after this that social critics and psychoanalysts could return to the vampire tales of the turn of the century and identify them as "naive, spontaneous" creations of the imagination, as "unconscious" expressions of the human psyche. As our culture "discovered" the "universality" of symbols whose psychological meaning had been established by the "science" of a previous generation, a cultural obsession that had very precise and clearly identifiable origins in nineteenth-century economic motives came to be seen as an "instinctual response." Intellectual circularity of this sort produces the "truths" of speculative disciplines.

The images and metaphors developed during the early years of this century still pervade every aspect of our consciousness. The social ideology of evolutionary inequality spawned by tendentious interpretations of Darwinian ideas rapidly became our "collective unconscious"—part of the sexual mythology of our popular culture. The vampires of gender antagonism proved to be shape-shifting monsters whose presence in the human imagination permitted the justification of virtually every sort of brutality, from domestic violence to mass murder. The monster of genocide was a product of the arrogance of early-twentieth-century science.

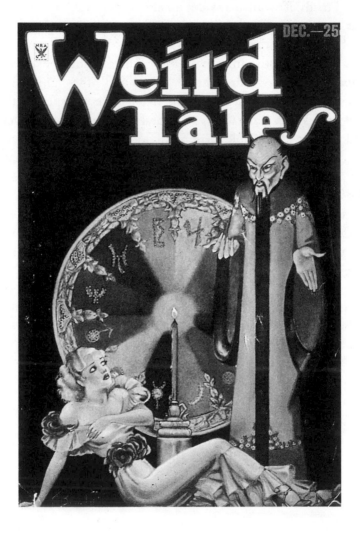

Margaret Brundage, cover of Weird Tales,
vol. 22, no. 6, December 1933

VII. REAL VAMPIRES: THE SEXUAL WOMAN AND HER ALLIES: BOLSHEVIKS, SEMITES, AND EURASIANS; THE YELLOW PERIL OF THE ARYAN IMAGINATION

Theda Bara was the American male's fondest nightmare: a sexual woman whose motives for seduction were not strictly economic, but "organic" as well. She was the invasive other of everyone's fears: Salome, Judith, Astarte; Lilith, the lustful, primal Eve who stole semen from sleeping men; Lamia, her daughter, the serpent queen. Semitic, masculinized, she was also Shylock, Svengali, Dracula: Arab Death. In *A Million and One Nights*, a witty two-volume early history of the rise of the movies as entertainment, published in 1926, Terry Ramsaye gave an eyewitness account of the Fox organization's publicity schemes to emphasize this connection as soon as *A Fool There Was* became a hit: "Immediately Miss Goodman began to acquire a most amazing atmospheric past." Publicists filled the newspapers with false biographical information: "Theda Bara was the daughter of a French artist and an Arabian mistress, born on the sands of the Sahara. 'Bara' was indeed a mere cypher, being Arab spelled backwards." "Theda" was, of course, an anagram for "death." Fox's intention was obvious: "This deadly Arab girl was a crystal-gazing seeress of profoundly occult powers, wicked as fresh red paint and poisonous as dried spiders. The stronger the copy grew the more it was printed. Little girls read it and swallowed their gum with excitement." (II, 703)

Meanwhile Theodosia Goodman, a pragmatic Jewish girl from the Midwest, did her best to play the part she had been given in the Aryan male's imagination. She realized from the start that she was merely a vehicle for the public's fears and dreams: "I do not consider that I look like a vampire-woman," she confessed in a two-part article published in *The Forum* in 1919. She had recently pointed out to her manager "that he could just as easily achieve that sort of appeal with any woman-of-curves-and-substance, as he could with me." (pt. 2, 88) She was a bit embarrassed by all the emphasis on her sexual nature: "in none of my vampire roles have I ever consciously shared their sensuous impressions." She just happened to be a good actress, she said, able to portray seductresses "due to an emotional strength in me, but not of me; an impersonal conception of what the Vampire-woman is." But because "realism in the movies is so essential," (pt. 2, 90) she had analyzed the type she had been chosen to portray as accurately as she could.

She was a quick study. As Ramsaye reported, Theodosia spent days

posing with skulls and crossbones, glass balls, and all the trademarks of Oriental desert mysticism. The motion picture public went to the theater to see about all this promisingly snaky stuff and found that the effect on the screen was up to the advance notices. Theda Bara of the screen, working her willowy way with men, became the vicarious and shadowy realization of several million variously suppressed desires. (II, 703)

But Theda Bara did not just pose with "skulls and crossbones," as Ramsaye indicated. She did better: Fox circulated a set of publicity stills, apparently in connection with the 1917 release of *Cleopatra* (one of Arabella Kenealy's touchstone "masculinized" regressors), in which she was shown crouching ominously over a—presumably male—skeleton. That depleted victim of her voracious appetite was shown reclining on the photographer's studio floor in grotesque final discomfort. One of the stills actually positioned her between the skeleton's legs, an ardent lover, unwilling to accept the fact that her prey had already done quite enough service to brute nature. Theda Bara herself was in these photos, as always, the picture of voluptuous health—except for the telltale darkly kohled rings around her eyes, symbolic of the continuing call of her seminal appetite.

One of these photographs showed her with her chin on her knees, a contented vulture in after-dinner repose. It paid tribute to what was probably the direct inspiration for this photo session: a painting by William Sergeant Kendall, prominent member of the National Academy and a perennial laureate of America's official art circles, as well as, from 1913 to 1922, the influential dean of Yale University's School of Fine Arts. The painting, not so enigmatically titled *A Sphinx,* had caused an uproar when Kendall exhibited it at the fall 1915 American Artists Exhibition of the Chicago Art Institute and subsequently at the spring 1916 show of the National Academy in New York. The artist, in turn, may have felt the stir of his predatory muse after seeing Theda Bara in *A Fool There Was*—although, perhaps to preclude such speculation, he had dated the painting 1914.

Kendall's painting was an unflinching delineation of the latest discoveries about woman's nature in the fields of biology and medicine. A contented, rosy-cheeked young woman in a snakeskin cap, her hips and thighs arranged like the jaws of a praying mantis, hovers above the woefully depleted skeleton of a hapless male. Though a "sphinx," this woman stripped of her civilized veneer, this predatory feline with a human face, was no mythological creature but an unorthodox portrait of the girl next door. The artist had obscured this mantis's mandibles under decorous draperies, but they remain the central feature of his composition, an almost palpable presence between the young woman's abrasively embracing thighs. Much like the half-eaten males of the mantises described by the period's naturalists, the skeletal shape of this young woman's well-picked-over lover seems almost physically attached to her loins. As if just alerted to the viewer's arrival, she looks up, flushed and satiated, but ready for more. "Do you want to be next?" her lively eyes inquire.

That one of the most prominent official painters of the period should have chosen to exhibit this provocative picture publicly in 1915 shows how common a knowledge of the biomedical effects of seminal depletion had come to be among sophisticates. The guardians of public morality were properly scandalized, but the public's outcry was directed against the painting's obvious vulgarity (certainly still a legitimate complaint) and against the sadomasochistic nature of its erotic focus (an equally reasonable objection), not against its subject matter as such.

The first two decades of the century were thus largely responsible for obliterating the distance between the symbolic vampires of fiction, who were still merely psychological monsters, and the tangible reality (after all, didn't we *see it happen?*) of the sexual vampires of the silent screen. The temporal trajectory that led from Stoker's novel, Philip Burne-Jones's painting, and Kipling's poem of 1897, through Porter Emerson Browne's play and novelization of 1909, to director Frank Powell and producer William Fox's film, as well as William Sergeant Kendall's painting of 1915, is indicative of the shifts in the public's perception of the role of the sexual woman during this period. If she had been a largely symbolic, unselfconscious, womb-driven predator at first, her pursuit of physical well-being was to bring her ultimately—just in time for the racist attitudes of the Twenties—directly in line with the criminally hedonistic, erotically effeminate, and intellectually undifferentiated "inferior races."

By 1915 the average citizen had come to accept what Gustave Le Bon had emphasized already in his *Psychological Laws of the Evolution of Peoples* (1894): the biologists had been able to determine that

> all the individuals of the inferior races, even as regards those of different sex, are on sensibly the same mental level. They all of them resemble one another, and they are thus a perfect exemplification of the equality dreamed of by our modern socialists. In the case of the superior races, on the contrary, the intellectual inequality of the individuals and the sexes is the law. (39–40)

Like Le Bon, most educated early-twentieth-century males saw a direct homology of purpose between, if not all women, then at least the sexual woman, and the "lower orders." The socialist agenda incorporated the desire of the vampire who refused to keep her place in the dimorphic advance of the Aryan elite. Both the sexual woman and the socialist insisted on pulling their victims down to the lowly mental level of the inferior races by destroying their capacity to function in the world of finance and industrial production. Like the socialists, these sphinxes, half animal, half woman, did so only in a selfish endeavor to add vigor and rosy, fleshy, full-blooded health to their own pleasure-loving constitutions.

Toward the close of the second decade of the century the term "vampire" was, therefore, no longer used to designate a symbolic, fictional creature. Instead it came to identify a medical condition: vampires were unevolved, constitutionally still mostly "masculine" women who had emanated from among the socialist masses to wreak havoc upon the male's intellectual and economic evolution. Soon the "vamps" of Hollywood would take these creatures out of the realm of serious socioeconomic theory and into the world of vulgar domesticity. But in June 1919, when the editors of *The Forum* presented Theda Bara's "How I Became a Film Vampire," subtitled "Self-Revelations of a Moving-Picture Star," they were still counting on their readers' scientific awareness of the link between biology and destiny, for they called her "the most celebrated exponent of emotional eroticism on the films" and identified her as an actress whose social mission it had been to "reveal the power of the wicked Vampire-women over men." *The Forum* was a semischolarly monthly aimed at the upper-management crowd (the Schuylers of the American establishment). It specialized in articles on economic development (Sumner's predatory laissez-faire evolutionism was God), statecraft (the utility of war was to ensure future peace), and biology (scholars searching for the "mental link" between the ape and man).

These "Self-Revelations" of Theda Bara's, which indeed appear to be in her own hand, are probably a mixture of truth and fiction—like almost everything else we know about her. They sketch a very wholesome Midwestern middle-class childhood, full of tomboy adventures straight out of Mark Twain and an adolescence devoted to acting, morally upright behavior, and dignified poverty (just about as Hollywood as such stories can get). All this was designed to prove what a fabulous "charlatan" of emotions, what a true actress, Theodosia was. Her dramatic abilities had allowed her to become "famous for the Vampire-woman I am not." (pt. 1, 727) Scattered through the two-part article were some very telling reflections upon the standard characteristics of the vampire woman of the 1910s—all from the period's unquestioned expert on the subject. Theodosia Goodman wanted her readers to understand that Theda Bara, the woman personifying "Arab Death," was an imaginative creation whose screen behavior was nothing but a "Kiplingesque" fiction, "not true to the life of any woman known to me, or to you." (pt. 2, 85) But she was proud to acknowledge her performance in *A Fool There Was* as a masterpiece of psychological realism. She considered it, given the "intensity of wickedness" she had been able to project, an accurate distillation of the soulless behavior of the actual vampire women of contemporary society.

These creatures were, she emphasized, first of all practical predators, businesswomen. Vampires never lost their heads in their encounters with their quarry. (pt. 2, 86) The "emotional abandon" Theodosia Goodman saw as her main strength as an actress was foreign to Theda Bara, the woman who was Arab Death. The vampires she portrayed were lawless erotic adventurers ("daring, recklessly sensuous, defiantly indiscreet") whose purely physical appetites she could only "intuit," for her success in portraying these women had been "due to an emotional strength in me; an impersonal conception of what the Vampire-woman is." (pt. 2, 88)

In a fascinating "aside" she insisted that, if within the context of civilization and the rules of dimorphic gender evolution, women had no longer any business publicly acknowledging any form of sexual arousal, such feelings nonetheless remained a fact of nature, for secretly "the good little girl is just as bad as the bad little girl is good—so why moralize." But the gender wars were real: "We were born to deceive, it is the way of a woman and a man." Society had taught women to be "charlatans," consummate actresses: "Women deceive themselves too, quite as much as they deceive others; for in imagination they defy all conventions. Why this should be is one of the secrets of the Sphinx." Still, "who can measure accurately the divine distance between what women try to be and what they are intended to be?" (pt. 1, 716)

The vampire was not socially acceptable as a woman because she refused to deceive herself. Her honesty about her own sexuality had allowed her to exploit the "idealizing" sensibility of the male. Although "any woman-of-curves-and-substance" could "look like a vampire-woman," only a very good and properly acculturated (dimorphically evolved) actress (a Theda Bara, clearly) who recognized the "primitive" sources of feminine motivation would be able to *fake* the vampire woman's erotic freedom convincingly.

Goodman, self-proclaimed mystic and faithful consulter of clairvoyants, decided that the "real vampire" who filled the hearts of Aryan industrialists everywhere with fearful lust during the 1910s represented no less than "the return on earth of Venus," pagan goddess of predatory sexual hunger. Kipling, by sketching the vampire as "the woman who did not know" and "could not understand," had failed to give the erotic woman enough credit. "No vampire would ever challenge Kipling. Though he may have inspired the verb 'to vamp,' he has only pointed at the Vampire, identified her type, whereas Swinburne has talked with her, established her age-old origin in Venus." (pt. 1, 716)

With that remark The[o]d[osi]a Goodman-Bara, the woman who had been made to personify Arab Death to her contemporaries by William Fox's publicity machine, demonstrated that she was also an astute literary critic. The interpretation of "pagan beauty" Swinburne had given in his long poem "Laus Veneris" (1866) was indeed not so much a hymn in praise of the goddess as a complex delineation of the *mons veneris,* the *Venusberg,* the "mound of Venus," the much delineated metaphorical perch of the *vagina dentata* of nineteenth-century male masochism—precursor to the "vampire's mouth" of the human praying mantis William Sergeant Kendall exploited in his portrayal of *A Sphinx.*

The archetype of the sexual vampire Theda Bara had found in Swinburne's poetry came to this: love between a man and a woman must always be a predatory exchange. The woman was "stung" into sexual awakening by her reproductive function. The onset of menstruation was brute nature's vampire attack on innocence (a conception soon to be anthropomorphized by Bram Stoker in the figure of Dracula, the primitive blood-lusting erotomane who symbolized the bisexual, pre-evolutionary "reproductive" element in nature: all those bitten by the vampire are "cloned," become vampires themselves, interchangeable "subdivisions" of the mothermonster). Menstruation turned the girl-child into a woman branded by nature with the mark of the vampire: "For her neck, / Kissed over close, wears yet a purple speck / Wherein the pained blood falters and goes out."

The woman now becomes hypnotized by her reproductive task and aroused by its accompanying sexual needs: "Deep sleep has warmed her blood through all its ways." Thus she becomes a creature of pre-Christian ardor. Even men whose lips were once "Stained with blood fallen from the feet of God" now "grow sad with kissing Christ." Enticed by "her clear limbs," they renounce their chance for salvation: "thou didst heal us with thy piteous kiss; / But see now Lord; her mouth is lovelier." Not surprisingly, "every thread" that helps weave the male's doom has in it "dry specks of red." The man bleeds vital essence as he slips into the sexual woman's watery domain.

It would be impossible here to decode all the metaphors and double entendres of Swinburne's very long poem, but in his perambulation of Venus's erotic topography, the poet touches upon virtually every cultural obsession that was to contribute to the creation of the woman-vampire of early-twentieth-century culture. In claiming "Laus Veneris" as the true source of her celluloid persona, Theda Bara therefore showed a remarkable depth of understanding—a genuine insight into the dynamics of the period's theories of "inherent sex-hostility" between males and females. This clearly belies her own decorous contention that she was not a "conscious" but an "intuitive" (and hence "truly feminine") participant in the primordial struggle between nature and culture.

Swinburne, on his part, anticipated Freud's discovery of the "death instinct" by a good fifty years. His generic masculine persona, "Love," the "I" of his poem, exhausted by his infatuation with Venus, yearns to return first to the preconscious, then to the inanimate, state: "would God that stems and roots were bred / Out of my weary body and my head, / That sleep were sealed upon me with a seal, / And I were as the least of all his dead." He fantasizes that he might at least scatter his vital essence to fertilize the earth herself: "Would God my blood were dew to feed the grass." But while he dreams that in this manner his self-destructive passion might be given a constructive function, so "That death were not more pitiful than desire, / That these things were not one thing and the same!" he soberly acknowledges that sex and death are two sides of a single equation that can only find its fateful resolution in the vampire mouth of the sexual woman. Swinburne's Venus, Theda Bara remarked, with brilliant understanding, "is the Vampire of Adonis." (pt. 1, 716)

Swinburne described his vampire-Venus as a creature of insatiable orifices: She "turns his kisses on her lips to sighs, / to sighing sounds of lips unsatisfied." Her "little chambers drip with flower-like red," and "Her gateways smoke with fume of flowers and fires." Poor Adonis does not stand a chance: "Her lips divide him vein by vein." The narrator is hesitant to come near her, "lest the kiss / Leave my lips charred." "There is a feverish famine in my veins," he exclaims: "Sin, is it sin whereby men's souls are thrust / Into the pit?" That pit is, without doubt, the *vagina dentata,* the hell-mouth of the vampire-Venus: "I see the marvellous mouth whereby there fell / Cities and people whom the gods loved well." This queen, "whose face was worth the world to kiss," has the "large pale lips" of Semiramis, the lustful woman who built Babylon. Her lips are "Curled like a tiger's that curl back to feed; / Red only where the last kiss made them bleed." A man tracked by Venus is

> *As one who hidden in deep sedge and weeds*
> *Smells the rare scent made where a panther feeds,*
> *And tracking ever slotwise the warm smell*
> *Is snapped upon by the sweet mouth and bleeds*
> *His head far down the hot sweet breath of her.*

In the end, Swinburne's narrator becomes a willing victim to the vampire-Venus's lustful enticements, feeling "About my neck your hands and hair enwound, / The hands that stifle and the hair that stings, / I felt them fasten sharply without sound." The narrator thereupon waxes "faint with fume of fruitless bowers"—a delicate admission that he has willingly squandered his vital essence out of wedlock upon a strong, sexually self-aware woman who is not about to bear him children.

Clearly Theda Bara knew exactly what Kendall's sphinx was after when she referred her readers to Swinburne's "Laus Veneris" for clues. When she became the cinematic expression of the early-twentieth-century male's nightmare conception of Woman, *any* woman, as vampire, she was therefore far more a conscious actor in the production of these nightmares than she was letting on. She captured the public imagination with lasting force because she was aware of the psychological sources of the masculine fears and desires Fox wanted her to exploit in her films. She had understood "the divine distance between what women try to be and what they are intended to be." To the public this meant that her cinematic persona had chosen sides, had truly become the personification of "Arab Death"—had struck an alliance with all those "primitive," benighted creatures of the non-Western world who had begun to invade the realm of Aryan transcendence and who, instead of being grateful to their masters, were demanding to be paid for their labors in support of the advancement of Western civilization. Theda Bara, the Semitic sexual woman, was therefore a very deliberate female version of Svengali, the hypnotic Jewish invader, and of Dracula, the sadistic yet effeminate vampire. All spelled the same fate to the Aryan male: dysgenic miscegenation. All were sexual terrorists, socialists, subversive agents of "Asia, in the guise of Bolshevism with Semitic leadership and Chinese executioners," emissaries of the continent that, Madison Grant insisted in 1920, in his foreword to Stoddard's *The Rising Tide of Color,* was fomenting a race war against "the Nordic states." (xxxi)

Aryan suspicions of an international "Eurasian" conspiracy had, by 1913, already spawned a new master of evil in Anglo-American culture: "Dr. Fu Manchu, the yellow peril incarnate in one man," as he was described by Sax Rohmer (a pseudonym of the British journalist Arthur Sarsfield Ward). In *The Hand of Fu Manchu* (1917), Rohmer identified his villain as "yellow-robed, immobile, his wonderful, evil face emaciated by illness, but his long, magnetic eyes blazing greenly, as though not a soul but an elemental spirit dwelt within that gaunt, high-shouldered body." Fu Manchu was an Asian Dracula—one of the earliest, and certainly one of the most infamous, incarnations of a new popular villain: the elusive fiend of a thousand disguises—product of irresponsibly mixed blood—constantly moving from place to place, virtually impossible to catch or to destroy; a devious, warped, criminally distorted mastermind whose unspeakable doings, always vaguely defined as politically motivated, were a direct "assault upon western civilization."

The doings of these Lombroso-inspired criminal minds, always surrounded by "she-devil" feminine accomplices and degenerate legions of "alien" followers, were to send chills through untold millions of readers of thousands of pulp-fiction spy-adventure narratives that would, in turn, spawn hundreds of Hollywood movies, to end up, finally, in the pages of post–World War II comic books. Here they became the supervillains who tried to thwart the good deeds of such heroes as Batman, Superman, and Dick Tracy. Today they continue to live on, if now at least on a superficial level racially defanged (though usually still physically deformed, according to nineteenth-century phrenological principles), in the ever more popular movie entertainments based on such comic books, and in numerous James Bond–styled spy dramas, where they are incarnated as sinister, heartless international conspirators.

"Secret and malign forces throbbed about us; forces against which we had no armor," (58) exclaims one of the main defenders of Anglo-Saxon civilization in *The Insidious Dr. Fu Manchu* (1913), the first novel in Rohmer's series. It was a statement that sounded the theme of three-quarters of all twentieth-century American pulp fiction. Fu Manchu was the "elusive invader" of the early twentieth century's race theorists, described by Norman S. Dike in *The Alien in Our Midst* (1930)—a collection of anti-immigration diatribes edited by Madison Grant—as "the alien who shifts his habitat" in order to elude the police. "There is no method of identification. He leaves one locality without regret, and takes up life wherever he finds it most promising." What characterized the "alien" nature of this interloper was that he basked in "the protection that comes from our utter and entire ignorance of his past." (83)

Fu Manchu, the alien invader, represented the immigrants who threatened to undermine the capitalist system of "hereditary continuities." In *Democracy and Liberty* (1896), William Lecky, one of the most highly regarded social historians of the period, insisted "that marriage and the family form the tap-root out of which the whole system of hereditary property grows"; it would "be utterly impossible permanently to extirpate heredity unless family stability and family affection were annihilated." Socialism was the destabilizing factor that might ultimately succeed in doing just that. Lecky was convinced that it had been devised by criminals who had risen from among the lower orders and were determined to reinstitute chaos. But these subversives also knew that the socialist system would "never approve itself to the masses of men unless all the foundations and sanctions of morality have been effectually destroyed." The socialist aim was therefore "to excite the worst passions of ignorant and suffering men." (II, 350)

Fu Manchu, like Dracula before him, was a criminal socialist, a monster who had no respect for the hereditary continuities, the racial "equilibrium," of the evolutionary elite. Also like Dracula, Fu Manchu personified the specter of dysgenic alien infiltration. In *The Rising Tide of Color* (1920), Lothrop Stoddard delineated the territorial ideology of early-twentieth-century race hatred:

> Our country, originally settled almost exclusively by Nordics, was toward the close of the nineteenth century invaded by hordes of immigrant Alpines and Mediterraneans, not to mention Asiatic elements like Levantines and Jews. As a result, the Nordic native American has been crowded out with amazing rapidity by these swarming, prolific aliens, and after two short generations he has in many of our urban areas become almost extinct. (165)

Major Frederick R. Burnham of Los Angeles warned, in *The Alien in Our Midst,* that "the Hawaiian Islands are already lost to us racially and the whole Pacific Coast would have been Asiatic in blood today except for the Exclusion Acts." (48)

If Fu Manchu embodied the "anti-individualistic" threat of the "Asian hordes," he also represented the threat of the Semite, for, as Stoddard's remarks indicate, the racist theorists of the early twentieth century considered Jews to be part of the Asian invasion. A turn-of-the-century French advertisement for the book *En Israël* by Charles Huard and J. Mably showed the caricatured heads of five Jews from different social strata, each clearly displaying what the phrenologists had identified as "criminal" physiognomies. Each also had heavily exaggerated, and thus very sinister-looking, "oriental slit eyes." The one on the far right, a degenerate, long-faced, aristocratic-looking Asian Satan, could have served as a model for Sax Rohmer's stock descriptions of Fu

Poster for En Israël, *1899*

Manchu, or of any number of the sinister agents of the Yellow Peril based on Rohmer's creation who populated the pulps of the Twenties and Thirties. Rohmer, too, portrayed his diabolical criminal as an Asian Shylock:

> Imagine a person, tall, lean and feline, high-shouldered, with a brow like Shakespeare and a face like Satan, a close-shaven skull, and long, magnetic eyes of the true cat-green. Invest him with the cunning of an entire Eastern race, accumulated in one giant intellect, with all the resources of science past and present. (*The Insidious Dr. Fu Manchu,* 17)

Mongrels were the result of an infernal mix of East and West, of "animal instincts" combined with the "debased" remnants of an intelligence that had become "diabolical cunning." Rohmer stressed that the struggle between Fu Manchu and his British opponents, Nayland Smith, a hardy veteran of the British colonial experience, and Petrie, a physician with "the ideas of a modern, ordinary middle-class practitioner," is a struggle between two worlds: "At last they were face to face—the head of the great Yellow Movement, and the man who fought on behalf of the entire white race." (86) The heroes are exemplary exponents of "the clean British efficiency which sought to combat the insidious enemy." (72) They are "the barrier between the White races and the devouring tide of the Yellow." (*The Hand of Fu Manchu,* 65)

In addition, Fu Manchu is artistic, and hence rather effeminate. He

is, in fact, an early version of Nosferatu, F. W. Murnau's vampire of otherness: "The hand that held my arm was bony and clawish; I could detect the presence of incredibly long finger nails—nails long as those of
some buried vampire of the black ages!" (62) He is taloned, a "grasper,"
a parasite, a criminal invert. Rohmer described him habitually in terminology usually reserved by his contemporaries for female sexual predators. He has eyes that are variously "reptilian" or "cat-like"; he speaks in
a "sibilant" voice; and his "gait," too, is both "serpentine" and "feline."
He is both phallic and feminine—a hermaphroditic manifestation of the
dysgenic forces of biological reversion. The defenders of the West could
therefore never sleep:

> Even at that very moment some venomous centipede might be
> wriggling toward me over the slime of the stones, some poison-
> ous spider be preparing to drop from the roof! Fu Manchu
> might have released a serpent in the cellar, or the air be alive
> with microbes of some loathsome disease! (*The Insidious Dr. Fu
> Manchu*, 90)

Not surprisingly, Fu Manchu was always surrounded by seductive
vampire women who, just like the mythical Theda Bara, were always
"Eurasian"—the evil issue of unholy liaisons between degenerate "oriental" men and vulgar white women. These Eurasians were direct descendants of the spermatophagous insects and reptiles described by the
biologists. In *The Insidious Dr. Fu Manchu,* for instance, Dr. Petrie in
vestigates the death of a licentious Schuyler-styled British gentleman
whose quarters are decorated with lurid pictures of women, which
prove it to be the "sanctum of a wealthy bachelor who was no misogynist"—an obvious mistake on his part, for the cause of death turns out
to be a "faint red mark, not unlike the imprint of painted lips." This
vampire bite, "A little mark upon the neck, face, or limb," popularly
termed a "Zayat Kiss," is the work of "a giant centipede," an "insect full
six inches long, and of a vivid, venomous, red color."

Soon after Petrie has discovered the liplike mark on the corpse, he is
accosted by a girl who, though she has "the skin of a perfect blonde,"
has "eyes and lashes as black as a Creole's, which, together with her full
red lips, told me that this beautiful stranger, whose touch had so startled
me, was not a child of our northern shores." She is Eurasian, of course,
and Petrie has an instant epiphany: "The grotesque idea momentarily
possessed me that were the bloom of her red lips due to art and not to

nature, their kiss would leave—though not indelibly—just such a mark as I had seen upon the dead man's hand." (9–21) Thus Rohmer, who in general tried to stick to the delineation of "real vampires" and to steer clear of stories in which women actually became spiders, praying mantises, or snakes, was nonetheless able to suggest the constitutional link between the sexual Eurasian woman and the insect predators of the jungle.

Even so, these Eurasians were generally characterized by what Rohmer in *The Green Eyes of Bast* (1920) was to identify as "psychic-felinism." (277) In *The Insidious Dr. Fu Manchu* he identified these beautiful "mongrels" as "one of the finest weapons in the enemy's armory." (15) Rohmer's descriptions of these predators often read exactly like Porter Emerson Browne's portraits of the Vampire in *A Fool There Was.* Together Browne and Rohmer may be said to have played a deciding role in developing the standard Hollywood iconography of the invasive seductress.

In *The Hand of Fu Manchu,* for instance, the dangerous Eurasian beauty Zarmi is presented to the reader in a set piece that was to find its echo in dozens of Marlene Dietrich seduction scenes of the Thirties and Forties. Indeed, Zarmi (a barmaid) could have been projected straight into Josef von Sternberg's *The Blue Angel* (1930). She was, Rohmer tells us, a "strange creature" with jet-black, frizzy hair, which was entirely innocent of any binding or ornament." She had a "lithe body" and a "sinuous gait," and her voice "had in it the siren lure which is the ancient heritage of the Eastern woman." Not only does she prefigure Dietrich's looks; she also anticipated her mannerisms:

> Zarmi placed the brass tray upon the table and bent down, resting her elbows upon it, her hands upturned and her chin nestling in her palms. The smoke from the cigarette now held in her fingers, mingled with her dishevelled hair. She looked fully into my face, a long, searching look; then her lips parted in the slow, voluptuous smile of the Orient. Without moving her head she turned the wonderful eyes (rendered doubly luminous by the *kohl* with which her lashes and lids were darkened) upon Fletcher. (18)

In Rohmer's voluminous output of adventure narratives the Eurasian woman was invariably the woman with the phallus, the vampire who had gained unlawful control over the masculine gun—or knife. No wonder she was almost invariably also a heavy smoker. In the iconography of early-twentieth-century sin, a cigarette in a woman's hand or mouth was as certain a sign of aggressive sexual promiscuity as a gun or knife. There was only one way in which such a woman could be controlled by Aryans (other than being killed outright for her transgressions, as Zarmi ultimately is). The knowledgeable colonialist Nayland Smith teaches a still somewhat timid Dr. Petrie this method in *The Insidious Dr. Fu Manchu:* the Eurasian woman, Smith informs Petrie, "would submit to capture by you if you would only seize her by the hair, drag her to some cellar, hurl her down and stand over her with a whip. . . . And she would adore you for your savagery, deeming you forceful and strong!" (80) The Eurasian, then, is a Kiplingesque leper woman, a "half-savage," a "mongrel," who must be whipped into submission. The male must take the phallus of primitive sexuality from her with whatever force necessary, and if there is any decency left in her, she will thank him for it. In that sense she comes to stand for all women—and all "Orientals"—in Rohmer's universe: man must conquer them, or they will take over the world.

Fu Manchu is the undisputed leader of this army of subversives. A diabolical cousin of Dracula, constitutionally effeminate and thus, according to the period's mathematics of atavistic traits, in a semibiological manner father to all masculinized Eurasian women (for female men had "given up" too much of their manhood in siring manly women), his appearances in the novels were usually brief. His female minions did most of the actual invading. For three decades he ruled the public imagination with his schemes for world conquest, always surrounded by flocks of these aggressive creatures, who, in turn, were most often directed in their attacks upon civilized manhood by the actual daughter of the marriage between Asia and evil. In *Daughter of Fu Manchu* (1931) this petal from a poisonous lotus mouths the invasive desires attributed to the Yellow Peril by Madison Grant and Lothrop Stoddard almost word for word. While her "magnetic fingers" are busy "soothing" the narrator's "hot brow" (these Eurasians did everything they could to get to the Aryan's store of vital essence), she gives him a thumbnail sketch of her political plans: "Her strange soul was wrapped up in world politics. Russia, that great land 'stolen by fools,' was ripe for her purpose. . . ." Once she had captured it, she would be poised to take over the world "backed by a New Russia, which then would be part and parcel of Asia—'*my* Asia . . .'" (104)

Rohmer's Eurasian female terrorists were always unrepentant spermatophages, dominatrices, updated versions of H. Rider Haggard's She Who Must Be Obeyed. Whether they appeared in the Fu Manchu series or in one of his numerous analogous novels, they were always prototypes of the characteristic twentieth-century pulp temptress. The description Rohmer gives of her in *The Yellow Claw* (1915) could be used interchangeably for her reappearance, in one guise or another, throughout dozens of his subsequent novels. Versions of this creature also played decoratively dangerous roles in thousands of volumes of a similar nature written by others, and in numerous Hollywood movies of the Twenties and Thirties. These were to provide gainful employment to stars such as Nita Naldi, Anna May Wong, and even a young, "Orientalized" Myrna Loy: "She wore a Chinese costume; a huge red poppy was in her hair. Her beauty was magnificently evil; she had the grace of a gazelle and the eyes of a sorceress." Like Haggard's two-thousand-year-old African She and Burroughs's La, the woman of ancient Atlantis, these Eurasians invariably had "witch-eyes wherein burnt ancient wisdom." (277) The Aryan ideologues had things worked out quite neatly: the evolutionary elite was gifted with "masculine reason," but evidence of intelligence among "inferiors" was mere "cunning," a sinister expression of primordial "feminine" instincts.

Rohmer in this manner always provided his readers with masochistic dreams of sexual involvement with the miscegenated Eurasian secret weaponry of Fu Manchu. But he also always took care to have the invasive sexual woman neutralized by his Aryan heroes before she could do any major damage. Sometimes, as in the case of his hero Nayland Smith's Karamandeh, she renounced her evil past to become a more devoted domestic slave than any dimorphically evolved woman of the Aryan master race. Such (rare) conquests crowned Rohmer's heroes' efforts to save Western civilization:

> Rebellion blazed up in her wonderful eyes instantly—and as quickly was gone, leaving them exquisitely bright. Two tears, like twin pearls, hung upon the curved black lashes. It made my blood course faster to watch this lovely Eastern girl conquering the barbaric impulses that sometimes flamed up in her, because *I* willed it; indeed this was a miracle that I never tired of witnessing. (*The Hand of Fu Manchu*, 85)

Generally speaking, however, the Rohmer Eurasian was virtually always a woman of death, who, as in *The Yellow Claw*, lives primarily to

Anna May Wong

tempt the Anglo-Aryan male "to gather the witch to his breast; to return that poisonous, that vampirish kiss, and then to crush out life from
the small lithe body." Indeed, sex, reproduction, and death were always
conflated among these spermatophages and their vengeful victims:

> "Oh, my beautiful dead-baby," she said, softly, and her voice was
> low, and weirdly sweet. "Oh, my new baby, how I love you, my
> dead one!" Again she laughed, a musical peal. "I will creep to
> you in the poppyland where you go . . . and you shall twine
> your fingers in my hair and pull my red mouth down to you,
> kissing me . . . kissing me, until you stifle and you die of my
> love. . . . Oh! my beautiful mummy-baby . . . my baby." (277)

Passages of this sort occur with astonishing frequency in early-
twentieth-century fiction—and certainly not only in the writings of
pop-fiction authors such as Rohmer. They are just as likely to be found
in the pages of a Nobel Prize winner like William Faulkner. When they
occur in such high-rent environments, critics tend to develop complex,
psychoanalytically based interpretations showing that the author in
question tapped into "universal" emotions expressive of the "archetypal" alliance between love and death in the human mind. But the
praying-mantis women of the period were, as this passage from Rohmer
clearly indicates, not merely "intuitive" expressions of "universal psychological conditions." Whether or not such universals in fact exist (be
they biological or psychological) is likely to remain a continuing topic
of legitimate debate. But the negative effects of the patently tendentious
and manipulative would-be "biological truths" about female sexual motivation uncovered by turn-of-the-century scientists are demonstrable
and incontrovertible. They had an immediate ideological influence on
men's conception of the feminine. These men *learned* to see sexuality as
a battlefield, a sadistic feast of fangs and whips. They *learned* to believe
that love could only lead to death, and that pleasure was another word
for economic incontinence. Those of us today who still measure love in
terms of the pain it brings to ourselves or to others are still political
prisoners of imperialist economics. The Vampire Lestat and his violent
pop-culture minions are not erotic revolutionaries but contemporary
businessmen with late Victorian dental work.

As we shall see, moreover, the social pressures of the early twentieth
century encouraged the average person to recognize the invasive polymorphous perversity of the sexual woman as a seductive expression

of the economic "effeminacy" of "the lower orders." The medically proven causal relationship between sexual intimacy and death made the "real vampires" of seminal spending into subversive operatives in the war between capitalism and "regressive" collectivism. In both the sexual and the economic realm, the middle-class male found himself required to share the temple of his body with an invasive other who brought death into his world. The sexual woman and the Bolshevik had fused in the evil beauty of the Eurasian temptress who was both a vampire and a socially subversive emissary of the "lower orders." This erotic terrorist demanded that the middle-class male let himself be drained of his vital essence (by "kissing me, until you stifle and you die of my love"). Once turned into her mummy (an artificially "dehydrated" corpse symboliz-ing the living dead), a paralyzed victim of the "lower orders," he must become a "new baby," a new recruit to the principles of miscegenation and collectivism, a "degenerated" being, *her* baby. Thus, by giving in to the Eurasian vampire, the evolutionary male lost his identity, his "indi-vidualism," and his hope for immortality. He now became a depredated, sterile "mummy baby" to the masculinized daughters of collectivism— who were themselves, in turn, the spawn of the "feminized masculin-ity" of the invader, the "evil being born of that secret quickening which stirred in the womb of the yellow races," as Rohmer put it. (*The Insidi-ous Dr. Fu Manchu,* 184)

The fact that Rohmer's politically subversive and economically voracious Fu Manchu was a Shylock in Oriental disguise made him all the more threatening as an alien interloper. His "criminal semitic effem-inacy" identified him as the biological missing link between the sexual woman and the "lower races." In *The Alien in Our Midst* Lothrop Stod-dard emphasized the alliance between Bolsheviks, Semites, and Asians. He warned that Eastern Europe was

> afflicted by a profound mongrelism revealing its disturbing effect in every phase of political and social life. It is next door to Asia, and periodically for two thousand years Asiatic hordes swept over it, upsetting its political and social equilibrium and diluting and mongrelizing its blood. The "Slavic" peoples who occupy most of Eastern Europe are all impregnated with Asiatic Mon-gol and Turki blood.

Impregnation, miscegenation, dilution: the Slavs were the "mummy-babies" of the Asian vampire.

Stoddard explained his contention that Eastern European Jews were Asians as follows: they are "not Semitic 'hebrews,' but are descended from West Asian stocks akin to the Armenians, and from a Central Asiatic (Mongoloid) folk, the Khazars." (227–8) In the same collection of essays, C. M. Goethe insisted that North America would still be a wasteland had it not been for the Aryans: "These strong ones, masterful Nordics, came. They conquered The Desert. But for whom?" (136) Henry Fairfield Osborn, president of the American Museum of Natural History (apparently a hotbed of Nordic pride: Madison Grant was on the Board of Trustees), was quite willing to answer that question, also in *The Alien in Our Midst*. The strong ones had done all the work so that effeminate Jews could move in and carry away the spoils, he wrote. "The entire control of the 'movie' industry and the larger part of the control of the stage industry in the United States are now in the hands of people of near or remote Oriental origin." The original Aryan principles of Americanism had been "alienated" (Osborn was an etymological literalist) from their roots by degenerate Oriental and decadent European influences. A "spiritual, moral and political invasion of *alienism*" in "some sections of the daily and weekly press, in the 'movies' and on the stage" had made Aryan survival "turn upon the struggle for existence between the Americans and the aliens whose actions are controlled by entirely different standards of living and of morals." "True Americanism" must gear up for a biological war—a war it was bound to win, Osborn confidently asserted, as long as the Nordic American stood firm and boldly withstood "the appeals of false humanitarianism and false sentimentality." (208–9)

The spawn of Fu Manchu, Eurasian sexual vampires, and their Semitic allies, Bolsheviks disguised as media moguls, were thus poised to overrun the world quite as melodramatically in the political imagination of the race theorists as in the pages of the period's favorite novelists. No barrier stood between them and world conquest other than the Western European and American white male's ability to withstand the hypnotic power of the sexual vampire. The Aryan male's seminal continence was all that kept civilization from being overrun by the agents of effeminacy ("false humanitarianism and false sentimentality"). But though this realization may have given the intellectuals sleepless nights, many of the evolutionary elite's rank and file clearly enjoyed the titillation provided by the imaginary "real" women of biomedically informed artists and writers. Popular culture became obsessed with the degenerative impulse to be found in every woman. But as Theda Bara had already intimated, most women, in turn, were readily seduced by the fantasies of power provided by the exploits of these interesting "real" vampires who syphoned off men's souls and turned them into "mummy-babies."

However, even if the general public did not seem unduly alarmed by the image of woman as vampire and by suggestions that she might be a "weapon" in the various wars of class, race, and gender, the vicious images of dark and deadly, catlike, man-eating women, effeminate Bolshevik Semites, and freakishly deformed mongrel races were nevertheless having a dramatic effect upon the average person's understanding of the nature of interpersonal relationships. Throughout the Twenties and Thirties proudly—and loudly—professed racial intolerance combined with brutal antifeminine rhetoric became a mark of good taste among the stylish. Concepts such as democracy and equal rights were declared to be dreams for fools, Bolsheviks, and naive humanists. The Darwinian "struggle for life among nations," which had offered the imperialist powers a satisfactory explanation for the carnage of World War I, soon began to make way for a more concrete and seemingly even more pressing "struggle for life among races," which set the stage for the genocidal realities of World War II.

The female sexual vampire, the early-twentieth-century male's unruly, self-consciously erotic evil sister, thus proved to be a product of the same general set of pseudoscientific principles that produced the threat of the mongrel invader. She once again ceased being the girl next door, this time to become a racial temptress, the sinister half sister of "degenerates." Both she and the immigrant hordes were agents of collectivism—that Semitic invention of a man named Karl Marx, who had made the call of "woman-rule" once again echo through civilization. Popular culture eagerly emphasized this link. Thus the sexual vampire became a political subversive who threatened the very survival of economic individualism.

Increasingly convoluted cultural obsessions such as this made the acculturated, dimorphically evolving women of the past a boring subject for early-twentieth-century audiences. Their tenacious determination to stand by their men, no matter what kind of moral or intellectual halfwits these men happened to be, had become an implicit social duty. But the seminal vampires made virtue look like just another household chore. The ever virginal wife might bear the future of the world on her shoulders, but she was not much fun to be with. Moreover, the newest intellectual fashion was to revolt against the "Puritan" past. Therefore one Lillian Gish was sufficient to draw out a whole flock of vampires. People rarely showed signs of remembering the "good" woman in a novel, play, or movie: the self-effacing woman was, by the very nature of her function, an invisible woman. In "high" culture, no less than in movie melodramas, good women were becoming little more than window dressing—unconvincing foils to the sexual vampire, the source of every man's dreams and fears.

The biopolitics of the first Darwinian era therefore forced the women of the 1910s and 1920s to exist in a highly paradoxical environment. Virtue was rewarded with invisibility, while vampirism got all the press. They were supposed to be helpless, but the practical economic realities of the period demanded that they learn to look after themselves. Theodosia Goodman, for instance, "being a feminist, convinced that a woman's private life should be economically sound before she should indulge in her own romantic impulses," was thrilled to discover "a public that would support me." ("How I Became a Film Vampire," pt. 2, 85) But to reach economic independence, she had to act out "sensuous impressions" she did not feel. And when she did what was expected of her, she would be denounced as a man-eating sexual animal, incapable of "romantic impulses."

To be accepted as an actress, therefore, she had to deny any *actual* interest in sensuous experience, even though, as a woman, her visibility in society depended on her constant enactment of a wide variety of such physical desires. But as she tried to deny any erotic feelings in her role-playing, she would find within herself precisely those erotic feelings she was so busy denying. "It may be that in every woman there is *Carmen* and *Cleopatra, Juliet* and *Salome.* In me they are frankly predestined," (pt. 2, 88) she finally admitted. She had come to terms with her realization that even the good girls of Western civilization were, in spirit, "bad girls" after all. But the Fox organization was not willing to countenance such complex perceptions in its favorite moneymaker. It was willing to grant that Theda Bara, properly brought to domestic submission (as she was in a variety of roles), could become a lordly Aryan's faithful Eurasian household slave, but it was resolutely set against having her play any roles that might reveal the existence of any latent psychological vampirism in a Lillian Gish–styled Western woman. As a result, her "real vampire" repertoire rapidly came to seem one-sided and dated. By 1921 her career was over.

The women of the early twentieth century, required by the bio-medical wisdom of the dominant ideology to behave like simpletons even while they knew themselves to be intelligent and practical—to be-have like virtuous household nuns while they recognized their yearning for sexual pleasure—thus found themselves surrounded by inescapable emotional and intellectual contradictions. These had been created by men who, afraid of sex but obsessed with it, longed to see the women in their lives as sexual beings, yet feared them when they freely expressed desire. In the end the woman was even blamed for not being a "real woman" whenever she tried to be what the men expected her to be. No wonder Freud discovered "penis-envy": being a man was, under such conditions, indeed a lot less conducive to "hysteria." That most women managed to maintain a modicum of sanity within this hostile social en-vironment is one of the still largely unsung miracles of the twentieth century—far more surprising than that some among them learned to manipulate the men's prevailing obsession to their own economic ad-vantage as efficiently as the vamps of the movies.

The "gold diggers" of the Twenties and Thirties, Theda Bara's do-mesticated vampire daughters, were an inevitable creation of early-twentieth-century social ideology. Most of these women were not heartless predators but laconic mirrors to men's minds; like Theda Bara, they became sexual entrepreneurs and dream merchants (which was why Hollywood became so obsessed with them: they were practical role models to the entertainment industry). The actresses who learned they could achieve a semblance of power by playing into men's erotic fan-tasies, much as Theodosia Goodman did when she became the person-ification of Arab Death, all knew they were playing parts in scenarios scripted by men. This knowledge helped them keep illusion and reality separate in the ever more baroque world of twentieth-century gender relationships. However, Theda Bara, the mystical—yet levelheaded—feminist of 1920, would no doubt be dumbfounded to find her vampire "role-playing" (that economically expedient concession to male fan-tasies) being turned into a form of "self-expression" by some of today's "revisionist" feminists.

The prevailing modernist temper of this century has encouraged us to believe that there is no causative link between art and social behavior, that art taps deeper sources of human motivation. But is there anyone who actually still believes that the "virtual reality" of the movies and television, with its relentless glorification of the masterful ejaculations of the man who rules with his gun, has had no influence on the mortality rate of inner-city youths? Theda Bara knew that the medium that made her fortune had also painted her into a corner. She pointed out that even if movie directors relentlessly pursued realism, this did not keep the cinema from being "an art of lies, because it is limited to primitive impulses, to barren emotions; because it is a record of the feverish pulse of life, instead of the normal pulse." (pt. 2, 90) Virtual reality, she emphasized, was a dangerous thing precisely because it seemed so real and was therefore all too easily mistaken for truth. A relentlessly repeated fiction all too often becomes a social reality in the long run. The vampire woman was a figment of the male misogynist imagination. To make her a positive erotic-fantasy figure expressive of "female sexuality" or of "the feminine creative imagination" is merely to solidify one of the most meretricious creations of turn-of-the-century misogyny.

Early-twentieth-century moviemakers, on their part, had come to understand very quickly that to reach the widest possible public, they should play into the socially directed fantasies of women as well as men. The movies enhanced the dreams, superstitions, and prejudices of the public by making these turn into reality before their very eyes. Fox and his cohorts understood that they had struck a gold mine when they began to show women as heartless erotic predators. By using the discoveries of science to equate female sexuality with the habits of the black widow spider and the praying mantis, they contributed immeasurably to the public's paranoia about gender relationships and "race-suicide."

Even so, by the beginning of the Twenties the "real" vampires of the World War I years had become so predictable in their one-dimensional simplicity of motive that the public was clearly beginning to get tired of watching their generally ham-fisted performances. The increasing social banality of their depredations had caused this flock of vampires to lose a good part of their credibility. The moral shock value that had made them so fascinating to moviegoers was gone. The public was ready to be titillated by even more explicit examples of the sexual woman's power over fools. The brief historical moment during which a woman could be regarded as a "real" vampire simply for showing an interest in sex was already passing. But the half-dozen years during which she reigned supreme would continue to cast their shadow over popular entertainment throughout the rest of the century. She was to live on almost unchanged to this very day as the stock "vamp" of thousands of movies and novels, and she became the standard evil woman of pulp fiction—an all-purpose blend of adolescent male-fantasy demons concocted by writers such as Sax Rohmer and Edgar Rice Burroughs, and further enhanced by the public's visual memory of Theda Bara's kohl-eyed appetites.

Increasingly convoluted cultural politics would require the sexual woman to take on a broader aura of "psychological" reality, to become "Freudian" in her motivation, so that she could appeal to the fantasies of the "sexually sophisticated" intellectuals of the Twenties. This psychological transformation encouraged an odd form of cellular self-division among the "real" vampires of the war years. Some returned to being creatures of direct fantasy: soulless, fanged, female animals (or insects, as the case might be). Others became spies—"Eurasian" terrorists. But most settled into being very average women, "innocents" unaware of their medical status as vampires but driven by mysterious forces in nature to depredate the vital economic essence of the middle-class male: Barbara Stanwyck was getting ready to buy a double-indemnity policy from a traveling salesman at just about the time Nosferatu had transformed himself into Jew Süss.

In the realm of fantasy the predatory vampire woman remained firmly linked with the imperial male's mixture of longing and fear for the "undiscovered territories" of the "primitive" world, just as she had been in Joseph Conrad's *Heart of Darkness*. The islands, rivers, and caves of as yet unconquered territories came to be equated with the mysterious cavities of the feminine body. In the minds of the early-twentieth-century colonizers, unknown lands exerted an attraction that seemed analogous to the erotic lure and unexplored temptations of the sexual (and hence "primitive") woman. Abraham Merritt, the period's most celebrated writer of "lost race" fantasies, proved this to be the case in no uncertain terms in the opening paragraphs of his novel *The Moon Pool* (1919). He showed that the same dangers lurked in the topography of not yet "civilized" lands as in the physiology of woman. "Papua" is an island, but the author's description turns it into a metaphor of universal femininity, in which the island becomes "she"—still another member of the She/La tribe of womb-driven primal feminine terrorists:

> Over the island brooded a spirit sullen, alien, implacable, filled with the threat of latent, malefic forces waiting to be unleashed. It seemed an emanation out of the untamed, sinister heart of Papua herself—sinister even when she smiles. And now and then, on the wind, came a breath from virgin jungles, laden with unfamiliar odours, mysterious and menacing. It is on such

mornings that Papua whispers to you of her immemorial an-
cientness and of her power. And, as every white man must, I
fought against her spell. (3)

The psychological analogues between the lure of "virgin" lands and
the siren-call of the "unevolved" sexual woman as an island of mystery
in the male imagination have rarely been expressed as effectively. The
book was Merritt's first novel of science and fantasy. An early section
had run in the June 22, 1918, issue of *All-Story Weekly*, the same magazine that made Edgar Rice Burroughs and Tarzan famous. *The Moon Pool*
created a sensation. In a recent account of Merritt's life, Sam Moskowitz
noted that many readers appear to have thought that the narrative was an
account of a real expedition. This suggests that Merritt had struck a
gender-ideological nerve. The author promptly wrote a six-installment
continuation, which was also published in *All-Story Weekly*, and subsequently, together with the original story, published as a book. Its popularity launched Merritt—a journalist (and real estate developer) who, in
1937, became the influential editor in chief of *The American Weekly*—on
a highly successful career as a writer of such "lost race" romances. Most
of these became classics of fantasy literature and have remained in print
virtually continuously ever since.

Merritt's influence on other writers of science fiction and fantasy
was to be enormous. Immediately after World War II, when his characteristic blend of anti-Bolshevist and antifeminine chauvinism seems to
have struck a particularly sensitive chord among American readers, his
popularity reached paperback best-seller proportions. Between the late
1940s and the early 1980s, paperback versions of *The Moon Pool* and the
half-dozen analogous narratives that followed it (with titles such as *The
Ship of Ishtar, The Metal Monster*, and *The Face in the Abyss*) each sold in
the millions of copies. By this time, however, Merritt's conscious use of
the medical theories that identified women as natural vampires of masculine essence had been long forgotten, and the author's narratives
instead came to be seen as proto-Jungian, "intuitive" expressions of
timeless, universal, psychological archetypes residing in the "collective
unconscious" of humanity. It is in such a fashion that the tendentious
speculations of science become psychoanalytic "truths."

The Moon Pool was intended to be *science* fiction: a heavily symbolic
exploration of the dangers that beset the masculine explorer of the uncharted territories of the feminine earth. Each woman-island, Merritt

suggested, was transformed into a mysterious door into the past by the energies of the moon. In their attempt to unravel the mysteries of the world, his explorers are quite literally made to enter into the body of Earth, the Great Mother. The moment the civilized female members of this group set foot on Papua, the island of primal femininity, they intuit their own link to the precivilized past. Thora, a Wagnerian Nordic goddess, "tall, deep-breasted, moulded on the old Viking lines," who "looked like some ancient priestess of Odin" (16), instantly registers "a curious sensitivity to what, I suppose, may be called the 'influence' of the place." (14)

The entrance into the body of the primal earth is an opening in a "moonrock" with a mysterious shape. Thora "cast herself upon its breast, hands and face pressed against it; we heard her scream as though her very soul were being drawn from her—and watched her fall at its foot." In the moonlight impulses related to primitive bisexuality overtake her. She experiences an "unhuman mingling of opposites," of impulses long suppressed by civilization. (20)

The moon rock itself, evidently aroused by all this reciprocal stimulation, splits open to reveal a quasi-vaginal entrance into the earth and a tunnel whose anatomical correctness is completed by a womblike basin at its lower end: "It was circular, perhaps twenty feet wide. Around it ran a low, softly curved lip of glimmering silvery stone. Its water was palest blue. The pool with its silvery rim was like a great blue eye staring upward." (29)

In the scene that follows Merritt wanted his readers to bear witness to an act of cosmic sexual intercourse. Into the circular Moon Pool "streamed seven shafts of radiance," which "poured down upon the blue eye like cylindrical torrents; they were like shining pillars of light rising from a sapphire floor." Even the seminal-nutrition theory is brought in: "the shafts did not illumine the depths. They played upon the surface and seemed there to diffuse, to melt into it. The Pool drank them!" (29) Clearly this pool was a true daughter of the moon, an example of the African womb in action: "It had grown milky, opalescent. The rays gushing into it seemed to be filling it." Soon a climax is near. "Over the surface of the Pool was a pulsating pillar of opalescent mist steadily growing stronger." The womb pool waits. "Into its center was passing the luminescence rising from the far depths. And the pillar glowed, throbbed—began to send out questing swirls and tendrils———." From this elemental marriage of moonlight and a mysterious, semen-like gray fluid that is not water but "vital" and "striated, streaked as though little living, pulsing veins ran through it," (76) emanates a shape that "was neither man nor woman; it was unearthly and androgynous." (31) This is the "Dweller" in the Moon Pool—but S/he disappears as soon as the moonlight that energizes the "pulsating pillar" loses its strength. "Moonlight," the narrator declares sententiously, "is, of course, reflected sunlight. But the rays which pass back to earth after their impact on the moon's surface are profoundly changed." (59)

The significance of this cosmic act of reproduction does not immediately reveal itself. Instead, the explorers are propelled into a gigantic dark cavern. This earth-womb is mother to the moon of sexuality: "Such a space in mother earth as we just glimpsed, how else could it have been torn but by some gigantic birth—like that of the moon?" Indeed, "it was not inconceivable that a film had drawn over the world wound, a film of earth-flesh which drew itself over that colossal abyss after our planet had borne its satellite—that the world womb did not close when her shining child sprang forth." After all, "the earth is child of the sun, as the moon is earth's daughter." (84) Passages such as this show that Merritt's tale was not an intuitive expression of archetypal symbols but a very self-conscious, would-be "scientific" exploration of the "earth body" of the primal feminine.

Indeed, Merritt wanted to make it clear to his readers that his Anglo-Saxon heroes' journey back to the primal womb had an immediate sociopolitical significance. He wanted to expose the hidden agenda of the androgynous "Dweller" in the womb pool of the primal feminine. The moon, as Mother Earth's first daughter, was also her most primitive creation—a product of cosmic "cell division." Hence, though clearly "feminine," it contained all the brute self-preserving tendencies of the life force at its most primitive: it was a true manifestation of humanity's bisexual ("androgynous") origins. In these early stages of primal sentience, the "feminine" element had dominated. The evolutionary biologists had established as much: "The male is an accident: the female would have sufficed. Brilliant as are the destinies of the male in certain animal species, the female is primordial," (43) Remy de Gourmont had said. Merritt's moon was the source of "woman-rule."

Thus, unwittingly, the sun, the masculine principle, and the earth, the reproductive womb of nature, had spawned the moon, Diana, the warrior, reflector of the sun's light, subverter of masculine creativity, "earth's daughter," the evil sister, the degenerative temptress, the dysgenic vampire of man's intellectual vitality. The moon was the death instinct itself, a product of the primordial reproductive drive of all organisms. When fused with the instinct for self-preservation—the aggressive, creative ("evolutionary"), "masculine" element—it took the form of a voracious monster, reproductive and destructive at once: it became the Dweller in the Moon Pool, primitive bisexuality made visible to the naked eye.

As if to forestall any later Jungian "archetypal" interpretations, *The Moon Pool* provided its readers with an extensive pedagogic recapitulation of the latest scientific theories concerning the origins of life. Merritt stressed that his narrative was based on "the idea of Arrhenius, the great Swede, of life starting on earth through the dropping of minute, life *spores,* propelled through space by the driving power of light." This solar "ejaculation" had been the source of "man and every other living thing we know." In the early stages of evolutionary development "all the face of the earth was covered with waters in which lived only tiny, hungry things that knew naught save hunger and its satisfaction." These primitive self-reproductive omniphages ("things which had begun as little more than tiny hungry mouths") in the course of the ages evolved into gigantic saurians, voracious in their matriarchal appetites. They were essentially ambulant devouring mouths, inhabitants of a primordial Jurassic Park, exclusively driven by the binary forces of eros and thanatos. (232–3) To illustrate that point, Merritt offered his readers a "frog woman" from the subterranean world: she "stood upright, her great legs bowed; the monstrous slit of a mouth slightly open, revealing a row of white teeth sharp and pointed as lancets." (80)

In the end, the creative influence of Father Sun, the original spore donor, had succeeded in establishing a creative counterpoint to the reproductive fervor of the primordial feminine. His energy made it possible for certain evolving beings to "conquer light—light that sprang at their bidding from the nothingness that gives birth to all things" ("nothingness" was the feminine principle, Weininger had pointed out some fifteen years earlier). This light was "self-realization," "consciousness." It signified the ascendancy of the masculine intellect.

This higher species grew into a "trinity" of supremely wise beings. Their masculine predominance expressed itself in a very Weiningeresque mathematical fashion: two were male, one female. The female's function, among this trio of middle-class sages, however, was strictly limited to the expression of motherly concerns and chaste conjugal sentiments: she was a true wonder of dimorphic gender evolution. But even so, her irrepressible womanly urge to reproduce, Merritt intimated, had led this evolutionary trinity to the creation of its own monster of reversion.

With the fatal hubris of scientists still partially deluded by feminine impulses, the Three, having brought "consciousness" to the Kipling-esque benighted creatures of the inner earth, "took counsel after this and said—'We have strengthened life in these until it has become artic-ulate; shall we not *create* life?'" Their hubris was punished with a return to the days of matriarchal evil, for they unwisely created the androgy-nous "Dweller" the travelers encountered in the realm of the Moon Pool: "Within the Universal Mother we shaped it, to be a voice to tell us her secrets, a lamp to go before us lighting the mysteries." The crea-ture's bisexuality was formed half with "the soul of light" and half with "the essence of life that ye saw blossoming deep in the abyss and that is the pulse of earth." (234–5)

But what the travelers had seen in that abyss was the feminine prin-ciple twice intensified, as it were, a womb *inside* the womb of the earth—primal femininity at its most dangerous and uncontrollable. Crossing a bridge over this witches' cauldron, the narrator had seen only despair: "I gazed down into depth upon vertiginous depth; an abyss in-deed—an abyss dropping to a world base like that in which the Babylo-nians believed writhed Talaat, the serpent mother of Chaos; a pit that struck down into earth's heart itself." (198)

This "feminine" element—blind instinct—inevitably turns the "Dweller" in the Moon Pool into a "debased" spermatophage. In trying to create life, the Three have rekindled the primordial energies of the feminine, the chaos of unorganized nature. Like all such nightmares of raw femininity unleashed in twentieth-century fiction, the Dweller soon breaks away from the Trinity's control and sets up its own domain, that of the Moon Pool. The Dweller, we now realize, is Merritt's ver-sion of Sax Rohmer's invasive Eurasian. The Trinity of the Intellect has, in its scientific hubris, resuscitated the vampire of vital essence.

Invigorated by moonlight, this androgynous creature is eugenics turned inside out—genetics gone wild, a voraciously self-cloning or-ganism from the earth's distant past. The Dweller is a vital-energy eater with a monstrous appetite. It incessantly vampirizes human beings:

> The core of the Shining One waxed—growing greater—as it consumed, as it drew into and through itself the life-force of these lost ones! So they spun, interlaced—and there began to pulse from them life, vitality, as though the very essence of na-

ture was filling us. Dimly I recognized that what I was behold-
ing was vampirism inconceivable! (141)

Numerous plot details now begin to intertwine in Merritt's convoluted narrative. Global politics weighed heavily on the author's mind.
Marakinoff, a Bolshevik terrorist—Merritt's version of Fu Manchu—
has managed to join the expedition. He recognizes the bisexual Dweller,
"the Shining One," as collectivism's ideal weapon in its conquest of the
civilized world. He therefore establishes a lewd alliance with Yolara,
priestess of the Dweller in the Moon Pool. Yolara is a standard-issue
man-eating spider of regressive feminine lust:

> The silken webs that half covered, half revealed her did not hide
> the ivory whiteness of her flesh nor the sweet curve of shoul-
> ders and breasts. But for all her amazing beauty, she was—sinis-
> ter! There was cruelty about the curving mouth, and in the
> music of her voice—not conscious cruelty, but the more terri-
> fying, careless cruelty of nature itself. (94)

In the end, however, as could be expected, these forces of evil are defeated by the chaste love that blooms between Lakla of the netherworld,
a fine specimen of passive acculturated femininity, and O'Keefe, a muscular Irishman, Rodin's *Thinker* with a sword, who is Merritt's version
of the golden Anglo-Aryan superman. The radiant aura of their devotion to each other proves sufficient to drive the Dweller back into the
mouth of chaos and free the world from regression.
    Virtually all of Merritt's subsequent novels and tales were to be in-
genious variations on this premise. They helped organize the fantasy
world of several generations of American boys and young men. The
hugely influential horror and fantasy magazine *Weird Tales* (1923–54)
soon began to mine the same field of symbolic adventure fiction. Like
Jack Williamson's "The Wand of Doom," such stories were always
full of sexual vampires, pulsating "worms," as well as an amazing flora
and fauna of man-eating flowers, spiders, and countless other death-
dealing insects. Hordes of degenerates, "mongrel races," and "diabolical
orientals" were also let loose upon the minds of eager, well-educated
young American males. The movies translated all this symbolism into
"virtual reality" for the masses. For neither Merritt's work nor the often
astonishingly sophisticated language and range of symbolical reference
of the best among the *Weird Tales* writers would have been easily acces-

Frank R. Paul (1884–1963), cover of Amazing Stories,
vol. 2, no. 6, September 1927

The calyxes of the same flowers that inspired some of the
most beautiful of Georgia O'Keeffe's abstractions held no
promise but death for most early-twentieth-century males.

sible to the rank-and-file readers of pulp fiction. Still, Merritt, *Weird Tales,* and other such publications can be said to have played a major role in contextualizing the scientists' biological discoveries in the fields of race and sex to an important, self-selected group of aspiring young mainstream writers and college-age males with febrile imaginations.

A number of these well-educated pulp-fiction readers, moreover, were to develop into the elite among fantasy and science fiction writers of the Forties and Fifties. The Merritt–*Weird Tales* legacy can therefore be seen as a major formative element in the thematic development of twentieth-century popular culture. In 1949–50, during the last days of the pulp-fiction era, just before these magazines were done in by television and comic books, there even appeared five issues of *A. Merritt's Fantasy Magazine,* an (unsuccessful) attempt to cash in on the popularity of this author (who had died in 1943). The latinate, baroque complexity of Merritt's language ultimately caused him to lose the larger part of his audience by the 1980s. Even educated young men by then no longer had the verbal skills to understand his flowery use of early-twentieth-century scientific information. Most retreated into watered-down *Star Trek* versions of Merritt-styled material, while *The Uncanny X-Men* and other such comic books have continued to crank out versions of "the Shining One" and his Yolara.

James Branch Cabell's *Jurgen* (1919) was another hugely influential, elegantly symbolic, erudite narrative that lost much of its readership when television began to make the practice of *reading* fantasy obsolete. Cabell's book, like Merritt's, was an elaborately symbolic narrative of a journey into the primal body of woman to find the vampire of seminal essence. *Jurgen* was a complex satire against women driven by a sensibility not unlike that underlying H. L. Mencken's *In Defense of Women,* which had been published just a year earlier.

It would be impossible to summarize the baroque twists and turns of Cabell's ironic, often flippant account of the adventures of the pawnbroker Jurgen in the subterranean realm of feminine perversity and foolishness, where he searches for his wife, whom the Devil has made disappear at Jurgen's behest. At first, content to let her be gone, Jurgen lives alone. When his neighbors take to gossiping about her disappearance, he begins to make halfhearted efforts to bring her back. To do so, he must enter the hellish cave of female sexuality.

Once he has entered the deep, dark body of the feminine, he encounters virtually every turn-of-the-century symbol of sexual abandon. A centaur, symbolic of primitive, prehuman masculinity, becomes his guide into this world of wombs: "In a trice Jurgen was on the Centaur's back and the two of them had somehow come out of the cave, and were crossing Amneran ["amnion"?] Heath." (10)

In this manner Cabell set up a symbolic narrative that allowed him to satirize the attitudes of a wide variety of fickle, irritating, venal, and materialistic females. Among these is Dorothy, the first of Jurgen's old flames, "Who Did Not Understand," as a chapter heading, deliberately echoing Kipling's "Vampire," announces. This once "pleasantest of play-fellows" of Jurgen's had, at puberty, unexpectedly turned into the ar-chetypal evil sister—the tomboy grown into the snake of sexuality, the object of every adult male's fears and fantasies. Handsome but "rather stupid," a "jill-flirt," she represents a temptation of the flesh Jurgen must learn to avoid. (16–28)

Very much in line with the findings of Freud and the other psycho-analysts of his time, Cabell argued that the only good sexual woman was a sublimated sexual woman, safely ensconced in the adult male's long-transcended erotic dreams. In Cabell's gallery of women Dorothy is therefore ultimately merely a harmless stimulant to the masculine imag-ination. In fact, the rest of *Jurgen* hammers home the lesson that women are to be looked at, and sublimated, but not to be met on their own ground by males who hope to survive the gender wars. While he is in the world of women ("all the women that any man has ever loved live here," the Centaur tells him), he establishes a variety of symbolic-erotic relationships with each of the feminine character types Cabell had de-cided men were likely to encounter in the real world. These encounters form the bulk of the book's satire against women.

Among them are Jurgen's mother, as well as Dorothy, once again, but now as an adult woman. Not surprisingly, she turns out to be exactly the temptress he imagined, but with none of the elegance he had given her in his imagination:

> She was leering at him, and he was touching her everywhere, this horrible lascivious woman, who was certainly quite old enough to know better than to permit such liberties. And her breath was sour and nauseous. Jurgen drew away from her, with a shiver of loathing, and he closed his eyes, to shut away that sensual face. (49)

A new Everyman, Jurgen finds himself "alone in a world of moon-light." Afraid to become a victim of "the witches of Amneran," the predators of the reproductive process, he reenters the vulval cave (oblig-ingly depicted as such by Frank Pape, Cabell's preferred illustrator) to re-trieve his previously unappreciated, boring wife. Upon entering this womb-tomb of femininity, he encounters there the dead bodies of all his former mistresses. Their condition emphasizes the inevitable link between eros and thanatos: "For each gay lover who concedes the lordship of love, and wears intrepidly love's liveries, the end of all is death." (52–4) Loss of vital essence spells death to the male. But if a man decides to retain his essence, as Jurgen has now learned to do, that decision means death to the women in his life.

However, as Jurgen descends ever further into the satanic chambers of woman's body, he continues nonetheless to meet, and romance, numerous famous females of myth and literature (thematic consistency was not Cabell's strong suit). This world of the eternal feminine is a composite of the pleasure principle and the death instinct. Heaven and Hell coexist in the house of coitus: to enter it, "you must knock two or three times" with a bronze knocker modeled from the genitals of Adam and Eve, "who were the first persons to open this gateway." As he touches the knocker, Jurgen remarks: "There is no earthly doubt that men degenerate, since here under my hand is the proof of it." (129)

Each of Jurgen's encounters gives Cabell an opportunity to develop various half-humorous, half-sententious double entendres of this sort about the morally corruptive sexual nature of the feminine. But the catalyst to Jurgen's grateful retreat into boring domesticity is his encounter with the ubiquitous vampire woman of his time. She is the absolute type of the sterile sexual female—a "normal" woman who, instead of being "a hideous creature with fangs and wings," is "very poisonous and seductively beautiful" and who, in her eagerness, represents "any number of vampires and succubi and such creatures, whom the flames do not injure at all, because these creatures are informed with an ardour that is unquenchable and is more hot than fire."

Jurgen "marries" this "most seductively beautiful creature," almost immediately after having declared he would certainly "have nothing to do with such unregenerate persons." She turns out to be the most prosaic, contemporary, and realistically presented of Cabell's women. She is rather lovable, very much a version of the girl next door. Presumably she became a vampire after a cat jumped over her coffin when she "chanced one day to fall ill and die." Her name is Florimel, and she is an odd mixture of realism and folklore. Jurgen—like Cabell, well aware of the antifeminine myths produced by the generation of 1890—surmises astutely that she "had been invented by his father."

Florimel spends her vacations in Hell, for as she remarks to Jurgen, "it is little rest a vampire gets on earth, with so many fine young fellows like yourself going about everywhere eager to be destroyed." Florimel is very much a contemporary young woman, a vampire of seminal essence

rather than of blood. To stress that point, Cabell offered his readers a sequence of images blatantly metaphorizing sexual intercourse. No doubt
these were principal exhibits in subsequent attempts by the authorities
to ban the book. The vampire, for instance, brings Jurgen to "a quiet
cleft by the Sea of Blood, which she had fitted out very cosily in imitation of her girlhood home; and she lighted a candle, and made him
welcome to her cleft." In obvious imitation of the double entendre of
the phrase *"ma chandelle est morte,"* from the French folk song "Frère
Jacques," Jurgen, upon entering Florimel's vulval lair, blithely remarks:
"Let us extinguish this candle!" Knowing that he was made an "em-
peror" during an earlier adventure, Florimel remarks that at first she was
"suspicious of your majesty," because "I had always heard that every em-
peror carried a magnificent sceptre, and you then displayed nothing of
the sort. But now, somehow, I do not doubt you any longer." And a bit
later on, Florimel remarks: "I always said your majesty had remarkable
powers of penetration, quite apart from your majesty's scholarship."
Freudian symbol analysis had clearly, by 1919, become a standard part of
the repertory of American wits.

But notwithstanding Jurgen's ability to wield his scepter with admirable prowess, Cabell made him not immune to the catabolic effects
of his "little deaths": "Jurgen would come out of Florimel's cleft considerably dejected, and would sit alone by the Sea of Blood." (234–51)
When Florimel's vacation in Hell is at an end, Jurgen, "forty-and-
something" and much the wiser for having sampled the various shortcomings of the world's sexual women, begins to long for Lisa, his
shrewish but sexually undemanding wife: he realizes at last "how much
more unpleasant—everything considered—life was without her than
with her." (310) Jurgen has learned that it is better to sublimate and fantasize about sex than to indulge and lose your position in the world. For
the sexual woman, who was thanatos personified, was always an agent of
economic, as well as seminal, perdition. As Mencken had pointed out
the year before in his "defense" of women, "a man may force his actual
wife to share the direst poverty," but he could not demand that from his
mistresses, for "even the least vampirish woman of the third part demands to be courted in what, considering his station in life, is the grand
manner." (159) A model for the gold diggers of the Twenties was beginning to take shape in the work of Mencken and Cabell. They had already reconfigured the sexual vampires of the 1910s into the primarily
economic vampires of the next decade. Amid such temptations a good

man spent wisely, and a wise man not at all. This was the crucial lesson Jurgen learned on his imaginary voyage.

Jurgen was a resounding popular success from the moment it was published. Various watchdog organizations prosecuted it for obscenity—a not unreasonable charge, even if it took a little effort to decipher Cabell's meanings. The intellectuals of the period feasted on the book's double entendres, and generations of boys and young men combed its pages for tidbits of sexual enlightenment. The book remained virtually continuously in print until the late 1970s, when the ready availability of far more direct sexual materials had turned the perusal of Cabell's often abstruse references to classical mythology and folklore into more of a journey of scholarly adventure than one of erotic innuendo.

Among several generations of early-twentieth-century readers, however, the author maintained a prominent reputation as an astute guide to the vagaries of "feminine nature." In a long series of follow-up volumes published during the Twenties, Cabell revisited the territory of *Jurgen* repeatedly, particularly in *Something About Eve* (1927), which offered Frank Pape a wealth of suggestions for thinly veiled genital references. Most of Cabell's fun at the expense of women inevitably fits directly into Western literature's long-standing tradition of satire against "the tribe of Eve," a tradition that stretches back through the medieval church fathers to Petronius, Juvenal, and Aristophanes. But Cabell's exploitation of the newly discovered medical bases for the link between seminal spending and death, and between feminine physical health and masculine "catabolic" depletion, proved him to be thoroughly "modern" in his take on the nature of the feminine. He therefore became a much quoted, immensely popular purveyor of half-whispered antifeminine commonplaces.

It was not until after World War II that his star began to wane. Not surprisingly, he still remains a cult favorite among hardy readers of Merritt-styled fantasies. For Jungian symbol hunters his work is a gold mine. Like Merritt's imagery of the *vagina dentata* of primal femininity, Jurgen's encounters with the vampire-women of his fantasies show that many of the period's males considered the sexual woman in a very literal sense anthropophagous, a man-eater.

This point was made even more directly in *Painted Veils* (1920), the sardonic swan song of James Gibbons Huneker's career as America's most sophisticated and knowledgeable arbiter of culture during the early years of this century. Huneker's good friend, the suave international littérateur and bon vivant Benjamin de Casseres, was to characterize him in the preface to a 1932 edition of *Painted Veils* as "a voracious shark of the intellectual and of the sensuous life." Set during the first decade of the twentieth century, the novel closely echoes the opinions of the New York intellectuals of this period. It is an uncensored evocation of the opinions and obsessions of this American cultural elite, written by a man who, de Casseres stressed, "lived its life, a man who made it his own, absorbing it with every breath, incorporating it in every cell of his body and brain." Huneker's provocatively "naturalistic" portrait of these intellectuals' behavior provides us with a cast of characters far more openly obsessed with issues of sex and gender than we are likely to encounter elsewhere.

Huneker's leitmotif was a progressive unveiling of the three faces of Eve. The experiences of three representative young American women illuminate "the universal nature of the feminine." The central figure of this trio is the talented Easter Brandes, who changes her name to Esther when she becomes an opera diva. On stage (and in spirit, Huneker makes clear) she is "Istar, daughter of Sin," who "bent her steps to the abode of the dead," where "she took and received the Waters of Life." The novel emphasizes that these magic waters are the male's "vital essence." Esther is a sexual predator whose "pre-evolutionary" masculine characteristics have provided her with "abnormal" creative energies, as well as a "dangerously high" level of intelligence for a woman.

Second in importance is Mona Milton, "over-sexed," as all women must be, but a truly "womanly woman." Huneker identifies her as a "maternal nymphomaniac." Like Esther, she is always after men's vital essence, always hungry for seminal fulfillment. But unlike Esther, who is a sterile egotist, Mona is driven in her yearning for the "waters of life" by her instinctive desire to reproduce, to give birth, to be a mother. She is perhaps the early twentieth century's most fully developed portrait of Kipling's "woman who did not know / and never could understand," the biologically predestined evil sister of the bourgeois male's fantasies.

The third of Huneker's Eves, Dora, is a very ordinary working-class girl, an example of "the average lust-cat of commerce," (94) representative of what Weininger had identified as the organic tendency to prostitution in every woman. In her, Esther's predatory masculinity and Mona's "maternal nymphomania" are combined and turned to commercial advantage: "A pretty vulgarian, her appeal was universal to males in rut." (95)

Together these three women formed a complete manifestation of womanhood. As in the case of Cabell's *Jurgen* and most other misogynist manifestos of the day, what separated Huneker's delineation of the "eternal feminine" from earlier forms of antifeminine thinking (such as the medieval characterization of woman as the "hell mouth" of temptation) was the aura of scientific and psychoanalytic legitimacy Huneker brought to his depictions of women's "constitutional nymphomania."

In her various modern manifestations, Easter/Esther/Istar, the eternal Eve, "the Great Singing Whore of Modern Babylon," (173) proved once again that to love woman is to love death. Woman was the vehicle of the male's urge to return to nothingness. She was the "death instinct" identified by Freud made flesh. The primal emotions that drove her were "Love and Death and Death and Love. First Things and Last." (38)

A minutely calculating predator, Esther is "coldly selfish." She has "the soul of a pawn-broker." (35) Alfred Stone, one of the novel's voyeuristic intellectuals looking in on the strange world of women, realizes that she is "hard as steel," a woman who does not hesitate "to use a man just as a man uses a woman." These primitive "masculine" qualities make Esther into the natural prostitute she soon proves to be. She is a creature of regression. Given the fashionable anti-Semitism of 1920, it therefore comes as no surprise that Stone identifies her as Jewish—although Esther herself, devious as ever, denies it.

Huneker intended to demonstrate that, no matter how civilized and talented they might be, Jewish women maintained at all times a much closer affinity to the "primitive races" than their Aryan counterparts. Jewish women had "inverted" the maternal nymphomania that made all women "think with their matrix," as Milton, a Jesuit in training, declares. They represented Merritt's "abyss" and were the sterile commercial "takers" among "the sexual sex." They were racial sisters to Theda Bara, the woman of Arab Death.

Milton reminds Ulick Invern, Huneker's fictional alter ego in *Painted Veils,* "of something your friend Remy de Gourmont told you," namely, "that mankind, all organic life, is the slave of its reproductive organs." Milton fervently (but, Huneker will show, futilely) declares that men should adopt religion, become celibate, and avoid women at all cost: "All the talk of psychologists about transposing the nervous fluid to the brain would be mere wind were it not for prayer."

But the suave and knowledgeable Ulick quotes Havelock Ellis and argues that men must rather learn *how* to let women harvest their seed than to avoid intercourse altogether. In a barrage of scientific learning largely taken from Ellis, Gourmont, and the popular sexologist Félix le Dantec, Ulick argues that, properly spaced, ejaculations in fact could be a boon to the ejaculator. Remember, Ulick points out, what le Dantec "says of the 'gamete,' the unfecundated sexual cells, poisoning a man swifter than does absinthe. . . . The sexes separated are unnatural, and joined, whether in wedlock or in concubinage—wedlock is the ultimate outcome—they are natural, healthy." But Ulick's ultramodern, "liberal" confidence in a lifestyle of free spending and sharing is not supported by his ultimate fate in the novel. On the other hand, Huneker let his readers know in no uncertain terms that Ulick was well aware of the health benefits to women of regular infusions of semen: "Waldstein, Ekler and other biologists have proved that the sperma of the male actually enters into the veinal circulation of the woman. 'Bone of my bone'!" (120–1)

With "the female ever in pursuit of masculine honey," men could easily become too generous with their allotment of vital essence, Alfred Stone points out. He recounts an anecdote his doctor told him about "a patient, an old chap of sixty," who had wanted to rejuvenate himself (1920 was, after all, the heyday of Voronoff's notoriety). The doctor had "bluntly told him a man isn't like a woman—toujours prête—but given by nature a certain number of cartridges which he is to use as suits his temperament. If he fires them off in his youth, in middle-age he will be empty-handed and must avoid targets and rifle-ranges." In the end, Stone tells his friends, "the doctor gave the poor old top a dose of some devilish compound, a Brown-Séquard cocktail containing picrid acid with mountain oysters, or lamb-fries, as a chaser." But after all this the "rejuvenated old goat," his "blood tingling with the passion of youth," had unwisely spent this "cartridge" on "the new rifle-range" of "a pretty puss of eighteen" instead of sharing it with his patiently waiting wife. (104–6)

In historical terms the significance of such an otherwise trivial instance of smoking-room humor is twofold: it reveals the sort of talk that was typical among intellectual males of the years around 1920, and it shows that the experiments of such now completely forgotten figures as Brown-Séquard and Voronoff were uppermost in these men's minds. But without a clear awareness of the "scientific" background to Huneker's characters' discussions, today's readers cannot possibly understand the "vital" significance of the ideas Huneker wanted to convey to his contemporaries.

Fortunately Huneker let his characters be scandalously blunt in their discussion of these issues. He deliberately broke a taboo, for though such topics might be on the mind of every educated male, and the subject of heated private debate, they were seen as beyond the pale of polite conversation in the realm of fiction. Where his fellow novelists tended to broach such issues in a more circumspect fashion (witness the proliferation of "real" vampire women), Huneker linked the actions of his women *directly* to the popular vital-essence theories of the moment. But ironically even these "straightforward" discussions are now likely to mystify the reader. Indeed, much of what we now see as "unconscious symbolism" in early-twentieth-century culture was—though it may since have become part of *our* unconscious—once a perfectly *self-conscious* part of social, economic, and scientific discourse. To see the socially constructed antifeminine imagery of *Painted Veils* or of such fictions as *Jurgen* and *The Moon Pool* as evidence of "inalterable" mental patterns is to succumb to the political motives underlying the proliferation of these prejudicial ideas of gender and race. To suggest that such images express "archetypal patterns" of the male psyche is to exploit them while rejecting any personal responsibility for their continued existence.

In the science-inspired trinity of Eves Huneker set up in *Painted Veils,* Dora, the eighteen-year-old working-class girl, represented the vulgar blending of sex and commerce in the minds of the average woman: "She was aware of her attractions and like the busy little merchant she was she sold her wares to the highest bidder." (95) Though the fact that she adores children is an indication that, obliquely at least, her worldly actions are guided by nature, she sees her relationships with men as business transactions. She is therefore another early sighting of the gold digger of the Twenties and Thirties, not, like Esther, a deliberate socialist terrorist of the gender wars. She is a small-minded sexual shopkeeper. "The psychology of Dora is as simple as a single-cell structure," Ulick announces. "She is of the genus prostitute, a superior prostitute." (121)

Also eighteen when we meet her, Mona Milton, the "maternal nymphomaniac," is Dora's bourgeois, "acculturated" counterpart. Though still a virgin, she is patently "over-sexed." In robust health, she is a born Anglo-Aryan "breeder": "Not even at the time when women are 'minions to the moon' did she relapse into that forlorn flabbiness noticeable even to the ordinary obtuse male." (66) Indeed, menstruation enhances Mona's unsuppressed hunger "for virility" (67); she is, to her naive, aspiring-Jesuit brother, Milt, therefore, the very personification of the evil sister: "He cherished profound affection for his sister, also profound distrust." But though Milt does not know it yet, he and his sister are very much alike. To identify the primitive bisexual erotic impulse behind all Mona does (and to explain the degradation to which her brother ultimately descends), Huneker has her exclaim: "He should have been the girl, I the boy." (68)

Ulick, though anything but a naif in the realm of sexual experience, is actually a bit embarrassed when Mona talks to him about the intensity of her reproductive desires. But Huneker goes out of his way to emphasize that she is not a "freakish" female; she is simply more spontaneous than most of her acculturated sisters. In fact, Huneker wants her to be seen as a very average specimen of modern middle-class femininity: "Her classmates at college had voted her desperately old-fashioned: worse—a womanly woman. Secretly she wished that her soul could be like a jungle at night, filled with the cries of monstrous sins. But it wasn't." (67) She is the archetypal mother-woman, whose loins impetuously clamor for the male seed. "Young men," Ulick decides, "have an easier time than girls, who must sit and sizzle while down in some subcellar of their being they hear the faint growlings of the untamed animal. Once unleashed it jumps all barriers." (75) Mona's "deep-set, passionate eyes" inevitably seduce Ulick, who, though dubious about the venture, "unleashes" the animal within her and "makes a woman out of her." Mona now instantly begins to bustle about like a mother in training and tries to make the two of them live together "like sensible married people."

For Mona, sex, like life itself, had only one meaning: it allowed her to "gather men's honey" so that she could breed. She

> saw in love but one object—children. Ulick realized now that it was maternity suppressed that had sent her to him knocking at his closed door. Love with her was not only a sensation but also a sentiment. She was not a sentimental girl. She loved Ulick, but she loved children more. "The sacred wound of maternity" was a phrase that appealed to her; it was thus she had heard called the semi-mysterious function of the lunar sex; that sex upon which the moon had impressed its rhythms. Mona, under the skin, was a matter-of-fact woman for whom Mother Nature could do no wrong. (136–7)

When she discovers that she is pregnant, she is ecstatic, even though Ulick and she are not married: "Nature, generous, glorious Nature, had performed this miracle in her behalf." (141) To get Ulick out of an awkward *mise-en-thèse,* which Huneker had originally designed primarily to teach us Weininger's dictum in *Sex and Character* that "most women have both possibilities in them, the mother and the prostitute," (217) the author conveniently disposes of this clinging vine's maternal aspirations by involving her in a car accident in which she loses her baby. This allows Ulick to leave the maternal stage quietly, his masculine "dignity" intact.

But for Huneker the mother and the prostitute in woman were merely secondary manifestations of that "real" vampire of the masculine essence, that most dangerous woman of all: Istar, who is Esther, who is Easter, in whom the sexual characteristics of Mona and Dora were conjoined, but whose primitive bisexual instincts were unleavened by the "normal" feminine elements of childishness and mental disability. Huneker depicts Esther as a masculinized monster of pagan lusts with utter disrespect for the precarious social balance created by man's painstaking efforts to bring forth a higher civilization of individuals in opposition to nature's collectivist reproductive chaos. Istar takes the essence of men's souls and steals their intellect. She is a terrorist of nature who wants to return to the chaotic world of woman-rule. She is not so much a feminist as a "feminine masculinist," in Arabella Kenealy's terms, a nonpolitical version of "the man-eating suffragettes" who, Mencken had insisted, were "almost male in their violent earnestness." (*In Defense of Women,* 197)

As a standard "man-woman" of the period, Esther/Istar is polymorphously perverse in her sexual choices. But though she likes to indulge, manlike, in "the sweet sin of Sappho," (175) her favorite pastime is to prey upon men. She absorbs their vital essence in great quantities, and this provides her with the masculine juices she needs to attain and maintain her position of supreme prominence in the performing arts. For Huneker the very fact that she is a woman *and* a brilliant opera singer establishes Esther's lowly position on the eugenicist and evolutionist scales of human development. He emphasizes this early on in the novel, by sketching her behavior during a "collectivist" ritual that was designed to shock, arouse, and terrify his readers.

During a vacation in New Hampshire years before the main action of the novel, Ulick comes across a scene taken almost directly from a painting by Bouguereau, featuring near-mythical nymphs and satyrs at play. "An irregular procession chiefly composed of women dancing, screaming, beating tambourines. Hysteria was in the air." In accordance with the racist iconography of "degeneration," which Huneker had accepted without question, "a gigantic noseless negro wearing a scarlet turban and dressed in a gaudy gown like a woman's wrapper, headed the throng." Behind him a young woman "carrying a banner shrieked: 'Holy Yowlers. Save your dirty souls. Dance into paradise. Holy Yowlers.' Her pretty eyes were bloodshot." She is "a poor deluded drunken creature under the control of this monstrous African."

Ulick decides to investigate the rituals of this primitive sect, composed of African men and white women, and he is joined in his investigation by another observer, a "tall beautiful girl in white," who spoke "in contralto tones that made him vibrate." All he notices about her at this time is that "the girl was dark and that her smile was fascinating." She is the woman who will later become Istar. Side by side they witness an orgiastic ritual. The African commands: " 'Lights out!' and darkness supervened." In the ensuing night of the spirit Ulick finds himself assaulted by "the importunate lascivious embrace of a woman." In vain he tries to ward off her attentions, but his flesh is weak and his assailant has her way with him. "The moaning ceased. From the pit below came a rutilant groaning and sharp exclamations of pain and ecstasy." Afterwards Ulick assumes that he has been raped by his beautiful dark-haired companion—that she was swept up in the primordial orgiastic spell created by the sinister African, for when the lights go on again, "her olive skin was drawn and yellow, her lips a sanguinary purple. Her great eyes were narrowed to slits and their hazel fire was like a cat's eyes in the dark." (29–33) Ever the gentleman, Ulick proposes marriage on the spot, but the beautiful young woman has an odd response: She cries, "You beast!" slaps his face, and flees, only to reappear later as the Semitic temptress Esther Brandes.

After that reappearance, Esther, who is still physically irresistible (though, Huneker emphasizes repeatedly to complete his iconographic presentation of Esther's "masculine" nature, unusually small-breasted), continues to flaunt her indiscriminate promiscuity. But the more outwardly beautiful she grows in her expropriation of the vital essence of the men around her, the more monstrous a man-woman she becomes psychically.

A woman with "hungry eyes," (40) Esther is not at all a "loving" woman. Instead, she has a "cold temperament. Brilliant, but hard." She moves from man to man, fortifying herself, and throwing them aside after she has depleted them. Meanwhile she works her way to international stardom. A true exponent of woman-rule, she finds her greatest pleasure in the arms of other women. Every time he sees her, Ulick is reminded of those predatory "lesbians, their sterile sex advancing," Swinburne and Baudelaire had written about. (84)

All the while Ulick continues to dwell upon his first carnal encounter with her, before she became the world-famous Istar, behind whose "robust physique," he knows, hides "the moral sense to be observed in a barnyard." (153) Though still refusing to sleep with him, Esther even makes love to Dora in Ulick's presence. At last provoked beyond tolerance, he dejectedly announces: " 'I think I had better go; go back to Paris. It can't be any viler there than here.' Jeering laughter followed him to the lift." (165)

Immediately after this Ulick's health takes a turn for the worse. He exhibits the period's favorite signs of unwise seminal management: "Ulick, my boy," Milt remarks, "you've got to stop your ways of living else land in a hospital, or worse—perhaps in a mad-house." Indeed, Milt is quite the amateur physician: "You look like a man with spinal trouble." Since the spinal column was generally thought to be the conduit by which a man's vital essence was distributed to the rest of his body, general sexual dissipation was thought to affect that organ of masculine rectitude first. But Ulick sees his problems as genetic: "I've inherited bad blood from my father."

Esther soon turns even Milt, the aspiring Jesuit, into her sexual slave. The constitutional effeminacy Mona had already diagnosed in her brother now rapidly does him in. When Ulick sees him next, Milt is a mess, with all the

> stigmata of a man on a protracted spree. He mumbled unintelligible words and with a shaky hand pointed to the decanter. A mortal weakness seized Ulick. He sank on the divan and endeavoured to shut out the repugnant picture. Milt! His critic, Milt of the lofty ideals, a besotted animal in the House of the Harlot! It was that devil-woman who had dragged him down. Dame Lucifer.

And Milton admits: "I've lost my purity, my manhood." Ulick now recognizes in Esther Brandes the mark of Theda Bara: "Only to gratify a caprice she had ruined the career of a weak man . . . she was a real vampire."

But Semitic Esther's psychological invasion of Ulick, the Aryan intellectual, is not yet complete. Like Istar, "who went down into hell and came back unsinged, only more evil," she reappears to torment Ulick once again. A perfect gentleman, he has always remained silent about the circumstances of their first encounter. But at last he calls her out: "You are a beast, Easter. You called me a beast that day at Zaneburg: Now it is you who are the beast."

Huneker's whole narrative was meant to build up to the revelation that now follows. Esther must be shown to be the ultimate "Whore of Babylon," the ultimate destroyer, the "real" sexual vampire, the Beast of the Apocalypse incarnate, the ultimate collectivist polyandrist. Esther therefore looks disdainfully at Ulick and says: "Ever since that day at Zaneburg, you have run after this beast as if you owned her. But you didn't—you never did, do you hear! You never had me." When Ulick, stunned, insists: "I did, I held you to me . . . ," Esther casually reveals that he had been assaulted, not by her, but by the noseless African's degenerate woman assistant: "I've never been anything to you." And as Ulick's world collapses around him, Esther now discloses that, rather than choosing to pair with the civilized Ulick, she had instead had commerce with the African: "I assented—physiologically," she acknowledges triumphantly.

Istar, the primitive "Eurasian" Jew, and the "childminded, half-witted African" were thus shown to have deliberately joined together in a single, unspeakably degraded, collectivist copulative ritual to defeat Ulick's dreams of transcendence. Horror-stricken to discover that the unfathomable depth of Esther's primordial depravity had been nourished by the abominable seed of "that black monster" who represented the lowest possible stratum of human life, Ulick now hastens "out of the accursed house" that harbors Istar, only to suffer a paralytic stroke. Broken and defeated, he dies a few months later.

Humanity, Huneker wanted to show, was being undermined by the Eurasian woman and her allies. The masculinized Semitic female who instinctively sought to mate with the effeminate males of the lower orders had become their agent—their port of entry into the world of the evolutionary elite. This Aryan elite's future seems dim at the end of *Painted Veils.* The differing fates of Esther and Ulick are placed into an ironic "negative eugenicist" context. While Esther continues to triumph as a world-famous opera diva, Ulick slips painfully into oblivion: "Euthanasia came to him wearing an ambiguous smile." (175–6)

Thus Huneker had shown his readers that to consort with woman for "pleasure" was ultimately a direct form of "race-suicide": "Like the tigress that has tasted human flesh and blood so is the woman who knows man; neither are satisfied but with human prey." (87) The three faces of Eve in *Painted Veils* are the three masks of a single predator. Choose your vampire, Huneker was saying, choose the manner in which you die, but die you must to keep the eternal feminine, nature's reproductive principle, alive. It matters little whether you fall to the masculinized woman, the "womanly woman," or the instinctive prostitute—Eve will deplete you in one fashion or another, for, indeed, each sexual woman is one of nature's man-eating spiders, and to perpetuate *her* species in the preevolutionary stasis of nature, she will gladly consume her mate. No wonder the intellectuals of *Painted Veils* quoted Remy de Gourmont at every turn.

Huneker's book thus demonstrates how little real difference in ideological focus there was between the "popular" imagery of a film such as *A Fool There Was* and the "philosophical subtleties" of the intellectuals. The latter may have brought in considerably more official "scientific" and "psychological" evidence to demonstrate that "real" women were also "real" vampires, but the overall result remained the same. Benjamin de Casseres showed how well Huneker's contemporaries had understood his message when he described Esther Brandes in his 1932 introduction to *Painted Veils* as a "Maw of Art and Sex," a creature who had made "every perversion" into the source of her art. She was "totally amoral, destructive, one of the Anthropophagi of Vice." The geneticists, biologists, and medical researchers had done their work well.

De Casseres's comments reflect the convenient dual function of misogyny among the intellectuals of 1920 in developing a single axis of race and sex prejudice. Even while these intellectuals raged against Puritanism as expressive of "the emasculated ideals of ancient Asiatic fanatics," they could declare the world to be "hag-ridden by sexuality." (158) While prattling like archcolonialist sons of Jules Michelet about "the unconcealed languorous passion" combined with "a touch of melancholy, a hint of fear, a sweet submissiveness, and the naivete of a child" to be found "only in the eyes of a negress," (94) they could portray African-American men as sexual monsters driven by "hysteria" and spouting "imbecile doctrines" compounded of "superstition and fornication." (29) And while railing against "woman, the eternal ninny," who had forced America to succumb to a politics of "sentimentality," they could show that the "struggle for life among nations" had reached a stage where (Huneker here deliberately echoed the words of Gustave Le Bon, Lothrop Stoddard, and Madison Grant) the country had been "eaten up" by foreign invaders who had taken advantage of that sentimentality: "The Jews are the last and deadliest locusts of all; when they finish with America not a green leaf, a blade of grass, an ear of wheat, will be left in the land," (100) exclaims Alfred Stone, the Weininger-styled anti-Semitic Jew of Huneker's narrative.

During the early years of the twentieth century, then, the metaphors of biology, which had made women into praying mantises and turned the non-Western world into a lair of rodents, were also used to turn the "effeminate Jew" into a locust, part of a plague of Eurasian anthropophages. And, like the sexual woman, the African was seen as a terrorist "contaminating" evolutionary culture with primitive passions driven by the womb of "brute nature." Science had established the new gospel of human inequality not by means of scientific evidence, but by using a host of subjective, ideology-driven metaphors to describe a wide range of still only dimly perceived organic processes. Prejudice had shaped the conclusions of early-twentieth-century science, and science had further falsified its own findings by using prejudicial metaphors to sway a gullible public. By adding the chimeras of eugenics and "natural selection" to their utterly speculative expositions of the workings of genetics, the scientists had convinced the public at large that immigration represented an "alien invasion" of "racial inferiors" designed to lure the evolutionary male into the lair of the Eurasian vampire of "collectivism" and genetic reversion. The prejudicial metaphors of men who regarded themselves as the first truly "objective" generation of scientists thus played directly into the worst antifeminine and racist fears of the average male. As a result, race and sex hatred came to blend ever further in Western culture during the two decades that followed the reign of the "real" vampires of the century's first twenty years.

The world of science and medicine is not at all eager to keep track of the historical evidences of its own mistakes; instead, it likes to project an aura of infallibility. Few of us therefore realize how important the faulty, subjective conjectures of science were in constructing popular notions about human behavior and gender relationships that still have a direct impact on our daily lives, many decades after such misinformation came to be discredited in the medical community itself. As a result, the Twenties—that first truly "modern" age of flappers, movies, gangsters, mass merchandising, and ready money—were in fact to be the triumphant breeding ground for an obsessive cultural equation of the prejudicial metaphors of sex and race. Something deadly had been added to the arsenal of images stored in the minds of the men who rang in the new age: many had become convinced that behind the enticing sexual woman, Istar, the woman with the African womb, stood the diabolical, effeminate blood lust of Dracula and Fu Manchu, chief agents of the reversive collectivism of the Jewish-Asian axis.

The robot from Metropolis *(1926), before being given the outward*
appearance of Maria

VIII. DOMESTICATING THE VAMPIRE: HOLLYWOOD AND SEMINAL ECONOMY

Metaphors are the gateway to genocide. Preposterous? Fear, hatred, and greed, the psychological tools of politics, lead to genocide. Metaphors are the instruments of poetry, beauty, and inner truth. Why blame the tool for how we use it? After all, "guns don't kill people, people do." But we use tools for what we don't want to do with our hands. Metaphors do the dirty work of ideology. They telescope complex ideas into simple imagery and encourage us to see others not as persons but as patterns. Social paranoia feeds on metaphor, because every image we form rapidly takes on a life and meaning of its own. "Once the human mind has created an image, it diligently attempts to paint it in ever more lurid colors," E. T. A. Hoffmann wrote in 1819. ("Das Fräulein von Scuderi," 294–5) Hoffmann, creator of some of the most fiercely obsessed characters in all of literature, knew that an image can kill. It can eat into reality and force our world to take on the shapes and colors of our fears. Metaphor, by establishing a bridge between image and act, encourages us to bypass common sense and reasonable doubt. Thus it hands us the gun that does our killing.

Among the "hard" sciences of the early twentieth century none were more obviously shaped by murderous metaphors than biology, genetics, and medicine. As soon as science resorts to metaphor, it acknowledges the unreliability of its speculations. The use of metaphor announces the abandonment of fact in favor of subjective interpretations of the morphology of human existence. Metaphor turns scientific theory into social propaganda. The researchers who came to see an overarching human significance in the reproductive experience of a variety of worms, spiders, and toads were expressing sociopolitical prejudices. They turned unreliable scientific data into tools of oppression. Metaphors depicting female vampirism and masculine spending in the insect or animal worlds as exemplary of the predestined "anabolic" and "catabolic" dichotomies of gender provided "scientific legitimacy" for the war on women. Science provided the cultural imagery of gynecide, for the metaphors it developed implied that the only way to withstand or overcome the vampire was to kill her.

But the period's preoccupation with the "battle of the sexes" also provided a convenient metaphoric framework for the social contextualization of the "race wars" many saw looming ahead. The metaphors that prepared the world for genocide depended heavily on the imagery of the battle of the sexes. The "deadly struggle between evolution and reversion" saw woman as the very center of racial combat: the proportions of "effeminacy" and "virility" scientists found in a nation's "productive energies" determined its rank in the racial pecking order, and therefore also its chances for survival in the coming "race wars." Thus early-twentieth-century biomedical speculation deliberately fed a social paranoia that was to prove far more deadly than any of the patterns of personal delusion once imagined by E. T. A. Hoffmann. The metaphors of genetics and biology, translated into provocative entertainments by the popular media, were beginning to prepare the world for the practical realities of genocide.

The role of the silent film in this process of indoctrination was perhaps crucial, though it has not been given much attention by historians. This is probably so because we tend to regard the era of the silents as a prelude to the "real" age of the movies, that of sound. But the visual impact of the silent film, its role in solidifying the prejudicial metaphors of sex and race, was quite different, and far more efficient, than that of the talkies. Without speech (other than the hints provided by scarce captions) to guide our reactions, what we see must be linked directly to the things we know—that is, to what we assume to be part of the nature of things. The silent film thus became a purely Bergsonian medium. Existence was validated only by constant action: "I move, therefore I am." To show two people sitting in a room and having a serious discussion for more than an instant would have required a dizzying string of captions. It would have turned the cinematic experience into merely another form of reading a book, and that would have cleared out the theater in minutes.

The early silents were therefore often not much more than salon paintings come to life. At a time in which still photography was struggling to rid itself of the dominance of "pictorialism" (traditional painterly concepts of composition), the movies were trying to establish a semblance of cultural legitimacy by reminding their audiences of the famous paintings they had seen. Consequently an awareness of the influence of painting on silent movies—a subject direly neglected by today's film historians—is crucial to any understanding of the links between this new popular medium and the psychosocial ideologies of the period. Within this context the movies' wholesale appropriation of the essential gender dichotomies characteristic of late-nineteenth-century art became a crucial factor in establishing the twentieth century's visual iconography of the "battle of the sexes." By disseminating the fin-de-siècle artists' symbolic representations to millions of viewers who had never even seen a painting, the movies were able to turn this often sardonic, science-informed imagery into a visual catechism of "inherent gender difference" for the edification of the masses.

The silents helped shape and standardize the general public's conception of gender roles, and particularly the "good girl–bad girl" dichotomies of sexual dimorphism. By turning static set pieces into continuous visual narratives, the silents brought a compelling sense of sequential logic and "objective" resolution to the suggestive (but, of necessity, suspended) gestures of nineteenth-century narrative painting. Moreover, in their efforts to bypass the written word, the silents had to rely on readily identifiable categories of visual characterization, which did not tolerate much shading, nuance, or ambiguity.

When sound came to the movies, the early talkies made their most distinctive mark by reclaiming the verbal complexities of the stage. In viewing movies from the Thirties, for instance, most of us are astonished—and taken aback—by the rapid-fire verbal exchanges of the protagonists. Those often complex exchanges are dramatically unlike the innocuous, captionlike dialogue used to dress up the neo-Bergsonian obsession with constant action of today's noisy but intellectually silent movies. Just as a lot of on-screen writing would have emptied the theaters in 1915, a lot of literate dialogue will today automatically relegate a movie to the art-house circuit. The near-elimination of coherent speech

Detail from an engraving of Georges Rochegrosse's The Death of Babylon,
ca. 1891; from L'Illustration, *no. 2514, May 2, 1891*

beyond expletives and grunts in Hollywood's cinematic choreographies
of fetishized movement has created a cultural environment in which our
popular "action" movies in particular (the ones that inspire—or are inspired by—comic books or video games) have once again obtained a
function nearly as nonverbal and totemic in nature as that of the silents.

The visual specificity, the "logical" sequencing of cause and effect,
characteristic of the silents was designed to remove any potential ambiguity of meaning. By demonstrating the practical validity of universally
understood moral and social verities, they attained a role in solidifying
the reigning truths of social reality on a scale never before achieved by
any public medium. Movie audiences want visual entertainment. They
won't pay to be told to change their minds. Existential uncertainty does
not entertain. The silents succeeded because they reliably reinforced
prevailing patterns of social behavior. They transformed the speculations
of prejudice into demonstrable truth before one's very eyes, and they did
so by using the imagery developed by the painters of an earlier generation. In the process they turned the battle of the sexes into as meretri-

cious a spectacle as the shoot-'em-up, cowboy antics of D. W. Griffith's
Ku Klux Klan.

Paintings are static and provide no more than a single instant of a
potentially widely variable sequence of events. Silent movies, however,
provide a sense of duration, of *reality* in motion. In ideological terms,
they provide "proof" by depicting apparently incontrovertible sequences of cause and effect determined by visual juxtapositions that,
given the inevitability of their unfolding (we *see* what happens), rapidly
establish themselves as quasi-objective presentations of the realities of
existence. Words, by adding narrative complexity, could only add ambiguity and uncertainty to the sequential clarity of *motion* pictures—for

Still from Cecil B. De Mille's Manslaughter *(1922)*
The visual world of the silents came straight out of
late-nineteenth-century academic art.

we all know that words are "abstract," that they are vehicles for our *speculations*. By substituting visual "fact" for verbal conjecture, the era of the silents consolidated the symbolic truths of gender dimorphism and the battle of the sexes with greater efficiency than any other form of cultural communication available during the early twentieth century. As a result, even today many of the visual conventions of nineteenth-century art appropriated by the silents continue to shape our notions of sexual difference. The movies helped turn the metaphors of fin-de-siècle art and science into the psychological realities of twentieth-century gender and race prejudice.

By 1915, for instance, the moviegoing public had already learned that the sexual woman was no less than the bestial god Moloch's feminine side. This had been the main point of *Cabiria,* an epic feat of silent-film propaganda championing nationalism and bourgeois happiness, by the Italian director Giovanni Pastrone. The film had opened in Turin on April 18, 1914, and began a highly successful run at the Knickerbocker Theatre in New York a few weeks later. D. W. Griffith was mightily impressed—much more so, it would appear, than this master of self-promotion was willing to admit. Perhaps as a result of Griffith's judicious understatement of his admiration for the film, the true significance of *Cabiria*'s influence on the development of American film has not yet been studied adequately.

Cabiria was constituted from texts by Gabriele D'Annunzio, the turn of the century's international star of symbolist fiction. In visual terms, it was inspired by the paintings of artists such as Jean-Joseph Benjamin Constant and Georges Rochegrosse (the Barnum and Bailey of fin-de-siècle academic "history" painting), as well as the often morbid and sadistic canvases of Aristide Sartorio (one of D'Annunzio's favorites). Like the visual world of D. W. Griffith's *Intolerance* and most of Cecil B. De Mille's films, it is a vivid example of the influence of fin-de-siècle "high art" on the visual language of object and gesture characteristic of the silent film.

Cabiria is a monumental (if historically confused and confusing) celebration of Rome's victories over Carthage during the third century B.C. The film's immediate affective function, however, was to provide its audiences with propaganda for Italy's much less heroic ventures into twentieth-century colonialism. It also celebrated the virtues of evolved, chaste, bourgeois (Italian) love in contrast to what it presented as the sexual evil of primitive African womanhood. These pseudohistorical and moral narratives were inextricably (and seamlessly) interwoven in the movie. The film therefore reflects the symbolic relationship between the politics of imperialism and the psychosocial fictions of dimorphic gender evolution.

In *Cabiria* the events of history become a sequence of individual acts: following social Darwinist principles, the simple homogeneities of the past are overcome by the ever growing social and emotional hetero-geneity of the evolving (masculine) intellect. The "physical" primi-tivism of Carthage's Hannibal is shown to be no match to Archimedes' intellect. The latter's scientific know-how destroys the Roman fleet. But in the end the Romans win because they are even better at using their heads. The events recorded in *Cabiria* also showed in no uncertain terms that female sexuality was a primary cause of political and personal fail-ure. Only woman's domestic submission to the male will made the mod-ern ideals of statehood triumph over the brute forces of regression.

By declaring chaste marital love to be the source of a nation's claim to global importance, *Cabiria* set the stage for the psychosocial propa-ganda of Griffith and De Mille. The film, leaning heavily upon the iconography of feminine evil established by the painters of the fin de siècle, developed much of the enduring cinematic symbolism still widely used to identify the perverse forces opposed to the manly heroes of civilization and gender dimorphism. The sinful idols of nineteenth-century academic art packed their scanty clothing and symbolic tools, left the sinking ship of narrative painting, and set up shop in the cinema, where they have flourished ever since.

D'Annunzio played a significant role in establishing the crucial gender-ideological theme of Pastrone's nationalistic epic. He proudly signed his name to the production, and the captions he wrote formed the conceptual basis for the imagery of the film. *Cabiria*'s most cele-brated and spectacular sequences—the ones that compelled Griffith to inflate the size of his own sets—showed the Carthaginians sacrificing little girls to the god Moloch. Artists had, since the 1862 publication of Gustave Flaubert's lurid description of the priestess Salammbô's amorous intercourse with a snake of remarkable proportions, become obsessed with the Carthaginians' regressive ritual eroticism. Guided by D'Annunzio's equally lurid imagination, Pastrone depicted Moloch, the god whose priestess Salammbô had been, as a monster of bisexual femininity.

In line with the latest discoveries of biology, Moloch became a gi-gantic anthropophagous *vagina dentata:* the entrance to the pagan god's temple is a fierce, gaping mouth complete with sharp, triangular teeth,

a latter-day revisitation of late-medieval depictions of the mouth of
Hell. Those who entered were clearly subject to immediate emasculation. Inside, a cavernous world of pillars and barbarous splendor anticipated Griffith's sets for *Intolerance*. At the center of it all, a gigantic statue
of Moloch breathed fire. The god is shown with a lion's head and a
woman's body. It sits, legs apart, enthroned and waiting. The text of a
priest's invocation to the god explained the statue's primitive bisexuality:
"Now consummate the sacrifice in your throat of flame, oh father and
mother, oh god and goddess, oh father and mother, oh father and son,
oh god and goddess! Voracious creator! Roaring, ardent hunger . . ."
After this even the most verbally deprived, lip-moving readers in the audience would have caught D'Annunzio's drift.

To demonstrate the withering power of the god/dess's devouring
womb, the statue's belly opens, revealing the fire within. A giant,
tonguelike slab slides out. On it the presiding priest places a naked girl-
child, still prepubertal and innocent. The slab closes like a drawbridge
(or a gigantic insect's prehensile tongue), throwing the girl into the belly
of the beast. The fire flares up, the lion's mouth breathes flame, and one
more virgin has been sacrificed to the vampire of female sexuality.
Moloch was the god/dess of primitive social collectivism, of all those
"homogeneous" male women and female men who had sacrificed the
future of the world to eroticism.

None of the Carthaginians seems particularly disturbed by the sacrifices—it's a fun-filled spectacle to them. But when the small, naked
body of Cabiria, a daughter of Rome, is raised to the fire to be devoured by the forces of regression, she is promptly rescued by Fulvius,
an undercover Roman patrician. Let primitives do what they must, was
Pastrone's message, but the children of civilization must not be defiled.
Fulvius is assisted by a devoted African slave (an Italian in blackface).

Enter Sophonisba, daughter of Hasdrubal, who is, a caption announces, a "passionate 'pomegranate flower.'" Three words, each sexually charged: both "pomegranate" and "flower" were widely used as
symbols of the female genitals. Like the invocation to Moloch, this text
represents the symbolic overkill typical of the silents' attempts to alert
audiences to the emblematic characteristics of their principal characters.
Sophonisba, the audience now knew, was a truly nymphomaniacal lass.
When we first see her, she is stroking a pet leopard, nineteenth-century
painting's favorite symbol of the devouring feminine.

Sophonisba's spirited carnal appetites had already caught the attention of seventeenth-century dramatists such as Pierre Corneille and

John Marston, and by the early twentieth century her name had become a byword for licentiousness. In *Cabiria* she stood for everything that was sexual—and hence evil—in woman. A born schemer, she uses her sexuality for political gain, but she is gratuitously lustful as well. Though she is to marry Syphax, she engages unhesitatingly in a tryst with Massinissa, king of the Numibians, who, mindful of Freud's lessons, has sent her a boxful of jewels.

In her chambers (filled with props familiar from dozens of the famous academic paintings of the time), about to meet with Massinissa (another Italian actor in unconvincing blackface), Sophonisba (acted by Italia Manzini, whose patriotic name was quite inappropriate to the character she portrayed) feeds her vanity. She looks into a large circular basin that serves her as a water-mirror (a favorite painterly prop symbolizing narcissistic feminine self-containment). A phallic, cobra-shaped faucet by her side spits water into this basin. The leopard is made to pace back and forth across the screen from time to time, lest we forget that connection. D'Annunzio makes Sophonisba invoke the moon, symbol of female sexuality: "Oh . . . nocturnal all-seeing goddess with bull horns . . . who walks in a circle . . . fertile, happy, radiant . . ." Uroboric, promiscuous, phallic, this sexual goddess of the night is Sophonisba's patron saint.

Appropriately the tryst between these primitive lovers (Africa as womb and phallus of the world) is interrupted by the properly colonized servant of an Italy-to-be: the patrician Fulvius's muscular, doggedly devoted African salve Maciste carrying Cabiria, who has just been rescued from Moloch's devouring mouth. Pursued by angry priests, Maciste leaves the child in Sophonisba's care, to grow up as one of her personal attendants. A lot of swashbuckling, running, jumping, and other such cinematic activity ensues, and all this commotion gives Cabiria the opportunity to grow into a demure young woman.

Sophonisba, meanwhile, has a prophetic dream: a gigantic arm hovers over her, snakelike fingers reach for her and grasp her breast. This image fades to reveal Moloch's wide-open Medusa mouth. Within it a young girl crawls forward in a desperate attempt to escape her fate. But at the last moment the monster's fangs lock her in, and she is consumed in its fire. Sexual awakening is stirring in Cabiria, and Moloch wants the sacrifice s/he was denied a decade earlier. Sophonisba, luxuriantly lustful herself, sees nothing wrong with such a pleasurable entry into womanhood, and orders her favorite slave to be offered to Moloch.

Fulvius and Maciste, of course, just happen to be in the area so they can come to Cabiria's rescue once again. Massinissa, meanwhile, has shifted his allegiance to the Romans and has conquered the city. Without hesitation the opportunistic Sophonisba offers herself to him. A man of some civilization now (Roman culture rubs off on everyone), he insists on a wedding ceremony—which takes place in front of another statue of Moloch, with an emphatic lion's head and pronounced breasts. The audience must not forget that this was a liaison between two African erotomanes, not a proper Italian wedding.

Their attempts to rescue Cabiria ineffectual, Maciste and the heroic Fulvius—who has predictably fallen in love with the demure young Roman beauty—return to the Roman encampment in despair, certain that she has fallen victim to Moloch. The Roman general Scipio, meanwhile, wants Massinissa to relinquish Sophonisba to him. But Sophonisba, loyal to her African master, takes the poison he has provided for her. During her lengthy, operatic death scene, she orders Cabiria, who, for some odd reason, has not yet been sacrificed, to be brought to her. She places the Roman virgin in the arms of Fulvius, who has shown up just in the nick of time. Having thus taken her own first steps on the road to dimorphic evolution, Sophonisba wisely does what repentant sexual women always do in the movies: she dies.

Cabiria ends on a stirring image inspired by the then-famous divisionist painter Gaetano Previati's *Dance of the Hours.* Fulvius, the Roman patrician, and his still-maiden bride—forever in his debt because he rescued her from the jaws of sexuality when she was still a child—embrace at last in virtuous wedded bliss on the surging bow of the ship that is to take them to Italy and civilization. While they are serenaded by their trusty slave Maciste, a swirling ring of identical white-gowned, prostrate women circles approvingly overhead. They are the submissive, harmonious, desexualized, acculturated female angels of a civilization well on its way to dimorphic transcendence. In the brave new world of bourgeois contentment looming ahead, the marriage of this happy couple (symbolic of the future unity of Italy) will leave all Italian women free to float about the home in diaphanous white, for Moloch, the man-woman of the African womb and the *vagina dentata,* and Sophonisba, his priestess, the vampire of sex, have been defeated. Who, having seen the happy effects of civilization on the sons and daughters of Italy, could henceforth disapprove of this country's ongoing attempts to bring its civilization to the benighted children of Africa?

Cabiria was, in its narrative, visual, technical, and propagandistic sophistication, far in advance of anything D. W. Griffith had produced up to its release. In their rush to turn Griffith into the "father of cinema," film historians have given Pastrone's work scant attention, but Griffith's debt to the Italian was clearly enormous. His lackluster pre-*Cabiria* historical epic *Judith of Bethulia* of 1913, for instance, was a poorly constructed biblical melodrama based on the popular Thomas Bailey Aldrich poem of that title, which, in turn, had been influenced thematically by the German playwright Friedrich Hebbel's *Judith* (1839). It offered a few very static battle scenes "on the ramparts of Bethulia" and a mechanically executed, badly contextualized secondary plot featuring Judith's sadistic-erotic beheading of Holofernes. Griffith's shoestring bacchanalia in illustration of Holofernes's dissipated nature were abjectly derivative, patched together from third- and fourth-rate "historical" paintings by hack second-generation "orientalist" artists—the sort of "art" the mass magazines of the period loved to feature to boost sales.

Griffith's cameras in *Judith of Bethulia* were largely inert, whether they were recording orgiastic dances or major assaults. The film contains none of the hyperkinetic cinematic sense of hop, skip, and jump, of run, dash, and clash, that made *Cabiria* so visually entertaining. It does, however, give us an early insight into Griffith's unwavering allegiance to the most regressive aspects of the period's gender-ideological bias.

His Judith (played by the talented Blanche Sweet, upon whom he could have relied to give a much more nuanced performance) had none of the psychological expressiveness that was to make Theda Bara's debut performance less than two years hence so remarkable. Instead, Griffith made Judith into an emotional automaton who could be read as a heroine only because she had been able to channel her lust in service to the fatherland. When Holofernes's military strategies are about to succeed (his troops are repetitively shown storming the same set of ramparts, filmed by a stationary camera), Judith decides to save the day by offering herself to him. But for no apparent reason other than that Holofernes happens to be a man, Judith actually falls in love with him the instant she sees him. Holofernes rather enjoys the idea of dallying with the Bethulian beauty and, rather foolishly, given his talents as a strategist in battle, consents to dismiss his guards for the night.

Holofernes's manly, intellectual side, Griffith implied, was fatally weakened by his carnal desires. On her part, Judith is, in the end, able to control her lust for the man she set out to defeat, but only by a hair. Wielding her sword in fierce erection above his head, she is touched by hot desire and hesitates. So much masculine gray matter, so close: why waste it, we see her think. But in the nick of time her starving compatriots flash before her eyes, and, forcing her substitute phallus to do patriotic service, she lops off Holofernes's head. Griffith had the camera linger on Judith as she held her long sword, angled downward now but still rigid, in the hollow of her loins. We see it pointing straight at the now-severed head of the sex-besotted Holofernes. Phallic women made men lose their heads, as Griffith had already learned from the symbolist painters.

In line with Griffith's protofascist celebration of exalted führers, intellectually evolved leaders who were to be the linchpins in any historical advance, Holofernes's Assyrian captains become totally ineffectual on the battlefield the moment they discover he is dead. Bethulia has been saved by a fickle female who was able to turn the remnants of her primitive feminine phallic lust into a temporary asset in the service of patriotism. *Judith of Bethulia,* then, demonstrated that promising boys who play with their swords instead of using them in the service of economic conquest are bound to lose their heads to the woman with the phallus. Nominally it was Griffith's first feature-length movie, but in fact it was, like his *Home Sweet Home* of the following year, little more than a group of conventional short films artificially strung together.

Home Sweet Home was based on the life of John Howard Payne, composer of the sentimental ditty that gave the film its title. In this film Lillian Gish, Griffith's steadfast paragon of virtue, spends most of her time pining faithfully for her philandering soulmate. Finally, surrounded by white lilies in typical late Pre-Raphaelite painterly fashion, she dies more or less spontaneously, soon after the only man who could have made her whole expires alone, among effeminate Middle Eastern fools. Griffith conveyed this salient detail by showing us Payne on his deathbed in a vaguely exotic setting, attended by two foppish, swarthy servants, one of whom selfishly orders the other to fan him rather than their fast expiring Aryan master. Griffith's racism was as ubiquitous as it was gratuitous; it was by no means only a somewhat naive, "incidental" feature of *The Birth of a Nation.*

Payne thus dies unredeemed by the soul his angel scrupulously kept pure for him—but all is not lost: a handful of subsequent stories demonstrate that the song he composed has brought virtue to many. At the end of the film, the philanderer is therefore rescued by a heavenly Lillian Gish, who has now evolved into a genuine angel in white. Accompanied by a cast of thousands of similarly attired winged women of excruciating virtue, Gish reaches out to "Man," though he wallow in the pit of "Carnality," "Brutality," and "Worldly" (oddly made into a noun). These hold him back. "Gish—pure, asexual, virginal-yet-motherly feminine self-negation personified—now helps "Man" out of the pit. Carried on her angel wings, he gains the intellectual transcendence her sacrifice has made accessible to him.

Home Sweet Home premiered in Los Angeles on May 4, 1914, just about when Cabiria opened in New York. It is therefore unlikely that Griffith had seen the Italian film's ending by this time, but the similarities are quite remarkable. Clearly the international evolutionary elite wanted its women to focus on the rewards of continence. Griffith's gender propaganda was successful because he placed himself squarely inside the existing framework of political and social prejudices. He always dedicated his films to such broad and conveniently fuzzy concepts as "Real Democracy," "True Tolerance," or the triumph of "Love and Charity." These slogans were designed to convince his audiences that he was not a bigot, a totalitarian, a hatemonger, or a misogynist, but a true Christian American, and that he and his viewers shared an unshakably correct moral viewpoint. God was on their side. It was therefore decidedly un-American not to cheer his Aryan heroes on when they thrashed the "criminally inferior" African; or when, disguised as French democrats, they guillotined, incinerated, or eviscerated the effeminate agents of "Bolshevism" or assorted masculinized working-class hags advocating "Anarchy" in Orphans of the Storm.

Griffith habitually disguised his social and political ideology as "moral truth." He liked to transform major human-rights issues into personalized, individual struggles between "good" (masculine self-control) and "evil" (effeminate lust). This practice made his films into extremely effective vehicles of imperialist propaganda. Even today his deliberate transformation of ideology into the visual reality of the movie screen continues to seduce many of his viewers, for in most cases (The Birth of a Nation is the obvious exception) it is difficult to recognize the propagandistic intensity of his films without a specialized knowledge of the intentional parallels between sex and race his contemporaries had established. These parallels have continued to affect every aspect of the popular imagination, in no small part due to filmmakers such as Griffith, who made them appear to be organic and "true," inherent in the nature of things.

Intolerance (1916) was an exemplary vehicle for the further propagation of this sort of social propaganda. Women must be portrayed either as properly acculturated passive vessels of virtue, as docile beasts of burden patiently carrying the evolving male upward toward intellectual transcendence; or as uncooperative termagants and vampires, as emotionally and spiritually inferior creatures, whose interest in sexuality proved them to be governed by the principles of "woman-rule," and who therefore revealed themselves to be primitive allies of the "lower races." All were lepers, still scarred by the mark of the beast, and largely responsible for human degeneration.

Intolerance once again patched together four very disparate stories. Only Griffith's ideological obsessions gave them a semblance of coherence. Their settings in different historical periods were designed to show the universality of human sentiments ("Today as yesterday, endlessly rocking, bringing the same human passions, the same joys and sorrows"), but in fact Griffith wanted to emphasize the *development* of civilization—and particularly the beneficial effects of feminine acculturation. The four stories illustrate the crucial stages of past, present, and future womanhood—another version of the three faces of Eve. Determined to out-Cabiria *Cabiria* in the realm of pagan spectacle, Griffith made his film longer, his sets bigger, his crowds of extras larger, and his violence more intense (we watch one warrior chop off another's head, for instance). The director's firsts were mostly quantitative or related to special effects (gee, didn't that head fly off realistically!). No doubt that gives him every right to be considered the father of Hollywood film. But his lofty reputation as an "artist" is more puzzling: here the issue of ideology steps center stage.

Griffith made sure there could be no ambiguity of allegiance in his viewers' reactions to his presentation of feminine virtue and feminine evil. In his films the message of *Intolerance* was repeated over and over again. The passive, dimorphically evolved "little mothers" he liked to see as representative of his own time always, either in spirit or in actuality, won out over the warrior women of the days of woman-rule. These "little mothers" paved the way for the White Angels of Mercy of future womanhood, who, Griffith argued, would herald an Aryan world order in which the lower races would gratefully eat the leftover crumbs off the white man's table.

Intolerance delineated a wide variety of characters Griffith was sure his audiences would love to hate. We shudder at the lascivious world of ancient Babylon. We are asked to make objective choices between lascivious Jews and Christ, the self-sacrificial servant to humanity; and between the lascivious, effeminate Roman Catholics of Paris "A.D. 1572" and courageous "Brown Eyes"—daughter of the frugal Huguenots—

child-hearted and well-meaning, though still something of a tomboy. Hateful postmenopausal (and hence, according to the medical logic of the time, masculinized) women with a stupid fetish for socialist meddling make life hell in the present for a "Little Dear One," a childlike, happy, innocent, all-giving, and helpless example of Griffith's ideal of the feminine. In each case the allegiance of only the most willfully perverse viewers could ever be in doubt.

In Griffith's variegated, multilayered spectacle, "historical" events become window dressing to the triumph of chaste love over eroticism. But his audiences liked to be rewarded for their sacrifices to virtue with graphic scenes of the sinful doings they had renounced. He therefore showed as many scenes of pre-Christian Babylonian debauchery as possible. He deliberately made his sets look like the celebrated late Victorian mural-sized canvases of Sir Edwin Long, who loved to paint slave markets cluttered with half-clothed, soon-to-be-sold-and-ravished women. The grand-opera canvases of Gérôme, Cabanel, Constant, and especially Georges Rochegrosse also helped him construct these scenes.

At Griffith's Babylonian slave market most of the captured women, "lips brilliant with juice of henna; eyes lined with kohl," are shown perfectly content to be as lewd as they need to be in order to be sold, but one Mountain Girl is a true firebrand in defense of her honor: "Touch my skirt and I'll scratch your eyes out!" Even so, she is clearly a still-far-too-masculine early female to be anything more than a distant promise of things to come. But the will to change is in her. She is in search of a man who will prove masterful and dominating enough to put her in her domestic place. A sentimental "Rhapsode," for instance, is much too effete for her taste. Shame on you, she taunts him: "Put away thy perfumes, thy garments of *Assinnu, the female man. I shall love none but a soldier.*"

Meanwhile, in the present, the "Dear One" totters on the brink of temptation. She pleads with her boyfriend to help her to be "a strong-jawed Jane." Flashback to Christ being scorned. In the sixteenth century "Brown Eyes" throws suggestive little bites of the apple on which she is nibbling at others: Eve has obviously still not quite been tamed (though she is already far more civilized than the Mountain Girl—or Mary Magdalen before her conversion). Flashing forward, Griffith now identifies the menopausal women harassing the "Little Dear One" as dangerous, misguided proto-Bolsheviks: "When women cease to attract men, they often turn to Reform as a second choice," his caption reads. Meanwhile, the boyfriend, "strongly braced in the Dear One's sweet human faith, sets his steps with hers on the straight road": at least one woman's existential task seems to be coming to fruition. But the boy is framed for theft and sent to jail.

More erotic doings in Babylon demonstrate what horrors are involved in human reproduction. But these dreadful concessions to nature, when properly channeled, can also bring rewards: in the present the pregnant Dear One becomes mom, only to find herself persecuted by the menopausal meddlers. In the sixteenth century, meanwhile, "the Old Serpent" Catherine de Medici, emblematic of phallic-erotic Roman Catholic femininity, foments hatred against the Protestants. The Mountain Girl, tired of the erotic effeminacy of her contemporaries, picks up a sword in defense of her beloved Belshazzar. She handles it a lot better than most of the men around her. The Babylonians go to war.

Histrionics, animated set pieces taken from academic paintings, and a barrage of killings ensue. Sex and violence, blended as entertainment, announce the era of Hollywood, with not a single "semitic-Oriental studio boss" of the sort Henry Fairfield Osborn was to accuse of plotting "the decline of original American standards of life" yet in sight. But somehow Griffith, that champion of Aryan values, who received so much praise for the cinematic innovations of others, never got the credit he deserves for taking sadism to an entirely new level in the filmic medium. There can be no question that Griffith, with a major assist from Cecil B. De Mille, inspired several generations of adolescent males with ever more tumescent dreams about the phallic power of swords and guns. His conception of the manly, cleansing power of violence was to be carried forward through the rest of the twentieth century by numerous admirers, until today violence has become the safe sex of entertainment. Robert Howard, the creator of Conan the Barbarian, learned indelible lessons from the sex-and-battle scenes of *Intolerance,* ones that shaped his self-shortened life as a pulp-fiction writer. Together, Griffith and Howard inspired an entirely new genre of impossibly muscular fantasy fiction that ultimately was to produce the overinflated Aryan pectorals and giant-size bullet-spurting metal-monster machines of Arnold Schwarzenegger and a host of others.

Belshazzar's Feast gave Griffith another opportunity to parade his knowledge of turn-of-the-century academic art. Belshazzar pets a growling leopard in abject imitation of the scene in *Cabiria* introducing Sophonisba, and the Mountain Girl is shown to have an orgasmic experience while milking a goat. She is erotically aroused as she manipulates the animal's udders and thinks of Belshazzar. Those who still prefer to

think of scenes such as this as "naive and unconscious" phallic symbolism are simply unaware of the art of sexual double entendre perfected
by early-twentieth-century artists and writers to skirt the censors. In
1945, in a different context, Geza Roheim delineated the very precise
reasoning underlying Griffith's imagery of the Goat Girl: "The woman
with the penis is the woman with the nipple"—the nipple she denied
the male. There certainly could be no more "penile" nipple than an
udder. Such symbols predicated that "sexual desire is not feminine" and
that "a woman who enjoys sex (has an orgasm) is a phallic woman, and
thereby deprives the male of his penis." (*Panic of the Gods,* 196–7)

To complete his symbolism of the Goat Girl's primitive yearning for
the phallus and its products, Griffith has Constance Talmadge, who
played her (and who was, Anita Loos was to insist later, "one of the few
genuine *femmes fatales* I have ever known"), drink the milk she has thus
gathered in a rough, brazen manner, "like a man," until the gray-
white fluid spills all over her chest. The symbolism gets even more maudlin when she playfully snuggles up to her goat (votary to the goat god
Pan) and nibbles at its ear. This primitive phallic woman was clearly in
every respect a better man than the effeminate sensualists who surround
her.

As Griffith's history of "intolerance" winds to a close, the Fall
of Babylon, Golgotha, St. Bartholomew's Massacre, and lots of proto-
Schwarzenegger bloodshed present themselves in rapid succession. First
to bite the dust of ages is the Goat Girl, who, sword-fighting with the
best of her male contemporaries, dies in defense of her phallic dream-
lover Belshazzar. Brown Eyes, the Reformation tomboy on the verge of
womanhood, is sacrificially impaled by Roman Catholics. The obstacles
placed in the way of dimorphic gender evolution come to seem insurmountable. But in the end the Little Mother of Griffith's contemporary
segment is reunited with her husband (in a last-minute reprieve, of
course), for even the Friendless Prostitute, her nemesis, has come to understand that she must sacrifice her sexual self so that love may thrive in
the purity of a bourgeois-capitalist household.

In the final frames of Griffith's history of the rise of Aryan "tolerance," we learn that "perfect love shall bring peace forever more." Soldiers magically drop their weapons. The reign of the phallic Goat
Girl—whose belligerent woman-spirit still animates the World War—
will be superseded by the properly castrated, dephallicized, terminally
passive Little Mother, whose final acculturation has made war unnecessary. Her ever tolerant motherly love, symbolized by a Whitmanesque

cradle endlessly rocking, is surrounded—once again in imitation of *Cabiria*—by a heavenly host of angels. Griffith's narrative fades on an image of the fates spinning their blessed lifeline toward the timeless heaven of Aryan domesticity.

World War I certainly provided Griffith with an excellent peg on which to hang his sermon. He could act, as he had at the end of *The Birth of a Nation,* as if all his blood and gore had been a part of a principled sermon against war. But even his moralizing tableau of war was tendentious. He had copied that image directly from a painting by Franz von Stuck, a popular, self-consciously "Aryan" German painter who was also instrumental in shaping the symbolic imagination of the young Adolf Hitler. Von Stuck (best known for a series of paintings personifying woman as "Sin") had depicted a lewd, stark-naked, clearly degenerate male riding arrogantly on a gigantic horse (undoubtedly not a gelding). This eroticized male brandished a monstrous sword over cowering masses of decent Aryans haplessly caught in earth's sublunary vale of sex-inspired violence. Clearly, if the *spirit* of war must always be

Franz von Stuck, The Battle over Woman, *1905, oil on canvas*

"feminine," the actual combatants were males who had been duped into mutual destruction by the erotic dissipations of woman-rule. *The Battle over Woman* was another of Stuck's widely known canvases, depicting two degenerate males about to get into a low-life wrestling match, all because of a very naked young woman who stands to one side, haughtily and triumphantly displaying her power over these fools.

With *Intolerance,* then, Griffith's prejudicial symbolism came full circle. If the sexual woman meant death to the male, and if men sought her out and fought over her even so, then war and violence must be her legacy to man. *Intolerance* set out to show that throughout history man's dreams of peace had been undermined by women's regressive erotic drive. The sexual woman was the goddess of war. War, degeneration, and death all had a single source: lust.

Cecil B. De Mille was to take more than a few pages out of Griffith's textbook of race-and-gender politics. *The Ten Commandments* (1923) professed to be about all ten of these "fundamental principles without which mankind cannot live together." But like Griffith before him, De Mille focused his audience-pleasing attention primarily on the "sex as violence" commandment of Hollywood's own Golden Calf. The celebrated sequences of *The Ten Commandments* professing to delineate the Bible's indictment of the worship of materialism are, in fact, a remarkably erotic presentation of woman's lust for man—for his vital essence as well as for his gold and his social power.

We are shown a young woman who uses her long hair, the familiar emblem of her primitive femininity ("the longer the hair, the smaller the brain," every wit of the period knew), to polish the gleaming surface of the Golden Calf of heathenish hedonism. She presses her face against it, lovingly, as if her skin were touching a lover's cheek. She is clearly an erotic materialist whose vicious desires are reflected in the idol's golden gleam. Then De Mille makes the gold-sex-war parallelism more explicit. A warrior stands behind her as she ecstatically caresses the gold. In a cunning close-up we see her glance upward at the warrior, the angle of her body blending into the angle of his own pose. For a moment their figures seem to mingle in an intensely eroticized image of desire and response.

De Mille wanted to reassure his viewers that he did not condone the pleasures of sex, and he therefore added a caption bewailing the "mischief and corruption" of the people. They "bowed down and worshipped the Golden Calf." But when we return to the scene, we find "the people" to be the same young woman, who, passionately extend-

*The Priestess of the Golden Calf, from Cecil B.
De Mille's* The Ten Commandments *(1923)*

ing her arms toward the Golden Calf, commences an orgiastic harem
dance taken directly from De Mille's memories of late-nineteenth-
century art. Like the sexual women who adorned the walls of the rich,
De Mille's sinner, too, was irresistibly drawn to any object of phallic
shape and substantial size. Soon we therefore see her rub her back like a
cat against the rigid foreleg of the bestial god. She is elevated above the
crowd: alone with her idol, she and the calf are one. Now she throws off
her veils and becomes Salome seducing Herod. Raising her arms in the
manner Theda Bara had adopted to announce the predatory intentions

of the vampire, she reveals the voluptuous outlines of her body (she's wearing a bra-and-panties-only vaudeville-styled costume). To apprise sluggish intellects of her intentions, she announces: "Come worship ye the golden god of Pleasure!"

We see her slide down to a prostrate position in knowledgeable imitation of the many late-nineteenth-century salon nymphs whose apparently sprained or broken backs had made them tempting targets of therapeutic rape in the world of academic art. Taking a beaker from an attendant, she drinks from it; then, writhing snakily into a standing position, she throws the rest of the fluid it contains over the multitudes, as if anointing them with the vital essence of pleasure itself.

Stimulated in this manner by the ejaculatory taunts of the phallic woman—votary of the Golden Calf—the worshipers go wild, and De Mille, with the same pious but titillating voyeuristic disapproval Griffith had popularized earlier, shows them engaging in a variety of orgiastic endeavors. Above them all we see the priestess worship the long, hollow snout of the Golden "Calf"—an ingenious instrument that is clearly both phallic and vaginal. The animal itself looks like a severely undernourished pig. As she hugs and nuzzles its vaginal phallus and rubs her body against the idol, she becomes the primitive bisexual feminine personified, a "golden calf" of lust.

A man approaches the lurid priestess while she continues to pay homage to the bisexual snout of her monstrous idol. Fervently he announces: "The people shall worship thy golden god—and call thee queen!" They hug and pet with abandon—but by this time De Mille had exploited the scene as far as he possibly could without publicly acknowledging the obvious hollowness of his own disapprobation. So much pleasure could no longer go unpunished. The ire of the righteous God of Christendom descends upon the licentious body of the priestess in the form of a sudden attack of leprosy, even while the revelers below continue to hug and kiss an assortment of supine, ready, willing, and extremely able nymphs.

It is now time for Moses to bring this world of revelling brutes to order, and for us to fade forward to the more subtle enticements of Modern Civilization. Here we encounter Dan, a skeptical son who doubts his pious mother's biblical exhortations concerning the horrors of sexual pleasure. Outmoded Victorian bunk! he tells her. He must be taught a lesson. The standard stuff of Twenties silents follows: missteps, penniless waifs, religious skepticism, even an attack on Elinor Glyn as apostle of the rotten values of the gold-digger crowd. Feckless youth dances wildly to "African" jazz: the Golden Calf still sticks its snout into everything.

Some underhanded business dealings and the doubting son of the religious mother is magically transformed into a millionaire. This means that it is time for the vampire of essence to do her erotic damage. Sally Lung, a characteristic Eurasian "mongrel" conflation of racial and sexual evil, makes her appearance in Dan's sumptuous office. "Go easy, son!" a henchman whispers. "This Sally Lung is half French and half Chinese. The combination of French perfume and Oriental incense is more dangerous than nitroglycerine!" De Mille had clearly read the recently published work of race theorists such as Lothrop Stoddard and Madison Grant very closely, and he was counting on his audience to understand the political significance of his metaphors.

When Eurasian Sally (Nita Naldi—secret participant in the erotic dreams of many young men of the early Twenties) sidles in, we know there is not a bat's chance in Hell that Dan will listen to such advice. Sally needs only murmur an invitation into his ear to come and try a "love-drink . . . distilled from a thousand lotus flowers!" and Dan is done for. Soon after, Dan's virtuous mom is killed by the collapse of a wall made from the inferior concrete he supplied to build an unsafe church. Silent-movie moralizing was nothing if not direct.

Back to Eurasian Sally, who seductively lounges in her lair of love, puffing provocatively on a cigarette to remind the audience of her direct link to the snout-worshiping priestess of the Golden Calf. Exotic trappings abound. The paper she is reading warns that a beautiful woman has escaped from Molokai Leper Island. Need we guess who she might be? Kipling, Rohmer, and De Mille: a mating of minds on silent celluloid. Now-dissolute Dan enters, short of cash. He wants his string of pearls back—he doesn't yet realize that a man's essence, once spent, is lost forever. Perhaps Freud would have added a jewelry box here, to offer the audience an even clearer clue.

Sally, of course, refuses to return Dan's pearls. He pulls them from her neck and shouts: "I'm through with you for good!" Sally takes another knowing glance at the Molokai headline and an evil smile falls over her face as Dan leaves. "You," she says, pointing at him dramatically, "you're not through with me! You'll never be through with me!" Openly mocking him, she shows him the article. *She* is the leper woman from the tropics, and she has sneaked into America from Calcutta hidden in one of his own bales of inferior imported jute to contaminate

America with her diseased Eurasian body. De Mille telescoped the racist diatribes of Grant and Stoddard into a single, astonishingly efficient gesture that told his viewers exactly how the leprous immigrant would decimate the Aryan elite. He meant his audiences to stand up at this point and shout: "Kill that woman!"

Dan at last realizes what has become of him. Traitor to the superior genes of the Aryan elite, he has, by renouncing the wisdom of God, slipped back down the evolutionary ladder into a world of Semitic and Asian modes of economic betrayal. Less than a decade later, in *Shanghai Express* (1932), Josef von Sternberg would further contextualize De Mille's point by having Warner Oland, as an evil Eurasian Bolshevik rebel leader, utter the Aryan dogma also at the root of De Mille's exposition: "You're in China now, Sir, where time and life have no value." Oland's acting career was itself a true Hollywood production: He was a Swede who habitually played "Orientals," starring as Fu Manchu in several silents and later gaining fame as Charlie Chan.

Once Dan understands that his unmanly business dealings and his licentiousness have unleashed the Yellow Peril, he knows he must try to do whatever he still can to stem "the rising tide of color against white world-supremacy" (the title of one of Stoddard's books, published in 1920). He shoots and kills Sally, the Eurasian vampire, who is death personified. Does he kill the woman, or does he eliminate the Yellow Peril? Is Dan's righteous act symbolic of civilization's dawning recognition of the need for genocide, or is it "just another" cleansing incident in Western civilization's rituals of gynecide? For De Mille and his audience that was no longer an issue: it was *both,* as a matter of course.

Dan ultimately finds his rightful reward in Hell, but De Mille could not let his audience leave without a better example. With the help of honest carpenter John (Dan's good brother), Mary, Dan's wife, seeks out the great carpenter of souls, the Man She Has Forgotten. She must be cleansed of the contamination she has received from the horrid string of seminal pearls worn by the leprous Eurasian prostitute who seduced her husband. For when the police came searching for him, they had casually handed her these pearls he left behind while trying to escape. Though Mary dropped them at once as if they were scorching her palm, she is now unclean; her womanly skin has been polluted by the eroticism of the vampire of seminal degeneracy. How can she ever be released from the leprosy of feminine eroticism? Carpenter John reads to Mary from the Bible: "And behold, there came to Him a leper, and worshipped Him." A scene of Christ in a barn follows. A young woman, blond hair, shunned by everyone, kneels before Christ. "Make me clean," she begs. "Be Thou Made Clean," he says, and she is clean.

In the modern world John and Mary are now ready to give immaculate birth to evolutionary Aryan humanity. Mary, having seen the light, looks at her hands: "Why, John—in the light, it's gone!" Yes, indeed, says John the carpenter, "in the light—it's gone!" Mary, newly sanctified by her renunciation of woman's instinctive yearning for the pearls of sex, shall henceforth be John's faithful footstool. As we watch her gratefully clinging to John's tolerant knees, the movie fades into silent hosannas.

Evolutionary cleansing of men and women carrying the leprous bite of the vampire, the mark of Kipling's degenerate child-minded colonized beast, took place in one form or another in hundreds of movies of this sort throughout the Twenties, quite a few of them directed by the rising De Mille or the fading Griffith. Two themes were churned over and over again: man's fateful pollution by the temptations of the sexual vampire and his redemption by the self-effacing love of the female saint.

The variations on this theme were endless. Nita Naldi, for instance, made another appearance, this time as Gina, an "Italian dancer," in John Robertson's 1920 version of *Dr. Jekyll and Mr. Hyde,* starring John Barrymore. Naldi, whose star ascended just as Theda Bara's had come to rest in the mud of history, became in this movie the catalyst to Jekyll's transformations into Mr. Hyde. In a den of ill repute, she first draws the virtuous Dr. Jekyll to her with a dance, and then she kisses him on the lips. It is as if she sucks his soul out of his body with that kiss. He is an instant goner: "For the first time in his life, Jekyll had wakened to a sense of his baser nature."

After much dashing about and a great deal of lurid evolutionary backsliding, Jekyll finds himself no longer able to control the incursions of the bestial Hyde within himself. We see the beast—symbolized by a gigantic tarantula—getting ready to take over. Jekyll realizes that to save his ever faithful, knee-clinging fiancée, Millicent, from a fate worse than death by his own hands, he must kill himself—and he does. The last shreds of humanity in him have saved the dimorphic organization of civilization. He has slain the tarantula of reversion called up by the dance of the sexual vampire. Millicent, in tears, clutches Jekyll's dear, dead feet. As the screen fades to black we find cold comfort in the realization that she will remain there forever, pure as the driven snow, a meek, self-sacrificial soulkeeper who can be counted upon to guide her mate belatedly toward a heaven he has earned by extirpating the mark of the beast in himself.

But only the worst male backsliders and female vampires needed to be killed. The silent film also initiated the durable Hollywood tradition requiring that tomboys, feminists, charming viragoes, and other such masculinized females be deprived of their phallic pretensions by masterly males. The actions of such termagants were always shown to be simply a factor of their repressed longing for babies. Women suffering from poorly sublimated forms of penis envy (Freud's amazing discovery was on everyone's mind) often tried to "grow" the male's erectile tissue by packing a variety of guns and knives, thereby denying that they were fragile women. All these deluded creatures needed was a firm regimen of masculine authority to renounce their own phallic ambitions forever.

Rudolph Valentino's starring vehicle *The Sheik* (1921), for instance, found its happy ending in the popular cliché that independent women were unhappy souls aching to be raped by a masterful male. Agnes Ayres played Diana Mayo, an arrogant "new woman" who dismisses a meek young suitor with outrageous feminist rhetoric: "Marriage is captivity—the end of independence." Subsequently Diana is denied entry to an Arab casino where, as part of a "marriage market," women perform exotic dances before being carted off "to the harems of the rich merchants—to obey and serve like chattel slaves." As yet unaware that in reality her body aches for the same treatment, Diana disguises herself as one of the exotic dancers and infiltrates the proceedings.

Discovered by Valentino, "Ahmed the Sheik," when she proves unwilling to go onto the podium and expose herself as "chattel," she whips out the requisite gun to emphasize her phallic self-sufficiency. But Ahmed is smitten anyway, charmed by "the pale hands and the golden hair of a white woman." Pretty soon he climbs into her bedroom to contemplate her while she is sleeping. When he sees her gun holster on a table, he picks it up, takes out the bullets, bites one, and smiles sardonically. The bullets in this phallic woman's weapon have more bark than bite. He already knows how to defang this vampire!

To prove her independence, Diana goes into the desert unaccompanied by other "Europeans." Ahmed chases Diana on horseback. The phallic incompetence of this pseudomasculinized female is obvious: she clumsily drops the gun she, for once, *should* have used to defend herself against the erotic incursions of Arab Death. Unconsciously she wants to be rid of this weapon that stands between her and the masterful male.

Valentino nimbly retrieves Diana's self-excised instrument of independence at full gallop, then plucks her off her horse as if she were a ripe fruit. The onlooking Arabs cheer. Caption: "Her exultant dream of freedom ended—a helpless captive in the desert wastes."

Of course the audience could not be expected to sympathize with a heathen Arab. The sheik therefore is soon revealed to be a decent European after all: "His father was an Englishman, his mother a Spaniard." With any suggestions of "miscegenation" out of the way, romance can flourish. But first the woman-as-defective-male gun symbolism is pushed to the hilt. The captive Diana asks: "Why have you brought me here?" and he responds: "Are you not woman enough to know?" But of course she *isn't:* after all, she is a *new* woman. He tauntingly weighs her gun in his hands, looks at it, and laughs deprecatingly. His own equipment is so much better! Diana panics and grabs a dagger in a last stab at phallic competency, but the sheik takes it from her effortlessly. A man in total control, he can now wait until Diana begs him to take her. "If I choose, I can make you love me," he says, grinning. Not yet completely tamed, she foolishly shoots back a pitiful new-woman blank: "I would rather you'd kill me."

But in fact Diana's passion is already double-edged. She loves the sheik, even if she doesn't know it yet. Lucky for her he's not a real Arab, for as a caption informs us: "When an Arab sees a woman he wants, he takes her!" The evil Omair is just such a savage. It is his role to make Diana realize that it is better to be taken by a European in Semitic disguise than by a real Arab in heat. But first Adolphe Menjou in the role of Raoul de St. Hubert, a suave French novelist and friend of the sheik, teaches her the facts of nature. Says Diana, her feminism fading: "The men in my life have been anything but tender and faithful." Raoul the Wise knows why: "Unfortunately, beautiful women provoke in some men all that is base in their characters." She: "And the woman pays for the beauty God has given her."

When it appears that an accident might have befallen the sheik who keeps her prisoner, Diana's response is that of a worried lover. She realizes that Ahmed is the sheik-Adonis of her dreams. He, meanwhile, returning unexpectedly, overhears her expressions of concern for his welfare and realizes that he has conquered. He therefore gives her back her gun. Diana, on her part, recognizes that from now on that gun is *his* gun, there to protect her from his competition. After all, there is still a world full of real Arabs out there, lusting after white womanhood. Rape was filmic fun for the viewers only when shown to be truly therapeutic, a ritual to bring a wayward woman back into the domestic fold. The "lower races" had no right to use such tactics. Diana therefore behaves like a doctrinal eugenicist when Omair manages to capture her. Being ravished by Valentino was one thing, but defilement by an actual Semite quite another. She orders Ahmed's servant to shoot her with the gun Ahmed has just returned to her. Ahmed's trusty servant, however, is killed before he can do so.

Omair, on his part, doesn't care a whit about eugenics. He takes Diana to his lair and is about to have his way with her when the sheik rushes in and kills him. Ahmed is conveniently wounded in the process, and this allows Diana to show that, notwithstanding her pseudophallic past, she can be as good a Florence Nightingale as any other subservient virgin. The film ends with the joyful recovery of the European sheik, who, upon waking, murmurs to his nurse: "Diana, my beloved! The darkness has passed, and now the sunshine." Once more we fade upon a world in which men have conquered the feminine night.

The film version of *The Sheik* was based on the British romance writer Edith Hull's potboiler of the same title. Published in January 1921, the book had gone through more than fifty printings by year's end. Hull had emphasized the young Diana's "manlike qualities." In the opening pages of the book a gossipy American remarks that Diana was "not a very human girl" and that "she was sure meant to be a boy and changed at the last moment. She looks like a boy in petticoats, a damned pretty boy—and a damned haughty one." Diana considers herself one of the boys: "A man to me is just a companion with whom I ride or shoot or fish; a pal, a comrade, and that's just all there is to it. God made me a woman. Why, only He knows." (11) Much of this is conveyed in the film by the convenient visual shorthand of the phallic revolver.

The setup of *The Sheik,* therefore, was a standard tomboy-on-the-verge-of-sexual-awakening ploy. All Diana needed to become a decent reproductive woman was the attention of someone more manly than she considered herself to be. This has remained one of the most popular of our cultural myths, designed to encourage women to think that they cannot be "complete" until they have been swept off their feet by "a real man," who will force them to face up to the iron will of "nature." The ravisher, of course, should always fall just short of actual rape in his attempts to transform his tomboy into a mother-woman. The Cary Grant or Clark Gable spanking-the-rebellious-leading-lady scene standard in

Thirties and Forties Hollywood comedies of manners was soon to become a convenient shorthand for the constant reiteration of this social
directive.

Diana's trajectory was no different from that of thousands of other
heroines who had to be slapped around a bit to learn their lessons of
submission. *The Sheik,* in book and film alike, exploited the period's fascination with sex as violence and its accompanying premise that "primitives," being "closer to nature," must be better at the roughhouse
behavior needed to jump-start a tomboy's sexual awakening than "civilized" men ("real" Arabs, in Hull's story, were invariably violent, childish, foolish, selfish, and lecherous). Such suggestions added just enough
spice to make this run-of-the-mill novel into a popular hit. Intimations
of violation were everywhere: the sheik, for instance, observes Diana
"with fierce burning eyes that swept her until she felt that the boyish
clothes that covered her slender limbs were stripped from her, leaving
the beautiful white body bare under his passionate stare." (56–7)

Hull made Diana—and her readers—wallow in lurid masochistic
fantasies of "therapeutic" rape:

> The flaming light of desire burning in his eyes turned her sick
> and faint. Her body throbbed with the consciousness of a
> knowledge that appalled her. She understood his purpose with a
> horror that made each separate nerve in her system shrink
> against the understanding that had come to her under the con-
> suming fire of his ardent gaze, and in the fierce embrace that
> was drawing her shaking limbs closer and closer against the
> man's own pulsating body. She writhed in his arms as he crushed
> her to him in a sudden access of possessive passion. His head
> bent slowly down to her, his eyes burned deeper, and, held im-
> movable, she endured the first kiss she had ever received. And
> the touch of his scorching lips, the clasp of his arms, the close
> union with his warm, strong body robbed her of all strength, of
> all power of resistance. (58)

Such overwriting has become the stock-in-trade of today's "bodice ripper" romances for women.

Hull was only one of numerous women writers who exploited the
cultural normalization of the dominance and submission imperatives of
late-nineteenth-century imperialism, a normalization that had forced
women to find erotic pleasure in being "colonized." Such celebrations

of feminine submission helped disguise the economic motives underlying the adolescent woman's confinement to the realm of reproductive domesticity as "biological predestination" and helped turn an ideological theorem into an inherent feminine rite of passage. These narratives told young women, over and over again, that what they craved was the "romance" of violent erotic seduction. A man unwilling to "assert" himself, a man who failed to take away the tomboy's gun, was a "female man," a wimp to be avoided for eugenic reasons. Untold numbers of books and movies patterned after *The Sheik* taught women to see the sexual violence done to them as a proof of their lovers' "manhood."

Thus the masterful rapist with a will and a phallus of steel, able to beat "the man" out of his woman with a loving daddy's concern for the "biological needs" of his wife, became the "romantic" idol of women everywhere. This Valentino syndrome required that a "true" man be passionate yet a transcendent "Aryan" at heart. He must have his "anima," his effeminate side, firmly under control and be sternly paternal in rationing his munificent contributions to her needs. The true male was both a ravisher and a father surrogate. He was the animus figure ("Beat me Daddy, Eight to the Bar" was the title of a popular hit of the Thirties), who soon came to be regarded by early-twentieth-century women as a shamanistic guide in their rite of passage to motherhood. Masochism, like sadism, is a metaphoric response, an imaginative adjustment of human expectations to environmental conditions. It is dependent on constant reinforcement. It is *not* an "archetypal psychological necessity" or a biological need.

The very survival of imperialism as a system of control depended on the evolutionists' dreams of a world of radical inequalities among individuals. In 1921, the year of *The Sheik*, Madison Grant, in his preface to the fourth edition of *The Passing of the Great Race*, proudly announced that genetics had taught Americans that "to admit the unchangeable differentiation of race in its modern scientific meaning is to admit inevitably the existence of superiority in one race and of inferiority in another." This project of education, he said, had at last "been accomplished thoroughly." The sociobiologists' unfaltering delineation of inherent social patterns of dominance and submission had even led "the Congress of the United States to adopt discriminatory and restrictive measures against the immigration of undesirable races and peoples." (xxviii–xxix)

The image of the sheik, the domestication of the Valentino syndrome, the psychiatric apotheosis of feminine masochism, of the need for feminine "castration," for mental (if not actual) clitoridectomy, for the social regulation of penis envy, the tomboy's rape, the ritual murder of women's creative erotic imagination—all were metaphoric representations of a gynecidal mind-set directly parallel to, and originating directly in, the racist agenda of imperialist evolutionist genetics.

The artificial separation between science and "the emotions" to which we have become accustomed in this century has thus seen to it that the tendentious evolutionist metaphors produced by biology, psychology, medicine, and genetics continue to interfere with the concept of true gender equality even today.

For if as the century progressed it gradually became acceptable to mistake the good woman for a woman of easy virtue at first, the good girl–bad girl dichotomy always remained in force. In the long run a woman might be permitted to be modern, vivacious, charming—even quick-witted sometimes—but only if in the end she revealed herself to be a sexual innocent who had merely been mistaken for evil. Vile vampires who might, at first, seem innocent and pure, only to be ultimately revealed as destroyers, were also added to the pop-cultural repertoire.

Fritz Lang's *Metropolis* (1926) played on both of these themes. The German director's science fiction parable contained dramatic imagery of the economic exploitation of the working classes, and this helped what was in fact a profoundly sexist and elitist film gain a reputation as a progressive social manifesto. But to point out that workers who are exploited can become dangerous is not necessarily an indication of humane intentions. In the decades around the turn of the century, numerous religious, politically conservative, or at most mildly socially aware writers had cautioned the Sumnerite captains of industry against limitless overexploitation of the working classes. Most were concerned that such ruthless social Darwinism would lead to a class war of major proportions. Workers treated like wild animals in chains and goaded beyond further endurance might break their bonds and make mincemeat of the evolutionary elite. The general tenor of such admonitions was: be kind to your servants, scratch their backs a bit from time to time, and they will be more productive, more useful to you. It was, in essence, a commonsense approach to slave management—still a popular argument in favor of social reform in political circles.

This was also the social message of *Metropolis*. Lang made use of the period's most egregious platitudes about the good girl–bad girl poles of species evolution and degeneration. Thea von Harbou, Lang's wife, who wrote the screenplay, was as adept as Edith Hull at exploiting the reigning social prejudices regarding the role of women in society. It is impossible to deny the visual power of *Metropolis*'s images. Within the context of modernist criticism, the success of those central images has been sufficient to establish Lang's film as a "work of art." One can argue about that assessment, but the film certainly is an extremely effective diatribe against women as active participants in political life. Its social values are no different from those of *Cabiria,* but instead of Cabiria, future hope of the Italian nation, we are offered Maria, whose saintly name indicates the religious nature of her maternal task as caretaker of orphaned children. Instead of Sophonisba, the woman with the African womb, we are offered the prototypical twentieth-century sexual Robot, a nightmare image of the "mechanistic" reproductive evil of woman. Even the Moloch of *Cabiria* makes a virtually unaltered appearance as a mechanized *vagina dentata,* when the young hero imagines the giant machines whose pistons chew up workers by the dozens to be a gaping and devouring mouth.

In *Metropolis* the standard soon-to-be-saintly mother-woman is identified as the "real Maria," while the robot, designed to be her double, is the "false Maria." The robot, even in its original, undisguised, form, is unmistakably feminine, with pronounced breasts and a stylishly bobbed hairdo. A creature of gleaming silver metal, she is the immediate precursor of, and no doubt also one of the sources for, the eroticized robot women of recent American comic books and heavy-metal album covers. The hyperdeveloped, polished-steel females designed by today's Japanese commercial artists probably also find their fetishistic roots in the robot vampire of *Metropolis.* This genealogy is significant, for it shows that the early twentieth century's virgin/vampire dichotomy helped shape today's pervasive male fantasy of the sexual woman as a Frankenstein creation—a robotic expression of nature's reproductive mechanisms. The point of such fetishization is always that if you awaken a woman's sexuality, you create a monster—a creature that should be mechanical and predictable in its responses, yet inevitably tends to get out of control after seminal lubrication. Man's "vitalizing electricity," could easily turn into a "Mother Jekyll" serum. Such potions awaken Mrs. Hyde, nature's erotic tarantula, the organic machine, the automatic lover who will bite your head off. The "awakened" woman is the contemporary metal monster, the gigantic, relentlessly egg-laying ur-mother of the H. R. Giger–inspired "aliens" Sigourney Weaver keeps trying to ward off in outer space.

The false Maria of *Metropolis* is a direct precursor to all these mechanical brides of the twentieth-century male imagination, and the story of her creation is a prototypical expression of the mixed sexual longing and fear that brought these mutant android women into being. Freder, naive son of the ruthless master of Metropolis, is stirred into action against his father by the appearance of saintly Maria (childlike, flat-chested, modestly dressed, and virginal). She is a Florence Nightingale who cares for orphan children. Smitten, Freder goes in search of her, discovering in the process the industrial stratification of Metropolis: the masters live above the machines, and the machines are hidden "far underground, yet high above the workers' city."

Deep down in this inhospitable womb of the earth, Maria edifies the worn-out masses with biblical stories that carry the message that "between the brain that plans and the hands that build there must be a mediator. It is the heart that must bring about an understanding between them." Freder has no doubt that Maria is this heart. Above ground, however, his dad, the brain, schemes to eliminate the heart. To this end, John Fredersen, master of Metropolis, visits Rotwang, the prototypical cinematic mad inventor, who has "created a machine in the image of man, that never tires or makes mistakes." More than an ideal worker, this is the ideal *woman* of every man's dreams: a robot with breasts and bobbed hair, a metal flapper. Rotwang needs just another twenty-four hours to produce "a machine which no one will be able to tell from a human being." Fredersen, annoyed by Maria's social activism, tells Rotwang: "make your robot in the likeness of that girl. . . . I will send the robot down to the workers, to sow discord among them and destroy their confidence in Maria."

A virtuous romance, chastely lit by the Cross, barely has time to bloom between Freder and Maria before Rotwang captures her. In an incredibly drawn-out sequence (it lasts a full three minutes), Lang exploited his audiences' various rape fantasies in every possible fashion: close-ups of Maria's panicking face as she realizes she is being stalked; shot after shot of her heaving, terrorized (yet modestly dressed) torso; the beam of Rotwang's flashlight almost literally "pinning" her to the wall. We see her desperately running, stumbling, and bouncing into rocks; the light beam exposes her body, "undressing" her as it crawls over her desperate form. This is one of the most implicitly violent, most exploitative "rape" scenes the movies have yet produced, a sequence that was to show several future generations of movie directors how to exploit sadomasochism in the name of virtue.

But Lang still had not finished his rape. We are shown poor, saintly

Maria, desperate in Rotwang's laboratory, continuing her struggle. Rotwang, grimacing, says, "Come, I'm going to make the robot look like you," as he throws his body on top of hers. Freder, passing by, hears her scream but is helpless against the mad scientist's tricks. Rotwang places the saintly Maria horizontally in a glass contraption and duplicates her outward form. Levers are switched, fluids bubble, electricity sparks. Rings of "magnetism" run up and down the robot. In her chest a heart begins to pound: the false Maria has come to life.

At once we realize that this Maria, unlike her holy namesake, is a lecherous, vicious creature, for her eyes are ringed with kohl. They glitter with feverish passion. The real Maria's head slips sideways: she is unconscious—the primal feminine element, held so virtuously under control by this heroically evolved woman, has been transferred to the metal body of the False Maria.

Thus begins the reign of the vampire woman over the workers of Metropolis. The robot Maria is brought to Fredersen, and though she is wearing the real Maria's virtuous dress, we suddenly realize that this Maria has breasts, and that her clothes are oddly disheveled. A provocative, lewd smirk distorts her vampire face. Her body loudly shouts "come hither." "She's perfect," Fredersen remarks, and he orders: "Now go down to the workers and undo Maria's teaching; stir them up to criminal acts."

It is clear that the false Maria won't have any trouble doing so. We see the evil, kohl-eyed vampire in close-up. She winks obscenely. When young Freder rushes in, he sees the would-be Maria and his father in a vile embrace (a last-straw perversion of woman's sacred motherhood role). Distraught, the young man faints. His ensuing fever dream turns fantasy into cinematic reality, and is meant to edify the viewers about the primal nature of woman stripped of all societal controls and inhibitions. We are shown a nightclub act attended by the bon ton of Metropolis. The false Maria begins a seductive dance, backlit to reveal the outlines of her body. The trappings are Art Nouveau sliding into Art Deco. The men of the elite are mesmerized. In the vampire woman's dance only her lower body moves—her loins become an image of the grasping womb of nature in action. Her breasts, even more pronounced now, are bare, except for what appear to be metal pasties. Freder panics in his sickbed: he has seen a sexual demon in the body of the virtuous mother-woman. Can this nightmare be as real as the mind's movie shows it to be?

True bestiality now drives the false Maria wild. Virtually naked, she takes on every pose the period's popular artists had been able to devise to convey the vampire's sexual hunger. She sits on her haunches and swirls her upper torso. Then the screen dissolves into a semiabstract nightmare of glittering vampire eyes. We see her open her legs and reveal the hollow portal of her loins. The mouth of Moloch is about to open. Freder sits bolt upright in bed, panic sweeping over him. He realizes civilization is about to be dragged back into the jungle. Again we see the false Maria, in a perfect Art Deco pose, her thighs wide apart, riding on a serpentine dragon, its venal mouth of lust wide open. Its coils are everywhere. The vampire Maria, legs still spread apart, her sex elevated to the center of the screen, has become the idol of eroticism enthroned as the leaders of Metropolis rush forward and stretch their arms out to her.

Metropolis, like so many ambitious silent movies, was over three hours long in its original form. About two hours of it have survived various cuttings. Even so, there are plenty of special effects and action sequences to keep its viewers from getting bored. But in the end the false Maria does what she was supposed to do—she drives the obtuse workers, male and female, into a revolutionary frenzy. Crazed, they destroy the machines that keep their living quarters from being flooded by groundwater. They are, after all, little more than savages and hence easily excited and deluded. They even forget their own children. These children are, of course, rescued by the real Maria, who has finally broken out of her confinement. She is aided by Freder: once more the bourgeois nuclear family saves the day—the heart has mediated between brain and loins.

The workers, thinking that their children have drowned, burn the vampire Maria as a witch. She laughs satanically while the fire consumes her. At last we see her return to her robotic metal shell. The witch of female sexuality is dead. Rotwang, meanwhile, realizing that he has been exposed, runs off with the real Maria, Hunchback of Notre Dame–style, to the top of the cathedral, only to be dispatched by Freder after much cliff-hanging. Tender embraces. Fredersen senior and the foreman of the workers confront each other. Maria pleads with the leader's son: "There can be no understanding between the hands and the brain unless the *heart* acts as a mediator." Saintly, sexless femininity, saved from the clutches of Rotwang, prevails: the son, enlightened by the real Maria, joins the hands of the foreman and his father. The millennium at hand, we fade to black.

Metropolis thus graphically illustrates how, toward the end of the Twenties, the themes of economic imperialism and gender depredation had come to overlap quite consciously in the thinking of many. The vampire woman had become a political subversive, determined to manipulate the inferior mind of the worker. Like the colonized "lower races," she was an incarnation of Kipling's rabid leper, a Sally Lung threatening to infect the Western male with the mark of the beast. The vampire woman and the worker were two of a kind, both driven by blind animal instinct. David Starr Jordan, the "liberal" first president of Stanford University, had already dismissed this stratum of labor in society in his treatise *The Blood of the Nation* (1902). He had ridiculed "the conventional literature of sympathy" for portraying this irredeemable segment of society as consisting of workmen "brutalized by machinery." The laborer was responsible for his own fate. "If it should be that his kind is increasing, it is because his betters are not. It is not that his back is bent by centuries of toil. He was not born oppressed. Heredity carries over not oppression, but those qualities of mind and heart which invite or which defy oppression." Therefore, the fact that the worker "is 'chained to the wheel of labor' is the result, not the cause of his impotence." (22–3)

The workers in Lang's film were exactly such "primitive, aboriginal" creatures as Jordan had sketched: "ox-like" and "gazing with lackluster eye upon the things about" them. They were undifferentiated mass-men. *Metropolis* does not advocate their liberation; it only argues that working them to death will drive them to desperate actions. Left alone, they are not even capable of tending to such fundamental human concerns as the care and well-being of their own children. Siegfried Kracauer pointed out as early as 1947 that though "on the surface, it seems that Freder has converted his father; in reality, the industrialist has outwitted his son. The concession he makes amounts to a policy of appeasement that not only prevents the workers from winning their cause, but enables him to tighten his grip on them." (163) Clearly these workers *needed* to be guided by a tyrant able to channel their primitive passions in a cost-efficient manner. Otherwise the vampire of socialism, the false Maria, would be able to rouse them to a blind revolt against authority and precipitate a cataclysm in which all would be lost.

Metropolis showed that socialism was an artificial creation, a robot designed by a subversive degenerate who combined masculine intellect with feminine cunning, a man whose half-evolved brain was capable of cabalistic scheming. This creature was Rotwang, the mad scientist, a man just far enough up the ladder of evolution to understand the uses of knowledge but not sufficiently advanced to be able to grasp that science must be used only to maintain social order in the service of the evolutionary elite. Rotwang had given the false Maria phony outward Aryan genetic credentials to obscure her perverse natural inclination to drive society back into the world of (feminine) chaos. As heathen thief of the real Maria's Christian virtue, Rotwang was clearly the most dangerous cog in the wheel of human evolution.

It has been suggested that Adolf Hitler was so impressed with *Metropolis* that, as soon as the Nazis had come to power in Germany, he told his propaganda minister, Joseph Goebbels, to ask Lang to make movies for the Reich. And why not? Lang's earlier Wagnerian films had been full of Nordic heroics. Presumably Lang declined and escaped to the United States. The story is most likely apocryphal, but it is, even so, a telling parable about the propagandistic implications of Lang's films. Moreover, Lang's wife, Thea von Harbou, who, as Kracauer pointed out, "was not only sensitive to all undercurrents of the time, but indiscriminately passed on whatever happened to haunt her imagination," (162) clearly understood that the glory days of Aryan expression still lay ahead. She split up with her husband, joined the Nazi party, and stayed with the dominant pulse of the moment.

Indeed, Harbou and Lang had sketched Rotwang just right for the mood of the times. He was an evil magician, an erotic necromancer, a sinister creature out of the past who straddled two cultures. He gave a clue to his nature when he decorated his door with a pentagram as if it were a mezuzah. When he placed a second huge pentagram behind the robot of sexuality, the false Maria he was about to create, most viewers undoubtedly confused the satanic sign with the Star of David, secret symbol of the worldwide conspiracy of Fu Manchu, Dracula, Svengali—and Rotwang, that most evil of interlopers, the eternal Jew.

In her novelization of the screenplay for *Metropolis* (1926), Harbou was even more explicit. She had described Rotwang's lair as a hotbed of reversive degeneracy in the midst of the modern city: "Set into the black wood of the door stood, copper-red, mysterious, the seal of Solomon, the pentagram. It was said that a magician, who came from the East (and in the tracks of whom the plague wandered) had built the house in seven days." (47) Harbou thus made it clear that Rotwang, as the contemporary incarnation of this pestilent magician—was a brother of Nosferatu, the plague-ridden semitic erotomane brought to the

screen just four years earlier by F. W. Murnau. Rotwang, Harbou emphasized over and over again, was an incarnation of the Wandering Jew,
poisoning the modern world with the womb-driven passions of Istar—
Huneker's Esther Brandes—whoremother of Babylon, infected carrier
of the past, emissary of a cursed race marked by the devil's sign, marked
by Solomon's seal.

Hollywood as the prowling ground of the Jew and his helpmate,
the sexual woman with her phallic snake. This 1939 handbill,
widely distributed on the West Coast by the "Anti-Communist
Federation," was reproduced in the March 6, 1939, issue of Life.
The handbill's text is an Aryan call to arms: "Christian
Vigilantes Arise! Buy gentile, employ gentile, vote gentile. Boycott
the Movies! Hollywood is the Sodom and Gomorrah where
International Jewry controls vice, dope, gambling."

IX. RIGGING THE GREAT RACE AGAINST THE BEAUTIFUL AND DAMNED: THE CULTURAL GENETICS OF UNCLEAN WOMEN AND EMASCULATE MEN

During the 1920s the "scientific" racism of genetics took center stage in the imagination of the "Nordic" world. Biology teamed up with medicine, psychoanalysis, and anthropology to codify the laws of evolutionary inequality separating the Aryan male from all other branches of humanity. In the United States a consensus was building that the tight legislative curbs being instituted on immigration from all areas beyond Western Europe would not be enough to protect America from contamination by the agents of reversion. Moreover, the scientists were worried that even the acculturated females of the master race could be turned into tools of the world's collectivist conspiracy. After all, it had been demonstrated beyond a reasonable doubt that "women in all human races, as the females among all mammals, tend to exhibit the older, more generalized and primitive traits of the past of the race," as Madison Grant emphasized. (*The Passing of the Great Race,* 27) Nordics could not rest easily next to their blonde goddesses, for if they did not watch out, these apparent angels might slip back into their primitive ways and drag the male of the Aryan species down with them.

This was a far more urgent matter than most people thought, for, as Edward M. East of Harvard pointed out in his book *Heredity and Human Affairs* (1927), manhood had not yet become fully triumphant in the battle of the sexes: "What we must hold fast is that the two sexual states, maleness and femaleness, are not mutually exclusive. They are quantitative characters like many others with which the geneticist has to deal." Consequently the sexual struggle and the racial struggle shared the same metaphors. "The germ-cells in numerous species," said East, had come to determine gender by inheriting specific "qualities which in ordinary circumstances hold the balance of power in the control of sex. Generally speaking, they cast the deciding vote; but there may be a recount."

Such homely social metaphors of human election suggested that "the balance of power" in the evolutionary struggle could shift at a moment's notice. If males failed to maintain their manly vigilance, they might wake up one day to discover that they had become female. Who could argue with the imagery of a Harvard professor? "One may think of men and women as possessing attributes both of maleness and femaleness," professor East pointed out. "The controlling power which makes one actually a man and the other actually a woman is the inherited constitution. The possessor of one *X* chromosome is a man, the possessor of two *X* chromosomes is a woman." This chromosome distribution had "shifted the balance of conditions" so much "that no environmental changes can reverse it." Yet "in some of the lower animals the balance of the sex complex is not shifted thus far by the particular inheritance received. Under extraordinary circumstances, conditions may be such that the sex is really changed." (81) East, who emphasized that he regarded African-Americans as a genetically deprived "lower species," in this manner meant to suggest that any sustained alliance of the sort James Gibbons Huneker had described between Esther Brandes and the "monstrous African" of *Painted Veils* could only result in a reversal of the balance of power in the great struggle for life among chromosomes and bring back the deficient world of "woman-rule." To the lay reader of the period, such suggestions intimated that even if humanity were not immediately in danger of reverting to the bisexual instability of the lower organisms, sexual "subversion" could still take a far more subtle route. Medical science had shown that indiscriminate indulgence permitted women to absorb ever more of their mates' "masculinity." Thus, from a biological point of view, women were growing stronger the more promiscuous they were, while men could only grow weaker with each encounter. Chromosomal war waged on the battleground of sex must therefore inevitably end in the triumph of regressive feminine characteristics.

Fortunately it was also true, Ellsworth Huntington of Yale reassured his readers in *The Character of Races* (1924), that given their hard-core hatred of men, "the women who stand strongly for women's rights are rarely the mothers of the next generation." Good, passive mother-women were the ones most likely to pass on "their qualities to the next generation." He suggested that feminism was a form of autogynecide.

> Let the present rapid process of selecting the strong-minded women for destruction and the gentler, less aggressive ones for motherhood continue a few generations, and the banner of feminism will have to be hung on the wall—an interesting trophy No type can persist long if it is rigorously picked out for destruction whenever it appears. (361)

In the phrasing of this last sentence there is an ominous intimation, to be found time and again in the writings of the period's academics, that if nature had any trouble weeding out "undesirables" by this process of "natural selection," science should step in and help speed up the process.

But if hard-core, man-hating feminists had already been "rigorously picked out for destruction" by natural selection—or rather by the absence thereof—what about the *man-eating,* praying mantis–like, masculinized *sexual* women? What about the biological spermatophages of human society—what about Istar, Huneker's transitional sexual vampire of race and sex, the lusting woman who constantly *gained* creative and economic strength by replenishing the primitive masculine energies within her? Men rather enjoyed thinking of themselves as providers, as long as they were in charge of disbursements and their women remained undemanding slaves to their sheiks. But Istar transformed herself into a flapper just around the time Huneker was writing about her, and became a new economic hazard in the day-to-day life experience of the average American male. In this new incarnation she took various shapes. She could be a heartless temptress with money on her mind, a fun-loving ingenue in search of a sugar daddy, a tomboy in need of reproductive comeuppance, or a social climber in search of "standing." But in all these cases she was no longer a mythic figure. Instead, she had settled into the house next door or, occasionally, the one across the tracks. Domesticated in this fashion, she lost her larger-than-life quality, if not her predatory nature.

Of course the materialistic, money-hungry social climber had by no means been a stranger to later-nineteenth-century culture. But she had been a familiar social type, well understood and posing little real danger to men, since her motives and her price were part of the general order of society. Edith Wharton, in *The House of Mirth* (1905), effectively documented the fading glories of this older type in the sad decline of Lily Bart. Medicine's "real" vampire of essence was beginning her ascendance at just about the time of Lily's demise. At first an almost mythic creature of evil herself, her secondary economic purpose had begun to take center stage by the time she came to be portrayed as Gloria, the beautiful and damnable principal female protagonist of Fitzgerald's novel of 1922. The Glorias of the Twenties were to combine the social skills of Lily Bart with the sexual prowess of the vampire of essence. But the new breed of domesticated predators began to show an ever more immediate preference for their victims' financial assets rather than their vital essence. This created consternation among the men of the period. Overtly sexual transactions, after all, had been a matter of conscious choice. If you let yourself be despoiled by the vampire of essence, you were going to have to pay the economic piper. The Lily Barts, too, had still engaged in a well-regulated social commerce with its own set requirements. Women who did not stick to the rules were thrown out of the game, as Lily learned the hard way.

But now women were changing the rules. They seemed to have come to understand that economic potency represented an even quicker avenue to social "manhood" than access to the male's precious essence, with its attendant reproductive hazards. If semen, blood, and "gold" formed the social measure of a man, why not start with the gold, they seemed to be thinking. This thoroughly modern entrepreneurial spirit among the seminal predators of men's fears undermined their fantasy quotient. Such an attitude was much too prosaic to invite direct translation into the sadomasochistic metaphors of masculine sociosexual self-justification.

Istar's other side, therefore, that "real" vampire of the 1910s personified by Theda Bara, the woman of "Arab Death," reverted to her symbolical roots and once again took up shop in the movies and the pulp culture of the Twenties as the favorite fantasy nemesis of growing boys and frustrated young men. Taking her cue from She, La, Salome, and the many other mythic decapitators of the fin de siècle, she followed H. Rider Haggard, Edgar Rice Burroughs, and Abraham Merritt into the abyss of the masculine imagination. Here, driven by the spidery hunger coursing restlessly through her blood, she could be found dancing wildly under the moon to the primitive rhythms of African drums—a fact amply documented in thousands of popular magazines, books, and movies. She became once more the spider woman, the tiger cat, the serpent goddess, the brain eater, the moon menace, the cat woman, the crawling curse, the eternal She Who Must Be Obeyed, the chameleonic female animal who turned men into beasts with her "maw of sex"—the fearful *vagina dentata* nestled in her loins.

But the "real" vampires of the first twenty years of the century, by fusing with the Lily Barts of the fin de siècle, also mutated into the domesticated, but very practical, materialistic "gold diggers" of the Twenties and Thirties. If the out-and-out sexual women of the earlier decade had been strict anthropophages, intent first and foremost upon satisfying the hunger of Gaia's African womb, the gold diggers of the Twenties took their cue from Undine Spragg, the antiheroine of Wharton's *The Custom of the Country* (1913). But where vulgar Undine had a wealthy father, the gold diggers mostly came from poor lower-middle-class and working-class backgrounds and had to use their ample intelligence in concert with their ample curves to gain the perquisites of wealth. Their conscious subversion of the erotic scenarios of their suitors was a factor of their recognition that the way to a man's bank account ran through his vanity.

Sometime during the late Twenties the Haldeman-Julius Company of Girard, Kansas, published a "Little Blue Book" with the title *Confessions of a Gold Digger.* These pamphlet-length, pocket-size "Blue Books" were among the period's most sensational publishing success stories. Widely read and ubiquitously advertised, they served as "how-to" manuals to millions, covering virtually every topic under the sun, from wood-working to spiritual enlightenment, and from stockmarket strategies to psychoanalysis. Even Havelock Ellis contributed a handful. They were the "home university" of many of America's "self-made" men.

The author of *Confessions of a Gold Digger,* Betty van Deventer (she also contributed such titles as *How to Get a Husband* and *Why Wives Leave Home*), set out to teach the undecided among her female contemporaries that gold digging was the best road to financial independence for a sensible young woman. She pointedly addressed the moral qualms a woman might have about the procedure required to extract coin from a man's trousers. She admitted,

> until I was old enough to vote, I had a romantic attitude concerning the relationships between women and men. I was, in other words, a feminist. "Fair play," "Equality of the Sexes" and "Economic Independence for Women" were sonorous phrases which captured my adolescent imagination. The world was a Garden of Eden in which Eve picked her own apple.

But she soon found out that the more independent a woman proved to be, the more certain it was she would fall on her face in the "warlike world of business."

"I know of many instances of women," she pointed out, "who are more competent than men in competition in business affairs, yet few of these women are offered the same opportunities as the men." (3–7) Van Deventer soon found out that an intelligent woman most often found herself having to settle for being a secretary—a badly paid intellectual prostitute to some dim-witted male—or be forced to act the clinging vine to a husband "who pats her head and thinks how dear and dependent his little girl is." (21)

Van Deventer knew that nature had endowed her "with tempestuous health and a prairie stature," as well as a cool and collected practical sensibility. If she played "the role of the drooping violet," that was not likely to produce "any but a laughing effect" in those who saw her. (7) Her career as a gold digger had given her a chance to use her intelligence, become financially independent, and demonstrate to herself that she could run rings around most men in the realm of emotional manipulation. It allowed her to regain a little self-respect in a world that characterized women as little more than helpless children. "I love nothing better than to outwit or outthink a man," she asserted with obvious pleasure. (10)

A sensible woman with a lust for life, van Deventer remarked, soon realized that "every man may be reached in his own way. If one is sagacious, one has only to discover the weakness of the particular man, and pounce upon that." (5) Her Little Blue Book was a compendium of handy hints for gold diggers, a sterling example of "a modern business method" adapted to the gender wars. There was no need to feel qualms about this manner of commerce: "A merchant is considered clever who outwits his opponent. Man and woman are opponents in this economic era." (30) Since men insisted on falling in love with women who played the shrinking violet, the dolts should be given what they wanted. "I trade not upon sex but upon femininity," van Deventer emphasized. (13)

Gold diggers were, she pointed out, merely modern women who had learned to roll with the punches of gender injustice: "Is there not some quality of beauty in their clever schemes to make the man, any man, pay for a change?" But to succeed in this project of revenge, the gold digger must "not fall heir to sentimentality which blinds her emotions." She must know what she wants and go "after it without apology, even to herself." Men who wanted to be fawned upon and flattered, or treated like a daddy or a son by the women in their lives got what they deserved in the arms of a gold digger. False values produced false emotions: "The really proficient gold digger is made, not born." (13–14) And van Deventer concluded her manifesto by asserting that gold digging had made her more realistic, more practical, more self-reliant:

> A woman is still at a great disadvantage in the economic world, and I think gold digging is a just compensation. Possibly as women begin to receive more equal pay for equal work, and as big business lets in more women into the big, paying executive positions, there will be fewer gold diggers. (31)

But for the moment there was little evidence that things would change.

Van Deventer's pamphlet effectively voiced the economic dilemma of intelligent early-twentieth-century women. As an exponent of "hard-boiled gold digging," (23) she exposed the economic basis for the period's conflicts of gender. Implicitly she also revealed the close similarities between the socioeconomic position of most women and the colonized "lower races," who were called upon to engage in similar patterns of flattery and deception to keep their heads above water, for she stressed that a gold digger, for all her machinations and apparent power, remained merely an upper servant in the household of the imperial male. She was forced to play the role of a silent subversive. She kept her willfully suppressed intelligence active by stealing crumbs from the master's table and thumbing her nose at him behind his back. She was a woman with sweetness on her tongue and disdain in her heart: "I always listen with almost reverence to any opinion which a man states, no matter how silly or erroneous I may know it to be." (13)

The gold digger of the Twenties and Thirties, then, was an economic terrorist invading the realm of the imperial male, a psychological
interloper, a true Bolshevik of gender—and there is every indication
that during the period of her reign she was often perceived as such by
the men around her. She was even becoming an actual political danger,
for in victimizing her masters, she mercilessly satirized their expectations of what a woman should be. By emphasizing this aspect, van Deventer's little pamphlet gives us a far better insight into the actual
mind-set of the Twenties' gold digger than Anita Loos's far more famous
Gentlemen Prefer Blondes of 1925.

It is not surprising that Loos's satire should have been a big hit, for
her portrayal of Lorelei Lee as "the dumbest blonde of all" allowed the
sophisticates of the Twenties to believe that they had their women well
in hand. Van Deventer made it a point to warn that Loos's Lorelei was
not a useful role model "for a young aspirant. Too many instances in her
experience are unreal." But Loos had adopted the male point of view,
reassuring the readers that the gold digger was indeed "as dumb as she
should be" to fulfill her function in boy-toy land. In retrospect, what is
perhaps most interesting about Loos's book is her scathing antifeminine
stance, which she had developed, as she was to admit in her retrospective preface to a 1963 reissue of her novel, partly in response to her
amazement at the sort of attention she, who carried her intelligence on
her sleeve, did *not* get from the men around her, while a woman she had
come to regard as "the dumbest blonde of all" had "bewitched" even
H. L. Mencken, her good friend and idol and "one of the keenest minds
of our era." Mencken, she added, "liked me very much indeed; but
in the matter of sentiment he preferred a witless blonde." When she
wrote *Gentlemen Prefer Blondes,* she used Mencken's current flame as
a model, "for I wanted Lorelei to be a symbol of the lowest possible
mentality of our nation." Thus Loos's "revenge" on the gold digger, eagerly appropriated by Hollywood, has deliberately skewed our perception of the motives of these female sexual entrepreneurs of the Twenties
and Thirties.

But when Loos declared, with what was meant to be heavy irony,
that she had "stumbled on an important scientific fact" (11–13) in her assessment of generic male attraction to blondes during the early Twenties, she was actually far closer to the social "truth" of the time than she
recalled in 1963. The Twenties were the heyday of the "Nordic" genetic
ideal. Mendelian biology insisted that proper dimorphic development of
men and women was of absolute importance to "race balance." The

dumb blonde was seen as the most genuinely advanced product of fe-male genetic evolution. She was the Twenties' equivalent of the mid-nineteenth-century women who had tried to prove their "value" in bourgeois society by adopting a "cult of invalidism."

The dumb blonde was the ideal Aryan reproductive female, the passive-instinctive maternal nymphomaniac whose long, *naturally* blonde hair (bleached blondes were obvious frauds) guaranteed her Nordic master-race credentials. Her public displays of inanity showed how far she had developed into pure "femininity." To be seen with one of these creatures on one's arm was, for the men of the Twenties, the ultimate sta-tus symbol, the purest indication of their right to belong to the evolu-tionary elite. The creation of the dumb-blonde stereotype, then, was a factor of the social demands racial thinking placed on "self-made men."

The American social structure had relatively little room for rigid patterns of social ostracism based on class. In *The Custom of the Country* Wharton had bewailed their absence. She had portrayed Undine Spragg as the subversive agent of an American blight whose vulgar materialist ambitions were even beginning to infect the values of the European aristocracy. The popular Sumnerite conception of "genetic excellence" based on the accumulation of wealth now gave Aryan Americans a chance to correct that situation and develop a "racial" class system. When Madison Grant emphasized in 1921, in the introduction to the fourth edition of his *The Passing of the Great Race,* that to accept the "sci-ence" of genetics was "to admit inevitably the existence of superiority in one race and of inferiority in another," he also triumphantly insisted that such an admission required that "inferior races and classes" be rele-gated once more "to their former obscurity and subordinate position in society."

Grant still saw wealth as the surest indication of a man's "election" to the ranks of the evolutionary elite, but the "lower races" were show-ing a disturbing ability to join that party when given half a chance (par-ticularly in Hollywood). Of course everyone realized that "stealth" was the technique used by these inferiors (as opposed to the moral rectitude of Aryan businessmen), but the increasing infiltration of Semites into the ranks of the wealthy, Grant warned, showed that degeneration had been creeping into every aspect of American society.

Lothrop Stoddard, too, emphasized in *The Rising Tide of Color* that things were not right for the Aryan: "Everywhere the better types (on which the future of the race depends)" were losing ground and permit-ting the "lower types" to infiltrate society. "This 'disgenic' trend, so ominous for the future of the race, is a melancholy commonplace of our time, and many efforts have been made to measure its progress in economic or social terms." Yet, noted Stoddard, the "tide of color" was still rising. (162)

Given this new race-is-class attitude sweeping through American society, it is hardly surprising that insecure men with new wealth thought they would gain status and "visibility" by associating with demonstrably "Nordic" women. What the racist geneticists of the period regarded as "sexual selection," practiced by males in search of genetically superior females, was thus in actuality little more than a semiconscious act of social climbing. No wonder that the "real" vampire of the 1910s, the dark—and dark-haired—exotic temptress, was seen as a "genetic" contaminant. She was too much a symbol of racial "deterioration" to be seen as anything but a destroyer. During the moneymaking years of the "roaring" Twenties, the entertainment industry exploited her sexual attraction while denigrating her personality at every turn. Sally Lung, the Eurasian leper, was loose in the streets, disguised as an immigrant's daughter.

But even the dumb blonde was from the very outset a focus of derogation. She might be "genetically superior," but as a companion she was dead weight, and financially she was a constant drain, with her fabled ability to spend money and drive her husband to drink. At best she was the blonde dreamgirl of male fantasy whose innocent "maternal nymphomania" would turn her into as voluptuous a mother to her man as she would undoubtedly be to the litter of kids she was bound to produce. The flappers of the Twenties, who were the real girls next door, inevitably took the behavioral directives provided by the entertainment industry much too seriously. They tried to hide their inexperience in the field of seduction by acting out the role of the vampire while bleaching their hair and trying to sound as dumb as they could. Forced to be culturally reactive, they remained regulated and exploited by male fantasy, although they saw themselves as having finally been liberated from Puritan constraints.

The gold digger was different. She combined the subversive mentality of Sally Lung with the looks of Lorelei Lee and came out Clara Bow, the "It" Girl of the Twenties, who used her smarts more than her looks to rope in the wealthy suitor of her choice. She was careful to invest her own money while she was out spending his. In the process she became emblematic of American moxie, and until she was killed by World

War II, she added a loud-mouthed, gutsy shimmer, a no-nonsense attitude, and so much vitality to this country's culture that she may well
have helped tip the balance toward democracy when her country was
flirting ominously with racial totalitarianism.

But if she triumphed for a while, that too was mostly thanks to Hollywood, where she had found support among the burgeoning culture of
"Semitic immigrants" who had—the racial purists were convinced—
deliberately begun to subvert the integrity of American values. But cultural imagery of the sort outlined here is, by its very nature, notoriously
unstable in its "ambient" significations, and the social environment of
the Twenties and Thirties inevitably produced a wide variety of recom-
binant mutations of these categories of femininity. But whatever
woman's social incarnations in the culture at large, one thing was certain: in the context of literature she was almost always treated with as
much disdain as Anita Loos brought to her portrayal of the dumb
blonde. And the less she was willing to do men's bidding, the more she
was shown to be a secret agent of the forces of degeneration.

To be a literary contender in the Twenties, you had to be a racist, an
ironist, a misogynist, male. F. Scott Fitzgerald's *The Beautiful and Damned*
is a prime example of this trend. The novel straddles the gender
metaphors of two generations, in both style and intellectual attitude. It
is therefore structurally confused, and for this reason it has never been
regarded as one of the author's more successful works. Its heavy-handed
symbolism and ponderous use of quasi-psychological exposition make
the novel forced, artificial, and self-indulgent. Stylistically it hovers between symbolism and modernist realism. But its transitional qualities
make Fitzgerald's narrative an exceptional record of the transformation
of turn-of-the-century scientific metaphors into the psychosocial con-
structs that would soon come to be seen as "universal archetypes" of the
"collective unconscious."

Published just two years after Huneker's *Painted Veils,* Fitzgerald's
novel featured a desultory version of the symbolic overlay of Huneker's
text by suggesting that Gloria, the main female protagonist of *The
Beautiful and Damned,* was the incarnation of Eve as "Beauty." But Fitzgerald quite deliberately moved away from Huneker's, and the previous decade's, general tendency to make sexual women into deviously
scheming devils of lust. To do so was to give women too much credit in
the intellectual realm for their depredations of men. Maury, the author's
philosophic mouthpiece, describes Geraldine, a passing infatuation of

his, as a "little usher at Keith's" who is a "peculiar little soul," "utterly stupid," and "a girl of nondescript and nomadic habits." Maury finds it "remarkable that a person can comprehend so little and yet live in such a complex civilization." Women like Geraldine were "timeless" in the most negative sense: "She's just been carried along from an age of spear-heads and plunked down here with the equipment of an archer for going into a pistol duel. You could sweep away the entire crust of history and she'd never know the difference." (45–6)

Fitzgerald is equally disdainful of flappers: Muriel Kane, daughter of a "rising family of East Orange," is characteristic of such clueless feminine upstarts:

> She was short rather than small, and hovered audaciously between plumpness and width. Her hair was black and elaborately arranged. This, in conjunction with her handsome, rather bovine eyes, and her over-red lips, combined to make her resemble Theda Bara, the prominent motion picture actress. People told her constantly that she was a "vampire," and she believed them. She suspected hopefully that they were afraid of her, and she did her utmost under all circumstances to give the impression of danger. (83)

Fitzgerald's remarks indicate why Theda Bara's career was destined to be short. Her petit-bourgeois imitators had taken the mystery out of her role:

> Muriel appeared in a state of elaborate undress and *crept* toward them. She was in her element: her ebony hair was slicked straight back on her head; her eyes were artificially darkened; she reeked of insistent perfume. She was got up to the best of her ability as a siren, more popularly a "vamp"—a picker up and thrower away of men, an unscrupulous and fundamentally unmoved toyer with affections. Something in the exhaustiveness of her attempt fascinated Maury at first sight—a woman with wide hips affecting a panther-like litheness!

The sophisticated men of Fitzgerald's novel were not about to be taken in by such ersatz vampirism. They all knew that wide hips identified a woman as a "breeder." (95)

Virtually all the women Anthony Patch, the novel's partly autobiographical, doomed hero, encounters are of Muriel's kind—harebrained grown children, "vividly dressed, overpainted girls, who chattered volubly in low, lazy voices." (321) Even so, Fitzgerald considers Anthony too generous in his assessment of women, too "tender-minded and pliable." (325) He is cursed with a generosity toward them that leads to his undoing. When Anthony, while in the military, has an affair with Dot, a nineteen-year-old daughter of the petit bourgeoisie, he sees more in her than he ought to: "She was a dark, unenduring little flower—yet he thought he detected in her some quality of spiritual reticence, of strength drawn from her passive acceptance of all things. In this he was mistaken." What makes Dot fall in love with Anthony is merely "that first hysteria of passion," (327) not discernment.

When Anthony takes up with Dot, he finds that he has to learn to exist "in the present with a sort of animal content." He is pleased by "her warm retarded kisses" (332–3) and her attitude of worship toward him. For the rest, "her violet eyes would remain for hours apparently insensate as, thoughtless and reckless, she basked like a cat in the sun." (338) Though more presentable, Dot is like the plebeian women Anthony sees leaning from tenement windows: "rotund, moon-shaped mothers, as constellations of this sordid heaven; women like dark imperfect jewels, women like vegetables, women like great bags of abominably dirty laundry." (283)

Fitzgerald's cynicism toward women, like H. L. Mencken's, was based on his perception that their "collectivist" humanism had succeeded in undermining the grand evolutionary designs of nature. Again Maury, the skeptic, was the author's spokesman: "Man was beginning a grotesque and bewildered fight with nature—nature, that by the divine and magnificent accident had brought us to where we could fly in her face." Maury's head was filled with the imperial ambitions of the master race. Nature "had invented ways to rid the race of the inferior and thus give the remainder strength to fill her higher—or, let us say, her more amusing—though still unconscious and accidental intentions. And, actuated by the highest gifts of the enlightenment, we were seeking to circumvent her." Humanism was obstructing the road to "racial" progress.

Instead of trying to subvert nature's attempts "to rid the race of the inferior," man should help *her* haphazard efforts by installing a Nietzschean master race of intellectual males who could give proper direction to *her* clumsy processes of "natural selection" by actuating "the highest gifts of the enlightenment." However, this glorious protofascist dream was being thwarted at every turn by effeminate, antiracial egalitarians:

In this republic I saw the black beginning to mingle with the
white—in Europe there was taking place an economic catastro-
phe to save three or four diseased and wretchedly governed races
from the one mastery that might organize them for material
prosperity. We produce a Christ who can raise up the leper—
and presently the breed of the leper is the salt of the earth. (255)

The leper, the salt of the earth, and nature—the colonized lower
races, the working classes, and woman—represented for Fitzgerald the
inimical trinity of atavism, social regression, and emasculation that kept
the master race from gaining its rightful ascendancy. This was the same
racist/sexist sense of unease underlying Madison Grant's *The Passing of
the Great Race:*

In the city of New York and elsewhere in the United States
there is a native American aristocracy resting upon layer after
layer of immigrants of lower races and these native Americans,
while, of course, disclaiming the distinction of a patrician class
and lacking in class consciousness and class dignity, have, nevertheless, up to this time supplied the leaders in thought and in the
control of capital as well as of education and of the religious bias
of the community.

Grant, like Fitzgerald, saw Sumnerite doom ahead: "We are now
engaged in destroying the privilege of wealth." Cultural literacy was
going by the boards: "In some quarters there is developing a tendency
to attack the privilege of intellect and to deprive a man of the advantage
gained from an early and thorough classical education." The lower orders of society, by spreading socialism and institutionalized ignorance,
were invading the body politic and making it "disregard the head with
its brains and eyes." (5–7)

The future must inevitably bring a race war, and the Aryan elite had
better throw aside its humanist pretensions if it wanted to maintain its
imperial superiority, for "no ethnic conquest can be complete unless the
natives are exterminated and the invaders bring their own women with
them. If the conquerors are obliged to depend upon the women of the
vanquished to carry on the race, the intrusive blood strain of the invaders in a short time becomes diluted beyond recognition." Guardians
of "superior" racial strains who failed to eradicate the inferiors around
them were doomed to eradication themselves:

It sometimes happens that an infiltration of population takes place either in the guise of unwilling slaves or of willing immigrants, who fill up waste places and take to the lowly tasks which the lords of the land despise, thus gradually occupying the country and literally breeding out their masters. (71)

Fitzgerald's novel, published almost simultaneously with the second printing of the fourth edition of Grant's immensely popular diatribe—and by the same publishers, Charles Scribner's Sons—chronicles the decline of one man belonging to America's "great race" of Aryan aristocrats. But by designating women as the primary source of degeneration, Fitzgerald went even further than Grant. In his work, issues of economics, racial inferiority and superiority, evolution and degeneration, and even sheer physical survival, all came to be mere factors of man's unceasing struggle against woman, who in all her incarnations remained the Eurasian daughter of Fu Manchu, the insidious agent of reversion and chaos. But ordinary women, the Geraldines and Muriels of the world, were no more than disfiguring Dots on the face of creative evolution. Only the exceptional, seemingly most fully acculturated ones, those personifying "Beauty," who kept their reversive masculinity hidden behind a deceptive air of vulnerability, posed any real danger. Masochistic existential agonists such as Anthony Patch (and Fitzgerald himself) became putty in their hands.

Such women were the undead revenants of being's urge to return to nonbeing. They were Freudian Doras, evil sisters in search of jewelry boxes full of their fathers' precious pearls. Spoiled Electras, they instinctively understood that semen and gold constituted the essence of a man's being and did not hesitate to deprive him of both: the mythical vampire Cristina of F. Marion Crawford's "For the Blood Is the Life" had multiplied into an army of gold diggers who understood that a man's bank account was his "manhood." These women frequently ended up depredating their suitors' savings more efficiently than their "blood." They had learned that to possess a man's money was to possess his penis.

Run-of-the-mill female erotics like Fitzgerald's Dot were no more than updated versions of the clinging vines who attached themselves blindly to a man's arms. In describing Anthony Patch's final meeting with Dot, Fitzgerald shows her to be "appallingly in earnest. Her violet eyes were red with tears; her soft intonation was ragged with gasping sobs." When Anthony repulses her, she shows herself to be a very "average" woman whose consummate masochism is a necessary component of her reproductive function: "'Hit me!' she implored him—wildly, stupidly. 'Oh, hit me, and I'll kiss the hand you hit me with!'" (445) Anthony obligingly throws a chair at her before his mind snaps, weakened beyond repair by this final evidence of woman's social perversity.

But natural gold diggers such as Fitzgerald's Gloria wanted to usurp the male identity altogether. They wanted his money—that is, his hierarchical penis rather than his actual "penis-baby." They had never reached the final stage of normal feminine acculturation Freud had identified in 1918, in his essay "The Taboo of Virginity," as the stage during which the girl finally learns to desire "instead of the penis—a child." (82) In 1925, in "Some Psychological Consequences of the Anatomical Distinction Between the Sexes," Freud was to clarify his position further: "The girl's libido slips into a new position by means—there is no other way of putting it—of the equation 'penis = child.' She gives up her wish for a penis and puts in place of it a wish for a child." (191) A woman who was unwilling to bear her husband children rebelled against this normal development. Instead, she actively usurped his manhood by taking his gold without giving him children in return. To become involved with a woman like that was thus, in effect, an act of "race-suicide."

This is exactly Anthony Patch's fate in *The Beautiful and Damned*. When we first meet him, in 1913, he is a worthy member of the financial and intellectual elite. He has a substantial income, "the interest on money inherited from his mother," and always enjoys his visits to his broker: "The big trust company building seemed to link him definitely to the great fortunes whose solidarity he respected and to assure him that he was adequately chaperoned by the hierarchy of finance." When his grandfather dies, Anthony stands to inherit some seventy-five million dollars. (12–13) The Aryan nation has reason to be proud of him.

Following the symbolist manner of the 1910s, but adding the ironic distance of modernism, Fitzgerald subsequently presented his readers with the Eve of paradise—"Beauty"—who engages in a dialogue with the disembodied "Voice" of the masculine intellect. The Voice tells Beauty that she is about to be sent to the United States, a world of henpecked husbands, a place where "women with receding chins and shapeless noses go about in broad daylight saying 'Do this!' and 'Do that!' and all the men, even those of great wealth, obey implicitly their women to whom they refer sonorously either as 'Mrs. So-and-so' or as 'the wife.' " Beauty, the Voice announces, will be incarnated as a society girl and be referred to as "a ragtime kid, a flapper, a jazz-baby, and a baby vamp." (27–9)

In the next chapter, titled "Portrait of a Siren," we are introduced to Gloria, Beauty's incarnation in the sublunary world. A young woman recently arrived from Kansas City, she is, according to one of Anthony's friends, "darn nice—not a brain in her head." Anthony, easily conversant with the details of Freudian analysis, misunderstands the young lady's name. He has to be told that it is "not Dora—Gloria." (37) Shadows of Freud's jewel box must have sounded an alarm in Anthony's mind.

Gloria enjoys talking about her legs, and about what sort of tan might go well with them. The gentlemen are intrigued. Maury reflects: "There was something about that little girl with her absurd tan that was eternally old—like me." (51) Anthony sees a girl "in a state of almost laughable self-absorption." She is the eternal child-brained woman, Beauty: "She talked always about herself as a very charming child might talk," yet "he understood what Maury had meant by saying she was very young and very old." "This *baby*" with hands "small as a child's hands should be," whose body is "amazingly supple and slender," is a "female Methuselah," a "timeless," archetypal woman. (60–3)

Gloria warns Anthony from the first that she does not "want to have responsibility and a lot of children to take care of." (64) But he, artist, "romanticist," and man of "deep sophistication," (73) falls in love with her anyway. This made it possible for Fitzgerald to parade his knowledge of psychoanalysis (Anthony made certain excuses "with Freudian regularity," we are told at one point [370]) by casting Gloria as a veritable case study of the regressive, masculinized woman. He carefully sketched out the "primal narcissism" of his antiheroine: Upon becoming the "most celebrated and sought-after young beauty in the country," Gloria "had fed on it ruthlessly," as an intuitive temptress who "struck to kill" while enjoying her notoriety "with a vanity that was almost masculine." (80–1) "Such women love only themselves with an intensity comparable to that of the man's love for them," Freud had said in 1912 in "A Note on the Unconscious in Psychoanalysis." (*General Psychological Theory*, 70)

A bit further on, Fitzgerald, constrained by the censors, dealt with the issue of Gloria's penis envy by means of a set of double entendres easily decodable by Freudian initiates. Soon after their marriage, Gloria and Anthony prattle playfully about the genetic disposition of their children-to-be (though by this time it is already obvious to the reader that Gloria has no intention of complying with Anthony's paternal desires). As Gloria enumerates the features she thinks their child should inherit from her, Anthony exclaims: "My dear Gloria, you've appropriated the whole baby." Then he adds: "Let him have my neck at least . . . your neck's too short." This attack upon her clitoral inferiority exasperates Gloria and makes her display the imposing length of her symbolic claim to phallic self-sufficiency: " 'Short? You're crazy!' She elongated and contracted it to convince herself of its reptilian sinuousness. 'Do you call *that* a short neck?' " Anthony tries to deflect the conversation into a practical discussion of eugenics, but Gloria cuts him short with masculine assertiveness: "Let's have them all with my neck." (183–5)

Although Anthony recognizes Gloria's archetypal femininity (her eyes "appeared to regard him out of many thousand years"), he fails to alert himself to the acute nature of his new wife's "castration complex." When her arms wrap themselves around him, "sweet and strangling," (209) it is the "sweet" he notices, not the "strangling." Infatuated beyond reason, he looks upon other women disdainfully as only "so many *females,* in the word's most contemptuous sense, breeders and bearers, exuding still that faintly odorous atmosphere of the cave and the nursery." But Fitzgerald carefully stresses Anthony's own growing feminization: "It never occurred to him that he was a passive thing, acted upon by an influence above and beyond Gloria, that he was merely the sensitive plate on which the photograph was made." (105–6)

In matching the "masculinized" Gloria with the "weak" Anthony Patch, Fitzgerald was following the era's fashionable notions about the masculine/feminine mix that determined the person's character. This was the notion Jung was about to appropriate as his animus/anima theory, by delving into a well-picked-over grab bag of derivative notions about the atavistic residues of "primitive bisexuality" to be found in humanity. As we have seen, notions of that sort had become an obsession among his older contemporaries. After outlining his theory in Keyserling's *The Book of Marriage* (1926), Jung subsequently returned to the notion at length in *The Relations Between the Ego and the Unconscious* (1928). His animus-anima theory is expressive of the tendency among psychoanalysts to construct theories that reflect rather than analyze the prevailing social prejudices. Popular fads such as the flapper flirtation with the idea of the "masculinized" female (tied-down, flattened breasts, pageboy haircuts, and waistless clothing) were far more subversive in their playful, satirical take on the ponderous "scientific" verities of the time. But psychoanalysis habitually cooperates with the dominant value system by interpreting such spontaneous popular commentaries as blind expressions of "universal" drives or "archetypal" patterns of human behavior.

Fitzgerald wanted to show that Gloria's "masculinity" was irresistible to Anthony because he was seeking to complement the female strain in his own personality, which made him "less of a man" and therefore undercut his right to be part of the Nordic evolutionary elite. Anthony was indeed dangerously weak:

> Instead of seizing the girl and holding her by sheer strength until she became passive to his desire, instead of beating down her will by the force of his own, he had walked, defeated and powerless, from her door, with the corners of his mouth drooping and what force there might have been in his grief and rage hidden behind the manner of a whipped schoolboy. (115)

Soon after this Fitzgerald has Gloria remark: "I've got a man's mind." And Anthony responds: "You've got a mind like mine. Not strongly gendered either way." (134) Even when it comes to making love, Gloria behaves in a very unladylike fashion. In sexual encounters she is only after "her own satisfaction." The hallowed feminine procreative impulse, the urge to be "plowed like the fertile earth," is absent in her. Her mood after sexual encounters is instead "the masculine one, of satiation and faint dislike." (344) She is not changed by a salutary desire for a "penis-baby." Instead, she continues her quest for the real thing. Even years after their marriage she still refuses to give "any show or sign of interest in children." (424)

Having established the phallic focus of Gloria's personality, Fitzgerald returns to the heavy-handed symbolic literary mode of the 1910s. During his last night as a bachelor Anthony has a nightmarish epiphany: the "Breath of the Cave" of female sexuality sweeps over him across "moon-flooded roofs." He hears "the noise of a woman's laughter. It began low, incessant and whining—some servant-maid with her fellow, he thought—and then it grew in volume and became hysterical." Soon it "reached a high point, tensed and stifled, almost the quality of a scream—then it ceased and left behind it a silence empty and menacing as the greater silence overhead." Anthony is "upset and shaken," for "some animal quality in that unrestrained laughter had grasped at his imagination." Aversion and horror sweep over him as he realizes that "life was that sound out there, that ghastly reiterated female sound." (148–50)

However, still in the thrall of regressive erotic impulses, Anthony is powerless to prevent his descent into the cave of sex. The marriage is consummated, and the outcome of Fitzgerald's novel is no longer in doubt. Anthony's dissolution begins almost immediately. Soon we learn that "Gloria had lulled Anthony's mind to sleep. She, who seemed of all women the wisest and the finest, hung like a brilliant curtain across his doorways, shutting out the light of the sun." (191)

Fitzgerald made Gloria's obsession with money characteristic of the "sterile" masculinism of the destroying women of the Twenties. The vampire women of the decade just past had still been driven primarily by a regressive sex drive. But these new vampires, having just been given the vote, were eager to usurp the daily affairs of their victims as well as their vital essence. Instead of merely "bleeding" their victims financially, the way Theda Bara's characters used to, they were beginning to show an active interest in maintaining the financial solvency of their mates. No wonder, for as Marie Stopes was pointing out, appropriation of that "substance, 'hormone,' 'vitamine' or stimulant" contained in man's contribution to the perpetuation of the race affected women's "internal economy in such a way as to benefit and nourish their whole systems." The anabolic energies of the female were thus enhanced with every infusion, lending new virility to her economic appetite, while the male's catabolic depletion could only contribute to the weakening of his financial resolve. As Freud had shown, woman's vital depredations, if not stimulated directly by a desire for motherhood, were an obvious attempt at appropriating, if not the male's actual phallus, at least its social fruits. Thus, with their "internal economy" steadily nourished at the expense of the masculine intellect, these women were growing strong enough to challenge the weakened male in the arena of his greatest phallic triumphs: his economic potency.

As Betty van Deventer was soon to make clear, the gold digger knew that to gain access to a man's material possessions, she must permit herself to be seen as a possession by her prey. But she always kept in mind that this was a transitional stage. Thus she used her position as possession to accumulate wealth even while her body accumulated health. The gold digger's existential goal was to be able to state: "I own, therefore I am." No wonder she began to exhibit humanity, spontaneity, and joyful energy within the context of the populist spirit of the later Twenties and the Thirties, when the rule of the economic elites seemed to have been broken. No wonder, as well, that in the realm of "high" literature, the private cultural domain of the Aryan ruling class, she remained a subversive, a destroyer, a piranha.

It is therefore also no surprise that in Fitzgerald's world of Sumnerite finance, where seminal continence and financial potency were interdependent, Anthony's "feminization" inevitably led to financial insolvency: "Of late their income had lost elasticity." (221) This alarms Gloria much more than Anthony, and the second half of the novel is largely taken up with Gloria's pursuit of the seventy-five million dollars Anthony should have inherited from his grandfather.

She rapidly degenerates into a sterile predator. Soon after Anthony returns from the army, drunk and defeated, he realizes that he has fallen "into the bottom of a deep and uncharted abyss" lit only by the moon. The breath of the cave has done him in: "All the distress he had ever known, the sorrow and the pain, had been because of women, it was something that in different ways they did to him, unconsciously, almost casually—perhaps finding him tender-minded and afraid, they killed the things in him that menaced their absolute sway." (444)

With clumsy irony Fitzgerald has Gloria announce the decision of the court just as Anthony's mind has finally and irretrievably snapped: "You're worth thirty millions!" When last we encounter Anthony, he is "a bundled figure in a wheel chair," on the deck of an ocean liner. Though defeated and permanently emasculated, a hollow shell of a man, he is still at heart a poet, dreaming of better days. By his side, Gloria holds court in "a Russian sable coat that must have cost a small fortune." An observer, a fresh young girl, just starting out in life, remarks: "She seems sort of—sort of dyed and *unclean,* if you know what I mean. Some people just have that look about them whether they are or not." (448)

The girl's perceptive evaluation of Gloria does not, however, promise new hope for womanhood in future years, for Fitzgerald emphasized that Gloria, too, was "intensely skeptical of her sex" and had always been preoccupied with

> the question of whether women were or were not clean. By uncleanliness she meant a variety of things, a lack of pride, a slackness in fibre and, most of all, the unmistakable aura of promiscuity. "Women soil easily," she said "far more easily than

men. Unless a girl's very young and brave it's almost impossible for her to go down-hill without a certain hysterical animality, the cunning, dirty sort of animality. A man's different—and I suppose that's why one of the commonest characters of romance is a man going gallantly to the devil. (234–5)

Gloria here reiterates an axiom of gender ideology that already had been articulated in an almost exactly analogue fashion more than fifty years earlier by the dedicated antifeminist Horace Bushnell in his book *Women's Suffrage: The Reform Against Nature* (1869):

Women often show a strange facility of debasement and moral abandonment, when they have once given way consentingly to wrong. Men go down by a descent—*facilis descensus*—women, by a precipitation. . . . When they do wrong, they have more to face, on which account they fall as much faster and lower. (142)

Thus Fitzgerald had his symbolical Everywoman neatly summarize the misogyny that shaped the antifeminine content of *The Beautiful and Damned*.

But the novel's documentation of the degeneration of Anthony Patch was more than an attack on woman as the vampire of man's golden soul. Time and again Fitzgerald emphasized that Gloria was linked, both emotionally and constitutionally, to the lower orders of society. True, she had "eyes whose irises were of the most delicate and transparent bluish white" and "yellow ripples of hair" and should therefore have been a prime Aryan breeding ground, but her unacculturated "masculinity" cancelled out all those "positive" qualities.

The treachery of the Eurasian was hidden under Gloria's deceptively Aryan skin. She had all the telltale evolutionary deficiencies of the lower orders: "childish" and without a brain in her head, she wanted "just to be lazy"—though she was able to win a major court case involving millions of dollars without any help from her husband. Like the "racial inferiors," Gloria is unable to accept her role in society: "I don't want to have responsibility and a lot of children to take care of." (57–64)

Fitzgerald, indeed, made Gloria express her instinctive kinship with Semites, Asians, and other "social defectives" at every opportunity. In a cheap cabaret, where out-of-tune musicians play "primitive" music, she murmurs obligingly: "I belong here . . . I'm like these people." Anthony is shocked: "For an instant this seemed a sardonic and unnecessary paradox hurled at him across the impassable distances she created about herself." Entranced by the music of "a Semitic violinist who swayed his shoulders to the rhythm of the year's mellowest fox-trot," Gloria remarks: "I'm like they are—like Japanese lanterns and crape paper, and the music of that orchestra." Now Anthony is appalled: "It was like blasphemy from the mouth of a child." When he upbraids her for her foolishness, she shakes "her blond head" and insists: "I *am* like them . . . You ought to see . . . You don't know me."

To forestall any thought that Gloria might be a political progressive with a humanist agenda rather than a typical woman responding to the sound of jungle drums, Fitzgerald made her add:

> I've got a streak of what you'd call cheapness. I don't know where I get it but it's—oh, things like this and bright colors and gaudy vulgarity. I seem to belong here. These people could appreciate me and take me for granted, and these men would fall in love with me and admire me, whereas the clever men I meet would just analyze me and tell me I'm this because of this or that because of that. (72–3)

You can keep your Freud, and I'll keep my phallus, Gloria is saying here.

Inevitably Anthony is horrified when he discovers that Gloria has freely associated with, and even taken money from, Joseph Bloeckman, a generic Jewish economic predator and "Hollywood Semite" straight out of the pages of the race theorists. In a cheap attempt at irony, Fitzgerald even tells his readers that Bloeckman, to hide his Jewishness, has changed his family name to "Black." In a drunken stupor of despair, Anthony bravely confronts Bloeckman/Black and calls him a "Goddam Jew." But Bloeckman beats him up and has him thrown into the street. *The Passing of the Great Race* is taking place before our very eyes.

In the downfall of Fitzgerald's semiautobiographical hero, we have thus witnessed exactly that "gradual dying out among our people of those hereditary traits through which the principles of our religious, political and social foundations were laid down," (ix) which Henry Fairfield Osborn had predicted in his 1916 preface to Madison Grant's racist diatribe. The "insidious replacement" of these traits by inferior ones, as Osborn had termed it, had been triggered in Anthony by Gloria, that perverse Everywoman, who had so emphatically asserted her kinship to the "lower orders." Fitzgerald clearly expected his readers to recognize in this "kinship" between woman and the agents of reversion one of the principal causes for "the decline of the west" (the title of Oswald Spengler's influential treatise of 1918).

The Beautiful and Damned indicates all too graphically that racist and sexist prejudices had begun to mingle inextricably in the minds of many during the 1920s. This blending had given rise to a set of images delineating a single, ominously spreading plague of sexual and racial degeneracy. An unholy alliance of lascivious, phallic women and weak, eroticized, racially inferior males was pitted against a beleaguered elite of spiritually evolving males and their immaculately maternal wives. The metaphoric speculations of science had succeeded in establishing an etiology of degeneration in which the gold digger, the sexual vampire turned economic parasite, had become the main undercover operative of the Jewish Eurasian Bolshevik conspiracy. Millions of genetic inferiors were waiting to invade the United States. When the initial poison of reversion, that "breath of the cave" dispensed by the women, had done its work, they would coax the sex-weakened Nordic-Americans into throwing open their borders to the waiting hordes of anti-individualistic foreign inferiors. Ultimately these agents of reversion would seize social and economic power and drag the country back into the Stone Age.

Fitzgerald was by no means the only literary light of the Twenties to follow this train of thinking. Ernest Hemingway's The Sun Also Rises (1926) is, like The Beautiful and Damned, based almost entirely on the author's implicit acceptance of the scientific logic of the "inherent" symbiotic relationship between racial and sexual "degenerates." The Sun Also Rises posits that one's manhood is absolutely determined by one's ability to cope with the temptation of woman. Hemingway's Jake Barnes is better at this than Anthony Patch because he has gained ultimate observer status in the battle of the sexes as a result of his own war wounds. Even so, he is clearly not man enough to overcome the vampire altogether. Hemingway's thinking about gender was no less rooted in turn-of-the-century fantasies about the evolutionary male's transcendence of woman than Fitzgerald's. But where Fitzgerald's narrative apparatus was perfectly adapted to the ironic, Menckenesque, self-styled symbolist "cleverness" of the smart set of the immediate postwar years, Hemingway had learned much from the flippantly voyeuristic show-and-tell of the period's pulp-magazine writers: "Brett was damned good-looking.

She wore a slipover jersey sweater and a tweed skirt, and her hair was brushed back like a boy's. She started all that. She was built with curves like the hull of a racing yacht, and you missed none of it with that wool jersey." (22)

Hemingway's celebrated "lean" writing could not have existed without the self-conscious modernity of such mysteries as Earl Derr Biggers's *Seven Keys to Baldpate* (1913): "She had cheeks like peaches and cream, but a heart like a lunch-counter doughnut" (214); the tough talk of early *Black Mask* writers such as Carroll John Daly: "She didn't do nothing but hang close to me and keep her head up against my chest as she clung to my coat" ("Three Gun Terry," 1923); or the "neutral observation" of Dashiell Hammett: "A plump maid with bold green eyes and a loose, full-lipped mouth led me up two flights of steps and into an elaborately furnished boudoir, where a woman in black sat at a window" ("Women, Politics & Murder," 1924).

In addition, Hemingway's experience as a journalist helped give *The Sun Also Rises* a reportorial tone. Exploiting the modernist tenet that less is more, he omitted any attempt to give his characters psychological nuance, instead relying upon his readers to project their own perceptions onto his hollow-shelled personalities. This approach suggested that he was unwilling to "judge" his characters, and therefore seemed to place him beyond facile moralizing. But by avoiding directive authorial commentary, he also gave many readers the impression that he was portraying things as they were without *any* interpretation. The novel conveys the human relationships it depicts with the inevitability of things *seen*. It has the imperative narrative organization of a good film script.

But by means of such conceits, *The Sun Also Rises* preaches more effectively than most other novels of the Twenties—by example rather than by statement. Its cinematic emphasis on descriptive exposition interspersed with lean dialogue recalls the catechismic verbal rituals of Porter Emerson Browne's novelization of *A Fool There Was*. Unfortunately Hemingway's catechisms about gender relationships are much the same as well. His vaunted slice-of-life approach is carefully orchestrated to make us accept the notion that the thoroughly modern, free-spirited Brett Ashley was, in fact, an unconscious vampire woman driven by needs beyond her control. At least Browne's scheming predator had still been a self-consciously evil creature. She had been a woman with a deliberately antimasculine agenda—a true "virago." Hemingway's modernist use of understatement highlighted the counterrational impulses characteristic of the women in his fiction. Thus he assured the further ascendancy of Fitzgerald's basically inane and unconscious, womb-driven evil females in American literature.

In *The Beautiful and Damned* Gloria had also been shown, time and again, to have no evil intentions. All she wanted was "to be young and beautiful for a long time, to be gay and happy, and to have money and love. She wanted what most women want, but she wanted it much more fiercely and passionately." (276) Like Freud's Dora, Gloria had still *known* what she wanted. She was a transitional woman, halfway between Browne's deliberate virago and Hemingway's unconscious destroyer. For Hemingway denied to woman even the *will* to evil, the satanic, deliberate power over men earlier generations of writers had given her.

Although Robert Cohn at one point declares Brett to be Circe, this merely emphasizes his own outdated symbolist mentality. In Brett even more than in Gloria, any suggestion of a conscious will to evil is transformed into a blind, benumbed expression of woman's "primordial needs." If Brett "turns men into swine," (144) she doesn't mean to; if she destroys men's lives, it is because she is no different from the bulls at the fiesta in Pamplona, blindly gouging all those who get in her way—she destroys men not because she wants to but because she has to.

Hemingway deliberately emphasized the kinship between Brett and the bulls. She enjoys watching their violent behavior: "'Funny,' Brett said. 'How one doesn't mind the blood.'" (211) That was a normal reaction for a woman, Hemingway implied. "Brett's not a sadist. She's just a lovely, healthy wench," (166) Mike, a man who "knows" her in the biblical fashion, declares casually. Moreover, Brett takes the equation of blood and semen very seriously. When she sees Pedro Romero, the bullfighter, dominate "the bull by making him realize he was unattainable," she instantly wants to have a go at Romero herself. Unconsciously she is seeking a man who can pierce her with his phallus the way the bullfighter pierces the bull with his sword. As Jake remarks early on, "Nobody ever lives their life all the way up except bull-fighters." (10) The sexual significance of Romero's intercourse with the bull is obvious: "His left shoulder went forward between the horns as the sword went in, and for just an instant he and the bull were one." (218)

So there could be no misunderstanding his intention, Hemingway soon after this repeated his description of the magic moment of union between the bull and his dominator: "The bull charged and Romero waited for the charge, the muleta held low, sighting along the blade, his feet firm. Then without taking a step forward, he became one with the bull, the sword was in high between the shoulders, . . . and it was over." (220) In the all-male world of bullfighting, Hemingway argued, the bull is a priapic underdog to the bullfighter, the real man, the imperial dominator, who, unlike the primitive bull, is in full control over his phallus. In Hemingway's ring the bull becomes Freud's clitoral-phallic female, a horned woman, acting out her futile masculine fantasies. The bullfighter dominates her, brings her to her knees, then drives her to an ecstatic death—excises her phallus with the cleansing penetrations of his sword. In Hemingway's world of "real men," only dominance is love. "The bulls are my best friends," Romero says. Skeptically Brett asks, "You kill your friends?" "Always," Romero answers, "so they don't kill me." Within minutes Brett and Romero are on their way upstairs to explore their new friendship. (186)

Jake wistfully remarks: "Pedro Romero had the greatness. He loved bull-fighting, and I think he loved the bulls, and I think he loved Brett." For Romero killing the bull and making love are simply two analogous processes in the domination of nature. Romero shows how a real man does "it":

> Never once did he look up. He made it stronger that way, and did it for himself, too, as well as for her. Because he did not look up to ask if it pleased he did it all for himself inside, and it strengthened him, and yet he did it for her, too. But he did not do it for her at any loss to himself. He gained by it all through the afternoon. (216)

The "it" here is bullfighting—metaphoric sexual dominance. The "her" is Brett, Hemingway's own version of Everywoman. No wonder Hemingway's novel has been a favorite among manly men for more than sixty years.

Indeed, Romero is such a good lover that "at the end of the pass they were facing each other again. Romero smiled. The bull wanted it again, and Romero's cape filled again." Brett, watching, is swept away by these intimations of tumescence. After Romero kills his second bull, he brings her the animal's "notched black ear." Proudly she holds it in her hand: "'Don't get bloody,' Romero said, and grinned." (221) But the blood is the life: Brett's loins are anointed with the blood of others. She too is a horned, instinctual creature eager to turn each of her men into a "cornuto," an amateur of love lying in the dusty village streets of Pamplona with "a horn through him. All for morning fun." (198)

Brett, then, like Gloria, is very much a phallic woman. She recognizes this in herself, and prides herself on it. She is the inventor of the pageboy hairstyle ("She started all that"), and like Djuna Barnes and many other creative women Hemingway knew at this time, she wears a "man's felt hat" or a "Basque beret." She calls herself a "chap." Romero (the book's only truly manly man) is ashamed to be seen with her because she looks so masculine: "He wanted me to grow my hair out," Brett remarks. "He said it would make me more womanly." (242) But then there is always Brett's remarkable racing-yacht bosom to compensate men like Romero for her masculine tendencies. Hemingway also gave Brett a Florence Nightingale strain: Jake and Mike both know by experience that "she loves looking after people." (203)

Indeed, Brett could have been every manly man's dream girl, had her rampant sexual hubris not exceeded even that of the bull. Her phallic desires are obvious, but she is not willing to exchange her penis envy for a proper baby. She clearly suffers from the "maternal nymphomania" Huneker had diagnosed in his portrait of Mona in *Painted Veils,* but she has none of Mona's blind passion for children. Thus Brett is Huneker's "female ever in pursuit of masculine honey" without the leavening effect of the phallic woman's appropriate self-castration through submission to the demands of motherhood. From the bullfighter's—the imperial castrator's—point of view, then, the "lost generation" of men who had seen their manhood, their lifeblood, destroyed by war was a sorry lot. Like Jake, these men were too fatigued to be able to supply Brett with the *Liebestod*—the deadly final love-ritual of domination and submission she so sorely needed.

Brett unflinchingly pursues her blind quest for liberation from phallicism even so. Her companions' inability to subject her is the tragic source of her personal failure to become a properly acculturated female (Romero, as a Latin lover, can only be a passing fling for an Aryan lass). We are to understand that Jake, Hemingway's approximation of a "thinking" man, would have been Brett's natural soulmate had it not been for his unfortunate war wound. But not having to share his vital essence with women anymore has made Jake into quite a philosopher. He compassionately observes how other men allow themselves to be devastated by women such as Brett. Thus he becomes the exemplary modern male hero, living a life of continent, strong-spined, quiet desperation.

At first Jake's spiritual manhood is entirely beyond doubt, particularly since he is disadvantaged only in the realm of tumescence and not in his transcendent "masculinity." Hemingway even had Jake express a manly urge to bash homosexuals who had the gall to be pleased with their own spiritual "inadequacy" as males: "I know they are supposed to be amusing, and you should be tolerant, but I wanted to swing on one, any one, anything to shatter that superior, simpering composure." (20)

Brett is more severely wounded than Jake. By not yielding to the maternal motive underlying her buxom sexuality, she is doomed to pursue a sterile seminal vampirism that only increases her masculine energies and undermines her intuitive quest for acculturation. She was meant to be Jake's natural ringside companion: "I simply turn all to jelly when you touch me," she admits. But when the philosophical Jake tries to argue that sex is not everything in a relationship ("it isn't all that you know"), the nymphomaniacal Brett shows that, for her at least, there can be no separation between sex and sensibility: "We kissed good night and Brett shivered. 'I'd better go,' she said. 'Good night, darling.' 'You don't have to go.' 'Yes.'" (26–34)

Hemingway was a firm believer in the medical validity of the seminal-nutrition theory. Consequently he portrayed Brett as fidgety, weepy, and weak whenever she had no sexual partner. She needs men to be healthy and to maintain her masculinized lifestyle. She depends on men more than men depend on her. Brett knows this very well, and the prospect of a life of perpetual depredation, of restless seminal vampirism, distresses her. Toward the end of the book, "shaking and crying" with what one is tempted to regard as seminal-withdrawal symptoms, Brett unconvincingly intends to turn over a new leaf. "I'm thirty-four, you know. I'm not going to be one of these bitches that ruins children." (243)

But in Hemingway's world bitchdom was the future of any woman not satisfied with the modest seminal energies meted out to her in measured quantities by a bullfighter male full of manly self-control. Brett simply cannot overcome her need for masculine vitality even to settle down to merely symbolic motherhood: "It's my fault, Jake. It's the way I'm made," she remarks bluntly when Jake suggests that they "just live together." (55) Jake begins his own descent from the lofty perch of spiritual manhood when he becomes her pimp to his friends—men with whom he otherwise bonds in bouts of alcoholism and other equally dangerous manly sports such as fishing and watching bullfights. "That was it. Send a girl off with one man. Introduce her to another to go off with him. Now go and bring her back. And sign the wire with love. That was it alright." (239) In effect he becomes Brett's steer, one of those castrated intermediaries who serve to quiet the constitutional aggression of a frisky bull until it is ready to be conquered by the bullfighter's sword.

Thus true manhood, as an abstract ideal, becomes the ultimate victim of this unholy alliance between Jake and Brett. Ideal manhood was a nirvana of testosterone distributed in carefully controlled gestures of racial mastery. It had been Jake's greatest pride that, notwithstanding his wound, he was counted as a genuine "aficionado" by the cognoscenti of bullfighting. He was part of their secret society, a closed boys' club of initiates.

But by accepting his role as Brett's pimp, Jake adds spiritual emasculation to his physical inadequacy. He becomes a traitor to the brotherhood of masculinity. Montoya, the book's undisputed arbiter of manhood, makes this very clear when he ostracizes Jake after Brett's fling with Romero: He "did not come near us. One of the maids brought the bill." (228) Having allowed himself to become a conduit for the forces of degeneration, Jake, the defective male of modern decadence, must henceforth remain locked out of the tower of true manhood forever.

In the figure of Brett Hemingway created the model for numerous subsequent female predators in fiction. But Robert Cohn, the racial inferior of the novel, is in many ways her mirror image. If the sun sets on Jake, if he becomes part of the passing of the great Nordic race, it is the destructive alliance between Brett and Cohn that is ultimately responsible for Jake's fall. Hemingway immediately established the symbolic importance of Cohn to his narrative by opening the novel with his name. Cohn is an economic parasite, an interloper in the world of the Nordics. Though he has gained wealth in this manner, he remains passive—a "drain" upon the system. A "fish out of water" among the Gentiles of Princeton University, he is enough of a "chameleon" (one of the Jew's most typical characteristics, according to the racist theorists) to adopt a semblance of their manly traits and become middleweight boxing champion, even though his heart is not in it. But his attempts to hide his otherness fail among the Aryan elite: "No one ever made him feel he was a Jew, and hence different from anybody else, until he went to Princeton." To the elite he is a true nonentity: "I never met any one of his class who remembered him."

Effeminate as well as passive, Cohn displays his genetic defects at every turn. Hemingway portrayed him as something of a wallflower in the sexual realm, by remarking that he "was married"—deliberately phrased to emphasize the passive tense—"by the first girl who was nice to him." Later, "just when he had made up his mind to leave his wife she left him and went off with a miniature-painter" (clearly the most "effeminate" sort of painter Hemingway could think of, but even so, "as a man," still clearly preferable to Cohn). Thereupon he "had been taken in hand by a lady" who hoped to profit from his connections. Throughout his novel Hemingway continued to describe Cohn's relationships with women in the most passive terms possible: "The lady who had him," "she led him quite a life," and so on. (3–7)

The ultimate proof of Cohn's "effeminacy" is his lack of interest in bullfighting. Jake hates him with particular intensity because, like the "effeminate homosexuals," he *chooses* to be what Jake has been *forced* to become. Indeed, Hemingway's more manly characters like to rib Cohn about his "steer-like" nature. " 'It's no life being a steer,' Robert Cohn said. 'Don't you think so?' Mike said. 'I would have thought you'd loved being a steer, Robert.' 'What do you mean, Mike?' 'They lead such a quiet life. They never say anything and they're always hanging about so.' " The decline of the West, Jake's spiritual emasculation, and the rise of the chameleonic Jew were inextricably intertwined.

Obviously Cohn is not man enough to keep from being gobbled up by the vampire: "*Is* Robert Cohn going to follow Brett around like a steer all the time?" Mike jeers. What rankles the Aryans of Hemingway's novel most is that Brett's sexual degeneracy is so all-inclusive that she is even willing to put up with half-males such as Cohn: "Brett's gone off with men. But they weren't ever Jews, and they didn't come and hang about afterward." (141–3) Mike is a consummate anti-Semite, vituperating against Cohn, "that kike," with his air of "Jewish superiority." Cohn, in fact, is less of a man than Brett herself. He becomes green in the face when he sees the slaughter of the bulls, and Mike ends up taunting him: "Do you think you amount to something, Cohn? do you think you belong here among us?" Finally Jake's upstanding Aryan blood brother tells the crawling Semite to leave him alone: "Go away for God's sake. Take that sad Jewish face away." (165–77)

The tendency among critics has been to accept these passages as integral to Hemingway's "realistic" portrayal of the widespread racism of his contemporaries. An "objective" reporter/novelist, they argue, could hardly be blamed for such passages, since this was the way people around him talked. But in *The Sun Also Rises* the denigration of Cohn is not presented critically. It is an organic element in the unfolding of the author's thesis. The decline of masculine values was the result of a two-pronged attack. The masculinized woman and the feminized Semite were eclipsing the sun. Mike and Jake are the two "true Aryans" in Hemingway's novel. But they both end up "damaged" by Brett's promiscuity and Cohn's unmanly behavior. Neutralized in this fashion, they become melancholy witnesses to the decline of manliness. But as Hemingway's title indicated, the sun also rises: if the Aryan could overcome his growing enslavement to feminine eroticism and chase away the sexual woman's Semitic acolytes, the golden light of masculinity might yet return to save the world.

William Faulkner, too, accepted the findings of the early-twentieth-century psychoanalysts and sexologists without hesitation. The vital-essence theory, and particularly the notion that young women suffered from a "Dora syndrome" they must overcome to become even halfway tolerable, was deeply imbedded in his near-paranoiac conception of gender relationships.

Faulkner's vicious portrayal of seventeen-year-old Temple Drake in *Sanctuary* (1931) adds a dense thicket of metaphoric and verbal complexity to what was otherwise unfortunately a very ordinary prejudicial ideology of gender and race. The key to the novel's antifeminine message is Popeye, Faulkner's version of what Lothrop Stoddard in the subtitle of his book *The Revolt Against Civilization* (1922) had called "the menace of the under man." Popeye, a violent killer, is like Hemingway's Jake, sexually impotent. But unlike Jake, Popeye has not lost his "natural manhood" in manly warfare. Instead, his impotence is a factor of the constitutional degeneracy of his parents. "An undersized, weak child," he was born to a dissolute, syphilitic father and a simpleminded mother who had been infected with her husband's disease at the time of her impregnation. As a result, Popeye "did not learn to walk and talk until he was about four years old." A doctor's assessment clarifies everything: "He will never be a man, properly speaking. With care, he will live some time longer. But he will never be older than he is now." (319–23) His degenerate ancestry has thus made Popeye into a "female man" and therefore, according to the quasi-phrenological black magic of the period's genetic theories, a born criminal.

Stoddard considered "under men" such as Popeye representative of "the workings of that fatal tendency to biological regression which has blighted past civilizations." This degenerative pattern had caused a "species separation" between "the high biological level" of the evolutionary elite and the lower orders of human society. The future of civilization depended upon the quality of its "racial stocks." The group "of superior individuals" at the top of the evolutionary scale had a natural right to rule the world. "At the other end a number of inferior individuals" made up the category of "the under man," while between the two extremes stood "the mass of intermediate individuals, who likewise grade up or down the scale."

Stoddard sketched a sadly recurring pattern of creeping humanism as the immediate cause of the destruction of past civilizations. Time and again "the successful superiors who stood in the vanguard of progress" would "divert human energy from racial ends to individual and social ends." Foolish attempts to improve the lot of the under man caused the "superiors" to neglect their "racial" responsibilities. "Late marriage, fewer children, and celibacy combined to thin the ranks of the successful, diminish the number of superior strains, and thus gradually impoverish the race."

In the meantime, of course, the dastardly inferiors could be counted upon to continue to breed uncontrollably. "No longer ruthlessly weeded by natural selection, the inferior survived and multiplied." Like Maury in *The Beautiful and Damned,* Stoddard saw only evil in humane behavior: "saturated with dullards and degenerates," the upper layers of the human foundation would wither away, leaving civilization to sink to a lower level or collapse in utter ruin. Once again humanity was at such a crossroads, Stoddard warned. More than ever, "the nemesis of the inferior" should concern Nordic Americans of the 1920s, for "the fatal tendency to biological regression" was always sparked by the "atavistic revolt against civilization" of the "Under-Man," that "congenital caveman" who instinctively hated the constructive order of society and who was therefore "always in trouble and usually in jail." (19–23) The "legions of the degenerate and the backward" were "spreading like a cancerous blight and threatening to corrode society to the very marrow of its being." Only the "racially superior" could still thwart their ascendancy: "It is this 'thin red line' of rich, untainted blood which stands between us and barbarism or chaos." (105–6)

Faulkner's Popeye has all the characteristics of Stoddard's "Under-Man." A murderous "anarchist," he represents the forces undermining "civilized society." Though a nondescript "lower-class" white man, he is a carefully constructed composite of society's "racial degenerates." "He smells black, Horace Benbow thought." This just after we have been told that "his skin had a dead, dark pallor. His nose was faintly aquiline, and he had no chin at all." Thus, implied Semitic traits mingle with phrenological evidence of "mental defectiveness" and "atavistic" signs of an African heritage to make Popeye into a Nordic's worst nightmare of miscegenated manhood.

Stunted and impotent, Popeye was of course also meant to evoke thoughts of the predatory, "penis-envious," prematernal female. Faulkner even tried to make his readers associate him with the man-eating arachnids: "Across his vest ran a platinum chain like a spider web." Popeye, as a "female man," was constitutionally closely allied with women in the throes of a "masculinity complex"—women who, as Freud had pointed out, still looked upon themselves as castrated males. Faulkner therefore saw him as a perfect foil to the very phallic Temple Drake. But while Temple is restlessly in search of her lost phallus, Popeye has compensated for his impotence by adopting a handgun as his symbol of phallic strength. The pistol's destructive power becomes his "masculine potency" substitute: "He squatted in his tight black suit, his right hand coat pocket sagging compactly against his flank." (5–7)

In Faulkner's morality tale of social degeneracy in action, Temple was still another Everywoman, much like Gloria had been for Fitzgerald and Brett for Hemingway. Horace Benbow, though himself not untainted by weakness, is the fascinated outside "observer" of *Sanctuary* who watches degeneration infiltrate the ruling class. In the opening scenes of the book, he enunciates the conflict between nature and civilization in traditional gender-ideological terms: "Nature is 'she' and Progress is 'he'; nature made the grape arbor, but Progress invented the mirror." The "conspiracy between female flesh and female season," Benbow adds, makes such a dichotomy inevitable. (14–16) In other words, woman is driven by her womb, and man by his reason. Woman reproduces and man creates. The future Nobel Prize winner's mind contained a plethora of such standard slogans of the gender wars.

Temple Drake, a judge's daughter, is a typical Anglo-Saxon upper-middle-class girl on the verge of womanhood. She is supposed to be a virgin when we first encounter her, though Faulkner makes Temple suggest otherwise in *Requiem for a Nun,* his 1951 continuation of Temple's story: "that is, a virgin as far as anybody went on record to disprove." (113) In the title of this sequel he also continued his play on the Renaissance double meaning of "nunnery" (whores' sanctuary) to highlight his heroine's "natural" aptitude for prostitution.

Temple, even at seventeen, is the standard sexual woman of the Twenties and Thirties. She has a "boldly scarlet" mouth (*Sanctuary,* 38) and a "soft chin"—an early phrenological indication of her spiritual kinship with Popeye—and her eyes are "blankly right and left looking, cool, predatory and discreet." Thus her appetite for sexual dissipation is adumbrated in every aspect of her appearance from the moment we first meet her: "Her face was quite pale, dusted over with recent powder, her hair in spent red curls." (30)

A quick bit of authorial artifice causes Temple to be abandoned by her boyfriend Gowan Stevens in a remote, dilapidated farmhouse amid the dregs of humanity, including, of course, Popeye. Faulkner spends the better part of the first hundred pages of his novel exploiting his readers' taste for voyeurism. We watch as, watched by the men around her, Temple runs about aimlessly for a good many pages, "like a trapped animal," still largely unaware of the nature of the passions stirring in her loins: "She whirled and ran. She ran right off the porch, into the weeds, and sped on. She ran to the road and down it for fifty yards in the darkness, then without a break she whirled and ran back to the house and sprang onto the porch and crouched against the door." (69) We watch the men watch her. We even watch her watch herself: She "saw within her fallen coat naked flesh between brassiere and knickers and knickers and stockings." (91)

Thus, for nearly the first third of the novel Faulkner does everything he can to make the reader complicit in the prurient anticipation of a rape Temple, he intimates, desperately longs for without knowing it. Only Ruby Lamar, mostly referred to as "the woman," an earthy, honest "motherwoman" and the closest approximation to a "good" woman anywhere in the book, has instantly understood what Temple's body craves. The girl stands before her holding the woman's child, and Faulkner's earth mother, whose "breast moved deeply and full," calls her a "little doll-faced slut." She "looked at Temple with cold, blazing eyes. 'Man? You've never seen a real man. You dont know what it is to be wanted by a real man. And thank your stars you haven't and never will, for then you'd find just what that little putty face is worth, and all the rest of it you think you are jealous of when you're just scared of it.'" Apparently Faulkner considered the concept of penis envy to be so ob-

vious that he did not think it out of place for a rural illiterate to refer to
"it." The woman knows exactly what the envious girl will do when she
is confronted with the real thing: "If he is just man enough to call you
whore, you'll say Yes Yes and you'll crawl naked in the dirt and the mire
for him to call you that." Furious at Temple's hypocrisy, she commands:
"Give me that baby." Temple is clearly not a mother-woman in training.
(62–3)

But grovel and say, "yes, yes," we shall see her do plenty. Popeye has
been parading around with his pistol showing. Young Temple at last goes
to sleep on an improvised mattress of "gnawed corncobs"—a grossly
symbolic resting place, not designed to quiet her unacknowledged physical longing. Later, recounting her experience to a horrified yet fascinated Horace Benbow, she recalls how lying on the cobs made her penis
envy run wild: "That was when I got to thinking a funny thing. You
know how you do when you're scared. I was looking at my legs and I'd
try to make like I was a boy. I was thinking about if I just was a boy and
then I tried to make myself into one by thinking." Hoping to conjure
up the desired appendage by sheer force of will, she had wondered "if I
could tell when it happened. I mean, before I looked, and I'd think I had
and how I'd go out and show them—you know. I'd strike a match and
say Look. See? Let me alone, now. And then I could go back to bed."

But Temple had not just wanted to be one of the boys. Recollect-
ing a chastity belt she had seen in a museum, she had imagined putting
it on: "I was thinking maybe it would have long sharp spikes on it and
he wouldn't know it until too late and I'd jab it into him. I'd jab it all the
way through him and I'd think about the blood running on me and how
I'd say I guess that'll teach you." Unlike Hemingway's Brett, Temple was
not merely waiting for the right bullfighter to come along; she wanted
to be a bullfighter herself. She had been unaware that "it was going to
be just the other way." (227–8) In consequence, Temple was to spend the
rest of Faulkner's novel trying to take revenge upon the men around her.

Two years after the publication of *Sanctuary*, Freud, in his *New Introductory Lectures on Psychoanalysis*, summed up his previous writings on
penis envy in a way that read like a direct gloss upon Temple's experience. Seeing the genitals of the other sex, Freud said, girls

> at once notice the difference and, it must be admitted, its signif-
> icance too. They feel seriously wronged, often declare that they
> want to "have something like it too," and fall a victim to "envy

of the penis," which will leave ineradicable traces on their development and the formation of their character and which will not be surmounted in even the most favourable cases without a severe expenditure of psychical energy. (125)

In *Sanctuary* Temple never relaxes her pursuit of the phallus. But Popeye, after shooting and killing Tommy, a half-wit who is naively trying to protect her, rapes Temple in a truly unorthodox fashion, presumably in an effort to accommodate his natural disability. Though at the trial that ends the book it is suggested that his instrument of violation is a corncob, it would seem that at this earlier point Faulkner wanted his readers to think that he had used his gun:

She sat there, her legs straight before her, her hands limp and palm-up on her lap, looking at Popeye's tight back and the ridges of his coat across the shoulders as he leaned out the door, the pistol behind him, against his flank, wisping thinly along his leg. He turned and looked at her. He waggled the pistol slightly and put it back in his coat. Then he walked toward her. (107)

Faulkner made it clear that Temple herself afterward associates her rape with Popeye's gun. He also wanted to make his readers doubt whether what happened was really a rape. Ruby's verdict was already in. But in *Requiem for a Nun* Faulkner went ever further, making the lawyer Gavin Stevens upbraid Gowan, by now Temple's husband, for continuing to dwell upon this episode in Temple's history and for taking the blame "for something your wife hadn't even lost, didn't even regret, didn't even miss." What was more, "she didn't even suffer, but on the contrary, even liked it." (63–4) What mattered to Faulkner was that Popeye's unorthodox defloration of Temple brought out the latent vampire in her.

Soon after the murder and rape, Popeye takes a passive, willing Temple to her "sanctuary," a Memphis house of prostitution. Here she maintains a passive, vegetative existence in what is obviously her "natural" environment, never attempting to escape. We are to understand that Popeye's gun has become the object of her phallic affection. The dark, degenerate owner of this instrument has taken to visiting her on a regular basis. In her room, in a closet, he keeps his black clothes. "Hanging from a nail was an automatic pistol in a holster of oiled silk. She took it down gingerly and removed the pistol and stood with it in her hand.

After a moment she went to the bed and hid it beneath the pillow." (237) Then, in an attempt to realize her dream of becoming a "boy," Temple directly "appropriates" Popeye's "manhood": "She felt the pistol through the pillow. She slipped it out and looked at it, then she slid it under her flank and lay motionless, her legs straight, her hands behind her head, her eyes focussing into black pinheads at every sound on the stairs." (242)

But just when she has made herself grow a penis-gun instead of a penis-baby, Temple is finally introduced to the real object of her obses-

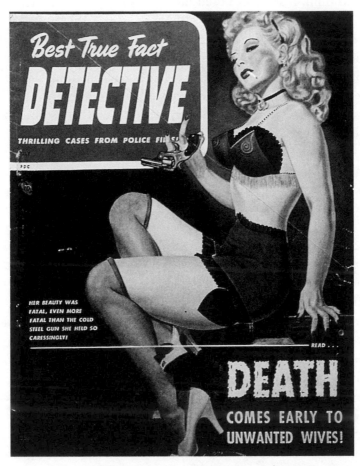

Cover of Best True Fact Detective, *July 1948*
Appropriating the phallus: Freudianism for the masses
in the wake of *Sanctuary*

sion, in a manner that allowed Faulkner to exploit his own obsession with voyeurism even further. Popeye brings Red, one of his criminal associates, to Temple and watches him have sexual intercourse with Temple. But the introduction of Red's personal endowment makes her furious at Popeye for "misleading" her: "Dont you wish you were Red? Dont you wish you could do what he can do? Dont you wish he was the one watching us instead of you?" Temple has finally understood what she'd been looking for all along. Popeye had misled her by offering her no more than a penis surrogate. " 'He's a better man than you are!' Temple said shrilly. 'You're not even a man! He knows it. Who does know it if he dont?' " (243–5)

Almost immediately after this, the sight of Red at a nightclub brings out the already none-too-latent nymphomaniac in Temple. Faulkner shows that, even so, she is still a somewhat confused "little girl," still not quite able to remember the difference between a real phallus and Popeye's gun:

> She put her hand on [Popeye's] shoulder. "Daddy," she said. Moving to shield them from the room, her hand stole toward his armpit, touching the butt of the flat pistol. It lay rigid in the light, dead vise of his arm and side. "Give it to me," she whispered. "Daddy. Daddy." She leaned her thigh against his shoulder, caressing his arm with her flank. "Give it to me, daddy," she whispered. Suddenly her hand began to steal down his body in a swift, covert movement, then it snapped away in a movement of revulsion. "I forgot," she whispered; "I didn't mean . . . I didn't. . . ." (249)

Her loyalty for Popeye gone, and in brute animal rut, Temple now rapidly becomes a true sexual vampire. When Red approaches her, all civilization falls from her and she turns into an uncontrollable predator: "When he touched her she sprang like a bow, hurling herself upon him, her mouth gaped and ugly like that of a dying fish as she writhed her loins against him." Then, "with her hips grinding against him, her mouth gaping in straining protrusion, bloodless," she begs him to take her with him. Focusing relentlessly on Temple's rapacious mouth, Faulkner stressed the primitive feminine "blood hunger" that made her act in this fashion: " 'Come on. What're you waiting for?' She strained her mouth toward him, dragging his head down, making a whimpering moan."

Red's true masculinity drives her beyond herself: " 'You're a man. You're a man.' She began to grind against him, dragging at his head, murmuring to him in parrotlike underworld epithets, the saliva running pale over her bloodless lips." (252–3)

Like every other vampire before her, Temple leaves dead bodies in her wake wherever she goes. Popeye kills Red, and Temple, for no detectable reason other than because Popeye happened to have been the man who showed her how she could have a phallus of her own, gives false testimony at a trial dealing with Tommy's murder and her rape. This allows Popeye to run free, while Goodwin, Ruby's common-law husband, is found guilty and is immolated by a vengeful mob. Temple, too, goes scot-free, to marry Gowan. In *Requiem for a Nun* we are to learn that she did go on to have children, but this information only serves to show her up as a truly terrible mother—a child-murderer, even. If Faulkner ever had any real qualms about the "sensationalism" of *Sanctuary,* as he later maintained, this revisitation of his vampire woman of the Thirties, twenty years after he created her, shows conclusively that he did not have any second thoughts about his characterization of this maniacal "Everywoman."

Faulkner's mixed erotic fascination with and hatred for Temple was patent, and it was very clearly focused. She was, he declared in *Requiem for a Nun,* the archetypal sexual woman, the agent of brute nature against whom society must struggle to survive, "insatiable and forever incontinent: demon-nun and angel-witch; empress, siren, Erinys." (225) As for Popeye, he was, in Faulkner's scheme of things, more a social pollutant than a truly satanic personage like Temple: he was therefore disposed of with cheap irony by being executed "for killing a man in one town and at an hour when he was in another town killing somebody else." But though Popeye was thus summarily dismissed, the modern world, Faulkner implied, continued to offer sanctuary to Temple, the real monster of society. Degeneration had therefore won another victory. In *Requiem for a Nun* Faulkner made it clear that Temple, as the draconian personification of the eternal feminine, aided by her team of degenerate male allies, had halted "the old brave innocent tumultuous" ascendancy of "the Anglo-Saxon, the pioneer, the tall man, roaring with Protestant scripture and boiled whiskey," who was "a married invincible bachelor." Aryan brotherhood lay in the dust, and woman was responsible. (89–91)

Sanctuary, then, showed that Temple Drake was Popeye's evil sister.

Both were murderous by nature, and their heritage of lust made each a vile and impotent drag on humanity. The novel's final message was that when society allows the "natural" maternal nymphomaniac in woman (Ruby) to be superseded by the terminally narcissistic, penis-envious, libidinally introverted and hence genetically regressive, masculinized women of decadent modern society, disaster must follow. Benbow sees the social beginnings of a "good," spontaneously evolving nuclear family (Goodwin, Ruby, and their child) attacked and destroyed before his very eyes as a result of the false accusations of Temple Drake, who perversely protects the raping degenerate who taught her to be phallic. In this she is aided and abetted by the mean-spirited women who rule Benbow's own feminized environment. Thus the evolutionary alliance between reproductive femininity and the creative masculine has been undermined once again in a vicious conspiracy between the dregs of human society: castrating women and emasculate men, the terrorist phalanx of social degenerates described by Lothrop Stoddard in *The Revolt against Civilization* as "the imbecile, the feeble-minded, the neurotic, the insane—all those melancholy waste-products every living species excretes but which are promptly extirpated in the state of nature, whereas in human societies they are too often preserved." (22) Humanism, liberalism—the "effeminate sentimentalism" of an "emasculate civilization"—had created the vampire of species degeneration personified by Temple Drake.

What to do, then, about these sterile vampire women who wanted to steal the all-powerful phallic gun and who, blinded by violent bouts of penis envy, had aligned themselves with the "mongrel" races? In *Requiem for a Nun* Temple acknowledges that her maid, "an ex-dope-fiend nigger whore" whom she casually sacrifices to save herself from being condemned as a child-murderer, "was the only animal in Jefferson that spoke Temple Drake's language." (136) And Gavin Stevens, Anglo-Saxon to the bone, also speaking in this drama published years *after* the genocidal revelations of World War II, directly voices the solution Faulkner had only implied in *Sanctuary*. Describing Popeye as "a little black thing with an Italian name, like a neat and only slightly deformed cockroach; a hybrid, sexually incapable," (121) Stevens declares that his formal execution had been too weak a punishment: "He should have been crushed somehow under a vast and mindless boot, like a spider." (126)

The spider woman, Temple Drake, and the mongrel, mixed-race

Italians, the hybrid Semitic, Eurasian, and black "under men," nature's degenerates, the emissaries of the Bolshevik revolt against civilization, should be summarily exterminated, this passage implied. And indeed, Faulkner's portrayal of Temple Drake in *Sanctuary* had, like so many characterizations that had come before it, been calculated to make his readers jump up once again and intone the social directive of Oscar Wilde's Herod: "Kill that woman!" His presentation was intended to stir the gynecidal impulse in the reader just as much as Stoddard's diatribes served to prepare the world for genocide. Faulkner's narrative closely followed the hard-line antihumanist social Darwinism of William Graham Sumner, which had also helped create the hard-line capitalist elitism of Lothrop Stoddard and Madison Grant. Proudly echoing Sumner's remarks about the "benevolent" passive extermination of the sick, the weak, and the poor, and further inspired by the categorical declarations of the geneticists, Grant took the line of thought to be found in Sumner's writings to its logical conclusion in *The Passing of the Great Race:*

> Where two distinct species are located side by side history and biology teach that but one of two things can happen; either one race drives the other out, as the Americans exterminated the Indians and as the Negroes are now replacing the whites in various parts of the South; or else they amalgamate and form a population of race bastards in which the lower type ultimately preponderates. This is a disagreeable alternative with which to confront sentimentalists but nature is only concerned with results and neither makes nor takes excuses. The chief failing of the day with some of our well meaning philanthropists is their absolute refusal to face inevitable facts, if such facts appear cruel. (77–8)

Exterminate the brutes, Grant was suggesting. But that was also the solution Faulkner placed in the minds of the readers of *Sanctuary:* exterminate these bitches! The imagery of the evil woman had blended with that of her degenerate allies. One could only fantasize about eradicating the sexual woman—after all, a man needed sons. But the Popeyes responsible for her awakening could be exterminated at will. Writers such as Fitzgerald, Hemingway, and Faulkner and innumerable other intellectuals and politicians in Western Europe and the United States thus helped prepare the world for the realpolitik of genocide. Their metaphoric excursions into the battle of the sexes were rapidly being translated into the language of global war. The "she" of nature and the "he" of progress were preparing for a decisive battle. The manly Aryan race must exterminate the "lower races," or be destroyed in a tide of ef-feminate regression. The Eurasian demon must be killed, or society would perish.

Nosferatu (*1922*)

X. DUALISM ENTHRONED: OAK TREES AND DESTROYERS; HITLER AND THE HAMMER OF DEATH; GENOCIDE AS GYNECIDE IN THE MYTHOLOGY OF POPULAR CULTURE

The sun god—the man whose closely guarded phallus was a shield against the lunar depredations of the vampire of effeminacy—was the patron saint of the Third Reich. Aryan men must avoid being drained by the moon and, with "bodies hard as steel," prepare for the coming millennium, Hitler argued in *Mein Kampf*. "Feminization of the man" and "masculinization of the woman," Carl Jung insisted at just about the same time, "must be regarded as regression in a young person." (*Symbols of Transformation*, 459) The anima in a man, he added during a 1930 lecture, "is always connected with the inferior function." "She" represented the misty world of feeling and sentiment rather than "Logos," steely reason, the man's "conscious principle." In *Mein Kampf* Hitler identified the hard body of the youthful male as the shining armor of spiritual masculinity: "What makes the Greek ideal of beauty immortal is the wonderful combination of the most glorious physical beauty with a brilliant mind and the noblest soul." (614)

Jung explained why the young Aryan needed physical armor: "The anima represents the primitive layer of man's psychology," and she is therefore "eternally a heretic and does not fit in at all, a perfect pagan, in more or less open revolt against the Christian point of view." It was "common for her to take on the quality of the Orient or an older civilization." After all, she was a negative entity, Jung reminded his audience, for she represented "the inferior Eros in man." To prove this point, the analyst discussed the dream of an Aryan man who had found himself in church, singing a hymn with the refrain "Rejoice, O Christendom." Behind him the churchgoer had heard somebody "singing the same words in a peculiar soprano voice, exceedingly loud and the melody quite different." The other's shrill, dissonant voice made the Christian worshipers sing "completely out of tune." After the service the dreamer heard the inferior singer remark to someone that, for once, he had been able to show that he too could sing. Though infuriated by the singer's clumsy insensitivity to his environment, the dreamer restrained himself from "making a disagreeable remark," observing that the other appeared to be "more masculine this time" and had "a Jewish type of face." The dreamer then "remembers that his son is a friend of his. Then the son suddenly appears and violently reproaches his father because he upset the hymn."

Jung was certain that the stranger represented the anima in this dream, but he corrected a member of his seminar who identified her as a "Jewess": "That she is feminine is probably quite clear to you, but why is she masculine too? This is a very unusual case. And mind you, afterwards she becomes a man, a Jew." This dream-Jew, Jung insisted, was an expression of the dreamer's own immature sexual ambiguity:

> If a man's anima is masculine, he is absolutely possessed—obsessed by her, and he cannot establish a relationship with her until she is feminine. To say he is effeminate means the same thing— that she has power over him. The fact that the dream expresses is: you are effeminate, you are possessed by your anima.

Both the dream and Jung's explanation are dramatic examples of the casual blending of prejudicial gender and race imagery by 1930. Jung took it for granted that, to the average Nordic male, effeminacy and Jewishness would be interchangeable concepts. The dreamer's irate son, he suggested, was his "Logos," his Aryan consciousness. This Logos rightfully blamed the father for having "disrupted" the Christian service with his "Jewish anima," the embarrassing public manifestation of his effeminate eros. The father, Jung concluded, could not expect to regain the friendship of his son until he ceased his disruptive Hebraic chant-ing—that perpetual disruption of Logos by eros that made Aryan soci-ety sing out of tune: "Such ideas would not fit in with the ideas of the Protestant church and would prove most disturbing. Obviously!" Jung exclaimed. The dreamer must conquer this "demon," this "phantom" of the feminine in himself, to give sacred masculinity, Logos, a chance to triumph and make him "whole." (*Aspects of the Masculine,* 127–39)

The casual domestication of anti-Semitism during the Twenties and Thirties could not have been expressed more dramatically than it was in this example of Jung's analytic technique. During the early 1910s Freud had broken with Jung over the latter's use of mythological imagery to explicate psychological states. Freud recognized Jung's constant use of such images as a facile attempt to falsify the patterns of causality under-lying the formation of neuroses. Jung's approach simplified complex crosscurrents of social, economic, ethical, and sexual conflict and turned these environmental influences into mere expressions of "universal" patterns of human behavior. By 1930, Freud, as a Jew, had been forced to take stock of the social impact of the prejudicially metaphorized ar-guments of medicine, biology, and genetics. In *Civilization and Its Dis-contents* he finally acknowledged that the condition of the world suggested "the diagnosis that, under the influence of cultural urges, some civilizations, or some epochs of civilization—possibly the whole of mankind—have become 'neurotic.'" (91) But Jung, caught in the prison of his own metaphors, considered "the cultural urges" that had made Western society by this time not just neurotic but psychotic, a normal part of its psychic "growth." Freud, at least, had belatedly real-ized that a *social* paranoia was sweeping the Western world.

Jung's contention that human behavior was organized by a "collec-tive unconscious" consisting of unchanging, primordial images actively encouraged the negative metaphors of sex, class, and race developed by the scientists. By positing the existence of "universal" psychological states and arguing that every "archetype" was linked to a specific stage of evolutionary development, he helped justify the reign of Logos over eros as the only reasonable outcome of humanity's internal battle of the sexes. In fact, he had merely adopted the racial-memory arguments of the genetic ideologues. Using a barrage of images and metaphors ten-dentiously imposed on a welter of myth and folklore, he argued the ex-istence of "ur-forms" of cognition that determined every aspect of human behavior. But his "archetypes" were all directly shaped by the prejudicial race and gender proposals of the scientists of the early years of this century. Masculine aggression became representative of the cultural "voyage of the hero," and feminine sexuality was an expression of the predatory call of the perpetually hungry and hence "deadly" womb of the "great mother." The hero was "the man who overcomes the Terrible Mother, breaks the teeth out of her vagina, and so makes her into a woman," as Jung's faithful follower Erich Neumann succinctly summarized the master's point of view in *The Great Mother: An Analysis of the Archetype* (1955).

Jung's system was thus tailor-made for the aggressive psychosocial paranoia of the Twenties. The self-liberating voyage of the "hero" could easily be read as a metaphoric representation of the evolutionary elite's genetic responsibilities. The Aryan must do to the "lower orders," the "effeminates" of modern society, exactly what the hero, the leader, the "Führer" of Aryan civilization, must do to the woman within. "Inferiors" could be subdued and made useful, but they should never be given equal rights with the ruling elite. "By mating again and again with other races, we may well lift those races out of their former cultural level to a higher one, but we sink down from our own high level forever," (637) Hitler exclaimed. To maintain racial purity was to overcome the reversive temptation of the "Terrible Mother."

But the members of "mongrel" races were not always easily identified. They often "passed" for white and could be counted upon to infiltrate the ranks of the Aryans and weaken them, "feminize" them, from within. The "Eurasian Semite," the hybrid most closely resembling the master race, was therefore also most likely to do serious genetic damage to the superior strains of humanity. The Aryan who had learned to assert his masculinity by breaking the teeth out of his woman's invasive vagina, must now learn to go further, and break the teeth—as well as the skull—of any inferior intent upon polluting the "racial purity" of the sons and daughters of the Aryan elite.

Frank Cowperwood, in Theodore Dreiser's *The Titan* (1914), already exhibited every aspect of the Jungian hero. A superman of capitalism, he knew that sexual and economic slavery were two sides of the same coin. He was, Dreiser noted, one of "a set of giants—Titans—who, without heart or soul, and without any understanding of or sympathy with the condition of the rank and file, were setting forth to enchain and enslave" all others. Cowperwood (and Dreiser with him) knew that it was every good woman's fondest dream to have a real man come along and bash her teeth out: "Say what one will, the wish buried deep in every woman's heart is that her lover should be a hero. Some, out of the veriest stick or stone, fashion the idol before which they kneel, others demand the hard reality of greatness." (478)

Membership in the master race of imperial masculinity required that one engage in drastic action to punish those who failed to "kneel." Cowperwood made this clear in his attitude toward Stephanie Platow, a mongrel of Russian Jewish and "southwestern American" descent, with whom, against his better judgment, he has a brief fling. This woman, who is an "unstable chemical compound," a "poison-flower," a "beautiful, enigmatic, immoral, and promiscuous woman," remains protected from his wrath only by the sappy effeminacy of modern times: in earlier days "he would have had her strangled, sewn into a sack, and thrown into the Bosporus." (218–21) The titanic males of the Aryan elite clearly longed for those days to return. Hitler understood their dislike of "feeble humanism":

> All these symptoms of decay are ultimately only consequences of the lack of a certain, commonly acknowledged view of life and of the general uncertainty in the judgment, and the definition of an attitude towards the various great questions of the time, resulting from it. Therefore, everything, beginning with education, is half-hearted and wavering, shuns responsibility and ends thus in cowardly tolerance of even recognized evils. Dreamy humaneness becomes the fashion, and by a weak surrender to the excrescences and in sparing the individuals, one sacrifices in turn the future of millions. (364)

Throughout Western Europe and the United States the ideologues of race agreed with Hitler. The steely resolve and "iron will" of the "higher man" were constantly threatened by women, liberals, Jews, and other do-gooders, whose "dreamy humaneness" served only to undermine the necessary evolutionary inequalities of race, sex, and class. Oswald Spengler, in his *Jahre der Entscheidung* (*Years of Decision*), published in the dark year of 1933, warned: "Western civilization of this century is being threatened by not just one but two world revolutionary movements of enormous proportions." The first came from "below," the other from "outside." They were "class war" and "race war." The poor, the weak, and the inferior had learned to take advantage of the "pacifism" of the humanists who had come to rule the West. The dregs of society, realizing that the white race no longer had the stomach to rule with an iron fist, were responding to this new form of cultural effeminacy by undermining the social order.

While the white leaders continued to prattle about "humane" behavior and "eternal peace," Spengler warned, the inferior "sniffed out the incompetence and the irresolution of the West's will to defend itself." Instead of grinding them down under its iron heel, the West was countering the "colored races" with a powderpuff of humane concerns. In consequence, those who had once feared the white man now simply despised him for his weakness. Russian Bolshevism—and let no one misunderstand, Spengler emphasized in a familiar refrain, "Russia is lord over Asia. Russia *is* Asia"—was fomenting the extermination of the white race under cover of its Marxist egalitarianism.

In addition, Spengler insisted, offering as incontrovertible proof of this contention Lothrop Stoddard's *The Rising Tide of Color,* The Japanese were teaming up with the Indians of Mexico, to whom they were racially akin, to foment a race war against the Aryans. Stoddard claimed that in 1914 the Japanese had devised a plot, a "Plan of San Diego," to destroy America. An army "composed solely of 'Latins,' negroes and Japanese" had been about to invade Texas in order to foment a race war. "The racial results were to be decisive," Stoddard said, "for the entire white population of both our South and Southwest was to be pitilessly massacred." Fortunately the plot had "completely miscarried." (133)

Spengler used Stoddard's claim to intimate that Russia and Japan—Bolshevism and the Yellow Peril—were conspiring against the white race in order to exterminate it. All this because the West had allowed itself to grow weak and mushy with humanism and sentimentality. But Spengler disapproved of "the anti-Semites in Europe and America among whom it is the fashion to see the issue of race solely in Darwinist and materialist terms." For him the future belonged not to those who worried about "race hygiene." Instead, what counted was the *strength* of the race. That strength manifested itself first and foremost in the fertility rate of the women. In the coming global race war, only hyperfertile nations could expect to triumph. The most valuable women of the race were not those sentimentally seen as "partners" or as "sweethearts," but those willing to devote themselves solely to the business of breeding. Only such women were worthy of the Aryan male's respect. The intellectual pretensions of big-city women were an expression of society's ongoing feminization. The increasing prominence of such women highlighted the weakening of the white race's will to survive. (147–65)

The innumerable theorists of race, class, and gender of the first thirty years of this century saw the betrayal of Logos by eros as central to a nation's moral and physical degeneration: the decline of the West started in the white man's lack of sexual self-control, which in turn led to a loss of "power" and "manhood." The main symptoms of social deterioration were "sentimentality," an emphasis on humanistic concerns over the exigencies of "nation building," and a weakness for egalitarian political systems. The iron heel of evolutionary masculinity must crush the spider of effeminacy or be crushed itself. The sexual woman, the main enemy of civilization, had many degenerate masculine allies. Everywhere Popeye's brothers were using Temple Drake's sisters as lures to tempt the rank and file of Western culture into perdition.

The notion that the "race war" must be fought first and foremost on the battlefield of human sexuality pervaded social thought. David Starr Jordan, generally credited with turning Stanford University from a "cow college" into one of the most distinguished American institutions of higher learning, is also still remembered for his opposition to the politics of war. But Jordan's reasons for opposing war were virulently racist. The title of his eugenicist manifesto of 1902, *The Blood of the Nation—A Study of the Decay of Races Through the Survival of the Unfit,* made his position crystal clear. More than a decade later Jordan elaborated upon his views in his book *War and the Breed* (1915). "War," he said, "leads toward racial decadence by the obliteration of the most virile elements, these being thereby unrepresented in heredity." The "War System of the world" was a dangerous "reversive" tendency in civilization, well up there with immigration and "unwise charity." A true believer in Sumner's no-nonsense attitude toward the "unfit," Jordan saw charity as weakness: "pauperism is helped to perpetuate itself, feeblemindedness becomes the heritage of future generations, and races of idiots and criminals have been created." (10–11)

The term "blood will tell" had the ring of racial truth, Jordan insisted. Genetics had shown that "the structure of the germ-cell and its contained germ-plasm" were the key to racial improvement. On the metaphoric level "blood which is 'thicker than water' is the symbol of race unity. In this sense lies the apparent paradox that blood determines history and history determines blood." Jordan was willing to admit that improvements in education and the quality of life might have a slight euthenic—"environmentally generated"—influence on the behavior of coming generations, but it would always remain the genetic inheritance of "the breed" itself that counted most. "Older, deeper set, more permanent than climate or training or experience are the traits of heredity and in the long run it is always 'blood that tells.' " (16)

Immigration should be drastically curtailed to prevent race suicide, for "everywhere under these conditions, the blood of the slave or the conquered had diluted that of the dominating race usually to its detriment." (29) Indeed, immigration was something of a genetic conspiracy among weaklings taking advantage of the foolish eradication of the truly able in the world war. As proof Jordan offered a remarkable synthesis of pseudohistory, pseudogenetics, pseudoanthropology, and pseudofolklore, all rolled into one fantastic theory exemplary of the ideological function of the period's academic scholarship. "An interesting phenomenon in London," this president of Stanford University began, without revealing his source,

> has been discussed as "The Return of the Fairies." It is a current theory that the fairy tales of Europe are based on persistent memories of pre-historic swarthy dwarf races which once lived on the continent. It is now claimed that these types, not yet extinct, are tending in the prevalence of military selection to reassert themselves and to "congregate in their old haunts." The "pygmies of London," undersized, darkskinned people, "clothed in rags and begging an existence," are now increasing in relative numbers. "The prehistoric small, dark types which were submerged by the Celtic and Teutonic invasions have been asserting themselves numerically, and have also been percolating back to the areas from which they were driven by those bigger, fiercer, blonde immigrants."

Jordan saw "the increase of these dwarfs" as the return of the genetically repressed—a direct result of "their immunity from military service." They were a racial menace, for in their case "we must be dealing with a matter of heredity," not merely with euthenic disadvantages. "Life in the slums causes deterioration in all types of men. But it is the weak and unstable who create the slums. Slum-life with its associations of liquor and vice constitutes at once a cause, an effect and a symptom of personal weakness." (17–19)

Jordan's obsession with these "dwarfs" of London is a clear example of the steadily more abstruse blending of metaphor and "science" during the early decades of this century. His dwarfs were clearly the children of Robert Louis Stevenson's Edward Hyde, who was, as a creature on whom evil had left "an imprint of deformity and decay," also "more of a dwarf" compared to Jekyll's "tall fine build." (67) The Western imagination was shopping for a scapegoat who might blend the fantasies of reason with the rationalizations of fantasy. It needed to find that "swart" and "dusky" being, "inherently malign and villainous," whose "bestial avidity" in pursuit of the pleasures of the flesh had begun to infect the "germ-plasm" of the Aryan, causing "the animal within" him to lick "the chops of memory" while his "spiritual side" drowsed. (86–92)

By the mid-1920s the social identity of this evil dwarf who dwelled in the slums was conclusively identified, not only by Adolf Hitler, but by most of the eugenicists, geneticists, racial theorists, and patriotic anti-Bolshevists of the Western world. He was, of course, none other than that Eurasian nomad, inventor of Marxism and seducer of the blonde daughters of the Aryan: Dracula, the ever invasive immigrant, the Wandering Jew. Wherever he went he made otherwise decent women his slaves, polluting their easily contaminated bodies and turning them into sensual predators.

Otto Weininger, who ought to know what he was talking about, had declared in *Sex and Character* (1903) that women were the Jew's natural minions. The Jew was a male with a female sensibility. Like woman, he was "always more absorbed by sexual matters than the Aryan." Both were instinctive dialecticians, intent upon undermining the progressively developing dualistic principles of rational thought. "The homology of Jew and woman becomes closer the further examination goes," Weininger insisted. "In the Jew and the woman, good and evil are not distinct from one another." Being "in constant close relation with the lower life," the Jew understood the desires of women instinctively and was able to manipulate them in ways Aryan males could not imagine. That was exactly why the Jew was Dracula. (307–20)

Far from being seen as a demented eccentric, Weininger, for several decades after the publication of the book, remained unquestionably one of the most highly respected and frequently quoted "authorities" on the subject of sex and race, in both Europe and the United States. An outsider himself, he had made the identification of "otherness" the central task of his life. The enduring popularity of his book was a tribute to the accuracy of his assessment of the prevailing racial sentiment among his predominantly "Nordic" audience. Recognizing his own otherness as a homosexual and a Jew, and masochistically accepting the "correctness" of the Aryan's antipathy to his "subversive" ambiguity of race *and* gender, he killed himself. Thus he remained a faithful slave to his Aryan masters, anticipating their every wish, even to the extent of his protogenocidal self-eradication.

But most Jews were not so accommodating. Lothrop Stoddard pointed out in *The Alien in Our Midst* that unless they were too obviously "descended from West-Asiatic stocks" and hence even more primitive than the superficially acculturated "Western" Jews, they instead appeared to be making every effort to "hide" themselves among the Aryans, sometimes even adopting Christianity. In *The Melting-Pot Mistake* Henry Pratt Fairchild recounted an "amusing" anecdote he had read in the work of Moses Hess about "the son of a rich German-Jewish banker, who would stand in front of his mirror for hours on end, desperately endeavoring to iron out the Semitic kinks of his hair." But, added Fairchild with calculated malice, "straight hair or curly locks, can any Jew ever hope to straighten out the 'kinks' of his oriental soul?" (224)

In their self-reflective vanity, Weininger had said, both the Jew and the woman tried to disparage the procreative function of sexual intercourse in favor of the act as an end in itself. The fin de siècle's preoccupation with sterile eroticism made it fair to say that "our age is not only the most Jewish but the most feminine." Jews and women had forged a lewd alliance, for woman had always understood "that her whole significance and existence depend on her mission as a procreating agent, and that she goes to the wall if man is allowed to occupy himself altogether with other than sexual matters." (335)

Though it was clearly not Weininger's report from the front but the prevailing temper of his time that gave Adolf Hitler the opportunity to create a common cause among Nordics, the Führer did keep a copy of *Sex and Character* in his library, no doubt as a guide to the devious feminine recesses of the Aryan enemy's mind. Weininger's insistence on very precise analogues between sexual and racial degeneracy probably helped Hitler to identify the Jew as a vampire-master. For in *Mein Kampf* Hitler promoted an image of the Jew as a sexual and economic aggressor who preyed on and infected Aryan womanhood and business indiscriminately. The Führer's Aryan manifesto was a rambling, two-volume tirade of nearly a thousand pages. It fulminated against "race-mixing," internationalism, "Jewish Marxism," and "cultural effeminacy." The first half was published late in 1925 and was later combined with the second half, which was first published in 1927. In *Mein Kampf* the socially constructed imagery of the sexual woman as vampire, which had already destroyed the lives of untold millions of women throughout Europe and the United States during the preceding decades, finally took an openly political turn when it became the organizing principle of Nazi anti-Semitism.

Hitler had gathered together all the clichés of early-twentieth-century science. He identified true masculinity as an exclusively Nordic trait. Effeminacy was a typically Jewish defect, and "good" femininity was characterized by a constant yearning for motherhood. The devious alliance between the Jew and the sexual woman could be seen in the parallel effects of the sexual woman's descent into sterile eroticism and the Jew's equally sterile lust for gold. Their combined depredations had undermined the Nordic nations' vitality with a "blood-sucking tyranny."

Over and over again in *Mein Kampf,* the Jew was identified as the ur-form of the sexual woman, as the master vampire who stood in the way of humanity's ascent toward a perfectly balanced dualistic nirvana of continent men and constantly breeding women. Guided by the "führer," the "strongest man," (752) humanity must patiently follow its upward path along the "endless ladder" to perfection. (405) The inferior could not hope to vault to the top by mating with superior specimens of evolved humanity. Blood was easily tainted, and hence blood-mixing was "blood-poisoning." (390)

Hitler's sources for such statements were the same as those used by the French and Anglo-American racist nationalists. He presented his readers with statements they could easily accept as factual, because an entire generation of biologists, geneticists, and physicians had paved his path to the politics of race hatred with a barrage of misogynist rhetoric. Hitler simply took their familiar vital essence and germ-plasm arguments and turned them into the basis for a policy for "national survival." Just as the sexual woman was the unevolved, still "masculine" primitive who depredated the continent male and siphoned off his gray matter with her *vagina dentata,* so the Jew was the still effeminate male sensualist who entered the nation by stealth and proceeded to pollute it through miscegenation. Thus the Jew and the sexual woman both plundered the national coffers of masculinity—for, as Carl Jung would write a few years after the publication of *Mein Kampf,* "we might compare masculinity and femininity and their psychic components to a definite store of substances of which in the first half of life, unequal use is made. A man consumes his large supply of masculine substance and has left over only the smaller amount of feminine substance, which must now be put to use." (*Aspects of the Masculine,* 32) Hitler used this reliable medical principle to conflate the racist imagery of the Jew as an economic predator with that of the sexual woman as a "consumer" of the steely masculinity German men so urgently needed for "the first half of life."

The metaphoric link between Hitler's rhetoric and the imagery of vampirism was unmistakable: the Jew, he stressed over and over again, was "always only a *parasite* in the body of other peoples," a "sponger who, like a harmful bacillus, spreads out more if only a favorable medium invites him to do so." (419–20) He was "the 'ferment of decomposition' of nations and races and, in a wider sense, the dissolver of human culture." (666) The Jew had lodged himself "inside the body of the other peoples during the course of the centuries" by appropriating the fruits of his hosts' labor. Thus he was "a real blood-sucker which attaches itself to the body of the unfortunate people," the "alien element" in the body of the Aryan state.

Like H. Rider Haggard's two-thousand-year-old She, and like women in general, the Jew had remained virtually untouched by the processes of evolution: "His character qualities have remained the same, whether two thousand years ago he spoke Roman as a grain merchant in Ostia or whether as a flour profiteer of today he haggles German like a Jew. He is always the same Jew"—an unchangeable mass-male. (427–30) None of Hitler's contemporaries would have had any difficulty recognizing these implied homologies between "the Jew" and "woman." As late as 1948, William Carlos Williams, still echoing Weininger, insisted that "every portrait of some woman comes out as woman; every portrait of man comes out as some man—or nothing." ("Woman as Operator," 182)

No wonder, then, that like Dracula, the Jew liked to hide and make women do his dirty work: "He poisons the blood of the others, but he guards his own. The Jew does not marry a Christian woman, but always the Christian a Jewess. Yet the bastards take to the Jewish side." (434) But as a consummate sensualist, the Jew liked to contaminate Aryan women whenever he could:

> For hours the black-haired Jew boy, diabolic joy in his face, waits in ambush for the unsuspecting girl whom he defiles with his blood and thus robs her from her people. With the aid of all means he tries to ruin the racial foundations of the people to

be enslaved. Exactly as he himself systematically demoralizes women and girls, he is not scared from pulling down the barriers of blood and race for others on a large scale.

Thus "he systematically tries to lower the racial level by a permanent poisoning of the individual." (448–9) Once polluted in this manner, a nation was lost, for "alone the loss of the purity of the blood destroys the inner happiness forever; it eternally lowers man, and never again can its consequences be removed from body and mind." (452)

To accomplish this permanent lowering of races, the Jew tried to turn the nations he had infiltrated toward eroticism. The "bolshevistic wave" used a febrile, effeminate "intellectualism" to undermine the Aryan male's iron control over his body. Indeed, "this Jewish disease" had caused the intelligentsia of the last several decades to become "physically completely degenerated." To combat the muscle-weakening intellectualism of the Jewish Bolshevist conspiracy, "theater, art, literature, movies, the press, billposters and window displays must be cleaned of the symptoms of a rotting world and put into the service of a moral idea of State and culture. Public life has to be freed from the suffocating perfume of our modern eroticism." (345–8) To counter the "poisoning of the soul" of the German nation organized by "this peoples' vampire," (451) the Aryan must pursue the rigorous "preservation of our people's health in body and soul. The right of personal freedom steps back in the face of the duty of the preservation of the race." (348)

But "Jewry, through its Marxist and democratic press," (374) was resisting any attempt to lead the Aryan out of "the swamp of a gradually decomposing world" (579) whose ongoing degradation was the product "of the Jew's attempt at excluding the overwhelming importance of the personality in all domains of human life and of replacing it by the number of the masses." (666) Thank God for the army, for "in this time of the beginning and slowly spreading decomposition of our national body," the army had become "the mightiest school of the German nation." Single-handedly it was bringing Aryan manhood back from the brink of perdition:

> In the face of the Jewish democratic idea of a blind worship of numbers, the army upheld the faith in personality. Thus it also bred what the newer times need most of all: men. Yes, indeed, in the swamp of a generally spreading softening and effeminacy,

out of the ranks of the army there shot up every year 350,000 vigorous young men who in two years' training had lost the softness of youth and had gained bodies hard as steel. (383–6)

The French, British, and American racist theorists, largely due to their countries' far more extensive colonial empires and relatively open immigration policies, had found a wide variety of racial inferiors in every corner of the world, and this had diffused the immediate effect of their venom toward any one group. Hitler, however, conveniently simplified the scattershot racial rhetoric of this group by concentrating the German people's racist energies on a single, easily identifiable, and already well-established object of hatred, thereby maximizing the political usefulness of prejudice.

In addition, Hitler deliberately fused the prevalent image of the fiendish, "gold-consuming" Jewish erotomane with that of the semen-consuming, darkly erotic sexual woman who depleted her man's bank account. He used the cultural mechanisms of metaphoric gynecide to foment a mentality of genocide against a single alien "bacillus" of degeneration eating its way into the Aryan body politic. Pure Aryan manhood, its blood defiled by Jewish temptresses and its bank accounts invaded by Jewish investors, must at last rise up against the agents of degeneration and recapture its destined position at the top of the ladder to perfection by driving a stake through the heart of the Eurasian.

The Führer was obsessed with the imagery of the sexual woman as personification of Sin, Sensuality, and Depravity to be found in the work of late-nineteenth-century artists such as Arnold Böcklin (singled out by Hitler in *Mein Kampf* as an artist "endowed with the grace of God"), Franz von Stuck, Lovis Corinth, Max Slevogt, Otto Greiner, Fritz Erler, and a host of others. These artists had already identified the sexual woman and the Jew as co-inhabitors of a world ruled by degenerate eroticism. Their work no doubt helped consolidate Hitler's obsession with the Jew as Dracula, as the pollutant vampire-master lording it over swarms of evil sisters—degenerate women whose only role in life it was to take the Aryan's mind off his voyage toward the sun of spiritual transcendence. The language of *Mein Kampf* indicates relentlessly that, in seeking to eradicate the Jew, Hitler also sought to eradicate the sexual woman.

The Führer's conception of a "good" woman was simple. The "folkish State" of the Aryan could brook only women who "are able to bring men into the world." Therefore "the *goal* of female education has invariably to be the future mother." (621) Strict Aryan matching would foil "the ice-cold plan of the Jews" to "begin bastardizing the European continent at its core and, through infection by inferior humanity, to deprive the white race of the foundations for a sovereign existence." (908) To prevent the Aryan woman from cozying with degenerates, she could only become "a State citizen when she marries." Until that golden day she should remain a "State subject" like others "without honor or character," such as "the common criminal, the traitor to the country, etc." (659) Hitler thus let it be known in no uncertain terms that the good Aryan woman must consider herself first and foremost a breeder. Any woman who indulged in sterile sexuality was likely to be a mongrel with a predisposition to prostitution.

Hitler's conflation of the issues of sex and race may well have been a deciding factor in solidifying his appeal to the German petit bourgeoisie. His demons were also their demons. His insistence that the Jew was a "parasite" or "bacillus" who had "invaded" the "national body" explained to them the social and economic disorder that had descended upon Germany following its defeat in World War I. In Hitler's pseudo-scientific terminology, the "national body" became every German's body. The fatherland needed to be tended by a good physician to counter the "degenerative disease" that had infected it. Turn-of-the-century neo-Platonic dreams of a world populated by an immortal elite of purely masculine souls served as the basis for his exploitation of his countrymen's sexual paranoia. The Jew, as the "peoples' vampire," leeched the gold of masculinity from his "host" by infecting all with his own erotic effeminacy. This "polyp," this "blood-sucker," had poisoned the nation's blood and was responsible for the eroticized social chaos of the Weimar years, which in turn had destroyed the Germans' domestic tranquillity.

Thus the rash mistakes and metaphoric half-truths of early-twentieth-century medicine and science served as the foundation for Hitler's appeal to the German nation. He cast himself as the stern doctor who would heal the nation with his leadership by overcoming the "blood-sucking tyranny" (426) of the Jews and by eradicating the sexual threat of these "peoples' parasites." (451) He became the Jungian hero Germany longed for: that exemplary führer of men who could end the erotic "spending" of the nation and reassert the hierarchies of masculine order by breaking the teeth out of the "male-female womb-gullet" of the Jewish Gorgon.

If the dominant themes of Western science and culture provided

Hitler with the metaphoric framework for his genocidal politics, the continuing emphasis of the popular culture of the later Twenties also contributed to the social legitimation of his conflation of the imagery of the sexual woman and the peoples' vampire. Josef von Sternberg, for instance, who showed in *The Blue Angel* (1930) that the sexual woman's erotic virus could invade a perfectly decent teacher and turn him into a slobbering subhuman almost overnight, was only one of a host of film-makers and writers who exploited the public's obsession with sexual depredation. For them the effects of erotic spending became a convenient way to explain a character's descent into social degeneracy. The blood is the life, the Bible had said; gold is a distillate of the brain, Sumner declared; the blood is the essence of the nation, Hitler shouted; lose your essence, lose your brain, lose your gold, lose your nation. The ideas swirled around and became ever more intricately mixed, until they produced a vicious miscegenation of half-baked pseudoscientific ideas—the stuff demagogues' dreams are made of.

Everyone got into the act. Novelists found Fagins everywhere and hastened to team them up with heartless, immoral, predatory women. Having already given in wholesale to the visual mix of racist and anti-feminine propaganda of D. W. Griffith and Cecil B. De Mille, Hollywood was easily seduced by the particularly Germanic brand of antifeminine imagery laced with anti-Semitism habitually concocted by F. W. Murnau, Fritz Lang, G. W. Pabst, Eric von Stroheim, Ernst Lubitsch, and Josef von Sternberg. These directors turned "serious" moviemaking during the late Twenties and early Thirties into a bastion of racist and misogynous clichés, languorously conveyed by Garbo and Dietrich, whose simmering feminine perversity was a far cry from the feisty, loudmouthed independence of such characteristically American pop gold-digger heroines as Clara Bow and Jean Harlow.

G. W. Pabst's *Pandora's Box* (1929) is a characteristic exposition of the sex-and-race equation Hitler was exploiting so effectively at just about this time. Pabst's self-conscious conflation of antifeminine and anti-Semitic images was an attempt to delineate the catastrophic downward spiral of degeneration visited upon a world that had given in to the "virus" of sex. He used Frank Wedekind's antifeminine characterization of Lulu in his plays *Earth Spirit* (1895) and *Pandora's Box* (1902) to give his film a very "current" anti-Semitic twist. His Lulu is, like Wedekind's, an "instinctive" prostitute without personal character, willing to be molded into any form the men around her might want to impose on her. She is a creature with no existence other than that conferred upon her by the male imagination. But Pabst expanded the role of Lulu's initial seducer, Schigolch, and turned him unmistakably into one of Hitler's peoples' vampires. To late-twentieth-century audiences the film would, no doubt, reveal its propagandistic nature more readily had the veteran actor Carl Goetz not played Schigolch, the "disreputable man who poses as Lulu's father to exploit her," with such gusto, or had a lesser talent than Louise Brooks been chosen to play the title role. In Brooks Pabst had found an actress brilliantly able to humanize Lulu's sense of innocent bewilderment at the moral agonies of the men (and the one man-woman, Countess Geschwitz) on whom she bestows her attentions with such a blissful lack of discrimination.

Pabst's Lulu was Pandora, the personification of woman as blind natural force, a creature sculpted out of the earth's primal clay, a pagan Eve, who, when she opened her legs to a man, unsealed the lid of the box that contained all the world's evils. She was the lascivious vessel into whom man poured his selfhood for the sake of reproduction. But she was also the personification of blind chaos, the uroboros, the phallic snake biting its own tail. She refused to succumb to the requirements of evolution to become the incubator of future generations of Aryan leaders. Instead, she naively pursued proto-Bolshevist fantasies of gender equality.

The parallel themes of misogyny and anti-Semitism established themselves in the film *Pandora's Box* with an aura of logical inevitability. They became a given, the sort of "higher truth" to be accepted as part of the "natural laws" of society—an expression of the uncritical social complacency that permitted someone like William Carlos Williams to write casually in his semiautobiographical novel *A Voyage to Pagany,* also published in 1928, that "a Jew of the usual objectional type made himself objectionable" (285) in a train compartment. No sensible reader, such a remark assumes, could possibly be expected to find fault with such a perfectly reasonable observation.

The racial assumptions underlying Pabst's work are of the same order: easily understood by its target audience but just as easily overlooked by those no longer driven by such concerns. Its opening scene is a case in point. It serves no useful function within the narrative progression of the film, but it was essential to Pabst's racial theme. A gas company meter inspector, in the vestibule to an apartment, is making some annotations in his ledger. He is a lower-echelon functionary who carries himself with a certain dignity, though he is clearly a man of the people. The slightly shabby cut of his clothing reveals this. Gray-haired and with a neatly trimmed moustache, tall, upright, and trim for his age, he is, though a menial, clearly an Aryan.

In the main doorway to her apartment, Lulu appears in a flouncy, formfitting dress. She is looking into her purse (*Pandora's* purse: everything in this film is symbolic) and rummages for money. Under her arm she carries a bottle of schnapps. The meter man's eyes light up as she pours him a glass. He expects this traditional public servant's reward on his appointed rounds. As he takes his first swig, well aware of the minor infraction of the rules his action represents, he cautiously looks at the seductive lady before him.

Flirting coyly, Lulu takes a bill and some coins out of her purse and hands them to the flustered meter man, who drops the coins, thus inadvertently spilling financial essence. Just then there is a knock on the door. "Allow me," the meter man gestures gracefully, still charmed by Lulu. He walks to the door and opens it. We see Schigolch with his back to us, outside the door. He is a shabby, dwarflike creature, one of David Starr Jordan's London "pygmies." As the meter man opens the door he faces the audience so that we may observe his reaction. In it disdain and astonishment mix. A close-up of Schigolch removing his bowler follows. Greasy, foul, smirking, stunted, with glittery eyes and a pronounced hook nose, Schigolch proves to be a typical "objectionable" Semite.

The meter man, suddenly taller, more dignified, and serious now, does not quite know how to react. Should he allow this horrid creature to enter this delightful young lady's apartment? But Lulu solves his dilemma. She joyfully shouts: "Schigolch!" and rushes toward him. With a big smile on her face, she wraps her arm around the dwarfish man's neck and excitedly hustles him into her apartment. Her flounces flutter about her as if she were a butterfly. The door abruptly closes upon the two. The meter man, tall and dignified but wide-eyed with astonishment, now stands alone in the vestibule. His face becomes contemplative. He grimaces knowingly, and looks down as he unfolds the bill Lulu handed him. Suddenly he remembers the coins he dropped a little earlier. We see a close-up of his hands as he gathers them up from the floor. The camera now pans to a chair on which his official meter-reader cap lies abandoned. He reaches for it, puts it on. Standing straight, a wizened Aryan soldier, a dignified member of the petit bourgeoisie of the most highly evolved race in the universe, he grimly, and with visible disdain, leaves this house of crass miscegenation as the screen fades to black.

But Pabst's mise-en-scène of the race/gender parallel was not yet complete. The next scene opens on the scruffy dwarf and the much taller, elegantly slender Lulu, whom we see whirling around the center of the room, arm in arm, in joyous celebration of their reunion. A head-and-upper-torso shot of Lulu, hands on hips, shows her saying, "Where have you been, you old rascal, you. I've missed you!" Beside her, prominently displayed against an otherwise empty background, so the viewer cannot possibly avoid seeing it, stands a menorah, the central religious symbol of the Jewish faith.

During the ensuing scenes this menorah remains one of the most noticeable background decorations, reappearing repeatedly and at crucial moments in the dramatic unfolding of the plot. Its function is not to suggest that *Lulu* is Jewish—Louise Brooks's features are far too "Aryan" to make that credible. The menorah is there to identify the man who "awakened" Lulu and set her up in her trade. It reveals the "degeneracy" of Lulu's physical environment, its "Jewish" character, and the racial nature of Schigolch's "polluting" influence.

We learn that Lulu is mistress to Ludwig Schoen, a pillar of the community, a wealthy publishing mogul. Schigolch is her pimp. We are

Lulu and her menorah confront Dr. Schoen in Pandora's Box *(1929).*

also made to understand that, even now, she would have absolutely no compunction about sharing her bed with him again—but the old man clearly has none of his paltry store of manhood left. Lulu is thus demonstrably amoral, a polymorphously and indiscriminately sexual woman, living always, as Weininger had put it, "in a condition of fusion with all the human beings she knows." (198)

She is Schigolch's conduit to the Aryan elite. That is why Lulu's apartment is the realm of the menorah. That is why Schoen, though radiant with the mature masculine *mens sana in corpore sano* his name reflects, turns into a mere donkey as soon as he enters Lulu's realm.

Everything that happens in the film after this opening segment is designed to bear out the validity of these assumptions. Schoen, upon surprising Lulu in the company of Schigolch, is determined to renounce her, but he is soon turned into her sexual slave. The scene of his catastrophic second seduction is set backstage during the premiere of a stage revue, which is to feature Lulu and has been organized by Alwa, Schoen's son, who is also visibly smitten by her erotic charms. The episode is deliberately cast to show that the otherwise authoritative evolutionary male does not stand a chance against the childish wiles of the sexual woman.

Acting like a spoiled little girl, Lulu gradually manages to overcome Schoen's steely disapproval. But as soon as Schoen has allowed himself to succumb to her charms, his Aryan intended and his son enter the dressing room. Unmistakably cast as a vampire at this point, Lulu looks up, a feeding predator glowering at them over her ecstatic prey. Her dark, kohled eyes are filled with triumph, and a sinister half-smile curves along the corner of her sensuous mouth. Louise Brooks is chillingly convincing during this scene, full of fire, erotic energy, and earthy power. The scene makes it very easy to understand why so many young women of the Twenties wanted to pattern themselves after the vamps of the movies. Marginalized and manipulated in real life, they imagined themselves in Lulu's place, in total control over men's bodies—sweet revenge for the damage these men had done to their inner sense of self.

When his intended silently bows her head and walks away, Schoen stumbles to the doorway and murmurs to his son: "This is my execution." He decides to marry Lulu, although just a reel earlier he had wisely warned Alwa that "men don't marry such women. It would be suicide." He will soon prove the accuracy of this assessment. Fade in upon the wedding reception. Only Lulu and Schigolch have cause for boisterous celebration. Countess Geschwitz, an artist (most Twenties lesbians were typecast as artists) and hence a "sexually intermediate" masculine female (even her name is a derisive sonic analogue to the vulgarity implicit in the name Schigolch), desires Lulu as much as any man. Among the dignified guests at the wedding reception, pillars of the community all, Geschwitz is an isolated island of oddity, her eyes hungrily devouring Lulu. Knowing better than anyone that Lulu, the eternal female, is "polymorphously perverse," Geschwitz makes a last-ditch attempt to lure Lulu into her own degenerative realm. She asks Lulu to dance with her, and, scandalously, before the eyes of the assembled dignitaries, they do. Geschwitz leading, a lover entranced, while the malleable, always willing, totally indiscriminate Lulu nestles herself in her arms. Schoen rushes in to break them up before the scandal becomes insurmountable. In his face we see a desperate recognition of Lulu's pansexual nature.

Meanwhile Geschwitz's pseudomasculine counterpart, Schigolch, has also been busy. The presence of this Semitic dwarf astonishes not only the openly appalled Aryan wedding guests but even the lowly servants, among whom he carouses drunkenly in the company of his newest discovery, the grossly proletarian trapeze artist Rodrigo Quast. Schigolch has cause to celebrate, for Lulu's marriage to Schoen represents a toehold for him in the world of the Aryan. The "invasion of the under man" has begun in earnest. No wonder he feels an urge to decorate the fateful marriage bed of his protégé with flowers, lots of flowers, the vulval symbols of Lulu as gateway to civilization's final degradation.

Schoen, depressed and glowering, is like a spectator looking in upon his own degradation. Awareness of the desperate future of civilization wracks his consciousness. He has sent Lulu into the bridal chamber, under the lustful eyes of his son and the desperate Geschwitz. In that bridal chamber, to her infinite delight, she meets the flower-strewing Schigolch in the company of Quast. Lulu soon finds herself on Schigolch's lap, blithely defiling her Aryan's husband's bridal bed with a vile kiss. This is how Schoen finds them: the decline of the West is documented right before his eyes. The blinders of lust fall from him. He knows what he must do. Gun in hand, his masculine potency no longer in thrall to the demon of eroticism, he chases the clownish Jewish vermin and the doltish emissary of the criminal proletariat from his house of Aryan dignity—but only to discover further sensual devastation when he returns. Alwa, his own son, has buried his head in Lulu's lap and declares his undying love. A tower of seething anger now, though in icy control over his emotions, truly a lord of creation at last, Schoen makes his son get up and leave.

Now, finally, the evolutionary male is ready to confront the sexual woman as she must be confronted. But Lulu, unaware of the turmoil she has caused, has begun to prepare herself for her wedding night in front of a long, oval mirror—the self-reflective emblem of her pansexual femininity. Schoen is appalled at her insensitivity. Ponderously, gloom personified, he appears behind her in the mirror. He speaks. Lulu is shocked. Terrified now, she backs into a corner of the room. His gun, emblem of true manhood on the rebound, is in his hand. He must teach Lulu to do what is right. To renounce her past and to become a true woman at last, she must kill herself—she must extirpate the reversive sexual woman within. Schoen tries to hand her his gun, to make her fingers wrap themselves around its barrel so she can turn the force of what she has appropriated inward for the good of the Aryan future. "NO," she gestures, "I won't!" But for once masculinity stands its ground. Fierce determination glowers in his eyes: "Take it!"

He succeeds in forcing the gun into her hand, then makes her turn the weapon's mouth against her own belly: "Kill yourself!" He moves very close to her, pleading now: "Kill yourself . . . it is the only way to save both of us." The death of the sexual woman meant life to the Aryan men of steel, for it would save woman's place in the evolutionary order as mother of us all. Pabst knew exactly what he intended to convey with this scene and was confident that his audience, too, would understand its significance: after all, he was expressing one of the cultural common-places of the Twenties.

But the phallic woman in Lulu—Diana of Ephesus, the pagan predator—rebels. She turns the gun barrel away from her body and fires. Instead of letting herself be slain by the phallus as a good woman should, she appropriates the phallus to kill the man. An imposing erotic apparition, her tightly clinging evening gown revealing every nuance of her sexual self, Lulu stands before Schoen. Mortally wounded, he staggers toward her. In a final, shameful gesture that reveals his inner weakness, he lovingly strokes her pitch-black pageboy hair. He tries to kiss her lips, but instead he slowly sinks onto his knees. As his arms slide helplessly down along her slender, sensuous body, he presses his head against her belly in mute erotic worship. Finally, having thus slipped down into the pit of deadly animality symbolized by Lulu's body, he finds himself on hands and knees, reduced to the condition of a dying beast—another

Schuyler in extremis. Alwa rushes in and tries to help his father, but Schoen is too far gone. "Beware, Alwa. You are next!" he warns his son—and dies. Pabst's point was unmistakable: when the Jew is allowed to become pimp to the sexual woman, humanity's course is locked into an ever more dizzying downward spiral.

The obligatory trial scene that follows allowed Pabst to belabor the "Pandora's box" theme. Pointing to Lulu, the prosecutor intones: "The Greek gods created a woman: Pandora. She was beautiful—enticing—well versed in the infatuating arts of flattery . . ." Lulu smiles enticingly at the prosecutor, who becomes flustered but finally manages to continue: "But the gods also gave her a casket in which they locked up all the evil in the world. The heedless woman opened the box and disaster overcame us!" Lulu, after having allowed her casket to be opened by the erotomaniacal Jew, has become the carrier of all evil—sister to the peoples' vampire. She is a "ferment of decomposition" herself. Having rejected the civilized world's cleansing ceremony of gynecide, Lulu now falls into a downward spiral of her own.

A ruse on the part of Alwa, Schigolch, and Quast allows her to escape the punishment of the law. But soon predatory lowlife encircle her everywhere. Schigolch's continuing influence can lead her in only one direction, for she is "hardly first class merchandise" anymore, as one character remarks callously. An erotic child, sitting on Schigolch's lap, Lulu cries at one point: "Everyone—everyone wants my blood—my life." The rapacity of the "lower orders" of society was emblematic of a world in decline, a world in which only Schigolch, the eternal Jew, the relentless economic schemer, could continue to survive. "He pursues his course, the course of sneaking in among the nations and of gouging them internally, and he fights with his weapons, with lies and slanders, poison and destruction, intensifying the struggle to the point of bloodily exterminating his hated opponents," Hitler had written two years before *Pandora's Box* was released. (960)

Schigolch was the "bacillus" who "consumed" the Aryan nation's blood, its vital essence, its "manhood." He used Lulu, as Dracula had used Lucy Westenra, as a conduit to the sources of his own rejuvenation. It was not "everybody," but only Schigolch, the leech, who wanted her blood—her life, for her blood was the blood of the Aryan nation she had consumed needlessly. But in the end even she must fall victim to the Jew's voracious appetite.

In London Pabst's tragedy of the world's erotic/economic depredation by the eternal Jew and his most dangerous instrument, the sexual woman, comes to a predictably grim conclusion. We see Lulu, Schigolch, and Alwa huddled in a miserable garret in the cold of winter. It is Christmastime. Outside the Salvation Army gathers alms. A young woman brimming with earnestness, a modern madonna, comforts the dispossessed. Within Pabst's universe, man's choice was clear: he must follow Christ's army. He must find his redemption in the soothing sexlessness of the acculturated woman cleansed by the fires of motherhood, or be doomed to follow the eternal prostitute, the blind tool of species degeneration.

These are also the alternatives that face Jack the Ripper, the archetypal conflicted male, who now emerges from the fogs of London to serve as Pabst's deus ex machina. In *Pandora's Box* he is a figure of melancholy, brooding introspection. Like Schoen, that other brooder, he is a man hopelessly torn between the knife and the cross. The Ripper is a man who, when waylaid by sexuality against his will, exorcises woman, the eternal vampire, by driving his knife through her heart in a desperate attempt to regain control over his precarious mental existence. But in the London fog the Ripper's own heart is temporarily warmed by the Salvation Army's daughter of mercy, who offers him a sprig of mistletoe.

Lulu has become a common prostitute. Schigolch has made sure of that. He even resents Alwa's feeble attempt to keep her from soliciting a bourgeois gentleman in the fogs of London: "A pity"—he grins at her—"I would so like to have eaten a Christmas pudding once in my life." Resigned to her task, Lulu walks deeper into the fog and solicits the Ripper. When she precedes the man with the knife up the stairs to her garret, he hesitates. "I have no money," he says. But Lulu is a sexual demon, not, like Schigolch, also intentionally an economic monster. Smiling, she answers: "Come just the same—I like you!" The Ripper's intellectual side is deeply moved by Lulu's charitable nature. Perhaps there is a mother-soul hidden within her after all. Surreptitiously he drops his switchblade over the railing of the stairs. This may be a salvageable woman.

In her garret, Lulu makes cozy with the Ripper. In his coat pocket she finds the mistletoe the Salvation Army madonna has offered him. She puts it on the table and lights a candle. Angelic in its light, she seems very far removed from sin. Instead, it is Christmastime for two of society's outcasts, driven to desperation by divergent forces. They hold hands. Lulu snuggles onto the Ripper's lap. The mistletoe on the table makes his inner torment recede. He picks it up and holds the modern madonna's holy sprig over Lulu's head. Becoming playful now, a thin, redemptive smile struggling about his mouth, he says: "You are under the mistletoe—now you must let yourself be kissed."

But he should have reread *The Golden Bough,* Sir James George Frazer's monumental study of the myths and rituals based on the symbolic meaning of mistletoe for primitive man. A one-volume abridgment by Frazer himself, published in 1922, had become hugely popular at just about the time Pabst was making his film. Mistletoe, Frazer had let the world know, was an ancient symbol of the feminine in all its forms. When not controlled, when not safely suspended above the womb of the earth but rooted in the soil, this parasitic evergreen was bound to wind itself ever more tightly around the oak of manhood. Ultimately it would suck the oak's soul into itself and turn into gold. Such rooted mistletoe was emblematic of phallic femininity. Only a woman who had accepted her ritual castration by "cutting herself loose" from her roots in the earth to become a loose sprig of mistletoe dependent for her survival on the oak of manhood (like the Salvation Army woman who had offered her sprig of mistletoe to the Ripper) could be considered a truly acculturated member of Aryan society.

A modest, acculturated daughter of Christ had given him this sprig, the Ripper remembers. The oak of manhood had been about to blaspheme the freely suspended mistletoe of passive femininity by anointing Lulu, a parasitic sexual woman with her roots still firmly planted in the soil of degeneracy who was winding herself around his loins at that very moment. We see this realization dawning in the Ripper's eyes. The madonna's Christmas gift has been a warning. For a moment Pabst keeps the audience in suspense: which of the two forms of feminine parasitism will the Ripper choose? The good or the bad? The desperate lovers kiss.

At this time in the development of twentieth-century cinematic symbolism, well before the advent of obligatory scenes of nude bodies cupped in bed-shaking simulated sex, a kiss of this sort was, just as Theda Bara's kiss had been, still a symbolic representation of THE KISS—"consummation"—which was why virtually every movie made during the Thirties and Forties still ended with THAT kiss. As late as 1943, the sweet and still innocent Elena of *Cat People* was—and for good reason—terrified of being "kissed" by her infinitely patient husband: she knew THAT kiss would bring out the Beast still latent within her. Yet *longing* for THAT kiss also made her claw the upholstery in their apartment to shreds.

THAT kiss, too, reveals Lulu to the Ripper as the emissary of the forces of degeneration that Wedekind, more than thirty years earlier, had shown her to be in his prologue to *Earth Spirit:*

> *created for every abuse,*
> *To allure and to poison and seduce,*
> *To murder without leaving any trace.*

THAT kiss makes the Ripper recognize Lulu as the parasitic phallic woman who, though rooted in the soiled energies of Schigolch, the eternal Jew, strives to fasten herself to the oak of Aryan manhood.

When the bread knife glistening in the candlelight of Christmas on the garret's rickety table catches the Ripper's eye, we know at once that it must pierce Lulu's body. In meretricious homage to the period's predictable equation of sex and death, Pabst shows her body tense in what seems to be orgasmic ecstasy. Then we see her hand drop in a mockery of postcoital relaxation. The Ripper, the melancholy, conflicted male adrift in a world of rampant degeneracy, in search of spiritual transcendence, has excised the sexual woman—cut her from the oak of manhood.

Thus the Ripper does for civilized society what neither Schoen nor his son have had the strength to do. Pabst sees him as a hero who has destroyed the link between the phallic woman and Schigolch, the effeminate Jewish seducer. When the Ripper disappears into the fog, we have learned to understand the reasons for his existential agony. The social tragedy of Lulu's necessary sacrifice is revealed to the viewer when, in the last frames of his film, Pabst shows Schigolch thriving "on the impotence of nations" while "guarding his own parasitic blood," just as Hitler had said. We see the Jew in a festive mood, celebrating his ascendancy in the Christian's world by blithely eating the Christmas pudding that is brought to him in a rowdy tavern. We watch him gingerly remove a sprig of mistletoe that has been placed on top—Lulu's wasted lifeline, cut from its roots at last by the Ripper. He discards it callously: it has served its purpose. The viewer understands that Schigolch will find other wombs to recruit in his campaign against civilization. Pandora has many boxes to spare.

While Lulu's blood seeps into the floor of her garret, draining into the dried wood of civilization, Schigolch joins the tavern's rowdy cheer. In a vile mockery of piety he removes his hat as the Salvation Army marches by. But his eyes glitter with base intentions. Pabst wanted his

Aryan audiences to understand that it could no longer serve any purpose to shout "Kill that woman!" until they had recognized that they must first learn to "kill that Jew!" The early twentieth century's circle of metaphor was closing. The imagery of gynecide had engendered the ideology of genocide. No wonder Pabst, in 1939, after first announcing his intention to move to Hollywood, abruptly chose to stay in Europe and make propaganda films for the Nazis. He had come to recognize that Hitler was the Aryan nation's own Jack the Ripper.

Though it is no doubt true that many of Pabst's film's original viewers would have missed many of his more abstruse symbolic allusions, general audiences could not help but be affected, at least on a semiconscious level, by the evil message hidden in *Pandora's Box*. Moreover, the film's blatant anti-Semitism had clearly identified the sexual woman's degenerate masculine ally as the dwarfish Jew of the Occidental imagination. Pabst's Hitlerite message was clear: the oak of manhood was, as Frazer had declared in *The Golden Bough*, "pre-eminently the sacred tree of the Aryans." Hitler, as *Mein Kampf* makes all too clear, had come to regard himself as the sacred priest of Nordic superiority, as the man who would sever the bond between the parasitic mistletoe of female sexuality and the invasive eroticism of the eternal Jew. The Nordic race had been chosen by God "to lift marriage out of the level of a permanent race degradation." The Aryan would at last use the reproductive process "to beget images of the Lord and not deformities half man and half ape." Man must replace "his lost instinct by perceptive knowledge" and in this manner transcend nature. The racial purity of the "great stocks of Nordic-Germanic people who remain unblended" was "the most valuable treasure of our future." But the Jew, that treacherous "peoples' vampire," was eager to contaminate the Aryan's blood. Race mixing was his tool. But the inferiors must "succumb in the mutual struggle for life, as long as there exists a higher race, that remained unmixed, as opponent." Therefore only the sacred marriage bond, cemented by the Aryan mother-woman's iron will to produce male offspring, stood in the way of the erotic onslaught of the Jew. (604–6)

Hitler, of course, had learned his racial-purity catechism primarily from German sources such as the eugenics of Wilhelm Schallmayer and Alfred Plötz and Oswald Spengler's rousing generalizations about the imminent "decline of the West." But the virulent anti-Semitism of such not so "Germanic" writers as Otto Weininger and the British-born nationalist-racist historian Houston Stewart Chamberlain were equally instrumental in giving his racial imagery focus. Hitler could also have

taken most of his arguments virtually verbatim from the likes of Lothrop
Stoddard, Madison Grant, Henry Pratt Fairchild, David Starr Jordan,
Henry Fairfield Osborn, and countless others who were widely considered to be among the lights of the American academic establishment
during the 1920s, and whose diatribes were cited frequently by their European counterparts.

From these sources Hitler had learned that genetic engineering was
the key to the eradication of the "unfit," the weak-blooded, the effeminate. The Aryan male must guard the Aryan female's health at all cost.
He should realize that the laws of evolution had forced him to leave
woman behind in the realm of brute nature. It was therefore his evolutionary responsibility to administer appropriate infusions of Aryan seed
to the sexually awakening female and turn her into a mother before she
was driven into miscegenation, prostitution, and disease by her blind reproductive needs. Young people must learn that marriage "cannot be an
end in itself, but has to serve the one greater aim, the propagation and
preservation of the species and the race. Only this is its meaning and its
task." (343)

"Sports and gymnastics" would help cultivate in the young Aryan an
"iron-like inurement" against "sensual gratification." Bolshevism was attractive to "the so-called 'intelligencia'" only because "the intelligencia
itself is physically completely degenerated." (345–6) Intellectual and
physical effeminacy, prostitution, Bolshevism: these were the ingredients
that constituted the "Jewish disease." These were, of course, also precisely the ingredients of Schigolch's contamination of Lulu, who had, in
turn, contaminated the Schoens—those fine specimens of Aryan manhood. A society that permitted such outrages demanded an Aryan Jack
the Ripper, a führer, to set things right.

"The homology of Jew and woman becomes closer the further examination goes," Weininger had said. "The Jew is always more absorbed
by sexual matters than the Aryan, although he is notably less potent sexually and less liable to be enmeshed in a great passion." Communism
was little more than a political version of woman's pervasive anti-
individualist carnality. Therefore "the Jew is an inborn communist."
(307–11) Hitler agreed wholeheartedly: "The destructive effect of Ju-
daism's activity" within the "national bodies" of Aryan Europe "must
basically be attributed only to its eternal attempts at undermining the
importance of the individual in its host nations and to put the masses in
its place." (666–7)

To prevent such social degeneration, the masses needed a führer just as much as a wife needed the steely determination of her husband: "Like a woman, whose psychic feeling is influenced less by abstract reasoning than by an undefinable, sentimental longing for complementary strength, who will submit to the strong man rather than dominate the weakling, thus the masses love the ruler rather than the suppliant." (56) The weak males of modern society who had abdicated their responsibility to rule their women with an iron fist had been infected by effeminate humanism, the "Jewish disease" that always made a shambles of proper gender separation. Advocacy of social equality for women was simply another version of Jewish Marxism's fey glorification of the masses, a typical example of "dreamy humaneness": "Therefore, everything, beginning with education, is half-hearted and wavering, shuns responsibility and ends thus in cowardly tolerance of even recognized evils." (364) The Jews had deliberately invented the flabby modern pacifist mentality to undermine the spiritual power of an Aryan nation ruled by real men with "bodies hard as steel."

The world needed a peace, Hitler said, "supported not by the palm branches of tearful pacifist professional female mourners, but founded by the victorious sword of a people of overlords which puts the world into the service of a higher culture." (599) Thus as long as Schigolch remained alive, the Ripper's attempts to cut Lulu from the tree of manhood would remain futile. For the Jew was the soil from which the mistletoe had grown. Without woman's sentimental cooperation in spreading the plague of miscegenation, the Jew was doomed. And since she had absolutely no identity of her own, the pendulum logic of dualistic thought dictated that woman could as easily be made into the madonna of the Salvation Army of Nordic purity as into a conduit for the Jewish poison.

The Aryan woman should therefore be supervised closely. She must be made to realize that her only role in life was to serve the state as the incubator of the Nordic race. The processes of sexual selection would, in this manner, produce an Aryan nation of beautifully proportioned blond males, whose bodies could glisten with that "steel-like versatility" characterizing the Greek ideal of beauty Hitler admired so much—that "wonderful combination of the most glorious physical beauty with a brilliant mind and the noblest soul." The Führer's suppressed homoerotic longing for a "truly masculine" beauty he himself patently did not possess became most apparent when he expressed his hope that the young Aryan male would learn to shed his clothes more often in public. That would be a character-building experience for the youth, as well as "a stimulant for his physical fitness," for it would make him self-conscious and arouse his vanity: "not the vanity in beautiful clothes which not everyone is able to buy, but the vanity in a beautiful, well-shaped body which everyone can help in building up." No wonder Leni Riefenstahl became the principal propagandist for the Nazis: Hitler and she shared the same erotic desire for steely bodies with shimmering swords.

Hitler emphasized that a greater measure of Aryan public disrobing had "use also for the future." Young women would be much less likely to latch blindly onto effeminate males if they were given ample opportunity to admire the manly musculature of the Aryan superman:

> The girl should become acquainted with her knight. If today physical beauty were not pushed completely into the background by our dandified fashionableness, the seduction of hundreds of thousands of girls by bow-legged, disgusting Jewish bastards would never be possible. Also this is in the interest of the nation, that the most beautiful bodies find one another and thus help in giving the nation new beauty. (619)

The artists of the Third Reich rushed in to satisfy Hitler's appetite for steel-bodied males and wax-coated women.

Hitler saw visual imaging—particularly the visual drama of oratory—as the central means to power. As *Mein Kampf* attests, he was acutely sensitive to the emotional impact of "public performance." The speaker, he pointed out, as opposed to the writer, "receives from the mass before which he speaks a continuous correction of his lecture, insofar as he can uninterruptedly read from the faces of his listeners how far they are able to follow his arguments with understanding, and whether the impression and effect of his words lead to the desired goal." This added "psychological finesse, and consequently suppleness," to the propaganda of the orator. The Führer's paeans to the seductive efficiency of the aural/visual media over the written word, as well as his shrewd delineation of the "difference in effect and impression" produced by even such apparent minutiae as the time of day during which audiences attend a theater piece (this "applies even to a movie," he emphasized) are still the most original (perhaps the *only* original) observations to be found in *Mein Kampf.* They are detailed prefigurations of the marketing strategies that dominate advertising today.

Hitler stressed that "traditional memories and images which exist in

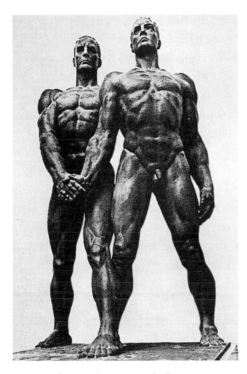

Josef Thorak, Comradeship, *1937*
Hitler's ideal of the steel-bodied Aryan
male, and the same dream transplanted to
America in the postwar era:

Cover of Astounding Science Fiction,
October 1948

man, are able to determine an impression decisively," thereby showing that he was quite as attuned to the social uses of "archetypes" as Carl Jung. Imagery and the spoken word, the Führer knew, were far more effective than print in swaying the emotions of the masses. What was printed could be scrutinized closely—it was subject to rational evaluation. Therefore it was of limited usefulness in the realm of propaganda. But theater, film, and the "public performance" of speeches were the bread and butter of indoctrination.

Those who criticized the *content* of propaganda failed to realize that it was only the *form* that counted. All propaganda needed to do was use the psychological power of the "traditional memories and images" that existed in the collective memory of the nation. Hitler disparaged the use of any image or turn of phrase whose meaning might be misunderstood by the general public. But any already existing image-structure could be reused, refigured, and enhanced for purposes of social indoctrination. Power, in the new world of aural and visual media, was dependent on familiar propaganda pitched as truth. Cultural prejudices, presented as "racial memories" common to all, as universal expressions of the "collective unconscious," would make Nazi ideology accessible to "the greatest layers of the people."

A "domineering apostolic nature" was needed, Hitler emphasized, to exploit the public's preexisting cultural assumptions. When used properly, the new media could effect unprecedented "encroachments upon man's freedom of will." A simple image was always preferable to words: "Far greater chances has the picture in all its varieties up to and including the motion picture." The fact was that "many will be far more ready to take in a *pictorial presentation* than to *read a lengthy piece of writing.*" (704–16) Hitler's rise to power was thus a factor of the burgeoning social influence of the visual media. He understood that the complexly nuanced imagery the human mind is capable of producing when left to its own synthesizing capacities represents a profoundly subversive anti-doctrinal force in society. He also understood better than most of his contemporaries that, to countermand this force, nothing was as effective as the pat gesturing, rote imaging, sloganeering, and pop-psychologizing characteristic of the new visual media. To establish a useable robot mentality among his ideal constituency, his propaganda machine therefore worked primarily in the visual realm (the mass rallies were visual theater) to create a simple imagery the people could understand. Even *Mein Kampf* can be seen as an experiment in "pictorial representation." Hitler knew that the modern demagogue's success was dependent upon an effective visual exploitation of assumptions already pervasively present in the public imagination.

Within such a framework the Jew was an ideal scapegoat. His graphic demonization could explain nearly everyone's sexual problems and money worries. A tribe of feminized Bolshevik erotomanes, of "black-haired," "blood-poisoning," "bow-legged bastards," had established a "Jewish machine of world conquest." By seducing the blonde, clean-limbed, buxom mother-women of Nordic Europe, they had "poisoned" the Aryan gene pool. Moreover, they had turned hordes of lowlife working-class women into prostitutes, sexual lures designed to sap the economic strength of the German nation. "An icy shudder," Hitler announced melodramatically, "ran down my spine when seeing for the first time the Jew as a cool, shameless, and calculating manager of this shocking vice." This recognition had taught him that behind the temptresses who were "spreading decomposition" and death through the nation with their diseased, syphilitic bodies stood the Jew, inventor of the false, leveling doctrine of social Democracy. (78)

The "peoples' parasites" of Marxism had, by the time of World War I, encircled the German nation in a sweeping, two-pronged attack, Hitler contended. Now "the spider began slowly to suck the people's blood out of its pores." (251) Thus, poisoned from within, God's nation had lost the war. Jewry's social tools, "syphilis and its pacemaker, prostitution," had polluted Weimar culture until "the Judaization of our spiritual life and the mammonization of our mating impulse" had caused that "prostitution of love" that now "befouls our entire new generation." (337) The task of National Socialism was therefore simple: "What we have to fight for is the security of the existence and the increase of our race and our people, the nourishment of its children and the preservation of the purity of the blood." (288–9)

Nosferatu, the still internationally famous 1922 film directed by F. W. Murnau, that probably gave Thea von Harbou the idea to make Rotwang into an incarnation of the plague-spreading son of Solomon of *Metropolis,* had already established the exact visual context for the racial melodrama Hitler, too, was to elaborate further in *Mein Kampf.* The film was thus, in a number of ways, to contribute forcefully, both directly and indirectly, to the Western world's store of anti-Semitic imagery by offering its viewers what may well be the most relentlessly evil incarnation of Dracula ever imagined.

Using the expressionistic techniques of the early German cinema, Murnau zeroed in on the xenophobic themes of Bram Stoker's original novel. Stoker had limited his delineation of Dracula's Semitic origins to a quasi-scientific enumeration of the vampire's criminal traits—derived directly from Lombroso's phrenological classifications: "His face was a strong—a very strong—aquiline, with high bridge of the thin nose and peculiarly arched nostrils; with lofty domed forehead and hair growing scantily round the temples but profusely elsewhere. His eyebrows were very massive, almost meeting over the nose, and with bushy hair that seemed to curl in its own profusion." (27)

Stoker had also emphasized that the unleashing of Dracula upon England was precipitated by the unstoppable Eastward push of the British Empire. This Kipling quotient of *Dracula* had been essential to its plot. Traveling to Transylvania, for instance, Jonathan Harker realizes that he is "leaving the West and entering the East." Harker himself is "a solicitor's clerk sent out to explain the purchase of a London estate to a foreigner." (25) This was the heart of the matter: to make money in the new world of international finance, decent Brits were being forced to deal with grubby aliens, and even allow them to buy property in England.

Stoker's message was that civilized society should think twice before selling the farm. Harker, being a loyal door-to-door salesman of British finance, had no choice but to complete his real estate transaction for his employer even when he realized that Dracula was evil: "What could I do but bow acceptance? It was Mr. Hawkins's interest, not mine, and I had to think of him, not myself." (40–1) Even so, the patriot in Harker was shocked at his own complicity: "This was the being I was helping to transfer to London, where, perhaps, for centuries to come he might, amongst its teeming millions, satiate his lust for blood, and create a new and ever-widening circle of semi-demons, to batten on the helpless. The very thought drove me mad."

Dracula was the product of a "cursed land, where the devil and his children still walk with earthly feet." He must maintain direct contact with that barren soil to survive: "There in one of the great boxes, of which there were fifty in all, on a pile of newly dug earth, lay the Count!" (57) He was rooted in the same dead, dusty womb of earth as the phallic mistletoe threatening to strangle the Aryan oak. Stoker's "blood sucker," was another Svengali, that "filthy black Hebrew" of George Du Maurier's *Trilby* (1894), who had been fashioned from the polluted clay of Eurasia, "the poisonous East—birthplace and home of an ill wind that blows nobody good." (377) A Semitic nomad, Dracula must take his "boxes, with their freight of earth," wherever he goes. (61)

No wonder, then, that, in the end, pierced by the knives of his Anglo-Saxon pursuers, Dracula simply "crumbled into dust": robbed of his parasitic life, he was nothing but barren soil.

By turning the women of Britain into gateways to species reversion, Dracula had been able to soak his foreign earth-body, "fertilize it," with the blood of the British nation. The blood transfusions Lucy Westenra received from four strapping Anglo–Aryan men had kept her alive only long enough to feed the "peoples' vampire." They had shown that woman was indeed the vampire's conduit to the blood of the men of the nation. But these transfusions were also bluntly symbolic of the economic parasitism of the poisonous alien interloper. Thus the theme of the Jew as financial vampire was already solidly embedded in Stoker's narrative, though this aspect of his story is usually overlooked by the novel's late-twentieth-century readers, who tend to be after sado-masochistic thrills rather than late-Victorian economic enlightenment. But Stoker's point had by no means been lost on Murnau. Indeed, in the filmmaker's hands this theme became central. In *Dracula* the erotic depredations of the Semitic vampire still took precedence. In *Nosferatu* the *economic* eroticism of the vampire took center stage.

Murnau's film, made twenty-five years after the book's publication, showed how much more intense and "directed" racism had become during the intervening years. For obvious ideological purposes (and to avoid having to pay royalties to Stoker's widow), the director had "localized" the events of the novel for his German audience and changed the names of the characters. Dracula became "Graf Orlok," Harker turned into "Hutter," and Renfield was rechristened "Knock." These adaptations were so transparent that when the film was released in the United States, the names of the principal characters were simply "re-translated" into those of Stoker's originals. Still, whoever did the transposition apparently relied on a somewhat clouded memory of the original source: Mina became "Nina" in the process. To facilitate comparison I have here used Stoker's, not Murnau's nomenclature, though it should be remembered that the "German Nationalist" message of the film was tied into the local significance of Murnau's alterations.

To enhance that aspect of the film, the director also changed the time and setting of the original. Where Stoker's Dracula attempted to subvert a self-consciously "modern" England replete with such newfangled inventions as dictaphones, shorthand, blood transfusions, rapid transatlantic travel, and so on, Murnau opted to present the German viewers of 1922 with a setting in 1843, a date with a historically important nationalistic Biedermeier setting. These were the years of the middle-class aesthetic's greatest triumph in Germany, just before the worker revolts and Marx's *Communist Manifesto* of 1848. Soon a fundamental political shift would begin to undermine the German bourgeoisie's proprietary self-confidence—a development that would ultimately result in the political ascendancy of Hitler.

It was also in 1843 that Marx wrote his essay *On the Jewish Question,* in which he attacked the concept of individualism and the glorification of man as bourgeois in capitalist democracy. Using the issue of religious freedom for the Jews as his point of departure, he argued for the gradual emancipation of humanity from the dictates of self-interest. The establishment of a society in which the masses had been liberated from the strictures of private property would bring about the cultivation of the genuine and harmonious species-life of man.

It matters little whether Murnau, his scriptwriter Henrik Galeen, or for that matter Hitler himself ever read this early essay of Marx. The Führer claimed that he had extensively investigated the "contents and the meaning of the life-work of the Jew Karl Marx," (289) but the average German's knowledge of Marx was limited to what had been written about him by his opponents. Central among such writings were attacks on Marx's "Jewish anti-individualism."

To see "the revenge of the under man" in the actions of Nosferatu required little specialized knowledge on the part of the film's original viewers. Nosferatu personified all the evils viewers had come to associate with the Jew. Hitler's focus on terms such as "bloodsucker" and "peoples' vampire" to identify the Jew deliberately exploited the same popular sources Murnau used to identify the horror of Dracula. Whether or not Hitler had seen *Nosferatu* when he wrote *Mein Kampf* is therefore of little importance to an identification of the film as a fundamental expression of the protofascist sentiments rampant throughout Western culture as the Twenties got under way.

Still, as a graphic delineation of the social prejudices that helped formulate the Nazi conception of the world, Murnau's social theater of fear undoubtedly contributed to Hitler's rise to power. The Führer's mind, like Murnau's, was a creation of German nationalism. Thus *Nosferatu* can be regarded as a remarkably accurate filmstrip of Hitler's "racial" imagination. The conflation of race, gender, and economics that formed the basis of Hitler's popular appeal was equally essential to the argument of Murnau's film. *Nosferatu* is therefore a remarkable indicator of the blend of cultural metaphors that would soon lead to the triumph of Nazism. The film joins Kipling's colonized leper with the destructive female "sexual vampire" of the 1910s, to bring about the birth of their miscegenated offspring: Hitler's emblematically destructive, disease-ridden, parasitic Jew.

As we have seen, the Führer's culturally constructed political imagination purposely echoed the fantasies of millions of ordinary people throughout Europe and America. It was his express purpose to use as ordinary a set of images as he could find. In *Mein Kampf* Hitler captured and exploited the racist spirit of the Twenties. He did not *produce* it. Truculent, mean-spirited, antihumanist, and obsessed by the rhetoric of sex-as-sin, but fiercely loyal to the "truths" of evolutionary science, he *was* the voice of the "Nordic" bourgeoisie of the period between the wars. *Nosferatu,* in turn, can be seen as a compendium of the visual sources Hitler exploited to gain his position of "leadership."

Murnau's anti-Semitic theme went Stoker's one better right from the start. In *Nosferatu* Harker is not a perfectly "normal" member of the British economic system but the unwitting pawn of an evil schemer. Renfield takes the place of the original novel's nondescript British Mr. Hawkins. A pronouncedly Semitic, greedy *real-estate agent* himself, he *knowingly* sends Harker off to unleash Dracula upon the unsuspecting German town of Wisborg (Bremen in the English version). Thus Murnau emphasizes the conspiratorial cooperation between the degenerates already within Germany and those still waiting to be invited in. The Jews in Germany, his implication is, cannot be trusted—they are constantly plotting to undermine the nation by expanding their clannish presence through immigration.

Stoker's Renfield and Dracula were linked only by Renfield's demented fascination with the "big-fish-eat-little-fish" principle of nature's food chain. Murnau's twosome, however, are explicitly linked by race. This gives an entirely new spin to Renfield's real estate dealings in *Nosferatu* and provides a direct focal point for Dracula's habit of carrying coffins full of native soil about with him wherever he goes. As the polluted, "prostituted" soil of the nomadic immigrant—the "syphilitic flesh" of the vampire—it becomes the visual focus of Murnau's symbolic presentation of Nosferatu's vile desire to mingle with the "clean, fresh" mother-soil of the fatherland.

The vampire's soiled earth of course also represented the danger of Bolshevism, the "Jewish social disease." The vampire's blood, when mingled with that of the fatherland, undermined the Aryan's "individuality," contaminating it with rat-infested Bolshevik egalitarianism.

A 1943 Nazi poster depicting Hitler's image of the
Jew as Nosferatu: the syphilitic disease of "oriental"
Marxism threatens the Aryan world—and in
particular the Aryan family—with extinction.

Murnau's Renfield is an only slightly less degenerate version of Dracula.
The latter proves to be an intensely emaciated, tall, talon-nailed,
skeleton-faced, bald creature with sharply pointed animal ears, a large,
bloodless, thin-lipped mouth, and sinister, deep-set eyes as deeply
kohled as those of any of the standard female film vamps of the time.
But the monster's central facial feature is an enormous, beaklike hook
nose—perhaps the largest ever produced by the anti-Semitic imagination. In the popular imagination noses were traditionally seen as indica-
tors of a man's phallic endowment, and Murnau was very well versed in
such lore. Nosferatu is thus quite clearly an unspeakably horrid, disease-
ridden, blood-sucking, Semitic satyr. Stills of this creature of death are

still among the most widely reproduced images in the history of the cinema.

If Renfield, the other Semite of Murnau's parable, initially still shows the civilizing influence of the Aryan environment in which he operates, he is presented in this manner only to offer the director a chance to chronicle the progressive degeneration of his facial structure toward Dracula's own level as the latter approaches German soil. By the end of the film, Renfield has taken on virtually every feature of Dracula's "Semitic degeneracy."

The coffins full of soil this Wandering Jew carries with him at least half the time we see him in Murnau's film are, inevitably, filled with pestilence. Crawling with plague-ridden rats, these coffins are portable emblems of Nosferatu's contagious syphilitic degeneracy. Once he has landed on German soil, Dracula's influence is felt immediately. The Aryans are poisoned by the alien plague-carrier. The nation's soul is weakened. The people die in the streets. The racial dissolution of the nation has begun.

But the economic pestilence accompanying the Jew's invasion is rooted in his sexuality. Nosferatu must therefore be shown to live in a state of permanent erection befitting the shape and size of his nose. Murnau hinted at the vampire's satyriasis whenever he could. When Harker first approaches Dracula's castle, for instance, we see it from a distance: The silver screen has never produced a more formidable and graphic, anatomically correct, erect penis. The Aryan's fascination with the Jewish vampire's sexual potency could not have been expressed more blatantly. Precariously poised, rock-rigid, fully engorged, this architectural manifestation of nature's primal need is topped with a glans we only slowly learn to identify as the walls and roof of a castle that is rimmed at its root by a scraggly pubis of pine trees.

It is the old story: the Jew's hypersensual erotic degeneracy creates the effeminacy that causes him to hunt for blood. In visual appearance Murnau's Nosferatu is a perfect match for the image of the habitual masturbator the generation of 1870 had been told to be on the lookout for in their children. He is thus precisely the sort of man Murnau's parents no doubt told him he would become if he indulged in that "vile effeminate practice." Murnau's Dracula has all the requisite symptoms: a "pallid, bloodless countenance, and hollow, sunken, and half-ghastly eyes." Indeed, he was clearly an extreme case, for the excessive indulger "will have black and blue semi-circles under his eyes, and also look as if worn out, almost dead from want of sleep, yet unable to get it." This passage from John Cowan's *The Science of a New Life* is characteristic of such medical directives to parents. The plague with which Dracula infected the men and women of his host country (Murnau's vampire no longer operated under Stoker's heterosexual strictures) was obviously of a syphilitic nature.

Murnau also depicted Nosferatu's body as something of a permanent erection itself: stiff, slow, elongated, and insistent. Even in this respect the mere sight of him signalized his sensual degeneracy, for many of the film's original viewers would have known that one could "detect a boy who is educated to this vice, by the peculiarity of the motion which is discernible at the junction of the locomotive organs with the body." Such a victim walked "as if he were stiffened. He does not show the peculiarity so much when walking slowly, or when running very fast, as he does when walking fast; then he impresses the looker-on that he is rheumatic, and suffering from stiffness in the small of his back." (Cowan, 361–2) Nosferatu exhibits exactly these characteristics when he walks.

Hitler knew what Murnau was trying to depict: Nosferatu was that "black-haired Jew boy" waiting, with "diabolic joy in his face," for unsuspecting Aryan girls to defile "with his blood." He was Fu Manchu crawling out of the Asian marshes to drag the Aryan woman back into the realm of primitive bisexuality. On Murnau's screen a title flashes: "Nina had promised never to open the book of the Vampires but she could not resist." The audience remembers Pandora—another woman who could not resist opening what should have remained closed. But once again Pandora's primal sin is about to be redeemed by a properly acculturated specimen of Aryan womanhood: "Only a woman is able to break the terrible spell—a woman pure in heart must offer herself to Nosferatu. The woman must remain at the side of Nosferatu until the crow of the rooster heralds the break of day." Stoker's Mina had still gained the upper hand over Dracula by remaining mentally independent until her male companions were able to kill the vampire. In Murnau's and scriptwriter Henrik Galeen's version, only a direct sexual confrontation will do.

Mina is the perfect Aryan woman. To remind us of this, Murnau shows her embroidering an "I love you" antimacassar as her last message to Harker. She will sacrifice herself for the nation. The pollution must stop. She will outwit the child-brained monster by doing what, after all, comes naturally to woman: she will seduce him into self-destruction. Thus Murnau's Mina becomes a kamikaze in the service of evolution by

sacrificing herself to Nosferatu's lust. At night, with the vampire lingering outside, she opens the window to her room—the symbolic entry to
her body. She performs Pandora's archetypal gesture of opening her box,
but this time she does so to redeem woman and lock the demon *in*.
Though visibly appalled by what she is about to do, she stumbles back
to bed, to receive Nosferatu's ambulant erection. This Aryan woman is
about to become a prostitute, not in service to, but to subvert, the pollutant ambitions of the invading Jew. Terrified, but demurely receptive,
she awaits her fate self-sacrificially upon her bed. This scene represents
the apotheosis of the sadomasochistic conception of sex as death in
Western culture.

Soon the Semitic monster of disease and pestilence hovers above her
loins; the shadows of the vampire's talonlike hands fall slowly, sadisti-
cally, over her barely covered breasts. Then the too heavily burdened
Mina's bed fades into darkness—until we see the cock crow, triumphantly announcing a new day. The sensualist slowly lifts his lustful
head: he has been caught off-guard after a night of effeminate dissipation. In punishment for this fatal weakness he now must wither in the
masculine light of the Aryan sun. His body is consumed in the blazing
furnace of a new day. The Nordic woman has exterminated the Jew:
Germany shall rise again.

Mina, polluted beyond salvation but sanctified by her sacrifice to the
fatherland, dutifully expires in Harker's arms: "And at that moment as if
by a miracle, the sick stopped dying and the oppressing shadow of the
vampire disappeared in the morning sun." A flame consumes the remains of the monster. Castle Dracula lies in ruins: the alien seed has
come to its final dissolution. "Only a woman, a woman pure at heart"
(though not in body), only the utterly passive mother-soil of the Aryan
nation proves to have greater anabolic strength than the Semitic de-
vourer, only the fire of the Aryan woman's self-sacrificial resolve can
keep the lid on Pandora's box. Equal partners in the underworld of
species evolution, the erotic forces of woman and Nosferatu ultimately
cancel each other out, leaving only Harker, the Aryan male. Alone, and
appropriately grateful to his departed helpmeet, he is now ready to
stride upward toward the Thousand Year Reich and immortality, toward
the ultimate triumph of the will.

At least that was the promise Murnau offered his audiences as his
drama of Aryan survival wound to a close. But he had left them with a
burning question: Renfield, the vampire-master's loyal human servant,
the everyday version of the monster's symbolic incarnation, who repre-

sented the atrocious commercial schemes of the Jewish merchant class, still lived. True, he had been imprisoned and was being restrained by a straightjacket. For the moment he had been neutralized. Even so, as Murnau's film had shown him doing once before, he might still escape from his confinement. If Nosferatu had been made to perish in the cleansing fire of the Aryan new day, would it not be better for mankind if Renfield, too, were given that fate? Wasn't it time for a final solution to the Jewish question?

Once again the implied solution was genocide. Fantasy, science fiction, pop endocrinology, medicine, biology, genetics, eugenics, anthropology—each of these sources of the twentieth century's pervasive rhetoric of class and race had helped to create a relentless barrage of metaphors and images that constantly circled back to this question: Shouldn't something be done about this spreader of disease? The many "scientific" quackeries that were doing the rounds during the early years of this century had all contributed to Murnau's imagery of the criminally invasive and subversive Eurasian Jew. The creator of *Nosferatu,* like G. W. Pabst and hundreds of other directors, writers, artists, journalists, and politicians throughout Western Europe and the United States, had taken up a strategic position next to Oscar Wilde's woman-hating Herod, so that when the time came for him to shout, pointing to Salome, the phallic decapitator, "Kill that woman!" they would be able to add to his gynecidal order their own genocidal call: "And kill that Jew, for he is the one behind all her abominations!"

The mentality speaking through much of the culture of the Twenties shows all too clearly that many intellectuals had been drifting toward the concept of genocide long before Hitler came to power in Germany. The colonial powers had been involved in brutal policies of suppression for centuries. But the "scientific" legitimation of policies of extermination had to wait for the ascendancy of the theory of evolution. The colonial leper now ceased being a nuisance, and became an active threat to "species survival."

The social, scientific, and economic causes for the spread of the genocidal mentality in twentieth-century culture are multifarious and convoluted. And it is true, metaphors don't kill, people do. But people need weapons to kill with: only animals and vampires use their own teeth. Hitler offered his followers the weapon of manhood to slay the dragon of effeminacy. He could not have done so without the metaphors of therapeutic gynecide that had become cornerstones of the male imagination during the early years of this century. The murderous animosities of gender cultivated during this period helped justify the climactic final scene of *Nosferatu* in which self-sacrificial Aryan femininity enthralls the Jewish vampire until he can be exterminated by the sunlight of manhood. As a brutal prefiguration of the monstrous realities of the Third Reich's "final solution," the scene remains emblematic of the psychosocial displacement of Western culture's demonization of female sexuality in the figure of the Jew. The all-consuming ovens of the Nazi concentration camps were first constructed in the gendered racist-evolutionist fantasies of turn-of-the-century males.

The chilling immediacy of this link is perhaps most strikingly expressed in Adolf Hitler's unbounded admiration for the art of symbolist painters such as Arnold Böcklin and Franz von Stuck. The latter's work in particular had a dramatic influence on the Führer's conception of feminine sexuality as a profound evil. This painter's widely reproduced canvases had documented woman's primitive bisexual lust for the phallus since 1889. His paintings could be seen in art magazines, books, and even on postcards—as well as in the form of posters suitable for framing produced by printing presses owned by the family of Hitler's friend "Putzi" Hanfstaengl. They fascinated Hitler. When he came to power, he quickly acquired several of von Stuck's paintings for his personal collection, including one of the many versions of the figure of "Sin" the artist had painted. This was von Stuck's most popular image—always a voluptuous naked woman, with thigh-long hair and a gigantic snake whose lower half was nestled between her legs while the rest of it curled upward around her body. A symbol of phallic female sexuality, the serpent would lean its *vagina dentata*–shaped head on the woman's shoulder and glare ominously at the viewer, its eyes a mirror image of those of the woman herself.

Von Stuck's women personified the temptation of "otherness" transformed into a sexual obsession. The artist eroticized the "phallic" power of these women to show that they represented an alien evil that must be destroyed. They were an invitation to rape as an act of domination and castration symbolizing the excision of these women's "phallic" independence, the destruction of their psychological and physiological identity. To perform this quasi-surgical rape, the male must be both "potent" and "continent"—in other words, he must destroy the usurper by using his phallus as a sword. By maintaining his erection and retaining his seed, the warrior proved his manhood. The phallus refusing to give up its seed was the hammer of the gods, the crown of species evolution. Loss of seed, ejaculation, signaled defeat—a loss of self, reverse castra-

Franz von Stuck, Depravity, *oil on canvas, 1894*

tion by the sexual vampire of masculine essence. Only effeminates, racial inferiors, and semibestial men freely joined von Stuck's sexual women in their revels.

In a painting of 1889, the year in which Hitler was born, von Stuck portrayed the Norse god Wotan as a caped avenger, an Aryan superman. As he gallops at top speed directly toward us we realize we are about to be trampled by this Nordic ur-führer's impetuous steed. The god's rigid, bloody sword is poised to thrust itself into whoever stands in his way. In the background voluptuous, newly conquered women are dragged along as booty by the god's marauding companions. In the middle distance we see the seemingly dismembered (symbolically castrated) figure of a male degenerate, justly overcome by Wotan's sword. His face presents a striking anticipation of Nosferatu's skeletal features. Wotan himself is, as Robert G. L. Waite pointed out in his book *The Psychopathic God* (1977), a meticulous portrait of Hitler, impossible as that might seem.

Von Stuck was not gifted with clairvoyance concerning the political future of Germany. But along with the majority of the intelligentsia of the age of imperialism, he *can* be held partly responsible for engendering the monster of Hitlerism. Given the future führer's obsession with this painter's art, it is, as Waite points out, highly probable that Hitler was familiar with this painting well before he came to power. Hitler dreamed of being Wotan, the true führer, the great Nordic leader of the Aryan advance. Most likely von Stuck's Wotan thus served Hitler as a

Franz von Stuck, The Wild Chase, *oil on canvas, 1889*

model for his own appearance, from his cowlick to his infamous moustache. But whether or not Hitler was actually familiar with this particular image is, frankly, of very little importance. The *mentality, the* cultural environment that allowed von Stuck to create this fantasy of a Nordic avenger, is what ultimately created the social phenomenon of Hitlerism. The confluence of patterns of prejudicial imagery produced by evolutionary theory, medical science, and genetics produced both von Stuck's imagination and the Nazis of twentieth-century politics.

Because Hitler was so intensely aware of the dramatic social power of imagery and metaphor, he knew better than anyone how deadly their power could be. Images were social directives. Even the main Nazi symbol itself, the swastika, had a significance in the gender wars that was certainly known to Hitler. O. A. Wall, in his book *Sex and Sex Worship* (1918), delineated that meaning as follows: in Norse mythology the symbol represented "lightning, and was called Thor's Hammer; but it also had a phallic significance, for with it Thor was supposed to bless or consecrate the newly married couples." (524)

In addition, the swastika, Thor's hammer, symbolized the continent Aryan phallus lost to the marauding sexual primitive, Nosferatu, Hitler's sinister "black-haired Jew boy," the priapic giant Thrym. As Wall pointed out,

> In the Eddas, it is related how the god Thor lost this hammer at one time, it having been stolen by the giant Thrym; the latter refused to surrender the hammer to its owner, except on the condition that the goddess Freya should be given to him for a wife. Upon this Thor disguised himself as a woman, pretending to be Freya, thus succeeding in meeting Thrym; he then slew the giant and recovered his hammer. (524)

Woman was the battleground of civilization. Thrym lusted after Freya ("Frigga," source of numerous colloquial terms for sexual intercourse)—the great mother—primal goddess of sexuality, Aryan fertility, and death. As mouth of the earth, she was the feminine principle personified, gentle mother or devouring monster. She was the conduit for all good and evil, keeper of Pandora's box. Thrym and Thor, Schigolch and Hitler, wasteful eroticism and Aryan continence, were locked in a deadly struggle over her possession. The future of the universe was at stake.

Hitler—Odin/Wotan/Thor—the Aryan avenger, was Freya's rightful husband. It was his task to protect her against the incursions of the vampire master who sought to make her his wife in order to possess the earth. But to protect her he must become her, and to become her was to succumb to sublunary dissipation and hence to "die"—unless he could eliminate the snake of primal eroticism, the Jew trying to possess her. Subverting Hitler's dreams of steely manhood was the reality of his slight, "effeminate" appearance—which had become a topic of frequent levity beyond Germany (and before his ascendancy, even within). He had *already* become Freya; to regain his hammer, to free masculinity from the yoke of eroticism, the Jew, the vampire master, must die.

Woman, most early-twentieth-century males believed, was man's "lower half." To be "with" her he also had to "be" her—descend to her level. Sex brought out the woman in man. Thus she drew him back into the realm of the "lower orders." Only Thor's hammer, the chaste phallus of Nordic masculinity, could conquer the serpent in woman, her degenerative link to primal bisexuality. That eternal peoples' vampire, the Jew, who fed on femininity instead of trying to transcend it, was the "ferment of decomposition" behind the sexual woman's attempts to appropriate Thor's hammer.

Woman, then, was the conduit to degeneration, the weak link in the evolutionary process. Only chaste motherhood could "kill" her, break the teeth out of her vagina. To slay the vampire, to excise the serpent that had wound itself around woman's loins, was also to excise the woman in man and bring on the Thousand Year Reich of Nordic masculinity's spiritual transcendence. Mina Harker, in Murnau's *Nosferatu,* had to die to prove herself a good woman, even though selflessly, purely in service to the fatherland, she had sacrificed herself to the sexual hunger of the vampire—to the woman in him. Thor had to become Mina to kill the monster of reversion, but to regain his manhood he had to kill Mina as well, for the feminine principle in nature was the root of all evil. Hitler no doubt perceived himself as a "hero" in the Jungian sense. He was "Mercurius, who was considered identical with the German national god, Wotan," (*Aspects of the Masculine,* 154) the personification of the great oak of Aryan manhood. Woman was Lilith, the serpent in his tree. Thus he contained both the Devil and "God's reflection in physical nature." (163) Only in his higher aspect could he be seen as a "Christ figure." A "loving belief in such a being" on the part of his followers "naturally involves cleansing one's own house of black filth." (165) Therefore the darkness of the body must be overcome by the spirit: only fire—the golden vengeance of the sun, the furnace of the intellect—could cleanse Mercurius and free him of his ambiguities.

Jung wrote this analysis of "The Spirit Mercurius" in 1943. Though it reads like a psychological profile of Hitler, it is, the Jungian analyst John Beebe pointed out in his recent introduction to *Aspects of the Masculine,* which includes Jung's essay, a *self-image:* "Mercurius was the patron of Jung's alchemical effort at self-unification, Jung's ultimate father-figure and masculine way through the psyche." Mercurius symbolized "the restless masculine spirit." In fact, Jung's Mercurius is the twentieth-century male, for it is a portrait of the *concept of masculinity* that had developed during the early decades of this century. Jung's archetype was a blatant *manipulation* of elements taken from ancient myth, a tendentiously constructed metaphoric delineation of the cult of manhood nineteenth-century science had created in the wake of economic change. It was not an *analysis* but an *expression* of the early-twentieth-century male's socially organized self-perception. But Jung's portrait of Mercurius is therefore also an exposition of the psychological *inevitability* of the Holocaust as a step on the road to the ultimate materialization of "the masculine spirit."

"Every spiritual truth," Jung maintained, "gradually turns into something material, becoming no more than a tool in the hand of man. In consequence, man can hardly avoid seeing himself as a knower, yes, even as a creator, with boundless possibilities at his command." Nazi Germany, he implied, had become "benighted" by its obsession with the evil feminine: "The growing darkness reaches its greatest intensity on the day of Venus (Friday [i.e., "Freya's day"]), and changes into Lucifer on Saturn's day. Saturday heralds the light which appears in full strength on Sun-day." Mercurius must relinquish the realm of Venus and return to his masculine instincts. But "modern man" was already "so darkened" by the feminine "that nothing beyond the light of his own intellect illuminates the world." That, Jung concluded, "surely is why such strange things are happening in our much lauded civilization, more like a *Götterdämmerung* than any normal twilight." (171–3)

In these remarks we reach the completion of the early twentieth century's uroboric circle of blame: though the effeminate Jew stood behind the corruption of modern womanhood, it was the feminine principle itself, the darkness of primal chaos, that stood behind the Jew. Genocide, Jung hinted, was a factor of man's failing illumination—a temporary aberration on the road to man's attainment of true enlightenment, which could only be achieved through the elimination of the anima, the mistletoe rooted in the earth, the primal *vagina dentata,* woman. Mercurius's millennium could dawn only in a cosmic act of gynecide.

As long as we allow the social fictions of past mythologies to shape our concept of the future, the present can be little more than an unlocked armory on the road to the next human disaster. When today's social mythographers try to "reinterpret" or "update" their sources, they invariably fashion their interpretations of gender to fit into the complex mix of social, political, and economic influences outlined in this book—influences that, in their turn, shaped the very premises of the mythographers and psychoanalysts these writers use as "authorities." The potential development of a truly humane social environment is still being undermined on an almost daily basis by new "scientific" revelations about the supposedly "fundamental," "genetic" differences between men and women. Every day we are told that we should bray in the woods or run with the wolves. In Hollywood the sagging fortunes of a studio boss can always be boosted by still another movie in which a phallic woman with a knife, a gun, a scissors, or a dolt for a husband is shown to be more aggressive than nature has given her the right to be.

The majority of us have come to see our adherence to such predictable structures of gender ideology as expressive of our "true" nature. Women in particular are still constantly encouraged to see compliance with market-directed male sexual fantasies as a spiritual assertion of the archetypal "woman within." Few realize how much of this supposedly "archetypal" creature they are trying to "liberate" within themselves is a male-constructed image—and a *negative,* deliberately condescending, manipulated male image at that. In almost every instance contemporary male attitudes hostile to successful women still express the convenient premise that such women resent being castrated males. Women who, tired of always being cast as the "receiver," try to do a "man's job" are disparaged as "ballbreakers." Like Faulkner's Temple Drake, they are still virtually always cast as being driven by a regressive desire to recapture the penis they lost in the evolutionary process. The dualistic mind thrives on such strict categories.

The social fictions governing the behavior of most Americans were no different from those that drove the Germans to mass murder. But fortunately, there was far less cultural homogeneity in this country than in Europe—a reality the ideologues of race never ceased to bewail. It was, ultimately, precisely this "racial chaos" that helped save the world from the Thousand Year Reich and its cultural hammer of death. For as the forces of hatred asserted their grim hegemony over the minds of the German people during the 1930s, the United States, *because* it was ideologically fragmented, for a brief historical moment welcomed a remarkably heterogeneous intellectual community in which the values of cooperation and integration were given nearly as much emphasis as any theory of mutual depredation.

That intellectual community was created in large part by the many immigrants and children of immigrants who first set foot on American soil during the years around the turn of the century. Caught between worlds, they were also caught between prejudices. Their integration into the American cultural environment encouraged an unprecedented flourishing of creativity in which "Aryans" and Jews, men and women, and humans of many races learned and worked together, exchanged ideas, and sometimes even recognized value in the products of those who saw a different pattern in the tapestry of the world. It was that complex variety produced by a "chaotic" immigrant society that saved America from Hitlerism.

During and after World War II, however, the dualistic mentality reasserted itself with renewed intensity, encouraged by the closing of the American mind *against* the values of complex multiplicity through the assertion of a narrow elitism of "national purpose." Nourished by the same multitude of evolutionist antifeminine, anti–Semitic, and racist prejudices that had fueled the excesses of Nazi Germany, the United States, after the war, entered what was perhaps its most static period of social homogenization, until that in turn began to fall apart in the Sixties under the oppressive weight of its own leaden predictability.

We are slowly beginning to realize that we are not two sexes, but as many as there are humans in the world. Difference and variety are the wellspring of all qualitative change. The false science of early-twentieth-century sex, race, and gender theory encouraged a privileged minority to seek to regulate the emotions of the entire human race. "For the good of all" this minority turned speculation into categorical "truth." The average person's all too hopeful belief in the infallibility of science permitted spurious categorical imperatives to serve as "proof" of humanity's "biological destiny." These still not adequately historicized "scientific" fictions of human predestination have made much of the century seem like the nightmare ward of an insane asylum strewn with Procrustean beds. On these, scientists driven by blatant prejudice have tried to stretch or shrink most others to make them fit their self-serving categories of excellence and inferiority.

Today we are in grave danger of repeating the intellectual mistakes of our grandparents. Every day we hear about one more scientist who has found "conclusive" genetic evidence for still another "bell curve" of "biological necessity." Darwinism is again riding high. "Evolutionary psychologists" are acting as if they had newly discovered the notion that we are still prisoners of "the caveman within us." Given the antihistorical bias of today's society, these new academic lights may actually be unaware that such an idea was already hackneyed when, in 1922, William J. Fielding used it as the title for one of his pop-psychologizing mass-market "how to think" manuals.

What we forget about history is what locks us into humanity's past mistakes. Demagogues and racists therefore almost invariably contend that history is bunk. Instead, they like the categorical imperatives of Jungian mythologizing and genetic puritanism. They hate the dangerous uncertainties and emotional pitfalls of a world guided by the polymorphous creativity of nongendered minds. That is why men have been so eager to turn "woman" into a political battleground. A world in which men are men and women housewives is a world without a future for most. Such a world would make us circle endlessly round as if we were inmates in the courtyard of a nineteenth-century prison.

True creativity depends on a recognition that we all have the potential to be different, that the architecture of life is infinite in its variety. The brilliant (and therefore forgotten) German feminist psychologist Rosa Mayreder said all this as early as 1905, in her book *A Survey of the Woman Problem*:

> Woman as an abstraction, as a figment of thought, exists only in the brain of the thinker, and is absolutely dependent upon this—as the nature of thought demands, but woman as an individual exists for herself, and is as noble and as vile, as gifted or as stupid, as weak or as strong, as good or as wicked, as like to man or as unlike him; in short, as diversified as is made necessary by the human species. [Therefore] nothing is of greater importance to women than to battle against the abstractions into which they are constantly being converted by masculine thought. If they wish to achieve power as real persons in the world they must battle against woman as fetish. (240)

All of us, women *and* men and every shade of self-conception in between, can escape from the fetishized gender imagery that surrounds us only by refusing to accept the mass media's lure of "evil sister" stereotyping. To fantasize about warlocks and witches, about vampires and werewolves, about Mars, Venus, and the caveman within, is to perpetuate the fantasies of a world eager for war and to remain complicit in the fetishization of others as "evil," as "alien," and as "inferior." To do so is to see difference as a disease.

Evil lurks *within* every social configuration—it is a product of our self-conception, not a result of "predestination." Groups are political; sex, race, and class are ethically and morally irrelevant physiological incidentals. But the media do everything they can to feed our desire to believe the reverse. Indeed, by turning gender and race conflict into the "virtual reality" of today's entertainments, they have effectively institutionalized the imagery of "scientific racism" developed during the early years of this century.

We are offered an ever more bloated menu of visual myths about the violence inherent in all forms of human interaction. The average living room has become a passive indoctrination chamber without any exits. By encouraging a renewed blind adherence to the early twentieth century's myths of gender, the media make money while they progressively entrap us further in sadomasochistic fantasies. As the early years of this century have shown all too clearly, every fantasy can become a reality if it is made to look like a natural law.

Fictions of personal regeneration through violence still organize our world. The homogenization of our visual media and the rapid decline of our capacity to read suggest that many among us will never be given the chance to realize that the images the media feed us are *not* part of "human nature," that they are *not* a mere expression of our "basic instinct" but a reinforcement of the early twentieth century's social fantasies of conquest. Today's films and music videos and most of our novels still glorify the "pleasures" of ecstatic submission or sadistic aggression. Few seem to realize that the glorification of such relationships represents not sexual liberation but an abject capitulation to the values of dualistic separation and the ideology of fear. As long as such conflicts are part of our social reality, they cannot be ignored in our arts—but why support the hucksters of gender and race by portraying violent acts as erotic? Why not celebrate the polymorphous interdependence of our lives and bodies instead of fetishizing the actions of those who seek pleasure in pain to express their anger about the falsely gendered inequalities of a cash-driven culture?

Any "formal order" imposed on our social imagination cannot but be profoundly repressive. We have deluded ourselves into thinking that the Nazi excesses of the early twentieth century were little more than an unfortunate "aberration" in the orderly "progress" of society. But the genocidal mentality was a product of ideas that continue to govern our sense of self. The monster of Nazism still roams among us—for the fictions of gender dualism that permitted it to gain power still darken our lives.

BIBLIOGRAPHY

Adams, Brooks. *The Law of Civilization and Decay* [1895]. With an introduction by
　　Charles A. Beard. New York: 1955.
―――. *The New Empire.* New York: 1902.
―――. "The New Struggle for Life Among Nations." *McClure's Magazine* 12
　　(April 1899): 558–64.
Angier, Natalie. "Feminists and Darwin: Scientists Try Closing the Gap." *New York
　　Times,* June 21, 1994, national edition, sec. B, pp. 7 and 12.
Anonymous. "A Visit to Movieland, the Film Capital of the World—Los Angeles."
　　The Forum 63 (January 1920): 17–29.
Appignanesi, Lisa, and John Forrester. *Freud's Women.* New York: 1992.
Arendt, Hannah. *The Origins of Totalitarianism* [1951]. New edition with added pref-
　　aces. New York: 1973.
Ash, Cay van, and Elizabeth Sax Rohmer. *Master of Villainy: A Biography of Sax
　　Rohmer.* Bowling Green, Ohio: 1972.
Atwell, Lee. *G. W. Pabst.* Boston: 1977.
Austin, Mary. "Sex Emancipation Through War." *The Forum* 59 (May 1918):
　　609–20.
Bara, Theda [Theodosia Goodman]. "The Curse on the Moving-Picture Actress:
　　Describing the Conflict in Her Artistic Experiences of the Moving-Picture
　　Art." *The Forum* 62 (July 1919): 83–93.
―――. "How I Became a Film Vampire: The Self-Revelations of a Moving-
　　Picture Star." *The Forum* 61 (June 1919): 715–27.
Barker-Benfield, G. J. *The Horrors of the Half-Known Life: Male Attitudes Toward
　　Women and Sexuality in Nineteenth Century America.* New York: 1977.
Barnes, Djuna. *Nightwood* [1936]. With an introduction by T. S. Eliot. New York:
　　1961.
Bauer, Bernhard A. *Woman and Love* [1927]. 2 vols. Liveright Library Edition. New
　　York: 1943.
Beaumont, Edouard de. *The Sword and Womankind* [1882]. New York: 1929.
Bierce, Ambrose. *The Devil's Dictionary* [1906 (originally published as *The Cynic's
　　Word Book;* retitled 1911)]. New York: 1958.
Biggers, Earl Derr. *Seven Keys to Baldpate.* New York: 1913.
Billeter, Erika, and Jose Pierre, eds. *La Femme et le surréalisme.* Lausanne: 1987.

Binion, Rudolph. *Love Beyond Death: The Anatomy of a Myth in the Arts.* New York: 1993.

Bleiler, Everett F. *The Checklist of Fantastic Literature—A Bibliography of Fantasy, Weird, and Science Fiction Books Published in the English Language.* Chicago: 1948.

Bloch, Iwan. *Anthropological Studies in the Strange Sexual Practices of All Races in All Ages, Ancient and Modern, Oriental and Occidental, Primitive and Civilized.* Trans. Keene Wallis. New York: 1933.

———. *The Sexual Life of Our Time.* London: 1903.

Bodeen, DeWitt. *From Hollywood: The Careers of 15 Great American Stars.* South Brunswick, N.J.: 1976.

Bonaparte, Marie. *Female Sexuality.* Trans. John Rodker. New York: 1953.

Borst, Ronald V., Keith Burns, and Leith Adams, eds. *Graven Images: The Best of Horror, Fantasy, and Science-Fiction Film Art from the Collection of Ronald V. Borst.* New York: 1992.

Bousfield, Paul. *Sex and Civilization.* London: 1925.

Bowler, Peter J. *The Mendelian Revolution: The Emergence of Hereditarian Concepts in Modern Science and Society.* London: 1989.

Brady, William A. "Have the Movies Ideals?" *The Forum* 59 (March 1918): 307–15.

Brennicke, Ilona, and Joe Hembus. *Klassiker des Deutschen Stummfilms, 1910–1930.* Munich: 1983.

Briffault, Robert. *The Mothers: A Study of the Origins of Sentiments and Institutions.* 3 vols. New York: 1927.

Brome, Vincent. *Freud and His Early Circle.* New York: 1968.

Brooks, Louise. *Lulu in Hollywood.* New York: 1982.

Browne, Lewis Allen. "Bolshevism in America: The Thing That Disrupted Russia and Has Been Seized Upon by Disloyalists in America." *The Forum* 59 (June 1918): 703–17.

Browne, Porter Emerson. *A Fool There Was.* New York: 1909.

Brownlow, Kevin. *Behind the Mask of Innocence: Sex, Violence, Prejudice, Crime: Films of Social Conscience in the Silent Era.* New York: 1990.

———. *The Parade's Gone By . . .* New York: 1968.

Bunson, Matthew. *The Vampire Encyclopedia.* New York: 1993.

Burgess, Gelett. *The Bromide and Other Theories.* New York: 1933.

Burne, Glenn S. *Remy de Gourmont; His Influence in England and America.* Carbondale, Ill.: 1963.

Burroughs, Edgar Rice. *Tarzan and the City of Gold* [1933]. New York: 1964.

Bushnell, Horace. *Tarzan and the Jewels of Opar* [1916]. New York: 1963.

———. *Women's Suffrage: The Reform Against Nature.* New York: 1869.

Cabell, James Branch. *Jurgen—A Comedy of Justice* [1919]. New York: n.d.

———. *Something About Eve: A Comedy of Fig-leaves.* New York: 1927.

Cain, James M. *Double Indemnity* [1935]. New York: 1978.

Card, James. *Seductive Cinema.* New York: 1994.

Carmichael, Joel. *The Satanization of the Jews. Origin and Development of Mystical Anti-Semitism.* New York: 1992.

Carnegie, Andrew. *Problems of Today; Wealth—Labor—Socialism.* New York: 1909.

Carpenter, Humphrey. *A Serious Character: The Life of Ezra Pound.* Boston: 1988.

Carrington, Leonora. "The Sisters." Trans. Charles Henri Ford. In *A Night with Jupiter and Other Fantastic Stories,* ed. Charles Henri Ford. London: 1947.

Carter, Margaret L., ed. *Dracula, The Vampire and the Critics.* Ann Arbor, Mich.: 1988.

Casseres, Benjamin de. Preface to Huneker, *Painted Veils* [q.v.]. Black and Gold Library Edition. New York: [ca. 1932].

Chamberlain, Houston Stewart. *Die Grundlagen des Neunzehnten Jahrhunderts (The Origins of the Nineteenth Century)* [1899]. 2 vols. Munich: 1932.

Chamberlin, J. Edward, and Sander L. Gilman. *Difference and Pathology: Stereotypes of Sexuality, Race and Madness.* Ithaca, N.Y.: 1985.

Chambers, Robert W. *The Crimson Tide.* New York: 1919.

———. *The Slayer of Souls.* New York: 1920.

Chesler, Ellen. *Woman of Valor: Margaret Sanger and the Birth Control Movement in America.* New York: 1992.

Chesterton, G. K. *Eugenics and Other Evils.* London: 1922.

Chideckel, Maurice. *Female Sex Perversion: The Sexually Aberrated Woman as She Is* [1935]. New York: 1938.

Chorover, Stephan L. *From Genesis to Genocide; The Meaning of Human Nature and the Power of Behavior Control.* Cambridge, Mass.: 1979.

Clarens, Carlos. *An Illustrated History of the Horror Film.* New York: 1967.

Cloete, Stuart. *Congo Song.* Boston: 1943.

Clute, John, and Peter Nichols. *The Encyclopedia of Science Fiction.* London: 1993.

Coblentz, Stanton A. *The Decline of Man.* New York: 1925.

Conrad, Joseph. *Heart of Darkness* [1899/1902]. Ed. Paul O'Prey. New York: Penguin Books, 1983.

The Control of Parenthood. Ed. James Marchant, with contributions by J. Arthur Thomson, Leonard Hill, Dean Inge, Harold Cox, Mary Scharlieb, H. Rider Haggard, A. E. Garvie, F. B. Meyer, and Marie Stopes. London: 1920.

Coppola, Francis Ford, and James V. Hart. *Bram Stoker's Dracula: The Film and the Legend.* New York: 1992.

Cowan, John. *The Science of a New Life.* New York: 1869.

Crawford, F. Marion. "For the Blood Is the Life." In *Wandering Ghosts.* New York: 1911. Reprinted in Ryan, *Vampires* [q.v.].

Crawley, Ernest. *The Mystic Rose: A Study of Primitive Marriage and of Primitive Thought in Its Bearing on Marriage* [1902]. Rev. and enl. ed., ed. Theodore Besterman. 2 vols. London: 1927.

Crofton, Algernon. *The Goat's Hoof.* Chicago: 1928.

Crook, Nora. *Kipling's Myths of Love and Death.* London: 1989.

Da, Lottie, and Jane Alexander. *Bad Girls of the Silver Screen.* New York: 1989.

Daly, Carroll John. See Nolan, William F. *The Black Mask Boys.*

Darwin, Charles. *The Descent of Man* [1871]. London: 1874.

———. *The Origin of Species By Means of Natural Selection, Or the Preservation of Favoured Races in the Struggle For Life* [1859]. With an introduction by Julian Huxley. New York: 1958.

Darwin, Leonard. *The Need for Eugenic Reform*. New York: 1926.

Deane, Hamilton, and John L. Balderston. *Dracula* [1927, stage version]. Ed. and annot. David J. Skal. New York: 1993.

Decker, Hannah S. *Freud, Dora, and Vienna 1900*. New York: 1991.

Degler, Carl N. *In Search of Human Nature: The Decline and Revival of Darwinism in American Social Thought*. New York: 1991.

Dell, Floyd. *Love in the Machine Age: A Psychological Study of the Transition from Patriarchal Society*. New York: 1930.

D'Emilio, John, and Estelle B. Freedman. *Intimate Matters: A History of Sexuality in America*. New York: 1988.

Deventer, Betty van. *Confessions of a Gold Digger*. Little Blue Book No. 1392. Girard, Kansas: [ca. 1929].

Dijkstra, Bram. "America and Georgia O'Keeffe." In *Georgia O'Keeffe—The New York Years*. New York: 1991.

———. "The High Cost of Parasols: Images of Women in Impressionist Art." In *California Light, 1900–1930,* ed. Patricia Trenton and William H. Gerdts. Laguna Beach, Calif.: 1990.

———. *Idols of Perversity: Fantasies of Feminine Evil in Fin-de-siècle Culture*. New York: 1986.

Dinnerstein, Leonard, ed. *Anti-Semitism in the United States*. New York: 1971.

Dixon, Thomas. *The Clansman—An Historical Romance of the Ku Klux Klan*. New York: 1905.

———. *Comrades—A Story of Social Adventure in California*. New York: 1909.

———. *The Leopard's Spots—A Romance of the White Man's Burden, 1865–1900*. New York: 1902.

———. *The Traitor—A Story of the Fall of the Invisible Empire*. New York: 1907.

Dorsey, George A. *Man's Own Show: Civilization*. New York: 1931.

Dracula (The Original 1931 Shooting Script). Production background by Philip J. Riley. Absecon, N.J.: 1990.

Dreiser, Theodore. *The Titan* [1914]. New York: 1965.

Dresser, Norine. *American Vampires: Fans, Victims & Practitioners*. New York: 1989.

Dreyer, Carl Theodor. *Vampyr*. In *Four Screenplays*. Bloomington, Ind.: 1970.

Drinka, George Frederick. *The Birth of Neurosis: Myth, Malady and the Victorians*. New York: 1984.

Durie, Alistair. *Weird Tales*. London: 1979.

Durkheim, Emile. *The Division of Labor in Society* [1893]. Glencoe, Ill.: 1933.

East, Edward M. *Heredity and Human Affairs*. New York: 1927.

Edwards, Anne. *The De Milles, An American Family*. New York: 1988.

Eisner, Lotte. *The Haunted Screen: Expressionism in the German Cinema and the Influence of Max Reinhardt*. Berkeley: 1973.

———. *Murnau*. London: 1973.

Ellis, Havelock. *Man and Woman: A Study of Human Secondary Sexual Characters*. London: 1894.

———. "The Psychology of Red." *Popular Science Monthly* 57 (August 1900): 365–75; part 2 (September 1900): 516–26.

————. *Studies in the Psychology of Sex* [1897–1928]. Complete in 2 vols. New York: 1936.

Elsaesser, Thomas. "Lulu and the Meter Man: Pabst's *Pandora's Box* (1929)." In *German Film and Literature, Adaptations and Transformations,* ed. Eric Rentschler. New York: 1986.

Erskine, John. *Adam and Eve: Though He Knew Better.* Indianapolis, Ind.: 1927.

————. *Helen Retires.* Indianapolis, Ind.: 1934.

————. *Penelope's Man; The Homing Instinct.* Indianapolis, Ind.: 1927.

————. *The Private Life of Helen of Troy.* Indianapolis, Ind.: 1925.

Essoe, Gabe, and Raymond Lee. *De Mille: The Man and His Pictures.* New York: 1970.

Estournelles de Constant, Baron d'. *Woman in the United States.* With a foreword by David Starr Jordan. San Francisco: 1912.

Etherington, Norman. *Rider Haggard.* Boston: 1984.

Evolution in Modern Thought—by Haeckel, Thomson, Weismann and Others. New York: [ca. 1919].

Fairchild, Henry Pratt. *The Melting-Pot Mistake.* Boston: 1926.

Farmer, Philip José. *The Lovers.* In *Startling Stories* 27, no. 1 (August 1952): 12–63.

————. *The Lovers.* Expanded ed. New York: 1980.

Farson, Daniel. *The Man Who Wrote Dracula; A Biography of Bram Stoker.* London: 1975.

Faulkner, William. *Sanctuary* [1931]. New York: 1987.

————. "Nympholepsy" [1925]. In *Uncollected Stories of William Faulkner,* ed. Joseph Blotner. New York: 1981.

————. *Requiem for a Nun* [1951]. New York: 1975.

Fausto-Sterling, Anne. *Myths of Gender: Biological Theories About Women and Men.* New York: 1985.

Féré, Charles Samson. *Scientific and Esoteric Studies in Sexual Degeneration in Mankind and in Animals* [ca. 1910]. Trans. Ulrich van der Horst. New York: 1932.

————. *The Sexual Urge: How It Grows or Wanes.* New York: 1932.

Ferrero, Guglielmo. *Between the Old World and the New: A Moral and Philosophical Contrast.* Trans. A. Cecil Curtis. New York: 1914.

Fielding, William J. *The Caveman Within Us.* New York: 1922.

————. *Woman: The Eternal Primitive.* Little Blue Book No. 901. Girard, Kansas: 1927.

————. *Sex and the Love Life.* New York: 1927.

Fiske, John. *American Political Ideas Viewed from the Standpoint of Universal History.* New York: 1885.

————. *The Destiny of Man Viewed in Light of His Origin.* Boston: 1884.

Fitzgerald, F. Scott. *The Beautiful and Damned.* [1922]. New York: n.d.

Forel, Auguste. *The Sexual Question* [1906]. Eng. adaptation by C. F. Marshall, M.D. Brooklyn, N.Y.: 1922.

Frazer, Sir James George. *The Golden Bough; A Study in Magic and Religion.* 1-vol. abridged ed. New York: 1922.

Freeman, Lucy, and Herbert S. Strean. *Freud and Women.* New York: 1987.

Freud, Sigmund. *Civilization and Its Discontents* [1930]. Ed. and trans. James Strachey. New York: 1962.

———. *The Complete Letters of Sigmund Freud to Wilhelm Fliess, 1887–1904*. Ed. and trans. Jeffrey Moussaieff Masson. Cambridge, Mass.: 1985.

———. *Dora: An Analysis of a Case of Hysteria* [1905]. With an introduction by Philip Rieff. New York: 1963.

———. *General Psychological Theory*. Ed. Philip Rieff. New York: 1963.

———. *Group Psychology and the Analysis of the Ego* [1921]. Ed. and trans. James Strachey. New York: 1959.

———. *New Introductory Lectures on Psychoanalysis* [1933]. Ed. and trans. James Strachey. New York: 1965.

———. *On Creativity and the Unconscious*. With an introduction by Benjamin Nelson. New York: 1958.

———. *Sexuality and the Psychology of Love*. Ed. Philip Rieff. New York: 1963.

———. "Some Psychological Consequences" [1925]. See *Sexuality and the Psychology of Love*.

———. "The Taboo of Virginity" [1918]. See *Sexuality and the Psychology of Love*.

Gardner, Augustus K. *Conjugal Sins Against the Laws of Life and Health*. New York: 1870. Republished, virtually unchanged, as *The Conjugal Relationships As Regards Personal Health and Hereditary Well-Being, Practically Treated*. New York: 1906. A British edition was published in London by Simpkin, Marshall, Hamilton, Kent & Co. as late as 1923.

Garner, Richard L. "Man-likeness in Jungle Beasts; Studying Animal Intelligence in Africa's Wilds." *The Forum* 62 (August 1919): 306–17.

Gilbert, Sandra, and Susan Gubar. *No Man's Land. The Place of the Woman Writer in the Twentieth Century*. 3 vols. Vol. 1: *The War of the Words*. Vol. 2: *Sexchanges*. Vol. 3: *Letters from the Front*. New Haven, Conn.: 1988–94.

Gilman, Sander L. *Difference and Pathology. Stereotypes of Sexuality, Race and Madness*. Ithaca, N.Y.: 1985.

———. *Freud, Race, and Gender*. Princeton, N.J.: 1993.

———. *Jewish Selfhatred: Anti-Semitism and the Hidden Language of the Jews*. Baltimore, Md.: 1986.

———. *The Jew's Body*. New York: 1991.

Gilman, Sander L., and Steven T. Katz. *Anti-Semitism in Times of Crisis*. New York: 1991.

Gish, Lillian, with Ann Pinchot. *The Movies, Mr. Griffith, and Me* [1969]. San Francisco: 1988.

Glyn, Anthony. *Elinor Glyn: A Biography*. Garden City, N.Y.: 1955.

Glyn, Elinor. *The Philosophy of Love*. New York: 1923.

———. *Three Weeks* [1907]. With an introduction by Cecil Beaton. London: 1974.

———. *Your Affectionate Godmother*. New York: 1914.

Gobineau, Joseph Arthur, Comte de. *The Inequality of Human Races* [1854]. With an introduction by Oscar Levy [abridged]. New York: 1915.

Gooddy, William. "Charles Edouard Brown-Séquard." In *Historical Aspects of the Neurosciences,* ed. F. Clifford Rose and W. F. Bynum. New York: 1982.

Goodstone, Tony. *The Pulps: Fifty Years of American Pop Culture.* New York: 1970.

Gould, A., and Franklin L. Dubois. *The Science of Sex Regeneration, or How to Preserve and Strengthen and Retain the Vital Powers* [1911]. 10th ed. Chicago: [ca. 1918].

Gould, Stephen Jay. *The Mismeasure of Man.* New York: 1981.

———. *Ontogeny and Phylogeny.* Cambridge, Mass.: 1977.

Gourmont, Remy de. *The Natural Philosophy of Love* [1903]. Trans. with a postscript by Ezra Pound. New York: 1931.

Grant, Madison. *The Passing of the Great Race, or The Racial Basis of European History* [1916]. 4th rev. ed. with documentary supplement [1921]. Second printing, New York: 1922.

Grant, Madison, and Charles Stewart Davison, eds. *The Alien in Our Midst, or Selling Our Birthright for a Mess of Pottage.* New York: 1930.

Haeckel, Ernst, et al. *Evolution in Modern Thought.* New York: 1922.

Haggard, H. Rider. *She.* Facsimile copy of first edition [1887]. New York: 1976.

Haller, John S., and Robin M. Haller. *The Physician and Sexuality in Victorian America* [1974]. New York: 1977.

Hamilton, David. *The Monkey Gland Affair.* London: 1986.

Hanna, Judith Lynne. *Dance, Sex and Gender.* Chicago: 1988.

Harbou, Thea von. *Metropolis* [1926]. New York: 1963.

Harrington, Anne. *Medicine, Mind, and the Double Brain; A Study in Nineteenth Century Thought.* Princeton, N.J.: 1987.

Harrowitz, Nancy A., ed. *Tainted Greatness: Anti-Semitism and Cultural Heroes.* Philadelphia: 1994.

Hecht, Ben. *The Kingdom of Evil.* Chicago: 1924.

Hemingway, Ernest. *The Sun Also Rises* [1926]. New York: [ca. 1954].

———. *To Have and Have Not* [1937]. New York: 1986.

Henderson, Robert M. *D. W. Griffith, The Years at Biograph.* New York: 1970.

Higashi, Sumiko. *Virgins, Vamps, and Flappers.* St. Albans, Vt.: 1978.

Higham, Charles. *Cecil B. De Mille.* New York: 1973.

Hirschfeld, Magnus. *Sittengeschichte des Weltkrieges.* Leipzig: 1930.

Hitler, Adolf. *Mein Kampf* [1925–7]. New York: 1939.

Hobsbawm, Eric. *The Age of Extremes. A History of the World, 1914–1991.* New York: 1994.

Hochman, Stanley, ed. *The Blue Angel: The Novel by Heinrich Mann; The Film by Josef von Sternberg.* New York: 1979.

———. *From Quasimodo to Scarlett O'Hara: A National Board of Review Anthology, 1920–1940.* New York: 1982.

Hoffmann, E. T. A. "Das Fräulein von Scuderi" [1819], in *Meistererzählungen.* Ed. Jürg Fierz. Zürich: 1963.

Hoffmann, Werner, et al. *Eva und die Zukunft: Das Bild der Frau seit der Französischen Revolution.* Munich: 1986.

Hofstadter, Richard. *Social Darwinism in American Thought* [1944]. Rev. ed. Boston: 1955.

Holmes, S. J. *The Eugenic Predicament.* New York: 1933.

Holt, Edwin B. *The Freudian Wish and Its Place in Ethics.* New York: 1915.

Hooton, Earnest A. *Apes, Men & Morons.* New York: 1937.

Hudson, Richard. *Sixty Years of Vamps and Camps; Visual Nostalgia of the Silver Screen.* New York: 1973.

Hughes, H. Stuart. *Oswald Spengler: A Critical Estimate.* New York: 1952.

Hull, E. M. *The Sheik.* Boston: 1921.

Huneker, James Gibbons. *Painted Veils* [1919/20]. With an introduction by Van Wyck Brooks. New York: 1964.

Hunter, Rev. W. J. *Manhood Wrecked and Rescued: How Strength and Vigor Is Lost, and How It May Be Restored by Self-Treatment.* New York: 1900.

Huntington, Ellsworth. *The Character of Races as Influenced by Physical Environment, Natural Selection and Historical Development.* New York: 1924.

Jacobs, Lewis. *The Rise of the American Film.* New York: 1939.

Johnson, Niel M. *George Sylvester Viereck, German-American Propagandist.* Urbana, Ill.: 1972.

Jordan, David Starr. *The Blood of the Nation.* Boston: 1902.

————. *War and the Breed: The Relation of War to the Downfall of Nations.* Boston: 1915.

Jung, Carl Gustav. "Anima and Animus," from *The Relations Between the Ego and the Unconscious* [1928]. Reprinted in *Aspects of the Feminine.* Trans. R. F. C. Hull. Princeton, N.J.: 1982.

————. *Aspects of the Masculine.* Trans. R. F. C. Hull. Princeton, N.J.: 1989.

————. *The Basic Writings of C. G. Jung.* Selected and introduced by Violet S. de Laszlo. Princeton, N.J.: 1990.

————. "Marriage as a Psychological Relationship." In Keyserling, ed., *The Book of Marriage* [q.v.].

————. *Symbols of Transformation.* Vol. 5 of *The Collected Works of C. G. Jung.* 2d ed. Princeton, N.J.: 1967.

Kallen, Horace M. *Indecency and the Seven Arts—And Other Adventures of a Pragmatist in Aesthetics.* New York: 1930.

Kammerer, Paul. *The Inheritance of Acquired Characteristics.* New York: 1924.

Kaplan, Louise J. *Female Perversions: The Temptations of Emma Bovary.* New York: 1991.

Katsainos, George M. *The Physiology of Love.* Boston: 1929.

Katz, Jacob. *From Prejudice to Destruction: Anti-Semitism, 1700–1933.* Cambridge, Mass.: 1980.

Kendall, Elizabeth. *Where She Danced: The Birth of American Art-Dance.* New York: 1979.

Kenealy, Arabella. *Feminism and Sex-Extinction.* New York: 1920.

Kevles, Daniel J. *In the Name of Eugenics: Genetics and the Uses of Human Heredity.* New York: 1985.

Keyserling, Count Hermann, ed. *The Book of Marriage: A New Interpretation by Twenty-Four Leaders of Contemporary Thought.* New York: 1926.

Kinsey, Alfred C., et al. *Sexual Behavior in the Human Female.* Philadelphia: 1953.

Kipling, Rudyard. "The Mark of the Beast." In *Life's Handicap* [1891]. New York: 1987.

Kisch, E. Heinrich, M.D. *The Sexual Life of Woman in Its Physiological and Hygienic Aspect*. Trans. M. Eden Paul. New York: 1916.

Klineberg, Otto. *Race Differences*. New York: 1935.

Kluckhohn, Clyde. *Mirror for Man: Anthropology and Modern Life*. New York: 1949.

Koehler, P. J. *Het Localisatieconcept in de Neurologie van Brown-Séquard*. Amsterdam: 1989.

Kopeloff, Nicholas and Lillian. "Glands: Fact vs. Fiction." *The New Republic* (July 19, 1922): 209–12.

Koestler, Arthur. *The Case of the Midwife Toad*. London: 1971.

Koszarski, Richard. *An Evening's Entertainment: The Age of the Silent Feature Picture, 1915–1928*. Vol. 3 of *History of the American Cinema*, ed. Charles Harpole. New York: 1990.

———. *The Rivals of D. W. Griffith*. Minneapolis: 1976.

Kracauer, Siegfried. *From Caligari to Hitler; A Psychological History of the German Film*. Princeton, N.J.: 1947.

Krafft-Ebing, Richard von. *Psychopathia Sexualis, With Especial Reference to the Antipathic Sexual Instinct* [1886]. Trans. Franklin S. Klaf. New York: 1965.

Lacan, Jacques. *Feminine Sexuality*. Ed. Juliet Mitchell and Jacqueline Rose. New York: 1982.

Lang, Robert, ed. *The Birth of a Nation*. New Brunswick, N.J.: 1994.

Le Bon, Gustave. *Les Lois psychologiques de l'evolution des peuples (The Psychological Laws of the Evolution of Peoples)* [1894]. New York: 1924.

Lecky, William Edward Hartpole. *Democracy and Liberty*. 2 vols. New York: 1896.

Le Conte, Joseph, *Evolution: Its Nature, Its Evidences, and Its Relation to Religious Thought* [1888]. 2d rev. ed. New York: 1897.

Leff, Leonard J., and Jerold L. Simmons. *The Dame in the Kimono: Hollywood, Censorship & the Production Code from the 1920s to the 1960s*. New York: 1990.

Leyda, Jay, and Charles Musser, eds. *Before Hollywood; Turn-of-the-Century Film from American Archives*. New York: 1986.

Liederman, Earle E. *The Hidden Truth About Sex*. New York: 1926.

Lindermann, Albert S. *The Jew Accused. Three Anti-Semitic Affairs (Dreyfus, Beilis, Frank), 1894–1915*. Cambridge: 1991.

Lombroso, Cesare, and William Ferrero. *The Female Offender* [1893]. New York: 1895.

Lombroso, Gina. *The Soul of Woman (L'anima della donna); Reflections on Life*. New York: [1923].

Loos, Anita. *Fate Keeps On Happening—Adventures of Lorelei Lee and Other Writings*. Ed. Ray Pierre Corsini. New York: 1984.

———. *Gentlemen Prefer Blondes* [1925] . . . *But Gentlemen Marry Brunettes* [1928]. New York: 1983. The 1983 reissue includes the retrospective preface.

Ludmerer, Kenneth M. *Genetics and American Society*. Baltimore, Md.: 1972.

Ludovici, Anthony M. *Man: An Indictment*. London: 1927.

Lundberg, Ferdinand, and Marynia F. Farnham, M.D. *Modern Woman, The Lost Sex*. New York: 1947.

Machin, Alfred. *The Ascent of Man by Means of Natural Selection*. London: 1925.

Malchow, C. W., M.D. *The Sexual Life: A Scientific Treatise Designed for Advanced Students and the Professions Embracing the Natural Sexual Impulse, Normal Sexual Habits and Propagation, Together with Sexual Physiology and Hygiene.* St. Louis: 1907.

Malinowski, Bronislaw. "Havelock Ellis," [1931] in *Sex, Culture and Myth,* 129–31. New York: 1962.

Mantegazza, Paolo. *The Sexual Relations of Mankind* [1885]. New York: 1935.

Markun, Leo. *The Mental Differences Between Men and Women; Neither of the Sexes Is to an Important Extent Superior to the Other.* Little Blue Book No. 731. Girard, Kansas: [ca. 1926].

Masson, Jeffrey Moussaieff. *A Dark Science: Women, Sexuality and Psychiatry in the Nineteenth Century.* New York: 1986.

Masters, R. E. L., and Eduard Lea. *The Anti-Sex: The Belief in the Natural Inferiority of Women—Studies in Male Frustration and Sexual Conflict.* New York: 1964.

Mayne, Judith. "Dracula in the Twilight: Murnau's *Nosferatu* (1922)." In *German Film and Literature, Adaptations and Transformations,* ed. Eric Rentschler. New York: 1986.

Mayreder, Rosa. *A Survey of the Woman Problem* [1905]. Trans. Herman Scheffauer. New York: 1913.

McCabe, Joseph. *The Key to Love and Sex.* 8 vols., including *What Sex Really Is; What Distinguishes the Male from the Female Sex, Physically, Emotionally, Intellectually; The Antagonism Between the Sexes; etc.* Girard, Kansas: 1929.

McDermott, John Francis, and Kendall B. Taft, eds. *Sex in the Arts; A Symposium.* New York: 1932.

McKee, James B. *Sociology and the Race Problem; The Failure of a Perspective.* Urbana, Ill.: 1993.

McNally, Raymond T. *Dracula Was a Woman: In Search of the Blood Countess of Transylvania.* New York: 1983.

Mencken, H. L. *In Defense of Women* [1918]. London: 1927.

Mendel, Gregor. *Experiments in Plant Hybridisation* [1865]. With an introduction by Paul C. Mangelsdorf. Cambridge, Mass.: 1965.

Merritt, Abraham. *The Moon Pool* [1919]. New York: 1951.

Money, John. *The Destroying Angel; Sex, Fitness & Food in the Legacy of Degeneracy Theory, Graham Crackers, Kellogg's Corn Flakes & American Health History.* Buffalo, N.Y.: 1985.

Moran, John C. *An F. Marion Crawford Companion.* Westport, Conn.: 1981.

Mordden, Ethan. *Movie Star: A Look at the Women Who Made Hollywood.* New York: 1983.

Moskowitz, Sam. *A. Merritt: Reflections in the Moon Pool; A Biography.* Philadelphia: 1985.

———. *Under the Moons of Mars: A History and Anthology of "The Scientific Romance" in the Munsey Magazines, 1912–1920.* New York: 1970.

Neumann, Erich. *Amor and Psyche: The Psychic Development of the Feminine.* Trans. Ralph Manheim. Princeton, N.J.: 1956.

———. *The Great Mother: An Analysis of the Archetype* [1955]. Trans. Ralph Manheim. 2d ed. Princeton, N.J.: 1963.

———. *The Origins and History of Consciousness.* Trans. R. F. C. Hull. Princeton, N.J.: 1954.

New York Times Film Reviews (1913–1968). 6 vols. New York: 1970

Nietzsche Friedrich. *The Philosophy of Nietzsche*. Ed. Geoffrey Clive. New York: 1965. (The material quoted in the text is from Nietzsche's *Thoughts Out of Season*, vol. II.)

Nolan, William F., ed. *The Black Mask Boys: Masters in the Hard-Boiled School of Detective Fiction*. New York: 1985.

Nordau, Max. *Conversational Lies of Our Civilization*. Chicago: 1886.

———. *Degeneration* [1893]. New York: 1895.

———. *The Interpretation of History*. New York: 1910.

Nova, Fritz. *Alfred Rosenberg, Nazi Theorist of the Holocaust*. New York: 1986.

Olmsted, J. M. D. *Charles-Edouard Brown-Séquard: A Nineteenth Century Neurologist and Endocrinologist*. Baltimore, Md.: 1946.

Ortega y Gasset, José. *On Love: Aspects of a Single Theme*. Trans. Toby Talbot. New York: 1957.

Palumbo, Donald. *Eros in the Mind's Eye: Sexuality and the Fantastic in Art and Film*. Westport, Conn.: 1986.

Panofsky, Dora, and Erwin Panofsky. *Pandora's Box: The Changing Aspects of a Mythical Symbol*. 2d rev. ed. New York: 1965.

Paris, Barry. *Garbo: A Biography*. New York: 1994.

———. *Louise Brooks*. New York: 1989.

Pendennis, "My Women Types—Robert W. Chambers." *The Forum* 59 (May 1918): 564–9.

Poliakov, Leon. *The History of Anti-Semitism*. Vol. 4, *Suicidal Europe, 1870–1933*. New York: 1985.

Porges, Irwin. *Edgar Rice Burroughs, The Man Who Created Tarzan* [1975]. 2 vols. New York: 1976.

Potter, Margaret Horton. *Istar of Babylon*. New York: 1902.

Ramsaye, Terry. *A Million and One Nights*. 2 vols. New York: 1926.

Reik, Theodor. *On Love and Lust: On the Psychoanalysis of Romantic and Sexual Emotions*. New York: 1941.

———. *Psychology of Sex Relations*. New York: 1945.

Review of *A Fool There Was*, by Porter Emerson Browne, stage version. *The Theatre* 9, no. 99 (May 1909): 135–6.

Rhodes, Frederick A. *The Next Generation*. Boston: 1915.

Richardson, Alan, ed. *A Theological Word Book of the Bible*. New York: 1951.

Richet, Charles. *Idiot Man, or The Follies of Mankind*. New York: n.d.

Ringgold, Gene, and DeWitt Bodeen. *The Films of Cecil B. De Mille*. New York: 1969.

Robinson, William J. *Married Life and Happiness, or Love and Comfort in Marriage*. New York: 1922.

———. *Sexual Truths Versus Sexual Lies, Misconceptions and Exaggerations* [1919]. New York: 1932.

———. *Woman, Her Sex and Love Life* [1917]. Enl. ed. New York: 1938.

Roheim, Geza. "Aphrodite, or the Woman with a Penis" [1945]. In *Panic of the Gods and Other Essays*, ed. Werner Muensterberger. New York: 1972.

Rohmer, Sax [Ward, Arthur Sarsfield]. *Daughter of Fu Manchu* [1931]. New York: 1964.

———. *Four Complete Classics: "The Hand of Fu Manchu" ["The Si-Fan Mysteries," 1917], "The Return of Dr. Fu Manchu" ["The Devil Doctor," 1916], "The Yellow Claw" [1915], "Dope" [1919].* New York: 1983.

———. *The Green Eyes of Bâst.* New York: 1920.

———. *The Hand of Fu Manchu.* See *Four Complete Classics.*

———. *The Insidious Dr. Fu Manchu (The Mystery of Fu Manchu, 1913).* New York: 1961.

———. *The Return of Dr. Fu Manchu.* See *Four Complete Classics.*

———. *The Yellow Claw.* See *Four Complete Classics.*

Ronay, Gabriel. *The Dracula Myth.* New York: 1972.

Rosen, Marjorie. *Popcorn Venus: Women, Movies and the American Dream.* New York: 1973.

Rosenberg, Alfred. *Blut und Ehre: Ein Kampf für deutsche Wiedergeburt.* Munich: 1936.

———. *Der Mythus des 20. Jahrhunderts; Eine Wertung der seelisch-geistigen Gestalten-kämpfe unserer Zeit.* Munich: 1930.

Ross, Edward Alsworth. *The Old World in the New; The Significance of Past and Present Immigration to the American People.* New York: 1914.

———. *The Principles of Sociology.* New York: 1920.

Ruch, Theodore C. "Charles Edouard Brown-Séquard (1817–1894)." *Yale Journal of Biology and Medicine* 18, no. 4 (1946): 227–38.

Russett, Cynthia Eagle. *Darwin in America: The Intellectual Response, 1865–1912.* San Francisco: 1976.

———. *Sexual Science: The Victorian Construction of Womanhood.* Cambridge, Mass.: 1989.

Ryan, Alan. *Vampires: Two Centuries of Great Vampire Stories.* Garden City, N.Y.: 1987. Also issued in paperback as *The Penguin Book of Vampire Stories.* New York: 1988.

Sadler, William S. *Race Decadence; An Examination of the Causes of Racial Degeneracy in the United States.* Chicago: 1922.

Saleeby, Caleb Williams. *Parenthood and Race Culture: An Outline of Eugenics.* New York: 1916.

Sampson, Robert D. *Deadly Excitements: Phantoms & Shadows.* Bowling Green, Ohio: 1989.

———. *Yesterday's Faces: A Study of Series Characters in the Early Pulp Magazines.* 4 vols. Bowling Green, Ohio: 1984–7.

Sanger, Margaret. *The Pivot of Civilization.* New York: 1922.

Sangster, Margaret E. *Winsome Womanhood: Familiar Talks on Life and Conduct.* New York: 1900.

Sexton, M. H. *Matrimony Minus Maternity.* New York: 1922.

Seymour-Smith, Martin. *Rudyard Kipling.* London: 1989.

Shaw, Leslie Mortimer. *Vanishing Landmarks: The Trend Toward Bolshevism.* Chicago: 1919.

Shipman, David. *The Story of the Cinema—An Illustrated History.* Vol. 1, *From the Beginnings to "Gone With the Wind."* London: 1982.

Shirer, William L. *The Rise and Fall of the Third Reich.* New York: 1960.

Showalter, Elaine. *Sexual Anarchy: Gender and Culture at the Fin de Siècle.* New York: 1990.

Silver, Alain, and James Ursini. *The Vampire Film from "Nosferatu" to Bram Stoker's "Dracula."* Rev. ed. New York: 1993.

Sinclair, Upton. *William Fox.* Los Angeles: 1933.

Skal, David J. *Hollywood Gothic: The Tangled Web of "Dracula" from Novel to Stage to Screen.* New York: 1990.

————. *The Monster Show: A Cultural History of Horror.* New York: 1993.

Slide, Anthony. "A Fool There Was." In *Magill's Survey of Cinema: Silent Films.* Vol. 2. New York: 1982.

Smith, Clark Ashton. *The Devil's Notebook.* Mercer Island, Wash.: 1990.

Spengler, Oswald. *The Decline of the West: Form and Actuality* [1918]. Trans. Charles Francis Atkinson. New York: 1926.

————. *Jahre der Entscheidung; Erster Teil: Deutschland und die weltgeschichtliche Entwicklung.* Munich: 1933.

Spillane, Mickey. *Five Complete Mike Hammer Novels: I, The Jury* [1947]; *Vengeance Is Mine* [1950]; *The Big Kill* [1951]; *My Gun Is Quick* [1951]; *Kiss Me Deadly* [1952]. New York: 1987.

Sterling, George. *Lilith; A Dramatic Poem.* New York: 1926.

Stern, Karl. *The Flight from Woman.* London: 1966.

Sternberg, Jacques. *Les Chefs d'oeuvre du kitsch.* Paris: 1971.

Stewart, Walter A. *Psychoanalysis, The First Ten Years, 1888–1898.* London: 1969.

Stoddard, Lothrop. *The Revolt Against Civilization: The Menace of the Under Man.* New York: 1922.

————. *The Rising Tide of Color Against White World-Supremacy.* New York: 1920.

Stoker, Bram. *Dracula* [1897]. New York: 1965.

————. *The Lair of the White Worm.* London: 1911.

Stopes, Marie Carmichael. *Contraception (Birth Control): Its Theory, History and Practice; A Manual for the Medical and Legal Professions* [1923]. Enl. ed. London: 1931.

————. *Enduring Passion* [1928]. 5th ed. London: 1934.

————. *Married Love: Or Love in Marriage* [1918]. New York: 1927.

————. *Married Love: A New Contribution to the Solution of Sex Difficulties.* Rev. ed. of 1918 work. New York: 1931.

Stout, Rex. *Under the Andes.* New York: 1984. Originally published in *The All Story Magazine* (February 1914).

Streatfield, D. *Persephone: A Study of Two Worlds.* New York: 1959.

Stroheim, Erich von. *Greed.* Ed. Joel W. Finler [1925]. London: 1972.

————. *Paprika* [1937]. Universal Giant Edition no. 2. New York: 1952.

Sullivan, Jack, ed. *The Penguin Encyclopedia of Horror and the Supernatural.* New York: 1986.

Sumner, William Graham. *The Challenge of Facts and Other Essays.* New Haven, Conn.: 1914.

————. *Earth-Hunger and Other Essays.* New Haven, Conn.: 1913.

————. *Essays.* Ed. Albert G. Keller. 2 vols. New Haven, Conn.: 1911.

————. *Folkways: A Study of the Sociological Importance of Usages, Manners, Customs, Mores, and Morals.* Boston: 1907.

———. *The Forgotten Man and Other Essays.* Ed. Albert Galloway Keller. New Haven, Conn.: 1919.

———. *Social Darwinism; Selected Essays.* With an introduction by Stow Persons. Englewood Cliffs, N.J.: 1963.

———. *War and Other Essays.* Ed. Albert Galloway Keller. New Haven, Conn.: 1911.

———. *What Social Classes Owe to Each Other.* New York: 1883.

Swinburne, Algernon Charles. "Laus Veneris." In *Collected Poetical Works.* 2 vols. London: 1924.

Talmey, Bernard S., M.D. *Love: A Treatise on the Science of Sex-Attraction for the Use of Physicians and Students of Medical Jurisprudence.* 2d rev. ed. New York: 1916.

Taylor, Brandon, and Wilfried van der Will. *The Nazification of Art, Art Design, Music, Architecture and Film in the Third Reich.* Winchester, England: 1990.

Theweleit, Klaus. *Male Fantasies.* Vol. 1, *Women, Floods, Bodies, History.* Trans. Stephen Conway, in collaboration with Erica Carter and Chris Turner. Minneapolis: 1987.

———. *Male Fantasies.* Vol. 2, *Male Bodies; Psychoanalyzing the White Terror.* Trans. Erica Carter and Chris Turner, in collaboration with Stephen Conway. Minneapolis: 1989.

Thornton, E. M. *The Freudian Fallacy; An Alternative View of Freudian Theory.* Garden City, N.Y.: 1984.

Thurer, Shari L. *The Myths of Motherhood: How Culture Reinvents the Good Mother.* Boston: 1994.

Tyler, John M. *Man in the Light of Evolution.* New York: 1908.

Variety Film Reviews (1907–1980). 16 vols. New York: 1983.

Veblen, Thorstein. *Theory of the Leisure Class* [1899]. With an introduction by John Kenneth Galbraith. London: 1973.

Velde, Th. H. van de, M.D. *Ideal Marriage: Its Physiology and Technique* [1926]. New York: 1930.

———. *Sex Hostility in Marriage: Its Origin, Prevention and Treatment* [1928]. New York: 1931.

Viereck, George Sylvester. *The House of the Vampire.* New York: 1907.

Viereck, George Sylvester, and Paul Eldridge. *My First Two Thousand Years: The Autobiography of the Wandering Jew.* New York: 1928.

———. *Salome, the Wandering Jewess: My First Two Thousand Years of Love.* New York: 1930.

Voronoff, Serge. *The Conquest of Life.* New York: 1928.

Voss, Heinrich. *Franz von Stuck: 1863–1928; Werkkatalog der Gemalde, mit einer Einführung in seinen Symbolismus.* Munich: 1973.

Waite, Robert G. L. *The Psychopathic God: Adolf Hitler.* New York: 1977.

Wall, O. A. *Sex and Sex Worship (Phallic Worship).* St. Louis: 1918.

Ward, Henshaw. *Evolution for John Doe.* Indianapolis: 1925.

Ward, Lester F. *Dynamic Sociology, or Applied Social Science, as Based Upon Statistical Sociology and the Less Complex Sciences.* 2 vols. New York: 1883.

———. *Pure Sociology: A Treatise on the Origin and Spontaneous Development of Society* [1903]. 2d ed. New York: 1907.

Wedekind, Frank. *The Lulu Plays and Other Sex Tragedies.* Trans. Stephen Spender. London:, 1972.

Weinberg, Robert. *The Weird Tales Story.* West Linn, Oreg.: 1977.

Weininger, Otto. *Sex and Character* [1903]. London: [1906].

———. *Ueber die letzten Dinge.* Vienna: 1904.

Weiss, Andrea. *Vampires & Violets: Lesbians in Film.* New York: 1992.

Weiss, Sheila Faith. *Race Hygiene and National Efficiency: The Eugenics of Wilhelm Schallmayer.* Berkeley, Calif.: 1987.

Westropp, Hodder M., and C. Staniland Wake. *Ancient Symbol Worship: Influence of the Phallic Idea in the Religions of Antiquity.* 2d ed., illustrated. New York: 1875.

Wharton, Edith. *The House of Mirth* [1905]. Ed. Cynthia Griffin Wolff. New York: 1985.

Wiggam, Albert Edward. *The Fruit of the Family Tree.* Indianapolis: 1924.

Williams, William Carlos. *A Voyage to Pagany.* New York: 1928.

———. "Woman as Operator," in *A Recognizable Image: William Carlos Williams on Art and Artists,* ed. Bram Dijkstra. New York: 1978, 180–3.

Williamson, Jack. "The Wand of Doom." In *Weird Tales, 32 Unearthed Terrors,* ed. Stefan R. Dziemianowicz, Robert Weinberg, and Martin Greenberg. New York: 1988. (Originally published in *Weird Tales* 20, no. 4 (October 1932).

———. *Wonder's Child: My Life in Science Fiction.* New York: 1984.

Willrich, Wolfgang. *Sauberung des Kunsttempels.* Munich: 1937.

Wolf, Leonard, ed. *The Essential Dracula.* New York: 1993.

Wood-Allen, Mary, M.D. *What a Young Girl Ought to Know.* Philadelphia: 1897.

Woody, Jack, ed. *Lost Hollywood.* Altadena, Calif.: 1987.

Wright, Henry C. *Marriage and Parentage: The Reproductive Element in Man, as a Means to His Elevation and Happiness.* 2d ed. Boston: 1855.

Wu, William F. *The Yellow Peril; Chinese Americans in American Fiction, 1850–1940.* Hamden, Conn.: 1982.

Wulf, Joseph. *Die Bildenden Kunste im Dritten Reich.* Gütersloh: 1963.

Wylie, Philip. *Generation of Vipers.* New York: 1942.

———. *Sons and Daughters of Mom.* Garden City, N.Y.: 1971.

Zierold, Norman. *Sex Goddesses of the Silent Screen.* Chicago: 1973.

INDEX

ILLUSTRATION CREDITS

frontispiece: Copyright 1986 Sotheby's, Inc.

page 8: Reprinted by permission of Contemporary Books, Inc., Chicago.

23: From *Fidus 1868–1948: Zur aesthetischen bürgerlicher Flüchtbewegungen.* Rogner & Bernhard, Munich, 1972.

48: From *Die Kunst für Alle,* volume 24 (1908–1909).

61: Unidentified turn-of-the-century magazine photograph.

65: From *Great Magazine Covers of the World,* Abbeville Press, New York, 1982.

82 (left): From *The Art of 1897,* supplement to *The Studio,* London, 1897. (right): Cover of *A Fool There Was,* The H. K. Fly Company, Publishers, New York, 1909.

126, 213, and 215: Copyright Alfred Kubin (Verwerungdgesellschaft, Bild Kunst, Poppelsdorfer Allee 43, D-53115, Bonn). Reprinted by permission of Graphische Sammlung Albertina, Vienna, Austria.

135: From *Die Kunst,* volume 25, 1912.

147: Cover of *Amazing Stories,* October 1949.

162: Oesterreichische Galerie, Vienna. From *Gustav Klimt, 1862–1918: The World in Female Form,* 1989. Benedikt Taschen Verlag, Cologne.

174: From *Jugend,* 1903, no. 51.

218: C. Allan Gilbert, popular print.

223: From the original cover of *Look* magazine.

242: Reprinted by permission of Muller & Kiepenheuer Verlag KG.

244: Etching by August Brömse.

257: From a cover of *Life* magazine, January 19, 1922.

260: From a cover of *Weird Tales,* December 1933.

272: From *Witness to History: The Jewish Poster 1770–1985.* Judah Magnes Museum, Berkeley, Calif., 1989.

277: From The Kobal Collection.

292: Cover of *Amazing Stories,* September 1927.

310: Copyright Edition Leipzig, 1986. From *The Illustrated History of Science Fiction,* Ungar Publishing Co., New York.

314: From *L'Illustration,* Paris, no. 2514, May 2, 1891.

315: From *The Films of Cecil B. De Mille.* Citadel Press, New York, 1969.

328: From *Die Kunst,* vol. 23, 1908.

330: From *The Man and His Pictures.* A. S. Barnes and Co., Inc., 1970.

348: Handbill reprinted in *Life* magazine, March 6, 1939.

386: From original cover of *Best True Fact Detective,* July 1948.

392: Reprinted by permission of David J. Skal, from David J. Skal, *Hollywood Gothic: The Tangled Web of Dracula from Novel to Screen.* W. W. Norton, New York, 1990.

411: From *German Film and Literature: Adaptations and Transformations,* ed. Eric Rentschler. Methuen, New York, 1986.

423 (top): From *Die Kunst im Dritten Reich,* vol. 7, no. 11, 1943.
(bottom): Copyright 1948 by Street and Smith Publications, Inc. Reprinted by permission of Dell Magazines, a division of Crosstown Publications.

430: Reprinted by permission of Bundesarchiv Koblenz.

436: From *Franz von Stuck: Das Gesamtwerk,* Munich, 1909.

437: Permission to reprint granted by Lenbachhaus, Munich.

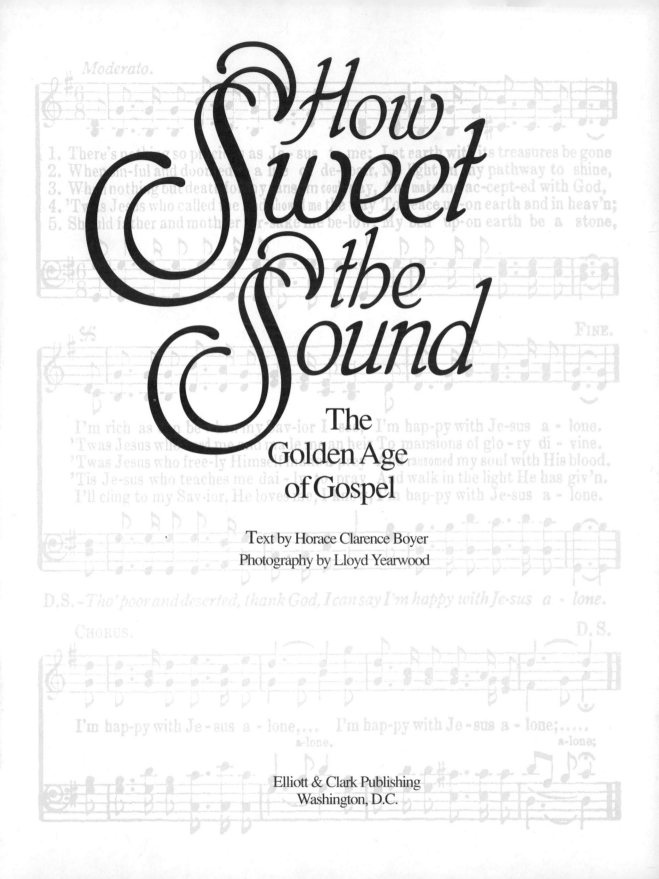

How Sweet the Sound

The Golden Age of Gospel

Text by Horace Clarence Boyer
Photography by Lloyd Yearwood

Elliott & Clark Publishing
Washington, D.C.

To my dear wife of thirty years, Gloria.
With heartfelt thanks to Eugene Smith and
my brother, James B. Boyer
—H.C.B.

Dedicated to my father Livingston Yearwood and
his deep concern for righteous living.
—L.Y.

Designed by Gibson Parsons Design
Edited by Maureen Graney
Printed in Hong Kong through Mandarin Offset

Any inquiries should be directed to:
Elliott & Clark Publishing, P.O. Box 21038, Washington, DC 20009-0538
Telephone (202) 387-9805

Table of Contents

The stars of the Ward Singers,
Clara Ward and Marion Williams

African American Sacred Folk Music: 1755–1945

n 1969 Edwin Hawkins, an Oakland, California, based pianist and choir director of the Church of God in Christ, reworked the nineteenth-century white Baptist hymn "O Happy Day" by Philip Doddridge (1702–51) and Edward Rimbault (1816–76). By placing the hymn in a bouncy tempo, emphasizing its inherent rhythmic possibilities with a drum set and congo drums, featuring the solo voice of a golden toned alto backed by a youthful-sounding energetic choir, and supporting the entire ensemble with piano accompaniment in a style that combined the harmonic variety of a Duke Ellington and the soulful accentuation of a Ray Charles, Hawkins (b. 1943) moved gospel into a new category. When the song was released on Buddah Records it quickly became number one on the Top Forty music chart, and gospel music, for more than sixty years the principal sacred music of many African American churches, became part of American popular music. Hawkins had synthesized not only what earlier great gospel musicians had developed but the entire sacred singing tradition of African Americans since they adopted Christianity, without which there would not be gospel music.

Early Sacred Singing

While a small number of slaves worshipped with their masters or attended services especially arranged for them as early as the seventeenth century, a larger number of slaves were converted to Christianity during the Great Awakening, the first great religious movement in the United States. The Great Awakening began as early as 1734 in New England (although reports of evangelical preaching in New Jersey surfaced in the 1720s). The leader of the New England movement, Jonathan Edwards (1703–58), was a forceful preacher who espoused logic, humility, and absolute dependence on God and divine grace, which alone could save a person. The fervent zeal Edwards demanded of his followers required a much livelier music than the slow, languorous long-meter hymns that were traditional. The music produced by the Great Awakening was the hymns that used text by such hymnists as Isaac Watts (1674–1748), whose significant publications include *Hymns and Spiritual Songs* (1707) and *The Psalms of David, Imitated in the Language of the New Testament and Apply'd to the Christian State and Worship* (1717); John Wesley (1703–91), who with his brother Charles (1707–88), founded the Methodist church in 1729 and who published *Collection of Psalms and Hymns* (1737) and *Hymns and Sacred Poems* (1739); and George Whitefield (1714–70), who published *A Collection of Hymns for Social Worship* (1753; 1765).

None were more eloquent in their hymns than Watts, who, for his 1707 publication of *Hymns and Spiritual Songs*, wrote:

> *Come, Holy Spirit, heavenly dove,*
> *With all Thy quickening powers;*
> *Kindle a flame of sacred love*
> *In these cold hearts of ours.*

Although mostly a New England and eastern religious movement, the fervor of the Great Awakening overtook the entire United States and had a profound effect on southern states, where attending church, reading the Bible, singing hymns, and a comportment of piety became the mark of a Christian. Slaves were permitted to attend these services with their masters, although they were seated in separate sections. Some slave owners arranged special services for their slaves during which the white minister who preached to slave owners in the morning would preach to

the slaves in the afternoon. Although the slaves sang like their masters when they attended services with them, reports of slaves singing sacred music independently began to surface in the 1750s. One of the earliest reports was based on letters sent in 1755 to church members in London by the Reverend Samuel Davies (1723–61), in which he comments on the singing of slaves in Virginia:

> *The books were all very acceptable, but none more so than the Psalms and Hymns, which enable them [the slaves] to gratify their peculiar taste for psalmody. Sundry of them have lodged all night in my kitchen, and sometimes when I have awaked about two or three-o'clock in the morning, a torrent of sacred harmony has poured into my chamber and carried my mind away to heaven. In this seraphic exercise some of them spend almost the whole night.*

The slaves were likely singing from one of the books of the Reverend Dr. Watts or from Wesley's 1737 hymn book. The style of singing would have been "lining out," a practice established in the United States in the 1640s. Adopted from the Church of England, this practice featured a song leader (precentor), minister, or church clerk singing (or reciting) each line of the hymn, immediately followed by the singing of the line by the congregation:

> *Leader: Praise God, from whom all blessings flow;*
> **Congregation: Praise God, from whom all blessings flow;**
> *Leader: Praise Him all creatures here below;*
> **Congregation: Praise Him all creatures here below;**
> *Leader: Praise Him above ye heavenly host;*
> **Congregation: Praise Him above ye heavenly host;**
> *Leader: Praise Father, Son, and Holy Ghost.*
> **Congregation: Praise Father, Son, and Holy Ghost.**

Among the slaves, lining out was called "raising" a hymn. The hymn would be raised by a minister ("exhorter" in slave language) or a devout male member of the community (who would later be called a deacon in the Baptist church or a steward in the Methodist church). Instead of singing the lines of the hymns as they were written or reciting them in an oratorical manner, the leader would chant the lines, often chanting two lines at a time to a tune unrelated to the tune the congregation would

sing. The congregation then sang the lines, decorating them with bends, slurs, slides, and held tones. The congregation would match or surpass the leader in ornamentation, although such songs were sung in a harmony composed of parallel intervals. This ancient style of harmony was reminiscent of that practiced in Western Europe during the ninth century.

The African American Methodist church replaced these hymns with standard Protestant hymns. However, raising hymns continued in the African American Baptist church, and the song type and genre are known today as Baptist lining hymns.

Around the turn of the nineteenth century, a new type of song entered the repertoire of African American sacred music. This new music was inspired by the second great religious movement in the United States. Variously called the Second Great Awakening, the Camp Meeting Revival, and the Revival Movement, this movement began in 1800 in Logan County, Kentucky. (However, reports show that its earliest activities date back to 1780.) According to Richard M'Near who chronicled the 1800 and 1801 services in the *Kentucky Revival* (1808):

A gospel concert flyer

> *Neither was there any distinction as to age, sex, color, or anything of temporary nature; old and young, male and female, black and white, has equal opportunity to minister the light which they received in whatever way the spirit directed.*

These nineteenth-century services, according to M'Near, encouraged singing, shouting, and leaping for joy. The music that promoted such behavior was the newer hymns with a certain "lilt and rhythm" and shaped-note melodies. Among the most popular of the revival hymnals were *Repository of Sacred, Part Second* (1813) by John Wyeth (1770–1858), *Village Hymns for Social Worship* (1824) by Asahel Nettleton (1783–1844), and *Spiritual Songs for Social Worship* (1831; 1833) by Lowell Mason (1792–1872) and Thomas Hastings (1787–1872).

According to John Fanning Watson, who published *Methodist Error or Friendly Christian Advice to Those Methodists Who Indulge in Extravagant Religious Emotions and Bodily Exercises* (1819), slaves would gather in their quarters at these meetings and:

> *sing for hours together, short scraps of disjointed affirmations, pledges, or prayers, lengthened out with long repetition choruses.*

Often unified by the inclusion of the word "hallelujah," these songs became known as camp meeting spirituals. William Frances Allen and colleagues recorded the following camp meeting spiritual in the 1867 publication *Slave Songs of the United States*:

> *What ship is that you're enlisted upon?*
> *O glory hallelujah!*
> *Tis the old ship of Zion, hallelujah!*
> *Tis the old ship of Zion, hallelujah!*

These songs were obviously set to a marching or sprightly tempo because Watson noted that:

> *With every word so sung, they have a sinking of one or other leg of the body alternately; producing an audible sound of the feet at every step, and as manifest as the steps of actual negro [sic] dancing in Virginia, etc.*

This stamping was called "shouting," a term used exclusively for this holy dancing, whether singly or with a group. In most instances such dancing was performed in a circle and has come to be known as the "ring shout." It is worth noting that the slaves did not shout with their voices but rather with their feet, reserving the voice for hollering or yelling. While African Americans may certainly have accompanied their sacred singing with body rhythm before the observation of the shout, singing in the African American church would henceforth include rocking or moving in time to the singing. The group shout did not continue long after the turn of the twentieth century, although according to James Weldon Johnson in the preface to his 1925 edition of *American Negro spirituals*, secret shout services were still being held in the first decade of this century.

The Camp Meeting Revival may have inspired other musical creations among the slaves, because shortly after the opening of this movement, a different type of spiritual surfaced in the slave community. Unlike the camp meeting spiritual with its emphasis on scriptural passages and praising God, the new music took on an extremely personal character. These religious folksongs, called Negro spirituals, not only spoke of the slaves' relationship to God but also gave special attention to their position on earth and the difficult fate that had befallen them. The songs combined

a recognition of the power of God and thanks for life, health, and strength, but more important they expressed the slaves' feelings about oppression, discrimination, and the struggle to survive. As such, references to sorrows, woes, hard trials, and the rewards they expected to receive in the next world were common themes. This is nowhere more poignantly expressed than in:

> *Nobody knows the trouble I see,*
> *Nobody knows my sorrow;*
> *Nobody knows the trouble I see,*
> *Glory, hallelujah.*

When life was extremely difficult for slaves they used these songs to inspire inner courage, for they had decided that freedom would come one day, either through emancipation or death:

> *Steal away, steal away,*
> *Steal away to Jesus;*
> *Steal away, steal away home,*
> *I ain't got long to stay here.*

So convinced were the slaves that they would be rewarded eventually for their trials on earth that they imagined what heaven would be like:

> *Plenty good room, plenty good room*
> *Good room in my father's kingdom;*
> *Plenty good room, plenty good room*
> *Just choose your seat and sit down.*

Feeling that they had no black heroes in the Bible and obviously unaware of other contemporary people who might be experiencing a similar slavery, the slaves adopted Old Testament heroes and celebrated them in song, often replacing the Israelites with themselves. Moses became the abolitionist and Pharaoh became the slave owner in:

> *Go down, Moses, way down in Egypt's land,*
> *Tell old Pharaoh to let my people go.*

"Joshua Fit [Fought] the Battle of Jericho," "Ezekiel Saw the Wheel," "Rock My Soul in the Bosom of Abraham," and "We Are Climbing Jacob's Ladder" are but a few of such songs. These heroes were often used to make direct supplication to God:

> *Didn't my Lord deliver Daniel?*
> *Deliver Daniel, deliver Daniel?*
> *Didn't my Lord deliver Daniel?*
> *Then why not deliver poor me?*

When slaves finally had a strong feeling that earthly freedom would eventually be theirs, especially around the middle of the nineteenth century, songs of celebration expressed their anticipation:

> *In that great gettin' up morning,*
> *Fare ye well, fare ye well;*
> *In that great gettin' up morning,*
> *Fare ye well, fare ye well.*

It was not the sophistication of the text nor the brilliance of the melody and harmony of these songs, most often consisting of a verse and chorus, that so inspired the slaves and caused wonderment among white listeners. Rather it was the release and satisfaction that the songs brought to the singer. Melodies had only a few tones, often as few as five, and were laden with blue (or flatted) notes that would later serve as one of the principal elements of the blues. Harmonies were those of Protestant hymns, but rhythms were the intricate patterns remembered from Africa. Singers made no pretense of placing the voice "in the head," as was the practice of European singing masters, but chose the voice of those "crying in the wilderness." While there were songs in which text was sung by everyone at the same time, the most characteristic practice was to divide the song into a part for the leader and a part for the other singers:

> *Leader: Have you got good religion?*
>   ***Others: Certainly, Lord,***
> *Leader: Have you got good religion?*
>   ***Others: Certainly, Lord,***

Leader: Have you got good religion?
        Others: Certainly, Lord, certainly, certainly, certainly, Lord.

The part taken by the leader was later named the "call," while that taken by the other singers was labeled the "response."

While it is known that these songs were used in work, religious meetings, and times of leisure as well as for teaching young and old the stories of the Bible and the values of the slave community, it is unknown exactly how and when they were composed. William Frances Allen, in *Slave Songs of the United States* (1867), reported the often quoted account given by a former slave:

> *My master call me up, and order me a short peck of corn and a hundred lash. My friends see it, and is sorry for me. When dey come to de praise-meeting dat night dey sing about it. Some's very good singers and know how; and dey work it in—work it in, you know, till they get it right; and dat's de way.*

Eileen Southern, author of *Black American Music: A History* (1983), supports the belief that many of these songs might have been composed first by congregations in northern African American churches. These congregations used the *sense* of some of the Protestant hymns and reworked the text to fit their needs but supplied original melody and harmony. In either case, the Negro spiritual not only shaped the composition and singing style of African American sacred music, but also became the first music considered "American" by people outside the United States.

THE AZUSA STREET REVIVAL
AND THE BIRTH OF PENTECOSTALISM

There was no great religious movement at the beginning of the twentieth century on the eastern seaboard, but California witnessed a series of religious meetings unlike any ever held before in the United States. This movement was called the Azusa Street Movement or Azusa Street Revival for the street where the church meetings were held.

A revival is a series of consecutive nightly church services for which, in most cases, a well known minister is brought in to preach and to provide religious counseling for church members or those seeking conversion from sin. Special choirs or

singing groups are sometimes imported, or the resident church choir provides music for each service. Since the services are designed to revive the current membership and attract new members, one of the important features of the revival is the "altar call." During this part of the service, those who have decided to join the church or seek membership through counseling or instruction come to the altar or, in sanctuaries where there is no altar, to the railing that would normally enclose the altar and kneel or stand to be welcomed by the visiting minister and the resident preacher. In earlier days specific benches or chairs ("mourners' benches") were provided where those seeking membership would sit. (Such seats were always located in the front of the church very near the pulpit or lectern, close to the preacher.) Most revivals are held for only one week, although some congregations hold two-week revivals. A nightly collection is taken in order to pay the preacher for his service.

The Azusa Street Revival, however, differed from previous revivals in four very important ways: the movement was initiated by and for African Americans; the principal element of becoming "saved, sanctified, and filled with the Holy Ghost" depended on the experience of "speaking in tongues"; African Americans invited white people into the service and insisted on complete interracial participation; and the principal music produced by the revival reflected African American religious concerns and musical sensibilities.

Although the 1906 Azusa Street Revival was initially a series of services by and for African Americans, the seeds of the revival were planted as early as 1867 when a small group of white Methodists, seeking a perfect relationship with Christ, organized the National Camp Meeting Association for the Promotion of Holiness with the goal of discovering "spiritual perfection." The zeal of this Holiness faction soon embarrassed and antagonized the larger body of Methodists. By 1903 Charles Parham (1873–1929), a leading minister in the faction, opened a Bible school in Houston to teach the tenets of this new theology. Despite the complete segregation of Parham's classes and religious services (African Americans had to sit outside the classroom and at the back of the room or outdoors at services), the new theology began to attract a few African Americans. One of the first was William Joseph Seymour (1870–1922), who learned of Parham's work from the Reverend Mrs. Lucy F. Farrow, an African American minister of the Holiness church.

In 1906 Neely Terry, who met Seymour while he was studying with Parham,

contacted Seymour and asked him to come to Los Angeles to serve as pastor of her twenty-member congregation of Holiness members. The invitation came at a time when there was a very small network of African Americans who believed in the Holiness movement. The Baptist and Methodist churches had served the needs of African Americans as far back as slavery, and by the turn of the century when these congregations were constructing their own church buildings and calling ministers from throughout the United States to serve as their pastors, it was not unusual for a Holiness preacher to relocate to a city thousands of miles away if he or she could minister to a faithful flock. The social situation in the South also contributed to physical movement. The Ku Klux Klan was conducting its night rides throughout the South, Jim Crow laws or practices were already in place in several towns, and the North, Midwest, and West were being touted as places where African Americans could find equality. These factors must have impressed Seymour for he accepted Neely's invitation.

When he arrived in Los Angeles (either in late February or early March of 1906), he preached Holiness and divine healing. Seymour was accepted with enthusiasm and gratitude by his small flock. His popularity began to spread in Los Angeles, which inspired him to introduce a doctrine in which he had long believed: baptism with the Holy Ghost, manifested by speaking in tongues. His belief was based on the description of Pentecost in Acts 2:4, which describes the activities of Christ's disciples fifty days after the Crucifixion when the Holy Ghost descended upon a gathering in the form of tongues of fire accompanied by the sound of the wind "rushing." Everyone present received the power to speak in a language understood by each member of the multilingual crowd. In the modern version of speaking in tongues, or glossolalia, the language is unknown, except to one or more of the group anointed to translate the message.

Seymour began a series of sermons that addressed this tenet. On April 9, 1906, he found a true believer with the manifested sanctification of Jennie Evans (1893–1936). Jennie Evans, whom Seymour married in 1908, had "come through"—she had been saved, sanctified, and filled with the Holy Ghost. She was saved when she made a conscious decision to lay aside "every weight that so easily beset" humans and to serve the Lord, treat her fellow human beings as children of God, pray constantly, and walk in a path that would lead to heaven after death. She became sanc-

tified when she chose to consecrate herself and live free from sin (or at least to make a great effort to do so). And she was filled with the Holy Ghost when her relationship to God and Jesus reached such a point of ecstasy that she was able to allow the Lord to speak through her in a tongue that has never been translatable. This incident was not the first time that speaking in tongues had been practiced (J. T. Nichols, in the book *Black Pentecostalism* (1982), reported that this phenomenon was quite common among those who "received the fire.") However, this was the first entire church doctrine that was based on speaking in tongues as proof that one had received the Holy Ghost.

Word of Jennie Evans' "coming through" spread quickly throughout Los Angeles and then to other parts of the United States. Crowds flocked to Seymour's church, the Apostolic Faith Gospel Mission, located at 312 Azusa Street, with people "falling under the spell of the Holy Ghost" in great numbers. *The Apostolic Faith*, a newspaper published by Seymour and his congregation, carried such headlines as "Los Angeles Being Visited by a Revival of Bible Salvation and Pentecost as Recorded in the Book of Acts" and "The Promised Latter Rain Now Being Poured Out on God's People."

1906 edition of **The Apostolic Faith**

While Seymour used the word "apostolic" in the name of his church, he considered himself and his congregation Pentecostal, distinct from Holiness congregations that did not believe that tongue speaking was necessary for entry into heaven. Pentecostalists also shouted (a holy dance, mentioned in Psalm 149:3), indulged in the act of humility (washed one another's feet, based on John 13:5), and experienced visions and trances. Such was the character of the services of the Azusa Street Revival.

It is ironic that while the African Americans of the Azusa Street Revival invited white people into the revival and treated them as religious equals, social racism eventually split the group into black and white congregations. Parham, a white man, had been Seymour's teacher and mentor. However, although Parham believed in sanctification, he did not like the emotionalism associated with speaking in tongues and would not advocate it in his preaching. Parham and many of the white attend-

ees withdrew in 1908, and Parham participated in the formation of the white Pentecostal congregation, the Assemblies of God, founded in Hot Springs, Arkansas, in 1914.

While the theology and practices of the Azusa Street Revival were new, they were in no way comparable with the unique music that accompanied these services. As members of the congregation "came through," they would celebrate their victory with a song. The congregation witnessed singing in tongues, much of which was never translated into English. *The Apostolic Faith* of September 1906 carried an article entitled "Holy Ghost Singing." The article stated that a song in an unknown tongue was interpreted as follows:

> *With one accord, all heaven rings*
> *With praises to our God and King*
> *Let earth join in our song of praise*
> *And ring it out through all the days.*

Beginning in the last quarter of the nineteenth century, white composers began publishing gospel hymns that were strictly organized with eight bars to the verse and eight bars to the chorus. The melodies were simple but attractive, and the rhythms were marked by an abundance of dotted eighth notes. Perhaps the most interesting aspect of these hymns was the pairing of soprano and alto against tenor and bass, with the female voices singing alternately with the male voices. But these hymns—always sung with the same notes, chords, and rhythms—contained no provisions for the improvisation so much a part of the African American musical style. Also, they did not contain the all important altered scale degrees and intricate rhythms that separate gospel hymns from the gospel songs sung in the African American congregations. One gospel hymn that was extremely popular during the revival was "In the Sweet By and By" by J. P. Webster (1819–75). The song is concerned with an overwhelming desire to go to heaven and be with the Lord, because once a person received the gift of the Holy Spirit, there was nothing more to seek on this earth. Among other popular Protestant hymns sung at the revival were those of Ira David Sankey (1840–1909), composer of "A Shelter in the Time of a Storm," and William Howard Doane (1832–1915), composer of "What a Friend We Have in Jesus" and "Pass Me Not O Gentle Savior."

Negro spirituals were often sung during the more emotional parts of the services. Songs that carried the message of a reward in heaven were especially favored for the shout:

> *Get on board, little children*
> *Get on board, little children*
> *Get on board, little children*
> *There's room for many-a more.*

"On board," a variation of "aboard," refers here to accepting Christ and the new religion by stepping onto the gospel train. During the slave era "get on board" would have meant to run away or would have been a call for help in the resistance effort. The last line of this song refers to "good room in my Father's kingdom"—the reward.

None of these songs, however, evoked the passion and frenzy produced by songs composed "under the spirit." Such songs usually consisted of one or two lines of poetry, a melody of only three or four tones, and harmonies as simple as those of a basic blues; they were delivered with a rhythm of both intricacy and complexity. These songs were led by soloists who had never considered studying voice and who, in most cases, neither read music nor gave much care to diction and articulation. But like the singers of the Negro spirituals of a century earlier, they sang with such power and conviction that their singing became as much of an attraction to the services and the religion as were the doctrine and practice. Often possessing voices that could be described as gravelly, whiny, or pinched, these singers nonetheless introduced a style of singing marked by a sincerity that was uncommon for the times.

Most of the songs composed spontaneously had no verse or contrasting section, but had a refrain in which the lead line would change with each call, while the congregation remained constant in its response:

> *Leader: Latter rain is falling*
> **Congregation: Falling from on high,**
> *Leader: Latter rain is falling*
> **Congregation: Falling from on high.**
>
> *Leader: It's falling with power*
> **Congregation: Falling from on high,**

Leader: Mighty, mighty power
Congregation: Falling from on high.

Leader: Holy Ghost is falling
Congregation: Falling from on high,
Leader: Holy Ghost is falling
Congregation: Falling from on high.

Some of the songs requested the gift of the Holy Spirit:

Leader: Power
Congregation: Power, Lord
Leader: Power
Congregation: Power, Lord.

Leader: We need your power
Congregation: Power, Lord
Leader: We need your power ·
Congregation: Power, Lord.

Leader: Holy Ghost power
Congregation: Power, Lord
Leader: Holy Ghost power
Congregation: Power, Lord.

When the spirit was especially high, the congregation would respond to these songs by shaking their heads, swaying their bodies, clapping their hands, tapping or stomping their feet, and interjecting individual tonal and rhythmic improvisations onto an already rich palette of sound. The song leaders were the ministers, preachers, or singers whose authoritative voices were developed out of the necessity to cut through the responsive singing, clapping, stamping, and shouting of large congregations.

PENTECOSTAL MINISTERS AND SINGERS

By the 1930s Pentecostalism had become entrenched in the African American community not only by those who felt the Baptist and Methodist denominations to be

inadequate but also by those who found traditional religion insufficient for their spiritual desires and needs. Despite protest and ridicule from the Baptists and Methodists—or perhaps because of it—Pentecostal denominations separated themselves from the Baptists and Methodists and created a service style, music, language, behavior, dress, and an attitude about their place among Christians. "Heaven or Hell" became their principal preachment.

Gospel music was selected as the illuminating force behind this theology and developed over all other types of sacred music. When hymns were sung by these congregations they were "gospelized." Services were nothing less than ecstatic with forceful and jubilant singing, dramatic testimonies, hand clapping, foot stamping, and beating of drums, tambourines, and triangles (and pots, pans, and washboards when professional instruments were not available). When a piano could be begged, borrowed, or bought, a barrelhouse accompaniment served to bring the spirit to earth. It was not uncommon for a shouting session to last for thirty or forty-five minutes, with women fainting and falling to the floor (where they would sometimes lie for twenty or thirty minutes) and men leaping as if they were executing a physical exercise or running around the church several times.

Members of these congregations addressed each other as "sister" (woman) and "brother" (man) and were collectively known as "saints." They greeted each other with a "holy" kiss and flavored their conversation with such phrases as "praise the Lord," "hallelujah," and "thank God." They found scriptures that supported a subdued style of dressing for women so that their arms, legs, and heads would be covered at all times. Congregation members were easily recognizable because the sisters wore long skirts long after they had passed from fashion; a dark suit, white shirt, and dark tie identified the brothers. They were never seen in places where many other Christians were seen: bars, theaters, movie houses, dances, parties, community picnics, or locations for "hanging out." Because they felt that they had found the one true way of connecting with the Supreme Being, they reduced their association with other Christians, often refusing to attend services at other churches or join other churches in ecumenical services. This behavior was perceived by some other Christians as a show of superiority or exclusivity. Strangely, this did not deter the other Christians from attending Pentecostal services (mainly to hear the singing and the preaching), although in many cases these services were viewed as a show and Mon-

day mornings were filled with comments about who "shouted the longest at the sanctified church last night." Despite the levity at the expense of the "saints," people returned to hear the new gospel music. It was not long before some of the same people who first found the services comical found themselves shouting and singing gospel.

Any discussion of the first group of minister-singers influenced by the Azusa Street Revival would necessarily begin with Charles Price Jones and Charles Harrison Mason. Jones (1865–1949) was born in Texas Valley (near Rome), Georgia, and reared in Kingston, located between Rome and Atlanta. His mother died when he was seventeen, and thereafter he wandered throughout Mississippi, Arkansas, Tennessee, and Oklahoma. He was self-taught and began preaching in 1885. In 1887 he settled for a short time in Cat Island, Arkansas. There he was licensed to preach in the Baptist church. Soon afterward he entered the Arkansas Baptist College at Little Rock, and after his graduation in 1891, taught for a short period. He later accepted the pastorate of several small churches. While serving as the minister of the Tabernacle Baptist Church (the college church) in Selma, Alabama, Jones found himself in need of a deeper experience of grace. After fasting and praying for three days and nights, Jones accepted sanctification—that is, he decided to live free from sin. On a trip to Jackson, Mississippi, in 1894, he came under the influence of the Holiness movement and consciously decided to serve the Lord.

Joining with other ministers of the Baptist denomination who were attracted to Holiness, Jones called a Holiness convention on June 6, 1897, in Jackson. Among those present were W. S. Pleasant, J. A. Jeter, and Charles Harrison Mason. During the next convention in 1898, this Holiness faction decided to change the name of the principal church within their faction from the Mt. Helm Baptist Church to the Church of Christ. They were sued by the Baptist Association and dismissed from the communion. They held their first independent convention in Lexington, Mississippi, in 1899.

When word of the Azusa Street Revival came to the members of the Holiness convention in 1906, the group decided to attend. Jones did not attend the Azusa Street Revival himself but supported the visit of the church representatives Mason, Jeter, and D. J. Young. After these three returned to Mississippi, Jones and Mason could not agree on the interpretation of some of the scriptures that served as the basis of the revival, and the two separated. Half the group sided with Jones, who

immediately organized the Church of Christ (Holiness); the other half sided with Mason, who organized the Church of God in Christ.

Jones was a self-taught but prolific composer of songs for his congregation, composing more than a thousand songs. He began publishing in 1899 with his hymnal, *Jesus Only*. This was followed with *Jesus Only, Nos. 1 and 2* (1901), *His Fullness* (1906), and *Sweet Selections* and *His Fullness Enlarged* (also 1906). The first official hymnal for the congregation, *Jesus Only Songs and His Fullness Songs*, was published in 1940. Among his most popular compositions are "I'm Happy with Jesus Alone," "Where Shall I Be when the First Trumpet Sounds," and "Jesus Only."

Jones's compositions are unique in early gospel because they cut through much of the rhetoric of late nineteenth- and early twentieth-century hymn writing. His songs move directly to the feelings and expressions of a group of people who, even after having been freed from slavery *by law*, still find no possible solution to problems on this earth, but who dismiss this earth and turn to the one still believable source of recompense: God in Christ. His attitude toward religion and the earthly life is eloquently expressed in his most famous composition, "I'm Happy with Jesus Alone":

VERSE
There's nothing so precious as Jesus to me,
Let earth with its treasures be gone;
I'm rich as can be when my Savior I see,
I'm happy with Jesus alone.

CHORUS
I'm happy with Jesus alone,
I'm happy with Jesus alone;
Tho' poor and deserted, thank God, I can say
I'm happy with Jesus alone.

Jones earned a respected position in gospel music. He was clearly the leader of one of the most respected Holiness groups in the South, and he was the first composer of gospel music to write for members of the Seymour movement. However, Jones based his entire doctrine on the New Testament in which no instruments are

mentioned in the worship of Jesus. For this reason Jones felt that instruments were unnecessary in his services, even though as gospel has developed, the piano has become the principal accompanying instrument. Although the congregations of the Church of Christ (Holiness) sang with enthusiasm, they used no instrumental accompaniment and discouraged excessive emotion. These congregations have not produced any professional gospel singers. Yet considering the number of Jones' compositions in traditional piano-accompanied gospel singers' repertoires, he is secure in his position as one of the pioneering composers of this music.

"I'm Happy with Jesus Alone" by Charles Price Jones

Charles Harrison Mason (1866–1961) was born in Prior Farm (near Memphis), Tennessee. He was educated in the public schools of Memphis, although his attendance at school was infrequent. In 1878, when Mason was twelve years old, the family moved to Plumbersville, Arkansas. A prolonged and intense fever overtook him in 1880, and after a miraculous recovery he was converted and baptized in the Mt. Olive Baptist Church near Plumbersville, where his brother was the pastor. He preached his first sermon in 1893 and immediately entered the Arkansas Baptist College. He remained there for only three months, then left to become a traveling evangelist.

Mason met Jones in 1895 and joined his small body of Baptist ministers who were seeking a greater spiritual involvement than the Baptists offered. At the insistence of this small body of Holiness believers, Mason attended the Azusa Street Revival and remained there for approximately five weeks. He spoke in tongues and thereby received the Holy Ghost in March 1907. Later that year he settled in Memphis, where he began a series of services that attracted a large following. After the dispute with Jones over doctrinal issues, which resulted in each minister founding his own congregation, the two founders worked together only intermittently. Mason was elected overseer (later bishop) of his denomination, the Church of God in Christ. By 1934 the denomination had a membership of 25,000; in 1971 the membership was listed as 425,000, and reached a total of five million members by the early

1990s. COGIC, as it is called, is now the largest predominately black Pentecostal church in the world.

Mason was not a musician but a preacher who felt the need to stir his congregations with thematic songs at crucial moments in the service or sermon. He never personally published his songs, even though during his long life he composed many and led his congregations in song fests. His songs were not written down until the first denominational hymnal, *Yes, Lord!*, was published in 1982.

Mason contributed two significant compositions to Pentecostalism and eventually to the African American church. The most popular is the shout song, "I'm a Soldier in the Army of the Lord." The other is "Yes, Lord," also known as COGIC chant because of its limited number of tones, unpulsed tempo, and simple harmonies. The chant became so popular in the 1970s that most gospel singers ended an extremely fast shout song with:

> *Yes, Lord, Yes, Lord*
> *Yes, Lord, Yes, Lord*
> *Yes, Lord, Yes, Lord.*
>
> *We need your help, we need your help*
> *We need your help, we need your help*
> *We need your help, we need your help.*

"I'm a Soldier" likewise became so popular that it moved into the folk music repertoire, and by the time of its publication in 1982, was sung by both African American Christian congregations and gospel singers:

> *Leader: I'm a soldier*
> **Congregation: In the army of the Lord,**
> *Leader: I'm a soldier*
> **Congregation: In the army.**
>
> *Leader: I'm a sanctified soldier*
> **Congregation: In the army of the Lord,**
> *Leader: I'm a sanctified soldier*
> **Congregation: In the army.**

Leader: The Holy Spirit is my rifle
Congregation: In the army of the Lord
Leader: The Holy Spirit is my rifle
Congregation: In the army.

Mason exerted a strong influence on the development of gospel music by encouraging its performance at his services and among his congregations. He learned church music and structure in the Baptist church, where two deacons would lead the Baptist lining hymns and the congregation would sing them, alternating songs with prayers. While in the COGIC, Mason fashioned a service in which each member of the congregation was encouraged to lead the other members of the congregation in a song. Even new communicants who had not sung in public were expected to lead songs as soon as they were "saved." This song was followed by a testimony, which was an elaborate statement of thanks for life, health, strength, a job, spouse, child, and family—interspersed with stories of having overcome serious trials—that ended with a plea for all who "know the worth of prayer" to pray for him or her.

At the conclusion of the testimony another singer would lead a song followed by another testimony. The responsibility of each member to lead songs resulted in the development of strong singers throughout the congregation. Familiar Pentecostal shout songs ("I'm a Soldier in the Army of the Lord," "Power, Lord," and so on), along with gospelized standard Protestant hymns, became the repertoire of the congregation. While there was no overt competition among the singers, early on those singers who were able to ignite the congregation into a shout became congregational celebrities. They were singled out and called on to sing a solo or sing with each other during special parts of the service (before the sermon, during the offering, and so on). It was in this manner that a style of singing, first conceived in Los Angeles, developed in such southern cities as Memphis, Jackson, and Little Rock. Performers of gospel music from COGIC would eventually include such luminaries as Sister Rosetta Tharpe, Andrae Crouch, Walter and Edwin Hawkins, the O'Neal Twins, the Banks Brothers, the Boyer Brothers, and Vanessa Bell Armstrong.

Of the thousands who traveled to California, hoards were from the East Coast and brought the message and the music back with them. Among the Pentecostal

denominations founded as a result of the Azusa Street Revival were the Church of the Living God; the Pillar and Ground of the Truth, founded by Mary L. Ester Tate (1871–1930); the Triumph Church and King of God in Christ, founded by Elias Dempsey Smith (c.1872–1908); the Church of the Living God, founded by William Christian (1856–1928); and the Church of God and Saints in Christ, founded by William Saunders Crowdy (1847–1908). The shout music of the Azusa Street Revival became the principal music of these congregations. Elder D. C. Rice (1880–c.1950) was a well-known Pentecostal minister from Alabama who recorded several of the songs sung during Pentecostal worship. Two of his most famous recordings are "Testify," in which he is accompanied by his congregation and a trombone and "I'm in the Battlefield for My Lord," in which he is accompanied by trumpet. All instruments were employed during his services.

In addition to Jones and Mason, two other Pentecostal ministers figured prominently in the development of gospel, although neither was a composer. They were Samuel Kelsey (1906–93) and Smallwood Edmond Williams (1907–92). Kelsey, born in Sandville, Georgia, received the Holy Ghost in 1915 and began preaching at the age of seventeen. After an association with the Pentecostal denomination called the First Born Church of the Living God, he joined COGIC in 1923. He moved to Washington, D.C., and founded the Temple Church of God in Christ where he not only encouraged gospel music within his congregation but also used his church as a performance venue for traveling gospel singers. Kelsey became a celebrity in 1947 when his recording of the gospelized spiritual "Little Boy," an elaboration of the story of Jesus preaching in the temple, became a gospel music hit.

Williams was even more dedicated to receiving traveling gospel singers than Kelsey. A native of Lynchburg, Virginia, he came to the Pentecostal church through a denomination known as the Church of Our Lord Jesus Christ of the Apostolic Faith, an organization in the direct apostolic line of Seymour and Robert Clarence Lawson (1883–1961). Lawson, from New Iberia, Louisiana, settled in Indianapolis in 1913 and came under the influence of Garfield Thomas Haywood (1880–1931), who championed Seymour's denomination. Lawson eventually moved to New York City where in 1919 he established the Refuge Church of Our Lord Jesus Christ of the Apostolic Faith. The Refuge Church became one of the principal performance venues for gospel music in New York City. Williams moved to Washington, D.C., in the early

1920s and founded the Bible Way Church of Our Lord Jesus Christ of the Apostolic Faith. Williams' daughter, Pearl Williams Jones, became a leading gospel singer, pianist, and scholar of the 1960s.

Pentecostal Music
Outside the Pentecostal Church

While most of the new music was being created and performed in Pentecostal churches of the Deep South, African Americans were leaving the South daily to find better jobs, cleaner houses, safer neighborhoods, and greater opportunities for their children. Wherever they went they took the music with them and introduced it into their new community. Beginning with the Great Migration immediately following the Emancipation Proclamation in 1863, African Americans began settling just north of the Deep South, or moving into the Midwest. Some traveled only as far north as Virginia, while others settled in Pennsylvania, New Jersey, and New York. Other routes that were followed were from Mississippi to Chicago and Arkansas and Texas to California.

This influx of African Americans from the Deep South inspired several composers to attempt to capture the fervor, energy, and anxiety of southern Christians' "old time religion" in song. Perhaps the first of these was William Henry Sherwood, who flourished during the 1890s. Little is known of Sherwood other than that he appears to have lived his entire life in Petersburg, Virginia, where he owned an orphanage for African American children, and that he was a composer who conducted both a choir and a band. He is significant in gospel music because he appears to have been the first composer to take advantage of the return to the roots movement of the small body of freed slaves that eventually flocked to Azusa Street.

In 1893 Sherwood published a collection of gospel hymns and other songs under the title *Harp of Zion*. Like most collections published during that time, Sherwood's included hymns by several other composers, as well as a substantial number of his own songs. Of further significance is the fact that Sherwood was the first African American to publish songs that were decidedly cast in the Negro spiritual, pre-gospel mode. The melodies, harmonies, and, to an extent, the rhythm, all forecast music that in less than thirty years would be called gospel. His most famous composition, "The Church Is Moving On," enjoyed popularity as late as 1927 as

evidenced by its inclusion in *Spirituals Triumphant, Old and New*, published that year by the National Baptist Convention Publishing Board. The publishing board was first drawn to Sherwood when news reached them in 1893 that he was about to publish his *Harp of Zion*. They contacted him and secured the plates, and with a few revisions, published his *Harp of Zion* as their *Baptist Young People's Union National Harp of Zion* in the same year.

Sherwood's songs are limited to few words, and call and response are written into the song. In his works the melody is simple but catchy, the harmony includes only three or four chords, and the rhythm leaves spaces for expansion. While the verses of the song attempt to tell a story, the refrain foreshadows that of a gospel song, with all of its concomitant parts, as in the refrain of "The Church Is Moving On":

> *Moving on,*   *moving on*
>   *(moving on)*   *(moving on)*
> *Oh, the church*   *is moving on*
>   *(Oh, the church)*   *(moving on)*
>
> *Moving on,*   *moving on*
>   *(moving on)*   *(moving on)*
> *Oh, the Church*
>   *(oh, the church)*   *is moving on.*

Less than a decade after Sherwood published his collection of gospel hymns, Charles Albert Tindley (1851–1933) of Philadelphia joined the ranks of preachers who would make significant contributions to the new music. Tindley, born in Berlin, Maryland, taught himself to read and write. At about the age of seventeen, he married Daisy Henry, and in 1875 they moved to Philadelphia to find a better life. While working first as a hod carrier and a sexton at the John Wesley Methodist Episcopal Church (the Methodist Episcopal Church, as it was then called, would become the United Methodist Church in the early 1970s), Tindley enrolled in correspondence school to complete his education and prepare for the examination to become a minister. He passed the examination, and beginning in 1885, he pastored congregations in Cape May and Spring Hill, New Jersey; Odessa, Delaware; and Pocomoke and Fairmont, New Jersey. He then received the call to Ezion Methodist Episcopal

Church in Wilmington, Delaware, where he was eventually appointed as presiding elder of the Wilmington District. Yet a greater honor awaited him: in 1902 he was called back to Philadelphia to the pastorate of the Bainbridge Street Methodist Church, the new name for the church where Tindley had served as sexton. Starting with a congregation of fewer than two hundred members, this eloquent, self-taught intellectual and, at the same time, spiritual-singing preacher built his membership to more than ten thousand members and amassed a budget of thousands of dollars.

"Leave It There" by Charles Albert Tindley

His fame as a preacher, orator, civil rights worker, and caretaker for the downtrodden of Philadelphia has been overshadowed by the more than forty-five gospel hymns—interpreted as gospel songs even during his life time—that he left as his legacy. Tindley was the first recognized composer of gospel music, whether they are called gospel hymns or gospel songs. In the 1940s and 1950s, when gospel was first recognized as an acceptable African American musical art form, Tindley's songs were the first to be presented. Among his most popular songs are "What Are They Doing in Heaven?," "Nothing Between," "Some Day" (more commonly called "Beams of Heaven"), "Stand by Me," and "Let Jesus Fix It for You." Two of his compositions are so important to gospel music that they are considered standard repertoire, meaning that if one is called a gospel singer, one must to be able to sing these songs from memory. The first of these is "Leave It There," of which the second and last lines of the refrain now serve as a popular religious response or catch phrase in African American speech:

Leave it there, leave it there,
Take your burden to the Lord and leave it there;
If you trust and never doubt,
He will surely bring you out,
Take your burden to the Lord and leave it there.

The second and by far the most popular composition by Tindley is his 1905 masterpiece, "We'll Understand It Better By and By":

We're tossed and driven on this reckless sea of time,
Somber skies and howling tempest oft succeed the bright sunshine;
In that land of perfect day when the mists are rolled away,
We will understand it better by and by.

Chorus

By and by when the morning comes,
When the saints of God are gathered home;
We'll tell the story how we've overcome,
For we'll understand it better by and by.

Like many of the songs created during slavery, this twentieth-century song spoke both to social and religious themes. Written during the rise of the Ku Klux Klan and before the Great Depression (which would further disenfranchise a group of people barely getting by), its refrain of "We'll Understand It Better By and By" struck a core chord in the hearts of African Americans and helped shape the music that would be called gospel. This was accomplished in no small way by the interpretation provided by the people who lived under the shadow and spirit of the Azusa Street Revival.

THE EMERGENCE OF THE JUBILEE QUARTET: THE JEFFERSON COUNTY SCHOOL

Almost simultaneous with the development of music and its performance style in the Pentecostal/Holiness churches was the development of another African American sacred music that was not born in the church, but in the workplace: the jubilee quartet. The impetus for creating this music was the 1905 decision of Fisk University to feature a male quartet singing Negro spirituals instead of the small mixed choir of male and female voices that had presented this music to the world since 1871. Fisk was not the only school to feature jubilee singers or a jubilee quartet, for such groups enjoyed great popularity. Hampton, Tuskegee, Utica, Mississippi, and Wilberforce universities were among the early schools that had jubilee singers.

As the men who sang in quartets while they were in school graduated or left, they went on to teach at less accredited schools or returned to their home communi-

ties. There they organized male quartets and modeled them after the Fisk Jubilee Quartet. James Weldon Johnson stated in 1925 that one could "pick up four colored boys or young men anywhere and the chances are ninety out of a hundred that you [would] have a quartet." Although they may not have been aware of it—though it is unlikely that they could remain ignorant of the Pentecostal/Holiness congregations springing up around them and the music sung there—they, like the singers from the Pentecostal/Holiness churches, were participating in the development of the African American gospel song and style. Even at this early stage of gospel, the Pentecostal/Holiness singers sang with more passion, seeming abandon, and consequently more improvisation than was sanctioned in the Baptist and Methodist churches, thus creating a unique style of singing. The early quartets avoided the most exaggerated vocal techniques for two reasons: of greatest importance was the fact that they could not, or would not, expose themselves to the ridicule that was heaped on and associated with Pentecostal/Holiness singers, who were often described as wild and savage. The quartet singers, were, in the main, Baptist, and following the admonitions of their denominational leaders, sought to "elevate the musical standards of the denomination." The Baptists had by the late 1910s developed their own style of singing, which, as exemplified in the Negro spiritual and the new white Protestant gospel hymn, was less frenzied and considered more refined than the Pentecostal/Holiness style. The Baptist singers remained close to the melody, only occasionally interpolating a stock phrase such as "yes, Lord," "thank you, Jesus," or "you know what I mean." A trained vocal sound was preferable to the rough "field" sound, and slow songs were favored over shout songs. A concert demeanor—standing straight and tall in one location with little use of the arms in gesturing—was considered proper, and standard Protestant hymns were more popular than the short and repetitive songs of the Pentecostal church.

Congregational response to the singing of the new church-directed quartets, who soon called themselves jubilee quartets after the Fisk Jubilee Quartet, was in the traditional church mode, with the congregation responding with "amen," "hallelujah," and "praise the Lord." It was impossible to maintain the Fisk Jubilee Quartet repertoire, style of singing, or stage behavior under this kind of religious enthusiasm. It was not long before these quartets began borrowing from the singing style of the Pentecostal/Holiness singers.

The quartet singers operated in the structure of a very disciplined club—that is, they elected officers, paid dues, had regularly scheduled rehearsals, wore uniforms, and arranged formal engagements for singing. The Pentecostal/Holiness singers were less formal, singing spontaneously during any church service and more as a participant in the service than as a special singer or guest. The quartet's organizational concept served the jubilee quartets well, for as Kerrill Rubman observed in *From Jubilee to Gospel in Black Male Quartet Singing*:

1. *Quartet singing (of both sacred and secular music) has been a widespread and respected pastime for Black men—a way for the musically talented to use and improve their skills without special training or instruments and*

2. *[Quartet singing provided] a way for Black men to travel and earn income, recognition, and status when few other avenues were open to them.*

To these observations could be added: .

3. *Quartet singers found another opportunity to express their belief in God and their Christianity in* public. *This was inspired by a desire—not to become famous but—to be another "witness" for the Lord.*

One of the university singers who went on to teach at a high school in Lowndes County, Alabama, was Vernon W. Barnett, a graduate of Tuskegee Institute (now Tuskegee University). One of his students in quartet singing was R. C. Foster (b. 1899), who came to Bessemer, Alabama, in 1915 to work in the mines. Foster formed a group of men into a quartet that sang as entertainment during their lunch period and in the evenings after work. Within a few months the group was singing in their local churches. The early quartets of Bessemer and Birmingham (Jefferson County), Alabama, found their audience from the beginning in the church and therefore created their music for the church rather than the concert hall.

Foster named his group the Foster Singers, after himself, and they featured a repertoire of Negro spirituals, standard Protestant hymns rendered in the jubilee quartet style, and the relatively new gospel hymns of both white and black composers. The Foster Singers were the first black male quartet formed in Bessemer, Alabama— and consequently the first quartet to begin the transition from the university-based

and European-informed quartet to what would become the gospel quartet. Foster became the founder of the black gospel quartet movement

The group's original members were R. C. Foster, tenor; Norman McQueen, lead; Fletcher Fisher, baritone; and Golius Grant, bass. Selected and trained by Foster, these singers, all employees of Woodwards Old Mine, were literally the first cousins of the university jubilee singers. They sang much of the same repertoire and dressed in the black trousers and dinner jackets of their forerunners, comported themselves on stage with formal behavior, and considered themselves practitioners of university-style quartet singing "brought home."

The jubilee style of the Foster Singers, and those who followed them, featured four male singers in vocal ranges from tenor to bass, with the second tenor often serving as the soloist on call-and-response songs; close barbershop-like harmony emphasizing sharp and clear attacks and releases; a relatively close blend, but not so close that certain individual vocal qualities could not be heard above the other singers; a variety of vocal devices such as scooping, sliding, and ending words with just a hum; and a dynamic level extending from the softest whisper to the loudest explosion. The original difference between the jubilee quartets and those of the universities was one of vocal color. The color preferred by university quartets was one associated with singing the European art songs of Shubert and Schumann or one that could be employed in singing opera. Without proper training in the technique of placing the tone "in the head," the jubilee quartets placed their tones as they would if singing in a regular church service and therefore brought a certain "homeness" to their sound. Free to be rhythmic, not in the university sense but in the church sense, the singers placed greater emphasis on rhythmic accentuation, and this accentuation was accompanied by a slight movement of the body (never allowed among the university-trained singers), eventually leading to marking time by moving gently from left to right and a quiet slap on the thigh. Negro spirituals were sung with more rhythmic accentuation than was applied by the university singers, and gospel hymns were soon featured in the repertoire of the jubilee quartets.

What these first jubilee quartets did not realize, however, was that they were influenced by the audience's loud vocal response to their singing, even during their singing. In fact, the quartets had gradually adjusted their style to fit the response of the audience for which they were singing, the African American church congregation.

Therefore, while they thought of themselves as a local Fisk Jubilee Quartet, they were in fact the first participants in a gospel music tradition. In retrospect, then, the Foster Singers, and those who followed, were the creators of the "folk" gospel style.

The significance and influence of the Foster Singers cannot be overestimated for they began and inspired the quartet movement in Alabama where they were soon joined by the Famous Blue Jay Singers and the Birmingham Jubilee Singers, both of which were organized in 1926, and in 1929 by the Ensley Jubilee Singers and the Ravizee Singers.

By 1926 Charles Bridges was recognized as the leading quartet trainer of Jefferson County. Bridges was born in Pratt City, a suburb of Birmingham, in 1901. After graduating from Parker High School in Birmingham, where he studied voice with high school music teacher Julia Wilkerson, Bridges sang with the Dolomite Jubilee Singers before he organized the Birmingham Jubilee Singers. Members of the original group were Bridges, lead; Leo "Lot" Key, tenor; Dave Ausbrooks, baritone; and the legendary Ed Sherrill, who, according to Doug Seroff, the historian of the Jefferson County Quartet Movement, was the "heaviest" (deepest-voiced) bass of all the Jefferson County singers. The Birmingham Jubilee Singers, known for their close harmony and the energetic leading style of Bridges, became Alabama's first professional quartet, beginning their recording career in 1926. One of their most famous recordings was "I Heard the Preaching of the Elders." As one of Columbia Records' most-recorded black vocal groups, they toured the vaudeville houses of New York City, Chicago, and elsewhere with stars like Ethel Waters in the 1920s. Until this group was disbanded in the 1930s (upon the death of Dave Ausbrooks), they were rivaled in gospel quartet singing only by the Silver Leaf Quartette.

The Ensley Jubilee Singers maintained Birmingham's reputation as a quartet town until early 1980 when they ended the live radio broadcasts they had presented since 1942. The group, always closely associated with the Williams family of Ensley, was formed while they were teenagers singing on the street corners of Ensley, in the local churches, and for "uptown" parties. By the 1930s they were regarded as one of the leading quartets of Jefferson County. Original members were brothers James, Rufus, and Leroy Williams and their cousin, Charlie Jamison. Over the years the group boasted such prominent lead singers as Willie Love, who later joined the Fairfield Four, and Lon "Big Fat" Hamler.

The Ravizee Singers was one of the first groups to include women, which was unusual but permitted here because the Ravizee was a family group. Original members of the group were Mary Ravizee, first tenor; Hattye Ravizee, second tenor; Reverend Issac C. Ravizee, lead and first bass; and William Ravizee, second bass. In later years sister Leola Ravizee sang second tenor. The group relocated to Bessemer in 1935 to be near brother Reverend S. H. Ravizee, whose location in Bessemer even before the group moved there entitled them to be a part of the Jefferson County singers. The Ravizees were known for their slow and moderate gospelized Baptist hymns.

Jefferson County was the home of many jubilee groups and enjoyed a reputation as the leading quartet center in the South for many years. The influence of the movement begun by R. C. Foster and his singers was soon felt throughout the South.

The Jubilee Quartet Movement Spreads

Jefferson County was not the only place where quartets began to flourish, for as early 1919 in Norfolk, Virginia, the seat of the Tidewater area, a community quartet from the Berkley section of town began singing in churches in Norfolk and Portsmouth. Named the Silver Leaf Quartet, it included in its membership Melvin Smith, first tenor and lead; William Thatch, falsetto voice; William Boush, baritone; and Ellis McPherson, bass. Like two other groups that helped to identify Tidewater gospel, the Harmonizing Four and the Golden Gate Quartet, the Silver Leaf Quartet sang in a smoother vocal style than the groups of Jefferson County and was more heavily influenced by popular music than were Jefferson County groups. Interested from the beginning in the harmonies of popular music—that is, harmonies other than the simple chords found in hymns and Negro spirituals—the Silver Leaf Quartet was one of the first to investigate the complex chords that later would be associated with vocal jazz groups. More interesting, however, was the inclusion of a falsetto voice in the quartet. The falsetto is an African Americanism inherited from African tribal singing (Richard Jobson discussed African falsetto singing in a 1623 book). Whereas most quartets employed a first tenor—some of whom were described as light as an "Irish" tenor—as the top voice, in the Silver Leaf Quartet the falsetto of William Thatch would often soar over the other voices of the group.

Their interest in popular music was instrumental in their decision to accept an extensive booking as the Cavalier Singers, the name under which they sang secular

The Harmonizing Four, the most popular gospel quartet of the Tidewater, Virginia, region

music, at the exclusive Virginia Beach Cavalier Hotel in 1947. From that time on the group sang both sacred and secular music, but they maintained their reputation as a jubilee quartet. The group retired in 1979, but reveled in the fact that they had influenced the Golden Gate Quartet, the most famous jubilee group of the 1930s and the 1940s.

A number of other quartets were formed in the 1920s. In 1921 in Nashville, Tennessee, a group of young boys organized a quartet and named themselves the Fairfield Four, in honor of their church, the Fairfield Missionary Baptist Church. In 1927 the Harmonizing Four was organized in Richmond, Virginia, while the Dixie Hummingbirds of Greenville, South Carolina, organized in 1928. The late 1920s witnessed the first of two halcyon times that the black gospel quartets would experience.

Church Singing Accompanied
by Piano, Guitar, and Other Instruments

The quartet movement of the 1920s coexisted with the Pentecostal movement, although there was one major difference: quartets celebrated the *a cappella* tradition while the Pentecostal/Holiness groups, generally, accompanied their singing with percussion instruments, banjos, harmoniums, melodiums, and eventually piano. The early 1920s witnessed the emergence of a group of gospel singers from the Pentecostal/Holiness movement, most of whom accompanied themselves, or were accompanied, on various instruments. Several of these singers served as song leaders for Pentecostal preachers and the emerging Pentecostal/Holiness church.

Blind Arizona Dranes

Arizona Dranes (c.1905–c.1960) was the most prominent of the early sanctified singers and the first-known gospel pianist. Dranes was known as the "Blind Gospel Singer" in the early 1920s. Her blindness is generally conceded to have resulted from an attack of influenza, an epidemic of which swept Texas in the early 1900s. She served as song leader and pianist for Emmett Morey Page (1871–1944), Riley Felman Williams (c.1880–1952), and Samuel M. Crouch, Jr. (1896–1976), all of whom became bishops in COGIC.

Page, a native of Mississippi, received sanctification in 1902. In 1907 when he met Charles Harrison Mason, Page received the Holy Ghost. In 1914 Mason assigned him to the Texas where he held his first state convention that same year. Within a few years Page was also assigned as "overseer" (superintendent) of Texas, Arkansas, Oklahoma, New Mexico, Louisiana, Missouri, California, and parts of Tennessee, Mississippi, and Wisconsin. On a visit to Texas he met Arizona Dranes, a singer in the new sanctified style who was developing a style of piano playing that did not detract from the fervor of the singing, but complemented it in an ecstatic way. Whenever Page was in Texas Dranes served as his song leader and pianist.

Williams, born in Memphis, Tennessee, was one of the second generation of ministers who joined Mason in "planting" or "working out" new churches for his denomination. "Planting" or "working out" a Pentecostal church involved finding a community that was even slightly ready to support a sanctified church, relocating to that community, becoming visible among the religious community, and after estab-

lishing a reputation as a devout Christian, introducing the new religion through services in homes (as Seymour did) or in converted storefronts. Church "planters" often held "street meetings" in front of popular businesses or borrowed the sanctuary or basement of an established church when the church was not occupied (this happened rarely but was significant in the development of Pentecostal churches). The planter remained until the new congregation had a strong identity and would then move to a new community and begin the process again. Planters were highly revered, to the extent that some churches took on the name of the planter, as did Flowers Temple Church of God in Christ in Winter Park, Florida, named after its planter, J. J. Flowers.

Williams traveled throughout the South conducting revivals and setting up churches, many of which were pastored by ministers whom he ordained. During his travels in Texas in the early 1920s he, too, encountered Arizona Dranes, who became his song leader.

After traveling with Williams, Dranes returned to her hometown of Dallas, Texas, and became the pianist and song leader for Crouch, who eventually became the First Assistant Bishop of COGIC. Crouch earned this honor through his travels throughout the United States preaching Pentecostalism and setting up COGICs, the activity which brought him to Dallas in the middle 1920s. In Texas he began an association with Dranes that lasted throughout her career as a recording singer. In the early 1930s Crouch moved to California where he continued planting churches. He eventually settled in Los Angeles, where he founded the Emmanual Church of God in Christ. In the early 1960s the pianist for his church was his nephew, Andrae Crouch (b. 1942).

While Dranes was serving as song leader for Crouch in Dallas, Richard M. Jones (1892–1945), pianist and a talent scout for Okeh Records, attended one of Crouch's services and heard her. Recognizing her talent and the sensation she would generate among black Christians, he negotiated a contract for Dranes with his record label after she made a test recording in Chicago. Dranes had secured a traveling companion and gone to Chicago where she recorded a Negro spiritual/gospel version of "My Soul Is a Witness for My Lord." The producers were highly impressed, not only with her singing, but with her piano playing as well.

Her piano playing was a combination of ragtime, with its two beats to the bar feel, octave passages in the left hand, exaggerated syncopation in the right hand, and

heavy full and ragged (syncopated) chords of barrelhouse piano, and the more traditional chords of the standard Protestant hymn. What Dranes brought to the style was what became known as the "gospel beat," emphasizing a heavy accent on the first beat in musical units of two beats and beats two and four in musical units of four. In addition to the accents on the primary pulses, Dranes filled in the space between the accented beats with octave and single note runs. The right hand's playing was characterized by repeated notes and chords and few—but well-chosen—single-note motives (runs), while the left hand played octaves. Most of her playing was in the center of the keyboard, with excursions into the very bottom and top of the keyboard during passages normally reserved for breaks in the music.

Her singing style, which influenced many later gospel singers, was remarkable for its piercing quality that cut through the clapping and stamping of church services. Located in range between a soprano and an alto, her voice was marked by nasality, but with clarity of pitch, and was treated like a drum when, with emotion and fervor, she shouted out the lyrics of songs. This is nowhere more clearly demonstrated than on her 1928 recording of "I Shall Wear a Crown." In addition to introducing a gospel piano style, Dranes sang with a true backup group, rather than a congregation, and rendered several songs in 3/4 time, which would become the 12/8 rhythm of gospel in the 1950s. Between 1926 and 1928 she recorded over thirty songs for Okeh Records and was one of their most commercial religious music artists.

Other Blind Gospel Singers

Dranes was only one of a cadre of blind singers who turned to gospel in the early 1920s, many of whom became recording artists. This is perhaps no coincidence: the Pentecostal/Holiness church placed heavy emphasis on healing and many of these singers were awaiting healing; the music was new and catchy; and donations were given with less pity and guilt when the blind person exhibited a talent.

Washington Phillips (1891–1938) was the second most popular blind gospel singer after Arizona Dranes. A Texas native who also died there after several years in an insane asylum, Phillips possessed a clear, but scratchy voice that could nonetheless melt the heart of the meanest man. His simple delivery, accentuation of key lyrical phrases, and crystal clear sincerity even on recordings made him a popular recording preacher and singer in the late 1920s. Accompanying himself on the

dolceola, one of several variances of the dulcimer (played like a piano), Washington is known today by the following lyrics:

VERSE
I want to tell you the natural fact,
Every man don't understand the Bible alike.

CHORUS
But that's all now, I tell you that's all;
But you better have Jesus now, I tell you that's all.

The opening of his 1927 recording of "Denomination Blues" was a sacred song based on the secular song "Hesitation Blues."

Blind Mamie Forehand, accompanied by her guitar-playing husband, A. C. Forehand, was one of the sanctified street singers from Memphis who did not fit the mold of the traditional Pentecostal shouter. Not only was her voice thin with a decided quaver not always used for vocal effect, her delivery was deliberate and measured. Yet she was one of the highly regarded sanctified singers of the 1920s, in spite of her advanced age at that time. She accompanied her singing by playing antique small cymbals (which are completely unrelated to the full-sized symphonic cymbals used in most gospel music accompaniment), while her husband accompanied her on guitar. When he sang, he accompanied himself on the harmonium, one of the earliest gospel keyboard instruments. The Forehands' legacy depends almost entirely on their recordings of "Wouldn't Mind Dying if Dying Was All" and the more famous "Honey in the Rock."

Among other blind gospel singers active during the 1920s was Blind Joel "Joe" Taggart, who recorded thirty gospel songs. Taggart possessed a strong voice, delivered lyrics with authority, and played guitar with noticeable skill. His recordings of "Handwriting on the Wall" and "I Wish My Mother Was on That Train" testify to his reputation as one of the strong singers of the 1920s. Blind Roosevelt Graves and Blind Willie Johnson, who often performed with his wife Angeline, made significant contributions to guitar-accompanied religious singing. Graves and Johnson both sang secular music as well. Charles Tindley's "Take Your Burden to the Lord" was recorded by both artists, first by Graves, then by Johnson one year later.

Sighted Gospel Singers

The gospel style of singing—though it was not yet called gospel but jubilee singing in public and sanctified singing in private—provided the perfect avenue for blind people to make a living and was preferred over selling pencils or standing on street corners with cups. The blind singers were joined by sighted soloists, duos, and quartets, some of whom, although inspired by the Pentecostal/Holiness singers, performed in a style not unlike that of the early jubilee quartets. The less frenzied, more controlled singing of the Baptists and Methodists coexisted with the energetic, florid, and "spirit-induced" singing of the sanctified saints. While Sister Sallie Sanders offered a rousing, spirit-informed version of gospel/spirituals in a 1923 recording session, the Nugrape Twins (Matthew and Mark), at the same session, recorded songs with a classically trained pianist who played a classically informed introduction, paused for the singers to commence, and carefully followed them through their songs. The difference between the two performances is so distinct that clearly, even without a name, *gospel* had become a distinct style of singing.

This style is more obvious in the singing of the legendary Sister Bessie Johnson, a Mississippi evangelist or a woman preacher (in COGIC or in similar denominations, women are not allowed to be called Elder or Reverend). Sister Johnson's voice, while that of the average alto, could summon up a deep and dark quality and assume the growling timbre associated with the African American folk preacher. Her singing partner, Sister Melinda Taylor, on the other hand, possessed a voice that was deep and resonant. Both Johnson and Taylor, along with Sally Sumler, were members of the Sanctified Singers. "He's Got Better Things for You" (1929) was one of their popular recordings. Sister Johnson's recording of "Telephone to Glory" illustrated the depth of her range and her ability to "growl," a technique that would not become popular among most gospel singers until the 1950s.

Sister Cally Fancy, a Chicago gospel singer and direct contemporary of Bessie Johnson, featured a repertoire of songs that commented on social issues of the day. Her recordings of "Everybody Get Your Business Right," about the rash of tornados that plagued the United States between 1928 and 1930, and "Death Is Riding through the Land," a realist's reaction to the perceived folly of the League of Nations in 1920, illustrate her style and repertoire.

Race Records

The preponderance of recordings of African American preaching and gospel singing as early as the mid-1920s testifies not only to the popularity among black people of this kind of African American religion and its music, but also to white people's fascination with it. The phenomenal sale of so-called "race records" (recordings produced using African American performers for the African American audience) between 1924 and 1949—when the term "rhythm and blues" was added to the Billboard list of records sold—is documented by Paul Oliver in *Songsters and Saints* (1984). This scholarly book on the popularity, sales, and importance of race recordings has a chapter on gospel singing and preaching but still does not tell the complete story. Gospel music and African American preaching were discovered by the record companies in the early 1920s, and as early as 1924, record companies began recording and marketing these songs. They often went to small towns and recorded in churches, homes, and bars. Companies small and large had two or three preachers or singers on their rosters. The major recording companies that recorded gospel in the 1920s and 1930s were Okeh, RCA Victor, Vocallion, Paramount, and Columbia.

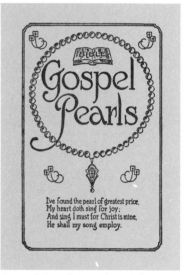

I've found the pearl of greatest price.
My heart doth sing for joy;
And sing I must for Christ is mine,
He shall my song employ.

Gospel Pearls (1921) with songs by Charles Albert Tindley, Lucie Campbell, and Thomas Andrew Dorsey

Gospel Pearls

Early gospel brought a new excitement to religion in the African American community. Like any sensation, it attracted new followers daily. The most genuine and inspiring music, however, was performed within Pentecostal and storefront Baptist churches. The music was infectious and mesmerizing, and the Pentecostal/Holiness movement presented a problem to the Baptists and Methodists. At first, because Holiness congregations waved their arms in exaggerated fashion at moments of ecstacy, shouted (executed a holy dance), and on occasion fainted or went into trances, few people sought membership in their congregations. However, in the late 1920s and early 1930s when the Holiness church began to make inroads into the membership of the major Baptist and Methodist established churches, the ministers of these churches saw the Holiness church as a threat, both to their membership and to their power.

At the same time, members of the budding African American middle class saw the Holiness church and its service as an attack on the accomplishments, positions, and progress they had worked so hard to attain.

Despite this feeling of shame and anger in the African American community, as early as 1921 the National Baptist Convention, the largest organization of African American Christians in the United States, formally recognized the power and beauty of this new music. In that year they published *Gospel Pearls*, the first collection of songs published by a black congregation using the term "gospel" to refer not only to the "good news" but to the new kind of song and singing that was stirring the nation. *GP*, as it is commonly called, was edited by Willa A. Townsend (1880–1947), a professor of church worship, music, and pageantry at Nashville's Roger Williams University. Townsend was ably assisted on the church editorial committee by such luminaries as Lucie E. Campbell, E. W. D. Issac, Sr., and L. K. Williams, all of whom played major roles in the development of music in African American Baptist churches after 1900. As musical associates, Townsend was flanked by a coterie of emerging Baptist gospel singers, as noted in the preface to this collection:

> *"Gospel Pearls" is a boon to Gospel Singers, for it contains the songs that have been sung most effectively by Prof. Britt, Mrs. J. D. Bushnell, Prof. Smiley, Prof. Nix, Mrs. Williams, and other prominent singers, telling of His Wondrous Love through song.*

While the music committee, the signatory of the preface, identified this group as "gospel singers," they did not mean singers in the tradition of Arizona Dranes and Sallie Sanders, but a new and different style of singing that sought to capture the ecstasy of the Holiness church singers but without the excesses. Excesses were interpreted as singing at the extremes of the register with a volume usually reserved for outdoor song, interpolating additional words into the text, hand clapping, and occasional spurts of shouting. This *GP* style of gospel singing leaned heavily on the nineteenth-century Baptist lining hymn tradition of singing songs in a slow tempo and elaborating each syllable with three to five embellishment tones.

Of the 163 songs in *GP*, 143 are standard Protestant hymns, gospel hymns by white composers, or patriotic songs such as "Battle Hymn of the Republic." In a section entitled "Spirituals," Townsend included "Stand by Me" by Charles Albert

Tindley and "Shine for Jesus" by E. C. Deas. In the first untitled section, Townsend included four other songs by Tindley, including "We'll Understand It Better By and By" and "Leave It There," several songs by E. C. Deas and Carrie Booker Person, "I'm Happy with Jesus Alone" by Charles Price Jones, and "If I Don't Get There," the first gospel song published by Thomas Andrew Dorsey. The late 1921 edition of *GP* (the first edition was published in early 1921) became so popular that the National Baptist Convention Publishing Board decided to use the original plates for all subsequent issues. The 1921 version of *GP* was still a saleable item in the early 1990s without any changes or additions. With the publication of the collection and the large membership of the National Baptist Convention, gospel music, as it was now called, began to spread among black Christians, endorsed by the respectability of the National Baptist Convention. *Gospel Pearls* crossed denominational music boundaries and by the 1930s was found in the pews of Baptist, Methodist, and Pentecostal churches.

Gospel Pearls and Gospel Singing

The publication of *Gospel Pearls* profoundly affected the singing of gospel music in the African American community because Baptists no longer had to attend Pentecostal, Holiness, or sanctified churches to hear the music. They could now hear this music in their own churches on Sunday mornings; for the shouting kind of gospel they still had to go to the source. There were now two styles of singing gospel: one that emphasized singing in which the spirit dictated the amount of embellishment, volume, and improvisation that was applied, and a second that, while attempting to incorporate the dictates of the spirit, tempered the rendition to the musical taste of the Baptist congregation. The Baptist style of singing gospel inspired the development of gospel groups and soloists who heretofore had been attracted to the music but found no way to participate, given their sense of moderate vocal and physical indulgence. One of the first groups to emerge was the Tindley Gospel Singers, also known as the Tindley Seven, organized in the Tindley Temple Methodist Episcopal Church in Philadelphia and named in honor of the pastor, Charles Albert Tindley. This group, organized in 1927, was unique in two respects: they were the first male gospel group to be accompanied by piano, although the piano accompaniment was much more like hymn playing than gospel singing, and while their basic repertoire

was the gospel hymns of Tindley, they sang other songs, principally those found in *Gospel Pearls.*

Golden Gate Quartet

Another group to emerge following the publication of *GP* was the Golden Gate Quartet, the most famous gospel quartet before the Golden Age of gospel. The Golden Gate Quartet, a name that had been used for African American high school quartets since the 1890s, was again used for a group that attended Booker T. Washington High School in Norfolk, Virginia, in the late 1920s. Its original members were Henry Owens, lead; Clyde Reddick, tenor; Willie "Bill" Johnson, baritone; and Orlando Wilson, bass. Reddick was later replaced by Willie Langford but returned to the group in the 1950s. Their style was, at first, similar to that of barbershop quartets and jubilee singers, emphasizing close harmony with precise attacks and releases (they were influenced by the Mills Brothers as well as by jubilee singers and gospel quartets). Most of their repertoire consisted of Negro spirituals, to which they applied a rhythmic beat, not unlike that associated with blues and jazz. In the late 1930s, they began to include songs of Thomas A. Dorsey, Lucie Campbell, and Charles A. Tindley and applied a few of the techniques of the sanctified singers.

Beginning in 1935 the Gates appeared in live radio broadcasts, first from the 50,000-watt station WBT in Charlotte, North Carolina. Their harmony, rich vibrato-laced tones, and rhythmic accentuation made them an early radio favorite among black and white listeners. In addition to other elements exploited by jubilee singers and gospel quartets, the Gates could imitate trains, boats, cars, whistles, and motors with their voices (probably inspired by the Mills Brothers). Often used as background for solos, these nonmusical sounds became a trademark that set the Gates apart from other groups. Their WBT broadcasts reached much of the eastern United States and brought them to the attention of Victor Records, for which they began recording in 1937. During their first session, they recorded a spirited version of the Negro spiritual "Jonah," and it became an immediate hit among race records.

The popularity of their recordings and radio broadcasts prompted John Hammond (1910–87) to feature them in the famous 1938 Carnegie Hall "From Spirituals to Swing" concert. By the end of the concert the Gates had become the toast of New York. They moved to a national CBS live broadcast, and in 1941 they performed

at Franklin Delano Roosevelt's inauguration (later they recorded "Why I Like-a Roosevelt," which became a big hit).

Because the Gates produced a sound that appeared to devote more attention to the techniques of polished barbershop/jubilee/popular music than to praising God, they were often mistaken for popular music singers (snapping their fingers for rhythmic accentuation and swaying their bodies in syncopated movement helped create the confusion). They soon attracted a large audience that had no particular interest in religion, only in music. After appearing at Cafe Society in New York in 1940 they began to perform more secular music—and gospel music presented in a secular manner—and eventually presented themselves as both jubilee and popular singers.

After World War II black gospel quartets began to proliferate, and the Gates were then only one of several popular quartets attempting to grab the same audience. Too involved in a style that had been more than twenty years in development, the Gates chose not to switch to pure gospel and around 1950 found themselves with a very small black audience. By 1955 the group had undergone several personnel changes and was not able to recreate their sound from the 1930s and 1940s. They thereby lost their entire black audience as well as much of their white audience. They made their first trip to Europe in 1953 where they became an instant hit (gospel quartets had not yet toured Europe). They immediately moved their headquarters to Paris where, through many personnel changes, they have remained, confining their touring to Europe. Some of their early hits include "Shadrack, Meshack, and Abendigo" and Tindley's "What Are They Doing in Heaven Today?"

The Southernaires

Another extremely popular quartet, one that often appeared with the Golden Gate Quartet in their early New York days, was the Southernaires. Organized in New York City in 1929, this group was formed to sing in local churches. During its early period the group rehearsed at Williams Institutional Colored Methodist Episcopal Church (CME) in Harlem and the following year began broadcasting over radio stations WMCA and WRNY. In 1933 the group began a series of broadcasts from the NBC Blue Broadcast under the title "The Little Weather-Beaten Whitewashed Church" that lasted more than ten years. Their broadcast "featured traditional spirituals and secular southern folksongs, as well as sermonettes, recitations, and guest speakers

The Dixie Hummingbirds

who emphasized the accomplishments of African Americans." Although they mixed secular and barbershop, jubilee, and gospel quartet styles into one musical melange, the Southernaires were most highly regarded as a gospel and jubilee quartet. From 1939 to 1941 they recorded jubilee and gospel songs on the Decca label.

GOSPEL MUSIC ON THE
EVE OF THE GOLDEN AGE

By the early 1940s gospel music was thoroughly entrenched in both the African American community and its churches. It did not go unnoticed, however, outside the African American community, and on December 23, 1938, when John Hammond staged the famous "From Spirituals to Swing" concert in Carnegie Hall, he included

the Mitchell Christian Singers and the Golden Gate Quartet, along with Sister Rosetta Tharpe, a gospel singer who accompanied herself on guitar. The next year Sister Tharpe recorded jazz versions of gospel songs with Lucky Millender (1900–66) and his band, and the Georgia Peach appeared with a quartet singing gospel songs at Radio City Music Hall. In the early 1940s, the Dixie Hummingbirds appeared at Cafe Society, and Ernestine B. Washington, the wife of a Holiness minister, recorded gospel with jazz trumpeter Bunk Johnson (1879–1949).

From the services held on Azusa Street in Los Angeles around the turn of the century evolved a music that began to challenge the Negro spiritual as the favored sacred music in the African American community. This new gospel music spoke in more immediate tones, both musically and textually, to the difficult life of being both black and Christian in the United States during the first two decades of the twentieth century. While the music began in the Pentecostal churches and moved into the community through jubilee quartets, it was spread throughout the nation by radio, recordings, and concerts by traveling gospel singers. The Sunday afternoon gospel concert was becoming a fixture in Baptist churches along with the pre-service gospel concert in Pentecostal churches. Occasionally even Methodist congregations received gospel singers into their sanctuaries.

By 1940 the *a cappella* male gospel quartet had been perfecting its style for more than twenty-five years, and this refinement was reflected in public preference at concerts. The newer piano-accompanied gospel singers coming into prominence at the middle of the century were less developed and still searching for a precise style of executing this music. On the one hand, the piano freed the singers from supplying the complete rhythmic foundation; on the other hand, it restricted absolute freedom of harmony because harmony was supplied by the piano. Between 1940 and 1945, the piano-accompanied group solved its accompaniment problems and was ready to challenge jubilee quartets for prominence within the emerging gospel audience.

Live broadcast of Mahalia Jackson at New York's WOV

Move On Up A Little Higher: 1945–55

Beginning as early as the mid-1930s, piano-accompanied gospel joined with the *a cappella* jubilee quartet to provide greater variety in this new music. The gospel choir, organized as early as 1932, could now be found in many Baptist and Pentecostal sanctuaries, with occasional performances in Methodist churches. By 1945 there were very few people in the African American community who had not heard gospel music. Jubilee quartets, who heretofore had only flirted with the virtuosic techniques of the Pentecostal gospel singers, now embraced those techniques and sought to create a music that would wreak emotional havoc. What exactly was this new music called gospel?

Gospel music was, by 1945, a sacred folk music that had its origin in the slave songs, field hollers, Baptist lining hymns, and Negro spirituals of the slave era and standard Protestant hymns and especially composed songs. These songs were adapted and reworked into jubilant expressions of supplication, praise, and thanks by the urban African American. The harmonies were as simple as those of a hymn or the blues, but gospel's rhythm, always personalized by singers into the accents

and cross-pulses of their speech, walk, and laughter, was intricate and complex—yet precise and clear enough to inspire synchronized movement. As important as the music were the practices employed in its performance. So great were these practices that by the mid-1940s they defined gospel style.

The gospel style features exaggerated improvisation as its driving force. Of special interest in gospel singing is the variety of timbres that make up the gospel sound, representing the diverse musical personalities of those singers who created the style: Arizona Dranes sang in a tense, almost shrill mezzo-soprano; Mamie Forehand had a contralto voice that she used in a low, almost lazy manner of singing; Washington Phillips and Joe Taggart possessed "dirty" baritone voices and were very much influenced by the blues in their singing; Willie Johnson sang in a hoarse, strained voice, not unlike that of a sanctified preacher. Yet each sang with the passion of a convinced Christian.

A gospel piano style had been developed based on the "rhythm section" concept, in which the middle of the piano is used to support the singers by doubling the vocal line in harmony; the left bottom portion of the keyboard serves as the bass fiddle, and the right upper portion acts as a solo trumpet or flute, playing countermelodies and "fill" material at rhythmic breaks.

The text of gospel songs speaks of the Trinity, blessings, thanks, and lamentations, and the manner in which the text is delivered is more important than the melodies and harmonies to which they are sung. Despite the fact that gospel songs were sung for others to hear, it was paramount that the singers *use* singing to communicate their feelings about Christianity. It was, therefore, not unusual to witness a singer *singing* through her problems. It was common for the congregation to become so moved that they forgot their own problems for days, while others transcended the weights of this world through the music.

During the first ten years of the Golden Age of Gospel (1945–55), the style of music reached a level of near perfection and amassed a devoted audience. Gospel moved from shabby storefront churches with a few untrained singers dressed in threadbare black or maroon choir robes to the gospel-group extravaganzas of New York's Joe Bostic or New Jersey's Ronnie Williams. The singers of the new generation exhibited extraordinary control and nuance, dressed in blazing pastel gowns and bright suits, and were accompanied by nine-foot Steinway grand pianos and

Hammond organs with Leslie speakers. A "singing," as gospel concerts were called, generated as much excitement as an appearance by Duke Ellington or Louis Jordan and provided an opportunity for the church folk in the African American community to view the finest in clothing, hair styles, and automobiles. But this new emphasis on opulence and grandeur did not interfere with the audience experiencing, through the music, a religious ecstacy heretofore unmatched in the twentieth century.

THE LEGACY OF WORLD WAR II: RADIO AND RECORDINGS

The years of World War II had stimulated unprecedented economic growth in the United States. Southern African Americans, mainly through benefits such as the G.I. Bill and its economic stimulus, were able to move to large northern and midwestern cities, secure high-paying jobs, buy homes, and send their children to better schools. However, many of these transplanted southerners were uncomfortable with the more formal worship services of the North and Midwest and felt the need to recreate the spirited and informal religious church services and music they had enjoyed back home. As enterprising record producers from labels such as Apollo, Gotham, Excello, Atlantic, Imperial, black-owned Vee-Jay, Savoy, Specialty, Peacock, Chess, Aladdin, and King scouted for the new secular music—soon to be called rhythm and blues— they also looked to the churches for music that would satisfy hard-shell Christians as well as lovers of rhythm and blues. Almost every major city boasted at least one gospel soloist, group, or quartet that was recording or waiting for the call to record.

Like the recordings of rhythm and blues, gospel recordings were, according to Portia Maultsby, a leading authority on rhythm and blues, first produced by "small, independent record companies founded by entrepreneurs. Some of the companies were established by white jukebox vendors who catered to black communities." In cities where there was no record store owned by African Americans, white record store owners stocked black gospel and would make special orders. James C. Petrillo (1892–1984), president of the American Federation of Musicians, led a strike in 1942 banning the union's members from making recordings until the record manufacturers agreed to pay the union a fee for every disc produced. According to Nelson George in *The Death of Rhythm and Blues*, "Records cut prior to the ban, plus some primarily vocal recordings and scattered bootleg sessions (falsely said to have been recorded before the ban), made up the bulk of record releases during the next two

years." The strike lasted until 1944, by which time many of the major record labels were no longer interested in gospel. New recording companies like Apollo and Gotham, eager to fill this void, stepped in and made African American gospel music a major business.

While gospel provided spiritual uplifting through the two or three songs rendered during a church service and the two hours of a concert, radio and recordings became the principal source for listening to gospel every day and all day. Gospel quartets had begun to perform live as early as 1933 when the Southernaires began a series of broadcasts on stations WMCA and WRNY in New York City. This musical diversion soon became so popular that it was picked up by stations in other cities. Such groups as the Golden Gate Quartet, the Swan Silvertones, the CIO Singers (from the Congress of Industrial Organizations union), the Soul Stirrers, and the Wings Over Jordan Choir joined the Southernaires for Sunday morning or weekday broadcasts. These early black gospel quartet broadcasts were not only an innovation in African American musical culture, but also in the history of American radio, for while African American swing bands had had live radio broadcasts in cities like New York and Chicago, African American sacred music had been confined to the church. Few black-owned radio stations were in existence in 1930, and the few that were active found greater sponsorship in playing jazz and blues recordings.

Radio in the 1940s was not yet the black-owned and black-programmed radio that became popular in the last quarter of the twentieth century. There were African American disc jockeys (DJs) on only a few stations, working three or four hours daily, while white DJs on other stations and at other times affected the timbre, rhetoric, and booming voice of African Americans. Regardless of who was broadcasting, radio had become the means through which small-town America could hear gospel on any Sunday and, in most cases, either before seven o'clock in the morning or after ten o'clock at night on weekdays. Gospel radio became a much desired reality in the mid-1940s, and stations from New York to Tennessee featured the gospel hour with Deacon Jones (a black DJ) or Brother Paul (a white DJ). Among the most prominent stations on which gospel could be heard were WDIA (Memphis), WXLW (St. Louis), WLOF (Orlando), WDBJ (Roanoke, Virginia), WNOX (Knoxville), WLIB (New York City), WIS (Columbia, South Carolina), WLAC (Nashville), WOKJ (Jackson, Mississippi), and WMMB (Miami). None of these stations were black owned.

While most of the stations covered a listening audience within a radius of twenty-five miles or less, WLAC of Nashville covered such a large area that it became the black radio station for the United States. With 1,510 kilocycles (the station was advertised as having 50,000 watts) in early 1940s, the station could be heard for thousands of miles during the day. After nine o'clock at night, when many stations left the airwaves, WLAC literally covered the nation. Playing easy listening music during the day, WLAC featured rhythm and blues and gospel at night. The station had three DJs who programmed music especially designed for black audiences. Each featured forty-five-minute segments of rhythm and blues alternating with fifteen-minute segments of gospel. The station was important not only because it featured race music at night but also because it was one of the first radio stations to sell items over the radio, expanding the mail-order industry. Through the mail from WLAC, African Americans bought baby chicks, hair pomade, recordings, garden seeds, choir robes, and skin-lightening cream advertised between the sounds of James Brown, LaVern Baker, and the Dixie Hummingbirds.

The three DJs (none of whom were black) that became "brothers" were Bill "Hoss" Allen, known as the "Hossman," Gene Noble, and John "John R" Richbourg. Depending on the hour of broadcast, the DJs were sponsored by Randy's Record Shop of Gallatin, Tennessee, or Ernie's Record Mart of Nashville. The principal gospel music DJ, however, was John R (b. 1910), who offered record packages of five records for $3.98, and for those who ordered within the next seven days, an additional free record.

At the height of WLAC's popularity in the early 1950s, the station covered thirty-eight states and had eight million to twelve million listeners. Kip Lornell, who studied gospel quartets in Memphis, reported that the Spirit of Memphis Quartet told him that it "was possible to drive from Atlanta to Los Angeles and never miss one of John R's broadcasts." John R and WLAC became part of the fabric of the gospel network early on.

The gospel radio programs needed an abundance of gospel recordings, of which there was no shortage. Not since the 1920s had record producers in such large numbers scoured the black community for religious music.

Few gospel recording artists ever received a fair accounting or money for the records sold. As was the case in other forms of black recorded entertainment, gospel

was a gold mine for ripping off the artists. The rip-off was manifested in several ways: record producers paid artists for fewer records than were sold (artists did not see the books), records were distributed in areas where the artists did not perform and therefore had no knowledge of the market, the artists were not advised that they themselves were paying for the recording session and they would receive no money until the cost of the session had been paid, and the reprehensible act of signing a group as a tax write-off and investing no money to promote their recordings. In order to offset their losses—singers had little leverage to negotiate more advantageous contracts—singers would purchase hundreds of recordings at a reduced price from the producer and sell them during their concert tours. The singers themselves left the stage or pulpit and moved through the audience selling records. This was often the only way they were able to make money from the recordings. While gospel artists knew they were not receiving the money they deserved from the recording industry, they were nonetheless grateful for recording contracts.

GOSPEL ON THE HIGHWAYS AND BYWAYS

A contract and the resulting recording could ensure singers a large crowd when they performed. Every singer sought to ensure a recording contract by courting gospel DJs (serious payola was not a major factor in the gospel recording industry), calling them from distant places on their tours, sending postal and Christmas cards, and making great ceremony when they attended concerts.

Despite many discomforts and problems, professional gospel singers—those who had given up their weekday jobs to sing—traveled throughout the United States during the rain, snow, sleet, or 120 degree temperatures to sing gospel before whomever would listen in any church or school auditorium. Having to perform in the African American church uniform of some combination of black and white (for economic reasons) or threadbare black or maroon choir robes and being accompanied on an old upright piano, often out of tune, these singers forged ahead to bring their message of "good news" in a new melodic, harmonic, rhythmic, and spiritual form. Often leaving home under the most dreadful circumstances, reaching their destination and converting new souls became more important to these singers than comfort during their travels. Soloists, quartets, and groups with their accompanists traveled in dilapidated cars, on trains, and in buses, and sometimes in a combination of all

these modes of travel. If cars broke down, singers would call sponsors or promoters and request financial assistance to make their engagements, or if they were relatively close to the place of performance, ask that they be picked up. Sometimes performers were up to two hours late.

Nonetheless, most singers preferred automobile travel. Riding buses or trains meant having to travel in the "colored" section. On trains only one porter (or none at all) was assigned to two or three cars. Seats in these cars were seldom in good repair, and luggage sat on passenger seats for lack of storage room above. Few food services were offered, and bathrooms were seldom cleaned. Many of the bus stops had no provisions for African Americans, requiring them to stand outside a side window of a restaurant for food service.

Many buses and trains arrived at a specific designated point at one or two o'clock in the morning. Upon arrival, singers had to find transportation to the "colored" hotels or rooming houses in town if no sponsor or friends could meet them. (During the 1940s and 1950s white taxi entrepreneurs began to dispatch taxis for the "colored" section of town, which alleviated this problem to a degree.) Except on visits to cities such as New York or Chicago, most singers had to stay in the one hotel or rooming house that would accommodate African Americans. If no rooms were available, friends or even strangers met on the street could direct singers to homes that took in "overnight" boarders. Rather than endure this travail, singers would use their church network or family and friends to arrange accommodation. In many towns where singers were performing for two or more days, dinner invitations from church members or concert attendees were eagerly accepted. Sometimes the sponsor of multiple concerts would arrange to have the singers dine at a different home each night.

When singers discovered that they would have to depend on restaurants and cafes for food, they would go to the local grocery store and stock their suitcases with crackers, potato chips, pork rinds, peanuts, potted meat, sardines, and pickled pig feet. Such action was necessary because many of the African American restaurants and cafes during the 1940s were run by people who worked at other jobs during the day and only opened their establishments after they completed their other jobs. Many restaurants did not open until six o'clock in the evening.

Whether singers lived in homes, hotels, or rooming houses, there was the

perennial problem of preparing their uniforms for the stage. Early on both men and women began to travel with one or two irons to press uniforms before a performance. While ironing in the home of a friend or family would be easy—often the host would volunteer to do the work—hotels and rooming houses usually made the singers pay extra for the electricity used. To make up for this extra charge, sometimes three and four people would sleep in one room, some in the one bed, some in chairs, and some on the floor.

Singers would bring extra posters or placards with them and, on the day before the concert, place them in stores and on signposts in the African American community to ensure proper advertising for the concert. This was especially crucial when the singers felt that the promoter was not sufficiently sophisticated in concert promotion. Many promoters—at first, all black—were gospel DJs who had no experience in concert promotion; some were ministers who assigned work to parishioners who were inept, and others were singers who thought that their names should be enough to guarantee a crowd.

By the early 1950s transportation problems had earned gospel singers such a reputation for late arrival at concerts that it became necessary to assure the public beforehand that the singers were indeed in town. In cities like Chicago, New York, and Detroit, a Sunday afternoon or evening concert appearance required that the singers be featured in one or two selections at one of the more popular churches so that the news of their arrival would spread before performance time.

Singers often performed with a guarantee of sixty percent of all collections or offerings. When paid admission to concerts began in the early 1950s, it was the custom for one or two of the singers to sit or stand at the door of the performance room or in the box office and collect (sometimes sell) tickets to ensure accountability for the number of persons attending a concert and the correct percentage they were due. Most singers required an advance two weeks before the concert. This advance, called a "guarantee," was necessary for two reasons: in many cases singers did not have the money to travel to the performance, and promoters were notorious for reporting a smaller amount of money than was collected, thereby cheating the singers of their full percentage of the money. Singers felt that if they were going to be cheated it would be better to get at least some money for the performance. If a group agreed to present a concert for a fee of $500, $200 would be the requested guarantee; the

remaining $300 was due at the intermission of the concert. While this plan appeared fail-safe, it seldom worked. Singers were left to collect whatever money they could. It was usually necessary to present the concert once they were in town so they would have enough money to return home.

While many professional singers appeared to be "on the road" in the 1950s, many more could have been had they not had to work so hard to bring their music and message to the people. The dedicated pioneers who persevered became part of American and world history. One of the first was Thomas Andrew Dorsey.

GOSPEL IN CHICAGO

The seeds for a gospel community had been planted in Chicago by COGIC minister William Roberts (1876–1954), a Mississippi native who was "saved" under Charles Harrison Mason. After serving as Mason's deacon for a few years, Roberts was called to preach and went to the Windy City in 1917 to plant a church, where he introduced sanctified singing to his small congregation.

Charles Henry Pace (1886–1963) had moved to Chicago from Atlanta at age thirteen, and although he studied the European masters in his piano lessons, he came under the influence of the new gospel music and composed and conducted a style of this music at the Beth Eden and Liberty Baptist churches. In 1925 he formed the Pace Jubilee Singers, a conservative gospel group that, with Hattie Parker as soloist, reached a new peak in gospel in 1930 with their recording of Charles Albert Tindley's "Stand by Me."

Chicago was thus primed for a genuine gospel movement, and Thomas Andrew Dorsey seized the day. With a group of gospel musicians from Chicago and the surrounding area (sometimes extending more than two hundred miles), Dorsey created a vigorous gospel community. The leaders of this community were Dorsey, Sallie Martin, and Theodore R. Frye.

Thomas Andrew Dorsey

By 1945, it was difficult to avoid gospel music in the African American community. Although gospel had been created in the Pentecostal/Holiness churches of the South, the National Baptist Convention formally adopted it in 1921. And because Chicago was the center of music making for the National Baptist Convention, this

city became the center for the development of gospel. For many years the leader of the "Chicago school of gospel" was Thomas Andrew Dorsey (1899–1993). Born in Villa Rica, Georgia, thirty-eight miles from Atlanta, Dorsey was the oldest of three children born to the Reverend Thomas Madison Dorsey, a graduate of what is now Morehouse College, and Etta Plant Dorsey, an organist. The Dorsey family moved to Atlanta in 1910, by which time young Thomas was able to play the pump organ for services at which his father preached, having first studied piano with his mother and then with a Mrs. Graves. Dorsey was encouraged in his musicianship by band

Thomas Dorsey and his female quartet, consisting of Bertha Armstrong, Dettie Gay, Mattie Wilson, and Sallie Martin, 1934

members who accompanied acts at the 81 Theater, a vaudeville house on Atlanta's Decatur Street, where, since age eleven, he had worked selling nickel soda pop.

Atlanta's 81 Theater, the principal performance house for black artists of the Theater Owners Booking Association (TOBA), presented the most popular black entertainers on the traveling circuit. Among the entertainers who performed there were Gertrude "Ma" Rainey (1886–1939), the first great female blues singer and leading blues

singer of the 1920s; pianist Eddie Heywood; and the comedy team of Butter Beans and Susie. Dorsey absorbed their influence, paying particular attention to the blues and to barrelhouse piano, and was soon able to duplicate their chords, riffs, and runs. He featured his new playing style at house and rent parties and teas sponsored by women's organizations.

Desiring a better musical education than he thought he could secure in Atlanta, Dorsey moved to Gary, Indiana, in 1916. His principal job there was working in a steel mill, but when he was not at the mill, he played piano in various local jazz bands. Settling permanently in Chicago in 1918, he enrolled for a short time in the Chicago College of Composition and Arranging. After only a few months in Chicago, he began playing with such well-known local jazz groups as Les Hite's Whispering Serenaders, a band that once included Lionel Hampton (b. 1909), and his own group, the Wildcats Jazz Band, the traveling band for Ma Rainey.

In 1925 he joined with Hudson Whittaker (1900–81), known as "Tampa Red,"

in a duo. The two produced "Tight Like That" in 1928, and the tremendous success of this double entendre song was the catalyst for several other duets, most of which were successful records. In late 1928, while working with Tampa Red, Dorsey suffered his second nervous breakdown in two years and decided to retire from music. During a two-year recuperation, a minister told him that he was "not as sick in the body as in mind" and that if he would use his music for God he would be healed. Dorsey accepted this as a warning that he should return to the music of his Christian roots.

This return would mean a radical change for Dorsey (Baptists, like Pentecostalists, did not believe that you could play blues, the devil's music, and still be a Christian), because for so long he had denied his "calling" to both the spoken and musical ministry. He had been converted as a small boy in Villa Rica and continued playing for church services even as he became involved with the blues. He kept his blues playing from his parents and most church members did not go to the places where he played, although if any had, they would not have mentioned his playing for they would not want it known that they had been to such places.

When Dorsey attended the National Baptist Convention in Chicago in 1921, he had no plan to return to the church, as he was having what he considered a successful career as a blues pianist. His intentions were changed when he experienced a second conversion during one of the services. The Reverend W. M. Nix, a Birmingham, Alabama, native, delivered a stirring gospel rendition of the 1907 hymn "I Do, Don't You?" by Edwin O. Excell (1851–1951) that was characterized by improvisation like that found in the singing of the sanctified singers. Dorsey, according to his biographer Michael W. Harris, declared:

> My inner being was thrilled … my emotions were aroused; my heart was inspired to become a great singer and worker in the Kingdom of the Lord—and impress people just as this great singer did that Sunday morning.

Despite this second conversion, Dorsey's return to the church lasted only a few months. During that brief time, however, he composed a gospel song, "If I Don't Get There," for the second edition of *Gospel Pearls*, published in late 1921. The song remains number 117 in the hymnal. Dorsey's first published gospel song, it is a fairly sophisticated indication of what his songs of the 1930s and 1940s would be, captur-

ing as it did the sonorous language of the common folk set to a melody of only six (scale) tones, four chords (one more than in the blues of the 1920s), and a refrain of repeated lines:

VERSE

Dear friends and kindred have gone from this world,
To dwell in that city so fair,
Hard trials and troubles no longer they share,
They'll be disappointed if I don't get there.

CHORUS

If I don't get there, if I don't get there,
They'll be disappointed with hearts in despair,
Dear father and mother, sweet sister and brother,
Kind kindred and others, if I don't get there.

When this gospel song did not propel Dorsey into the forefront of gospel singers, he felt there was nothing to do but return to the world of secular music. Then the minister's words "not as sick in the body as in mind" finally struck a chord with Dorsey in 1928, and in 1930 he renounced secular music and became a full-time gospel musician. It was a tumultuous two years between 1928 and 1930 for Dorsey because he had no church community to replace the community he had established in blues. At the same time his blues-playing friends were regularly offering him jobs. He had no occupation other than music and without his blues and jazz engagements he could not make a living. But after playing only a few blues jobs, Dorsey set about meeting church musicians and attending sacred music concerts. To earn a living, he began composing gospel music and peddling song sheets throughout Chicago, although he was often the butt of jokes and humiliation.

Determined to serve the Master through his gospel music, he organized one of the first gospel choirs at Chicago's Pilgrim Baptist Church in 1932 and secured as his pianist the young adult Roberta Martin, who would become a leading force in gospel within ten years. In the same year he opened the first publishing house for the exclusive sale of gospel music by African American composers, and the following year, along with Sallie Martin, Magnolia Lewis Butts, Theodore R. Frye, and

Beatrice Brown, organized the National Convention of Gospel Choirs and Choruses, Incorporated (NCGCC). The members of Dorsey's NCGCC were directors and choirs in Baptist churches throughout the United States. Each annual convention, held in a different city, brought forth a new batch of songs that choir directors could teach to their local church choirs.

Dorsey was particularly skilled at writing songs that not only captured the hopes, fears, and aspirations of the poor and disenfranchised African American but also spoke to all people. Marked by catchy titles, many of which became part of the religious rhetoric of African American Christians, these songs had simple but beautiful melodies, harmonies that did not overshadow the text, and open rhythmic spaces for the obligatory improvisation that identified gospel. Indeed, during the 1940s there were periods when all gospel songs were referred to as "Dorsey."

There has been no more imposing figure in gospel than Thomas Andrew Dorsey, and for his contribution to the music, he was named early on "Father of African American Gospel Music" and was celebrated as such in the 1983 documentary *Say Amen, Somebody*. His most popular composition, "Take My Hand, Precious Lord," second only to "Amazing Grace" in popularity in the African American community, has been translated into more than forty languages and has even been used as a prayer.

It is ironic that one of the most beloved of all Christian hymns, "Take My Hand, Precious Lord," was born of tragedy. In 1932 Dorsey and Theodore R. Frye left Chicago en route to St. Louis, Missouri, to organize a gospel choir. After traveling only a few miles Frye remembered an important engagement and requested that Dorsey return him to his home. Dorsey took the trip to St. Louis alone. Upon his arrival at the church in St. Louis, he found a telegram waiting for him. The telegram said that his wife had suddenly become extremely ill and that he should return to Chicago at once. Dorsey's wife was in the last stages of pregnancy, and when he finally returned home he found that his wife had died. The baby had been born without difficulty but unfortunately died within two days. He retired to his "music" room and remained there for three days. Dorsey said that when he came to himself after three days he went to the piano and, using as inspiration a white Protestant hymn, "Must Jesus Bear the Cross Alone" by George N. Allen (1812–77), composed this song:

Precious Lord, take my hand,
Lead me on, let me stand,
I am tired, I am weak, I am worn;
Through the storm, through the night,
Lead me on to the light,
Take my hand, precious Lord, lead me on.

It was one of several Dorsey compositions sung at his funeral in Chicago on January 28, 1993.

Sallie Martin

The first genuine gospel singer to attract Dorsey's attention was Sallie Martin (1896–1988) of Pittfield, Georgia. Martin arrived in Chicago in 1927, by way of Cleveland, Ohio, with her husband and son after a hard life in her small Georgia town. From baby-sitting, cleaning houses, cooking, and washing clothes, Martin became a church singer, singing hymns and spirituals for Sunday morning services, Wednesday evening prayer meetings, and revivals. When she moved to Chicago she became affiliated with the Pentecostal church, but retained an association with the National Baptist Convention, the denomination into which she was born. When Dorsey began his gospel movement in 1930, Martin attempted to become his associate. Dorsey considered her singing style unrefined, filled with whoops, slides, groans, and most abominably, physical steps while singing, a practice associated with shouting in the Pentecostal church.

Another bone of contention that Dorsey had to reconcile was Martin's inability to read music and her complete disinterest in learning to do so. While Martin had been brought up in the Baptist church and had sung there as a young girl, her mature singing had developed in the Pentecostal church. At that time the Pentecostal church did not use hymn books, preferring to sing relatively simple refrains such as those of the Azusa Street Revival. Since such music could be learned so quickly and improvisation was so important to the style, reading music was unnecessary. Dorsey was aware that most choir members did not read music, but many soloists did, especially those who were good enough and sang enough to develop favorable reputations. Even though he did not care for Martin's singing he recognized her celebrity

as a local singer. Dorsey would soon discover that the ability to read music was extremely rare in gospel choirs, and that teaching music without reading it would become his method of working with gospel choirs.

Martin devised a plan to win Dorsey's attention. Whenever she knew that Dorsey was to appear at a local church, she arranged to appear on the program or lead a song during the service. Singing a repertoire of sanctified songs, she was able to stir the church into a frenzy. She auditioned for Dorsey three times but was rejected each time. Through the intervention of Theodore R. Frye, Dorsey agreed to accept her as a member of a trio he formed in 1932 to demonstrate his songs. It was a year before Dorsey assigned her a solo, and although he objected to the dark color of her voice, her tendency to purposely insert a break in the voice at the beginning and ending of phrases, and her curt manner of addressing him, he could not deny the fact that she possessed a special relationship with church audiences: they responded enthusiastically to her singing of his songs.

Sallie Martin had a keen sense of finances: at the height of her career in the 1960s she was reportedly the wealthiest woman in gospel, having accumulated more money than either Roberta Martin or Mahalia Jackson. She knew how to market sheet music, save on printing, charge for voice lessons, and save money. Dorsey was little concerned with such matters, delegating such responsibilities to Martin once their partnership was solidified. She organized his music store, hired assistants to work at the counter, and kept records of the inventory. After a few short months of working with Dorsey, she was able to show a profit for his business—a feat that had eluded Dorsey. This success was not achieved without many stormy sessions between Dorsey and Martin. Martin was argumentative and adversarial by nature and was constantly on the attack. Their heated discussions were often caused by Martin's statement to Dorsey that "you have something here [his compositions] but you just don't know what to do with it [he was not an aggressive salesman]." The same kind of tenuous relationship was to mark her association with Willie Mae Ford Smith, her partner in Dorsey's convention, as documented in 1983 in *Say Amen, Somebody*.

In 1932 Martin joined Dorsey in organizing the NCGCC, and served as first vice president from its organization until her death. In 1940, with gospel song composer Kenneth Morris and with financial backing from the Reverend Clarence H. Cobb, she opened the Martin and Morris Music, Inc. in Chicago, a publishing company she

codirected until 1975. In 1940 she also formed the Sallie Martin Singers with whom she traveled throughout the United States and Europe (the singers disbanded in 1975). She was an active supporter of Martin Luther King, Jr., and represented him at the 1960 ceremony marking independence in Nigeria. Her visit to Africa inspired her to make financial contributions to the Nigerian Health Program. As a result, a state office building in Isslu-UKA, Nigeria, was named in her honor.

Martin was unlike other Chicago singers in that she never attempted to smooth out her rough-hewn voice. She adopted the sanctified style of shout singing and was known for her Holy Ghost jerks and steps. When taken over by the spirit, her dark alto would soar above a shouting crowd on such songs as "I Claim Jesus First and Last" and Dorsey's "It Don't Cost Very Much" and "I'll Tell It Wherever I Go." Of all her recordings, she is best known for her duet with Alex Bradford of "He'll Wash You Whiter Than Snow" in which she matches Bradford note for note and nuance for nuance as he, with a voice much like that of a young Louis Armstrong, wailed and squalled through one of the most joyous jubilee songs of the 1950s.

Despite her adversarial relationship with Dorsey that endured until the 1980s, when Dorsey retired from composing, Martin was Dorsey's right hand in his gospel ministry. In recognition of her contributions to gospel music and her work with Dorsey, she was accorded the title of "Mother of Gospel" by the NCGCC.

Theodore R. Frye

The third person in the triumvirate established by Dorsey was Theodore R. Frye (1899–1963). Born in Fayette, Mississippi, Frye moved to Chicago in 1927. Having studied piano and voice as a child and having served as soloist and choir director in his hometown, Frye eagerly sought a musical camaraderie in Chicago with musicians who not only read music but who were not afraid to sing with the "spirit." He found this in Dorsey. With Dorsey as his pianist, he quickly developed a reputation as a singer who could "move a house," meaning that he was generally successful in arousing the emotions of a congregation. His light baritone was perfectly suited to the new gospel songs: enough volume in the low register to give a solid reading of the theme and enough notes in the upper register to display varied techniques while improvising. He and Dorsey became close friends and served as codirectors of the junior choir at Chicago's Ebenezer Baptist Church; Frye became sole director in 1932

when Dorsey assumed the directorship of the gospel choir at Pilgrim. In 1933, a year after cofounding the NCGCC, he and Roberta Martin formed the Martin-Frye Quartet of young boys from Pilgrim's Junior Choir. Although Frye composed the popular "Sending up My Timber up to Heaven" (1939) and "God's Power Changes Things" (1949), he is more popularly known as the revisionist of "I'm Going to Walk That Milky White Way" (1948), first recorded by the CBS Trumpeteers in 1948 and a popular hit again in the late 1980s through a recording by the gospel/jazz *a cappella* group, Take Six. His compositions, like Dorsey's, are characterized by a poetic use of black rhetoric, singable melodies, and syncopated rhythms.

In the 1940s Frye became an associate of Mahalia Jackson and figured prominently in her second recording session for Apollo Records in 1947 that produced her greatest hit, "Move on up a Little Higher." He was a cofounder of the National Baptist Music Convention (1948), an auxiliary of the National Baptist Convention that was organized to train musicians for the denomination. Frye worked with Lillian Bowles and Dorsey in their publishing firms and finally opened his own publishing house in 1948.

Magnolia Lewis Butts

A close associate of both Dorsey and Frye was Magnolia Lewis Butts (c.1880–1949). Butts had served as the director of the Youth Choir of the Metropolitan Community Church since 1928, and when Dorsey organized the gospel choir at Pilgrim, she followed his lead and adopted gospel music for her group. She changed the name of her choir to the Metropolitan Community Church Gospel Chorus in 1932 when she became a cofounder of the NCGCC. While Butts was known then as a great gospel soloist whose small but prominent alto voice could fill a large hall with spirited singing, she is remembered today principally as the composer of "Let It Breathe on Me" (1942), a composition that even in the early 1990s was still being sung during the call to prayer and meditation in many African American services:

> *Let it breathe on me, let it breathe on me,*
> *Let the breath of the Lord now breathe on me;*
> *Let it breathe on me, let it breathe on me,*
> *Let the breath of the Lord now breathe on me.*

Unlike most of Dorsey's associates, Butts never opened a publishing firm, but published her songs through the Bowles Music House, whose catalogue was purchased by Sallie Martin in 1959 for the Martin and Morris Music Company.

Roberta Martin

Dorsey's Chicago school of gospel inspired many younger musicians to adopt his style and join his followers. Roberta Martin (1907–69) had been with Dorsey since he organized the gospel choir at Pilgrim in 1932. She had heard gospel before she met Dorsey, however, and in a 1964 interview Martin described her introduction to gospel:

> I've been playing in churches nearly all my life, ever since I was so high. I started down at Pilgrim where I was the pianist for the Sunday School. At that time I was just interested in church hymns, anthems, choir music and secular songs. The first time I heard gospel singing as such, was this lady and the men—Bertha Wise and her Singers [from Augusta, Georgia]. Miss Wise played the piano for them. They came to our church, and oh, did we enjoy them. Actually, they were famous—they would go around to the National Baptist Convention and sing. They were not exactly singing gospel songs, but spirituals like gospel songs and the one that interested me the most was "I Can Tell The World About This." This was in 1933 [1932?].

Martin's experience with the Wise Singers was evidently before her assignment as the pianist for Dorsey's choir. In either case, in 1933 she and Frye organized the Martin-Frye Quartet, and by 1935 when she changed the name of the group to the Roberta Martin Singers, she had become a convert to gospel.

Roberta Evelyn Martin was one of six children born to William and Anna Winston in Helena, Arkansas. She moved with her family to Cairo, Illinois, when she was ten, by which time she had studied the piano with her oldest brother's wife and had already been a pianist for the Sunday School. While attending the Wendell Phillips High School in Chicago, she was inspired by her teacher, Mildred Bryant Jones, to study to become a concert artist. However, when she was invited to become the pianist for the Young People's Choir at Ebenezer Baptist Church, she began to devote her talents to church music.

Eugene Smith, Archie Dennis, Delois Barrett, Roberta Martin, and Gloria Griffin as the Roberta Martin Singers

After working with both Dorsey and Frye, she decided to enter the field of gospel and selected several young boys from Ebenezer and Pilgrim to become the Roberta Martin Singers. The original members were Eugene Smith (b. 1921), Norsalus McKissick (b. 1925), Robert Anderson (b. 1919), James Lawrence (1925–1990), Willie Webb (b. 1919), and Romance Watson (b. 1925). Inspired by Bertha Wise and her singers, and undoubtedly because even as a youngster Martin possessed a dark, rich contralto that could easily mix with the male timbre, she set about developing a gospel sound with no bass, but rather a dark treble sound with the vocal elasticity that the new music required. Eugene Smith, who was only twelve years old when Martin first assembled the group, sang first tenor, Watson sang second tenor, Webb was the high baritone, and Anderson the low baritone. Martin filled in when one of the boys took the lead. In the early 1940s when Martin decided to add female voices to her group, she selected Bessie Folk (b. 1928) and Delois Barrett (b. 1926) and refined the "Roberta Martin gospel sound and style."

The Martin style was one of refinement in songs, singing style, and piano and

organ accompaniment. Although her inspiration came from the Pentecostal shouters, she felt that she could not duplicate this fiery kind of singing and instead attempted, with great success, to capture their zest with well-modulated voices. She began the tradition of each member serving as both soloist and background singer. Rather than encouraging a lead voice with increasingly aggressive background singing, she took the opposite approach, assigning a hum as response instead of an energized repetition of the lyrics. This practice encouraged the audience to pay more attention to the delivery of the text and melody by the lead singer. This technique worked well with slow, lyrical gospel ballads; for jubilee or fast-paced songs Martin returned to the original Pentecostal/Negro spiritual practice of call and response with the background voices spurring the leader on to a vocal frenzy.

Martin was equally well known for her piano style, which was marked by nuance and refinement rather than virtuosity. She played mainly in the middle of the piano, introducing chords—magnificently voiced—that she borrowed from the Western European classical music she had studied and that were new to gospel. She emphasized the first beat of each musical unit in the middle of the piano and provided her own response by answering this beat with secondary beats at the upper ranges of the keyboard. One of her trademarks was bringing a song to a "ritard" (slowing down) at the end, followed by cascading chords all the way to the upper extremes of the keyboard.

She opened the Roberta Martin Studio of Music in 1939, and one of her first publications was the gospel standard "He Knows How Much We Can Bear." Her first composition to become a gospel standard, "Try Jesus, He Satisfies," was written and published in 1943. Among her other famous compositions are "I'm Just Waiting on the Lord" (1953) and "God Is Still on the Throne" (1959). Unlike Dorsey, who published only his own compositions, Martin published songs by other composers, as long as they were songs her group sang. In this way she advertised her inventory. She published and her group sang compositions by James Cleveland, Lucy Matthews, Sammy Lewis, Kenneth Woods, Alex Bradford, and Dorothy Norwood. Her most famous publication was her theme song, "Only a Look" by Anna Shepherd.

Martin began recording in the late 1930s, and during the thirty-six-year career of the Roberta Martin Singers, she earned six gold records for selling a million copies of a song or an album. She was one of the first singers to refuse to permit her

group to perform in secular venues. She did, however, accept an invitation to perform at Gian-Carlo Menotti's Spoleto Festival of Two Worlds in Spoleto, Italy, in 1963. She was honored for her groundbreaking work in gospel by a colloquium and concert at the Smithsonian Institution in 1982.

Eugene Smith and Gospel Blues

In 1941 Eugene Smith, a member of the Roberta Martin Singers, composed "I Know the Lord Will Make a Way, Oh Yes, He Will." His composition became extremely important because it gave another formal structure to composers of gospel and would continue to intrigue composers even into the 1980s.

Smith, the most flamboyant of the Martin Singers and the manager of the group from 1947 until it disbanded in 1969, could have easily led his own group. With his penchant for caressing the lyrics and tones of a gospel ballad (a slow gospel song that often tells a serious or melancholy story) and his ability to deliver a shout song not unlike his Pentecostal preaching friends, Smith was approached on several occasions to leave the Martin Singers and form his own group. He chose not to but made a contribution to gospel that was possibly greater than the formation of a group. "I Know the Lord Will Make a Way, Oh Yes, He Will" is now recognized as *gospel blues*. While, at first hearing, gospel blues bears none of the formal characteristics of the blues made famous by Bessie Smith (1884–1937) or B. B. King (b. 1925), their structural relationship becomes clearer on closer examination.

The most obvious characteristic of the blues is its constant harmonic progression. That is to say, whether the blues is "Fine and Mellow" by Billie Holiday (1915–69) or "Everyday I Have the Blues" by Memphis Slim (Peter Chatman, b. 1915), each with a different melodic line, the harmony that supports the melody for each is the same. The harmony, explained in musical textbooks as I-IV-V and embellished with as many additional chords as there are performers, is the harmonic foundation over which each composer lays a new or different melody.

"I Know the Lord Will Make a Way, Oh Yes, He Will" is as true to the gospel blues structure as "Everyday I Have the Blues" is to the secular blues. Both use a constant harmonic scheme: secular blues is composed of a three-line poem with an AAB rhyme scheme, while gospel blues is composed of a four-line poem with an AABA rhyme scheme. Secular blues requires three units (three four-bar phrases) of

musical time to express its poetry, while gospel blues requires four units of musical time. Also, a different middle and closing section are incorporated into gospel blues. Secular blues text treats a dire situation that worsens in the last line, while gospel blues speaks of a hope that is guaranteed and celebrated in the third line with the first line repeated as the last, giving symmetry to the poem. For example:

SECULAR BLUES—"STORMY MONDAY"
They call it stormy Monday, but Tuesday's just as bad
[rhyme—A; musical time—four bars]
They call it stormy Monday, but Tuesday's just as bad
[rhyme—A; musical time—four bars]
Wednesday's worse, and Thursday's oh, so sad
[rhyme—B; musical time—four bars]

GOSPEL BLUES—"I KNOW THE LORD WILL MAKE A WAY, OH YES, HE WILL"
I know the Lord will make a way, oh yes, He will
[rhyme—A; musical time—four bars]
I know the Lord will make a way, oh yes, He will
[rhyme—A; musical time—four bars]
He will make a way for you, He will lead you safely through
[rhyme—B; musical time—four bars]
I know the Lord will make a way, oh yes, He will
[rhyme—A; musical time—four bars]

"I Know the Lord Will Make a Way, Oh Yes, He Will" revived interest in the first gospel blues composition, "When the Storms of Life Are Raging, Stand by Me" by Charles Albert Tindley, and inspired such later compositions as "I'm Going to Die with the Staff in My Hand" and "Lord, I've Tried."

Robert Anderson

While Eugene Smith remained with the Martin Singers, three other members left to organize their own groups. The first was Robert Anderson, followed by Willie Webb and Delois Barrett. Having come to Chicago from his native Mississippi as a small child, Anderson followed other young, musically inclined children to Metropolitan

Community Church where Magnolia Lewis Butts directed the children's choir. He never studied piano formally but, like many other pianists and organists in the African American church of the period, learned to play by ear and often assisted Roberta Martin with the Sunday School choir. Anderson cared little for traveling so when the Martin Singers began to do so full time in the early 1940s, he decided to establish a solo career. This was a momentous step for Anderson, because he had one of the most unusual voices in gospel, a true baritone singing in a style similar to such then-popular singers as Billy Eckstine and Bing Crosby. Although he came from Mississippi, the adopted home of Charles Harrison Mason, Anderson never adopted a shouting style of singing gospel. His style was marked by fullness of tone, few embellishments, and little physical activity while singing. Yet his attention to phrasing, purity of tone, and dynamic style brought the same kind of response from audiences as Eugene Smith did using the theatrics of the Pentecostal church.

Anderson organized several groups to sing with him even as he continued his solo career, hoping to find other singers who would bear some of the responsibility of leading songs. Most successful was the Gospel Caravan, which he organized in 1947. Unlike those he organized before and after, this group was composed of all women and included seventeen-year-old Albertina Walker, who within a few years would leave Anderson to organize her own group. Serving as his own accompanist, Anderson developed a reputation as a stirring singer, conductor, and composer. While he performed the compositions of Dorsey, Frye, and Martin with enthusiasm, none of these performances equaled the renditions of his own compositions. The 1950 recording of his 1947 composition "Prayer Changes Things" has yet to be equaled in its reading of the lyrics and forceful delivery of the melody, especially in its sing-a-long style chorus:

> *Oh yes, I know prayer changes things, oh yes, I know*
> *Prayer changes things,*
> *When I was out on the stormy, raging sea;*
> *I was hungry, I was sick, I was filled with misery,*
> *Along came Jesus and He rescued me,*
> *That's why I know that prayer changes things.*

Like Dorsey, Roberta Martin, and Sallie Martin, Anderson opened a publishing

house, Robert Anderson's Good Shepherd Music House, in Gary, Indiana, in 1942, through which he published his compositions. Anderson was the only member of the Chicago school of gospel to publish outside Chicago. Among his other popular compositions were "Why Should I Worry?" (1945) and "Oh Lord, Is It I?" (1953).

Norsalus McKissick

Norsalus McKissick was not a composer, but as the second youngest of the original Roberta Martin Singers, he was so instrumental in presenting the gospel ballads sold by Martin that he deserves special mention. Like Eugene Smith, McKissick came to Ebenezer Baptist Church from Metropolitan to join the Youth Choir organized by Roberta Martin and Theodore R. Frye in 1933. Slight of stature and the quietest member of the Roberta Martin Singers, McKissick did not possess a golden baritone like that of Robert Anderson, but rather a slightly brassy baritone, extraordinary breath control, and a sense of phrasing unmatched in gospel even into the 1990s. Called a "deliberate" singer, that is, one who is always slightly behind the beat, allowing time for each syllable to become an independent unit within itself, McKissick could work through a ballad in such a way that the listener was transported into the situation about which he sang. Throughout his long career with the Martin Singers (1933–69), there was always a rush of audience emotion when he sang, "I was lost in sin and sorrow," the opening line of Dorsey's recasting of the Negro spiritual "Old Ship of Zion." He was no less at home with Roberta Martin's gospel arrangement of the white Protestant hymn "The Old Account Was Settled." He reached new heights of interpretation with Alex Bradford's "Saved Till the Day of Redemption" in the mid-1950s.

Kenneth Morris

Although he never worked directly with Dorsey, Kenneth Morris (1917–88) came under his influence early on and patterned much of his career after Dorsey's. Morris was born in New York City and took piano lessons from grammar school through high school. Like most child pianists of the church, he occasionally served as pianist for the Sunday School, but by his teen years, his interest was focused on impromptu jam sessions with other teenage boys from his neighborhood. After graduating from high school, Morris entered the Manhattan Conservatory of Music where he studied traditional Western music theory—but with the hope of becoming

a jazz musician. While he was at the conservatory, the Kenneth Morris Jazz Band, which grew out of the jam sessions, received an invitation to perform in Chicago at the 1934 World's Fair. His group was a success, but Morris contracted tuberculosis and had to leave the band.

Rather than return to New York to recuperate, Morris decided to remain in Chicago. For entertainment during this period he occasionally "sat in" with a group of Chicago jazz musicians, all of whom could read and write music. The news of the group reached Lillian Bowles, owner of Bowles Music House, who approached Morris in hopes that he could recommend a scribe to write down in musical notation the songs composed by those who were technically illiterate and could not do so themselves.

Mrs. Bowles (c.1884–1949), originally from Memphis, Tennessee, but a long-time resident of Chicago, had opened a publishing house in the late 1920s. Gospel was one of several types of music she published, along with blues, jazz, and ragtime. Although Bowles' publications were mainly skeletons of what an improvising performer was expected to play, the scribe who wrote out the music needed to know the several styles. In most cases scribes did not alter in any way what composers sang or played for them—people who did that were called "arrangers." However, Morris did not know this when Mrs. Bowles approached him and he took the job, which he considered a good find since it was not strenuous and was indoors. Although he was initially disappointed, Morris worked at the Bowles Music House from late 1934 until 1940. He filled a position that had been previously held by Charles Henry Pace, who left Chicago in 1936 for Pittsburgh, Pennsylvania, where he established the Pace Music House shortly afterwards.

During Morris' tenure with Bowles he transcribed such popular gospel songs as "God Shall Wipe All Tears Away" (1935) by Antonio Haskell, "I'm Sending My Timber up to Heaven" (1939) by Theodore R. Frye, and in the same year, a 1937 composition attributed to Mrs. Bowles—and in 1937 the first song recorded by Mahalia Jackson—"God's Goin' to Separate the Wheat from the Tare." Although he transcribed other kinds of music during his years at Bowles, Morris reported in an interview for a 1986 symposium of his music held at the Smithsonian Institution that he was transcribing so much gospel music that he began to lose interest in the other types.

The Reverend Clarence H. Cobb (1907–79), known as "Preacher," often visited the Bowles store to select new music for his church choir. As founder and pastor of Chicago's First Church of Deliverance, Cobb was one of a few preachers in the town who welcomed gospel music. Mrs. Bowles felt that Preacher should meet her new scribe, who could not only play gospel music, but transcribe it as well. Preacher was so impressed with the musicality of Morris that he persuaded him to become choir director at his church. Morris not only accepted the position, arranging for and directing the choir, but in 1939 he revolutionized gospel singing by introducing the Hammond organ as a gospel instrument. When the piano and Hammond organ were paired, they created the ideal accompaniment for gospel: one instrument would sustain tones while the other was rhythmically active; one instrument could affect the vibrato of the voice while the other instrument could be struck like the patting of feet; and one instrument could imitate a bass fiddle while the other instrument tinkled the highest keys like a harp being plucked. These two instruments became the standard accompaniment for traditional gospel until 1970, when a newer style of gospel, called "contemporary," introduced the synthesizer.

Morris became almost as significant a publisher as he was a composer. When he and Sallie Martin realized that Dorsey was publishing only his own compositions and Roberta Martin was publishing only what her singers sang, they saw a tremendous opportunity. By publishing the music of those who had no connection to either the Dorsey or Roberta Martin publishing houses, they could serve a large number of new composers. Their company, Martin and Morris Music, Inc., became the leading publishing house in Chicago. Among their composers were Alex Bradford, James Cleveland, (composers sometimes published with as many as five houses), Sam Cooke, W. Herbert Brewster, Lucie Campbell, and Dorothy Love Coates. Morris transcribed all their compositions, although some composers, such as Lucie Campbell, could notate their own music.

Morris would pay fifteen dollars for each song that he accepted from new or relatively known composers. Well-known composers such as Cleveland and Bradford would haggle over song fees and, depending on their fame at the time of their song submission, could receive as much as fifty dollars for a song. This was an important victory for the composers, for that payment was all that they received from Martin and Morris. On the other hand, Morris would copyright the song in the composer's

name and would sell song sheets or books that included the song to the composer at a reduced rate.

Morris, responsible for demonstrating and selling music at the store in addition to transcribing music, still found some time to compose, and from 1940 until the mid-1960s produced some of the most important songs in African American gospel. His first hit came in 1940 with "I'll Be a Servant for the Lord," made famous by the popular Ohio-based choir Wings Over Jordan. On a train trip from Kansas City to Chicago, Morris exited the train on one of its stops to get some fresh air and heard one of the station porters singing a song. He paid little attention at first, but after he reboarded the train the song remained with him and became so prominent in his mind that at the next stop, he left the train, took another train back to the earlier station, and asked the porter to sing the song again. Morris wrote down the words and music and published the song "Just a Closer Walk with Thee" that year, 1940, adding a few lyrics of his own to provide more breadth. Within two years the song became a standard in gospel music, eventually becoming a standard in jazz, and then moving into the realm of American folk music, known and sung by many.

In 1944 Morris published his most popular song, "Yes, God Is Real." The song opens with a strong declaration of the inability of mortals to understand the universe and to survey all its wonders:

> *There are some things I may not know,*
> *There are some places I can't go.*

The song then immediately shifts to an equally strong statement of confidence, proclaiming what people can understand and their joy in such knowledge:

> *But I am sure of this one thing,*
> *That God is real for I can feel Him deep within.*

In 1946 Morris published the second most popular song in his catalogue, "Christ Is All." Following the Morris formula for lyric writing—that is, stating the problem in the verse of the song, it begins:

> *I don't possess houses or land, fine clothes or jewelry,*
> *Sorrows and cares in this old world my lot seem to be;*

Continuing the formula he brings the verse to a close in the last two lines of the inevitable solution:

> But I have a Christ who paid the price way back on Calv'ry,
> And Christ is all, all and all this world to me.

Morris songs are distinguished from Dorsey and Roberta Martin in this problem-solution aspect of verse writing. His melodies and harmonies were those of 1940s gospel whereby three or four chords supported the melody of five or six tones, limiting the tones of the melody so that the words would not be overshadowed by any musical elements. His "Eyes Hath Not Seen," composed in 1945, goes beyond his usual harmonic language to introduce new and modern chords into gospel that were not completely adopted by gospel composers until the 1960s. Among his more than five hundred songs are several gospel standards, including "Jesus Steps Right in When I Need Him Most" (1945), "Dig a Little Deeper in God's Love" (1947), and "King Jesus Will Roll All Burdens Away" (1947).

Emma L. Jackson

Emma L. Jackson, who flourished from 1940 to 1960, was a staunch supporter of the music of the National Baptist Convention. Deciding to follow the "sound of gospel," she relocated from New Orleans to Chicago in the early 1940s. She first made an impression on the city as a soloist capable of "rocking a church" with both the old Baptist moan and the newer gospel songs. She is credited with introducing Dorsey's "Take My Hand, Precious Lord" at the National Baptist Convention, a song she kept in her repertoire throughout her performance career. Encouraged by Dorsey to write her own songs, in 1942 she composed "I'm Going to Die with the Staff in My Hand":

> I'm going to die with the staff in my hand,
> I'm going to die with the staff in my hand;
> Sometimes I reel and I rock from side to side,
> I'm going to die with the staff in my hand.

Jackson wrote her song for a choir rather than a small group, and when it was performed in the mid-1940s by nearly a thousand voices at the National Baptist Convention, the organists, pianists, and choir directors were participants. They

brought the song back to their local choirs, and it soon became extremely popular.

"I'm Going to Die with the Staff in My Hand" served to introduce Jackson to the gospel public. However, by far her most popular song was "Don't Forget the Family Prayer," composed in 1945 and published in her newly formed publishing house, Jackson Studio of Music:

VERSE

Prayer will keep your home together,
Bring your wand'ring child back home;
Prayer will make you love your neighbor,
Don't forget the family prayer.

CHORUS

Don't forget the family prayer,
Jesus goin' to meet you there;
When you gather round the altar,
Don't forget the family prayer.

Jackson's lyrics were set to a melody that could be remembered and sung after only one rendition. The song captured the essence of Chicago gospel: a simple solution to a difficult problem, but a solution that requires total trust in God; singers who delivered songs with a conviction that would normally be confined to the privacy of one's home; a beat that would not permit a listener to remain uninvolved in the singing; and vocal virtuosity that had not been imagined before the Azusa Street Revival. Jackson's song evoked a passion that had not been experienced by African Americans since slave meetings. The African American nuclear family had been given no respect during the slave era, and families were often broken up, with mother going to one plantation, husband to another, and the children to yet another. In post-slavery times husbands often had to work away from home (sometimes as far as a hundred miles), coming home only on weekends. Often families were, for one reason or another, fatherless. Jackson's song presents, if only for the length of the song, a family obviously composed of both mother and father eagerly awaiting the return of their child from some wayward journey. "Don't Forget the Family Prayer" was and still is popular because of strong African American belief in family and prayer.

Willie Webb

The second singer from the original Roberta Martin Singers to form a group was Willie Webb. Webb (b.1919), like Frye and Anderson, came to Chicago from Mississippi as a small boy. Hearing of the opportunities afforded young musical talent, he joined Anderson, Smith, and McKissick at Metropolitan and sang under Magnolia Lewis Butts. Like Anderson, he did not wish to travel; but unlike Anderson, Webb developed into a virtuoso pianist and organist and was soon recruited to play for and direct local church choirs in the Chicago area. Before "Little" Lucy became the substitute pianist for the Roberta Martin Singers, Webb often replaced Martin at the piano.

He never felt secure enough about his solo voice to lead songs, but he was skilled at arranging songs to fit any voice, teaching all the parts of the chord to singers, and accompanying them on piano or organ. He organized an all-male group in the late 1940s that sang in the Chicago area. In 1949 he founded a mixed group not unlike that of his mentor Roberta Martin, that could express his compositions with an attention-getting flair. The group was composed of, among others, such well-known singers as new Chicago resident Alex Bradford, Ozella Weber, Oralee Thurston, and Webb himself. While Webb has been accorded a certain celebrity for having introduced Alex Bradford to the gospel world—Bradford was the lead singer on Webb's 1951 recording of "Every Day and Every Hour"—many gospel music lovers remember him as the composer of his "I'm Bound for Higher Ground" (1945), a popular gospel standard for twenty years, as was his 1947 composition entitled "He's All I Need."

"Little" Lucy Smith

The Reverend Lucy Smith (1874–1952), founder and pastor (1920–52) of Chicago's All Nations Pentecostal Church, arrived in Chicago in 1910 from her native Athens, Georgia, with ten children. While working as a dressmaker to support her family, she became active in the Olivet Baptist Church. In 1914, however, reacting to the news of the Azusa Street Revival, Smith received the baptism of the Holy Ghost. She founded a healing ministry in 1916 and four years later built one of the first churches in Chicago to receive sanctified singing. Her granddaughter (b. 1928) was known as "Little" Lucy.

Little Lucy showed spectacular musical aptitude from age four when she got on the piano stool and began picking out tunes that she had heard in church. At age ten her grandmother sent her to Roberta Martin for piano lessons. Little Lucy mastered the gospel style in two years and transferred her piano skill to the organ. At age twelve, she became the organist at her grandmother's church and was as much a drawing card as her grandmother.

When she was sixteen, Little Lucy suggested to Roberta Martin that Martin meet her father, who by that time was divorced from her mother. The meeting took place, and through a strange set of circumstances, Martin married Little Lucy's father. Martin then began to teach Little Lucy music theory and voice. In the mid-1950s Little Lucy organized the Lucy Smith Singers, whose members were Catherine Campbell, Sarah McKissick (wife of Norsalus McKissick), Gladys Beamon, and Smith. Her most famous composition was "I'll Never Let Go His Hand," while the most famous recording for the Lucy Smith Singers was "Somebody Bigger Than You and I." In the early 1960s she became the official pianist for the Roberta Martin Singers.

Other Composers Associated with Chicago Gospel

Dorsey and his associates (which did not include the Pentecostal gospel singers because they seldom associated—even musically—with non-Pentecostal singers) inspired others to turn to gospel. One of the most important of these second generation associates of Dorsey was Sylvia Boddie.

SYLVIA BODDIE

Sylvia Boddie, wife of the Reverend Louis Boddie, pastor of the Greater Harvest Baptist Church of Chicago (one of the principal venues for gospel performance during the 1940s and 1950s), composed more than one hundred songs, many of which became gospel standards. Because the choir of her husband's church was the principal vehicle for the performances of her songs, she composed most of them for large groups. Chief among her compositions is the gospel standard "Now Lord" (1948), in which she delivers a prayer to the Master as if talking to a neighbor across the back yard fence:

Chorus

Now Lord, now Lord, now Lord, now Lord,
You've been my burden bearer, you've been my all and all;
I need you when troubles grieve me, I need you when friends deceive me,
Now Lord, please hear me when I call.

VIRGINIA DAVIS

Virginia Davis' "I Call Him Jesus, My Rock" (1950) bears a close relationship to Sylvia Boddie's "Now Lord" and was dedicated to Sylvia Boddie's husband. Davis (b. 1904) occasionally served as a choir director and soloist in Chicago but earned her living as a musical scribe for most of the major publishing houses in Chicago. (She perfected this skill while serving in the same capacity for Lillian Bowles.) She opened a publishing house for a short time but found that all her potential customers had lucrative contracts with other houses at an advance of fifteen or twenty-five dollars per song, so she returned to working with Frye, Jackson, and others as a freelance scribe. She was at her best in arranging songs for gospel singers. She also wrote several songs that enjoyed huge popularity for a short time. Her most famous song, recorded by Clara Ward and the Ward Singers among others, has a sing-a-long chorus built of few words but attached to a memorable melody supported by the sparse harmony that the gospel of the 1940s and 1950s required:

Chorus
Calling Jesus
      My rock
I need you Jesus
      My rock
Hear me Jesus
      My rock
I'm calling Jesus
      My rock
I know He won't deny me
      Jesus—Jesus
For He's walking right beside me
      Jesus—Jesus

Church, I call Him Jesus—
    My rock
I call Him Jesus
    My rock.

The lyrics literally sing the call and response and elicit the kind of audience participation that invariably results in a shout.

VIOLA BATES DICKINSON

A choir director and organist in Chicago churches since the early 1940s and still working in such a capacity in the early 1990s, Viola Bates Dickinson opted for texts that were more progressive than the resurrected Negro spiritual/Pentecostal texts commonly associated with early gospel. Despite what was considered a large number of words, the chorus of her 1942 composition "It's My Desire to Do Thy Will" was a popular hit:

> CHORUS
> *It's my desire to do Thy Will, bear my cross up ev'ry hill,*
> *Tho' the way is sometimes drear, still I know that Thou art near.*
> *You can righten ev'ry wrong, you can change a heart of stone,*
> *Lord, you know it's my desire to do Thy Will.*

BEATRICE BEALE

Beatrice Beale, an associate of Dorsey's since the early 1930s, made no pretense of a progressive slant in her most famous composition "Great Day" (1951). A choir director and pianist who successfully made the transition from standard Protestant hymns to gospel, Beale enjoyed reaching a wide audience through songs that would immediately invite participation:

> VERSE
> *The saviour's face we'll see, with the Lord we shall be,*
> *In that land beyond the sea when we all gather home;*
> *No more sorrow will we know, peace and joy shall overflow,*
> *We shall rest for evermore when we all gather home.*

CHORUS

It will be a great day when we all gather home,
It will be a great day when we all cease to roam;
We will shout hallelujah, over in the land of Beulah,
It will be a great day when we all gather home.

To be sure, Chicago resonated with gospel in the 1940s and early 1950s. While Dorsey had been ridiculed and even turned out of a few churches, not ministers, the burgeoning middle class, nor music conservatories could halt the speed at which gospel was growing. When main-line or old-line churches, as they were called at that time by the educated and the black intelligentsia, refused in the 1920s and 1930s to allow gospel music in their sanctuaries, many young men and women withdrew from established congregations such as Quinn Chapel African Methodist Episcopal (AME), Bethel AME, Olivet Baptist, and others, some of which were members of the National Baptist Convention. These young people organized independent congregations where the principal music was gospel. Of extreme significance is the fact that these new gospel churches were being organized by the generation that had rejected gospel in the first decade of the twentieth century when they heard it in its rawest form in the Pentecostal church. These were also the same people who nonetheless did not protest when a more refined and sedate style of gospel singing was touted by the National Baptist Convention after the publication of *Gospel Pearls*. By the mid-1930s, they had adopted gospel and were willing to fight for its presence in their churches.

Such concerns, however, were far from the minds of Dorsey and his associates in the late 1930s and early 1940s, and without a backward glance they forged a path into American music and culture that allowed gospel to enter the mainstream. But first they needed to find one person or group who could break through the stalwart resistance presented by, of all people, the African American church.

Almost unnoticed by Dorsey and his associates were a cadre of soloists and groups who were more than capable, ready, and willing to stake their reputations on the presentation of this music. Chief among them was Mahalia Jackson.

MAHALIA JACKSON

Mahalia Jackson (1911–72) was the only child born to Charity Clark and Johnny Jackson, Jr. Mahala, as she was christened at birth, grew up in a tightly knit family of devout Baptists who could be found every Sunday morning at the Plymouth Rock Baptist Church in New Orleans. The family enjoyed the music of the church, and although none showed the interest or talent to join the choir, like the other worshippers they participated in the singing of the Baptist lining hymns, standard Protestant hymns, and Negro spirituals, accompanied by a keyboard instrument, usually a harmonium, melodeon, pipe organ, or piano. The singing inspired church members to get "happy" on occasion, but that music did not prepare them for the style of music that they heard on the Sunday morning when little Mahala made herself known to the congregation. According to Jackson's biographer Laurraine Goreau in *Just Mahalia, Baby* (1975):

> At four, with a voice twice as big as she was, Halie ranged before the Plymouth Rock pulpit in its children's choir, singing loud and clear … *Jesus Loves Me.*

By twelve she was a member of the junior choir at the Mount Moriah Baptist Church, where members regularly requested her to sing "Hand Me Down My Silver Trumpet, Gabriel."

It would be many years before Mahala realized the most important influence on her singing style—the singing she heard in a sanctified church a few doors from her house. Unlike the Baptist churches with their single weeknight service, the Wednesday night prayer meeting, the early sanctified saints would meet two or three evenings each week for services that lasted almost until midnight. In her 1966 autobiography *Movin' on Up*, Jackson described her relationship to those sanctified churches:

> I know now that a great influence in my life was the Sanctified or Holiness Churches we had in the South. I was always a Baptist, but there was a Sanctified Church right next to our house in New Orleans.
>
> Those people had no choir and no organ. They used the drum, the cymbal, the tambourine, and the steel triangle. Everybody in there sang and stomped their feet and sang with their whole bodies. They had a beat, a powerful beat, a

Mahalia Jackson sings "Move on up a Little Higher"

rhythm we held on to from slavery days, and their music was so strong and expressive it used to bring tears to my eyes.

I believe the blues and jazz and even rock 'n' roll stuff got their beat from the Sanctified Church.

Although Mahala had been unaware of its influence, her ability to sing with the seeming abandon of the sanctified shouters was apparent to the congregation at Plymouth Rock and would become more apparent through the years.

As Mahala's voice changed from soprano to alto, she listened for hours to the recordings of popular blues singers Mamie Smith, Bessie Smith, and Ma Rainey and attempted to capture their nuances and volume. She then blended this sound with that of the sanctified singers, and by the age fifteen her vocal style was formed: from Bessie Smith and Ma Rainey she borrowed a deep and dark resonance that complemented her own timbre; from the Baptist church she inherited the moaning and bending of final notes in phrases (what W. C. Handy called "worrying over a note"); and from the sanctified church she adopted a full-throated tone, delivered with a holy beat and the body rhythm to accent that beat. While it may appear strange that none of her influences came from gospel singers, it should be remembered

Three gospel divas: Sister Rosetta Tharpe, Madame Ernestine B. Washington, and Mahalia Jackson

that gospel was only arriving in New Orleans as Mahala was leaving, and other than the sanctified church, the only singing she heard outside of the Baptist church was that of the emerging gospel quartet. That sound would also have a lasting influence on her style.

Mahala's Aunt Hannah, who lived in Chicago, invited her to that northern city, and shortly after Thanksgiving of 1927, Mahala made the journey. She accompanied her aunt to church on her first Sunday in Chicago, and as reported by Goreau in *Just Mahalia, Baby,* "as the spirit rose up in her, Halie stood up to witness, her way: 'Hand me down my silver trumpet, Gabriel.'" The big Chicago church, with its formal service not unlike the solemn dignity of the white Baptist church, was shocked

Gospel promoter Johnny Myers and Mahalia Jackson

by the unsolicited solo from the congregation, but they could not deny the beauty of the voice nor the sincerity of the singer.

In 1929, dissatisfied with the reception of her singing in the old-line churches of Chicago, Mahala accepted the invitation of the three Johnson Brothers—Robert, Prince, and Wilbur—to join their singing group, which had one other female singer, Louise Lemon (Jackson had joined the Greater Salem Baptist Church because of this group). The Johnson Singers became not only the stars of Greater Salem Baptist Church, pastored by the father of the Johnson Brothers, but also the first organized gospel group in Chicago.

After only a few years with the Johnson Singers, Mahalia, as she now chose to call herself, became exclusively a soloist. Her style of singing, full throated, bending

a note here, chopping off a note there, singing through rest spots and ornamenting the melodic line at will, confused trained pianists but fascinated those who played by ear. Teenager Evelyn Gay from COGIC, who with her sister, Mildred, would become one of the major gospel duos of the 1950s, played for Mahalia for the sheer pleasure of it. Mahalia soon became a fixture on local gospel concerts. She also served as a soloist for politicians, often traveling to surrounding towns to accompany them or to sing at rallies in their stead.

She met Thomas A. Dorsey in 1928, and he attempted to secure her as his song demonstrator, although he was a little concerned about the melodic liberties she took with his music. In retrospect, it is crystal clear that Mahalia Jackson was never a Baptist singer, except when she sang songs in the Baptist lining hymn tradition. Such songs as "Even Me," "Amazing Grace," and "In My Home over There" show the kind of treatment of the melody line, restrained improvisation, and most of all the legacy of the older styles of African American religious music that the Baptists treasured. If Jackson sang a song that had a solid beat serving as the rhythmic foundation, she exhibited the aggressive style and rhythmic ascension that was found only among the Pentecostal singers. And for all his credit as the "Father of Gospel," Dorsey was a Baptist at heart and fostered a Baptist style of singing.

Jackson was not always inclined to follow the Baptist style of singing, especially when she was caught up in the spirit. Dorsey was legitimately concerned with what she would do to his songs. On the other hand, Jackson was taking Chicago by storm, and Dorsey wanted to be a part of that storm. The decision, however, was not for Dorsey to make, and it was not until 1930 that she accepted his invitation. In 1937 the two became a team for fourteen years, during which time Mahalia would accompany him to his concerts and sing his songs whenever she was not giving concerts of her own. Their relationship was a warm one, although in later years Jackson came to resent Dorsey's insistence that she learned everything she knew about gospel from him.

Realizing that certain doors were not open to her because she had no voice training and could not read music, she was persuaded by one of her friends to audition for a voice teacher, Professor Kendricks, for voice lessons at four dollars an hour. In 1932 their first and only meeting resulted in an admonition from Professor Kendricks:

Young woman, you've got to stop that hollering. That's no way to develop a voice, and it's no credit to the Negro race. White people could never understand you. If you want a career, you'll have to prepare to work a long time to build that voice.

Mahalia left his studio, and that was as close as the lady who sang gospel at one of the inaugural parties of President John F. Kennedy ever came to a voice lesson.

Despite Professor Kendricks' opinion, by 1937 her reputation as a gospel singer had become so great that J. Mayo "Ink" Williams (1894–1980), artist and repertoire director for Decca Records, Race Division, and producer of many of Ma Rainey's recordings, approached her to record four songs with piano for the Decca label. She and her pianist for the past two years, Estelle Allen, had their first recording session on May 21, 1937, in Chicago. Mahalia wanted to use organ on gospel, which she thought would enhance the slow songs, although it had not been tried before. She recorded "God's Goin' to Separate the Wheat from the Tare" by Lillian Bowles and "Oh, My Lord" with piano. Then Allen moved to the organ and pumped away on "God Shall Wipe All Tears Away" by Antonio Haskell (from her hometown of New Orleans) and the standard Protestant hymn "Keep Me Every Day." These recordings received little attention and despite the pleas of Ink Williams, Decca would not record Mahalia again. In fact it was seventeen months before Decca recorded another gospel artist (on October 31, 1938, they held their first session with Sister Rosetta Tharpe).

Despite the commercial failure of her first recorded songs, Mahalia set about to cultivate a national career. She traveled throughout the Northeast and to several states in the South, in addition to appearing annually at the National Baptist Convention. When she felt that the revenue from these concerts did not provide sufficient income, she enrolled in the Chicago branch of Madame C. J. Walker's famous beauty school. After completing her course, she opened a beauty salon in Chicago and confined her traveling to weekends. Ever the entrepreneur, she opened a two-chair shop and rented out the second chair so that she could afford to pay the rent even when she traveled.

While she was a beautician, Johnny Meyers, the most prominent African American concert promoter in New York City, booked Mahalia into New York's Golden

Gate Auditorium. One of the attendees at this concert was Bess Berman, owner of Apollo Records. Berman had under contract at the time such African American secular music performers as Billy Daniels, Arnett Cobb, and Dinah Washington and gospel singers including Clara Hudman Gholston (the Georgia Peach) and the Dixie Hummingbirds. Despite a few problems between the two strong-willed women, they agreed to one recording session of four sides. On October 3, 1946, Mahalia, with her pianist Rosalie McKenny, recorded "I Want to Rest," "He Knows My Heart," "I'm Going to Tell God All about It," and "I'm Going to Wait until My Change Comes." Although these recordings did not garner much public attention, Mahalia's interview on the Studs Turkel radio program from Chicago created a wave of interest and, because of this publicity, Berman was persuaded to record her again.

Gospel DJ Joe Bostic and friend presenting flowers to Mahalia Jackson after her performance at a Baptist Church in the Bronx

Producer Art Freeman was dispatched to contact Mahalia, and the two agreed that she would record a song that she had used as a warm-up before her first recording session. The song had been surreptitiously secured for Mahalia by Theodore R. Frye from a concert that the Brewster Ensemble of Memphis had given the year before in Chicago. (In the 1930s and 1940s copyrights were not secured until a number of years after a song had been introduced—for example, Dorsey composed "Precious Lord" in 1932, but it was not copyrighted until 1938.) Using an early tape recorder, Frye recorded the leader of the group, Queen Candice Anderson, singing "Move on up a Little Higher." Freeman hit upon the idea of recording the song in two parts since the 78 rpm recordings of the time could accommodate only three to three and one-half minutes per side. With James "Blind" Francis (b. 1914) on organ and James Lee (b. 1915) on piano, Mahalia recorded "Move on up a Little Higher" on September 12, 1947. The recording made gospel history, and the career of Mahalia Jackson was established.

The piano part was left off the recording, leaving the tremolo-based Hammond organ as the only accompaniment. This sound had not been heard in gospel before. Francis set up a moderately slow tempo, unifying the accompaniment with a triplet figure that would emerge each time Mahalia would take a rest. The result was an extraordinary display of call and response—but not between soloist and choir, but between soloist and instrument. Mahalia, in the time-honored southern black tradition, "stands flat footed and sings this song." She employs a scooping technique so that there is no clear movement from one note to the other; instead, she connects each note to the other by sliding through all the notes of the melody.

Side One set up the story of the journey from earth to heaven, while Side Two related Mahalia's meeting with all of the heroes of the Bible, as well as family members and friends. The journey is characterized by an ascending melody line from a low to a high tone, bringing the phrases to a close with the voice dropping down the tones of a blues like scale as easily as water falling over a rock. In her usual style, she brings Side One to a close with obligatory ritard. Side Two of the record opens with the voice completely open and soaring above the accompaniment:

> *Move on up a little higher, meet with Old Man Daniel.*
> *Move on up a little higher, meet with Paul and Silas.*

Since each one of the statements melodically travels a short distance and turns on itself to be repeated, the melodic action is held in place for several phrases, while the element of repetition serves its function to get the message across. Each full chorus is ended with Mahalia shouting, "It'll be always 'howdy, howdy,' and never goodbye." The rhythm is so freely intricate that only after hearing the song is one capable of appreciating the number of rhythmic strains that were simultaneously combined, while the embellishments rival those of a coloratura soprano (think of birds chirping). The big, dark, liquid, burnished contralto of Mahalia signaled this recording as a masterpiece. And this is exactly how it was received by the public when it was released in January 1948.

The success of the recording secured for Mahalia a weekly network radio show. She became the first gospel singer to broadcast the pure sanctified gospel as host and star of her own CBS radio program, which premiered on Sunday, September 26, 1954. With Mildred Falls on piano, Ralph Jones on organ, and a white quartet con-

ducted by the show's music director, Jack Halloran, Mahalia began a series of broadcasts that would ensure her career into eternity.

A successful number of recordings at Apollo followed. Among the most popular were "Just over the Hill," "These Are They," and "In the Upper Room." Mahalia was by this time so popular that Columbia Records felt that she could become a crossover artist, and on November 22, 1954, she had her first recording session with that powerful company. Columbia Records made Mahalia Jackson an international star and the "World's Greatest Gospel Singer," but many gospel singers and people from the African American church felt that the singing was not the same as it had been on Apollo Records. Much of this criticism was due to the repertoire assigned to Mahalia on Columbia. The popular music market wanted "Rusty Old Halo" and "You'll Never Walk Alone," while the African American church audience wanted "When I Wake Up in Glory" and "If We Never Needed the Lord Before." Mahalia solved the problem by creating two performance styles: one for the recording studio and the other for live performance.

With Mildred Falls she went on to star on the "Ed Sullivan Show" in 1956, at the Newport Jazz Festival in 1958, and at one of the inaugural parties for President John F. Kennedy in 1960. She sang just before Martin Luther King, Jr., delivered his famous "I Have a Dream" speech at the March on Washington in 1963 and sang Thomas A. Dorsey's "Take My Hand, Precious Lord" at King's funeral in 1968. She sang all over the world before church people, kings, and queens and at her beloved National Baptist Convention. She was on a concert tour in Germany in 1971 when her heart began to beat so slowly that she knew it was her last performance. Through beauty of voice, extraordinary technique, and through her Christian conviction, Mahalia Jackson, more than two decades after her death, is still considered the world's greatest gospel singer.

JAMES LEE

While Mahalia Jackson earned success as a soloist—and she was most often presented as such—she enjoyed singing with choirs, groups, and in duets. One of her favorite singers was her hometown compatriot, James Lee. Lee came to Chicago as a teenager in the early 1930s and quickly aligned himself with emerging gospel singers Robert Anderson, Eugene Smith, and Theodore R. Frye. He always held a unique

position among these men and in the gospel movement because of his unusual voice. Lee could sing tenor but only with great effort, and shortly after arriving in Chicago he turned to his true voice, that of a counter-tenor, with the range of a soprano. He became one of the principal soloists in the Greater Harvest Baptist Church gospel choir and in 1949 persuaded Robert Anderson to direct the choir. His greatest popularity, however, rested on his singing soprano to Mahalia Jackson's alto on such compositions as Lucie Campbell's "He Understands, He'll Say 'Well Done'" and the hymn "I Can Put My Trust in Jesus."

SALLIE MARTIN SINGERS

With the opening of their music publishing company in 1940, Sallie Martin and Kenneth Morris had to devise a method of advertising their inventory. Dorsey advertised his music during his convention and Roberta Martin featured her music with her singers. Some consideration was given to organizing the Kenneth Morris Singers, for which Sallie would be the lead singer and Kenneth would serve as pianist, composer, and arranger. But because Kenneth could both transcribe and play music, while Sallie was only able to sing, they decided that Sallie would organize a group of singers and feature the inventory from the Martin and Morris Music, Inc.

In late 1940, Martin selected four young women and formed the Sallie Martin Singers. Among the early members were Dorothy Simmons (b. 1910), who with Doris Akers would later form the Simmons-Akers Duo. The others were Sarah Daniels, Julia Mae Smith, and Melva Williams. The pianist for the first group was Ruth Jones (1924–63), who in 1943 left the group to build a career as a secular music singer under the name Dinah Washington.

Cora Juanita Brewer (b. 1927) joined the group in 1942, and even though her parents were alive and living in Chicago, Martin adopted her and she became famous as Cora Martin. Although Brewer's parents loved her and could well afford to bring her up, they saw her dreams for a gospel singing career coming true only with someone like Sallie Martin. They gave up their daughter willingly to Martin; however, Brewer continued to maintain a close relationship with them. Brewer and Martin enjoyed a loving relationship until Martin's death at age ninety-two.

In the fashion of the day, most of Sallie Martin's songs featured a lead soloist with the rest of the group providing the response. Simmons possessed a brilliant

soprano; Ruth Jones, who sang and played the piano, had a brassy light alto; Cora's alto was strong and capable of rapid embellishments; and Sallie's "bass" could soar into her upper register when she delivered a shouting song.

The group's signature sounds, however, were the unrefined, uneven, and yet warm voice of Sallie and the brilliant alto of Cora. While Cora could deliver the sweet gospel ballad with sincerity and conviction, Sallie was known to "rock the house" with explosive attacks, releases, and soaring slides, occasionally accented by a quickly executed shouting step. Under the name of the Sallie Martin Colored Ladies Quartet, the group gained notoriety when, in 1944, they appeared as special guests in the crusades of the legendary evangelist Aimee Semple McPherson (1890–1944). One newspaper review stated that "The Sallie Martin Colored Ladies Quartet possess [sic] … exceptionally fine voices blended together." And indeed this blending, along with tightly arranged harmonies (initially arranged by Kenneth Morris) and the solo voices of Sallie and Cora, became the trademark of the Sallie Martin Singers. Among their most outstanding recordings are "Eyes Hath Not Seen," a Kenneth Morris composition in which Cora shows the full range of her voice and technique, and Sallie's aggressive handling of "Thy Servant's Prayer, Amen."

THE GOSPEL QUARTETS IN CHICAGO

The male quartet movement, while created and developed in the South, had become so popular by the mid-1940s that it could no longer be contained at home. In the 1920s and early 1930s, such cities as Bessemer, Alabama, Richmond, and Nashville served as fertile ground for gospel quartets, in part because of their proximity to the African American colleges and universities where the quartet movement began. But by the early 1940s, quartets began springing up in the North and Southwest, where there was not only an audience desperate for "home grown" church music, but an economy that could import southern singers. Another drawing card was the the manner in which the male quartet had created the quartet world.

When southern quartets began leaving the South to take their music throughout the United States, they presented themselves not only as upstanding and talented members of the community, but as a group of African American men who could and did serve as role models for other African American men. When they arrived at the church or school auditorium for a concert, they were dressed exactly

alike in sharply pressed business suits with white shirts and respectable ties (the tuxedos and white dinner jackets of earlier times had been discarded). Each member of the group sported a fresh haircut or a freshly marceled hairdo, and the breath of each singer was kept fresh by the constant use of Sen-sen, a breath freshener. To maintain this freshness, it became a rule that smoking was not to be permitted outside the car that brought the singers.

Inside the performance hall, quartet members sat together in the pews or on stage, and when they were announced for performance, while still seated they began singing their "theme song." In many cases theme songs dealt textually with the group and included such material as where and when they were organized, who the members of the group were, and the kinds of songs they sang. In other cases, theme songs were favorite compositions of such composers as Dorsey and Lucie Campbell, or a Negro spiritual. After one or two choruses, the quartet would sing its way to the stage and offer an A and B selection. As the B selection neared its end, the quartet would proceed back to its seats, continuing to sing while standing in place, and at the end of the song the group would turn to the audience and bow.

While quartets featured more four-part harmony singing than leader-group singing until the middle 1940s, they were still able to elicit a feverish response from the audience. On slow gospel ballads women showed their approval by "getting happy"—shaking the head in agreement, saying "amen" or "hallelujah," crying, screaming, or even fainting. On jubilee (moderately fast songs) or shout songs (very fast songs) women would clap their hands and execute a shout. Social restrictions (and even church restrictions) dictated that men only smile and "talk back" to the singers. Many singers insisted that while singing they were actually in a service rather than a concert and therefore encouraged the congregation to act as if they were in church. Usually, little encouragement was needed for the congregation to act in a churchly manner because they had come for that exact reason. During this period female gospel singers made their entrance on the national gospel scene and were beginning to elicit the same kind of audience response that the male groups drew. Within the next ten years, they would challenge the male groups for the most aggressive audience response.

In addition to their dress, behavior, and four-part singing, male quartets brought to audiences their experiments in the development of the soloist-oriented quartet.

Realizing that a soloist—out in front of the group—would require a rhythmic foundation over which he could spin his tune, quartets found the perfect background rhythm for slow gospel songs: seven even-punctuated sounds with one-beat rests. The problem was one of finding syllables to fit the seven pulses but not detract from the text of the soloist (most songs did not lend themselves to seven equal divisions). The problem was solved by the creation of a number of syllables that had no meaning, but possessed a *sound* over which the soloist would be free to spin a web of sorrow, joy, happiness, thanks, or any number of textual themes. The syllables selected were: "Oom-ma-lank-a-lank-a-lank." When these syllables were sung giving each syllable the same amount of time, a viable and much-beloved background chant was established:

> *Soloist: Just*   *a*   *closer*
> **Quartet: Oom-ma-lank-a-lank-a-lank**   *Oom-ma-lank-a-lank-a-lank*
> *Soloist: walk with thee*
> **Quartet: Oom-ma-lank-a-lank-a-lank**

For variety some quartets began using the phrase "Oh my Lord-y, Lord-y, Lord."

Armed with the newest sound in African American sacred music the black male jubilee quartets—soon-to-be gospel quartets—decided to present themselves in the gospel music center, Chicago. The first two such groups to venture into that piano-accompanied gospel territory were the Soul Stirrers from Texas and the Famous Blue Jay Singers of Alabama.

REBERT H. HARRIS AND THE SOUL STIRRERS

While the Soul Stirrers, perhaps the most famous and innovative of all gospel quartets, can hardly be discussed in gospel circles without some reference to Rebert H. Harris (b. 1916), the group was already ten years old in 1937 when Harris became a member. By 1926 gospel quartets had spread to Trinity, Texas, where baritone singer Silas Roy Crain organized a quartet at the Mount Pilgrim Baptist Church. This group of teenagers sang in a style close to that of the Fisk Jubilee Quartet and the other quartets that famous group inspired. Crain experienced frequent turnover in his quartet as young men graduated from high school and moved to larger cities for college and more profitable employment.

Around 1931 or 1932, Crain decided to move to Houston, one hundred miles away, to work in a rice mill. There he found several gospel quartets, but none impressed him as much as the New Pleasant Grove Singers that had been organized by Walter LeBeau in 1928 and named after the church they attended. Because their baritone had recently died, the New Pleasant Grove Singers asked Crain to join the group. Crain agreed, provided they change their name to the Soul Stirrers, the name of his former group, since "at one of the first performances of his teenage group, a member of the audience came forward to compliment them on how much they had stirred his soul, and from that day they adopted the name, Soul Stirrers." The New Pleasant Grove Singers accepted his request, and the group that was to set many trends in modern gospel became the Soul Stirrers.

The members of the original Soul Stirrers were Edward R. Rundless, lead; LeBeau, tenor; Crain, baritone; O. W. Thomas, bass; and Harris as first tenor. Quartet singing was not new to Harris. At ten he had formed a family group, the Friendly Five, to sing at the Harris Christian Methodist Church (named after his father, the pastor) in his hometown of Trinity, Texas. The group was composed of his brothers and cousins, and their repertory included a song Harris composed at age eight, "Everybody Ought to Love His Soul," and another he composed a year later that was to become a classic, "I Want Jesus to Walk around My Bedside."

While Harris attended Mary Allen Seminary in Crockett, Texas, for two years and was exposed to the Western European art music tradition of using the voice in a formal or subscribed manner, he resisted the operatic "head tone" of the quartet singing at his school and chose to place his voice between the head and chest so he could call on the power of his lower voice and the falsetto, in which he could essay his high range but without the opera-singer sound. His was a vocal sound never before heard in gospel—nor has it been heard since.

The addition of Harris to the Soul Stirrers signaled a change in gospel quartet music history. Harris precipitated or helped develop many new trends in quartet singing. His deep religious grounding, developed while attending his father's church, inspired him and the Soul Stirrers to approach their singing with an emotional intensity that until then had been considered too sanctified. He encouraged the singers to move around the stage as they sang, unlike the Fisk Jubilee Quartet and the quartets who had adopted their stage presence, and although he retained the tight

harmonies that had been the trademark of gospel quartets, he encouraged a less rigid ensemble so that individual parts could develop integrity. Jesse J. Farley, who joined the group one year before Harris, was a bass with the ability to "thump" a bass line in the style of Jimmy Bryant of the Heavenly Gospel Singers, and while Harris moved the group's entire singing range higher than it had been, he still found the harmonic depth for Farley to provide a thumping bass. Finally, he persuaded the group to change their repertoire from Negro spirituals, biblical songs, and standard Protestant hymns to the songs of *Gospel Pearls* and such composers as Thomas A. Dorsey and Kenneth Morris.

The Soul Stirrers introduced the "swing lead," which amounted to two singers leading one song. In most cases one singer, usually a baritone, would sing the verses while the choruses would be assigned to a tenor. The swing lead style was most effective when one singer brought a song to a high level of intensity and the second lead (the swing leader) would work the audience into a frenzy. The swing leader, sometimes called a "utility" man—in such cases one singer would move from tenor to baritone to bass to lead—enlarged a quartet to a quintet; however, groups continued to use the designation quartet. In time additional members were added to quartets so that by the mid-1950s a quartet seldom involved only four singers but would often involve five to seven singers.

The Soul Stirrers made their first recordings under John Lomax at the Smithsonian Institution in 1936; their first recordings with Harris were made in 1939. One of the songs in that first session was the Harris composition "Walk Around." This recording, different from those being made at the same time by the Golden Gate Quartet, appeared less concerned with polished precision and popular music techniques and more concerned with touching some element in the soul that would bring a tear to the eye. The recording also was instrumental in distinguishing the gospel quartet from the jubilee quartet. The Soul Stirrers were able to arouse audiences to a feverish pitch, not only through their soulful singing, but also when Harris, overcome by the spirit, would jump from the stage and continue singing without missing a beat. Their popularity became so great that by 1944 they had concertized through forty-eight states. The Soul Stirrers were among the first religious group to have a sustaining weekly radio show of their own, broadcasting each Sunday morning for over ten years from Chicago's radio station WIND. To ensure the spread of the gospel quar-

tet movement, Harris, along with several other quartet leaders, organized the National Quartet Association of America in 1947. Harris served as president of this group for many years, during which he patterned the organization on the Dorsey convention, setting up chapters in cities throughout the United States, conducting training sessions, and fostering the organization of teenage gospel quartets.

Harris' pure and clean tenor, along with his sincerity and coolness of storytelling in song, influenced the gospel quartet movement in a way that has yet to be paralleled. He not only inspired innovations in quartet singing but directly influenced the singing style of several gospel and soul singers, the most popular of whom was Sam Cooke, who took over the solo leadership of the group when Harris retired. Among others who credit Harris with directly influencing their style were Johnnie Taylor, Bobby Womack, and Paul Foster.

SILAS STEELE AND THE FAMOUS BLUE JAY SINGERS

While they did not rival the Soul Stirrers—their lead singers were not as commanding nor was the group as innovative—the quartet that came closest to capturing the public's fancy in the late 1940s and early 1950s was the Famous Blue Jay Singers. They earned their greatest popularity while based in Chicago, although they were formed and had honed their skills in Jefferson County, Alabama, which included such towns as Bessemer and Birmingham. Jefferson County was fertile territory for gospel (then still called jubilee) quartets. Among the groups organized in the area during the 1920s were the Sterling Jubilee Singers, the Shelby County Big Four, the Birmingham Jubilee Singers, the Ensley Jubilee Singers, and the Blue Jay Singers.

Sometime between 1925 and 1926, Charles Bridges of Pratt City, Alabama, who had moved to Birmingham to work in the mines, organized the Birmingham Jubilee Singers. They soon gained a local reputation as leaders of the new group of quartets that sang with the spirit, and in April 1926 they went to Atlanta for a recording session for the Columbia Record Company. Several of the songs recorded in that first session, including "Southbound Train," "He Took My Sins Away," and their signature song, "Birmingham Boys," met with only modest success among race record sales. But that success was sufficient to inspire several other groups to form and develop local and regional careers. Gospel quartet members maintained their day jobs and concertized in local areas during the week, but on weekends they would travel

as far as two hundred miles for performances. The success of the Birmingham Jubilee Singers recording lit a fire under the Blue Jay Singers who decided that they too would seek a regional, if not national, career.

Around the same time that the Birmingham Jubilee Singers was formed, Silas Steele (b. 1913) from Brighton, Alabama, joined forces with Clarence Parnell, a former bass singer with the Pilgrim Singers, another local quartet, to form the Blue Jay Singers. Parnell had already gained local celebrity as a quartet singer, and Steele, a young baritone and the younger brother of James "Jimmie" Steele, leader of the Woodwards Big Four Quartet, was beginning to gain a reputation as an outstanding soloist in his church choir. Parnell and Steele "stole" (a tradition in gospel quartets) James "Jimmie" Hollingsworth, tenor, and Charlie Beal, bass, from the Dunham Jubilee Singers to form their group. Within a very short time the Blue Jays, featuring young Silas as the lead (he was only thirteen when he joined the group), were the biggest rivals of the Birmingham Jubilee Singers. Because Steele possessed extraordinary charisma and began to adopt the preaching style of singing introduced by the sanctified singers, the Jays usually "took the program" when they appeared on the same bill with the Birmingham Jubilee Singers.

The Jays' style was one that would influence gospel quartets for the next fifty years: they celebrated the beauty and character of the natural male voice with its low sounds and brassy, but warm, timbre; they sang with the power of the African American Baptist and Pentecostal preachers; they celebrated the African American tendency of gathering resonance from the fatty tissues of the mouth rather than placing the tone close to the bridge of the nose; and they were not afraid to celebrate the body in their rhythmic accompaniment to their singing. These are the qualities that they brought to their 1931 recording of "If You See My Savior," the first Dorsey song ever recorded by a gospel quartet.

The gospel quartet movement had spread to Dallas, Texas, and the Blue Jays began to divide their time between Dallas and Birmingham. On one of their trips home they recruited Charles Bridges, former lead singer of the Birmingham Jubilee Singers. He agreed, because since the death of Dave Ausbrooks, the stalwart baritone of the Birmingham Jubilee Singers, that group had become inactive for long periods, and Bridges felt that they would find no suitable replacement to revive the group. With the addition of Bridges, the Jays became one of the most popular quar-

Prominent Chicago Gospel Women

Although men most often organized gospel events and ceremonies, women were always the facilitators of such activities. This trend started in Chicago, the first center of gospel, with a group of gospel women who composed, sang, conducted vocal groups, played piano and organ, and published music for themselves and others.

Sylvia Boddie

Lillian Bowles

Magnolia Lewis Butts

Virginia Davis

Viola Bates Dickinson

Mollie Mae Gates

Emma L. Jackson

Mahalia Jackson

Roberta Martin

Sallie Martin

Albertina Walker

tets in the quartet network. Their 1947 recordings of "I'm Bound for Canaan Land" and "Standing on the Highway" are perfect examples of the Jays' style, illustrating the swing lead technique between Steele and Bridges.

While in Texas the Jays became close friends and frequent performers with the Soul Stirrers (whom they might have influenced in the early days, although the Soul Stirrers surpassed them in popularity within a few years) and followed the Stirrers to Chicago in the mid-1940s. After settling in Chicago and seeing the development of a battalion of gospel quartets, Steele adopted the sanctified preaching style of talking through a song, which later became known as the "sermonette" before or during a song performance. His preacher shouts became legendary and marked a clear break with their original style of sweet singing in the jubilee style and a pronounced entry into gospel. They were one of the first quartets outside the Tidewater gospel quartets (Golden Gates, Silver Leafs, Harmonizing Four, and so on) to employ the "clank-a-lank" response as a rhythmic and syllabic accompaniment to a solo lead.

Although the Blue Jays flourished until the 1960s, by the late 1940s other groups had surpassed them in innovation and popularity, causing Steele to seek more current and fertile ground for his talent. By 1948, James Darling, one of the leaders of the Spirit of Memphis quartet, was able to report:

Silas Steele talked with me long distance and told me that his fellows was getting old and not well. They couldn't go on the road anymore and he didn't know nothing but singing…. He asked me if I thought I could get him with the Spirit of Memphis…. So I talked with the boys and they said yes.

Silas Steele left the Famous Blue Jays, the name they used by this time, and joined the Spirit of Memphis Quartet. While it meant a new career for Steele, it sounded an impending death knell for the Famous Blue Jay Singers, one of the most important musical organizations in the history of African American sacred music.

More Chicago Musicians

Three other Chicago-based musicians played prominent roles in the development of gospel though they never took to the road.

ALVIN A. CHILDS

Alvin A. Childs (1908–c.1972) was born to a Baptist preacher and his wife in Missouri. The family moved to Des Moines, Iowa, when Childs was an infant, and it was there that he received his education, which was tempered by the strictness of his Baptist household. Childs was fascinated by the joyous and rhythmic music of the Pentecostal church and without his parents knowledge began to attend services there. He was saved in 1922 and became a member of COGIC, in which he was ordained to preach in 1934. After several pastorates in Iowa and Illinois, Childs settled in Chicago in the early 1940s and became a member of the gospel community, often singing with Theodore R. Frye and Robert Anderson. He is known today chiefly as the composer of three gospel standards: "How Much I Owe," a song that became so popular in the late 1940s and early 1950s that it moved into the folk music realm and was adopted as a shouting chorus; "Sow Righteous Seeds," made famous by Robert Anderson; and "He's My Lord."

RALPH GOODPASTEUR

Ralph Goodpasteur (b. 1923), a native of Columbus, Indiana, came to Chicago in 1948 after having learned gospel music from the Los Angeles gospel community where he lived from 1942 until his move to Chicago. He, along with J. Earle Hines,

Chicago Music Publishing Dynasty

In the mid-1950s there were at least ten gospel music publishing houses in Chicago. Chicago held a virtual monopoly on gospel music publishing. Although Clara Ward had a firm in Philadelphia, Eugene Smallwood and Doris Akers had houses in Los Angeles, and Arthur H. Hughes had a small company in Miami, they all relied on Chicago to provide their major inventory. Gospel music publishing was so successful during the 1950s that according to Kenneth Morris, in an interview given to culture historian Bernice Johnson Reagon in 1986, during the 1950s he averaged $100,000 annually.

Robert Anderson's Good Shepherd Music House
(located in Gary, Indiana, but considered part of the Chicago school)

Bowles Music House
(Lillian Bowles)

Thomas A. Dorsey, Music Publisher

Theodore R. Frye Publishers

H & T Music House Publishers, Inc.
(Theodore R. Frye and Georgiana Rose)

Jackson Studio of Music
(Emma L. Jackson)

Martin and Morris Music, Inc.
(Sallie Martin and Kenneth Morris)

Roberta Martin Studio of Music

Sallie Martin House of Music
(1965–75—concurrent with Martin and Morris)

Pace Music
(1910–35—Charles Henry Pace)

carry the distinction of being the first two celebrated gospel choral conductors after Thomas A. Dorsey. Goodpasteur was brought to Chicago by C. H. Cobb to succeed Kenneth Morris as choir director at the First Church of Deliverance. (In the early 1950s Cobb began a series of midnight broadcasts of services from his church that could be heard in most parts of the United States because few radio stations broadcast after midnight.) Goodpasteur brought the same kind of harmony, precision, and intensity to his choir of seventy-five voices that Roberta Martin brought to the Martin Singers. The choir became a model for many gospel choirs around the nation (the

group was selected to accompany Nat King Cole on a 1959 recording) and was responsible for introducing Kenneth Morris' "Jesus Is the Only One." Goodpasteur composed several songs for the choir, which received modest popularity. Among these songs were "Joy Bells Ringing in My Soul," "Precious is He," and "To Me He's So Wonderful."

CLAY EVANS

Clay Evans (b. 1925) began his public career as a singer, gained fame as a preacher, and since the 1970s has combined the two. As a child Evans often sang with his family group, led by his mother who was a gospel singer and pianist. As a teenager he was a member of the Lux Singers, a piano-accompanied gospel group, and the Soul Revivers, an *a cappella* male quartet that was often presented in concert with the Highway QCs when Sam Cooke was its lead singer. In 1950 Clay founded the Hickory Grove Baptist Church in Chicago with five members. The church soon changed its name to Mount Carmel and then to Fellowship Baptist Church, the name by which it has become famous. With a membership of five thousand (among whom were Sam Cooke, J. J. Farley, and Johnnie Taylor) and a recording choir of two hundred voices, Evans secured his sister LeDella Reid as his choir director and, since the mid-1950s, this choir has been one of the principal gospel choirs in the United States.

GOSPEL IN PHILADELPHIA

The Chicago school of gospel resonated throughout the nation. Male gospel quartets had been springing up around the country since the mid-1920s, and the 1940s saw the organization of a group of female singers that would bring gospel into the mainstream of American music. The rise of gospel throughout the United States owed no small debt to the Pentecostal church since they were "duty bound" to lift up their voices like a trumpet. Following the Azusa Street Revival virtually every small town in the United States found itself host to some branch of the Pentecostal church. Cities of 50,000 or more supported two or three Pentecostal congregations. Pentecostalism began its claim as the religion of the twentieth century as early as the 1920s. It was during this period that Ozro Thurston Jones (1891–1972) settled in Philadelphia. A native of Fort Smith, Arkansas, Jones was saved at age ten and began preaching in the COGIC shortly thereafter. He organized the youth depart-

ment in that denomination in 1914 and in 1925 moved to Philadelphia and assumed the pastorate of the newly organized Holy Temple Church of God in Christ. Sanctified singing became a feature of church music in Philadelphia.

Elizabeth Dabney (c.1890–1967) came to Philadelphia from her native Virginia to attend college. After hearing a sermon preached by Jones she joined his church and became known in the city as one who could "get a prayer through." After marrying Thomas Dabney, a minister in her denomination, she helped him in his newly founded COGIC in the city. Upon Jones' death, Dabney became spiritual advisor for the congregation (COGIC laws prohibited her from assuming the pastorate). Her constant fasting and praying drew visitors from throughout the United States to her church, the Garden of Prayer Church of God in Christ. Both Jones and Dabney featured gospel music during their regular services and presented concerts of this music as a feature of their Sunday evening Young Peoples Willing Workers activities.

Gertrude Ward and the Ward Singers

Clara Ward and the Ward Singers

Gertrude Ward (1901–81), originally of Anderson, South Carolina, and her daughters, Clara (1924–73) and Willarene (b. 1922), were constant visitors to the services of Jones and Dabney and wanted to sing the kind of music featured in their services, but had no one to teach them. Staunch Baptists that they were, they considered it improper to request lessons from the pianist and soloist of churches to which they did not belong. However, Mrs. Ward knew that Thomas A. Dorsey and Sallie Martin were traveling throughout the nation organizing gospel choirs and groups and that the annual National Baptist Convention was held each year in a different city, so she hoped they might come to Philadelphia. Mrs. Ward was not able to get the convention into Philadelphia in 1935, but she was able to get Dorsey, Sallie Martin, and Ruth Jones (Dinah Washington) to be the guests for her special concert commemorating the number of years she had been singing in public, or her "anniversary" as it was called. (She had no special guest for her anniversary in 1934, opting to present for the first time the

Ward Trio, composed of Gertrude, Clara, and Willarene, who was called Willa). Mrs. Ward's singleness of purpose and tenacity—as exhibited in her quest for gospel music skills—would become her hallmark in later years.

Although in 1935 Mrs. Ward had been singing publicly for only four years, she delighted in recounting (and stating in her printed programs) the story of her beginning:

> The year was 1931 when standing before a steaming tub at work, I heard the Master's voice say "Gertrude, leave this place and go sing the gospel." The rest is history.

To her, gospel meant the word of the Lord and not the style of singing that she would adopt four years later during Dorsey's 1935 visit. The Ward Trio, with Clara playing the piano, adopted the music of Dorsey and began singing in Philadelphia churches with the gospel sound and style. They gained a local reputation as the leaders of the new music and by 1943 were ready to launch a national career. They chose the 1943 National Baptist Convention as the venue for their debut. With Clara playing the piano and leading one of the old Baptist lining hymns so dearly beloved by this congregation, the Ward Trio became the sensation of the convention. From that single appearance they were able to schedule a year of concert and revival dates throughout the National Baptist Convention network. Following that year of travel they entered the network of the entire African American church.

By 1947 Willa had married and begun to raise a family and was therefore not able to travel with the trio. Mrs. Ward added two singers to the group that helped create the Ward Singers' sound. Henrietta Waddy (1902–81), a South Carolinian like Mrs. Ward, possessed a rough and unsophisticated alto but was able to blend with the rather pure voices of Mrs. Ward and Clara. Drawing on her southern church behavior, Waddy would move throughout the audience as she sang, accenting the rhythm of songs with arm gestures. This activity brought a much needed physicality to the group, who had until then been considered great singers but too "stiff."

The second new member was Marion Williams (b. 1927) of Miami, Florida. Brought up in a Pentecostal church, Williams was well grounded in singing shout songs at very fast tempos, using fill-in words at points where the melody called for a rest, repeating words and melodic motives for intensity, and singing with a volume like few other singers. Her unique and most outstanding talent, however, was her

The Ward Singers, the first to replace choir robes with elaborate gowns

ability to soar effortlessly into the top of the soprano register with purity and volume. It was not unusual for Williams to sing eight or nine consecutive high Cs and then drop to the bottom of her register and deliver a growl in the manner of sanctified preachers. Her high notes were delivered most often on the syllable "ooh," although she occasionally used "ah." To give the sound more of a percussive accent, Williams would place a "wh" sound in front of "ooh," thereby producing the syllable "who." This device, now known as the "high who," became a standard practice in gospel and is used when going from the end of one chorus into the beginning of another, producing a seamless sheet of sound. The high who became a signature of the Ward Singers, as they were now called, and was sung by the entire group on their recording of Mary Lou Coleman's 1948 composition "Jesus."

The Ward Singers began recording in 1947, but it was not until 1949 that they found "Our God Is Able," the song that was to make them the most famous female group of the 1950s. The song's composer, W. Herbert Brewster, a Memphis-based minister in the National Baptist Convention, wrote elegant songs based on scriptural texts. Most of his music was performed by his own group, the Brewster Ensemble, led by Queen Candice Anderson. The Ward Singers appeared in a concert with the Original Gospel Harmonettes and heard them sing "Our God Is Able," which they had learned from the Brewster Ensemble.

Clara took the song and completely reworked it for the 1949 recording, dividing the lead between Williams and herself and adding a repetitive section at the end. The arrangement was unique and completely new to gospel. After five single notes played in the middle of the piano as an introduction, Clara sang the last four bars of the chorus to begin the song:

> *Clara: Surely*
> > **Group: Surely**
> *Clara: Surely*
> > **Group: Surely**
> *Clara: He's able*
> > **Group: He's able**
> *Clara: To carry*
> > **Group: To carry**
> *All: You through.*

The word "through" is sung to seven different tones on the two chords used in singing the "amen" at the end of a hymn. Each member of the group moved up and down in parallel fashion, creating simultaneous improvisation, another Ward Singer trademark that soon became a standard device in all gospel. After singing one verse, Clara begins a chorus during which she rehearses biblical situations in which the Lord worked miracles:

> He was Daniel's stone a-rolling
> And Ezekiel's wheel turning,
> He was Moses' bush burning
> He was Solomon's "Rose of Sharon,"
> He was Joshua's mighty battle ax.

As the chorus comes to an end, Williams begins a high who and holds a high A-flat until the second chorus begins, which she now leads. While Clara addressed previous miracles, Williams speaks to miracles the Lord will affect for those who follow Him:

> He'll be your friend when you are friendless,
> He's a mother for the motherless, a father for the fatherless;
> He's your joy when you're in sorrow,
> He's your hope for tomorrow;
> When you come down to the Jordan
> He'll be there to bear your burdens,
> He's going to step in just before you
> At the judgment He's gonna know you.

Where Clara ended her chorus singing the word "surely," pronouncing the word as it is spelled, Williams pronounced the word "showly." She repeats the word several times, each time with a response of the word from the group. "Surely, God Is Able" became one of the biggest hits in gospel and was sung by choirs and local groups throughout the nation.

Several new elements, while not being new to gospel, were made famous and became standard gospel music devices with this recording. Williams use of such

Clara Ward and the Ward Singers

phrases as "He's going to step in just before you, at the judgment He's gonna know you" is a practice held over from Negro spirituals in which a group of rhyming couplets are catalogued and when a variety of text or words for a contrasting section are needed, the singer selects an appropriate or favorite couplet and inserts it into the song. Among other famous couplets are:

> *I went in the valley, I didn't go to stay*
> *My soul got happy and I stayed all day.*
>
> *My hands got stuck to the gospel plow,*
> *I wouldn't take nothing for my journey now.*
>
> *If you get to heaven before I do,*
> *Look out for me 'cause I'm coming too.*

While less popular than couplets, quatrains are also a part of the folk poetry singers insert into songs:

You may not sing like Angels,
You may not preach like Paul;
But you can tell the love of Jesus
And say He died for all.

These "wandering" couplets and quatrains became standard practice after their use by Brewster in "Move on up a Little Higher," recorded by Mahalia Jackson, and the Ward Singers' version of "Surely, God Is Able." (Brewster originally published this song as "Our God Is Able." After Williams emphasized the word "surely" in the recorded version, he republished the song with the title "Surely, God Is Able.")

The third device employed by the Ward Singers in "Surely, God Is Able" was the repetition of the same musical elements to different words, bringing the progress of the music to a halt for a period resulting in a section of repetition called a "vamp." Clara knew that repetition is the most important element in African and African American music for getting its message across and employed it judiciously in this recording. The vamp became so important in gospel that for the next forty years there would be very few gospel songs that did not employ the device.

Another practice made famous by the Ward Singers was that of the immediate reprise. During the mid-1950s when the Ward Singers were at the height of their career, they would sing only six songs at each concert. Four songs were delivered before intermission, each of which was immediately followed by a reprise that was often longer that the initial performance. After the intermission came the two additional songs, each of them reprised, which brought the concert to a close. On those occasions when the spirit was exceptionally high, as many as two or three reprises would follow the initial performance.

The Ward Singers set the standard for all female gospel groups. They led the way in vocal arrangements, uniforms, dress (the Ward Singers eventually sang in sequined gowns), and mode of travel (Cadillacs with trailers). They were the first gospel group to wear exaggerated coiffured wigs at a time when women were ridiculed for wearing "false" hair. Mrs. Ward jealously protected her singers, demanded grand fees for performances, juggled programming so that the Ward Singers would appear in the most lucrative places on the program, and even resorted to taking up special collections when she felt they had been underpaid. These tactics would be employed

by other groups in the future. She was also an entrepreneur, seizing on the idea of creating a second group of Ward Singers in 1951 that she called the Clara Ward Specials. This group traveled with the Ward Singers on double-billed concerts and also appeared in solo concerts, from which Mrs. Ward received a percentage. In 1954 Mrs. Ward and Clara opened the Clara Ward House of Music and published Clara's songs as well as those of Brewster that they featured in their concerts.

In 1958 Williams, Waddy, Kitty Parham (b. 1931), along with Frances Steadman (b. 1928), who had recently joined the group, withdrew from the Ward Singers and formed the Stars of Faith, a group that would enjoy tremendous celebrity for the next few years. With the loss of the original group, Clara never regained her status in gospel even though she organized several groups of singers after 1958. Her influence is still felt in gospel even more than twenty years after her death. She influenced many gospel and soul singers, among whom were Aretha Franklin and Della Reese.

Angelic Gospel Singers

Philadelphia's second gospel group, organized in 1942, began as a gospel choir called the Spiritual Echoes. They toured Philadelphia's churches on Sundays, gaining a citywide following. During the height of the choir's popularity, the leader of the group, Margaret Allison, had a dream in which her pastor asked her why she hadn't formed her own group. When she answered that she didn't know how to launch a group, her pastor replied, "The Lord will bless you in whatever you do, as long as you keep Him first."

Margaret Wells Allison was born in 1921 in McCormick, South Carolina, fifty miles north of Augusta, Georgia. When she was four, Allison's family moved to Philadelphia so that her father could find a better job. They prospered until the Great Depression, when the family went on welfare briefly until her father secured employment with the Works Progress Administration (WPA). Allison's parents attended the Little Temple Pentecostal Church in Philadelphia, and although she never sang in a choir, it was the training camp for most gospel singers (Pentecostal churches did not have choirs until the late 1940s). Allison was fascinated by the congregation's joyous gospel singing.

Allison studied piano for a short time when she was twelve and transferred her membership to the B. M. Oakley Memorial Church of God in Christ (the church that

Marion Williams would later join) where she had an opportunity to play for services. By 1942 the twenty-one-year-old Allison was ready to enter the gospel field. During her tenure with the Spiritual Echoes, she learned how to arrange for female voices, compose songs, play and sing at the same time, and introduce a song to an audience. Even though she had lived in Philadelphia since she was small, her musical contacts celebrated the old-fashioned southern style of church music, gospel, and hymns in which elements of slave singing were quite prominent: percussive attacks, sliding from one pitch to another, vocal interjections by each member of the group, and repetition of any portion of the song that struck a spiritual chord. By 1945 the tours of such groups as the Sallie Martin Singers (conducting singing revivals) had made this gospel style seem dated; however, many gospel music lovers still knew it and wished to hear it again. Allison built her new group on this old-time sound.

The name Angelic Gospel Singers came to her in the same dream in which her pastor had encouraged its organization. In 1944 Allison recruited two South Carolinians who had also relocated to Philadelphia—Lucille Shird, originally of Ashville, and Ella Mae Morris, a native of Greenville. The fourth member was her sister, Josephine McDowell.

The Angelics were to the Pentecostal congregations what the Ward Singers were to the National Baptist Convention. They sang in their denominational circuit throughout the United States, and by 1949, they were not only known throughout gospel circles but had scored the greatest success of their career with their rendition of Lucie Campbell's "Touch Me, Lord Jesus." (Although Allison states that the song was recorded in 1947, records indicate 1949 as the date of the session.) The Angelics were to have many hits during their long recording career, but no other record ever equaled the success of their first. Among their other hits were "When My Saviour Calls Me Home," which was the flip side of "Touch Me, Lord Jesus"; "Jesus, When Troubles Burden Me Down," the revival meeting song; "There's Not a Friend Like the Lonely Jesus"; and "Back to the Dust." Although not apparent from its early modest success, "Glory to the New Born King" (1950), became as popular in gospel music circles as "White Christmas" is in the popular music world:

> *Jesus, Jesus, oh, what a wonderful child.*
> *Jesus, Jesus, so holy, meek and mild;*
> *New life, new hope to all He brings,*

> *Listen to the Angels sing:*
> *Glory, glory to the new born King.*

Although the Angelic Gospel Singers introduced many gospel standards, their name is irrevocably associated with "Touch Me, Lord Jesus":

> *Touch me, touch me, Lord Jesus, with Thy hand of mercy,*
> *Make each throbbing heartbeat feel Thy pow'r divine.*
> *Take my will forever, I will doubt Thee never,*
> *Cleanse, cleanse me, dear Saviour, make me wholly Thine.*

Not only was the old time or early gospel music style presented in the Angelics' arrangement of this song, but Allison's piano gave the voices the kind of support that 1940s gospel required: basic accompaniment doubling the voice parts in the middle of the keyboard, rhythmic licks in the upper portion of the keyboard during the singers' rest periods, and percussive attacks with explosive releases at every open space in the rendition. "Touch Me, Lord Jesus" was picked up by radio stations across the country and reached Billboard's R & B Top 20 that year. It also became a silver disc selling well over 100,000 copies—a phenomenal success for the time. Ernie Young of Ernie's Record Mart, broadcast over WLAC, the principal national gospel radio program during the 1950s, used the song as its theme for over a decade.

Even though "Touch Me, Lord Jesus" was accompanied by piano, it possessed a male gospel quartet character. This may be because when she first organized the group, Allison knew no female groups other than the Ward Singers, so she patterned the Angelics after the Fairfield Four. The quartet element in the Angelics' sound prompted their management to couple them for several tours with the Dixie Hummingbirds, who had recently relocated to Philadelphia. The Angelics and the "Birds" toured as a package during 1950 and 1951 and recorded six singles together. Most outstanding among these recordings were "Dear Lord, Look Down upon Me" and "In the Morning."

The Angelics suffered a great loss in the late 1950s when both Shird and Morris retired from the group. For a while Allison traveled with her sister, Josephine McDowell, and a new singer, Bernice Cole; in later years, she added men to the group. The Angelics, however, remain one of the historic female groups of gospel.

The Davis Sisters

Another Philadelphia female group was the Famous Davis Sisters. Like the Angelics, this group from the Pentecostal church brought the spiritual and musical intensity of that congregation to their singing. Like the Ward Sisters, members of the Davis Sisters were born and reared in Philadelphia but inherited their parents' appreciation for southern religion and its music heritage. Additionally, they captured—and to a degree attempted to refine—the intensity of the sanctified church. However,

"Baby Sister" Ruth Davis, the leader of the Davis Sisters

when Ruth (Baby Sister) was given free reign in shout songs, the congregation ultimately responded as if they were in that "little wooden church out on a hill."

The Davis Sisters were members of the Pentecostal sect called Fire Baptized. The Fire Baptized Holiness church, founded in 1908 by Bishop and Sister W. E. Fuller in Atlanta, Georgia, is a small, but prominent, congregation within the Pentecostal/Holiness apostolic denominations organized after the Azusa Street Revival. The Davis family was one of the first members of the Mount Zion Fire Baptized Holiness Church in Philadelphia after its founding in the late 1910s. And there the Davis children developed into great gospel singers. On special occasions the Mount Zion pastor would highlight the talent of his membership and called upon the young women to sing a selection. The Davis Sisters, organized in 1945, was initially led by the eldest sister, Ruth (1928–70), known as "Baby Sister." The other sisters in the group were Thelma (1930–63), Audrey (1932–82), and Alfreda (1935–89).

After establishing a reputation as "house rockers" in the Philadelphia area, the sisters made their official debut in 1946 at their parents' home in Port Deposit, Maryland, and then followed the Pentecostal circuit, performing in churches and schools

in the Northeast. They began recording in 1947, by which time they had been joined by pianist cousin Curtis Dublin (1928–1965). Dublin provided an accompaniment style midway between the sanctified church and the nightclub, characterized by occasional jazz riffs. The group's first hit, Alex Bradford's "Too Close to Heaven," was released in 1953 shortly after Bradford's own version. The Davis' version was overshadowed by the composer's performance, even though Baby Sister brought a genuine sanctified approach to her determination to complete the journey to heaven, despite innumerable problems. In their "Twelve Gates to the City," Baby Sister delved into the Book of Revelations and began her journey with such lines as "twelve gates to the city and twenty-four elders to the kingdom" so that the Negro spiritual was transformed into a gospel song.

Many songs of the Davis Sisters were taken directly from the church services they attended and experienced while growing up, and hence a number of so-called congregational songs were staples in their repertoire. Some of these songs were "In the Morning when I Rise," "Get Right with God," and "God Rode in a Wind Storm." They were not unfamiliar, however, with other music. One of their most popular recordings was a gospel version of the Christmas carol "The First Noël."

The Davis Sisters became a force in gospel when they recorded Lucie Campbell's "He Understands, He'll Say 'Well Done'." By the time they recorded this song in 1955, it had been recorded by more than a dozen gospel singers, including Sister Rosetta Tharpe, whose recording was a popular hit. The difference in the Davis Sisters' interpretation and all the other recorded versions of the song was attitude. While Lucie Campbell envisioned a contemplative and meditative interpretation of the song—and indeed all recordings to the time of the Davis Sisters followed this idea—the Sisters came to the song with an aggressive pronouncement of joy, and even victory. "The battle was won and though I have not yet received the prize, I have overcome" was the attitude that Baby Sister conveyed when, in the tempo of a sprightly jubilee song, she declared:

> Oh, when I come to the end of my journey,
> Weary of life and the battle is won;
> Carrying the staff and the cross of redemption,
> He'll understand, and say "Well done."

The Davis Sisters

This affirmation of faith and conviction would never be heard with the same prayerful ears after Baby Sister squalled victory in those famous words.

The song that cemented the Davis Sisters in the minds of gospel music lovers, however, was their 1952 recording of Kenneth Morris' "Jesus Steps Right in When I Need Him Most." Set again in a jubilee (moderately fast) tempo, Baby Sister wailed on the line "Jesus Is with Me when I Need Him Most." As the chorus ended, she repeated the word "steps." Her recasting of the line came out as:

> *Don't you know the man steps, steps, steps*

When she was particularly excited, she would deliver the line as:

> *Don't you know the man steps, yeah! yeah!*
> *Can't you see Him come stepping, stepping, stepping*

stating each syllable with a choreographed step forward by the group.

With Baby Sister in the lead—although Thelma, as second lead, could illuminate a gospel ballad and bring energy to one of the Pentecostal shout songs—the Davis Sisters emerged as the first female group to sing "hard" gospel. Hard gospel, which made its appearance in the early 1950s, was totally different from the Baptist style of singing, which emphasized beauty of tone, precise rhythm, and occasional ornamentation. Hard gospel, first introduced by the saints of the sanctified church, is characterized by straining the voice during periods of spiritual ecstacy for spiritual and dramatic expression, singing at the extremes of the range, delivering perpetual text, in some cases repeating words or syllables or developing the text through the employment of wandering couplets or quatrains or stock interjections ("Yes, Lord," "Don't You Know," "Listen to Me," and so on), and "acting out" songs with scrubbing motions for washing, stooping shoulders for "bearing the cross," and a military-like precision march for "walking up the King's highway." This style would soon be adopted by Dorothy Love Coates and Shirley Caesar and make another distinction between Baptist and Pentecostal gospel.

During the 1960s, the Davis Sisters added nonfamily members Imogene Green (1930–86), a Chicago-born singer with a leaning toward hard gospel, and Jacqui Verdell, who had a special talent for essaying the gospel ballad. As the sisters passed away, their deaths, averaging one a decade, were considered tragic losses in the African American church community.

Mary Johnson Davis

There were few pure soprano gospel soloists during the Golden Age. The ideal gospel sound was one of authority, symbolized by the alto voice. To be sure, Marion Williams and Delois Barrett were sopranos but in moments of high intensity each of these singers would reach into the bottom of their registers and growl. The only soprano who retained her soprano register and quality at all times—and yet evoked the spirit as easily as Mahalia Jackson—was Mary Johnson Davis (1899–1982), a native of Pittsburgh, Pennsylvania. Known for her ability to rouse any church with her Baptist lining hymn renditions of such favorites as "Come, Ye Disconsolate" and "I Need Thee Every Hour," Davis could also generate foot tapping and hand clapping with her rhythmic rendition of jubilee songs.

From age six she was a local singing celebrity in Pittsburgh and continued

singing into adulthood, specializing in classical, Negro spiritual, and hymn interpretations. Upon hearing the songs of Thomas A. Dorsey in the late 1930s, she changed her style to that of the new gospel music, and in 1937, when the National Baptist Convention met in Los Angeles, she was accorded the title of "National Gospel Singer" for her spirited rendition of "Holy Spirit Surely Is My Comforter."

In the late 1930s she married an aspiring gospel songwriter, E. Clifford Davis, composer of "Holy Spirit." In order to help his career, she organized the Mary Johnson Davis Gospel Singers and in the 1940s secured a recording contract with Atlantic Records. Among the members of her group were the Banks Brothers—Jeff (pianist) and Charles—her sister Bernice Johnson, and Lucie Banks.

A longtime friend and colleague of Gertrude Ward, Davis moved to Philadelphia in the 1950s after the death of her husband. Remarried to the Reverend B. J. Small, she renamed her group the Mary J. Small Singers. She and Gertrude Ward were instrumental in developing young gospel groups throughout Philadelphia and the surrounding area. Davis retired from traveling in the 1970s but continued to sing in the Philadelphia area until shortly before her death. She is best known for her recordings of "These Are They" and "Walk in the Light."

The Dixie Hummingbirds

Like Chicago before it, Philadelphia was a piano-accompanied gospel town. Charles Albert Tindley used organ and piano for his gospel hymns (although at "Prayer Meet-

ing" gospel hymns occasionally turned into gospel songs). Orzo Thurston Jones and the Dabneys used piano for sanctified singing, as did the congregation at the Mount Zion Fire Baptized Holiness Church. Clara Ward played piano for the Ward Singers, and Margaret Wells Allison played piano for the Spiritual Echoes choir. Philadelphia was indeed a piano-accompanied gospel town until the Dixie Hummingbirds moved there in 1942.

The Birds were unique in gospel: they could shout with the best of the shouters, but they always cherished and developed what quartets called the "minors." The Birds were one of many quartets that, according to Ray Allen in a 1984 study of Philadelphia quartets, subscribed to four song types:

> Sentimentals—*moderate to slow tempo; smooth, extended vocal phrasing; most major harmonies.*
>
> Minors—*slow tempo; smooth, extended vocal phrasing; generous use of minor, diminished, and augmented harmonies [called "off chords"].*
>
> Jubilees—*moderate to rapid tempo; short vocal phrasing; major harmonies.*
>
> Chop Jubilees—*very rapid tempo; short vocal phrasing; chopped, staccato-like attack on lyrics; major harmonies.*

While the piano-accompanied gospel singers called sentimentals "gospel ballads"; minors, "Baptist lining hymns"; and chop jubilees, "shout songs"; by any name the Dixie Hummingbirds could sing them all, and with the spirit. What the Birds brought to Philadelphia gospel was variety—and that variety would bring two Philadelphia male gospel quartets to the forefront (the other group would be the Nightingales).

The Birds were organized by James Davis in Greenville, South Carolina, and drew its original members from the junior chorus at the Bethel Church of God in Greenville, calling itself the Sterling High School Quartet after the high school they attended. When Fred Owens replaced the short-term J. B. Matterson shortly after the group's organization, Davis changed their name to the Dixie Hummingbirds (they had decided to leave school and sing professionally). The members were Davis, tenor; Barney Gipson, lead; Barney Parks, baritone; and Fred Owens, bass. After gaining a local reputation as a "smooth" singing group (specializing in sentimentals,

The Dixie Hummingbirds

minors, and jubilees), the Birds, like other quartets in their area, made their way to the National Baptist Convention in Atlanta where they met with only modest success but garnered enough engagements to keep them singing in and around the South Carolina area.

By the 1930s the Birds were popular enough to be invited to participate in "battles of song," a favorite church and entertainment activity throughout the South. During one such battle in 1939 in their hometown, they competed against the Heavenly Gospel Singers, whom they had met at the National Baptist Convention, and the Carriers, a group from Spartanburg, South Carolina, led by Ira Tucker (b. 1923). The battle was monumental, for not only did the Dixie Hummingbirds win (determined by applause from the congregation), they also gained two new members: Willie Bobo, bass of the Heavenly Gospel Singers, and Tucker.

Tucker, who had been heavily influenced by the Norfolk Jubilee (Jazz) Quartet and the Golden Gate Quartet, quickly became the major musical force in the group. They began to meld the jubilee quartet style with that of the jubilee jazz quartets (some of the Tidewater gospel quartets had switched to jazz singing). For the next fifty years the Dixie Hummingbirds' style would be characterized by a genuine gospel sound, but one with a nod toward jazz and show tunes.

The Birds' style was actually not unlike the quartets of the day: well-modulated tones between the head (lyrical quality) and chest (church-style), tight and sweet harmonies, explosive releases, and slight body movements. After the group moved to Philadelphia and came in contact with local church groups who possessed the same abilities, Tucker took on additional musical and show business attributes. There was no melodic or harmonic device that he could not execute: his lyric tenor voice was capable of cascading up and down not only the diatonic (seven-note) scale but the chromatic as well. Not only did he put his voice and vocal technique to use, he also became the model for the "activity" singer. He ran up and down aisles, jumped from the stage, and spun around without sacrificing one iota of the pure musical sound that he first brought to the quartet. Indeed, he served as the model for many of the rhythm and blues and soul singers from Jackie Wilson and Clyde McPhatter to Bobby "Blue" Bland and the Temptations.

Throughout the first fifteen years, the group went through several personnel changes, but by the late 1940s it had settled into a quartet with Tucker on lead,

Beachy Thompson (from the Five Gospel Singers and the Willing Four) as first/second tenor, Davis as second/first tenor, and Bobo as bass. Second to Tucker in significance to gospel was Bobo, who early on helped move the bass from its ungrateful position at the bottom of the harmony to that of co-soloist, thumping bass in each song at every opportunity. James Walker joined the group in the early 1950s, alternating lead with Tucker, and his semihard gospel technique helped the Birds move to the forefront of gospel quartets.

Ira Tucker, with William Bobo on guitar, leading the Dixie Hummingbirds to the pinnacle of gospel

The artistry of their first twenty-five years is magnificently illustrated in their recordings of "Lord, Come See About Me" (1949), on which Tucker takes the lead but at the end of each chorus Bobo interpolates a deep velvety bass anticipated note that gives the song its real character, and "Search Me, Lord" (1950) on which Tucker shows the full range of his vocal beauty and pyrotechnics.

Beginning in 1951 the Birds toured with the Angelic Gospel Singers in the first pairing of an all male quartet with an all female piano-accompanied gospel group. They toured at intervals during 1951 to 1953 in a series of highly successful gospel concerts. Their most popular joint recordings were "Jesus Will Answer Prayer" and "Dear Lord, Look Down upon Me," both recorded in 1950.

When the popularity of the gospel quartet movement began to fade in the mid-1960s, the Birds found a home on the folk music circuit and performed in major folk music festivals, including an appearance at the Newport Jazz Festival in 1966. When pop singer Paul Simon (b. 1941) wanted a gospel quartet to sing background on his 1973 recording of "Loves Me Like a Rock," the Birds were chosen. Their contribution to the popularity of the recording was so great that they later recorded the song on their own and it became a hit for them. The Birds went on to appear on such television shows as "The Merv Griffin Show"

and "Soul Train," and by the late 1970s they had revived their career. Their popularity was still growing in the 1990s in large part because of the continuing popularity of their 1953 recording of "Let's Go Out to the Program" on which Tucker leads the group through imitations of the Soul Stirrers singing "Jesus Gave Me Water," the Blind Boys of Mississippi singing "Our Father," the Pilgrim Travelers version of "Mother Bowed," and the Bells of Joy singing "Talk about Jesus."

The Philadelphia gospel sound was helped in no small way by the fact that the Gotham, Savoy, and Imperial record companies had major studios in Philadelphia and Mary Mason, Walter Stewart, Louis Williams, and Charles Williams were extremely powerful DJs who favored a hometown sound. When the African American DJs around the country met with each other, they encouraged their friends to play the recordings of their hometown artists. The Philadelphia gospel singers were aware of this fact and treated their DJs accordingly.

GOSPEL IN DETROIT

While Philadelphia was the first major city to follow Dorsey in gospelizing the music of the African American church, cities much closer to Chicago were also responding, although not with the speed and power of the City of Brotherly Love. Pentecostal congregations had begun planting churches in Detroit as early as the mid-1920s, and Dorsey had established a chapter of his convention there in the mid-1930s. However, gospel in Detroit existed primarily in the Pentecostal/sanctified churches until the mid-1940s. Because of Detroit's proximity to Chicago, gospel musicians from Detroit moved easily between the two cities. But in the 1940s three people who were to shepherd the gospel movement in Detroit moved to that city.

Anna Broy Crockett Ford

The first to arrive was Anna Broy Crockett Ford (b. 1916), who moved there in 1942 from her native Lexington, Mississippi. She affiliated with COGIC, pastored by John Seth Bailey (c.1891–c.1986), and because of her natural talent for singing and her training at Chicago's American Conservatory of Music (1935–36), she was able to identify herself early on as one who would champion gospel music. While Ford was a powerful singer, possessing a strong but light alto voice, her greatest contribution came through her organization of gospel groups. Elder Bailey, later Bishop Bailey,

recognized this strength in her and commissioned her to organize a gospel choir in his church in 1945. Her success with this choir inspired her in 1949 to organize the Music Department for the national Church of God in Christ. Additionally, Ford has served as the director of music for the Women's International Convention of the COGIC since 1951. Ford later moved to Chicago and continued her musical activities.

C. L. Franklin

Reverend C. L. Franklin

On the first Sunday in 1946, Clarence LaVaughn Franklin (1915–84), known as C. L. Franklin, preached his first sermon as the pastor of the Bethlehem Baptist Church in Detroit and thus began a thirty-five-year promotion of gospel music. And while Tabernacle Baptist Church, pastored by Charles Craig (flourished 1950–70), and a number of Pentecostal congregations, including Bailey's, were major venues for gospel in Detroit, Franklin was clearly the major force.

Born in a rural area of Mississippi near Indianola (the birthplace of legendary blues singer B. B. King), Franklin grew up near the village of Doddsville. When he was very small, his father served in World War I and returned only to abandon the family. His mother remarried, and her second husband's name is the name Franklin carried throughout his life. His mother and stepfather had one child, Aretha, and Franklin passed this name on to his own daughter. That name has since become famous.

In tenth grade, Franklin quit school and became a "season worker," that is, a migrant farm laborer who follows the planting and harvesting season throughout the United States. He became a preacher at age seventeen. Eventually he was able to relinquish the season work for the ministry, pastoring churches in Clarksdale, where he married Barbara, the mother of his children, and Greenville, as well as several other small parishes. He eventually moved to Memphis, where he pastored, then to Buffalo, New York, and finally to Detroit. The latter moves were not happy ones for

before he moved north, Barbara died and he was left to care for his four children. In Detroit, female members of the church looked after the children, leaving Franklin free to care for his church flock.

Franklin was a singer, and while his singing was first rate, it did not match his "gospel" preaching. During Franklin's lifetime he recorded more than sixty of his sermons on double-sided LP records, each side lasting four or five minutes. On side one he would illustrate his oratorical ability, often being dramatically verbose. On side two he would shift into a musical key and virtually sing the remainder of the sermon. When his daughter Aretha began to sing, she mimicked the Franklin style of preaching in her singing.

Mattie Moss Clark

Although there is no doubt that James Cleveland was to gospel in the 1960s and 1970s what Thomas A. Dorsey was to that genre in the 1930s and 1940s, he was not alone in the necessary shift from Golden Age gospel to a more modern interpretation. One other choir director, Mattie Moss Clark (1928–94), had a major impact on the gospel choir in its new form. And even after her death, Clark continues to influence the direction that the gospel of the 1990s is taking.

The importance of gospel singers appearing before audiences at the National Baptist Convention diminished after the death of Lucie Campbell (who had made the convention the most important venue for introducing new gospel singers for forty years). The principal denomination for the introduction of new gospel singers became COGIC through its Midnight Musicals at the annual convention, under the direction of Mattie Moss Clark. Some of the singers who came to prominence through these musicals include Rance Allen, the Hawkins Family (Edwin, Walter, and Tramaine), Andrae and Sandra Crouch, Beverly Glenn, Donald Vails, Keith Pringle, and gospel saxophonist Vernard Johnson. Though presented in a COGIC forum, the Midnight Musicals became a nondenominational showcase for new gospel talent deemed worthy of presentation by Clark. Such power and prestige testified to the hard work and long miles traveled from her meager beginning in Selma, Alabama, to that of the most powerful woman in black gospel in the last decade of the twentieth century.

Born the second of six boys and two girls to Edward and Mattie Moss, Moss was

brought up in the Methodist church, in which her mother was a singer (she was also a guitarist) and a licensed minister. Two of her brothers played instruments, and all sang. Moss began piano lessons at age six (she was taught by her older brother), and by age ten she played for services at the three small parishes pastored by her mother.

In preparation for entering Fisk University as a music major, Moss sang and studied piano throughout high school. Between graduation from high school and the opening of the next college term—when she was to enter Fisk—her father died. Wary of leaving her mother during such a crucial period, she elected to remain at home and attend Selma University. After one year at Selma, she decided to relocate to Detroit to live with her sister.

Coming into a strange town with musical talent but no venue for exhibiting it frustrated Moss, and she looked for a congregation with which to affiliate. She first served as pianist for a Baptist church but did not find the religious and musical expressions she craved. Within one year of her arrival in Detroit, she discovered COGIC, sought and found the Holy Ghost, and became director of the choir at what is now the Bailey Temple Church of God in Christ, pastored by John Seth Bailey. Her ability to compose music, play piano and organ, and direct choirs quickly led to her appointment as director of music of the Southwest Michigan Jurisdiction (diocese) of COGIC, and then president and director of the music department of COGIC, International.

She married Elbert Clark, a native of Gary, Indiana, a guitarist and Pentecostal minister who had come to Detroit shortly before her arrival, and bore him one son, Elbert Junior, and five daughters, Elbernita ("Twinkie"), Jackie, Denise, Dorinda, and Karen. In the 1970s the five sisters would become gospel superstars as the Clark Sisters. Elbernita, the leader of the group, became one of the leading organists and composers of the 1970s and 1980s and official organist for her mother's Midnight Musicals.

As the composer of more than one hundred songs, Clark was able to insinuate her musical ideas on a whole denomination of musicians. She eschewed a choir with a vibrant and aggressive sound with a fully opened throat—sometimes resulting in volume that destroyed purity of tone—for a choir with close harmonies and crisp rhythms. She began recording in 1963 with the Southwest Michigan State Choir of

the Churches of God in Christ, and their first recording of her composition "Save Hallelujah" was enthusiastically received. This was followed by her most popular recording, "Salvation Is Free." She also recorded with the 1,500–member Church of God in Christ Convocation Choir, and through her recordings introduced such singers as Esther Smith, Betty Nelson, the Clark Sisters, and Douglas Miller. Her brother Bill Moss leads the gospel group known as Bill Moss and the Celestials.

Moss was not without the certain temperamental qualities known in people of such extraordinary talent. She was as well known for her temper tantrums as she was for her music. It was not unusual for Moss to throw books or musical scores— even during concerts—at singers who displeased her. Unfortunately, her name can hardly be mentioned without a discussion of the tantrum that resulted in her physical assault on Twinkie during a performance. And yet, she is remembered today as one of the most talented and innovative women in music, and singers flocked to her for training and guidance until her death.

Della Reese, Earnestine Rundless, and the Meditations

C. L. Franklin's influence on gospel in Detroit was great. Among those he influenced were Delloreese Patricia Early, popularly known as Della Reese (b. 1932), who was the second lead for a female group from Detroit known as the Meditation Singers. The Meditations were organized by Earnestine Rundless in 1947 and quickly became to Detroit what the Ward Singers and the Davis Sisters were to Philadelphia, what the Caravans were to Chicago, and what the Original Gospel Harmonettes would become to Birmingham: singers who made cities into gospel centers.

Indeed, between 1953 and 1959 in Detroit and the surrounding area, the Meditations personified the gospel sound. While their influence has not been generally acknowledged, within gospel circles it is commonly held that the Meditations had a great influence on the Motown Sound. Earnestine Rundless notes that in the early days of the group "a young fan named Diana Ross" got the front seat at most of their concerts.

Rundless came to Detroit from the historic Mount Bayou, Mississippi, but was reared in Chicago. After marrying E. A. Rundless, who relinquished his position as a singer in the Soul Stirrers to enter the ministry and move north, she formed a group of singers from her husband's Detroit church. These singers included Rundless, Della

Reese, her sister Marie Waters, and Lillian Mitchell. The Meditations were indistinguishable from other female groups of the time except in its lead singers Rundless and Reese.

Della Reese, one of the major popular music entertainers from the 1960s on, was born in Detroit. She attended high school there and studied at Wayne State University until she was recruited by Rundless to join the Meditations. She brought a great deal of gospel-singing experience to this group: she had been singing in church choirs since age six and toured with Mahalia Jackson during the summers of 1945 to 1949. She sang for short periods with Beatrice Brown, Roberta Martin, and Clara Ward before she left gospel in 1954 to pursue a career in popular music. In 1955 she began recording, showing the influence of Dinah Washington, who also began as a gospel singer. While Rundless leaned toward the sanctified style of singing, Reese, with her brassy yet crystal clear alto, always maintained a Baptist style with a solid melody line. Essaying myriad colors, she sustained tones while resorting to a drum-like sound when she delivered a song in the declaratory style. Her style is eloquently illustrated on her 1953 recording of "Jesus Is Always There." With unabashed homage to the style of the Ward Singers and W. Herbert Brewster's multimetered songs, this rendition begins in the tempo of a gospel waltz, during which Reese shows her ability to paint pictures with a gospel ballad. As she nears the end of the verse, however, she picks up the tempo and suddenly the group is singing in the jubilee style, prompting Reese to do a little preaching. She handles this like the old gospel hand that she is.

The Meditations were later accompanied and coached by James Cleveland, during which time they adopted the style for which the Caravans would later become famous. Despite all their changes of personnel and song styles, the Meditations remain one of the premier female gospel groups of Detroit.

Harold Smith and the Majestics

Harold Eugene Smith (1934–93), like Della Reese, was born in Detroit. As a teenager he came under the influence of Mattie Moss Clark and sang with her in choirs and small groups in the Detroit area. In August 1963 he organized the Majestics, a gospel choir of fifty voices, which made its debut the following year at the Henry and Edsel Ford Auditorium in Detroit. In addition to giving concerts, the group presented

gospel music dramas in the style of those of W. Herbert Brewster, which incorporated dance.

The group appeared in concerts or rallies with Martin Luther King, Jr., Mahalia Jackson, and Duke Ellington and performed in Buffalo, New York, Boston, Philadelphia, and Chicago. Smith was a founder-member with James Cleveland of the Gospel Music Workshop of America in 1968 and was known for his flamboyant direction of choirs. His recording of Cleveland's "Lord, Help Me to Hold Out" is largely responsible for the song becoming a gospel standard.

Aretha Franklin

Like Sam Cooke, Della Reese, Lou Rawls, and Johnnie Taylor, Aretha Franklin (b. 1942) came to soul music after a distinguished career in gospel. Born in Memphis, Tennessee, to the Reverend C. L. Franklin and his wife, Barbara, Franklin grew up in Detroit and learned everything she knew about music in her father's church. While Franklin is known worldwide as the "Queen of Soul," the church still refers to her as "Aretha, Reverend Franklin's daughter." By connecting her with her father, the church registers a deep-seated hesitancy to dismiss Franklin from the church as it had done with Sister Rosetta Tharpe, Sam Cooke, and Lou Rawls. And part of this hesitancy is due to Franklin's attitude and behavior since she made the move to popular music.

Franklin never pretended to be anything other than a gospel singer, as clearly exhibited in early 1994 when she was given a Grammy Award for "Lifetime Achievement in the Recording Industry." She began her acceptance speech for the award with "I want to first give thanks to God Almighty, and then to my father, the Reverend C. L. Franklin, for you all know where I'm from." Only four years old when her father became pastor of New Bethel Baptist in Detroit, she literally sat at the feet of such gospel luminaries as Mahalia Jackson, Clara Ward and the Ward Singers, Rebert H. Harris, and James Cleveland. Her idol was Clara Ward.

She reacted like a sponge to gospel, and out of this wellspring of talent, she created a style that has influenced an overwhelmingly large number of African American female popular and soul music vocalists as well as a respectable number of non-African American female popular music singers. Only Bessie Smith, Dinah Washington, and Ella Fitzgerald can claim as many musical "daughters and grand-

daughters" as Aretha, and as late as the early 1990s she was still the Queen of Soul. Despite these accolades, none of her singing matches the pure and unadulterated soul of her gospel recordings at age sixteen when she poured forth with heartfelt renditions of "Never Grow Old" and "There Is a Fountain Filled with Blood." Her 1972 gospel album with James Cleveland entitled "Amazing Grace" has become the best-selling gospel album in history, and yet it does not capture a glimpse of the sound that Aretha gave when she sang gospel at her father's church during gospel's Golden Age.

Wynona Carr

By a strange twist of circumstances one of the greatest gospel composers and singers from Detroit spent only a short time there, although the tours and recordings she made while in Detroit certified her celebrity. Sister Wynona Carr (1924–76), born the same year as Clara Ward, was an enigma in gospel, as was Sister Rosetta Tharpe, after whom Carr's record producers patterned her and with whom she appeared in concert later in her career. During the early and mid-1950s, Carr served as one of the choir directors at C. L. Franklin's Bethlehem Baptist Church in Detroit. It was during her tenure there that she recorded her most popular hit, "The Ball Game," and her other "sports" song, "15 Rounds with Jesus."

With a progressive sound in the same category as Sister Rosetta Tharpe, though much more refined and hence less assaulting, Carr was too far ahead of the gospel world in which she lived. The major emphasis of her songs dealt not with Jesus and thanks, but with the metaphors and similes of the Christian religion. Additionally, her singing style did not evoke tears and sighs at her expression of heartfelt passion, but hand clapping and cheers at the sophisticated beauty of her jazzy singing style. Nowhere is this more eloquently illustrated than in her composition "The Ball Game" (1952):

> The first base is temptation (you know) the second base is sin,
> (The) third base tribulation, if you pass you can make it in;
> (Old man) Solomon is the umpire, and Satan's pitching the game,
> He'll do his best to strike you out, keep playing just the same.

Unlike most of the gospel singers of the Golden Age, Wynona Carr was not born in the Deep South but in Cleveland, Ohio, of Beulah and Jess Carr who had recently

moved from the South. Her mother remarried when Carr was quite young, and she was brought up in the household of her mother and her stepfather, Arthur Summers, who encouraged the musically talented child to begin piano lessons at age four. At age thirteen she entered Cleveland Music College where she studied voice, harmony, and arranging. During her teens she played for several Baptist church choirs and at age twenty began to commute between Cleveland and Detroit, directing church choirs in both cities.

After serving a tenure as a member of the famed Wings Over Jordan Choir in Cleveland, she organized her own group, the Carr Singers, in 1945 and toured throughout the Midwest. Her life changed when the group served as the opening act for J. W. Alexander and the Pilgrim Travelers at one of their concerts in Cleveland. While Carr only directed the choir and served as an occasional soloist, Alexander was impressed enough to pay for a demonstration tape, which he took back to Art Rupe, the owner of Specialty Records, for which his group recorded. The demonstration tape landed a contract for Carr and through her ten-year affiliation with the recording company, she became a popular star. The Five Blind Boys of Mississippi made her "Our Father" a national hit. Her recordings of duets with Brother Joe May and her own compositions secured her place in gospel history.

Always attracted to popular music, rhythm and blues, and jazz as much as she was to gospel, Carr combined a career of the church and the club for a number of years. However, in 1955, with a letter to Rupe stating that "I've tried singing spirituals [gospel] for fourteen years when all the time my real thoughts were in the show world," Carr left gospel. She had one hit in secular music, "Should I Ever Love Again" in 1957, but by that time she knew that she had contracted tuberculosis. She retired to her family's home in Cleveland for two years and took to the road afterward as a rhythm and blues singer. She never regained the popularity she had won while with Specialty Records, which she left in 1959. She signed with Reprise Records. They released only one of her albums during her lifetime; others were released after her death. During the 1960s she appeared at several plush nightclubs, but was always plagued by ill health. She finally retired in 1970 and died in May 1976.

It is ironic that Carr's music made more money after her death. In the 1980s her composition "Operator, Operator" was recorded by Manhattan Transfer, the pop jazz

group of the decade, and became a major hit. Had Carr been alive during that time she would no doubt have been a major star in either jazz or gospel.

The Gospel Quartets in Detroit: Flying Clouds and Evangelist Singers

Despite the fact that Detroit did not produce a male gospel quartet that achieved a national impression during the Golden Age of black gospel quartets, they have thrived in the city since the 1930s. As in most American cities, black gospel quartets abound, but like New York City, many of these groups elect to become community-based, singing more for pleasure than for money and limiting their performances to their hometown and traveling no more than two hundred miles for weekend engagements. This was the situation in Detroit except for two groups: the Flying Clouds and the Evangelist Singers.

FLYING CLOUDS

Like the Fairfield Four of Nashville, the Flying Clouds began as a teenage quartet in 1929. They were originally called the Russell Street Usher Board Four for their benefactors, the Usher Board of the Russell Street Baptist Church. Personnel changed so often in the early days that few remember the original membership of the group. By 1942 they had changed their name to the Flying Clouds, after a popular automobile that had recently been introduced. During the 1940s membership included original member Horace Simmons, John Evans, Joe Union, and Elmer Stallworth, former lead singer of the Friendly Brothers of Houston, Texas. Until the middle 1940s the Flying Clouds were considered a sweet gospel group, emphasizing tight harmonies, controlled voices, and little physicality in stage decorum. Then, in order to compete with such famous singers as the Soul Stirrers and the Dixie Hummingbirds, the Flying Clouds recruited Joe Union, formerly of the Loving Brothers of Omaha, Nebraska. Union brought an aggressive lead to the group, providing a startling contrast to the understated lead of John Evans.

Even though the group had a weekly broadcast for more than a decade at Detroit's WJR and later sang over CLLW in Windsor, Ontario, and recorded for several Detroit labels, a national reputation eluded them. Two of their popular recordings of the 1940s are "Savior Don't Pass Me By" and Lucie Campbell's "Something within Me."

EVANGELIST SINGERS

Oliver Green, an experienced quartet singer by 1938, organized his own group that year, basing their style on quartets he had heard and sung with in his hometown of Dennison, Texas. After several changes, membership in the Evangelist Singers came to include Green, Jimmie Bryant, Bob Thomas, and Larry Barnes. Receiving their greatest popularity as the Detroiters, a change of name suggested by a talent scout for radio personality Horace Heidt who felt that the name Evangelist Singers was too spiritual, the group recorded several sides for the Specialty label. Their style combined both the sweet singing of the Alabama quartets and the shouting songs of the Pentecostal church. "Don't Drive Your Children Away," featuring the growling bass lead of Jimmie Bryant, is one of their most popular recordings.

Other Detroit Singers

Among other singers from Detroit who made an impression on gospel during its Golden Age were Cissy Houston, mother of the 1990s popular music star Whitney, who was a member of the Drinkard Singers, along with Mancel Warwick, the father of Dionne and DeeDee Warwick. Both Dionne Warwick and Whitney Houston sang gospel at one time but switched to popular music through which they gained fame. The partially blind Princess Stewart, who had trained for concert and opera but who eventually succumbed to gospel, and Sammie Bryant were also well-known singers. "Prophet" Jones, coming from Bessemer, Alabama, as did Alex Bradford, gave up playing the piano and singing to become one of the most flamboyant gospel preachers of all time.

Detroit Pianists and Organists

Detroit produced several esteemed keyboard artists, the most outstanding of whom was Herbert "Pee Wee" Picard (b. 1933), who served as pianist and organist for Dorothy Love Coates and the Original Gospel Harmonettes when Evelyn Starks, the original pianist, returned to public school teaching. Thomas Shelby (1900–72) served as minister of music for C. L. Franklin's Bethlehem Baptist Church for over forty-five years. This Memphis, Tennessee, native came to the attention of the Reverend Franklin during his tenure as pianist for E. W. D. Isaac and Lucie Campbell's Good Will Singers of the National Baptist Convention. Also, Shelby was the first pia-

nist to teach Aretha Franklin gospel. Alfred Bolden (1937–70), a classically trained organist who was able to turn that technique into gospel, recorded several albums of organ gospel, hoping to identify that instrument as a solo voice in gospel.

GOSPEL IN ST. LOUIS

Records of the Pentecostal church show no strong influence in the introduction of gospel music in St. Louis, Missouri. Nonetheless, the 1920s, the period of the introduction of gospel music through the Pentecostal churches, also saw the rise of gospel in St. Louis. It is therefore noteworthy that by the early 1950s, when St. Louis was recognized as a gospel center, it was the Pentecostal singers who brought this recognition. Willie Mae Ford Smith, brought up in the Baptist church, had joined the sanctified church; Joe May was from the Church of God, one of several Pentecostal denominations; and in the middle 1950s the O'Neal Twins of COGIC joined other duos of gospel (although the twins, like Brother Joe May, were from East St. Louis, Illinois, they were considered part of the St. Louis, Missouri, school—as Robert Anderson of Gary, Indiana, was considered part of the Chicago school). In the last ten years of the Golden Age, when gospel was the most arresting music in the African American community, Tennessean Cleophus Robinson, a COGIC singer, joined the St. Louis school.

The National Baptist Convention influenced several of its St. Louis members to sing and compose gospel. Two of the most outstanding were A. B. Windom, composer, and Martha Bass, singer. But regardless of the denomination, all gospel singers sooner or later wanted to get to know a woman who was as strong as she was gentle: Willie Mae Ford Smith.

Willie Mae Ford Smith

The leader of gospel music in St. Louis and the surrounding area was Willie Mae Ford Smith (1904–94), who later earned the title of "Mother." She was born in Rolling Fork, Mississippi, but as a child moved with her family to Memphis. Piano-accompanied gospel was resonating throughout what was to become Mason Temple Church of God in Christ in Memphis but received little attention from Smith, because at that time, as she was later to recall, she was: "Baptist bred, Baptist Born, and when I die it will be a Baptist gone." In the 1920s, when her father could no

longer work in Memphis, he moved his family to St. Louis, where young Willie Mae served as the leader in a family group organized by her father. The Ford Sisters, as they were called, soon garnered a local and regional reputation as one of the finest female quartets of Missouri and Illinois.

The female quartet, patterned after the male quartet—even to the extent of using the male vocal designations of tenor, baritone, and bass—had been a part of the African American religious music scene since the 1930s. And while they were comparable with the male quartets, often competing against them in battles of song, the piano-accompanied female group was the *new* sound in gospel. The Ford Sisters compromised by rendering some of their songs with piano, while others they performed *a cappella*.

Smith was the most talented of the sisters, possessing a dark contralto and an easy style of delivery. She could have performed in opera as easily as gospel, which would have been gospel's loss. The Ford Sisters sang at the 1922 National Baptist Convention and created a sensation. Thereafter Willie Mae, because of her extraordinary voice, was sought after as a soloist at each convention.

In 1929 Smith married James Peter Smith, who owned a small moving company. Shortly after her marriage the stock market crashed, and in order to assist with family finances, she began traveling to other cities and conducting musical reviv-

Mother Willie Mae Ford Smith, with her adopted daughter Bertha at the piano

als. Dorsey heard her on one of these trips in 1931 and invited her to Chicago in 1932 to help him organize the NCGCC. In 1936 he appointed her director of the soloist bureau and the principal teacher of singing. In 1937 she set the standard for solo singing with her rendition of her own composition "If You Just Keep Still" at the National Baptist Convention. Smith joined the Church of God Apostolic, a Pentecostal denomination in 1939, and her singing thereafter had the added elements of rhythm, bounce, and the percussive attacks of the sanctified singers.

Although her fame began to spread she made very few recordings, and those that she made met with little success. Without the recording success of Mahalia Jackson and Roberta Martin, both of whom considered her a superior singer, Smith could concentrate on preaching and singing at revivals. As she traveled she would also

teach gospel singing and in this capacity met Edna Gallmon Cooke, Martha Bass (the mother of soul singer Fontella Bass,) Myrtle Scott, the O'Neal Twins, and her most famous student, Brother Joe May, who was the first to call her "Mother."

Mother Smith, as she was affectionately called, possessed a chameleon-like personality, and could be alternately sweet or sour. From years of traveling on buses and trains (most often alone) to teach gospel soloists, attempting to make a community of gospel singers in the St. Louis area, and continuously working to express her sanctification through song—as well as preaching—without the support of the "brethren of the church," Smith had built up defenses that could be volatile. She had to, in her words, "beat down" pastors of churches who would not permit her to sing from the pulpit, deacons who objected to her moving her body as she sang, and, most important, those who gave her little money for her singing. While she was, in the language of the church, "saved, sanctified, and filled with the Holy Ghost," she did not like to be crossed. Sallie Martin, with whom she worked for over sixty years in Dorsey's convention, was one of the few people who could disturb her sanctification, perhaps because they both saw themselves as the first assistant to Dorsey. Their on-again, off-again relationship was documented in the 1983 documentary *Say Amen, Somebody*.

Her most notable contribution to gospel, however, was the introduction of the "song and sermonette" into gospel music whereby a singer delivers a five- or ten-minute sermon before, during, or after the performance of a song. This device was later brought into standard gospel practice by Edna Gallmon Cooke and Shirley Caesar. Smith appeared at the Newport Jazz Festival and Radio City Music Hall, was celebrated in *Say Amen, Somebody*, and was featured in Brian Lanker's 1989 book of photographs called *I Dream a World: Portraits of Black Women Who Changed America*.

Brother Joe May

Mother Smith's most famous student, Brother Joe May (1912–72), was born, like her, in Mississippi. Hailing from the small village of Macon, May was brought up in the Church of God. He began singing at age nine and soon became a member of the Church of God Quartet, which traveled throughout Mississippi and Alabama. After marriage he and his wife and the first two of their seven children moved to East St. Louis, Illinois, in 1941 to be closer to Mother Smith and to find work.

As director of the soloist bureau of Dorsey's convention, Smith had run a revival (not of preaching but of singing) in Macon and had met May during that visit. Not only did she encourage May to sing, but mentioned to him that there was a great deal of work in the St. Louis area that would help him care for his family. May found work in St. Louis—he worked as a janitor but at a much higher salary than he was drawing in Mississippi—and visited Smith nightly to learn new songs. This led to concert appearances with her. Knowing that May was, at that time, extremely shy about his singing, Smith had to use all her powers to persuade him to accompany her to the National Baptist Convention and audition to sing a solo at the concert of new singers.

Trusting Smith, May auditioned at the National Baptist Convention in Los Angeles, was accepted, and became an immediate hit. He impressed J. W. Alexander, who was instrumental in securing a recording contract for him with Specialty Records. His first recording, Dorsey's "Search Me, Lord," became an instant hit. The popularity of the recording was due as much to May's voice as to Dorsey's song. May possessed a huge and powerful tenor with the agility of an Ira Tucker. Although he had been brought up singing the shout songs of the sanctified church he had learned to moan on an Isaac Watts hymn as well as any Baptist preacher. His powerful voice and Dorsey's songs, which he favored, made him a popular singer on the gospel circuit, and in 1950 he quit his job as a janitor at the Monsanto Chemical plant in St. Louis to go on the road as a professional singer. He was often paired in concert with Mahalia Jackson because of the similarity in their singing styles. Such concerts, often billed as a battle of song between the "World's Greatest Gospel Singer," a title then held by Jackson, and the "Thunderbolt of the Middle West," a title given to May by Smith, always generated huge crowds and powerful singing.

Although May presented solo concerts, he was most often part of a package of singers, among whom were the Pilgrim Travelers, the Sallie Martin Singers, Wynona Carr (all part of the Specialty stable), and May's son and daughter, Annette and Charles. While May never became the crossover artist that Jackson was—his singing style was considered too churchy for white audiences in the 1950s and 1960s—he was one of the most financially successful gospel singers of his day, often earning up to $50,000 a year. In 1957 May moved to Nashboro Records, a company that distributed mainly in the South. Without recordings in the West, Midwest, and North-

east, his popularity waned. Concerts became fewer, but May continued to travel and sing until 1972 when he suffered a fatal stroke. His recordings resurfaced in the late 1980s, and May became once again one of the most popular soloists in gospel.

Other St. Louis Singers

Two other St. Louis natives who were important figures in gospel between 1945 and 1955 were Martha Bass and A. B. Windom. Bass, who possessed a dark contralto, was known as a "house shouter" because of her ability to rouse a church into pandemonium. She sang with Clara Ward and the Ward Singers for several years. Windom, a one-time accompanist for Mother Smith, composed several gospel songs; her "I'm Bound for Canaan Land" and "I've Got the River of Jordan to Cross" became gospel standards.

GOSPEL IN TENNESSEE

Memphis was the city selected by Charles Harrison Mason as the headquarters of his Church of God in Christ, one of the congregations in which gospel was developed. Not only was there congregational singing of gospel during Sunday and weekday services, but special concerts of this music were presented during the annual convocation held in the city each November. Mason's church quickly became one of the places visitors to Memphis insisted upon frequenting, and word of the music spread throughout the state. Tennessee produced several important figures in gospel's Golden Age, none more important than Lucie Eddie Campbell.

Lucie E. Campbell

Lucie E. Campbell (1885–1963) has the unenviable distinction of having been born on a train just outside of Duck Hill, Mississippi. Her father, Burrell, worked on the railroad, and her mother, Isabella Wilkerson Campbell, would deliver him his lunch each day on the train that carried workers back and forth. While Isabella was returning from this lunch delivery one day, Lucie decided to enter this world. Miss Lucie, as she was called by members of the National Baptist Convention, delighted in telling this story, because it testified to her uniqueness.

Shortly after Lucie was born her father was killed in a railroad accident, leaving Mrs. Campbell to bring up nine children. Hoping to find work in a large city she

moved her family to Memphis. Lucie attended elementary school in Memphis and graduated from Kortrecht High School in 1899. Her high school record was so extraordinary that she was named valedictorian of her class, and after graduation she was immediately hired by the Carnes Grammar School. She taught there from 1899 until 1911 when she was hired as teacher at Kortrecht, by then renamed the Booker T. Washington High School, where she taught for the next thirty-three years.

Campbell was just as dedicated to the Baptist church as she was to teaching and served as a national officer for the National Baptist Convention from 1916 when she was elected music director of the Sunday School and Baptist Training Union (BTU) until her death in 1963. In this capacity she arranged pre-convention musicals and directed the choir during the one-week series of services. From 1919 until 1960 Campbell wrote a song each year for the choir of the convention. Within weeks of the introduction of each new song, choirs around the country added the song to their repertoires. Several of the more than fifty songs written by Campbell have become gospel standards—quite a singular feat for a woman who never studied music.

Campbell's interest in music began in the 1890s when she listened to her elder sister's piano lessons. Campbell would go to the piano as soon as her sister was finished and play the pieces she had heard. She not only taught herself to play but taught herself to write out songs in music manuscript. As a college student at Rust College in Holly Springs, Mississippi, from which she graduated with a major in liberal arts in the summer of 1927, Campbell sang in the choir and was occasionally assisted in her composition by the choral director.

She was a lyricist who chose simple words to express her great Christian conviction. With melodies of simple beauty transporting lyrics of deep sincerity, Campbell was able to write songs that struck at the very heart of gospel music lovers. It is commonly acknowledged that "Amazing Grace" by John Newton is the most favored song among African American Christians and Thomas A. Dorsey's "Take My Hand, Precious Lord" is the second most popular song. There is little doubt then that Campbell's "He Understands, He'll Say 'Well Done'" comes in third:

> *If when you give the best of your service*
> *Telling the world that the Savior is come;*
> *Be not dismayed if men don't believe you*

He understands; He'll say, "Well done."
Oh, when I come to the end of my journey
Wearied of life and the battle is won;
Carrying the staff and the cross of redemption
He understands; He'll say, "Well done."

This 1933 composition was long a favorite for funerals but gradually moved into the gospel mainstream where it has been performed both as a gospel ballad at a slow tempo and as a fast shout song. Campbell's most famous shout song, "Jesus Gave Me Water," equally as effective when performed in the slightly slower jubilee tempo, tells the story of the woman who met Jesus at the well:

The woman from Samaria once came to get some water
And there she met a stranger who did her story tell;
He spoke, she dropped the pitcher, she drank and was made richer,
When Jesus gave her water that was not from the well.

Campbell was known as a feisty and authoritative woman who exercised a great deal of power in the National Baptist Convention. Mahalia Jackson could always inspire howls of laughter when she recounted how, during her audition before Miss Lucie for a spot on a concert during the National Baptist Convention, Miss Lucie interrupted her with great ceremony only to say very curtly, "Stand up straight, young woman." J. Robert Bradley, who succeeded Miss Lucie as director of music for the National Baptist Convention, could be equally hilarious when he reminded singers that Miss Lucie was so powerful that ministers' wives would give her the front passenger seat of the family car (with their husbands driving) while they sat in the back. Miss Lucie never refused such honors, thinking rather that the women were behaving properly. She maintained her high spirit until the end of her life, as evidenced by her marriage at age seventy-five.

W. Herbert Brewster

Memphis boasted a second important Golden Age composer, William Herbert Brewster (c.1898–1987). Brewster was the first gospel music composer to write songs that, when recorded, sold a million copies. Often called the "eloquent poet," he was

born in the small village of Sommerville, Tennessee. After graduating from high school he entered Roger Williams College, from which he graduated in 1922. He moved to Memphis that year to become the dean of a proposed African American seminary sponsored by the National Baptist Convention. When the school did not materialize he accepted the pastorate of the East Trigg Baptist Church in Memphis and remained its pastor until his death. In addition to pastoring, he founded and directed the Brewster Theological Clinic, which had branches in twenty-five cities. His greatest joys, however, were writing biblical dramas, for which he also wrote the music, and composing gospel songs. During the 1940s Brewster wrote a drama each year and presented it at one of the auditoriums in the city. These presentations became sacred highlights of the year. It was for such a drama that the song "Our God Is Able" was composed. His *From Auction to Glory*, written in 1941, was the first nationally staged black religious play to feature gospel music written for the production. Previously, Negro spirituals had been used in religious plays.

Brewster composed his first song, "I'm Leaning and Depending on the Lord," in 1939, but it was not published until 1941. From this first composition it was obvious that Brewster was a learned and eloquent person with an extraordinary knowledge of the Bible. He drew on these attributes for his songs. In fact, much of what the African American community heard about the Old Testament in music during the Golden Age of Gospel might very well have come from Dr. Brewster (he was awarded an honorary doctorate by Bennett College of Greensboro, North Carolina). In addition to serving as a tour guide through the Old Testament in "Move On Up a Little Higher," Brewster provided a mini-atlas of the cities of God in "I Never Heard of a City Like the New Jerusalem":

> *I have heard of Babylon, with its walls and towers grand,*
> *With its temples and its gardens, palaces that once did stand;*
> *Where the three Hebrew children won over wicked men,*
> *And where Daniel held his own in a lion's den.*
>
> *I have heard of mighty Sodom, Ninevah and Jericho*
> *How they reveled in their splendor till their sins brought them low;*
> *I have heard of Tyre, Sidon and wicked old Gomorrha and*
> *How God snatched away their glory.*

While lyrics were the most outstanding feature of Brewster's songs, his sense of gospel tempos ushered in a new sense of foot patting and hand clapping. Growing up during the era of the "Dr. Watts" hymns and the Baptist lining hymn, he had a keen sense of emotion brought about through wringing each syllable and tone through several rhythmic variations. He combined the slow nineteenth-century hymn with the more rhythmic gospel song by dividing many of his songs into two parts. Like the operatic combination known as recitative and aria, the slow and unmetered section of the song unfolded the serious part of the song, while the rhythmic portion commented on or gave the moral of the whole. "Just over the Hill" begins with a slow and unmetered section:

> *There is a land of fateless day*
> > ***Just over the hill***
> *Beyond the rainbow and the sky*
> > ***Just over the hill;***
> *It's a land beyond compare, free from sorrows, pain or care*
> *And they tell me there's no night there*
> > ***Just over the hill.***

He then moves into a sprightly gospel tempo with the refrain:

> *Just over the hill, just over the hill,*
> *I'm on my way to the land of day just over the hill;*
> *Soon below I'll cease to roam, for I shall outrun the storm,*
> *And make my way to my happy home, just over the hill.*

During the slow section, the singer would embellish and elaborate at will, while during the faster sections rhythmic devices such as syncopation and double time (singing twice as fast) became outstanding features. These devices became all the more sensational when Brewster assigned a song three different tempos, as he did with "Faith Can Move Mountains" in which the verse is sung at a very slow and unmetered tempo, while the refrain is delivered in a lively tempo, and a special chorus is sung at the fast tempo of a shout song.

The vamp, a section of a song based on repetition, was Brewster's most popular

compositional device. The vamp serves as the basis for "Our God Is Able" and "Move on up a Little Higher" but is most ingeniously employed in "Let Us All Go Back to the Old Landmark." Not only does Brewster show his skill at repetition, but his sense of rhyming is at its best in this composition of a chorus and three stanzas, each stanza ending with a four-line vamp:

Verse I	Vamp
He will	hear us
And be	near us
We'll be	given
Bread from	heaven

He will feed us until we want no more.

When the vamp from each of the three stanzas was sung successively, it provided an extended vamp of sophisticated gospel.

Brewster was honored at a weekend seminar at the Smithsonian Institution in December 1982, where his songs were presented in several concerts and he was the star of his own biblical drama *Sowing in Tears, Reaping in Joy*.

Queen Candice Anderson

Brewster was fortunate to find the precise voice he wanted to interpret his songs. That voice belonged to a young member of his singing group, the Brewster Ensemble. While still in her early teens the young girl, whose original name seems to have been forgotten, joined Brewster's church, and he heard her sing. (During the 1982 seminar in his honor at the Smithsonian Institution, Brewster told the audience that once he accepted Anderson as one of his singers, she literally divorced her family and spent most of her time at the church and with his singers. Her family appeared to have no problem with this and until her death Anderson was considered part of the Brewster family.) Because she was so beautiful and so talented Brewster decided that she should bear the name of a queen. He chose Queen Candice of Ethiopia, mentioned in the Bible in Acts 8:27–39, who was the queen of the eunuch converted to Christianity by Philip. He retained her last name and most of his published compositions bear the note: "As Performed by Queen C. Anderson."

Anderson (1913–59) had a light but powerful alto voice and appeared to have had an affinity for Brewster songs. According to Brewster, he could begin teaching her a song and before he could finish she would take over and complete that which she had never heard before. She was responsible for introducing such Brewster songs as "Move on up a Little Higher" (Mahalia Jackson learned the song from her); "Our God Is Able," as it was called when she sang it; and "Lord, I've Tried," made famous by the Soul Stirrers. Although she recorded with the Brewster Ensemble in 1950, none of the records have been located as of this writing. Queen Candice traveled little, and so only those around Memphis can speak with any authority about the voice that the "eloquent poet" chose to sing his songs.

J. Robert Bradley

At Lucie E. Campbell's death in 1963, John Robert Lee Bradley (b. 1920), known as J. Robert, became director of music for the National Baptist Convention. Bradley seemed destined for this position; he was discovered by Ms. Campbell when he was twelve years old, sang principal lead in a quartet organized by her for the National Baptist Convention in the 1930s, was selected by English composer Roger Quilter (1877–1953) during the late 1940s to introduce his new songs, and garnered a worldwide reputation as "Mr. Baptist," the most renowned singer within the Baptist denomination, both black and white.

Bradley was born to—in his words—"one of the poorer families in North Memphis." He attended elementary school there, but he disliked formal education and missed classes on a regular basis in third grade. Thereafter he attended school intermittently, never graduating from high school. At age twelve he was standing outside the city auditorium in Memphis on Christmas Eve when the area Baptists were holding their annual musicale. Bradley began to sing along with them. A policeman who was monitoring the crowd heard this lovely voice and took him inside to the director of the musicale, who happened to be Lucie E. Campbell. In one of those strange strokes of circumstance, Miss Campbell decided to have Bradley sing on the program. She was so impressed that she took the young singer under her wing and began to teach him her songs (among the Campbell songs dedicated to Bradley are "Even a Child Can Open the Gate," "Signed and Sealed with His Blood," and "Heavenly Sunshine"). Under Campbell's tutelage Bradley not only developed a voice that

would be compared with the great Russian bass Chaliapin, but also learned how to sing a gospel song with all the fire of a sanctified preacher and delivered with all the care and cunning of an opera singer.

During the 1930s the Reverend E. W. D. Isaac, Jr.—who brought Campbell into the Baptist Training Union in 1916—and Campbell organized a male gospel quartet (with piano accompaniment) to travel around the country and appear at the National Baptist Convention singing songs that Campbell and others composed for the denomination. The Good Will Singers, one of the most popular gospel groups of the 1930s and 1940s, was composed of Bradley; Odie Hoover of Cleveland, Ohio; J. Earle Hines of Atlanta; and Charles Simms of Nashville. Thomas Shelby of Memphis served as the first pianist, and Elmer Ruffner (1913–88) followed him in this position.

Always interested in European art music as much as gospel, Bradley was encouraged by Dr. A. M. Townsend of the National Baptist Convention to study voice seriously in New York. He left the Good Will Singers in the early 1940s and began studying with Madame Edyth Walker (1870–1950), the famous Wagnerian mezzo-soprano, at her studio in New York. He later moved to London where he remained for six years studying and singing throughout Europe. He made his debut at London's Albert Hall in 1946 in a concert of German, French, and Italian songs; Negro spirituals; and Lucie Campbell's "Heavenly Sunshine."

Bradley has been praised for his controlled intensity, evenness of tone, and the sheer beauty of his voice. His earthy bass has a power unheard of in gospel. While some gospel singers decry him for his penchant for singing the slow gospel hymn and ballad, in 1975 his singing so inspired President William Richard Tolbert, Jr., of Liberia that he knighted him "Sir" Robert. Both Lucie Campbell and Mahalia Jackson requested that he sing at their funerals. In his quiet but extremely moving singing style, Bradley honored their requests.

Spirit Of Memphis

Quartet singing in Memphis has been a pastime and vocation for men and women since the early 1920s. Groups organized in the 1920s include the I. C. Glee Club, the Harmony Four, and the Mount Olive Wonders. Along with Jefferson County, Alabama, Memphis shares the record for having the most female gospel quartets.

Among the female *a cappella* quartets in Memphis were the Golden Stars, the Southern Junior Girls, and the Songbirds of the South, whose leader, Cassietta George, later became famous as a member of Albertina Walker's Caravans.

The most outstanding quartet from Memphis, however, was the long-lived Spirit of Memphis Quartette (by the early 1950s they dropped "Quartette"). The seeds of the group were planted in 1927 or 1928 when several members of different quartets would get together informally and sing. In 1930 James Darling, A. C. Harris, Forrest Terrel, and Arthur Wright formed a quartet but gave themselves no name. One evening when they were to appear on a program and had to be introduced, the group was discussing a name when Darling began to wipe his face with a handkerchief that had written in the corner "The Spirit of St. Louis" (in honor of Lindbergh's 1927 flight across the Atlantic in an airplane of the same name). Darling changed "St. Louis" to "Memphis," and this group was born.

Heavily influenced by the Famous Blue Jay Singers, the first professional quartet the group saw, they featured precise attacks and releases with harmony reminiscent of the university jubilee quartets. Their strength lay in the several leaders they had over the next thirty years.

Memphis was the home of Sam Phillips' Sun Records and Hallelujah Spiritual, a local label. Galatin, Tennessee, was home to Dot Records, and Excello Records was located in Nashville. Only the Hallelujah Spiritual label appeared interested in the Spirit of Memphis. Their first recording was released in fall 1949, and, although recorded in Memphis on Hallelujah Spiritual, it was immediately leased to Deluxe, a regional label. "I'm Happy in the Service of the Lord," backed with "My Life Is in His Hands," became regional hits.

The success of this recording inspired the group to leave their day jobs and go on the road as professionals. When the group became full-time singers, their membership included Early Malone, Jethroe "Jet" Bledsoe, Theo Wade, James Darling, Robert Reed, and the Reverend Robert Crenshaw. With the release of their recording they began to accept invitations to appear throughout Alabama, Arkansas, Mississippi, and Tennessee. Silas Steele from the Famous Blue Jay Singers and William Broadnax, known as "Little Ax," soon joined the group, and the Spirits boasted two of the greatest leaders in gospel quartets. Gospel music historian Anthony Heilbut described the Spirits during their heyday:

The group's powerhouse was the ever dependable Alabaman, Silas Steele, late of the Blue Jays and Bright Stars. Steele's thunderous baritone could shake a church, the subdued lead of Jet Bledsoe and the ringing tenor of Willie "Little Ax" Broadnax blended gloriously with his roars. Often James Darling, the group's baritone, would improvise a melodic counterpoint to Steele's lead, while the bass "boom-de-boomed" in accustomed style.

This description captures, in ringing sonority, the Spirits' singing of Wynona Carr's "Lord Jesus" in a live performance at Memphis' seven-thousand-seat Mason Temple in October 1952. While the quartet provides a solid harmonic and rhythmic background to compete with the solo—a beloved competition in gospel—Jet Bledsoe literally preaches his solo. The delight at this exchange is apparent from the shouts, encouragements, and screams of the audience (captured on the recording), providing an indication of the kind of ecstacy apparent at live performances of beloved gospel groups. Jet Bledsoe, the manager of the Spirits during the 1950s, took the group off the road in 1960, but they appeared locally for the next several years. In 1980, the group celebrated its fiftieth anniversary.

Samuel McCrary and the Fairfield Four

In April 1991 the Fairfield Four performed in concert at Carnegie Hall, helping to celebrate the one hundredth anniversary of the finest performance house in the United States. Two months later this group celebrated an anniversary of its own—its seventieth—as one of the world's leading male *a cappella* gospel quartets.

In late 1921 the Reverend J. R. Carrethers, assistant pastor of Nashville's Fairfield Missionary Baptist Church and a well-known musician, organized and trained a trio of young boys from the Sunday School to sing during services and special programs held at the church. When the trio became a quartet in 1925, the Reverend Stratton, then pastor of the church, and Mrs. Annie Clay, mother of the church, gave them the name Fairfield Four. The group sang "in their home church, at local churches and at teas and social gatherings for friends and acquaintances." Samuel McCrary (1911–91) joined the group in the mid-1930s and by the late 1930s the group had secured its first radio broadcast over WSIX. Doug Seroff, their biographer, comments on the addition of tenor McCrary to the group:

His silver-toned tenor voice, a marvel of projection and control, set the Fairfield
Four apart from other local gospel groups. Young Sam McCrary was the most
outstanding gospel quartet lead singer Nashville has ever produced.

In 1941 John W. Work III, the venerable composer and music educator from
Fisk University, came to the Fairfield church to record a sermon by the Reverend
Stratton for the Library of Congress. Work recorded the Fairfield Four as well, and
thus the group began a recording career that would last more than fifty years.

As the prize for winning a promotional contest held by the local Colonial Coffee
Company, the Fairfield Four began broadcasting over Nashville's 50,000–watt
WLAC in 1942 and continued their broadcasts for almost a decade. During their
broadcasting years, the members of the group were Samuel McCrary, first tenor and
lead; John H. Battle, alternate first tenor; George Gracey, second tenor; Harold L.
Carrethers, baritone and pianist (like many other quartets during the late 1940s and
1950s the Fairfield Four occasionally used piano accompaniment); and Rufus L.
Carrethers, bass. Their repertoire consisted of Negro spirituals sung in the style of
the university jubilee singers, jubilee songs, and the newer gospel songs composed
by Dorsey, Campbell, and Brewster. In 1946 the group signed a recording contract
with Bullet Record Company, and over the next fifteen years recorded more than one
hundred titles on such labels as Bullet, Delta, Dot, Champion, and Old Town.

The Fairfield Four, like the hundreds of black male *a cappella* quartets of the late
1940s and early 1950s, thought and spoke of their singing groups as "clubs." As
such, although a great deal of time was spent socializing and having fun with other
men who were all nearly the same age and had the same interests, they were ruled
by strict bylaws and, in some cases, a constitution. Doug Seroff published the following document of the Fairfield Four for a 1988 Gospel Arts Festival Day, held at
Fisk University in Nashville:

BYLAWS OF THE FAIRFIELD FOUR (c.1943)

1. *Business meeting and rehearsal twice weekly—Tuesday and Friday, 10:00*
   o'clock until. All not present on time will be fined 50 cents, absent—$1.00.
2. *All discussions be made in meeting and not in public. Anyone caught*
   arguing with anyone in public—$2.00.

3. *Members of quartet must be in church at all programs at 8:15 or be fined $1.00 without a lawful excuse.*

4. *For members caught drinking within 8 hours of program—be fined $5.00.*

5. *When in church any time during program no member should look at others, argue on stage or appear to look angry. Stage etiquette—no unnecessary talk, sitting out of order—if any clause be disobeyed—fined $1.50.*

6. *Any member caught with alcohol on breath while on duty—be fined $2.50.*

7. *When program is out of town make special place to meet at a certain time. If not present without lawful excuse—fined $1.00.*

8. *When money is in treasury after weekly division, no money will be given to any member unless necessary.*

9. *Any member accepting drinks from any strangers—be fined $5.00.*

10. *Any member that doesn't respect members of group or any outside person—saints or sinners—be fined $5.00.*

11. *Any member that tries to arrange or fix a song for the group and the others don't assist will be fined $1.00.*

12. *Any member caught with chewing gum while in service—be fined $1.00 upon entering church.*

13. *All fines must be paid at the end of week and divided among other members.*

14. *All members be in studio 30 minutes before going on air or be fined $1.00—absent $2.50.*

15. *Each member fined $2.50 for the word G. D. and $1.00 additional for each offense.*

16. *Any member that argues when fine is presented to be fined double.*

The Fairfield Four's fame spread throughout the United States, and they were in great demand. A split following a dispute within the group in the late 1940s resulted in two different quartets using the same name. By 1950 McCrary had pulled together a single group of singers that continued to sing into the 1990s. One of the newer members was bass Isaac "Dickie" Freeman from Johns, Alabama. While McCrary reigned as the supreme lead of the group, with the Reverend W. L. Richardson (1913–93) succeeding him in the 1980s, much of the Fairfield Four's reputation was

based on the booming voice and skill of Dickie Freeman, often described as the "thumpingest bass in all of gospel."

A 1952 recording of the group, whose membership at that time included Samuel McCrary as first tenor and lead, Willie Love as second tenor, Willie Frank Lewis as baritone, and Isaac "Dickie" Freeman as bass, captures and illustrates their sound and style. The title of the song, "Tree of Level," bears the misunderstanding of the word "Lebanon" as it was pronounced on the original recording by the Dixie Hummingbirds. Despite this mispronunciation, the rendition shows McCrary at the height of his powers and provides an indication of how Freeman can "thump" bass.

Under Freeman's leadership the Fairfield Four continued to sing into the 1990s at folk music festivals, country fairs, and on the European folk and gospel circuits.

Cleavant Derricks

A new gospel song burst on the scene in the late 1930s and by 1945 had become such a popular favorite of gospel singers and Christian denominations that it was regarded as a folk song. The song was "Just a Little Talk with Jesus," composed in 1937 by Cleavant Derricks (c.1900–76), a pianist and choir director from Chattanooga, Tennessee. The phrase "a little talk with Jesus makes it right" has been one of the popular folk sayings in the African American community since the turn of the century. Because the phrase is used in the song, few people realized that there was, in fact, a Negro spiritual called "A Little Talk with Jesus Makes It Right." James Weldon and J. Rosamond Johnson published an arrangement of the spiritual in their 1927 *Volume Two of American Negro Spirituals*. The words, as contained in that arrangement, are:

> CHORUS
> *O, a little talk wid Jesus, makes it right, all right;*
> *Little talk wid Jesus makes it right, all right.*
> *Lord, troubles of ev'ry kind, thank God, I'll always find,*
> *Dat a little talk wid Jesus makes it right.*

While there are minor similarities between the harmonic structure of the Negro spiritual and Derrick's composition, the melody is totally different and the lyrics bear no relationship save the title:

Chorus

(Basses)	(Choir)
Now let us	*have a little talk with Jesus*
Let us	*tell Him all about our troubles*
He will	*hear our faintest cry*
And He will	*answer by and by;*
Now when you	*feel a little prayer wheel turning*
And you	*know a little fire is burning,*
You will	*find a little talk with Jesus makes it right.*

Verse

I once was lost in sin but Jesus took me in,
And then a little light from heaven filled my soul;
It bathed my heart in love and wrote my name above,
And just a little talk with Jesus made me whole.

Derrick placed the song in a jubilee—sprightly walking—tempo, assigned the bass lyrics to the triadic tones of a doorbell answered by the choir in a melody that alternates an ascending portion with a descending portion, and found that he had composed a song that was one of the first gospel songs to cross over into the jazz repertoire.

W. Herbert Brewster reported that in the early 1930s before Derrick began composing he came to Memphis and worked with him for a short time. Derrick's style of lyric writing attests to this association. Moreover, he borrowed one of Brewster's rhythmic devices in "Just a Little Talk with Jesus"—every syllable is set to a single tone, creating the kind of "patter song" made famous in Gilbert and Sullivan operettas.

Derrick was born in Chattanooga and grew up singing in the Orchard Knob Baptist Church. As a young man he and his wife, Cecelia, directed the choir at Orchard Knob. In his early thirties he was called to the ministry and moved first to Knoxville and then to Beloit, Wisconsin, founding a church in each place. He later settled in Washington, D.C., pastoring a church there until illness forced his retirement in the early 1970s.

Derrick continued to compose throughout his life, writing more than three hundred gospel songs. Others of his songs that have become gospel standards are "When God Dips His Love in My Heart," "I Trust Him on My Journey All the Way,"

and "We'll Soon Be Done with Troubles and Trials." Derrick realized a long-held desire when in 1975, after the song was more than forty years old, he recorded "Just a Little Talk with Jesus."

GOSPEL IN NEW YORK

Despite its prominence as an African American world cultural center and its role in the development of African American secular music after the 1920s, New York City has a less-than-illustrious place in the development of gospel music. It is ironic that this mecca of talent has not produced that major star, group, composer, publishing house, pianist, or organist who would set the standard in gospel and therefore entice gospel performers to the city because "things were happening there." The one exception was the Selah Jubilee Singers led by southern-born and musically initiated Thurmon Ruth. And while New York has always been considered a gospel city—every gospel singer must eventually appear there—during the Golden Age it was not a gospel center where the music was created and produced. However, New York City, like the other cities, began to participate in the same way as a "center."

Charlie Storey, who has sung with both the Jubilee Stars and the Brooklyn All Stars, witnessed the gospel movement in New York City from the late 1920s. He observed that when he moved to the city, he started on the road to gospel the same way his brothers and sisters had in the South. Born in Camake, Georgia, he moved with his family to Brooklyn in 1928. His father, a Holiness preacher, "set up a church in the family's small house at 711 Gates Avenue." Soon after their arrival Storey and his sisters formed a vocal "spiritual" group and began singing in neighborhood churches.

The Storey family arrived in New York at about the same time as Otha M. Kelly (c.1897–1986). Kelly, a Mississippi native, was saved under the Elder I. E. MacFadden in Hattiesburg, Mississippi, in 1914 and shortly thereafter moved to Chicago, coming under the tutelage of Williams Roberts, who later became the first Overseer (then Bishop) of the Chicago Jurisdiction of COGIC. After working fourteen years with Roberts, Kelly relocated to New York, eventually becoming Overseer and then Bishop of the New York Jurisdiction. Like other ministers in the Pentecostal denomination, Kelly brought this sanctified style of singing to New York.

This sanctified music filled homes, small churches, and storefronts throughout

New York, but it was not the only sacred music to make an impression on the city. The jubilee quartet movement had entered the city in the mid-1920s. Before that the original Golden Gate Quartet had been inspired by the Fisk Jubilee Singers to present concerts of Negro spirituals and folk songs before nonchurch audiences. College-trained quartets began settling in the city in 1927 when the Utica Jubilee Quartet, originally students from the Utica Normal and Industrial Institute in Utica, Mississippi, relocated to New York City. Ray Allen, in his study of New York quartets, reported that "in 1927 they began broadcasting over WJZ of the National Broadcasting Company, becoming the first African American quartet to be featured on a nationally syndicated radio program." While many of the jubilee quartets relocated to New York City—including the Virginia-based Golden Gate Quartet, the Dinwiddie Singers, and the Norfolk Jubilee Singers—few elected to make the switch from jubilee to gospel.

One of the first quartets to do so was the Southernaires. Representing the several southern colleges where they had been trained in the jubilee tradition, the Southernaires were formed in New York City and made their first appearance at the Williams International CME Church in Harlem that same year. The original membership included first tenor Homer Smith of Florence, Alabama; lead soloist and second tenor Lowell Peters of Cleveland, Tennessee; baritone Jay Stone Toney from Kentucky; and bass William Edmondson from Spokane, Washington. Although they sang the traditional jubilee songs, they were also able to make a house "shout" with the newer gospel songs. In the late 1950s this group made another switch—to popular songs and rhythm and blues—and stopped singing religious songs.

Soloists and groups who had nourished their talent in their southern hometowns, however, began to move into New York City in the 1930s. This second group of transplanted southerners were thoroughly steeped in the gospel tradition. The first of these was also the first superstar in gospel, Sister Rosetta Tharpe. Sister Tharpe was also the first of the sanctified saints who kept one foot in the church and one foot in the clubs.

Sister Rosetta Tharpe

At age four in her hometown of Cotton Plant, Arkansas, Rosetta Nubin (1915–73) stood on boxes playing a guitar only slightly smaller than herself and singing "Jesus

on the Main Line, Tell Him What You Want." While there was no doubt that she had an extraordinary voice—bright and clear, sonorous, warm, slightly brassy—and an easy delivery, she also knew at that tender age how to sing. Her pitch was solid; she knew the melody and could even add extra notes of her own. Her rhythm was as accented, syncopated, and intricate as any of the blues singers "in the bottoms."

None of these vocal qualities, however, matched her guitar playing. To be sure, she played her share of strummed chords, as most amateurs do, but she also played individual tones creating motives, runs, riffs, and melodies. This was all the more interesting because before the mid-1920s very few African American women played the guitar, opting instead for the piano, which was considered the appropriate instrument for women. Only one other African American woman gained prominence as a guitarist before the 1930s: "Memphis" Minnie Douglas (1896–1973), who began on the banjo but switched to guitar by age fifteen. The guitar family was not strange to Rosetta Nubin, for one of the first sounds she heard was her mother, Katie Bell Nubin (1880–1969), strumming the mandolin and singing sanctified songs, but Rosetta's string technique had surpassed her mother's even at age four.

Clearly, Rosetta Nubin was a prodigy, exactly what Katie Bell Nubin needed to do her work: carry the word of the Lord. As a woman preacher in the sanctified church, she was not able to call herself "Elder," the title used by ministers, nor was she able to oversee a congregation as the senior spiritual officer. Yet she felt that she was "called to preach." The one avenue left open for her was to teach. A female preacher who taught was called a missionary or an evangelist and could teach in any sanctified church and even conduct revivals. Unable to acquire the status of elder, Katie Bell Nubin became a missionary who, in traveling from church to church and town to town, acquired the status of evangelist. Her hook for drawing people to her services was "Little Rosetta Nubin, the singing and guitar-playing miracle." This duo—Katie Bell Nubin, woman preacher, singer, and mandolin player, and her daughter, Little Rosetta, singing and playing guitar—as members of the tent-meeting troupe of male evangelist P. W. McGhee, preached and sang their way through Arkansas, Mississippi, Florida, Georgia, and Tennessee before settling in Chicago in the late 1920s.

In Chicago the Nubins became participants in the growing Holiness movement

and Rosetta earned a reputation as a "sweetly saved" young woman. Opportunities to demonstrate her talent abounded, and she accepted every opportunity offered. She began appearing in multiact concerts with performers of blues, jazz, and folk. Her close association with the sanctified church had mellowed her interest in secular music, but she could not deny that her guitar playing and certain aspects of her singing style had been strongly influenced by the blues singers she heard in Arkansas and the jazz she heard on every corner in Chicago, where both King Oliver and Louis Armstrong were holding forth. While she sang and played blues and jazz in the privacy of her home and at the homes of friends, she performed only gospel music in public.

On the advice of several Chicago promoters, Rosetta moved to New York in the mid-1930s and settled in Harlem, once again affiliating with the sanctified church. She soon married a minister from that denomination. This marriage did not last long however, because, like the sanctified church, her husband did not realize she had to be a free spirit. In 1934 Nubin married Wilbur Thorpe—he later changed the name to Tharpe—in Chicago, and he seemed to approve of her career. Upon arriving in New York, however, he began to publicly object to some of her professional action in public, perhaps in an effort to control this great talent. For example, he objected to her appearing without a hat (a necessity within the black church tradition).

Encouraged by her fellow singers in the sanctified church, Rosetta made a demonstration tape for Decca Records in their New York studio in mid-1938. Although she sang her usual repertoire of gospel songs, the producers felt that she could have a wider audience if her songs were less gospel and more worldly. While Katie Bell Nubin, now called "Mother Nubin," objected to any change in her daughter's style, Tharpe agreed to a four-record session in which the producers were free to record her according to their desires. On October 31, 1938, Tharpe recorded four sides for Decca: Thomas A. Dorsey's "Hide Me in Thy Bosom," but with the title "Rock Me"; "That's All"; "My Man and I"; and "Lonesome Road." The record company immediately released "Rock Me," billing the performer as "Sister Rosetta Tharpe." In addition to her own guitar accompaniment, she was backed up on the record by the full Lucius "Lucky" Millinder (1900–66) jazz orchestra.

The members of the sanctified church were shocked, but the record-buying pub-

lic went into a frenzy for this new singer with the new sound. Her popularity was so great in New York City that she was included in John Hammond's first extravaganza of African American music, "From Spirituals to Swing," staged at Carnegie Hall on December 23, 1938. The concert was a sensation and was reported in newspapers throughout the United States. Sister Tharpe took advantage of this publicity and concertized throughout the Northeast but was not yet able to make the impact on her beloved South that she desired. This problem was erased with her second recording session for Decca in 1944.

The uproar over her accompaniment by a jazz orchestra was so strong that Sister Tharpe requested that Decca permit her to record with only her guitar. They refused this request but agreed to have her accompanied by a trio of piano, bass, and drum. The house boogie-woogie pianist for Decca during the 1940s and 1950s was Samuel "Sammie" Blythe Price (1908–92).

Price was born in Texas and as a child played alto horn in a boys' band in Waco. When he was ten his family moved to Dallas, where he began studying piano with Portia Washington Pittman (1883–1978), the celebrated musician daughter of Booker T. Washington (1856–1915), the educator and statesman. Price settled in New York in 1935 and in 1937 became staff pianist and arranger for Decca. Sammie Price was Tharpe's accompanist and arranger from her September 26, 1944, session with Decca until 1951.

The Rosetta Tharpe-Sammie Price sound blanketed juke boxes, victrolas, and turntables throughout the nation. Every skill that Sister Tharpe had honed since age four shone brightly with the bouncy boogie-woogie and pure blues accompaniments set up by Price on piano, Billy Taylor on bass, and either Wallace Bishop or Henry Cowans on drums. Other such drummers were Ed Burns, Kenny Clarke, and Kansas Fields. She was at her most illustrious on medium fast and fast songs. "Strange Things Happening Everyday" was set to a medium tempo and became the song that made Sister Tharpe famous. Her rendition begins with a few strumming chords on the guitar to solidify the harmony; she then follows with elongated phrasing of single tones. The unique element in this solo is not the single tones in themselves, but that in places where one single tone would normally suffice, Tharpe uses four. For each beat then, she plays four notes, giving each bar sixteen different tones. This is no easy task for any guitarist.

She begins the song with a line directed at the membership of the sanctified church that attempted to scandalize her name because she mixed blues and jazz with gospel. She asserts that they are committing what could be considered greater sins:

Oh, we hear church people say
They are in the "Holy way,"

and inserts an internal refrain:

There are strange things happening everyday.

She pronounces "every" as "ev-vuh-ree" for rhythmic division. She follows with:

On that last great judgment day when they drive them all away,

followed by the internal refrain:

There are strange things happening everyday.

The independent refrain of the song with its call-and-response delivery follows. Surprising to some, Tharpe did not choose one of the established gospel quartets such as the Soul Stirrers or the Dixie Hummingbirds to serve as the congregation to her preaching. Instead, she used the trio accompanying her, which sang in voices suggestive of cynicism, satire, and levity. In the final analysis it was a perfect mixing, because "Strange Things Happening Everyday" was on the borderline between African American sacred music and secular music. This state of near ambivalence was noted by the people of the church, yet Sister Tharpe became the biggest star of gospel to that time, surpassing the Golden Gate Quartet in popularity.

Unfortunately, among church folk, Tharpe's talent could not be separated from her lifestyle. She would attend services with COGIC saints and within a few weeks or a month appear in concerts with such jazz stars as Cab Calloway, Benny Goodman, and Count Basie and at such establishments as Cafe Society. Her popularity became greater among nonsaints than with saints. And then Sister Tharpe received a boost to her gospel career.

On July 3, 1951, she married Russell Morrison, a former manager of the Ink Spots, in an extravagant ceremony at Griffin Stadium in Washington, D.C., for which

she charged admission (since the marriage ceremony was to end with a concert). Before and after the ceremony, Sister Tharpe not only sang, but presented as her guests her new backup group, the Rosette Gospel Singers (four female singers); soloist Vivian Cooper; the Sunset Harmonizers; the Harmonizing Four; and a trio of bass, drums, and piano. The Bishop Wyoming Wells (1909–74) and the Reverend Samuel Kelsey, both ministers in COGIC, officiated during the ceremony. (Marie Knight, Tharpe's frequent partner, was not invited to sing because Morrison wanted to present Tharpe again as a soloist, a move that caused a breakdown in an almost sisterly relationship between Tharpe and Knight.) *Ebony* magazine published a photo layout of the wedding.

Given a new career through the wedding publicity, Sister Tharpe began another series of concerts. It was during this time, however, that the "anniversaries" and "extravaganzas" became popular. These multi-starred concerts sometimes had as many as twenty different singing groups on the same bill. When Sister Tharpe, with what was now called "secular-style" gospel, was pitted against such singers as Dorothy Love Coates and the Original Gospel Harmonettes, the Davis Sisters, and the Pilgrim Travelers, she appeared to be out of her league. Not only was her singing jazz inflected, her stage decorum was more reminiscent of a nightclub than of a church service. Her concert dates dropped off, and she lost her recording contract. In 1970 she suffered a debilitating stroke. Her attempts to concertize from a wheelchair after a slight recovery garnered more sympathy than cheers.

Marie Knight

Although Tharpe's fame as a solo artist was secure in 1947, Decca decided to pair Tharpe in duets with Marie Roach Knight (b. 1918). The two recorded and concertized together from 1947 to 1952. Knight, who became known as Madame Marie Knight, was born in Sanford, Florida, to a sanctified deacon and his wife and grew up in Newark, New Jersey, singing and playing piano. After establishing a local reputation in New Jersey as a gospel singer who possessed a solid and strong contralto and a delivery close to the one that Della Reese would make famous twenty years later, Knight went to New York. After singing with local groups for a number of years, she auditioned at Decca Records. Rather than offering her a solo contract they arranged duets for Knight and Tharpe.

Their most outstanding recording was "Up above My Head" from a November 1947 session in which Tharpe provides the call and Knight the response. Although Knight's voice is darker than Tharpe's, they made the perfect gospel duet, even on the chorus after Tharpe's solo interlude where Knight assumes the role of the male bass from gospel quartets, essaying her range from the top to the bottom.

Sister Rosetta Tharpe and Madame Marie Knight became the rage of the nation. They were able to provide variety in their concerts through several exchanges: Knight would play the piano while Tharpe sang; Tharpe would play the piano while Knight sang; they both stood and sang while Tharpe played the guitar; and Knight would stand as still as a concert artist while Tharpe treated every song as if it were an activity song for small children.

The Georgia Peach: Clara Hudman Gholston

The year after John Hammond presented his first Carnegie Hall "From Spirituals to Swing" concert, Radio City Music Hall, the recognized bastion of movies and music in the United States, presented a similar show. The gospel star for this presentation was "The Georgia Peach."

Clara Hudman Gholston, The Georgia Peach.

It was a long route from Atlanta's Mount Moriah Baptist Church to Radio City Music Hall for Clara Hudman Gholston (1903–66), and she made the trip against what appeared to be insurmountable odds. There is apparently no record of a Mr. Hudman, but her mother Esther was always known as the devout woman who brought up three children in Mount Moriah. According to the Reverend C. J. Johnson (1913–90), the venerable singer of lining hymns and other congregational songs, he and Clara Hudman were brought up in the same church and often sang together, although Clara was about ten years older than Johnson. She began singing as a teenager and was known throughout Atlanta as the girl who could sing "Daniel in the Lion's Den." She and her brothers Luther and Ralph, both younger, formed a trio and would deliver stirring renditions of this missionary hymn (a Baptist song patterned after such Pentecostal songs as "I'm a Soldier" but performed at a slower tempo) on local programs:

Clara: It was Daniel in the den
  Brothers: In the den
Clara: Daniel in the den
  Brothers: In the den
Clara: And He locked
  Brothers: He locked
Clara: The lion's
  Brothers: The lion's
All: He locked the lion's jaw.

It was not unusual for ministers to see Hudman in the audience at a concert and ask her to come to the choir loft and sing. These invitations were more like pronouncements, and Hudman always obliged, singing "Daniel in the Lion's Den" or "What a Friend We Have in Jesus."

When Hudman was sixteen years old, the wife of the Reverend T. T. Gholston, pastor of Mount Moriah, became ill, and upon the request of Gholston and the deacons of the church, Mrs. Hudman gave permission for Clara, who no longer attended school, to take care of Mrs. Gholston and her two young boys during the day while the pastor cared for his flock. Clara cared for Mrs. Gholston until the pastor's wife died two years later. She then stayed on to care for the pastor's young children and prepare his meals. Six months after Mrs. Gholston's death, the minister married Hudman and moved her permanently into his home. Mount Moriah was split apart by the marriage; the deacons and older church members objected to such an early marriage, and the middle-aged women of the church were angry because the minister became a lost "catch" and his new wife was only eighteen years old and had "lived in the house with his wife." Gholston preached a sermon addressing all the public concerns about this marriage, but forgiveness did not seem forthcoming from his congregation. Within a few years he became an alcoholic, and on one Sunday when he was too inebriated to complete his sermon, the congregation "voted" him out of the pulpit. According to the Reverend C. J. Johnson who witnessed the episode, Hudman felt that she was a vehicle for the Lord's work and therefore stood by her husband. It would be several years before her youthful loyalty would wear thin.

Gholston accepted an appointment at a church in Detroit and after a few years

there decided to move to New York City. Shortly after their arrival in New York City, Gholston and his wife separated, and she left the Baptist church and affiliated with Bishop Lawson's Refuge Church of Our Lord (a Pentecostal denomination). It was with this congregation that she found her "new voice" in gospel.

She began recording as early as 1930, and judging from one of her first recordings, "Lordy, Won't You Come by Here," she sang superbly in the Baptist tradition with conviction, clear delivery, and beauty of tone in a light contralto capable of smooth runs and explosive attacks. Her 1942 recording of Kenneth Morris's "Does Jesus Care," however, shows a matured, "tried and true" gospel singer with a fully developed dark contralto, filling empty spaces in musical time and making not only a sincere appeal to the listener to "accept Jesus because He cares," but showing herself to be one of the early great gospel singers.

Although she came to New York City from Detroit, her audience heard her Georgia roots in her singing and therefore dubbed her the "Georgia Peach," not only because of that popular name for southern women but because her style gave the title meaning: sweet, smooth, melodious singing fueled by the same intensity that the sanctified singers brought to their shout. She recorded extensively and traveled throughout the United States as a soloist and leader of a quartet. She made several appearances in New York on the same bill as Mahalia Jackson and Ernestine B. Washington. The three were the leading soloists in New York in the 1940s (Willie Mae Ford Smith was not well known in that city). She is regarded as a pioneer in gospel music.

Madame Ernestine B. Washington

Like so many of her compatriots, the "Songbird of the East," Ernestine Washington, was actually from the South. Although the program for her funeral in Washington Temple Church of God in Christ in Brooklyn on July 5, 1983, bore the caption:

Service of Victory for the late
Mrs. Ernestine B. Washington
The First Lady of Washington Temple
& Eastern New York Jurisdiction
Church of God in Christ

what was really being celebrated was a life of music and good deeds that had been nurtured in Arkansas and by the music of Arizona Dranes.

Ernestine Beatrice Thomas Washington was born in 1914 in Little Rock. She attended school in Arkansas and began singing at age four. Her mother was a popular sanctified singer in the Little Rock community, and she and little Ernestine were known for their duet of "I Come to the Garden Alone." Ernestine completed high school in Little Rock and was engaged in domestic work while singing at the annual Convocation of the Church of God in Christ, where she met and married the Reverend Frederick D. Washington (1913–88). Washington, who attended the Moody Bible Institute and later was awarded an honorary Doctorate of Humanities from Trinity Hall College and Seminary, traveled with his new wife to Montclair, New Jersey, where he founded the Trinity Temple Church of God in Christ. In the early 1940s the couple moved to Brooklyn, New York, where Washington founded the Brooklyn Church of God in Christ, which was later named Washington Temple in his honor, where he pastored until his death. He also served as Auxiliary Bishop of the Jurisdiction of New York.

Madame Washington had been strongly influenced by Arizona Dranes, and the resemblance in their singing style was uncanny. Dranes possessed a high-pitched mezzo-soprano-alto voice with a fast vibrato that would soar in the upper register; in the lower register she would adopt a soft growl. She approached her attacks with a percussive bent that set beginning words in phrases apart from other words, and she had a sense of melody and rhythm that was so secure that she simply rode on the meter that had been established, setting a rhythm to fit the text and mood of the song. The same description applied to the style of Ernestine B. Washington. If there was a difference between her style and Dranes', it was that Madame Washington lived in an age when singing at range extremes was accepted and expected, and she indulged the expectation. This style is evident in her 1946 recording of "Does Jesus Care" with the legendary William Geary "Bunk" Johnson (1872–1949) and his jazz band. Despite the traditional New Orleans-style jazz band, complete with an active drummer, behind her, Washington begins the song in a contemplative move, controlling voice and range while delivering a meditative soliloquy of questions and answers regarding the love of God. When she reaches the chorus, however, she spins forth the full range and power of her voice in a statement of affirmation: "Oh yes, I know He cares."

By 1946 the Reverend Washington had become a fixture in Brooklyn, one of the most respected ministers in COGIC, and Madame Washington was the official soloist of the denomination, singing the solo before the sermon of the presiding bishop in the flagship service of the annual November convocation in Memphis. Yet, she recorded with a "sinner" like Bunk Johnson. Unlike Sister Rosetta Tharpe, Madame Washington was not subjected to the contempt of the church membership for working with secular musicians. However, Madame Washington only recorded with Bunk Johnson and did not seek a relationship with him or his musicians (who played secular music) outside the studio. Also, the people of the church somehow felt complimented that such a star as Bunk Johnson was called upon to accompany one of their own.

Her 1957 recording of W. Herbert Brewster's "I Thank You, Lord" shows Washington in her sanctified style. Accompanied by her longtime pianist and organist Alfred Miller (b. 1920) and the members of her church choir, she unleashes the full power of her voice and the style that made her famous. This type of performance brought Washington fame as she toured throughout the United States, often appearing in concerts with the Roberta Martin Singers, Mahalia Jackson, and the Selah Jubilee Singers from her own neighborhood. At her death she was mourned in two crowded, overflowing services at Washington Temple, complete with all of the dignitaries of COGIC. To this date, there has been no replacement for the "Songbird of the East."

Thurmond Ruth and the Selah Jubilee Singers

Only one quartet was able to break through the New York syndrome and become a major force in gospel during the Golden Age. That group was led by Thurmond Ruth (b. 1914), who moved to that city at age eight and by twelve had organized the group that he would lead for the next forty-five years. The Selahs started out as disciples of the Fisk Jubilee Quartet style; moved to the Jefferson County, Alabama style; and within ten years of their organization adopted the gospel music of Chicago and the sanctified churches of the New York area. During their first decade their home was St. Mark's Holiness Church and from there they performed throughout the five boroughs of New York, taking occasional trips to New Jersey, Pennsylvania, and as far south as Baltimore. Inspired by the Soul Stirrers, the group approached J. Mayo Williams, a scout for Decca records, regarding a contract.

The Selah Jubilee Singers

By the time their first recordings were released in 1939, the group included Crip Harris and Melvin Coldten, both former members of the Norfolk Jubilee Quartet; Bill "High Pockets" Langford, formerly of the Golden Gate Quartet and the Southern Sons; Allen Bunn, who later gained recognition as a blues artist; Gene Mumford; and, of course, Ruth. Like many other groups of their time that began their recording career with an already recorded song, the Selahs' first recording was a "cover" of the Soul Stirrers' recording of a few months earlier, Rebert H. Harris' "Walk Around." The Selahs called their song "I Want Jesus to Walk around My Bedside." While the Selahs' version is interesting for its sophisticated editing of this southern testimony, it does not capture the sincerity, urgency, and old-time fire and brimstone of the original.

Once the Selahs came into their own, however, they were hard to beat. An example of their mature style is the 1958 recording of Thomas A. Dorsey's "Today." Rendered almost exclusively in the Baptist lining hymn tradition of unpulsed singing in which the highly embellished syllable created a phrase, the Selahs injected new life into this beloved song. True to tradition, they delivered the first line of the song in the Baptist lining hymn tempo, but beginning with the second line, they moved into a foot-patting jubilee tempo, complete with a call and response. The re-

sponse was not merely a repetition of the call but a return to earlier days with the refined "oom-ma-lank-a-lank-a-lank" response of "Yes, my Lord" at every turn where rhythm was needed. The climax was a vamp at the end of the chorus, accompanied by guitar. The guitar accompaniment showed the influence of not only the Golden Gate Quartet, the major influence on Ruth, but the gospel style of the period, in which few quartets dared to sing *a cappella* at concerts where other gospel singers used piano or guitar accompaniment.

Other New York City Singers

New York City had a very active community of local singers who made a career of traveling from church to church within the five boroughs. Most of these groups never recorded, and few traveled farther from the city than Philadelphia. Yet they kept New York City gospel music lovers supplied with concerts, radio broadcasts, anniversary programs, and local representation on concerts when famous traveling singers appeared in the city. One of the local favorites was the Sunset Jubilee Singers, organized in 1940. According to Ray Allen, author of *Singing in the Spirit: African American Sacred Quartets in New York City*, they were among the most popular groups in the city in the early 1940s. Although the Sunsets made a few recordings for the Hub and Okeh labels, they were unable to garner a national reputation.

As children, sisters Fay (b. 1936) and Anna (b. 1938) Scruggs both sang piano-accompanied gospel in New York City. By age seventeen Fay had landed a contract with and cut two sides for Atlantic Records. Within a year she had gone to record producer Arnold Shaw, and under the name Fay Adams cut a song called "Shake a Hand." This song became one of the biggest hits of 1953. Her sister, Anna, known as Anna Tuell, remained with gospel and became one of the premier gospel soloists in New York City.

New York City's Daniels Singers, while not singing much outside of the city, was the favorite local group to open concerts for traveling gospel stars during the 1950s. Organized by leader-pianist-arranger Jackie Daniels (1910–56), the group was composed of leaders Evelyn Price and Anna Quick Griffin, and the husband-and-wife team of Connie and Becky Burruss. Daniels, a pianist and organist who also accompanied other singers, was well known as an organist throughout the Northeast. Along with Alfred Miller, James "Blind" Francis (b. 1914), and Herman Stevens, he

was one of a handful of organists who truly could play gospel. In 1948 he organized the Daniels Singers and for the next decade they ruled the piano-accompanied gospel wing of New York City, often in direct competition with the Herman Stevens Singers. Two of their best-known recordings on the Savoy label are "Jesus," their theme song, and Thomas A. Dorsey's "Search Me, Lord."

James "Blind" Francis was the regular organist for the tent revivals of A. A. Childs in the early 1950s and accompanied Mahalia Jackson on several recordings. He also traveled with her while she concertized in the Northeast.

Alfred Miller, organist and choir director at Washington Temple Church of God in Christ in Brooklyn in the early 1950s, was the favorite organist of Madame Ernestine B. Washington, and traveled with her on occasion as her pianist and musical director. Miller organized the Miller Singers in the 1950s and recorded several songs that met with modest popularity. However, the group had a fluctuating membership—always dependent upon the engagement—and would often serve as the local group that opened for traveling singers. Miller was often called on to accompany, both on recordings and in concerts, such singers as Mahalia Jackson, Clara

Sunset Jubilee Singers

Fay Adams and Anna Tuell

Ward, the Davis Sisters, and Bishop F. D. Washington. He, along with Francis, Daniels, and Stevens, constituted the New York Gospel Organ Guild.

Gospel DJ Joe Bostic

By the early 1950s, gospel music was the music of the working-class African American Christian, and performers, producers, and promoters of gospel made an honest attempt to touch the religious mood of these people as rhythm and blues had touched the secular mood. Concerts were presented, recordings were made and sold, and gospel DJs became plentiful, although few were able to have a career outside the radio station, since most had no skill in concert production or artist management. Along with such luminaries as "Hoss" Allen, John Richburg, and Jean Noble, New York City's Joe Bostic could ensure a career by playing and commenting on certain recordings. While the other DJs ruled the South, Joe Bostic ruled New York City.

Joe William Bostic (b. 1909) was born in Mt. Holly, New Jersey, attended public schools in the city and graduated from Morgan State College (now University) in 1929. After conducting radio programs in Baltimore and serving as a sports correspondent for the *Afro-American*, he settled in New York in 1937. Working in both journalism and radio, he hosted "Tales from Harlem" for WMCA from 1937 to 1939 and was a DJ for WCMW from 1939 to 1942. He joined the staff of WLIB in 1942 where, in addition to his radio programs, he produced weekly talent shows with live performers. It was during this time that Bostic became aware of the gospel audience and devoted his energies to the new sacred music.

He began to produce concerts of gospel music in some of the most respected venues in New York City and created a sensation in 1950 when he presented his first "Negro Gospel and Religious Festival" at New York's Carnegie Hall. Among the guests were the Selah Jubilee Singers and the Herman Stevens Singers. The pièce de résistance, however, was the star attraction: Mahalia Jackson. While succeeding Carnegie Hall presentations were festive occasions, featuring such singers as the Roberta Martin Singers, James Cleveland, and Professor J. Earle Hines, none carried the significance of the first Mahalia Jackson concert, for Bostic had introduced pure gospel into Carnegie Hall. To be sure, John Hammond had introduced a kind of gospel with Sister Rosetta Tharpe and the Mitchell Christian Singers, but Bostic's was a

different gospel. His was gospel for a primarily African American audience, and his audience wept, clapped, shouted, and fainted to a music that was not rendered for form and fashion, but for "soul salvation."

Bostic was considered the "Dean of Gospel Disk Jockeys," because he was among the first and the most successful of the DJs to use radio to gather large crowds for gospel singers. As late as 1959 he produced his "First Annual Gospel, Spiritual and Folk Musical Festival" in Madison Square Garden before an audience of eleven thousand, thereby opening up yet another venue for gospel.

GOSPEL SPREADS ACROSS THE NATION

As the 1940s came to an end, gospel had insinuated itself so strongly on the African American community that it was no longer necessary for aspiring gospel singers to move to major gospel music centers like Chicago and Philadelphia. Every major city wanted to be identified with gospel, and groups began to spring up in all areas, making such cities as Richmond, Birmingham, and Los Angeles as sonorously gospel as those called home by Roberta Martin and Clara Ward. The Tidewater area of Virginia, which had produced such groups as the Silver Leaf Jubilee Singers and the Golden Gate Quartet, contributed yet another group that would become one of the leaders of the quartet movement: "Gospel Joe" Williams and the Harmonizing Four.

Joseph Williams and the Harmonizing Four

Joseph "Gospel Joe" Williams (b. 1916) was born in Richmond, Virginia, into a musical family. His mother was a singer at the Second Baptist Church where the family worshipped, and his father was a singer with the Zion St. John Jubilee Singers, a local *a cappella* quartet. Williams remembered that as a very small boy, "I used to stand up beside him and sing the best I could." It was not long before Williams began to stand on his own; when he was eleven years old and attending Richmond's Dunbar Elementary School, he was invited by three school mates who had been gathering after school to sing jubilee songs to join with them in organizing a quartet. Thomas "Goat" Johnson, Levi Handly, Robert Simpkins, and Joseph Williams became the Harmonizing Four on September 27, 1927, and gave their first public performance on October 27, one month later, at the Dunbar School.

Like the Zion St. John Jubilee Singers, after whom they patterned themselves

(along with other male *a cappella* quartets of the time), the Harmonizing Four specialized in singing Negro spirituals, hymns, and the new gospel songs of Charles Albert Tindley and Lucie Campbell. From the beginning the group emphasized what Kip Lornell called "a full, sweet vocal blend that became their hallmark." As they developed and experienced personnel changes over the years, they continued to give special prominence to close harmony, precise attacks and releases, and a smooth sound.

Jimmy Jones of The Harmonizing Four

They made their first recordings in 1943 for the Decca label, a contract probably secured for them by Sister Rosetta Tharpe, the label's principal gospel singer at that time. In addition to recordings of their own with Decca, the group recorded several sides with Sister Tharpe. Her close performance associates, they appeared with her on the "Ed Sullivan Show" in the 1950s and sang at her wedding to Russell Morrison in 1951. Their reputation as church singers was so secured that they, unlike Sister Tharpe, were not ostracized by church members.

By the time of their first recording, the group had acquired guitarist Lonnie Smith (the father of jazz pianist Lonnie Liston Smith), who joined the group in 1941. They recorded and traveled for the next decade as a solid, dependable group with a reputation based on close harmony and country-style singing. By 1957 when they began recording for the Vee-Jay label, their personnel consisted of original members Williams and Johnson, plus Smith and new member Jimmy Jones.

Jones, formerly of the Texas-based Southern Sons Quartet, provided a bass foundation for the Harmonizing Four that few other groups could claim. Not satisfied to simply support the group, Jones became a soloist and an obbligato bass, singing his part in the harmony and at the same time singing above, around, and outside the others. With a full, flat, virtuoso voice, Jones was one of that small group of basses who could compete with any lead, whether he was Joseph Williams, R. H. Harris, or Ira Tucker. Jones' skill and the style the Harmonizing Four had developed over thirty years were nowhere more thoroughly demonstrated than on the group's

1957 recording of "Farther Along," a standard in the African American church since its publication in 1937. The song is cast in a call-and-response arrangement, and in it Jones celebrates the basso profondo by singing the melody at the very bottom of his range but with the power of his middle register. He begins in a slow, almost contemplative mood, and by the end of the chorus, has moved the entire melody up an octave. While Jones thunders in and around the melody, the other singers set up a harmonic and rhythmic response that is constant in its movement, leaving Jones free to explore with his considerable talent.

There was no doubt, as gospel music historian Anthony Heilbut observed, that "Joseph Williams is one of the most sincere and subtle readers of a lyric this side of R. H. Harris," and the other members of the Harmonizing Four blended their considerable talents with his to produce memorable performances.

CBS Trumpeteers

A little to the north of the Tidewater region another gospel quartet was making history. Joseph Johnson, who learned his quartet skills as a member of the Golden Gate Quartet and the Willing Four Quartet, decided to organize a group that he could influence in both repertoire and style. In 1946 in Baltimore he formed a group called the Trumpeteers with Joe Armstrong, baritone; Raleigh Turnage, tenor; James Keels, bass; and himself on lead. The Trumpeteers were the personification of the jubilee quartet: tight and sweet harmony, tenor voice lead, and attacks and releases that were perfectly coordinated. Shortly after they were organized the Trumpeteers began singing over WCAO radio in Baltimore and were noticed by the Columbia Broadcasting System, whose executives signed them to a daily radio show. In honor of this collaboration, the group added CBS to their name. They, along with the Golden Gate Quartet and the Wings Over Jordan Choir, were among the few jubilee and gospel singers to have a network radio program.

Their contract with CBS lasted only two years, but the radio show gave the group national celebrity and helped them land a contract with Score Records. The first recording session on September 12, 1947, produced their greatest hit, Theodore R. Frye's arrangement of "Milky White Way," a gospel blues song like Tindley's "Stand by Me" and Eugene Smith's "I Know the Lord Will Make a Way, Oh Yes, He Will." Each of the three stanzas are sung to the same melody. Although the group often

performed *a cappella*, this particular rendition begins with the guitar playing each note of the chord of the song. Johnson begins in a quiet mood, as if speaking to a neighbor, over a humming background by the group (one of the outstanding features of this rendition:

> STANZA 1: *I'm going to walk that milky white way some of the days*
> STANZA 2: *I'm gonna tell my mother howdy, howdy when I get home*
> STANZA 3: *I'm going to meet God the father, God the son.*

Like the lead singer of other jubilee quartets who were making the transition to gospel, Johnson sings with equal amounts of vigor and restraint, permitting the beauty of his voice and singing style to carry the message of the song. While the background voices maintain an even hum behind the soloist, at the second stanza the bass singer adds just enough interpolated thumps to give the performance the lilting rhythmic quality it needed to make listeners pat their feet. Not until 1952, when the Bells of Joy released their "Let's Talk about Jesus," would there be another quartet recording that commanded the attention of every gospel music lover as "Milky White Way" did in late 1947 and 1948.

Joseph Johnson kept the Trumpeteers together until shortly before his death in 1984. Since that time the group has been managed by Calvin Stewart, a native of South Carolina, who joined the group in 1949. They no longer sing in the jubilee quartet style but have succumbed to the hard gospel techniques of singing at the extreme ranges and seeking more to overpower than to soothe. But every so often the sweet style of the CBS Trumpeteers comes through again, reminding the listener of their sound from the first decade of the Golden Age of Gospel.

James "Woodie" Alexander and the Pilgrim Travelers

While the African American quartet movement began in Jefferson County, Alabama, just before the beginning of the second decade of the twentieth century, it was not long before Houston became the center of the Southwest for jubilee/gospel quartets. The Soul Stirrers had become the leading quartet in the Southwest, and young African American males who could only sing a chorus of "Mary Had a Little Lamb" were attempting to form groups and duplicate the success of Rebert H. Harris and the leading quartet from Houston. Of the many groups that were formed in Houston as

a result of the success of the Soul Stirrers, the most popular was a group only a few years younger than their idols.

Joe Johnson gathered together a group of young men from Houston's Pleasant Grove Baptist Church and formed the Pilgrim Travelers in 1936. As a community-based group, personnel, style, and repertoire changed frequently as they appeared in the area, usually on weekends at church and quartet concerts. Their membership began to stabilize in 1944 when, after winning a quartet competition, they were given the opportunity to travel with the Soul Stirrers.

In 1947 Johnson decided to move the group to Los Angeles rather than to Chicago to avoid direct competition with the Soul Stirrers. When the group arrived in Los Angeles, James "Woodie" Alexander became the manager. Seldom featured as a song leader, Alexander selected the repertoire, composed several songs for the group, coordinated stage behavior, selected uniforms, replaced singers when needed, and booked the group. Alexander was born in 1916 and reared in Coffeyville, Kansas, home of the legendary African American choral director Eva Jessye (1895–1992) and sang both gospel and popular music during his youth. Before joining the Pilgrim Travelers in 1946 he played professional baseball in the Negro League and sang with the Southern Gospel Singers. With more than a bit of the "smooth operator" blood in his veins, Alexander was almost a dictator, but his style was so understated that, when in conversation or association with him, one was completely unaware that he was, with cultivated skill, directing the entire encounter. Because he did not appear to be malicious in the slightest way, singers and promoters forgave his understated dictatorship where his group was concerned. Alexander used this skill to push the Pilgrim Travelers into the forefront of gospel quartets.

By the time the group had their first recording session in late 1946, the membership was composed of Alexander, tenor; cousins Kylo Turner and Keith Barber, who until they joined the Pilgrim Travelers had worked as farmers in Cleveland, Texas, leads; Jesse Whitaker, who joined the group in California, baritone; and Rayford Taylor, bass. Their first recordings show the influence of the Golden Gate Quartet and the Soul Stirrers, the reigning quartets of the day. Tindley's "What Are They Doing in Heaven" and Kenneth Morris' "Dig a Little Deeper in God's Love" both show the precise attack, close harmony, rhythm execution, and even the timbre of the Gates and the Soul Stirrers.

In 1948 the Travelers scored successes in the gospel market with their two biggest hits. Brewster's "Thank You, Jesus" and Mary Lou Coleman's "Jesus" (with which the Ward Singers also scored a major success in 1949) showcased the group in two of their three styles: gospel jubilee and gospel ballad. While "Thank You, Jesus" sets up a toe-tapping tempo over which the group literally spits out their thanks to Jesus for bringing them "a mighty long way," "Jesus" is cast in somber colors and tempo—one of those instances where tempo and mood belie the text.

The text of "Jesus" is a rehearsal of the goodness of the Lord and could very well have been delivered as a jubilee or a shout. The ballad tempo, however, ensures strict attention to the lyrics; a more sprightly tempo might have drawn the listener to the beat. The song begins with an anticipation by Turner on the word "oh," to which he assigns nine different tones, followed by the entrance of the group on the word "Jesus." To give the fullest accentuation to the word, the group pronounces it as "Cheesus" and delivers it in dark and resonant harmony. Before continuing with the text, bass singer Raphael Taylor inserts a riff (bum-bum-bum-bum-bum) of five tones (which would become a standard gospel "lick"), as the group continues with "when troubles burden me down." A similar phrase is then delivered, including Taylor's insertion, with the words "I know your love's all around." The Travelers then deliver one of their signature melodic and harmonic devices on the word "oh." While the group holds a single tone, Turner begins his word an octave (eight tones) higher and shimmers down an octave where he will sing the remainder of the phrase. (This device would become associated with Ira Tucker in the early 1950s.) While Turner became much more vocally active during the two stanzas of the recorded version, the song remains a prime example of the mixture of jubilee and gospel, for which the group became famous. They scored several major hits in the next few years, including "Jesus Met the Woman at the Well," "Jesus Gave Me Water," and the immensely popular "Mother Bowed"; however, few of their recordings captured their talent and conviction as well as "Jesus."

In addition to his work with the Pilgrim Travelers, as talent scout for Specialty Records, Johnson secured recording contracts for Wynona Carr and Dorothy Love Coates and the Original Gospel Harmonettes. He also recommended singer-pianist Jessy Dixon (b. 1938) to Brother Joe May as his pianist.

Claude Jeter and the Swan Silvertones

Male falsetto singing, a cherished practice in African singing since ancient days, became associated with rhythm and blues and soul singing in the United States. Long before it became popular as a secular music device falsetto was thoroughly entrenched in gospel singing, and the credit for this all-important technique, which every male singer attempts at some point, can be attributed to two quartet singers, Rebert H. Harris and Claude Jeter (b. 1914). More striking than the beauty of his falsetto is Jeter's judicious use of the device. Not content to discard the natural voice altogether, like Eddie Kendricks and the Bee Gees, Jeter essays his beautiful and firm lyric tenor voice in most of his singing. But for special climaxes and emotion he turns to his falsetto, one of the purest and strongest among singers to date.

Claude Jeter (in white), the inspiration for many soul music singers, and the Swan Silvertones

Jeter was born in Montgomery, Alabama, to a middle-class family whose father was a lawyer and held a professional position for the Tennessee Coal and Iron Railroad. His interest in music was kindled early by his mother, who had a local reputation as a "singer of note." Unfortunately, his father died when Jeter was eight years old and his mother was left to rear the children. Shortly after his father's death, the family moved to Kentucky where Jeter completed high school and sang in the church choir and with informal quartets. He then began working in the coal mines across the border in West Virginia, and to provide entertainment he organized a quartet of his fellow mine workers and named them the Four Harmony Kings. In 1938, the Four Harmony Kings, consisting of Jeter, his brother, and two miners, began singing locally. Within a few months they had garnered a reputation as "some of the sweetest singing boys in the world." While they worked in the mines during the week their weekends were reserved for short singing trips throughout West Virginia and nearby Kentucky and North Carolina.

In the early 1940s the group relocated to Knoxville, Tennessee, and underwent some personnel changes, the most important of which was the addition of Solomon Womack as second lead. The group then was composed of Jeter, first tenor and lead;

Womack, second lead; John Myles, baritone; and Henry Bossard, bass, who would emerge, along with Jimmy Jones, Isaac "Dickie" Freeman, and Raphael Taylor, as one of the leading bass singers in gospel. They performed in the traditional barbershop style, in which Jeter's light and lyrical voice contrasted well with Womack's heavier tenor. *A cappella* singing was the rage at this time, although a few quartets used guitar, and the Four Harmony Kings were masters of the art. According to Jeter:

> *When they [the Four Harmony Kings] sang ... it wasn't too emotional. They would just stand flat-footed and sing, because they tried to specialize in harmony. They wanted the music to be right.... In those days, it was more like barbershop harmony.*

The group was offered a sustaining Sunday morning spot on WDIR, a 25,000-watt station that could be heard as far away as North Carolina and Florida. Just before they began broadcasting their name changed to the Silvertone Singers to avoid confusion with the more popular Four Kings of Harmony. The show was sponsored by Swans bakery and, in order to provide additional publicity for the company, the group again changed its name—this time to the Swan Silvertone Singers.

Through their radio broadcasts, the Swan Silvertones became one of the most popular quartets in the South, which led to a recording contract with King Records in 1946. Over the next five years the group recorded more than one hundred titles for the label. From these titles one of the most characteristic performances as well as one of their most popular songs was "All Alone." Kerrill Rubman, in her study of this group, describes their performance:

> *In "All Alone" the group uses two other approaches. The verse is sung in barbershop-style blended harmony, without rhythm, with pauses to emphasize individual chords. In the chorus, Claude Jeter and later Solomon Womack exhibit "gospel"-style lead singing, improvising vocal flights with snatches of the lyrics as the group sings the chorus in a steady rhythm. Underneath, Henry Bossard adds bass runs.*

The group relocated again in 1948, this time to Pittsburgh. With a new membership consisting of Jeter; Louis Johnson, second lead; Paul Owens, alternate lead and second tenor; Myles; and William "Pete" Connor, bass, they switched to the Spe-

cialty label in 1951 and to Vee-Jay Records in 1955. Their biggest hit, "Mary, Don't You Weep," was recorded on the Vee-Jay label in 1959. This gospel song underwent an almost complete change from its first incarnation as a Negro spiritual:

> *Oh Mary, don't you weep, don't you mourn,*
> *Oh Mary, don't you weep, don't you mourn;*
> *Pharaoh's army got drown(d)ed,*
> *Oh Mary, don't you weep.*

The Swans slowed the tempo down from a jubilee to a sprightly gospel ballad tempo, gave it a call-and-response arrangement, and opened up the form to include an extended vamp. Jeter begins the song contemplatively, singing the chorus and verse, each set to the same tune, to sixteen bars rather than the eight to which it was sung in the Negro spiritual:

> *Jeter: Oh, I'm singing Mary*
> **Group: Oh Mary don't you weep**
> *Jeter: Tell Martha not to mourn*
> **Group: Tell Martha not to mou—rn**
> *Jeter: Listen, Mary*
> **Group: Oh Mary don't you weep**
> *Jeter: Tell Martha not to mourn*
> **Group: Tell Martha not to mou—rn**
> *Jeter: Pharaoh's army*
> **Group: Pha—a—raoh's army**
> *Jeter: Got drowned in the sea one day*
> **Group: Drowned in the Red Sea**
> *Jeter: Listen, Mary*
> **Group: Oh Mary don't you weep**
> *Jeter: Tell Martha not to mourn*
> **Group: Tell Martha not to mou—-rn.**

After leading the verse, Jeter turns the remainder of the song over to Paul Owens who delivers the vamp (the "working out" section) during which he repeatedly sings the word "Mary." The song reaches its climax after Owens has raised the pitch and

volume several notches, creating a vocal frenzy. "Mary, Don't You Weep" was accompanied by guitar, as were many other songs recorded after Linn Hargrove became guitarist for the group in 1955.

Jeter felt the call to the ministry and was ordained in Detroit's Church of Holiness Science in the mid-1960s. He then left the group and settled in New York City where he occasionally preaches and continues to sing both as a soloist (he had a successful recording of Brewster's "Lord, I've Tried" in 1972) and as a member of "reunion" quartet concerts. After his retirement from the Swans, the group continued singing with new leaders James Lewis and Carl Davis.

Other Early Golden Age Singers

THE RADIO FOUR

The Radio Four, a Nashville group, was so named because they, like many groups in the 1930s and 1940s, had weekly broadcasts over a hometown radio station. These five brothers probably sang over WBDL of Bowling Green, Kentucky, according to Chris Smith, annotator of the 1982 re-release of "There's Gonna Be Joy" by The Radio Four. Organized in the late 1940s, the group was composed of George, Ray, James, Claude, and Morgan Babb. While Morgan, probably the youngest, began as a substitute and guitarist, he became the principal singer in the group; later he switched to a solo career in the 1970s. Their first recordings were made in 1952 and show the group having a special ability to execute jubilee songs. Among their most popular recordings are "How Much I Owe" and "When He Calls."

THE SWANEE QUINTET

Like the Harmonizing Four, the Swanee Quintet was a prime example of the down home unaffected quartet. Led by the Reverend Reuben W. Willingham, the group's membership remained constant for decades. Along with Willingham, members were Charlie Barnwell, James "Big Red" Anderson, Rufus Washington, and Johnny Jones, with guitarist William "Pee Wee" Crawford. Unlike most quartets who gained popularity in gospel, the Swanee Quintet kept Augusta, Georgia, as their home base. Although Augusta has been a metropolitan city for many years and the group was organized there, they consciously cultivated the rural sound of early quartets.

Their hard gospel style is demonstrated on their recording of "In My Savior's Care."

THE BELLS OF JOY

This group made their debut with what turned out to be the most popular recording of their career. "Let's Talk about Jesus," led by A. C. Littlefield, was the most popular gospel song during 1953. Alternating between jubilee and hard gospel techniques, the Bells personified the changing quartet. The jubilee style, with its emphasis on harmony, attacks, and releases, and time and tune, was replaced by much louder singing, extreme range investigation, and faster tempos.

SISTER O. M. TERRELL

A group of female vocalists made significant contributions to the development of gospel during 1945 through 1955. Among them was Sister O. M. Terrell, about whom little is known other than that when she began recording she was living in South Carolina and had a Sunday radio program at station WPAL in Charleston. Her affiliation with the First Baptized Holiness Church is apparent from her 1953 rendition of "God's Little Birds." Terrell shows a kinship to Sister Rosetta Tharpe: although her guitar is far less sophisticated than Tharpe's, her timbre and her Dranes-like delivery (also apparent in Tharpe's voice) are a testament to the influence of the early gospel singer.

SISTER JESSIE MAE RENFRO

Completely unlike the Arizona Dranes school of singers, Sister Jessie Mae Renfro is a product of modern gospel, complete with hard gospel techniques. Born in 1921 in Witchataxee, Texas, Sister Renfro was brought up in the COGIC in Dallas. Although attracted to secular music she chose to sing gospel and traveled with the Sallie Martin Singers during the mid-1940s. Although she began recording in 1946, it was not until the early 1950s that she found songs and a style that attracted public attention. While her voice is lighter in color than Clara Ward's, she possesses the same metallic hue and even has a delivery similar to Ward's, eschewing embellishments for sustained tones. Her rendition of the gospel blues (a 16–bar harmonically schematic composition) in "I've Had My Chance" demonstrates her fondness for resorting to the hard gospel technique of broadening tones as she enters her higher register. Her compatriot in COGIC, Emily Bram, was different from her in several ways.

MADAME EMILY BRAM

Emily Bram (c.1919) a Texan, began singing in her youth in COGIC and as a young adult began preaching. Evangelist Bram conducted revivals in which she alternated singing and preaching. Her voice, like that of traditional African American preachers, has the ability to stretch into a growl at will, and she has the power of a quartet. She is an aggressive singer who can build a climax in only three or four notes, as amply demonstrated on her 1951 recording of "Blessed Assurance," rendered in the style of the long-meter Baptist lining hymn.

ETHEL DAVENPORT BANNISTER

Jacksonville, Florida, produced a singer, who, with a wider audience, might well have rivaled Wynona Carr. Ethel Davenport Bannister (1910–85) possessed a brassy alto with a delivery halfway between the sanctified shouters and the Baptist moaners. Known principally as a soloist, Bannister often teamed with *a cappella* male quartets for the harmonic and rhythmic support they provided. Always delivering her lines halfway between the Baptist moaner that she was and the sassy declamations of a jazz singer, Bannister was as much show person as gospel singer. This style, however, did not prohibit her from settling into real gospel when the spirit or the competition demanded it, which was the case on July 22, 1955. On that day she appeared in concert at the Shrine Auditorium in Los Angeles on a bill with the Pilgrim Travelers, Dorothy Love Coates and the Original Gospel Harmonettes, the Soul Stirrers featuring Sam Cooke and Paul Foster, the Caravans with Albertina Walker and James Cleveland at the piano, and Brother Joe May with his children Annette and Charles. Anthony Heilbut, annotator for the recorded version of the concert, reported that Bannister rendered a "haunting version of 'My Troubles Are So Hard to Bear,' supported vocally by Brother Joe May and his children."

Bannister earned a national reputation through her recordings on the Coral, Gotham, and Herald labels and for many years hosted a Sunday evening gospel program over Jacksonville's radio station WJAX.

Herman James Ford

Herman James Ford (c.1898–c.1958) is considered the "mystery" composer in gospel, for although he wrote several of the most popular gospel songs of the 1950s, he

was not a singer, pianist, or conductor, nor was he considered a part of any gospel community. It is known that he lived and copyrighted his songs from Washington, D.C.; that he was a member of the Vermont Avenue Baptist Church in that city; and that he lived on G Street. Almost thirty years after his death, the older members of Vermont Avenue Baptist remembered Ford as a quiet man who was regular in his attendance at services, but few remembered him from gospel concerts held at the church.

Nonetheless between 1946 and 1956 Ford published twenty-six songs through the publishing houses of Roberta Martin, Martin and Morris, and Andrea (New York). His songs were recorded and made famous by singers such as Mahalia Jackson, the Angelic Gospel Singers, and the Pilgrim Travelers. Three of his most popular compositions were the jubilee song "This Same Jesus," the gospel waltz "Somebody Save Me," and "In My Home over There." This last song was made famous by Mahalia Jackson in the tempo of a Baptist lining hymn:

> *When my work on earth is done at the setting of life's song*
> *I am going to my home over there;*
> *I shall walk the golden stairs free from sorrow, pain or care,*
> *I'll be happy in my home over there.*
>
> *In my home over there that the Lord has prepared,*
> *There will be peace, there will be joy everywhere;*
> *I shall see His face so fair and a starry crown I'll wear,*
> *I'll be happy in my home over there.*

Mysterious or not (it was possible to mail compositions into publishers), Ford ranked with Dorsey, Morris, and Brewster as a principal composer of the first part of gospel's Golden Age.

The Gospel Choir

Groups of four, five, or even six singers could travel by car, train, or bus around the country singing gospel, but groups of twenty-five or more found it too expensive to travel. The large groups—the relatively new gospel choirs—were, nonetheless, popping up throughout the United States. Very few choirs recorded during the first ten

years of the Golden Age of gospel, and the better gospel choirs, those directed by the leaders of the gospel movement, could be heard only at the National Baptist Convention, when singers from all over the United States were formed into a mass choir, or at one of the Dorsey conventions. There were, however, three choirs that recorded, and one had a national weekly radio program heard by a large part of African American society each week.

Wings Over Jordan was unique in the annals of gospel, for as William Talmadge reported in his study *From Jubilee to Gospel*, this choir was "neither a trained nor folk-style" group. They performed each song in the style in which it was composed. While the choir was a group of very talented singers, the soloists in particular "projected a sophisticated awareness of all of the elements of black music from folk through popular." They sang Dorsey's and Campbell's compositions as if they were members of the National Baptist Convention, as indeed many were.

A choir of thirty to forty voices, Wings Over Jordan was organized by the Reverend Glenn T. Settle (1895–1952) in 1937, shortly after he was assigned to the Gethsemane Baptist Church in Cleveland. Upon discovering that the church had no choir with any degree of excellence, Settle studied music and served as the first director of the group. Within a few months the choir auditioned for local radio station WGAR. Their popularity became so great that they were picked up by the CBS radio network for whom they presented a Sunday morning program entitled "Wings Over Jordan" from 1937 to 1947. Under the direction of Worth Kramer, their second director, the choir featured a repertoire of "skillfully arranged" Negro spirituals, hymns, and gospel songs ("He Understands, He'll Say 'Well Done'," recorded in 1948; "When I've Done The Best I Can," recorded in 1953; and "Somebody Touched Me," recorded in 1960). The Wings sang in a gospel style reminiscent of that of Mother Willie Mae Ford Smith, in which beauty of tone, extension of breath, and clarity of diction were all combined with passion and flair.

The most fully developed gospel choir of the first decade of the Golden Age was the St. Paul Baptist Church Choir of Los Angeles. Like the Reverend Settle in Cleveland, when the Reverend John L. Branham was assigned to the St. Paul Baptist Church in Los Angeles, he found no choir that could sing the music to which he had become accustomed in his native Chicago. In 1947 he organized the Echoes of Eden Choir with J. Earle Hines as director and Gwendolyn Cooper Lightener as pianist.

Hines had served as baritone soloist for the National Baptist Convention's Good Will Singers, and Lightener had been pianist for Emma L. Jackson, composer of the gospel blues "I'm Going to Die with the Staff in My Hand" and with whom she composed "I Can See Everybody's Mother, but I Can't See Mine" (1945). These were gospel musicians who knew the tradition, and together they developed the Echoes of Eden into the premier gospel choir in the nation.

Drawing from the compositions of the Chicago school of composers—Dorsey, Roberta Martin, Sallie Martin, and Emma L. Jackson, and Lucie Campbell of Memphis—and augmented by the budding California school of composers, Hines and Lightener developed a choir that sang with "open" throats (a necessity in gospel singing), that could learn parts, and that was not afraid to get "happy" as they sang. Shortly after its organization the choir was featured on a Sunday evening broadcast from St. Paul Baptist Church that could be heard in "seventeen states with an audience of one million people (the largest audience on the West Coast)." Their early 1946 recordings sold regionally, but at their second session in April 1947 they recorded Thomas A. Dorsey's "God Be with You" and the missionary hymn turned gospel song "I'm So Glad Jesus Lifted Me," both of which became gospel standards. "God Be with You" by Dorsey and Artelia Hutchins replaced the beloved "God Be with You Till We Meet Again" by Jeremiah E. Ranks and William G. Tomer (1832–96) as a benediction song. The choir had several other popular recordings, among them Kenneth Morris's "What Could I Do if It Wasn't for the Lord?" and Dorsey's "If We Never Needed the Lord Before, We Sure Do Need Him Now."

The choir of C. H. Cobb's First Church of Deliverance in Chicago was perceived as a laboratory for composers in Chicago; as soon as a song was published it was featured by this choir. Ralph Goodpastor was a hard taskmaster with the choir and his strict directional manner resulted in a well-trained and ready choir for each Sunday's midnight radio broadcast from the church. The 50,000–watt station carried this choir throughout the Midwest and on clear evenings into New York City. Many of Dorsey's, Morris', and Roberta Martin's songs were introduced over this broadcast, but none was as popular as Goodpastor's semigospel rendering of Albert Hay Malotte's (1895–1964) arrangement of "The Lord's Prayer."

Like jazz lovers visiting New York and working a night at Small's Paradise, a premier jazz spot of the 1940s and 1950s, when gospel music lovers traveled around

the country, they included in their activities a church service where they could hear one of the several choirs who had developed national reputations, some even without the benefit of recordings. Among these were services at Chicago's Greater Harvest Baptist and Salem Baptist churches, New York's now Childs Memorial Church of God in Christ, and Mason Temple Church of God in Christ in Memphis.

The Gospel Band

As if the introduction of gospel music into the Azusa Street Movement were not enough to shock the conservative Christian, the Pentecostalists went one step further and accompanied this music with tambourines, drums, and cymbals (the piano was not introduced into gospel until the early 1920s). Basing their practice on Psalms 150, the Pentecostalists felt that all instruments belong to God and were made for the expressed purpose of serving Him. The use of instruments other than the organ provided further fodder for those who felt that the preaching and singing in the Pentecostal church was primitive. The Pentecostalists were undaunted; in fact, they encouraged the playing of all instruments in their service. This practice resulted in the organization of gospel bands in the 1920s. These bands were unique for two reasons: very few, if any, of the players could read music and were therefore taught their parts by rote, with the leader playing a part over and over until the student eventually learned to play the tune as it was played for him. Also, the bands did not play in the style of Duke Ellington's or Count Basie's bands where the trumpets had one part while the saxophones had another and the two parts were put together to make an arrangement. The gospel band played like a choir with one instrument acting as soloist and the other instruments acting like the choir. The result was a band that played like a choir sang.

While gospel bands occasionally accompanied the congregation during praise services, they were at their best when they played alone. It was common during the 1940s for larger Pentecostal congregations to have a gospel choir and a gospel band. As the Hammond organ with powerful Leslie B-3 speakers became popular in Pentecostal churches, the gospel band gradually lost its popularity. The one denomination that continued to cultivate the gospel band was the United House of Prayer for All People, Church on the Rock of the Apostolic Faith, Incorporated.

This congregation was founded by Bishop Marcelino Manoel de Graca, better

known as "Sweet Daddy Grace" (1884–1960). Born in the Cape Verde Islands, Grace began preaching in 1925 after moving to the United States. He was a flamboyant and charismatic leader who demanded that his followers worship him as God, but was instrumental in feeding and lodging thousands of African Americans during the Depression. Like most Pentecostal services, Grace's services were heavily laden with music. Nick Spitzer, historian of the gospel bands of Daddy Grace, observed that in order "to propel his energetic services and attract a congregation, Daddy Grace established brass bands, modeled in part on the instrumental jazz of the era, to perform gospel hymns. Today [1992] there are more than 130 Houses of Prayer, each with one or more large brass bands."

Perhaps the best known of these bands is the Kings of Harmony of the national headquarters of the United House of Prayer. According to Nick Spitzer this band, like others, has a sound created by a lead trombone and a "choir of twelve trombones, a baritone horn, a sousaphone, and drums and tambourine." Two other popular bands are McCollough's Sons of Thunder of Brooklyn, New York, and the Sounds of the South of Savannah, Georgia. In addition to playing for services and presenting concerts, these gospel bands perform at funerals, parades, groundbreakings, and anniversary services.

Sam Cooke

And The Walls Came Tumbling Down: 1955–65

*W*hereas the first ten years of the Golden Age of Gospel testified to the emergence and inclusion of gospel music in the African American Baptist and Methodist churches, the second decade of the Golden Age witnessed the crumbling of the firm walls that had kept gospel from the larger part of American society. During the first ten years of the Golden Age the gospel network comprised a comparably small group of churches and singers; the second decade was marked by a national gospel community that included not only most black churches, but also reached others through radio, recordings, television, and theater. Indeed, the second decade witnessed the crumbling of the wall that had forbidden performance in nonsacred venues.

Sister Rosetta Tharpe sang gospel at Carnegie Hall in 1938, the Georgia Peach and her quartet sang at Radio City Music Hall in 1939, and Sister Tharpe and the Dixie Hummingbirds sang at Cafe Society in the 1940s. But those appearances were looked upon with disdain, because at that time Christians were admonished to follow the dictum to be "in the world but not of the world." They believed that

associating with non-Christians (much less going into a theater) would lead to temptation, and if Christians refrained from associating with the "unsaved," whether at work or elsewhere, the likelihood they would backslide was remote.

In the mid-1950s, however, black Christians, and especially gospel singers, began to feel an obligation to spread the word to the unsaved. The question was how to get the word to the unsaved if the unsaved would not come where the word is preached and sung? They solved this problem by taking gospel music into "nonsacred" places, turning these venues into sanctified, Baptist, and Methodist places of worship. Gospel singers developed a new attitude: it became a compliment to be invited to sing outside the church. Mahalia Jackson was one of the first gospel singers—with this new attitude—to step over the crumbling walls when, on October 1, 1950, she presented her first concert at Carnegie Hall.

In the mid-1950s, Jackson was persuaded to sing on Dinah Shore's television show. Jackson chose songs that captured the best in gospel, and her demeanor was consistent with that of the saints. The show included the obligatory duet with the hostess. The duet, while entertaining, was not a good mixture: Shore was trying too hard to sing gospel, and Jackson was visibly uncomfortable because of the restriction of singing gospel with a nongospel singer. But Jackson's appearance was viewed as a success and led to an appearance on the "Ed Sullivan Show." This time the audience was treated to pure gospel with only Jackson and her longtime accompanist, Mildred Falls.

In 1957 Clara Ward and the Ward Singers invaded the Newport Jazz Festival, which attracted jazz lovers and critics from all over the world. Richard Gehman, music critic for *Coronet* magazine (July 1957), offered this appraisal of the Ward Singers performance at the festival:

> *They seemed nervous as they arranged themselves around a microphone and the woman at the piano, Clara Ward, played a few bars of introduction. They glanced at each other as though to muster strength. And then with a smiling placidity—they sang.*
>
> *Rhythmic, high, clear, in perfect harmony they sang, the words in metered, driving cadence, underscored by piano. They began to clap their hands; and within seconds, hundreds in the audience were clapping with them. The singers*

threw back their heads and went into a second chorus, fervent and joyous. The voice of one, a young girl of ample girth [Marion Williams], soared above the others whose voices beat a counterpoint behind hers.

Mahalia Jackson sang at the festival in 1958 with equal success. Jackson's 1959 appearance at Carnegie Hall drew gospel aficionados as well as gospel novices. Marshall Sterns, critic for the August 1959 *High Fidelity*, must have held membership in the latter group:

The effect is something for which my rather Puritanical New England background never prepared me. Gentle old ladies on all sides start to "flip" like popcorn over a hot stove. Directly in front, an angular woman springs to her feet, raises her arms rigidly on high, and dances down the aisle shouting "Sweet Jesus!" A white-clad nurse, one of thirty in attendance, does her best to quiet her. This is a religious possession, as old as Africa itself.

Sterns could have written his description with only three words: they had church!

By the 1960s a completely new audience for gospel had developed. This was an audience composed of people who liked music, especially music with a beat. But this new audience's unfamiliarity with the music or with African American cultural traditions produced some interesting reactions. In 1963 business leaders, more concerned with making money than with cultural mores and folkways, began moving gospel to nightclubs. Gospel nightclubs soon opened in New York, Miami, and Los Angeles. The music critic for the May 24, 1963, issue of *Time* magazine visited such a club and wrote this review:

For months (and in the record business, months are decades), desperate music hustlers have been searching for the new groove. Exceptional huntsmen confined their attention to Negro music, which, with the single exception of country, has supplied them with every new idea since the blues. Last week, with appropriate fanfare, they proclaimed they had found the sound: pop gospel. Waving contracts and recording tape, Columbia Records moved into a new Manhattan night club, the Sweet Chariot, and began picking such devotional songs as "He's All Right" for the popular market. "It's the greatest groove since rock 'n roll," said Columbia pop A & R Director, David Kapralik. "In a month or two, it'll be all over the charts."

"TV Gospel Time," a one-hour national television show of gospel singers, lasted two seasons and attracted an African American audience. It also introduced gospel to a large white population that would not normally attend churches where it was performed. The format of the program was built around a guest host (soloist or group) and a group of gospel singers who appeared once or twice during the hour, offering sometimes as many as three songs. The studio audience was all black, and the sponsors were, in part, black-owned businesses. The program was treated like a church service with the host acting as the preacher and the audience as the congregation. Most of the major stars appeared on the program including Sister Rosetta Tharpe, the Soul Stirrers, and Alex Bradford and the Nightingales. But "TV Gospel Time" aired on Sunday mornings before noon when the largest part of the gospel-loving audience was in church. The ratings were low, and sponsors received little for their investment. Consequently, the program was dropped.

"Hootenanny" was a national radio program that aired in the late 1950s and 1960s. The Saturday afternoon broadcast had a format similar to that of "TV Gospel Time," but the host was permanent. During this part of the 1960s, gospel groups, especially *a cappella* male quartets, found a new audience. Male quartets, such as the Fairfield Four, Dixie Hummingbirds, Swan Silvertones, and the Soul Stirrers, and piano-accompanied gospel acts, such as Alex Bradford and the Caravans, appeared on this show.

In 1962 the Apollo Theater, a bastion of African American entertainment, began to book gospel acts. Around that time the Apollo had begun to lose its audience. This was partially the management's fault: the theater booked the same performers year after year, and the new talent it presented couldn't compare with such contest winners as Ella Fitzgerald or Sarah Vaughn. But the rest of the blame lay with integration. The days when a black entertainer in New York could only find work uptown were fading fast. Even though black entertainers had always worked downtown, there was always a certain indignity that accompanied downtown work. Even major stars felt so unwelcome in predominantly white venues that once they were off stage, they lived and socialized in Harlem. Black stars were not feted with the grand parties given to white stars, and many were paid less than white stars of comparable reputation and celebrity. But in the 1960s black entertainers approached their work

downtown feeling, "I can perform here legally now, and if you want me you will have to treat me with the same dignity given to Patti Paige."

Considering the money that could be made by booking top black acts, downtown managers began according a new respect to black stars who appeared in their venues. While this was good for African Americans in general, it meant that the Apollo had lost its previous advantage in attracting quality acts. It was feared that all the music created by African Americans had been co-opted by the moneymen downtown. So the management of the Apollo decided to turn to one area still untouched by white entrepreneurs: gospel. They selected the summer months—when New Yorkers escape their apartments in whatever way they can and the city is overrun with tourists—as gospel months. At first gospel acts were paired with secular ones. When the management discovered that gospel acts could stand alone, the Apollo soon began to present entire gospel weekends. The Caravans were one of the first groups to be booked; then the Dixie Hummingbirds appeared; Clara Ward and the Ward Singers followed; and Dorothy Love Coates and the Original Gospel Harmonettes made an appearance.

These shows yielded great financial rewards for the Apollo for almost two years, until the market became saturated. But the appearance of gospel singers at the Apollo—between movies that often negated the very message of gospel—opened up new venues for gospel performance that could never be closed off again.

In the early 1950s, gospel music's popularity did not go unnoticed by singers aspiring to a career in rhythm and blues. The emotional singing of such groups as the Soul Stirrers, Pilgrim Travelers, and Dixie Hummingbirds, with their versatile and charismatic lead singers and tight harmony background singing, was the impetus behind early rhythm and blues vocal groups, many of whom sang gospel when they were first organized. The Larks were originally the Selah Jubilee Singers, who appeared in public as a gospel group but who also had a successful recording career as a secular group.

Billy Ward, the son of a preacher father and a choir-singing mother, began composing classical and gospel songs at age fourteen when the family relocated to Philadelphia from Los Angeles. When Ward organized the Dominoes in 1950, the group sang both gospel and rhythm and blues. The other leader of this group was Clyde McPhatter.

The Five Royales, led by the brothers Lowman and Clarence, started out as the Royal Sons Gospel Group of Winston-Salem, North Carolina, in 1945 and delighted churchgoers throughout the South until 1951, when they went to New York to develop an eastern following. There they recorded first as the Royal Sons Quintet, a gospel group, and also as the Five Royales, a secular group. By the mid-1950s they were so popular as a rhythm and blues group that they stopped recording gospel.

Both the Ravens, organized in New York City in 1945 and the first rhythm and blues group to incorporate dance steps into their act, and Sonny Til and the Orioles, organized in 1946 in Baltimore, Maryland, were not only inspired by gospel quartets but created their sound by combining jazz, blues, and gospel.

The early rhythm and blues soloist Jackie Wilson replaced Clyde McPhatter as lead singer of Billy Ward and the Dominoes and easily moved into the gospel/blues sound that this group had developed. Little Richard (Richard Penniman), one of twelve children, grew up in a devout Seventh Day Adventist family. While the Seventh Day Adventists did not sing gospel music at that time, Little Richard sang gospel while serving as the pianist for a Baptist church in his hometown of Macon, Georgia. He was particularly impressed with Clara Ward and the Ward Singers and adopted Marion Williams as a singing model, going as far as incorporating her "high who" into his own songs. Little Richard joined several other blues shouters, including Big Joe Turner, Big Bill Broonzy, and Jimmy Rushing, whose singing style was based on that of sanctified singers.

In the mid-1950s the influence of gospel quartets among secular singers began to decline. This decline coincided with the rising influence of piano-accompanied gospel. Nowhere was this influence exhibited more clearly than in the singing of Ray Charles, Aretha Franklin, and James Brown, all of whom came to prominence during the last decade of the Golden Age of Gospel. These three people literally created the style of music known as "soul," and they created it by borrowing from gospel music. Ray Charles (b. 1930) was brought up in a Baptist church in Albany, Georgia, and played for Sunday School and church. Although he did not play gospel, between 1945 and 1955 Charles became so inundated with gospel that he abandoned his desire to be the next Nat "King" Cole and found his calling by combining gospel style with the blues and popular music, delivering his songs in the voice and style of a sanctified preacher. Charles has acknowledged that Alex Bradford and the

Pilgrim Travelers had tremendous influence on his post-1950 music. James Brown (b. 1933), too, was reared in the Baptist church where gospel had found a home. Brown, like Charles, was not a gospel singer. But the emotional intensity and delivery of his "Please, Please, Please" (1956) sounds for all the world like a gospel singer pleading for the grace of God. And Aretha Franklin has never pretended to be anything other than what she is: a gospel singer. As late as 1994, when she was named to the Grammy's Hall of Fame, she declared "You know, I'm nothing but a gospel singer."

Jazz musicians also came under the influence of gospel. In the 1950s, when secular music began to return to its blues roots, gospel techniques and devices recreated the "feeling" (soul) that had been lost. Among the most famous jazz compositions in the gospel style were Horace Silver's "The Preacher," Bobby Timmons' "Moanin'," and Jimmy Smith's "The Sermon."

GOSPEL AND THE TRADITIONS OF AFRICAN AMERICAN FOLK MUSIC

With the mixing of gospel and several kinds of secular music, it is clear that African American sensibilities about music changed radically during the second half of the Golden Age. Some critics have mistakenly judged African American sacred music by Western European standards: they try to find distinct differences in *sound* between what is considered secular and what is considered sacred. They find the melodies, harmonies, rhythms, instruments, timbre, and behavior of secular music unworthy of expression in the service of the Lord. When they apply these constrictions to what is sacred and secular in African American music, they create an artificial division. As with other cultural manifestations of African American society, it is not the medium in itself that carries the message but how that medium is used and the response it receives.

All African American folk music is drawn from the same wellspring of musical materials. This wellspring includes scales, melodies, harmonies, timbre, and rhythm, as well as a person's behavior during performance and while listening. If the wellspring offers "blue notes" for use in folk music, both secular and sacred music will employ blue notes. If rhythmic motives and riffs are the only folk elements in African American music, sacred music will use these motives and riffs. Otherwise the music would have to draw from outside the culture—and be less true to itself. The

African American musical wellspring is as important to its culture as material from the European wellspring is to the descendants of European culture. This does not mean that music making is limited only to materials from a single cultural source, but it does mean that musical traditions should not be judged by the standards of another culture's folk materials.

When people call gospel music spiritualized secular music, they usually are thinking of the blues. But only those ignorant of the fact that the Negro spiritual, the progenitor of gospel, was almost one hundred years old before the blues arrived make such a claim. Blues and jazz employ the same materials that spiritual music employs—and in most cases in the same way. Because they come from the same wellspring, they are sisters and brothers under the beat. The mood of the performer and the listener determines the effect that the music produces. Albert Murray, in his book *Stomping the Blues*, notes that:

> *Downhome church music [gospel] is not fundamentally less dance-beat-oriented, it simply inspires a different mode of dance, a sacred or holy as opposed to a secular or profane movement, a difference which is sometimes a matter of very delicate nuance.*

There is a difference nonetheless. As recognized by no less eminent a scholar than W. E. B. DuBois, there is a "twoness" that accompanies being an African American, and salvation is attained only by those who know which part of their culture to exhibit at which time. This problem of "twoness" was nowhere greater than in the mid-1950s when gospel invaded the African American church. Murray responded to this situation in this way:

> *There is, after all, a world of difference between the way you clap your hands and pat your feet in church and the way people snap their fingers in a ballroom, even when the rhythm, tempo, and even the beat are essentially the same.*

In the 1930s and 1940s, when African American parents were struggling to send their children to piano lessons, it was most likely so they could play in church, not in a juke joint. However, the person who played in the juke joint on Saturday night might also be the pianist for church on Sunday. Inevitably, the residue of Saturday evening's performance would drain out on Sunday morning, just as it was inevitable

that Friday night's choir rehearsal would see its demise on the dance floor Saturday night. James Cone, in his book *Spirituals & the Blues*, goes as far as to say:

> The blues are "secular spirituals." They are secular in the sense that they confine their attention solely to the immediate and affirm the bodily expression of black soul, including its sexual manifestations. They are spirituals because they are impelled by the same search for the truth of black experience.

Thomas A. Dorsey is called the Father of Gospel Music and rightly so. Even if he had not composed more than five hundred gospel songs, traveled around the country teaching them, and opened the first publishing company for the express purpose of publishing African American gospel music, the fortitude with which he met the resistance of African American ministers when he sought to introduce gospel music into their congregations was sufficient to earn him that title. It should be remembered that Dorsey was not well received in the 1930s when he presented a kind of music that ministers termed "all jazzed up." Michael Harris, in his book on Dorsey, recounted the story of a minister who promised Dorsey a spot in the Sunday morning service to present his songs yet dismissed the congregation at the end of the service, all the while looking directly into Dorsey's eyes. There were ministers who permitted gospel in their services, but it had to be sung by the junior choir, a group that was more cute than musical or serious. Dorsey, undaunted, persevered.

THE NEW AND NEWLY REVISED GOSPEL QUARTETS

There was no doubt in 1955 that gospel music was here to stay and that it wanted the recognition that other American music enjoyed. Gospel musicians felt that they had earned and deserved the respect of the music world because they had paid their dues. They were as talented, musical, and well presented as any other musicians, and they felt they were as innovative as any music group in the country. In fact, gospel singers opened the last decade of the Golden Age with an innovation that at first met with great resistance in the gospel world: piano-accompanied male gospel quartets. The success of keyboard-accompanied quartets reached its peak with the advent of Sam Cooke as the leader of the Soul Stirrers, one of several groups that became prominent or was reborn during the years 1955 to 1965.

Sam Cooke and the Soul Stirrers

Sam Cooke appeared destined to lead the Soul Stirrers and make them once again the leading quartet in the country. Every musical activity from his early years until 1951 when he assumed the group's leadership pointed in that direction. One in a family of eight boys and two girls, Cooke (1931–64) was born to the Reverend Charles and Mrs. Anna Mae Cooke in Clarksdale, Mississippi. Shortly after his birth the family relocated to Chicago's South Side where the Reverend Cooke had accepted the pastorate of a church. The Cooke children all sang in the church choir and later formed a group consisting of Sam, his two sisters, and a brother. Calling themselves the Singing Children, they performed at their father's and other churches on the South Side.

Cooke received his musical education in Chicago's public schools, and sang in the glee club of Wendell Phillips High School. While still in high school he was invited to join the Highway QCs, a neighborhood quartet named after the Highway Baptist Church and Q.C. High School in Chicago. The quartet, prominent in its own right, had been organized by Soul Stirrer baritone R. B. Robinson and served as an unofficial training camp for the Soul Stirrers: not only did Sam Cooke and Johnnie Taylor come to the senior group from this neighborhood quartet, but Willie Rogers, who remained a gospel singer until his death, was the third leader to graduate to the Soul Stirrers.

Even as a teenager Cooke showed an unusual talent for gospel. He possessed a light lyrical tenor voice, an easy and smooth vocal delivery, and an ability to improvise that never overpowered the melody with its embellishments. Cooke was particularly adept at textual interpolations, adding or subtracting words from the original text of the song to fill in spaces occupied by rests in the melody or as a prefix to the text. In a performance of the song "What a Friend We Have in Jesus," Cooke would lead into the opening with a phrase such as, "Sometimes when I'm lonely I just say to myself 'What a Friend We Have In Jesus.'" When he switched to popular music he carried this device with him, and it was never more strategically employed than on his first hit, "You Send Me" when he led into the chorus of the song with "I know, I know, I know that YOU SEND ME." Cooke also wrote beautiful songs and knew how to "work" an audience without resorting to stage histrionics—the same qualities possessed by Rebert H. Harris, then leader of the Soul Stirrers.

The Soul Stirrers

As Cooke neared his twentieth birthday Harris noticed a change in gospel that went totally against his grain. In his paper "Sam Cooke: Soul Stirrer," Dave Law, a 1992 graduate student at New York's Brooklyn Conservatory of Music, elaborates:

> *All the hysterical "carrying-on," gimmickry and showboating from the perform-ers, which caused equally hysterical reactions from the female audience in par-ticular, became too much for Harris to handle. In disagreement with this new direction in gospel performance, Harris took his high morals and gentlemanly ways and left the sinful temptations of the road and the Soul Stirrers in 1950.*

Cooke inherited Harris's position in January 1951. At first sounding and acting like a clone of Harris, Cooke gradually evolved into a thoughtful and creative singer as

well as a prolific songwriter. When Cooke had completed the creation of his new persona, he easily won the hearts of the congregation with his beautiful voice, extraordinary vocal technique, youthful good looks, and, as far as women were concerned, according to Law, "irresistible charm and sexuality." Cooke brought the Stirrers to the forefront again but with a difference: no longer were they the reverent semirural *a cappella* quartet of Harris's day, but a sophisticated, pop-oriented performing group, accompanied by guitar in concerts and by guitar, piano, and organ on recordings.

In March 1951 J. W. Alexander, the leader and manager of the Pilgrim Travelers and a talent scout for Specialty Records, brought the new Soul Stirrers to the Specialty label and from their first session produced a fine version of Campbell's "Jesus Gave Me Water." The recording met with immediate success. The Stirrers noted the success of Cooke's arrangement, and as he had matured musically and developed his own distinctive style, they agreed to his becoming the group's leading arranger and composer. One of the first songs Cooke wrote for the group was "That's Heaven to Me."

His most famous composition is "Nearer to Thee," in which Cooke's ability to write lyrical poetry is evident from the opening verse:

> *The minister was preaching*
> *And the crowd was standing near,*
> *The congregation was singing a tune*
> *In a voice that was loud and clear...*
> *They were singing "Nearer My God to Thee."*

With Cooke leading the song in his distinctive voice, complete with the repetition of words and singing the word "oh" on five or six tones, the Stirrers gave new life to quartet singing—and incidently brought the quartet several steps closer to the style of piano-accompanied groups.

Cooke's success with the Stirrers did not go unnoticed by record producers and popular music promoters. Alexander, hoping to leap ahead of other record labels that might attempt to entice Cooke into rhythm and blues, began recording Cooke singing secular music under the name Dale Cooke. One of these songs, "I'll Come Running Back to You," became a minor hit. It was about this time, in late 1956, that

Alexander's contract as talent scout for Specialty was sold by the gospel division to the rhythm and blues division. Specialty rhythm and blues producer Bumps Blackwell directed Cooke's second recording for the Keen label. Cooke soon moved to RCA and became an extremely successful crossover artist. His engagements moved from small clubs to theaters and eventually to the Copacabana in New York City. He even did a screen test on October 2, 1964, for a part in the movie *In the Heat of the Night*. The world will never know whether Sam Cooke the singer would have become Sam Cooke the actor, for he was shot and killed under mysterious circumstances in a Hollywood motel on December 10, 1964. Nonetheless, Cooke's contributions to gospel and the many soul singers who adopted his techniques and sang his songs, even thirty years after his death, are still recognized and applauded.

Archie Brownlee and the Five Blind Boys of Mississippi

One of the most familiar sights of gospel concerts in the 1950s was five or six blind men, each with his hand on the shoulder of the man in front, being led by a sighted man to the performance space. And the most familiar sounds at gospel concerts in the 1950s were the wails, shrieks, and hard gospel singing of Archie Brownlee and the Original Five Blind Boys of Mississippi.

Archie Brownlee (1921–60) holds the title of the "hardest singing" man in gospel. This title is due in part to the hard gospel techniques he adopted after his group left Mississippi and moved to Chicago. In Mississippi the group was, like most other quartets at that time, practiced in the cardinal rules of jubilee singing—time, tune, and tenor—and gave special emphasis to blending and nuances. After moving to Chicago and noting the excitement generated when fellow singer J. T. Clinkscale interjected strident moans and wails into his singing, Brownlee adopted this technique and took it to a higher level that was enjoyed by many. Others, however, thought it overly exaggerated: it was not uncommon for Brownlee to insert wails, shrieks, screams, strident falsettos, yells, and grunts all into one song. In most cases these devices brought a certain excitement to a rendition; at other times, they appeared to disrupt what had been a beautifully developed vocal line. There was never full agreement on Brownlee's singing style, but that lack of consensus did not hinder the group from becoming one of the most popular quartets of the 1950s.

In 1932, while attending the Piney Wood School for the Blind in Piney Wood,

Archie Brownlee and the Five Blind Boys of Mississippi

Mississippi, Brownlee formed a gospel group, the Cotton Blossom Singers, from among his classmates. The original members of the group were Brownlee, Sam Lewis, Lloyd Woodard, Lawrence Abrams, and Joseph Ford. When the group began to earn enough money from singing in local churches and at parties to pay their own tuition (they were originally scholarship students), they changed their name to the Jackson Harmoneers, after the largest city in Mississippi. During this time they traveled with the International Sweethearts of Rhythm, an all-female orchestra from the Piney Wood Country Life School, a school for sighted students, and sang Negro spirituals and novelty songs.

In 1944 the group turned professional, changed their name to the Original Five Blind Boys of Mississippi, and relocated to Chicago where Brownlee could be closer to Rebert H. Harris, his idol and mentor. The membership at this time consisted of Brownlee, Abrams, Woodard, J. T. Clinkscale, and the Reverend Percell Perkins. The group began recording around 1951 and had many hits during the next decade. Among their popular recordings are "I'm Willing to Run" and "Will Jesus Be Waiting," in both of which Brownlee sings solidly but uses hard gospel techniques; "I'm Going to Tell God," in which he modulates his voice and gives a simple and refined

reading to the lyrics; and "I'm Going to Leave You in the Hands of the Lord," a "mother" song. Mother songs invariably recounted the story of ungrateful children who had mistreated or disappointed their mothers. Such songs usually ended with no remorse being shown by the children. In "Leave You," Brownlee wonders if he treated his mother right during her life, because as she was dying she told him she was "leaving him in the hands of the Lord," a black church statement meaning "I can do no more with you."

The Blind Boys' most popular hit was a 1952 recording of Wynona Carr's "Our Father." This rendition finds the Blind Boys at their very best and illustrates a blending of the jubilee and gospel styles. The background voices repeat the words "Our Father" as constant as the ticking of a clock throughout the rendition in deep vocal colors with tight harmonies and crisp attacks and releases, not unlike that of the better jubilee quartets of the 1930s. Over this drumlike accompaniment Brown delivers two verses separated by a chorus. In a full fleshy voice Brown sings the Lord's Prayer as the first verse using minor, but attractive, ornamentation. However, when he reaches the chorus he cannot resist inserting one of his signature screams and delivers two more during the second verse. Screams notwithstanding, "Our Father" illustrates the singing of one of the finest male quartets.

Clarence Fountain and the Five Blind Boys of Alabama

At about the time that the Blind Boys of Mississippi were organized, a group of blind students in Alabama were also organizing a gospel quartet. In 1937 Clarence Fountain (b. 1929) was an elementary school student singing in the Talladega Institute for the Deaf and Blind Glee Club. Fountain and a friend, Johnny Fields (b. 1927), selected George Scott (b. 1929), Olice Thomas (b. 1926), and Velma Bozman Traylor (1923–47) from the Glee Club and formed the Happy Land Jubilee Singers.

Their early style was influenced by the Golden Gate Quartet, to whom they would listen during the Gates' national broadcasts. They borrowed the Gates' repertoire as well. As soon as they learned enough songs, they began to sing at churches and social functions in Talladega, Tuskegee, and Birmingham, and because they could hear people say "there go the blind boys," they changed their name to accommodate their audience. The name change caused many problems for the group: sometimes they were advertised as the Blind Boys and other times as the Happy

Clarence Fountain and the Five Blind Boys of Alabama

Land Singers. Further, in the 1940s they heard Brownlee's group that was also called the Blind Boys. When the two groups toured together in the early 1950s, they each added the name of their home state to their names.

The Alabama Blind Boys left Talladega in 1944 and became professionals. Fountain, the leader of the group, had a strong high baritone voice with a slow vibrato, which he used to color slow Negro spirituals and hymns. The background singers supported Fountain with a resonant barbershop harmonic foundation. The Blind Boys brought this sound to Coleman Records when they began to record in 1948. By 1949 they had their first hit record with Emma L. Jackson and Gwendolyn Cooper Lightener's "I Can See Everybody's Mother, but I Can't See Mine." Their being blind added additional meaning to the song. The success of this "mother" record consciously or unconsciously affected their repertoire, because during the next decade they would record a number of mother songs, all of which became popular. Among them were "Living on Mother's Prayers" and "When I Lost My Mother." Fountain, after hearing that Brownlee was "tearing up churches" with his screams and shrieks, adopted the technique with the same results. In the mid-1950s, when the two blind groups toured together, all their concerts were characterized by extremely hard singing.

Because of misunderstandings and anger, Fountain left the group twice but returned each time. He first left in 1969 and toured as a solo act until he returned to the group in 1975. In 1983 the Alabama Five Blind Boys and J. J. Farley and the Soul Stirrers starred on Broadway in a musical version of Sophocles' drama *Oedipus*.

Julius "June" Cheeks and the Sensational Nightingales

Julius "June" Cheeks (1929–81), who later became the Reverend Julius Cheeks, was the personification of the hard gospel singer. By the time of his death he had very little voice left, but he could still "bring a house down."

Cheeks was born in Spartanburg, South Carolina, and was attracted to gospel as a child by the recordings of the Dixie Hummingbirds, the Fairfield Four, and the Soul Stirrers. He began to sing in the second grade, at which time he also left school permanently to work in the cotton fields and at service stations. He spent his leisure time singing with a local quartet, the Baronets. He was singing with this group when the Reverend B. L. Parks, a former member of the Dixie Hummingbirds, approached him to sing with a new group he was forming, the Nightingales. (The original group called the Nightingales was formed in 1942 in Philadelphia with members Howard Carroll of the Hummingbirds, Paul Owens of the Swan Silvertones, Ben Joiner, and William Henry. At the height of their popularity they cut several sides for Decca Records but disbanded shortly after the session.

The Reverend Julius "June" Cheeks and the Sensational Nightingales

Gospel Quartets of the Golden Age

In the early 1950s gospel quartets were known as much by their leaders as by their repertoire and harmony. Within a few years these leaders wove their groups into a sweet (close harmony, precise attacks and releases, and understated—yet firm—rhythmic accentuation) or hard (energetic and extremely intense solo and background singing, a preaching style of delivery, and exaggerated physical gestures) gospel group.

Sweet Gospel

CBS Trumpeteers
Dixie Hummingbirds
Harmonizing Four
Pilgrim Travelers
Soul Stirrers
Swan Silvertones

Hard Gospel

Blind Boys of Alabama
Blind Boys of Mississippi
Mighty Clouds of Joy
Sensational Nightingales
Spirit of Memphis
Swanee Quintet

Sweet and Hard Gospel

Fairfield Four

In 1946 Parks changed the personnel to Cheeks, Joseph "JoJo" Wallace of Wilmington, North Carolina, and Carl Coates, a Washington, D.C., native living in Birmingham. (His wife was Dorothy Love Coates of the Original Gospel Harmonettes.) The group went to Goldsboro, North Carolina, where they spent a month in rehearsal for their first appearance. The Nightingales were an immediate sensation. In fact, they were called sensational so often that they added the word to their name. Much of their success was due to Cheeks' overpowering vocal style. Possessing a thick baritone voice, he approached singing as he did preaching (to which he turned in 1954). Like Archie Brownlee, he employed falsetto, growls, and screams in his singing, much to the delight of the audience. Two of his most popular recordings are "Somewhere to Lay My Head" (1955) and "The Last Mile of the Way," recorded in the last year of his life when his voice was ragged, his breath was short, and he had

difficulty reaching the notes he heard in his head. And yet, "The Last Mile of the Way" shows Cheeks at his most poignant, sincere, and, considering what little voice he had left, his most versatile:

> If I walk in the pathway of duty,
> If I work till the close of the day;
> I shall see the great King in His beauty
> When I've gone the last mile of the way.

Cheeks left and returned to the group several times. In 1960 he formed his own group, the Knights, with which he recorded "The Last Mile of the Way." In the late 1960s he disbanded this group and sang for a while with the Mighty Clouds of Joy. After 1970 he spent his time preaching in Baltimore, Newark, and Miami. The Nightingales continued to sing into the 1990s under the leadership of Calvert McNair, Jr.

THE CALIFORNIA SCHOOL OF GOSPEL

African American gospel music developed in the South and Midwest despite its start in Los Angeles. After the close of the Azusa Street Revival in 1909, the people who had moved to Los Angeles disbanded and returned to their hometowns or staked out new territories in Mississippi, Tennessee, Arkansas, Texas, and other southern states where they could plant churches. Since only the people who had attended the revival services knew of the new sanctified singing, the old-line churches of Los Angeles continued to sing the hymns, Negro spirituals, and anthems they had sung before the revival. Even the Apostolic Fifth Gospel Mission, Seymour's church, returned to singing "spirited" hymns and Negro spirituals. Not until the 1930s did gospel (as it was known on the East Coast) return to California, and Los Angeles was its most receptive city. Dorsey, Sallie Martin, the Roberta Martin Singers, Robert Anderson, and Thomas Shelby made frequent visits, sometimes remaining in the city for five weeks at a time, while ordering sheet music from Chicago. In the 1940s, when a coterie of California gospel composers developed, several opened publishing companies. These were local and regional companies that lacked the distribution of Dorsey or Martin and Morris, so California continued to seek the latest gospel songs from the East Coast and the Midwest.

J. Earle Hines

The first important gospel singer from the East Coast to settle in Los Angeles was James Earle Hines (1916–60), a native of Atlanta, Georgia. He attended Atlanta public schools and participated in the musical activities of the churches, the city, and the college community of Atlanta University, and Spelman, Morehouse, Clark, and Morris Brown colleges. Most of these activities featured Western European art and music. After high school he moved to Cincinnati where he attended the Cosmopolitan School of Music and later matriculated at Columbia University in New York City. After two years at Columbia he returned to Cincinnati and began directing local church choirs.

During the 1930s Hines was recruited by Dr. L. K. Williams, president of the National Baptist Convention, to sing in a male quartet that Lucie Campbell and E. W. D. Isaac were putting together to travel to National Baptist Convention churches and represent the convention in song. Hines accepted the invitation and for several years sang with the Good Will Singers along with J. Robert Bradley and Thomas Shelby, among others. He received a thorough grounding in the African American sacred music tradition at the annual National Baptist Convention as a member of the convention choir during the early 1940s.

In 1947 Hines was hired as the director of the newly founded Echoes of Eden Choir at St. Paul Baptist Church in Los Angeles. The choir quickly became the most outstanding gospel choir in the city and was the first black church choir to have a weekly radio broadcast. The choir also has the distinction of being the first true gospel choir to make records. In the late 1940s and early 1950s, they produced several hits, among them Kenneth Morris' "He's a Friend of Mine," Dorsey's "God Be with You," and the two songs that made them famous, "Yield Not to Temptation" and "Just Look for Me in Heaven."

With a baritone voice that sounded as if it were made of steel, Hines was an aggressive singer, at times literally shouting out lyrics. He was particularly adept at realizing older hymns in the Baptist lining hymn tradition. His flamboyant stage mannerisms helped, rather than hindered, his ability to "upset" a church; the sisters would execute a holy dance or faint, while the men attempted to inconspicuously wipe the tears from their eyes.

Cora Martin-Moore

Singer, pianist, and choir director Cora Juanita Brewer Martin-Moore was born in 1927 in Chicago. She was the oldest child of Lucius and Annie Claude James Moore, but as a youngster she was adopted by gospel pioneer Sallie Martin and thereafter used the name Cora Martin. She attended public schools in Chicago and began her musical career as a child at that city's Mount Pleasant Baptist Church. She joined her adopted mother's group, the Sallie Martin Singers, as a teenager and toured with them throughout the United States, even after 1947 when she made her home in Los Angeles and affiliated with the St. Paul Baptist Church. As a soloist in the Sallie Martin Singers, Martin-Moore gained fame through a recording of Robert Anderson's "Eyes Hath Not Seen" on which she displays an alto voice of even tone, highly developed breath control, and restraint in embellishments. She was equally at home with jubilee music, illustrated when she sang the Alex Bradford part in "He'll Wash You Whiter than Snow" while on tour with the Sallie Martin Singers.

After moving to California, Martin-Moore attended California State University at Dominquez Hills and earned a bachelor's degree. She served as minister of music and director of the Echoes of Eden Choir and worked as a religious music DJ, in addition to owning a music studio and record shop.

Eugene Douglass Smallwood

Until the arrival of Doris Akers in Los Angeles, Eugene Douglass Smallwood (b. 1920), born in Guthrie, Oklahoma, was the principal gospel music composer in Los Angeles. He began composing and publishing his music in 1939, the year he came to Los Angeles City College as a music major. While attending college, he served as the minister of music at the Zion Hill Baptist Church and sang tenor with the Three Sons of Thunder. Smallwood also organized, along with Earl A. Pleasant, the Interdenominational Chorus, the venerable Smallwood Singers, and a music school with James Lewis Elkins, a former member of the Wings Over Jordan Choir. His crowning achievement was the founding of Opportunity Baptist Church, where he has served as senior minister since 1946. Gospel musicians who have worked with him at his church include Albert A. Goodson, Robert Anderson, the Simmons-Akers Singers, Thurston G. Frazier, and Raymond Rasberry.

The composer of more than one hundred gospel songs, Smallwood is most fa-

mous for his composition "When He Spoke," which has been recorded by Mahalia Jackson, the Davis Sisters, the Robert Anderson Singers, and the Clara Ward Singers. Smallwood, who still possesses a bright tenor voice, was honored in February 1994 at the Smithsonian Institution for his contributions to gospel music. During the ceremony, Smallwood sang several impassioned renditions of his own songs.

Doris Akers

By the 1990s several Christian hymnals (including the United Methodist and the African Methodist Episcopal) contained either "Sweet, Sweet Spirit" or "Lead Me, Guide Me." Both songs were composed by the most prolific composer in gospel music since the days of Dorsey, Campbell, Brewster, Morris, and Roberta Martin: Doris Mae Akers.

When she arrived in Los Angeles in 1945, Doris Akers (b. 1922) was not only a seasoned singer, pianist, and choir director, but a composer as well, having written her first composition at age ten. Akers was born in Brookfield, Missouri, but her family moved to Kirksville, Missouri, when she was five. She studied piano, sang in her high school glee club, and while still a teenager, organized a five-piece band called Dot Akers and Her Swingsters that featured swing jazz and other popular music of the 1930s and 1940s.

In Los Angeles she sang and played for the Sallie Martin Singers and later organized her own group with Dorothy Simmons, the Simmons-Akers Singers, which concertized throughout the United States. Akers won special prominence in the late 1950s and 1960s when she became the soloist and director of the Sky Pilot Choir, one of the first racially mixed choirs in Los Angeles, which featured African American gospel music.

Akers' 1947 composition "I Want a Double Portion of God's Love" became the first of many hit songs that she would write. Others are "Lord, Don't Move the Mountain," which was made famous by Inez Andrews, "You Can't Beat God Giving," "Grow Closer," and "God Is So Good to Me." Akers' compositions are unique for their elegant and sophisticated lyrics and for their melodies, which draw less from Negro spiritual and gospel characteristics and more from European art music and American popular music. Her most famous composition, "Lead Me, Guide Me," is a gospel song set as a lullaby:

Verse

I am weak and I need Thy strength and power
To help me over my weakest hour;
Help me through the darkness Thy face to see,
Lead me, oh Lord, lead me.

Chorus

Lead me, guide me, along the way
For if you lead me, I cannot stray;
Lord, let me walk each day with Thee,
Lead me, oh Lord, lead me.

The title of this song was chosen as the title of the African American Catholic Hymnal in 1987.

Dorothy Vernell Simmons

For many years Akers' singing partner was Dorothy Vernell Simmons (b. 1910), a gospel singer and choir director. A native of Louisiana, Simmons moved with her family to Chicago when she was seven years old. After high school she worked in the Martin and Morris Music, Inc. where she came into contact with gospel music. Martin discovered Simmons was a singer and engaged her as a member of the Sallie Martin Singers when they were organized in 1940. Simmons visited California in 1944 with the Sallie Martin Singers and in 1947 decided to move there. Her association with Akers began in 1948. Her lyric soprano, agile and with a high range, blended sonorously with the mezzo-soprano-alto of Akers. Akers' compositions and the singing of the Simmons-Akers Duo were the inspiration for Edwin Hawkins' arrangement of "O Happy Day" and the new gospel sound from Los Angeles.

Thurston Frazier

The most important California gospel choral conductor after J. Earle Hines was Thurston Gilbert Frazier (1930–74). Frazier was born in Houston, Texas, and moved to Los Angeles in the late 1930s. His introduction to gospel music came when he met J. Earle Hines and sang in one of his choirs. He studied repertoire and conducting with Hines and found gospel more demanding and more inspiring than, and just

as difficult as, the music he studied as a music major at Los Angeles City College.

Frazier gained fame as the director of the Voices of Hope Choir, a community gospel chorus that he and Gwendolyn Cooper Lightener, former pianist for Mahalia Jackson, organized in 1957. Their first album, released in the early 1960s, included Frazier's composition "We've Come This Far by Faith." The song became extremely popular and was soon being sung by choirs throughout the United States. Frazier's choral style, much closer to James Cleveland's than Thomas A. Dorsey's, anticipated the style of the 1970s and 1980s, with its three rather than four parts, a full bright sound, and rhythms closer to those of rhythm and blues than to those of Negro spirituals.

Frazier served as director of music at Phillips Temple Christian Methodist Church and Opportunity Baptist Church. His most popular compositions are "Come Holy Spirit" and "Let Us Sing Praise," both of which show traces of the Western European art music that he studied in college. Frazier was widely praised for his ability to direct and command gospel choirs of five hundred voices.

Albert A. Goodson

Albert A. Goodson was born in Los Angeles in 1933 and acquired his musical education in the church. Although he was raised in the Pentecostal church, he joined St. Paul Baptist Church at age twelve to learn the music and technique of J. Earle Hines and Gwendolyn Cooper Lightener. While studying with Hines, he served as assistant pianist for the Echoes of Eden Choir and the Hines Good Will Singers. He later served as choir director at Grace Memorial Church of God in Christ and Opportunity Baptist Church. During the early 1950s he toured and recorded with the Sallie Martin Singers, as well as served as their pianist. He moved to Chicago in 1955 where he was engaged as minister of music at Fellowship Baptist Church, pastored by the Reverend Clay Evans. At the invitation of Thomas Wyatt, director of the Wings of Healing Ministry, he returned to Los Angeles in 1961 to direct the interdenominational Wings of Healing Gospel Choir.

While living in Chicago he composed the song that would catapult him to fame within a few short months of its release. "We've Come This Far by Faith," recorded by the Voices of Hope, became as popular a processional for the gospel choir as Dorsey's "God Be with You" was a benediction song for congregations:

We've come this far by faith, leaning on the Lord,
Trusting in His holy work, He's never failed me yet;
Oh, oh, oh, can't turn around,
We've come this far by faith.

Arthur Atlas Peters and Dave Carl Weston

Two important but lesser-known gospel musicians from the California school are Arthur Atlas Peters and Dave Carl Weston. Peters (c.1907–75), born in Slidell, Louisiana, began playing piano at age seven and studied piano with the local school teacher. He attended Southern University and after graduating taught school in Mississippi for several years before moving to Los Angeles in 1936. He immediately immersed himself in music, singing spirituals, anthems, gospel, and Western art music. Later he served as director of the choir at Phillips Temple Christian Methodist Church and simultaneously opened a music store where he taught gospel singing. In 1939 along with Eugene Smallwood and Amos Pleasant, he organized the Three Sons of Thunder, a gospel trio.

Victory Baptist Church, a prominent church in Los Angeles, was founded by Peters in 1943, and in 1949 he began "Voices of Victory," a weekly radio broadcast. The first television broadcast of his church services began on April 5, 1953, and continued for a number of years. Victory Baptist Church was among the first to welcome gospel into its sanctuary.

David Carl Weston was born in Lufkin, Texas, in 1923. After attending Prairie View A & M College (now University) for one year, he relocated to Santa Monica in 1942 where he joined Calvary Baptist Church. At the same time he entered the University of California, Los Angeles, from which he graduated in 1947 with a major in English and a minor in music.

He served as pianist for the gospel and youth choirs at Calvary and organized the Merri-Tones, a community gospel choir. His own group, the Dave Weston Singers, toured with the Jordanaires, the Sallie Martin Singers, and Brother Joe May. Between 1951 and 1955 Weston lived in Chicago and directed the choir at the First Church of Deliverance. In 1955 he returned to California where he became Calvary's first minister of music.

PIANO-ACCOMPANIED GROUPS

Piano-accompanied gospel demanded virtuoso piano playing. The gospel piano style of the 1950s, with its heavy chords played in the center of the keyboard, rolling bass, and punctuated riffs in the upper part of the keyboard, was so distinctive that one had to be grounded in gospel in order to execute the style. Quartet gospel, older than piano-accompanied gospel, was at the peak of its popularity during the early 1950s. Gospel supported by piano emerged as the public's favorite, and singers took great pains in selecting pianists, because no group could be strong if its pianist was weak. Having worked at developing a style since the 1926 recordings of Arizona Dranes, by 1955 gospel pianists were as popular as the groups they were with. Some groups even mentioned the pianist in their name, such as the Davis Sisters and Curtis Dublin and the Original Gospel Harmonettes and Herbert "Pee Wee" Pickard. Several pianists were considered phenomenal. In addition to Dublin and Pickard, Mildred Falls, Mildred Gay, Jessy Dixon, and James Herndon were sought-after pianists. Most pianists in gospel during the 1950s were also the leaders of their group and created piano styles to fit the singers. The most outstanding among these were Clara Ward, Roberta Martin, Alex Bradford, James Cleveland, Edgar O'Neal, Raymond Rasberry, Charles Taylor, and Lucy Smith. The art of gospel piano and pianists developed to such a degree that quartets, heretofore accompanied by guitar (and before that singing *a cappella*) began using piano accompaniment at first for recordings only and gradually in concerts. The Soul Stirrers with Sam Cooke was one of the first quartets to use piano; by the late 1950s, however, nearly all quartets used piano at one time or another. Piano gospel finally came into its own.

Dorothy Love Coates and the Original Gospel Harmonettes

The 1940 National Baptist Convention met in Birmingham, and a local pianist was called on to play for the convention choir. Her friends sang in the convention choir and when the convention was over she and those friends decided to form a group to sing some of the songs they had learned. The pianist was Evelyn Starks (b. 1922), who would serve also as composer and arranger; the singer who proposed the formation of the group was Mildred Madison Miller (b. 1923), who was a member of the William Belvin Singers as second soprano. The other singers were Odessa

Dorothy Love Coates and the Original Gospel Harmonettes performing live to a church audience

Glasgow Edwards (b. 1921), second alto; Vera Conner Kolb (b. 1924), first soprano; and Willie Mae Brooks Newberry (b. 1923), first alto.

They named themselves the Gospel Harmoneers, but later became the Original Gospel Harmonettes when a record producer suggested they find a more feminine name. Within a few months of their organization, they were approached by A. G.

The Original Gospel Harmonettes: Willie Mae Newberry, Vera Kolb, Mildred Miller, Odessa Edwards, and Dorothy Love Coates

Gaston, the leading African American funeral director in Alabama, to sing for a half-hour weekly radio broadcast on station WSGN, with Gaston Funeral Homes as their sponsor. The Harmonettes sang on the weekly program for a year and became regional stars. They toured Alabama and several states in the East and West and served as the local group to open concerts when famous stars appeared in town.

Their first recording session took place in New York City in 1949. During this session they recorded, among other songs, "Move on up a Little Higher" and "In the Upper Room." The recordings from this and a second session yielded little results, but the group continued to travel, drawing huge crowds through word-of-mouth publicity. J. W. Alexander, of the Pilgrim Travelers and a talent scout for Specialty Records, became interested in the group and arranged an audition for them in California. The group decided they wanted Dorothy McGriff Love, who had substituted for individual members of the group on several occasions in the early 1940s, to join them for the recording session. They went to Nashville and persuaded Love, who was living there with her husband, Willie Love of the Fairfield Four, to make the trip with them.

Their first session for Specialty produced two songs, equal in popularity, that immediately placed the singers in the forefront of female gospel groups. Love was given the lead in "I'm Sealed," a gospel ballad set to a gospel-waltz tempo. From the first note it was apparent that this soloist was extraordinary: a singer with a sanctified timbre and a preacher's delivery. As the song unfolded, the passion became

Dorothy Love Coates and the Original Gospel Harmonettes

greater and by the end of the recording more than a few listeners would be weeping. The other side of the recording was a semishout song, "Get Away, Jordan," with the lead shared by Miller and Love. Miller proved to be a formidable singer and matched Love nuance for nuance. What was of particular interest was the minivamp inserted toward the end during which Love, using African American folk axioms and phrases, describes a peaceful death. The public soon discovered that Love had written the additional lyrics and music, and they were primed for more of her songs.

The Harmonettes followed this first release with a string of hits that were new to gospel. Most Love compositions bore a relationship to Brewster's songs, which were wordy and historical. Love's songs were wordy but bursting with well-known folk sayings that tugged at the hearts of listeners. Her compositions include "You Can't Hurry God," "That's Enough," and "I Won't Let Go." Perhaps her finest composition is "You Must Be Born Again," in which the chorus says:

> *You must have that fire and Holy Ghost, that*
> *Burning thing that keeps the prayer wheel turning;*
> *That kind of religion you cannot conceal, it makes*
> *You move, it makes you shout, it makes you cry when it's real;*
> *Keep your head right in the winding chain (till your)*

Soul's been anchored in my Jesus' name (you know I'm)
Filled with it, free from sin, don't you see, you must be born again.

With Love, who by this time had married Carl Coates of the Nightingales, improvising on the solo, the group delivered this chorus in short staccato punches. And the longer they sang, the more excited Love became. She would then add

Gospel Pianists

Combining ragtime, barrelhouse, and Protestant hymns, Arizona Dranes and those who followed her created one of the most distinctive piano styles in music: gospel. By the end of the Golden Age of gospel its piano style had been refined and had begun to permeate American popular music. While there were many more progressive gospel pianists than can be mentioned here, a few of the most prominent are listed below.

Early Period
(Development)
Estelle Allen
Thomas A. Dorsey
Arizona Dranes
Kenneth Morris
Bertha Wise

Middle Period
(Refinement)
Margaret Allison
Jeff Banks
Curtis Dublin
Mildred Falls
Evelyn Gay
Ruth Jones (Dinah Washington)
Gwendolyn Cooper Lightener
Roberta Martin

Evelyn Starks
Clara Ward

Late Period
(Virtuosity)
Doris Akers
James Boyer
Alex Bradford
James Cleveland
Jessy Dixon
James Herndon
Edgar O'Neal
Herbert "Pee Wee" Pickard
Raymond Rasberry
Lawrence Roberts
Charles Taylor
Eddie Williams

growls, shrieks, and grunts to match the rhythmic and perpetual motion of her body.

The Harmonettes brought a new intensity to gospel that could only be matched by the frenzy of a joyful sanctified shout. At the same time they brought a quiet dignity and simple elegance to gospel that belied its inherent emotional capabilities. They performed in pastel robes, and when they otherwise appeared in public, they were always clad in fashionably styled, tailored suits. They were soft spoken, exhibited a refinement not seen since the days when Roberta Martin traveled with her group, were always seen together, and comported themselves as the Original Gospel Harmonettes—but without the artificial pride they could have assumed.

When they hit the stage, however, they were something else. While the others maintained an almost subdued stage presence, when Coates began to reach back into her life's experience as one of God's disenfranchised children and recount "how she got over," the group's demeanor changed. Without acting like the sanctified saints and giving up their entire presence to God, the Harmonettes began to "have church." Often performing with only one microphone, that microphone would be right in front of Coates' mouth, and the other members of the group would huddle around it and answer Coates note for note. When overcome by the spirit, Coates' eyes would open wide and remain open without blinking for minutes on end. As she sang, jerked, jumped, shouted, waved her arms, and moved through an audience, the lyrics of the song she was singing sprang vividly to life. On several occasions at the end of a song, the group would have to lead Coates back to the stage because she was completely out of herself, having given herself over to the Master.

In fact, as the supreme hard gospel singer, Coates could "take a house" and have everybody standing up, swaying, shouting, crying, or fainting like no one else, including her near-equal, Ruth Davis of the Davis Sisters. She would leave in the dust such hard singers as Silas Steele, Archie Brownlee, Clarence Fountain, and Julius Cheeks. When the Harmonettes made their first appearances with Coates, the audience was unprepared for what they eventually came to love. Coates brought more than fifteen years of gospel singing and passion to the Harmonettes.

Born in 1928 in Birmingham, Alabama, into a musical family, by age ten Coates was playing piano for her church Evergreen Baptist. As a teenager she sang with the Royal Gospel Singers and the McGriff Singers, a family group composed of three sisters and one brother. The group had a weekly broadcast over WJLD, one of the first

live radio gospel concerts in the city. It was for the McGriff Singers that Coates began to compose, but it was not until she was a Harmonette that her compositions began to rival those of her idol, W. Herbert Brewster. What Brewster was able to say in the eloquent language of a sage, Coates was able to say in the homespun language of a weary traveler. In her 1953 composition "You Can't Hurry God," she spoke like a deacon from the Amen Corner:

> You can't hurry God, oh no, you just have to wait.
> You have to trust Him and give Him time, no matter how long it takes;
> You know He's a God you just can't hurry, He'll be there, don't worry,
> You know He may not come when you want Him, but He's right on time.

The Harmonettes appeared at Carnegie Hall in 1953, then at the Apollo Theater, Madison Square Garden, and concert halls throughout the United States and the Bahamas. After the Original Gospel Harmonettes disbanded in the 1960s, Coates organized the Dorothy Love Coates Singers and made several tours of Europe and in the late 1960s appeared in concert at Harvard University.

Albertina Walker and the Caravans

The Roberta Martin Singers were fantastic in that each member was such a great soloist that a concert could have been built around them individually. Albertina Walker and the Caravans were also fantastic, because not only could concerts be built around each singer, they eventually were. The Caravans have produced more gospel superstars than any other group or choir. Among their alumnae are Bessie Griffin, Shirley Caesar, Inez Andrews, Cassietta George, and Dorothy Norwood. Each of these singers was given the opportunity to develop herself by the Caravans' leader, Albertina Walker, one of the finest gospel singers of all times.

ALBERTINA WALKER

Walker was born in Chicago in 1930 and began singing at West Point Baptist Church at age eleven. By the time she was seventeen, she had joined a group led by Robert Anderson. In 1952, with Ora Lee Hopkins, Elyse Yancey, and Nellie Grace Daniels, who were also members of Anderson's ensemble, she organized the Caravans. The original Caravans were timid singers in comparison to the group that would emerge

Albertina Walker and the Caravans

in three years, but they were good timid singers. Their recordings of "Think of His Goodness to You," "Blessed Assurance," and the Negro spiritual "All Night, All Day" bear witness to close, earthy harmony, percussive attacks, and a precise rhythm unlike any other female gospel group. Tina, as Walker is called, was responsible for most of the solos in the original group, and it was the beauty of her voice and singing style to which others were attracted. Her voice is a husky contralto with a characteristic crack of three or four descending tones as she moves through a melodic line, a feature also heard from soul singer Gladys Knight. The sincerity with which Walker sings can turn a dry Protestant hymn into a jubilant testimony of faith.

By 1953 and with the addition of Bessie Griffin, the Caravans began to change into an ensemble of soloists. Walker, who has always believed in a kind of musical democracy, began to share the spotlight with each new singer. Yet none matched the

soulful Albertina Walker, as illustrated on her 1980 recording of "Please Be Patient with Me."

BESSIE GRIFFIN

Bessie Griffin (1927–90), like her more famous compatriot Mahalia Jackson, was born in New Orleans, and the rich musical heritage of her birthplace exuded from every note she sang. After her mother died, Griffin was brought up by her grand-mother. This meant church all day every Sunday and one day during the week. Early on Bessie began singing the songs she heard in church, and by the time she reached high school she was considered to be one of the best soloists in New Orleans.

Griffin moved to Chicago in 1951 and became part of that city's musical scene. Comparisons were often made between Griffin and Mahalia Jackson, although few similarities, save power, existed between their style. Griffin possessed a contralto that was lighter in texture than Jackson's and much more fluid. Griffin was capable of executing pyrotechnics such as sustaining tones for long periods, inserting growls, essaying a coloratura-like run, and singing for long periods of time (it was not un-usual for her to sing one song for twenty minutes). She brought these assets to the Caravans in 1953. Her special song with the group was an extended version of Alex Bradford's "Too Close to Heaven." Griffin sang the song in such a way that each stanza brought the listener closer to heaven as she increased pitch, embellishments, and volume. In 1954 Griffin left the Caravans and thereafter followed a solo career, concertizing in the United States, Europe, and Africa, and singing gospel in night-clubs on the West Coast.

SHIRLEY CAESAR

"Baby Shirley, the Gospel Singer," as she was called by age ten, was born in Durham, North Carolina, in 1938 to a mother who was a great church worker and a father, known as "Big Jim," who was a legendary quartet singer. One of her greatest joys as a young child was attending the rehearsals of the Just Come Four, the *a cappella* quartet in which her father sang lead. Her father died when she was twelve years old, and she was thereafter responsible for her invalid mother. To help with finances, she joined the traveling group of the "one-legged preacher," Leroy Johnson, and she appeared regularly on his television show out of Portsmouth, Virginia, in the early 1950s. She also cut several records for the Federal label.

After graduating from high school, she enrolled in North Carolina State College (now North Carolina State University) seeking a major in business education. In 1958 she attended a concert by the Caravans and was so mesmerized by their singing that she wanted to join the group. Through a strange set of circumstances, and with the assistance of Dorothy Love Coates, Caesar withdrew from college in 1958 and joined the Caravans whose members at that time included Walker, Cassietta George, and Inez Andrews.

Caesar has a light alto voice with a rapid vibrato marked by its agility. She possesses an extensive range, the upper part of which she uses at the climax of a song. Her songs are delivered in a style not unlike that of a preacher (which she is), and she can energize an audience. Indeed, most audiences are on their feet several times during a Caesar concert. She first demonstrated her ability to completely mesmerize an audience in 1961 with her rendition of "Hallelujah, It's Done." During the choruses of the song she ad-libs in the style of African American folk preaching tantamount to a short sermon or sermonette. This song and sermonette form was also

Gospel Organists

From its introduction into gospel in 1939 by Kenneth Morris, the percussive sound and myriad colors of the Hammond organ were eventually adopted by rhythm and blues and jazz performers. Among the several prominent gospel organists performing during the Golden Age were Alfred Bolden who, in addition to gospel, played European art music, and Billy Preston, who became the premiere soul music organist.

Alfred Bolden	"Little" Lucy Smith
James "Blind" Francis	Gerald Spraggins
Ralph Jones	Herman Stevens
Alfred Miller	Louise Overall Weaver
Kenneth Morris	Willie Webb
Billy Preston	Maceo Woods

practiced by Mother Willie Mae Ford Smith and Edna Gallmon Cooke. In later years Caesar would perfect this practice to such a degree that she had no peer.

Her other special talent was the dramatization of songs, as first demonstrated in 1958 with "I've Been Running for Jesus a Long Time" and "I'm Not Tired Yet." Each time the word "running" appeared in the lyrics, Caesar would run up and down the aisles to the delight of the audience. She surpassed her dramatization of that song in 1962 when, while singing "Sweeping through the City," she pantomimed sweeping, moving through the auditorium and giving special energy to the corners of the hall.

Caesar left the Caravans in 1966 and organized her own group, the Caesar Singers. While in this group she developed a repertoire of mother songs, the first of which was "Don't Drive Your Mama Away" in 1969. Other such songs recorded by Caesar are "No Charge" and "Faded Roses," her first crossover piece.

Caesar became an evangelist in 1961 while with the Caravans, and in the 1980s, upon her return to Durham, she established the Mount Calvary Work of Faith Church, of which she is the pastor and her husband, Harold I. Williamson, is the presiding bishop. She also returned to college and earned a degree in business education in 1984, served on the Durham City Council, and founded the Shirley Caesar Outreach Ministries. In 1972 Caesar was the first gospel singer to be nominated for a Grammy Award, which she won. In addition to awards from the Gospel Music Association and the NAACP, she has been inducted into the Gospel Music Hall of Fame. Caesar is the most popular gospel singer since Mahalia Jackson.

INEZ ANDREWS

Inez McConic Andrews (b. 1929), like Dorothy Love Coates, was born in Birmingham, Alabama, to a Baptist preacher father and a sanctified singing mother. Her mother died when she was two years old, and she was raised by her father. She received her education in Birmingham public schools and sang in the junior choir of her father's church. She sang locally as a soloist and joined the Carter Choral Ensemble, which traveled around the Alabama, Mississippi, and Georgia region. She also sang for a short period with the Raymond Rasberry Singers and intermittently substituted in the Original Gospel Harmonettes.

In 1957 James Cleveland, while serving as pianist and arranger for the Caravans, persuaded Andrews to move to Chicago and join the group. Her addition sparked

new energy because Andrews, like Caesar, was a singer and "preacher." There the similarity ends. While Caesar was a light mezzo-soprano-alto, Andrews was a metallic contralto; while Caesar had the rapid-fire delivery of an impassioned sanctified preacher, Andrews chose a slower, majestic delivery characteristic of a presiding bishop. Yet they were equally fiery.

Andrews had her first hit with the Caravans singing Cleveland's "Soldiers in the Army," which develops the ideas contained in the sanctified congregational song "I'm a Soldier in the Army of the Lord":

> *We are soldiers in the army,*
> *We've got to fight although we have to cry;*
> *We've got to hold up the blood-stained banner,*
> *We've got to hold it up until we die.*

Andrews turned "Soldiers" into an order, sung with the authority of a commanding general. However, that emotion in no way matched her passionate pleading to Mary in the Claude Jeter arrangement of "Mary, Don't You Weep." After four or five stanzas of gently requesting Mary to cease weeping, Andrews turns the song into one of the most compelling vamps in all gospel. She begins to call Mary's name gently at first; the second time she calls with a louder and higher tone; and with the third call she ascends into the very top of her register and wails "Ma—a—a—ry!"

In the early 1960s Andrews left the Caravans and organized her own group, the Andrewettes. With this group she toured Europe in 1965. Since that time she has concertized and recorded as a solo artist. "Lord, Don't Move the Mountain" by Doris Akers was a big solo hit for Andrews in the late 1970s. Occasionally Andrews reunites with other former members of the Caravans for concerts.

DOROTHY NORWOOD

If Shirley Caesar and Inez Andrews are preachers, then Dorothy Norwood is the master storyteller. This Atlanta, Georgia, native (b. 1930) blanketed the 1960s with gospelized stories of ungrateful children, boys who have circuitous meetings with Jesus, and old ladies with houses.

Norwood grew up in the Baptist church and honed her singing skills in choirs and groups in Atlanta before moving to Chicago. By 1955 she was a member of the

Caravans. Norwood's voice is a burnished alto, capable of great warmth and yet elastic enough to produce a preacher's growl. Although outstanding with the Caravans, Norwood did not seem to come into her own until she left the group in the late 1950s. Then, she sang with a number of groups including James Cleveland's Gospel Chimes. It was as the leader of her own group, the Norwood Singers, that she became a superstar, not because of her singing but because she knew how to tell a story.

Her four most famous stories are "Johnny and Jesus," "The Boy and the Kite," "The Old Lady's House," and the overwhelmingly popular "The Denied Mother." On her recording of "The Denied Mother," perhaps the saddest of all mother songs, Norwood begins her story in this manner:

> A mother who, having sent her daughter away to college, goes to the train station to meet her at the end of a year of school. Though the mother is standing at the station with her arms open wide to greet her daughter, her daughter looks right at the mother, turns in another direction and walks away. Though feeling rejected and hurt the mother runs after the daughter and asks her why she did not greet her as the other daughters did their mothers. The daughter answers that she didn't greet her because she didn't want anyone to know that the old lady with all the burns and scars on her face was her mother. Her mother told her that when she was a baby three months old, she left her in the house to go outside and hang up her washing. When she looked around she saw that the house was on fire, and though her neighbors tried to keep her from going inside, she could only think about her baby, went in the house and not only saved her baby, but put her hands over the baby's face so that the baby would not be scarred.

At the end of the story the mother says "that's all right though; I know a man [Jesus] who sits high and looks low." In this live recording, the audience roars their approval for the mother's fail-safe salvation. Throughout the recording the audience has participated as if they were responding to a preacher, and that is the role Norwood takes in the performance. Like C. L. Franklin would, she begins the story in her normal speaking voice. As the story progresses and the spirit arises, she moves into the key of the organ and piano that accompany her with sustained and staccato chords and begins to chant the story. By the time she reaches the end, she has turned her narra-

tive into song. She and her singers immediately begin Dorsey's famous prayer "Take My Hand, Precious Lord." Norwood moved to New Jersey and sang with a number of choirs but in the 1970s returned to her native Georgia.

CASSIETTA GEORGE

Cassietta George was born in 1928 in Memphis, Tennessee, and died in Los Angeles in 1995. She graduated from McKinley High School in Canton, Ohio, where she lived for a number of years. After she finished school, she returned to Memphis and sang for a while with the Songbirds of the South, one of the many female *a cappella* quartets in Memphis during the 1940s and early 1950s. She later sang with the Brewster Ensemble. In the early 1950s she moved to Chicago, and in 1954 became a member of the Caravans.

Short in stature and slight of build, George astounded audiences with her thin and clear but huge voice. Having been brought up in the *a cappella* tradition, she was particularly sensitive to attacks and releases. In public performances it was clear that despite piano accompaniment she marked the rhythm in her singing with physical gestures. Her most popular song with the Caravans was a spirited arrangement of "Somebody Bigger than You and I" that carried such a popular music character that it just missed becoming a crossover hit for the Caravans.

George began composing while with the Caravans and has composed more than twenty-five songs, including "To Whom Shall I Turn?" and "I Believe in Thee."

OTHER CARAVAN PERFORMERS

Several other singers made their own contributions to the Caravans. Imogene Green (b. 1931), a Chicago native and schoolmate of James Cleveland, began singing gospel in high school with Cleveland accompanying her on piano. During the course of her transition from a soprano to a robust sounding contralto, she sang with the Caravans (1955–57), Cleveland's Gospel Chimes, and the Davis Sisters. Delores Washington, Josephine Howard, and Louise McDonald each sang with the Caravans during the 1960s.

Among the pianists who played for the Caravans were James Cleveland, Eddie Williams, and James Herndon. Herndon wrote the group several compositions that became famous, among them "I Won't Be Back No More," "No Coward Soldier," and "He Sits High and Looks Low."

Professor Alex Bradford

Almost twenty years after his death, Alex Bradford (1927–78) is still considered one of the most talented singer-composers in gospel and certainly its most flamboyant. In a relatively short while, Bradford moved from his hometown of Bessemer, Alabama, to the front line of the national gospel scene to become the toast of Broadway and the "Darling of the Continent." This task would seem difficult for a "whiskey sounding" baritone who was "always on stage," but it came easy for Bradford.

Born to a father who was an ore miner and a mother who was a cook, seamstress, beautician, and stage mother, Bradford was given piano and dancing lessons at age four, even though this was during the Depression. Within a few short months of his dancing lessons, he was appearing on stage. The admiration and applause he received during his short-lived vaudeville career stayed with Bradford forever. The excitement of the theater, the overwhelming admiration of the audience, and the congeniality among the performers inspired six-year-old Bradford to join a sanctified church near him—the ambience seemed the same as vaudeville's to him. However, his Baptist mother brought him back to the family church in short order. At age thirteen Bradford joined a children's gospel group, the Protective Harmoneers, and within a year he had his own radio show on which he sang, played the piano, and presented other talented youth.

Bradford attended elementary and junior high school in Bessemer but after what was perceived as a racial altercation, he was sent to New York City to complete high school. He did not remain there long, and on his return to Bessemer, his mother enrolled him in a prestigious African American private school, Snow Hill Institute, approximately 160 miles from his hometown. Founded in 1893 by William James Edwards, the great-grandfather of film director Spike Lee, Snow Hill was comparable to such African American boarding schools as Palmer in North Carolina and Fessenden Academy in Ocala, Florida. Bradford was an extremely bright student, excelling in English, history, and music. Only slightly interested in European classical music, Bradford led jam sessions with other students in the latest blues hits. He would also lead them in the latest songs of the groups that visited Bessemer: the Kings of Harmony, the Swan Silvertones, the Famous Blue Jay Singers, and Arizona Dranes—who were singing sanctified gospel as early as 1926—and the Brewster Ensemble, featuring Queen Candice Anderson. Bradford's musical activities did not

Professor Alex Bradford and the Bradford Specials

deter his teachers from appointing him a teacher's assistant. As a result his classmates named him "Professor," a title he used throughout his career.

After graduating from high school Bradford served a tour in the armed services
during World War II and upon his release in 1947 moved to Chicago, the center of
gospel. His great desire was to join the Roberta Martin Singers. Although Martin welcomed him to Chicago and presented him at her concerts, she offered him no spot
in her group. Robert Anderson presented him in concert with his group but made no
attempt to make him a star. Bradford became friendly with Mahalia Jackson who
hired him for a short period as her secretary and traveling companion. During one
of their tours, he copied down the names of promoters from her address book for use
at a later time. While traveling with Jackson, Bradford received a call from Willie
Webb informing him of a vacancy in his group. Bradford joined the Willie Webb

Singers, and at their next recording session Webb permitted Bradford to sing the lead on Bradford's arrangement of the nineteenth-century white Protestant hymn "Every Day and Every Hour." While this recording was not a hit, in it devout gospel lovers recognized not only a new voice, but a new style. This recording opened the door for Bradford.

On the minor, but ultimately significant, success of "Every Day and Every Hour," Bradford organized a group called the Bradford Specials and recorded nine songs, all composed by Bradford, for Specialty Records' gospel division under the supervision of Art Rupe on July 19, 1953, in Chicago. On the advice of Rupe, "Too Close to Heaven" was selected as the first release. The gospel world—save the few who had noticed "Every Day and Every Hour"—was taken by surprise when this gigantic husky overseer-type voice stated that:

> I'm too close to my journey's end,
> I'm too close to shaking hands with all my friends,
> And I wouldn't take nothing for my journey right now,
> Lord, you know I've got to make it somehow;
> I'm so close—almost reach my goal,
> (I said) I'm so close to finally saving my soul,
> I'm too close to heaven to turn around.

If the beauty of Bradford's rough voice and his ability to make it toss and turn at will was not sufficient, halfway through the verse of the song he inserts a real high C in falsetto and immediately drops back to his gruff baritone.

Bradford was supported on "Too Close" by the Bradford Specials—James Brendon, Jonathan Jackson, Billy Harper, Louis Gibson, and Charles Campbell. Bradford was to have several hits during the next decade. Among them were "Lord, Lord, Lord," "I Won't Sell Out," and "He'll Wash You Whiter than Snow," a duet with Sallie Martin. By this time in Martin's career her voice had deepened almost to the range of Bradford's.

Just at the point at which Bradford's popularity began to wane, he was approached by Broadway producers to star in one of the earliest gospel musicals. *Black Nativity* opened in 1961. The play was highly successful and went on to have a run in London. Later he starred in the musical *Don't Bother Me, I Can't Cope*. He and

Vinette Carroll were preparing a new production, *Your Arm's Too Short to Box with God*, when he died.

Raymond Rasberry

Raymond Rasberry, pianist, composer, and choral director, was the first child of Gertrude and Raymond Rasberry, born in 1928 in Akron, Ohio. Learning to play the piano completely by ear at age eight, he became something of a sensation in his hometown because of his ability to hear songs only once and then duplicate them almost exactly. As a member of a Pentecostal church, Rasberry had ample opportunity to develop his talent by accompanying hymns and shout songs led by the congregation. (In Pentecostal churches the congregation begins the song; the pianist must find their key and create an accompaniment.)

Wynona Carr heard him play piano while he was still in his teens. Impressed with his virtuosity, she hired him as her pianist. Carr was her own best accompanist but wanted to stand and sing for greater contact with the audience. Rasberry traveled with Carr on weekends through high school, and after he graduated from East High in Akron, he moved to Cleveland to work with her and one of the choirs she was directing. His fame as a pianist spread, and he began accompanying other singers as well. He accompanied Mahalia Jackson on one of her tours and played piano for Clara Ward and the Ward Singers on several of their recordings.

In the mid-1950s, Rasberry organized the Rasberry Singers, a group of five men. His was the first major all male piano-accompanied group since Alex Bradford had formed the Bradford Specials. What made the Rasberry Singers unique, according to Anthony Heilbut, was that the group contained the finest male soprano in gospel, Carl Hall. The Rasberry Singers had several hit recordings, among them "No Tears in Heaven" and "We're Crossing over One by One," composed by Rasberry. His composition "Only What You Do for Christ Will Last" became a gospel standard and was recorded by several singers including Mahalia Jackson.

Marion Williams and the Stars Of Faith

Clara Ward and the Ward Singers had the perfect combination of voices and styles in Clara, Marion Williams, Henrietta Waddy, and Gertrude Ward and undoubtedly could have gone on singing as a group until they were too old to perform. However,

Marion Williams had come too far from scrubbing floors during the week and singing in local churches on weekends to take a back seat.

By the mid-1950s, Marion Williams had become gospel's leading lyric soprano and one of its greatest growlers. She had appeared at Carnegie Hall, Boston's Symphony Hall, and almost every Baptist church that had a piano, but she did not lead the Ward Singers, nor had she reaped the financial benefits that came to the group in large part because of her talent. She was, in the old vernacular, a "side man," and she needed either to go out as a soloist or to form her own group so that she could develop her ideas.

Kitty Parham leading the Stars of Faith in "Looking to Jesus"

In 1958 after being refused a raise and reimbursement for hotel expenses, Williams and Henrietta Waddy quit the group. Mrs. Ward was so certain that neither singer could make a living without her management that she gave little concern to their departure; she had organized a second group of singers who performed independently as the Clara Ward Specials, and she replaced Williams and Waddy with two singers from this group. But without Mrs. Ward's knowledge, Williams contacted the remaining members of the Clara Ward Specials—Kitty Parham, Frances Steadman, and Esther Ford—and invited them to become members of a group she was organizing. Like Williams and Waddy, the three felt Mrs. Ward was mistreating them. They immediately accepted Williams' invitation, and Mrs. Ward was left without the Clara Ward Specials. Williams never worked with the Ward Singers again. Audiences, however, delighted in witnessing the two groups during the same concert, especially since Williams' group now had the most exciting singers.

Kitty Parham (b. 1931), a native of Trenton, New Jersey, grew up in COGIC and was a leading soprano soloist in that denomination. From her experience as a song leader in congregational singing, Parham had cultivated every nuance of shout singing and could execute them all for long periods. Esther Ford (b. 1925) from Detroit, another COGIC singer, had long been an associate of Mattie Moss Clark and the na-

Marion Williams and Henrietta Waddy of the Stars of Faith

tional music scene. The gospel ballad, with which she could "paint a picture" and send audiences into hysteria, was her specialty. Frances Steadman (b. 1915) a native of Greensboro, North Carolina, who later lived in Baltimore, was brought up in both the Baptist and sanctified churches. She knew how to handle the shout and the Baptist lining hymn. Steadman, one of the most talented contraltos in gospel, when performing in the Baptist lining hymn tradition would, as Mahalia Jackson used to say, "take you back to slavery days."

Each of the five women was a powerful soloist, but none had the voice of Williams, and none could weave a musical spell like she could. One of their most successful recordings was a remake of the Ward Singers' song "Packing Up." The song deals with preparation for meeting Jesus, and in performance Williams would walk through the audience collecting as many as twenty purses. On her way back to the stage, she would return each purse to its rightful owner to the amazement and delight of the audience.

A special honor came to Williams in 1961 when she and the Stars of Faith were asked to appear on Broadway in Langston Hughes' *Black Nativity*. In 1971 Williams recorded Dorsey's "Standing Here Wondering Which Way to Go," which was selected as background music for the popular television commercial for the U.S Army "Down and Out," and in 1980 Barney Joseph, founder of the famous Cafe Society and owner of the New York nightclub The Cookery, called on Williams to substitute for the ailing Alberta Hunter. Two more great honors came to Williams in the early 1990s. She was selected as a MacArthur Fellow, an award that carries a $350,000 stipend, and she was the first gospel singer to receive a Kennedy Center Award for outstanding contribution in the arts.

The Lockhart Singers

One of the most popular gospel songs of 1954 and 1955 was "Own Me as a Child," composed, sung, and recorded by Esther Lockhart, two of her sisters, and one cousin who sang as the Lockhart Singers. Although their two recordings were popular, these teenagers seldom traveled out of their native Chicago. They became, instead, a fixture on many of the concerts of traveling singers in Chicago, and although they attempted to introduce other songs from their repertoire, audiences demanded that they sing their hit:

Oh Lord, hear my voice, a long time ago I made my choice
Trying to walk in this gospel way, you said you'd hear me whenever I pray;
You know that Satan has set a trap for me but when I call your name he
    lets me be,
I'm saying Lord when I come to die I want you to own me as a child.

The group disbanded in 1957.

Rosie Wallace and the Imperials

Philadelphia gave the gospel world a powerful group in Rosie Wallace and the Imperials. Wallace (b. 1932), the leader and pianist for the group, could sing in the traditional as well as the newer style of gospel with equal effect. "Reach out and Touch Him" and "Show Me the Way" were popular hits for the group.

Wallace was also a composer, writing most of her songs for her group. Among her most popular compositions are "Can't Turn around Now" and "Just to God Be True."

The Imperials

The Herman Stevens Singers

Herman Stevens (1928–70) is better known as one of the finest organists in gospel, serving as the gospel organist for Savoy Records. He was also the leader of a gospel group that he organized in 1952 with members Helen Bryant, Evelyn Archer, and Dorothy McLeod.

Right before her death, Dorothy McLeod (1927–61) was emerging as possible competition for Mahalia Jackson. A native of Florida, McLeod possessed a lighter

The Herman Stevens Singers

voice than Jackson's but enjoyed the same vocal qualities: evenness of tone, an extraordinary range allowing her to essay a bass quality in the bottom of her range without losing her soprano-like top voice, the ability to shout a house (she was a life-long member of COGIC), and the newly developed technique of "moaning like a true Baptist." In the late 1950s when she married Herbert Carson, a shouting baritone from North Carolina, he joined the Herman Stevens Singers, and the two were often featured in duets.

The Stevens Singers traveled little because Stevens was so active in the New York-Philadelphia-New Jersey area. The group became an opening act for traveling groups in New York and were celebrated for their renditions of "Peace in the Valley" and "Somebody Touched Me," which they recorded.

Professor Charles Taylor and the Gospel All Stars

While Raymond Rasberry adopted Alex Bradford's all-male piano-accompanied sound for his all-male singers, Charles Taylor inherited Bradford's performance flamboyance. Taylor (b. c. 1932), an Alabaman, arrived in New York in the early 1950s and affiliated with several Pentecostal churches in the capacity of soloist, pianist, and choir director. He was so interested in gospel that he absorbed everything that was happening in the field. Although Taylor was a talented and interesting performer, he was without a unique voice. His piano style was heavily based on Bradford's with Roberta Martin runs and chordal explosions and Bradford's penchant for dropping "bombs" (a very loud chord in the middle of an otherwise rela-

tively quiet section). He trained his background singers in the Roberta Martin sharp attack, precise harmony, and slightly cultured timbre of the Baptist church, yet his lead was pure sanctified singing, complete with the high volume, explosive releases, and preaching style of delivery. The recordings of "On the Battlefield" and "New Born Soul" capture Taylor at the height of his style.

Other Piano-accompanied Groups

Several other piano-based groups were acclaimed during the last decade of the Golden Age. Two of the most popular were the Argo Singers and the Patterson Singers. While neither of these groups attained the stature of the Caravans or the Stars of Faith, they were solid gospel groups with the ability to stir a house during concerts. The Argo Singers had several successful recordings, including "He's Alright with Me." The Patterson Singers recorded on the Savoy label, producing such hits as "Throw out the Lifeline," "Going to Canaan," and "Christ Is Coming."

Professor Charles Taylor and the Gospel All Stars

The Highway QCs

Described as a farm team for the Soul Stirrers, the Highway QCs were organized in 1945. Their original membership consisted of Sam Cooke, Spencer Taylor, Lee Richardson, Creadell Copeland, and Charles Richardson. Original member Sam Cooke left the group in 1950 to join the Soul Stirrers and was replaced by Johnny Taylor, who at that time sounded very much like Cooke. In 1955 the group signed with Chicago's Vee-Jay Records and scored a success with their first release, "Somewhere to Lay My Head," with Taylor on the lead. In 1956 there were some personnel changes, and the group was dormant for a few years. In 1958, however, Overton Vertis Wright spent time as a lead with the group before he moved to the Sunset Travelers. Wright gave up gospel music for a career in secular music in 1964.

The QCs were heavily influenced by the Soul Stirrers, and their sound was a cross between the Soul Stirrers and the Swan Silvertones: a smooth, sweet style with an aggressive lead. Among their many popular recordings were "He Lifted My Burdens," "Do You Love Him?," and "Teach Me How to Pray." While the QCs were always a solid gospel group, they leaned toward popular music: their sound was smooth, with little of the grit associated with earlier quartets, and their stage manner was as close to a routine as possible without stepping across the invisible line between secular and sacred stage deportment. Their dress was ultrafashionable for their time, and they were one of the most popular gospel acts presented at the Apollo Theater.

The Skylarks, Violinaires, and Norfleet Brothers

By the mid-1950s it was evident that piano-accompanied gospel had replaced the purity of unaccompanied voices. Not only did all-male quartets travel with piano-accompanied groups, but they would also use the same accompanists for their own selections.

Only a small group of piano-accompanied quartets made their mark during the second decade of the Golden Age. Among them were the Skylarks. Organized in the late 1940s, the Skylarks were indistinguishable from the major quartets. They had powerful leaders, but not powerful enough to give the group real integrity, except in the thumping bass of Isaac "Dickie" Freeman, who later joined the Fairfield Four.

The Violinaires, on the other hand, created a big splash at their introduction into

Wilson Pickett singing pop later in his career

the mainstream of gospel. Organized in 1955 by Wilson Pickett (b. 1941), the Violinaires, despite having the smooth harmony of the Soul Stirrers and Dixie Hummingbirds, featured the hard lead of Pickett, who was emulating his idol, Julius Cheeks. After Pickett left the group in 1959 to become a soul singer, the group had several different lead singers but would not become a major force in gospel until the 1970s.

The Norfleet Brothers, composed of family members and friends, are a Chicago-based group that quickly earned a reputation as a solid gospel quartet that could easily stir up a house. The group has done little outside of Chicago and therefore has had little national influence.

Edna Gallmon Cooke

Edna Gallmon Cooke (1918–67) was born in Columbia, South Carolina. She studied music at Temple University and subsequently became a school teacher. In 1938 she heard Willie Mae Ford Smith sing gospel in Washington, D.C., and decided to

adopt the style. She began singing in the area around Washington, D.C., and soon became known as the "Sweetheart of the Potomac," a title that remained with her throughout her career. She began recording in the early 1950s and by 1953 was a major gospel star, specializing in the song and sermonette. She performed most often with the support of a male quartet, beginning a song softly and subtly, then building in volume and drama as the song progressed.

Her most popular recordings, all made during the 1950s, include "Amen," "Evening Sun," and "Stop Gambler." In "Stop Gambler" Cooke recounts the story of the crucifixion of Christ and the gamble for his robe. She discusses the gamble in the contemporary parlance of a radio sports announcer and begins the countdown from the deuce to the ace like someone familiar with casinos:

> I can see the first gambler as he throws down the deuce, the two spot—representing Paul and Silas bound in jail. They didn't do any wrong, God delivered them.

> The next gambler throws down the trey, the three spot—representing Shadrach, Meshach, and Abednego. God delivered them from a fiery furnace.

> Look at that next gambler, he is throwing down the four spot now—representing the four gospel writers, Matthew, Mark, Luke, and John.

> The next gambler is throwing down the five spot now—representing the fifth commandment: honor thy father and thy mother.

> The next one is throwing down the six spot—representing the six days God worked to create the earth.

Cooke addresses each card in the deck with the same kind of biblical reference. By the time she arrived at the ace, representing the Father, Son, and Holy Ghost, her audiences would be standing and waving, clapping their hands, and generally acting as if they were at the sports event that she had created through her oration, which was always accompanied by soft organ music.

Jessy Dixon

Jessy Dixon was born in San Antonio, Texas, on March 12, 1938. He studied piano at St. Mary's College there with the aim of becoming a concert pianist. He first heard

gospel music as a teenager through the recordings and concerts of Clara Ward and the Ward Singers and Dorothy Love Coates and the Original Gospel Harmonettes. Leaving college after two years, he served for a time as accompanist for Brother Joe May. In 1960 Dixon joined James Cleveland's Gospel Chimes. After five years with Cleveland, Dixon became director of the Thompson Community Singers, recording with them under the name of the Chicago Community Choir.

In the late 1960s he organized the Jessy Dixon Singers, modeling their sound and style on that of Cleveland and his group. Dixon provided a baritone lead, employing high falsetto in a repertory of call-and-response songs.

From his piano study, Dixon developed an interest in progressive harmony. In the early 1970s he left the Savoy label and moved to Light Records. There his style changed to that of contemporary gospel, in which the emphasis is on pure vocal sounds with melodies and harmonies borrowed from the popular music tradition and accompaniment is provided by electronic instruments. In June 1980 Dixon was selected to represent contemporary gospel at the Golden Jubilee Year Celebration of Gospel Music held in Chicago. His best-known compositions include "The Failure's Not in God," "Bring the Sun Out," and "Satisfied."

Joe Ligon and the Mighty Clouds of Joy

Willie Joe Ligon was born September 11, 1942, in Troy, Alabama. In 1959, while in high school in Los Angeles, he helped organize a male quartet, the Mighty Clouds of Joy. The original members were Ligon as lead, Elmore Franklin, Johnny Martin, and Richard Wallace; Paul Beasley joined in 1980. The group negotiated a recording contract with Peacock Records and by 1962 was one of the leading male gospel quartets. They began performing in the hard gospel style, singing loudly and rhythmically at the extremes of their vocal range, but later became one of the first groups to embrace the softer, contemporary gospel style. At the same time they employed a backup group of two guitarists, an organist, and a drummer, although their later recordings would include full orchestral accompaniment.

The group performs many traditional gospel songs, but in the 1970s they added "message" songs to their repertory—songs with lyrics that can be interpreted as either sacred or secular, for example, "You've Got a Friend." This made the group popular with multiracial and secular audiences. They have appeared with such artists as Earth, Wind, and Fire, the Rolling Stones, James Brown, Gladys Knight and

the Pips, and Smokey Robinson and have performed in major concert halls throughout the country as well as on television.

Ligon's unique voice with its gritty timbre is capable of displaying many different colors and emotions; his range encompasses several octaves. His solo lead has earned the group two Grammy Awards.

OTHER SINGERS

A number of soloists made significant contributions to the development of gospel through difficult times. The ideal gospel sound in the late 1950s and early 1960s was that of a large group of singers led by an energetic and commanding soloist: the gospel choir. All the major soloists had begun to record with a backup group: Mahalia Jackson was with the Jack Halloran Singers, Brother Joe May sang with the Pilgrim Travelers, and Cleophus Robinson was recording with his church choir. The soloists who brought something new to gospel or were unique in their presentation of the old were able to survive the public's change in taste. Blind Harold Boggs (b. 1928) of Port Clinton, Ohio, and Singing Sammy Lewis (b. 1929) of Chicago both earned national reputations as singers before they entered the ministry.

Other soloists, while never attaining the status of a Mahalia Jackson, continued to offer the single voice that has been with gospel since the 1920s. Several of these singers gained new popularity after a period of dormancy, including the venerable R. L. Knowles; Brother John Sellers, who frequently performed with Mahalia Jackson; the Reverend Gary Davis, who continued to sing both gospel and blues; Gloria Griffin, who had been one of the leaders of the Roberta Martin Singers; Morgan Babb; Willie Morganfield; and Elizabeth Lands, who switched from gospel to rhythm and blues at the height of her gospel career. Chicago singers Myrtle Jackson and Myrtle Scott resurfaced, as did Molly Mae Gates, a longtime associate of Dorsey. An indication of the widespread acceptance of gospel was the organization of the Nashville-based BMC Choir, composed of Baptists, Methodists, and Catholics. Two young musicians who made a great impression on the gospel world through their singing, composing, and directing were Robert Fryson (1944–94) and Donald Vails (b. 1947). Pearl Williams Jones (1931–91) developed a cult following after the release of her recording of "Jesus Lover of My Soul," sung to the accompaniment of Bach's "Jesu, Joy of Man's Desiring."

FAMILY GROUPS

During the 1930s and 1940s, before television became a fixture in American homes, family singing sessions were a chief form of entertainment for many churchgoers. While most of the groups were community based, singing for their own church services and those of others, several of these family groups, parents and children, brothers and sisters, sisters alone, and brothers alone earned national reputations and became recording artists.

The Staple Singers

The Staple Singers are the only famous gospel group composed of a father and his children. The leader of the group is Roebuck "Pops" Staples of Winona, Mississippi, who with his wife, Oceola, moved to Chicago in 1935, bringing with them their one-year-old daughter Cleotha. In Chicago the couple had four more children: Pervis, Yvonne, Mavis, and Cynthia, all of whom eventually sang with their father as the Staple Singers. Often described as down-home gospel singers, the Staples' sound is

The Staple Singers

characterized by folk style and simple harmonies rendered in a country and western twang, supporting a lead by the tenor voice of Roebuck or the hard gospel voice and style of Mavis. With Roebuck's bluesy guitar, "Will the Circle Be Unbroken" and "Unclouded Day" were huge hits for these singers.

The Banks Brothers

The first gospel duet singing goes back to the beginning of the sanctified church when, in most cases, the preacher and his wife would hold "street meetings," singing to attract people and recruit new members. But the first modern male gospel duo was Jeff (b. 1927) and Charles (b. 1929) Banks. The Banks Brothers had the task of discovering the type of harmony, the kinds of songs, and the sort of style appropriate for two dark voices in gospel.

The Banks owe the development of their duo to Mary Johnson Davis, who organized her first group in the 1930s in Pittsburgh, Pennsylvania. The Banks Brothers became members of the Mary Johnson Davis Singers in 1947, although they began singing in their home church, the Christian Methodist Church (CME) in Pittsburgh, in 1943. Jeff was also the pianist for the group, and both brothers were song leaders. They remained with Davis until 1953, when they left the group to perform as a duo. Their first record, "I've Got a Witness," brought them into the national gospel scene.

The Banks Brothers' style involved one of the voices singing a harmony three tones above the melody in the other voice, using call-and-response technique, and occasionally singing in unison on the melody. These characteristic features would be adopted by other male duos, including the Boyer Brothers and the O'Neal Twins.

Both Banks brothers became ministers. Jeff became a bishop in COGIC and the pastor of Revival Temple Holiness Church of God in Christ, while Charles became the pastor of the Greater Harvest Baptist Church. Both churches are located in Newark, New Jersey. They continue to sing on occasion and celebrated their fiftieth anniversary of professional singing in 1994.

The Gay Sisters

Gospelizing standard Protestant hymns has been a part of the gospel movement since the Azusa Street Revival, but at no time was it more popular than in the 1950s. The Ward Singers produced a hit with "I Need Thee Every Hour"; the Caravans

scored a hit with "Think of His Goodness to Me"; and Alex Bradford made his recording debut with a gospel-waltz version of "Everyday and Every Hour." None of these recordings could match the popularity of the gospelized version of the 1905 white Protestant hymn "God Will Take Care of You." The recording of this hymn introduced another group of family singers, the Gay Sisters.

Mildred (b. 1926), Evelyn (b. 1924), and Geraldine (b. 1931) were born to Jerry and Fannie Gay in Chicago. Fannie Gay and her children attended services at the Reverend Lucy Smith's All Nations Pentecostal Church. Inspired by the talent of "Little" Lucy, Evelyn and Mildred began singing as a duet, with Evelyn playing piano. Geraldine was an even more talented pianist than Evelyn (and as a youth Evelyn had accompanied Mahalia Jackson), and soon she played piano while Evelyn and Mildred sang. After Reverend Smith died, the Gay family moved its membership to the Church of God in Christ pastored by Elder William Roberts, where the three sisters became pianists and directors of music for the church. They concertized throughout the Midwest and made an annual trip to Memphis to sing at the Convocation of the Church of God in Christ.

In 1951 Evelyn and Mildred had their first session at Savoy Records (Geraldine had retired from the group). The first song sung during the session was also their first release, "God Will Take Care of You." With Mildred singing soprano and Evelyn singing and playing the piano, the sisters changed the hymn from the somber and lifeless performance usually given it to a rollicking 12/8 song of conviction and assurance. Particularly effective is the "high who" that Mildred inserts to introduce the last phrase. Evelyn's talent as a pianist was evidenced by her work on this recording, and the lyric soprano of Mildred was equal to that of Delois Barrett or Marion Williams. The Gay Sisters sang with Mahalia Jackson on Joe Bostic's annual Carnegie Hall concert bill in 1954 and made several tours throughout the United States in the 1950s and 1960s.

The Boyer Brothers

The Boyer Brothers, James Buchanan (b. 1934) and Horace Clarence Boyer (b. 1935), are two of eight children of the Reverend Climmie and Ethel Boyer of Winter Park, Florida. They received their education in the public schools of Winter Park and Eatonville and graduated from Bethune-Cookman College. The brothers were

brought up in Faith Holy Temple Church of God in Christ, where their father was the pastor. Both played piano for services, and Horace directed the choir. They formed the Boyer Brothers when they were teenagers and sang throughout Florida.

When they were still in high school, they began recording on Excello Records, which was owned by Ernie's Record Mart of Nashville, one of the major distributors of gospel recordings in the 1950s. With Horace singing tenor and James singing baritone, the brothers sang two-part harmony on slow songs and used call and response on jubilee and shout songs. Singing in the sanctified style, they were adept at building tension through the use of the vamp. Among their popular recordings are "He Understands, He'll Say 'Well Done' "; "Step by Step"; and "Oh Lord, Be My Protector," composed by James.

"Step by Step," their first release, was their signature song and was performed with a mixture of harmony singing and call and response:

HARMONY

Step by step I'm nearing the kingdom
Step by step I'm going home.
Jesus will welcome me into His kingdom
Step by step around the throne.

I know this world is not my home
Horace: *And I cannot*
    James: *I cannot*
Horace: *Make this journey*
    James: *this journey*

HARMONY

Alone, Oh
Step by step I know Jesus will greet me
Welcome me home around the throne.

In the late 1960s the brothers returned to college for graduate study. Each holds a Ph.D. and teaches at the university level, James at Kansas State University and Horace at the University of Massachusetts–Amherst. Because of the distance, the Boyer Brothers have sung only occasionally since 1980.

The O'Neal Twins

Edgar (b. 1938) and Edward (1938–93), the O'Neal Twins, were the most successful gospel duo since Sister Rosetta Tharpe and Madame Marie Knight. The twins were born in East St. Louis, Illinois, and received their education in the public schools there. They were brought up in the COGIC and as teenagers came under the influence of Mother Willie Mae Ford Smith, who introduced them at one of her concerts and with whom they traveled for a time thereafter. They were also influenced by Mattie Moss Clark.

Edgar served as their pianist and arranger, while Edward was the song leader and announcer. Like the Banks Brothers and the Boyer Brothers, their style was one of close harmony, call and response, and occasional unison singing. The twins both possessed robust and attractive grainy baritone voices equipped with the timbre that was particularly effective in the hard gospel style.

Among their most popular recordings were "The Lord Is My Shepherd" and "I Have Decided to Follow Jesus." Their recording of "I'd Trade a Lifetime" placed them in the front ranks of gospel singers:

> *I sure would love to see loved ones*
> > ***who've gone on before,***
> *Shake hands with the elders,*
> > ***the twenty and the four;***
> *In that holy righteous place*
> > ***I'll see my Master's face,***
> *I'd trade a lifetime*
> > ***for just one day in paradise.***

The O'Neal Twins traveled widely and were one of the first gospel groups to appear at New York's Apollo Theater. Along with Thomas A. Dorsey, Sallie Martin, Mother Willie Mae Ford Smith, and the Barrett Singers, they were featured in the 1983 documentary film *Say Amen, Somebody*.

Cleophus Robinson and Josephine James

Cleophus Robinson (b. 1932) and his sister, Josephine James (b. 1934), were born in Canton, Mississippi and moved to Memphis as teenagers. Robinson attended

LeMoyne-Owen College for two years, then withdrew to pursue a career as a professional gospel singer. Robinson's early musical influences were Mahalia Jackson, from whom he adopted deliberate phrasing, and Brother Joe May, from whom he borrowed the technique of growling in the upper part of the tenor register. While Robinson recorded mostly as a soloist, he and James made several successful recordings including "Pray for Me" and "When I Cross Over."

Brother and Sister Pugh: The Consolers

The Consolers

Not since the days of Blind Mamie Forehand and A. C. Forehand has a husband and wife singing team generated as much enthusiasm as Sullivan Pugh and Iola Lewis Pugh of the Consolers. The youngest of four brothers and one sister, Pugh was born in 1925 in Morehaven, Florida. His mother, like hundreds of others, was lost in the massive hurricane that passed through Florida shortly after his birth. He, his sister, and youngest brother were adopted by James and Virginia Pugh and brought up in the south-west Florida coast town of Punta Gorda where he attended school. As an adult he moved to Miami to find work.

Iola Lewis (b. 1926), the third oldest of four daughters, was born in Cottonton, Alabama. When Lewis was three her mother died, and she was subsequently raised by her maternal grandmother. When Lewis was eleven, the family moved to Columbus, Georgia, where she completed high school. After attending Claflin College in Orangeburg, South Carolina, for a short period of time, Lewis moved to Miami. She met Pugh in 1949, and they were married in 1950. They began singing as the Consolers in 1953.

Pugh shared in the singing and was the composer for the Consolers. He wrote a number of highly successful songs on the fallibility and frailness of mankind: "May the Work I've Done Speak for Me," "I'm Waiting for My Child to Come Home," and "Thank God, They Are as Well as They Are." Delivered in the "old timey" style of the Angelic Gospel Singers and the country sincerity of the Staple Singers, the

Consolers' most popular song was based on an old African American church saying—Give me my flowers while I can smell them:

> Give me my flowers while I can see them
> So that I can see the beauty that they bring;
> Speak kind words to me while I can hear them
> So that I can feel the comfort that they bring.

"Give Me My Flowers" brought superstar fame to the Consolers and drew to a close the duet tradition of the Golden Age.

THE SECOND GOSPEL TRIUMVIRATE

As Thomas A. Dorsey, Sallie Martin, and Theodore R. Frye constituted that triumvirate of the 1930s that took gospel from dubious status to its place as the principal music of the African American church, the triumvirate in gospel during the 1960s moved gospel from being a music of the church to a music of the nation. James Cleveland, Edward Smith, and the Reverend Lawrence Roberts were the second triumverate of gospel. Like Dorsey, Cleveland had the talent; like Sallie Martin, Edward Smith possessed the business acumen to make money. And the Reverend Lawrence Roberts, a gospel record producer for Savoy Records, provided the conduit to the music-loving public.

James Cleveland

James Edward Cleveland (1931–91), gospel singer, pianist, composer, and conductor, was born in Chicago and began piano lessons at age five. By age eight he was a soloist in Thomas A. Dorsey's Junior Gospel Choir at the Pilgrim Baptist Church. At age fifteen he joined a local group, the Thorne Crusaders, with whom he remained for the next eight years. As a leader of this group, he strained to reach high notes and, in the absence of sound systems, sang louder than his vocal cords could accommodate. This vocal strain resulted in a throaty and gravelly quality that increased with the years. During his tenure with the Thornes, he began composing and by age sixteen had composed "Grace Is Sufficient," which was recorded by the Roberta Martin Singers and is now part of standard gospel repertoire.

After leaving the Thornes, Cleveland served as pianist and arranger for Albertina

Walker's Caravans and recorded several sides with that group. He later joined other groups, including the Gospel Chimes and the Gospel All Stars, eventually organizing the James Cleveland Singers. In 1960 Cleveland joined with the Reverend Lawrence Roberts and his choir at the First Baptist Church in Nutley, New Jersey, to make a number of successful recordings, the first of which was "Peace, Be Still" (1963). Cleveland liked a treble sound and dispensed with the bass voice in the gospel choir. He also preferred the call-and-response delivery when singing in concert, and on all his choir recordings he played the role of the preacher to the choir's congregation. Further, he felt that gospel was in its element with a congregation and made all his choir recordings live.

During the 1950s and 1960s Cleveland was most prolific as a composer, writing more than five hundred songs. Many have become gospel standards, including "Oh Lord, Stand by Me," "He's Using Me," "Walk on by Faith," and "Lord, Help Me to Hold Out." He continued to compose into the 1980s and scored a huge success when the Mighty Clouds of Joy recorded his "I Get a Blessing Everyday."

The Cleveland style, which he employed and taught his singers, was half crooning, half preaching the verses, and then moving into snug refrains. His hard gospel technique of singing at the extremes of his register evoked a heavy contrast with the rich falsetto that he employed. He was particularly fond of the vamp in gospel music, over which he would extemporize variations. Like his model, Thomas A. Dorsey, he had the ability to write and sing in the everyday language of his audience, dealing with such subjects as paying rent, buying food, and heating the home in winter.

Cleveland's greatest contribution, again like Dorsey, was the organization of a gospel choir convention. In August 1968 he organized the Gospel Music Workshop of America (GMWA), an organization that had several hundred thousand members by the mid-1980s. Each large town had a chapter of the GMWA, and Cleveland would make periodic visits to chapters to teach new songs and techniques and to critique the work of the local choirs. An annual convention was held for one week, each year in a different location. Since many members of GMWA would choose this week for their vacation, attendance at these meetings was large. Each year's convention released a recording of the outstanding groups in attendance, with Cleveland leading one or two songs. One of his most successful recordings was with one of his

protégés, Aretha Franklin, singing "Amazing Grace"; she had studied his style when he was the director of the Radio Choir at Detroit's Bethlehem Baptist Church, where her father was pastor.

Cleveland had many gold records and won three Grammy Awards, appeared at Carnegie Hall and many other prestigious performance venues around the United States, worked with Quincy Jones in the television production "Roots," and recorded the opera *Porgy and Bess* with Ray Charles and Cleo Lane. In 1980, along with Natalie Cole, he starred in the television special "In the Spirit," filmed in Northampton, England, for Granada Television (BBC). On August 12, 1981, Cleveland was awarded a star on the Hollywood Walk of Fame. In August 1983, accompanied by the Southern California Community Choir, Andrae and Sandra Crouch, and Shirley Caesar, Cleveland performed live in concert at the Sultan's Pool amphitheater in Jerusalem.

In November 1970 Cleveland had organized and become the pastor of the Cornerstone Institutional Baptist Church in Los Angeles with sixty charter members. When he died in February 1991, membership at the church totaled more than seven thousand.

Lawrence Roberts

The Reverend Lawrence Roberts was born in 1939 in Newark, New Jersey. He learned to play the piano at an early age, and by age fifteen he was the pianist for the junior choir at the Zion Hill Baptist Church in Newark. For the next ten years Roberts served as pianist for Newark gospel groups and organized his own group, the Gospel Chordettes, whose members were Bernadine Walls, Delores Best, Freida Roberts, Gertrude Deadwyler, and Margie Rains. In October 1954 he became a producer for Savoy Records and in that capacity supervised recordings for such groups as the Roberta Martin Singers, Dorothy Love Coates and the Original Gospel Harmonettes, the Five Blind Boys of Mississippi, the Gay Sisters, and the Ward Singers. He met James Cleveland in the late 1950s, and in 1960, at Cleveland's request, he began recording with Cleveland, backed by the choir of the First Baptist Church of Nutley, New Jersey, of which he had recently become pastor.

As a record producer always searching for new and different talent, Roberts attended Cleveland's GMWA convention each year and selected a choir to sign with

his label. Over the fifteen years of his association with Cleveland, he not only introduced many choirs into the national gospel scene but made Cleveland's workshop the springboard to a recording career. He and Cleveland worked closely in establishing new gospel devices, such as variations on the standard vamp and polyphonic call-and-response patterns.

Edward Smith

Edward M. Smith (1935–94) was born in Detroit, Michigan, attended Northwestern High School, and graduated from Highland Park Junior College. His gospel career began in 1962 as cofounder and business manager for the Harold Smith Majestics. The owner of two florist shops, Smith developed a keen sense of business, which he applied to his management of the Majestics and other gospel groups in Detroit.

Smith met Cleveland in the early 1960s and sang in several of his choirs during Cleveland's stay in Detroit. When Cleveland organized the GMWA, he asked Smith to act as its executive director, a position Smith held from 1975 until his death. It was through Smith's management skills that the workshop became one of the most successful financial ventures in gospel music.

Gospel on Broadway

Religious dramas, complete with costumes, lights, scenery, and music, have been part of African American church activities since the first quarter of this century. Labeled by scholars as "recreational dramatics," the plays served several purposes: fund raising, sacred entertainment, opportunities for actors and singers to display their talents, and the introduction of new songs. William H. Wiggins, Jr., in a 1982 paper entitled "'From Auction Block to...Nativity': A Study of the Evolution of Black Gospel Drama," noted that in 1937 *Heaven Bound* became the first of these church dramas to be taken from its original church stage and performed on a professional stage. (While Hall Johnson's *Run, Little Chillun* played on Broadway in 1933 and used spirituals and folk songs for music—the usual music for these dramas—it was not conceived nor presented as a church drama.)

Wiggins further noted that 1941 was the year that gospel musical made its debut:

> In 1941 W. Herbert Brewster, a Baptist minister from Memphis, Tennessee, had his religious drama, From Auction Block to Glory, produced at the National

Baptist Convention's annual meeting [in Memphis]. On the surface, there would not appear to be much to suggest that this would turn out to be a watershed event in Black American culture.... But Brewster's From Auction Block to Glory *broke...old dramatic molds. It was the first nationally staged black religious play that featured gospel songs written to be sung during that production.*

Brewster continued to write and stage gospel musicals and introduced several of his most popular songs within the drama. Among these were "Move on up a Little Higher," "How Far Am I from Canaan?" and "They Are They." In many instances church dramas were the only live theater many churchgoers saw since most traditional Protestant denominations frowned upon attending films and dramatic plays. These congregations adopted church dramas and inserted well-known gospel songs for music.

While Brewster moved the church drama from the church to the auditorium and composed gospel songs especially for the production, Langston Hughes (1902-1967), a prolific author and poet, moved the gospel song-play from small city theaters to the *great white way*. Hughes approached popular music composer Jobe Huntley in 1956 and asked him to write music for a play about a "store-front church and how it got started." As Hughes wrote scenes and song lyrics for the play he would pass them to Huntley who set them to music. The musical was completed in early 1957 and entitled *Tambourines to Glory, A Musical Melodrama*. Hughes pitched the play from early 1957 until March 1958 when he was notified that the Theater Guild would stage the play in summer stock in Westport, Connecticut. Among the actors and singers contracted for the summer stock performances were Hazel Scott, Nipsey Russell, John Sellars, Joseph Battles, Theresa Merritt, and, to provide an authentic gospel flavor, Clara Ward was cast as Birdie Lee. Eva Jessye conducted the choir and Sam Price led the orchestra.

The show opened in Westport on December 5, 1958 and ran through September 10, 1959. The opening night reviews were glowing, but despite the reviews and positive responses to audience questionnaires Hughes could not find a producer willing to gamble on a gospel musical for Broadway. Hoping that a producer would come forth in a few months, Hughes turned his attention to a gospel song-play celebrating the birth of Christ. Using dialogue, pantomime, dance, and song, Hughes

fashioned *Black Nativity: A Gospel Song-Play* into a tapestry of African American religious and musical expressions. Fully aware of the rich legacy of Christmas Negro spirituals and Christmas gospel songs, Hughes chose well-known songs rather than new compositions for the production. The cast included gospel singer Alex Bradford and the Bradford Singers who were still riding high on "Too Close to Heaven"; Marion Williams and the Stars of Faith; the partially blind former concert singer Princess Stewart, with the entire production under the direction of Vinnette Carrol; and with dances staged by Louis Johnson. Although each of these groups and soloists sang separately, when they formed a chorus they turned New York's 41st Street Theater into a Pentecostal church. Among the well-known songs in the production were "Sweet Little Jesus Boy," "Mary, What You Gonna Name That Pretty Little Baby?" and "Children, Go Where I Send Thee." *Black Nativity* ran on Broadway for two years. After closing in New York the play had a successful run in London, toured throughout Europe, and filmed for television in Cannes, for which it received the Catholic Dove Award. Although the play has not returned to Broadway, it has become a Christmas staple in large cities throughout the United States, often involving casts of hundreds.

While *Black Nativity* ran in London Hughes turned his attention again to *Tambourines to Glory*. It was not until 1963, five years after its original summer stock production, that producers Joel Schenker, Hexter Productions and Sidney S. Baron agreed to take *Tambourines* to Broadway. Huntley wrote in his 1983 book *I Remember Langston Hughes*:

> When casting was completed, Louis Gossett and Hilda Harris were in the leading roles, Rosetta LeNoire played the mother, Clara Ward, Joseph Attles, and Anna English signed to play the roles they had created at Westport. Newcomers to the cast were Micki Grant and Robert Guillaume who played the young lovers. Lyn Hamilton played the Deaconess, Al Fann and Ruby Challenger were the policemen.

Vinnette Carrol directed for the second time and developed a first-rate production. The show opened on November 2, 1963, again to excellent reviews. To promote the play and ensure a continued big box office, Clara Ward and some of the singers from the show were scheduled to appear on the Ed Sullivan Show on Sunday night,

November 24. Jobe Huntley reported that he went to the theater late on Friday, November 22 and was sitting in a dressing room watching television when the news announced that President John F. Kennedy had been shot. In a dramatic show of respect all theaters on Broadway closed for the weekend, and Ms. Ward's appearance on the Ed Sullivan Show was canceled. *Tambourines to Glory* never regained momentum and closed after only twenty-six performances.

Black Nativity and *Tambourines to Glory* have not returned to Broadway but they inspired several gospel Broadway musicals and musicals that featured gospel songs. Of more importance is the continued influence of these two gospel musicals; they set the singing style for black Broadway musicals. Whether in *Purlie* (1970), *Don't Bother Me, I Can't Cope* (1972), *Raisin* (1973)—a musical version of *Raisin in the Sun*, *The Wiz* (1975), or *Dreamgirls* (1982), Broadway has been shouting to the gospel sound.

GOSPEL ABROAD

African American sacred music became the sensation of Europe in 1873 when the Fisk Jubilee Singers sang before Queen Victoria and other European royalty. A number of jubilee quartets went to Europe in the 1920s, and although Negro spirituals were featured in their concerts, the popular music of the period occupied the center of their repertoire. Gospel music as composed by Dorsey, Martin, Brewster, and Bradford did not reach Europe until 1953, when Mahalia Jackson toured Europe and made a sensational debut at Albert Hall in London.

The Golden Gate Quartet made their first tour of Europe in 1953 and although they had changed the Negro spiritual from sacred to popular music, spirituals were nonetheless included in their concerts. Likewise, J. Robert Bradley went to Europe in the 1960s to study and sing, but he divided his concerts between European art music, Negro spirituals, and the music of his mentor Lucie Campbell and other gospel composers of the National Baptist Convention.

Clara Ward and the Ward Singers made a much publicized tour of Europe in 1962, which culminated with a heavily attended concert in the Holy Land. In the same year Alex Bradford, Marion Williams, and Princess Stewart appeared in *Black Nativity* in several countries on the continent.

For the 1963 Spoleto Festival of Two Worlds, Gian-Carlo Menotti invited the Roberta Martin Singers, Madame Ernestine B. Washington, the Lorraine Ellison

Singers, the Twilight Gospel Singers, and Professor Albert Miller to perform. Presenting gospel in Italy suggested that gospel was no longer a ghetto music.

With their fondness for African American music in Europe, and especially gospel—a music so foreign to their culture—it was not surprising that Europeans accepted this music as another American innovation.

DESERTERS AND JOINERS

In the late 1950s, promoters of acts that appeared at Carnegie Hall, Radio City Music Hall, and Madison Square Garden approached gospel singers about appearances in those hallowed entertainment halls. Some promoters went further and described a utopia if gospel singers would only change their repertoire and performance attire—not their style—and become soul or popular music performers. Many were approached, but few accepted the offer. Ironically, those who accepted the invitation were some of the best performers in gospel.

Lou Rawls and the Pilgrim Travelers

Wynona Carr, for example, spent the last five years of her life performing in supper clubs and theaters where gospel was never mentioned. In addition to the love songs that she composed, she included such standard jazz repertoire as "Satin Doll" and "For All We Know." But Carr was not nearly as successful as Della Reese of the Meditation Singers who, with her 1954 release of "Don't You Know," moved from the choir loft to plush supper clubs and theaters.

Male *a cappella* quartets yielded a host of singers who switched to popular or soul music. The first singer during the last half of the Golden Age to make the switch was Sam Cooke, leader of the Soul Stirrers. His replacement in the Soul Stirrers, Johnnie Taylor, switched from gospel to soul music in the late 1950s, while Bobby Womack and the Womack Brothers quartet, who had sung gospel professionally for ten years, changed their name to the Valentines and sang soul music before Bobby left to become a single act. Lou Rawls sang with the Pilgrim Travelers from 1950 to 1960 when he left to begin a career as a nightclub singer. Wilson Pickett, who served a tenure with the Detroit-based Violinaires, left to join the rhythm and blues group the Falcons and eventually went on to a solo career. O. V. Wright scored a success with his pop recording of "Little Green Apples," after a tenure with the Spirit of Memphis. Brook Benton had learned his craft as a lead singer with the Bill Langford, and Joe Hinton left the Spirit of Memphis for the world of soul. Marie Knight, like her one-time partner Sister Rosetta Tharpe, recorded and performed popular music before returning to the church and becoming a minister. Imogene Green, the Pilgrim Travelers (under the name of the Travelers), and the Selah Jubilee Quartet (under the name of the Larks) all recorded secular music.

Conversely, a number of rhythm and blues and blues artists had "born-again" experiences and turned to gospel. Among these are Solomon Burke, Candi Staten, and Gatemouth Moore. Little Richard and Al Green both announced a born-again experience but that experience did not forbid their still singing secular music.

James Cleveland, the
crowned prince of gospel

Conclusion: I Looked Down the Line and I Wondered
1965 and Beyond

James Cleveland followed his 1963 hit "Peace, Be Still" with a string of successful recordings unlike any gospel artist before. He introduced choirs from around the nation in a series of recordings called "James Cleveland Presents," and by the end of the 1950s the choir, often with as many as 500 singers, had become the ideal sound in gospel. While Brother Joe May, Mahalia Jackson, Edna Gallmon Cooke, and other soloists were still in demand, gospel adopted a "more the merrier" attitude, and the gospel choir finally came into its own. The gospel audience grew by leaps and bounds, and it was not unusual for a gospel concert to garner an attendance of five to seven thousand; major record labels—before recording only white gospel singers and popular music artists—began contracting black gospel singers, and television beckoned gospel singers both current and past (Della Reese, Al Green, Little Richard). Major auditoriums, once hesitant to book gospel singers, sought out gospel packages for Sunday afternoons. Black gospel became big business, and artist fees, modest by any comparison only a few years earlier, rose astronomically. Cleveland, who by 1965 had earned the title "Crown Prince of Gos-

pel," presided over gospel's new status in a princely fashion. And he should have.

He had inherited the mantle of singers who began their struggle for musical acceptance in store-front churches, dressed in threadbare robes, and singing to untuned upright pianos. These same performers' position elevated to presenting concerts in the Hollywood Bowl and Albert Hall, with limousine service to the stage door, large audiences, and fees that would satisfy rock stars. Equally important as the trappings was the development of the music and the style of performance. What began as experimentation in melody, harmony, and rhythm had evolved into a refined gospel song and style attractive enough to be performed at the inauguration of a president of the United States. But all was not well, for even though gospel was beloved in 1965, there was a faction within the group that was a decade or more younger than the leaders. This new generation wished not only for a modern sound in gospel but also more access to the popular music market. They wanted to drop choir robes and business suits and don the latest in casual fashions; they wanted to add synthesizers, drum machines, and other instruments from popular music, and they wanted a greater association with popular music performers. Popular songs were given religious words in order to attract a popular music market (Paul Anka's "My Way" became "His Way" and "I Had a Talk with My Man Last Night" became "I Had a Talk with God Last Night"), and gospel singers became the opening act for popular and blues singers. What once had been a genuine expression of ecstasy in responding to gospel soon became vocal and physical cliched responses to the music. In fact, gospel was bursting out of the world it had created.

It was at this time, 1969, that Edwin Hawkins rescued the uneasiness with "O Happy Day." Unfortunately "O Happy Day" had its largest sale among new gospel music lovers who wanted more of the same and with few references to God, Christ, and heaven. Important to note is that the audience that clamored for more of the Hawkins gospel was not composed of anthropologists, sociologists, or ethnomusicologists who wanted to observe the music in its natural habitat. Instead it was made up of music and dance loving people who cared nothing for the gospel background or significance; the music just had to be catchy and rhythmic. A group of gospel singers were willing to comply with this demand but did not understand that in so doing, they presented music that did not necessarily further God's kingdom in the land. The next generation of gospel musicians would be challenged to

bring back together the secular and religious sides of gospel. While there would always be singers who would attempt to carry on the legacy of Thomas A. Dorsey, Mahalia Jackson, and Roberta Martin—most notably Delois Barrett and the Barrett Singers, Vanessa Bell Armstrong, and Walter Hawkins—there would also be a cadre of singers who would fuse the Dorsey legacy with the music of jazz, rhythm and blues, and popular music. Chief among them would be the Winans, Take 6, Commissioned and BeBe and CeCe.

Like New Orleans traditional music (Dixieland), traditional gospel—the kind that Dorsey espoused—will survive as *one* type of gospel, for in the near future there will surely be many types of black gospel music. Like the blues, gospel will become part of the fabric of American music and will become synonymous with American music. It will be heard in elevators, over telephones, in department stores, movies, and commercials.

But while it is being used for advertising and dancing, it will also be used for meditation and worship. As the Reverend C. L. Franklin said, "Gospel music mends the broken heart, raises the bowed-down head, and gives hope to the weary traveler." Indeed, each time gospel serves such a function, it will surely create a "Happy Day."

BIBLIOGRAPHY

Allen, Ray. *Singing in the Spirit: African American Sacred Quartets in New York City*. Philadelphia: University of Pennsylvania Press, 1991.

Allen, William Francis, Charles Pickard Ware, and Lucy McKim Garrison. *Slave Songs of the United States*. New York: Freeport Press. (reprint; Books for Libraries Press, New York, 1971).

Anderson, R. and G. North. *Gospel Music Encyclopedia*. New York: Sterling Publishing, 1979.

Baker, Barbara Welsey. *Black Gospel Music Styles*, Ph.D. dissertation. Baltimore: University of Maryland, 1978.

Boyer, Horace Clarence. *An Analysis of Black Church Music with Examples Drawn from Rochester, New York*, Ph.D. dissertation. New York: Eastman School of Music (University of Rochester), 1973.

Boyer, Horace Clarence. *The Gospel Song: An Historical and Analytical Survey*, Master's thesis. New York: Eastman School of Music (University of Rochester), 1964.

Boyer, Horace Clarence, ed. *Lift Every Voice and Sing: An African American Hymnal*. New York: Church Hymnal Corporation, 1993.

Cobb, Charles. *A Theoretical Analysis of Black Quartet Music*, Master's thesis. Madison, WI: University of Wisconsin at Madison, 1974.

Cobbins, Otha B. *History of the Church of Christ (Holiness) U.S.A.* New York: Vantage Press, 1966.

Cone, James H. *The Spirituals and the Blues*. New York: Seabury Press, 1972.

Corum, Fred T. and A. Harper Sizelove, eds. *Like As of Fire: Newspapers from the Azusa Street World Wide Revival*. Washington, D.C.: Middle Atlantic Regional Press, 1985.

Davis, John P., ed. *The American Reference Book*. Englewood Cliffs, New Jersey: Prentice-Hall, Inc., 1966.

Dixon, Robert M. W. and John Godrich, comp. *Blues and Gospel Records, 1902-1942*. London: Storyville Publications and Co., 1963.

DuPree, Sherry Sherrod and Herbert C. DuPree. *African American Good News (Gospel) Music*. Washington, D.C.: Middle Atlantic Regional Press, 1993.

DuPree, Sherry Sherrod. *Biographical Dictionary of African American Holiness: Pentecostals, 1880-1990*. Washington, D.C.: Middle Atlantic Regional Press, 1989.

Goreau, Laurraine. *Just Mahalia, Baby*. Waco, Texas: Word Books, Publishers, 1975.

Harris, Michael W. *The Rise of Gospel Blues: The Music of Thomas Andrew Dorsey in the Urban Church*. New York: Oxford University Press, 1992.

Hayes, Cedric. *A Discography of Gospel Records, 1931-1971*. Copenhagen, Denmark: Knudson Music, 1973.

Heilbut, Anthony. *The Gospel Sound: Good News and Bad Times*. New York: Limelight Editions, 1985.

Hillsman, Joan. *The Progress of Gospel Music: From Spirituals to Contemporary Gospel*. New York: Vantage Press, 1983.

Hine, Darlene Clark. *Black Women in America: An Historical Encyclopedia*, Vols. 1 and 2. Brooklyn, New York: Carlson Publishing, Inc., 1993.

Hitchcock, H. Wiley and Stanley Sadie. *New Grove Dictionary of American Music*, Vol. II. New York: Grove's Dictionaries of Music, Inc., 1986.

Huntley, Jobe. *I Remember Langston Hughes*. New York: Huntley Press, 1983.

Jackson, Irene V. *Afro-American Gospel Music and Its Social Setting with Special Attention to Roberta Martin*, PhD. dissertation. Middletown, CT: Wesleyan University, 1974.

Jackson, Irene V., ed. *Afro-American Religious Music: A Bibliography and Catalogue of Gospel Music*. Westport, CT: Greenwood Press, 1979.

Jackson, Mahalia and Evan McLeod White. *Movin' on Up*. New York: Hawthorne Books, 1966.

Jones, Ralph H. *Charles Albert Tindley: Prince of Preachers*. Nashville: Abingdon Press, 1982.

Levine, Lawrence W. *Black Culture and Black Consciousness: Afro-American Folk Thought from Slavery to Freedom*. New York: Oxford University Press, 1977.

Lincoln, C. Eric and Lawrence H. Mamiya. *The Black Church in the African American Experience*. Durham, NC: Duke University Press, 1990.

Lornell, Kip. *Happy in the Service of the Lord: Afro-American Gospel Quartets in Memphis*. Urbana, IL: University of Illinois Press, 1988.

Lornell, Kip. *Virginia's Blues, Country, and Gospel Records 1902-1943: An Annotated Discography*. Lexington, KY: University of Kentucky Press, 1989.

M'Nemar, Richard. *The Kentucky Revival*. Cincinnati, OH: E. and E. Horsford, 1808.

Murray, Albert. *Stomping the Blues*. New York: Schirmer Books, 1976.

O'Daniel, Therman B. *Langston Hughes, Black Genius: A Critical Evaluation*. New York: William Morrow and Company, Inc., 1971.

Oliver, Paul. *Songsters and Saints: Vocal Traditions on Race Records*. New York: Cambridge University Press, 1984.

Paris, Arthur E. *Black Pentecostalism: Southern Religion in an Urban World*. Amherst, MA: University of Massachusetts Press, 1982.

Patterson, J. O., German Ross, and Julia Atkins Mason. *History of Formation of the Church of God in Christ with Excerpts from the Life and Works of Its Founder—Bishop C. H. Mason*. Memphis: Church of God in Christ Publishers, 1969.

Payne, Wardell J., ed. *Directory of African American Religious Bodies*. Washington, D.C.: Howard University Press, 1991.

Raichelson, Richard M. *Black Religious Folk Song: A Study in Generic and Social Change*, Ph.D. dissertation. Philadelphia: University of Pennsylvania, 1975.

Reagon, Bernice Johnson, ed. *We'll Understand It Better By and By: Pioneering African American Gospel Composers*. Washington, D.C.: Smithsonian Institution Press, 1993.

Roberts, Lawrence C. *The Gospel Truth*. Pittsburgh: Dorrance Publishing Company, Inc., 1993.

Rubman, Kerrill L. *From "Jubilee" to "Gospel" in Black Male Quartet Singing*, Master's thesis. Chapel Hill, NC: University of North Carolina at Chapel Hill, 1980.

Sherwood, William Henry. *Harp of Zion*. Petersburg, VA: Sherwood Orphan School, 1893.

Southern, Eileen. *Biographical Dictionary of Afro-American and African Musicians*. Westport, CT: Greenwood Press, 1982.

Southern, Eileen. *The Music of Black Americans: A History*. 2nd ed. New York: W. W. Norton & Company, Inc., 1983.

Southern, Eileen. *Readings in Black American Music*. New York: W. W. Norton & Company, Inc., 1971.

Spencer, Jon Michael. *Protest & Praise: Sacred Music of Black Religions*. Minneapolis, MN: Fortress Press, 1990.

Titon, Jeff Todd, ed. *Reverend C. L. Franklin—Give Me This Mountain—Life History and Selected Sermons*. Urbana and Chicago, IL: University of Illinois Press, 1989.

Townsend, Willa, ed. *Gospel Pearls*. Nashville: Sunday School Publishing Board, 1921.

Tyler, Mary Ann Lancaster. *The Music of Charles Henry Pace and Its Relationship to the Afro-American Church Experience*, Ph.D. dissertation. Pittsburgh: University of Pittsburgh, 1980.

Walker, Wyatt T. *Somebody's Calling My Name: Black Sacred Music and Social Change*. Valley Forge, PA: Judson Press, 1979.

Warner, Jay. *The Billboard Book of Singing Groups—A History 1940-1990*. New York: Watson-Guptill Publications, 1990.

INDEX

A NOTE ON THE TYPE

This book was set in a version of the well-known Monotype
face Bembo. This letter was cut for the celebrated Venetian printer
Aldus Manutius by Francesco Griffo, and first used in
Pietro Cardinal Bembo's De Aetna of 1495.

The companion italic is an adaptation of the chancery
script type designed by the calligrapher and printer
Lodovico degli Arrighi.

Composed by NK Graphics, Keene, New Hampshire

Printed and bound by Quebecor Printing, Martinsburg, West Virginia

Designed by Iris Weinstein